Democratizing
Artificial Intelligence
to Benefit Everyone

Democratizing
Artificial Intelligence
to Benefit Everyone

*Shaping a Better Future in the
Smart Technology Era*

Jacques Ludik

Dr Jacques Ludik
Visit my websites at jacquesludik.com, sapiens.network,
cortexlogic.com, cortexgroup.ai, miiafrica.org

Printed in the United States of America

First Printing April 2021
Amazon Kindle Publishing

ISBN- 9798723055261

DEDICATION

To my family

Contents

1. Introduction

We live in tremendously exciting times where we already experience the disruptive and far-reaching impact of a smart technology revolution that seems to be on track to comprehensively change how we live, work, play, interact, and relate to one another. And it is happening fast, almost at break-neck speed, especially in relation to what we see in homo sapiens' rear-view mirror. It is like being on a run-away train or imagine driving a car that keeps on accelerating where we only have control of the steering wheel. It is therefore also extremely dangerous times, where it is critical to think on our feet and make the right choices to not only "save" our lives and get control of the situation, but also shape a better future for all of humanity. That is a daunting task that requires visionary leadership, wisdom, innovative thinking across multiple disciplines, and comprehensive collective collaboration of all stakeholders and levels of society. Whereas some people feel helpless or choose to ignore or deny or are even blissfully unaware of the full extent of these developments, we cannot afford to rest on our laurels. As humans we experience time in a linear way and sometimes struggle to see the speed of technology change, driven by a combination of exponential technologies such as artificial intelligence (AI), the Internet of Things (IoT), autonomous vehicles, robotics, 3-D printing, nanotechnology, biotechnology, materials science, energy storage, distributed ledger technology and quantum computing. The possibilities of people connected by mobile devices, with unprecedented processing power, storage capacity, and access to knowledge, are not only unlimited, but can be multiplied and amplified by these exponential technologies. The more we instrument the world, the more data are being generated to feed our artificial intelligence algorithms, which in turn leads to intelligent automation, more powerful solutions, and significant technology disruption. With AI spearheading the smart technology revolution, we see fundamental changes happening simultaneously with new opportunities through infinite data, efficiencies through self-learning, and the ability to bring machine interaction closer to human interaction. The smart technology revolution could either pull the "bottom billion" out of poverty, speed up personalized education, help us to be healthier through personalized wellness and precision medicine, and transform dysfunctional institutions or it could entrench injustice and increase inequality (almost sixty percent of the people in the world own less than \$10,000 — or roughly less than 2 percent of total wealth in the world).[1] The outcome will depend on how we manage the coming changes. It is clearly not in the best interest of humanity to have regions of the world left behind or get involved in a smart technology driven arms race. With wisdom, a deep understanding of reality and the systems that we have created, and proper use of our ever increasing smart technology toolbox, we have the opportunity to re-engineer and calibrate a more equitable, safe, and prosperous world where we not only see economic growth and other positive effects of intelligent automation, labor productivity enhancement, and innovation diffusion, but also decentralized smart technology-driven governance, meaningful work and relationships, people incentivized to make positive contributions to society, and a new type of sharing economy that benefits humanity as a whole.

My massive transformative purpose is to help shape a better future in the Smart Technology Era, and specifically to help business and society thrive in this incredibly disruptive fast changing period where the fusion of multiple exponential technologies is impacting all industries, disciplines, and economies. As a smart technology entrepreneur and ecosystem builder, I have been fortunate to not only have my whole career so far shaped by AI and related smart technologies but witnessed firsthand the transformative impact of AI on real-world applications for more than two decades through my business ventures (helping to operationalize AI for enterprises to increase revenues, reduce risks and save costs as well as AI-driven platforms for health and financial wellness). Apart from the wonderful learning experience and having experienced the world moving from an AI winter period to the incredible hype of the so-called AI era, it has been a rewarding career so far that started as an AI researcher and academic before embarking on my entrepreneurial journey in applying AI and Machine Learning across multiple industries around the globe.

It is important for me to have a mission that matters. Passion is absolutely key to forward progress. When the going gets tough, will we push on or give up? Even in my little corner of the world, how can I apply my skills, experience, knowledge, and talent to make a meaningful contribution? I have been passionate about AI and its applications for a long time. The journey began at Stellenbosch University where I also did my Ph.D. and M.Sc. in AI and Machine Learning and started to collaborate with a broad spectrum of researchers to apply AI and Machine Learning across various disciplines such as Computer Science, Chemical Engineering, Electronic Engineering, Business School, and Psychiatry (the latter which, amongst others, led to *Neural Networks and Psychopathology*, a book published by Cambridge University Press)[2]. But it was only after spending 14 years at CSense Systems, my first AI company that I co-founded in 1998, where I have been directly involved in developing and delivering impactful AI software solutions in a number of industries (e.g., minerals, metals and mining, manufacturing, semiconductors, food and beverages, financial services sector, etc.), to clients in Europe, North America, South America, Africa, and Australia in collaboration with our international reseller and solution partner network. I then already realized that AI is an exponential technology that can not only help businesses thrive, but also be used to help shape a better society for everyone. After selling CSense Systems to General Electric in 2011 (as far as I know it was the first AI company on the African continent sold to a multinational corporate) and gaining some more multinational corporate experience and Silicon Valley exposure at GE as Big Data and Analytics Leader and Director of GE Intelligent Platforms, as well as at Jumo in executive management capacity to help build the next generation mobile money marketplace in Africa and other emerging markets in Asia, I had time to reflect on my next entrepreneurial move that is driven by a massive transformative purpose that matters - helping business and society thrive in the Smart Technology Era. I had opportunities to do this in Silicon Valley but got inspired by some visionary leaders in Africa and people at the World Economic Forum to continue my entrepreneurial journey to help transform Africa (and contribute to ensuring that the continent and its people is not left behind) through Smart Technologies such as AI and building AI communities and exponential organizations to help accelerate the transformation and from there rollout solutions globally (as we have done with CSense Systems). As a result, in 2016, I founded Cortex Logic, as next generation AI and smart technology solutions provider that operationalizes state-of-the-art AI in an end-to-end fashion, which now forms part of the Cortex Group that besides AI solutions for enterprises also builds scalable platform businesses that disrupt traditional value chains in healthcare and finance. At the same time, I also founded the Machine Intelligence Institute of Africa

(MIIA) as a non-profit organization to be an innovative community and accelerator for AI and Data Science Research and Applications to help transform Africa. These are all vehicles to contribute to help shape that better future in the Smart Technology Era.

So, what is the Smart Technology Era? It is my term for the fourth industrial revolution (4IR), which builds on the third, the digital revolution, to amongst others, create smart automation and is characterized by the fusion of new smart technologies that are "blurring the lines between the physical, biological and digital worlds" as mentioned by Prof Klaus Schwab, founder of the World Economic Forum.[3] The 4IR effectively has a global impact that touches all aspects of business, government and society, and even challenging ideas about what it means to be human as we will explore in a later chapter. Whereas the first industrial revolution used water and steam power to mechanize production and the second used electric power to create mass production, the digital revolution used electronics and information technology to automate production. What we now see in the smart technology revolution, is the exponential speed of technology change and breakthroughs which has no historical precedent, disruption in almost every industry in every country, and the transformation of entire systems of production, management, and governance. To help shape this better future we need a collective, integrated, and comprehensive response that involves all stakeholders of the global system of governing, from the private and public sectors to civil society and academia. In this book I am arguing for a more decentralized beneficial human-centric future where AI and its benefits can be democratized to as many people as possible. I have also proposed a massive transformative purpose for humanity and associated goals that complement the United Nations' 2030 vision and sustainable development goals to help shape a beneficial human-centric future in a decentralized hyperconnected world. As a practical step towards a building block in support of this purpose and goals, I am introducing here an initiative and an invitation to people around globe to participate in the development, deployment and use of a *decentralized, human-centric, and user-controlled AI-driven super platform* called *Sapiens*.

I also mentioned shaping a "better future", but what does this mean in the context of the Smart Technology Era? Given the current trajectory and path that we are on, what does a good outcome for humanity look like within, say, the next 20, 50 or 100 years to really set us up for beneficial outcomes for the centuries and millennia ahead? This book explores some likely outcomes and potential ways to get there, with a specific focus on shaping AI and its applications to be human-centric and beneficial for homo sapiens and life on Earth. It is reasonable to assume that we are not going to get the smart technology future that we dream of or the one that we fear, but the one we plan for. That is where the massive transformative purpose for humanity and goals fits in. As Ray Dalio says, "Truth - or, more precisely, an accurate understanding of reality - is the essential foundation for any good outcome".[4] It is important to have dreams, but it needs to be grounded in reality, molded by collective intelligence and wisdom, and converted into clear realistic goals and plans that can be relentlessly executed in an adaptive and agile fashion with passion and determination. That would lead us to success.

We therefore also need to be hyper realists and make sure that we have a good grasp of the current reality and trajectories that we are on with respect to smart technologies such as AI and its applications. To put ourselves in the best possible position to be visionary, practical and wise as we plan and build this "better future", we need to make individually and collectively sense of our current phase of civilization, AI as key exponential technology in the Smart Technology Era, how current business enterprises are becoming digitally transformed and AI-driven, how AI is currently impacting and disrupting all industries and business sectors, the current impact of AI on society and the public sector, as well as the progress and likely future paths of AI. Furthermore, as part of this sense-making journey, we need to consider what it means to be human and living meaningful in the twenty first century, we need to understand the problematic trajectory of our current civilization, analyze issues and ideas for reshaping our civilization for beneficial outcomes, and understand the various potential outcomes for the future of civilization given the current information that we have. We therefore also need to develop a deeper understanding of the risks that we are facing on this planet. Apart from job loss due to technology disruption and technology risks such as hostile artificial intelligence and destructive biotechnology or nanotechnology, we are also confronted by other potential global anthropogenic risks such as those within the domain of earth system governance (such as global warming, extinction of species, environmental degradation, human overpopulation, famine as a result of non-equitable resource distribution, non-sustainable agriculture and crop failures) and harmful or inadequate global governance in the social and political domain (such as nuclear holocaust, cyberterrorism destroying critical infrastructure like the electrical grid, bioterrorism using genetically modified organisms, or the failure to manage a natural pandemic of which COVID-19 is at the very least a painful example that caught civilization by surprise and where our success in handling the pandemic varied significantly across the planet). We also need to be a lot more agile. In a Forbes article, *Why Only the Agile will Survive,* the COVID-19 pandemic is described as a crisis that both accelerate positive and negative trends, will likely have significant repercussions on an economic, political, social, biological, and moral level for many years to come, and will require continuous agility to adapt to the new way of interacting, learning, working, playing, leading, and living.[5] The same holds for AI's transformative impact on society, business and the public sector.

So, although the aim of the book is to help with the drive towards democratizing AI and its applications to maximize the beneficial outcomes for humanity, a big part of the book has also been dedicated to this sense-making journey as a foundation for democratizing AI and to more accurately understand where we are heading given all the current dynamics on a global and national economic and political level as well as across ideologies, industries, and businesses. There is lot of fantastic thought leadership, information, ideas, and research out there that we can tap into and benefit from if we can properly synthesize the material, make sense of it, be clear about what we want to achieve, plan properly, collaborate and then execute. This book therefore also acts as a filter on those thoughts, information, ideas, and research to enable as many people as possible to not only interpret and make sense of this, but also participate in helping shape a better future for ourselves, our children and humanity going forward. It also provides a snapshot of our current reality across the spectrum and the varied insightful opinions out there. Where relevant and in the spirit of decentralized knowledge sharing and sense-making, I also highlight or emphasize certain perspectives from some of the best resourced research and consulting organizations and thought leaders as well as ideas and thoughts from people that might not be well known in many circles but have important perspectives that needs to be considered as part of synthesizing a more balanced view. To get a proper grip on and understanding of other people's point of view, it is important to steel man their opinions instead of straw manning it. In this book I share many different perspectives on AI's impact on society and its potential benefits, risks, concerns, challenges, progress, lessons learnt, limitations, future paths, and research priorities. One example is making sense of the debates on AI's future path and impact on humanity, which is like a roller-coaster ride of disparate ideas and thoughts from a wide spectrum of experts and people of all walks of life and driven by a combination of trepidation and enthusiasm about the monumental risks and opportunities that AI presents in the 21st century and beyond. I also share specific solutions to address AI's potential negative impacts, designing AI for social good and beneficial outcomes, building human-compatible AI that is ethical and trustworthy, addressing bias and discrimination, and the skills and competencies needed for a human-centric AI-driven workplace.

We all have many questions surrounding smart technology. We want to know what it is, how it is being used, how it affects us. But we are missing something rather important, something that we need to ask before the "what's" and "how's" of AI can have any meaning to us. We need to know why. Why should we care? Why should we embrace AI? Why should we buy into it enough to care about what it is and how it is being used and what it can do for us? Smart technology of which AI is a major building block are our latest tools. We can essentially use these tools to achieve any goal we set our mind on. We can incorporate them into most businesses, products, services, and offerings - replacing the old materials, processes or tools or imagining completely new solutions because of the new tools at our disposal. This still does not tackle the question of why. The general why - not an organizational sense of why which may involve wanting to offer affordable transport or to change the way people travel. In these instances, what the organization does may change each time there is a new idea or new tool that allows the organization to keep fulfilling their sense of why.[6] Using the latest tools is usually a given for organizations with a strong sense of why. The new tool will allow them to achieve their purpose more effectively. They are less focused on what they do and more on why they do it, so when there is another way to achieve why they do it, the natural choice is to explore it. Ask them why they would use AI and other smart technologies and they will likely tell you it is because these new tools offer them new opportunities to expand on, create, transform, or simplify their offering. Again, they are less focused on what they do and more focused on why they do it, and in this innovation and change do not scare them. Changing what they do may take time and will likely require effort, trial and error and an interesting journey, but as long as they are inspired by why they are doing it, this is all worth it. Without a guiding purpose, changing what we do is difficult. We are comfortable in what we do, in how we live our lives and how we recognize and place the world around us. If change is forced on us, of course it will be our instinct to reject it. Especially if this change threatens to uproot our sense of reality and comfort. Especially when this change affects our daily lives, the processes we are used to, the jobs and tasks we are used to, the products and interactions we are used to. So, what we need when it comes to AI and smart technology, and all the changes to reality that we face, is a strong sense of why. Why change?

When we are focused on what we do and what our routine is and what we are used to and what reality looks like, change is often unwelcome. When we are focused on why we exist, on our life's purpose on why we started that company or why we go work for this company or why we even bother getting out of bed in the morning then what we do matters less. We will follow, advance, and even chase whatever fulfills our sense of why. For why people, change may not be easy, but it is a part of life. So, why start using or developing AI?

Because it is a tool to help you achieve your why. AI is one of the most incredible tools at our disposal to shape the world we want. Forget innovation or development or transformation. Forget all the fancy words you have been hearing and the fear they may bring to the surface and think about why you get up in the morning. For some it is to ensure their families are always safe and happy. For some it is to see equality and freedom; see an end to poverty and desperation and a rise in opportunities for all people. For some it is growth, for some love, for some connection. For some it is solving problems that make life better and easier. For some it is having more time to revel in and enjoy the wonders of life. Whoever you are, whatever you want from the world, you are either seeking to be happy with what you have or to have more or better of what you have and what you see around you (sometimes implying less of the horrors or sadness's you face). What does this have to do with smart technology? Everything. Smart technologies are the tools we have to help us improve, solve, and develop everything we have ever dreamed. And without understanding, embracing, and directing smart technology and where we apply it, we are merely ignoring an almost miraculous way to actualize our whys. AI and its counterparts can leapfrog socio-economic development and inclusion, instill transparency in the systems we have lost faith in, insist on public service delivery, allow us to protect, preserve and save our natural resources, exponentially improve access to education, enhance and automate business intelligence, personalize our education, consumption and tasks and free up time for the more important things in life - the things we can really only get from other humans - love, commitment, meaningful communication and community.

Also, no one wants to be left behind. The more we fear the changes that the Smart Technology Era brings, the more we reject it. The more we reject it, the more we are at risk of being left behind and the more we leave it up to others to dictate where society is going. Without knowledge, we cannot be a part of the discussions, solutions, developments, and changes that are coming anyway. We fear becoming irrelevant or of things too fast for our sense of comfort, but by rejecting something that is coming anyway, we are ensuring exactly that. Now that we know why, we must empower ourselves with the knowledge and thinking that will shape our future. We now need to ask specific questions related to AI - starting with the simplest and culminating in the deep or complex; like how to create laws surrounding AI or how organizations and people can adopt it. In this book, the aim is to not only understand AI's transformative powers, benefits, risks, and future direction, but explore the beneficial outcomes that we want for humanity, a vision of the future, real projections forward, real smart technology-driven solutions, and how we can address the problems that prevent us from achieving beneficial outcomes for humanity. In this, we ask our own questions, offer an analysis that aims to diagnose and a framework to propel action and solve problems on multiple levels. To do this, first, we must ensure we are deeply thinking about the questions that may set the world on a path to a sustainable future. We ask and answer the questions that the world is asking, in this way, and the questions we do not yet know to ask. Each chapter of this book will directly or indirectly ask and answer a few questions, which carry different levels of depth and various purposes. Sometimes, the aim is simply to provide information for background purposes, sometimes to explain why it matters and provide several vantage points for sense-making and sometimes it is to challenge. Throughout, the aim of this book and the questions it tackles are to help guide every leader, every problem solver, and every individual towards a fruitful, ethical, sustainable, and beneficial human-centric future and democratizing AI to benefit everyone.

Although I have tried to keep the content throughout the book at a level that is simple enough for layman's understanding, there might be some sections in some of the chapters that are slightly more technical and information rich that can be skipped for readers that choose to do so. The key is to get an overall sense of where we currently are on our AI journey as a civilization so that we can maximize participation of as many people as possible to help shape that better future that we collectively want for ourselves and humanity.

In the next chapter, I focus on the Smart Technology Era to give a broader perspective of where AI fits in with respect to our past and current revolutions and start thinking about some of the challenges and rewards that AI presents in this new era. In Chapter 3 the focus is on AI as key exponential technology and how it is transforming our world in the Smart Technology Era. It also provides a brief historical overview of AI, which is followed by an unpacking of AI in terms of its many subfields, the man-machine intelligence continuum with respect to assisted, augmented, and autonomous intelligence, and how AI relates to the Internet of Things, blockchain and the future of computing. The chapter is concluded with a section on our responsibility in directing AI for beneficial outcomes. Chapter 4 does a deep dive into what AI-driven digital transformation of the business enterprise looks like, discussing the importance of being agile, how AI solutions and technology partners can help accelerate companies on their AI-driven transformation journeys, and how AI is changing business processes. AI's significant impact on the workplace, employment, and the job market is discussed next along with AI-driven human-computer interfaces such as intelligent virtual assistants that are becoming the new face of customer-centric businesses and customer services. As cybersecurity is becoming an increasing risk especially as business are becoming more digitized, AI has a huge role to play to help defend against a spectrum of evolving cyber-attacks that might also be AI-driven. The focal point of the next three chapters 5, 6, and 7 is on AI applications across multiple industries. Whereas Chapter 5 highlights how AI is revolutionizing personalized engagement and other applications for consumer facing businesses, Chapter 6 gives an overview of AI-powered process and equipment enhancement and other applications across the industrial world. Chapter 5 specifically considers AI's comprehensive impact on financial services, retail, ecommerce, telecommunications, media, entertainment, transportation, travel, and tourism. Chapter 6 examines the impact of AI on utilities and the energy sector, as well as AI applications in resources, manufacturing, and agriculture. Chapter 7 explores AI applications in key areas of civilization namely education, healthcare, and wellness, and specifically how AI is transforming these sectors as they become more instrumented which in turn enables better personalization and accuracy in the delivery of tailor-made solutions. Chapter 8 considers AI's impact on society, governments, and the public sector, the potential benefits of AI for society and social good, as well as the risks, concerns, and challenges of AI for society. This chapter is concluded by showcasing some AI applications in the public sector, and an overview of governmental AI strategies, policies, and adoption across the globe. In Chapter 9, I am making sense of the AI debates on AI's future path and impact on humanity, a fascinating comparison of human intelligence versus machine intelligence, AI lessons learnt, and the limitations of the current AI technology. I conclude that chapter with an overview of the current state-of-the-art AI techniques and the progress, research priorities, and likely future paths of AI. All these chapters are laying the foundations for the next three chapters which is the crescendo of this book and discusses beneficial outcomes for humanity, democratizing AI to help shape a beneficial human-centric future, and introducing Sapiens, the human-centric user-controlled AI-driven super platform for humanity. Chapter 10 specifically explores what it means to be human and living meaningful in the 21st century, the problematic trajectory of our current civilization, issues, and ideas for reshaping our civilization for beneficial outcomes, and various potential outcomes for the future of Civilization. That chapter is then wrapped up by discussing beneficial outcomes for humanity and introducing a proposed massive transformative purpose for humanity and its associated smart goals that complement the United Nations' 2030 vision and sustainable development goals. In Chapter 11 various aspects of democratizing AI to help shape a beneficial human-centric future is unpacked such as solutions to address AI's potential negative impacts, a framework for strategic planning, designing AI for social good and beneficial outcomes, building human-compatible, ethical, trustworthy, and beneficial AI, addressing bias and discrimination, and the required skills, competencies, and jobs for a human-centric AI-driven workplace. The final chapter concludes with an introduction and invitation to people around globe to participate in the development, deployment and use of Sapiens, a decentralized human-centric user-controlled AI-driven super platform with personalized AI agents that not only empower individuals and monetizes their data and services, but can also be extended broader to communities, businesses, and city-states. In the Appendix I highlight a specific project of the Machine Intelligence Institute of Africa (MIIA) on democratizing human-centric AI in Africa.

2. The Smart Technology Era is Here

Before highlighting how AI is transforming the world, let us dig into the Smart Technology Era that we have entered. One of the amazing things about this time, which already has a significant impact on our lives, is that it has only just begun. Each adult and even each teenager has grown up in a relatively different time to the Era that has just begun. Of course, teenagers will experience less of an adjustment because they were not born in a time where dial-up internet or even no internet was a part of their realities. They have not experienced the changes that personal technology and digitization brought. They were simply born into a time where they already existed. They were born into a digital world where digital interactions and transactions are relatively commonplace in most parts of the developed world. This aptitude for digital life might make the changes that are coming simpler to adopt and consume, but this does not mean that these changes will be small, and it does not mean that they will be slow. In fact, they are coming fast. Faster than we have ever seen before. These smart technologies like nanotechnology, robots, IoT, drones and intelligent, cognitive machines, all used in conjunction and powered by the speed and processing abilities of advanced technology, cloud technology and huge amounts of online data available, are all coming together to give us the tools dreamed possible in Science Fiction. These tools, as will be described in detail throughout this book, are the enablers to transform the world. Of course, we cannot predict the future, but we can steer it intentionally in a direction that can help, protect, and enhance all life. To do this, however, we need an accurate understanding of where we are. We need to be informed, empowered to learn from history and equipped with how fast and with how much range these changes are coming. In the broader context, the human revolutions started with the cognitive revolution about 50-80,000 years ago with communications skills. This was followed by the agricultural revolution 12,000 years ago when foragers turned into farmers, humans gained mastery over animals and the rise of cities. With the industrial revolution coupled with the enlightenment and scientific method, homo sapiens started to gain mastery over the planet which led to ending the perpetual tyranny of famine, starvation, and extreme poverty. We are currently in an information revolution, where smart technologies such as AI will likely ensure more profound impacts than any of the other major human revolutions.

Let us begin by understanding history and using this as a way to help us place ourselves in the Transformation that has begun - the Smart Technology Transformation. Of course, this transformation has been given many names or is discussed in various contexts. Klaus Schwab, of the WEF, calls it IR4 or the 4th Industrial Revolution. Steve Case calls it the 3rd Internet Wave.[1] *The Economic Singularity*'s Calum Chace discusses this new transformation within the context of the Information Revolution where the dramatic growth in the capability of AI leads first to an economic singularity and then possibly a technological singularity.[2] Yuval Harari, in *Sapiens, Homo Deus* and *21 Lessons for the 21st Century*, discusses the twin revolutions in information technology and biotechnology within the context of the Scientific Revolution.[3] Richard Baldwin calls it *The Globotics Transformation*.[4] Erik Brynjolfsson and Andrew McAfee call it *The 2nd Machine Age* which started with the Digital and Information Revolution.[5] Each of the names given to the Era that has just begun are all in relation to the transformations or revolutions that preceded them. And each transformation or revolution in history has affected not only work and production, but agriculture, politics, economics, social climates, and the very way people go about their lives. We know these best as the 1st, 2nd and 3rd Industrial Revolutions throughout which globalization and automation have been creeping their way into our existence. We may have started off as local, rural, community driven creatures, more focused on our immediate survival and trading only what was immediately available in our proximity, but with each transformation we became more globalized, more connected and tasks, processes and services became increasingly more automated.

Let us take a brief look at the history of the revolutions or transformations over the last few centuries that have led us to where we are today:

- The First Transformation (the start of the Industrial Revolution) used technologies such as water and steam power to mechanize production. This began in the early 1700s where societies effectively switched from agriculture to industrial and from rural to urban. From 1712 onwards, we saw for example the age of primitive steam engines, textile manufacturing machines, and the canals, whereas from 1830 onwards the age of mobile steam engines and the railways. These technologies (along with electricity soon thereafter) unleashed the disruptive duo of automation and globalization which led to an economic transformation and economic and social upheavals. However, technology impulses launched new forms of automation long before they launched new forms of globalization (a century later) where we for example saw steamships and railroads dramatically reduced the cost of moving goods.

- The Second Transformation used electric power to create mass production. This began in the late 1800s, where we saw the age of steel and heavy engineering and the birth of the chemicals industry and from 1910 onwards the age of electricity, oil, mass production, cars, planes, and mass travel. During the second industrial revolution we witnessed how technology produced technology with a cluster bomb of innovations on the advanced economies where each explosion produced a chain reaction of innovation, rising productivity, and income growth.[6]

- The Third used electronics and information technology to automate production and connect the world. The digital revolution turned analogue to digital and began around the 1950s and led to the Services Transformation which for all practical purposes started in the early 1970s. Whereas the past globalization and automation is mostly about making and shipping goods, globalization and automation in the Services Transformation is about processing and transmitting information (that is linked to the laws of physics that apply to electrons and photons, and not matter which is more restrained). We have effectively moved from things (which includes land to capital) to thoughts. Computers and other digital devices are doing for mental power (ability to use our brains to understand and shape our environments) what the steam engine and its descendants did for muscle power. Information and knowledge became increasingly important factors of production (alongside capital, labor, and raw materials) and acquired economic value in its own right. Although the industrial revolution is still ongoing, there was a shift in focus from industry to services, which mostly disrupted the manufacturing sector. Services became the mainstay of the overall economy, pushing manufacturing into second place and agriculture into third.

- And the Fourth Transformation, the Smart Technology Era, is building on the information and digital revolution to not only create smart automation, but new forms of globalization and robotics that taps into a wild combination of smart technologies where the distinction between the digital, physical, and biological realms are not clear. We can probably date this back to 2010s (although the exact times will likely be dictated by history books of the future). Richard Baldwin has coined these new forms of globalization and robotics into a new word called "globotics", where tele-migrants and white-collar robots coming for the same jobs at the same time are driven by the same digital technologies. This globotics transformation applied to the services sector has an amazingly fast and unfair impact on societies, effectively disrupting the services sector in a significant way. The result is an upheaval, a so-called Globotics Upheaval, and a backlash for which we need a resolution.

It is interesting to note that some of today's thought leaders do not see these transformations or revolutions as broken up into four. Calum Chace, author of *The Economic Singularity* believes that there have only been two real Revolutions in modern times.[7] The first one that began in the 1700s and evolved as the domino effects saw one revelation or invention leading to another and then another. The second revolution was an Information Revolution that began when information and knowledge became such important parts of production and services, that it pushed manufacturing and agriculture into second and third places, respectively.[8] That began with the age of computing - the digital revolution if you would like to call it that. On the other hand, Erik Brynjolfsson and Andrew McAfee in *The Second Machine Age* believes that we can look at the transformations in modern history as divided between the 1st Machine Age (also beginning with the steam engine in the early 1700s) and the Second Machine Age where computers, digital devices and the flux of information changed the very nature of our existence yet again.[9] Jeremy Rifkin, in *The Third Industrial Revolution*, divides the world's transformations into three.[10] The First Industrial Revolution, powered by the steam engine, took us from rural into urban. The Second Industrial Revolution changed the landscape of urban life with the telephone, fossil fuels and automobiles and the aspirational Third Industrial Revolution which is unfolding with the convergence of ultra-fast 5G communication technologies, a renewable energy internet and driverless mobility internet all connected by IoT. He is advocating for a 21st century smart digital infrastructure to give rise to a radical new sharing economy that is transforming how we manage, power, and move economic life.

There is much to learn from the patterns of previous transformations (call them industrial, economic or technological revolutions); from the developments that changed the course of the world and left those who feared, rejected or were geographically or economically sidelined in, what Richard Baldwin, calls "upheaval".[11] Whatever the defining nature of our revolutions, whether they have been seen to be primarily production-based, services-based and now, information-based - upheaval is one thing that they have in common. Their domino effects are predictable because of how these changes (in what may seem to affect only one industry in the beginning) spread into every part of life. This common factor of economic, social, or political upheaval is an important thing to note, as it reminds us that what is happening now has happened before in some way. But our urgency to understand this now is greater than it ever was before because our technological advances and powers mean that the speed of these changes, and their capacity to spread into every part of our existence means that there is no time not to be thinking about solutions, ways to manage these changes smoothly and the parts we will play in steering the information-powered Smart Technology Era. The commonly termed Industrial Revolutions have been a whole lot more than industrial. Yes, they have transformed industries, but they have also transformed economies, politics, societies, and individual lives.[12] They have changed the world as we know it and presented an entirely different one. Sometimes the new world has taken centuries to shape, but as we become more developed, the time it takes for revolutions to affect mass change grows smaller.

Understanding the Past

Generally, revolutions begin with a technology, discovery or invention offering a new solution that changes how an industry or industries worked, sometimes, with time, rendering entire industries obsolete. This has economic and social effects - making some skills, services, or products irrelevant. Also, with the effects of the invention and its application, we are given new ways to live as well. Our daily lives are disrupted by the new overtaking or replacing the old. Some businesses and people thrive, and others become overwhelmed, left behind, socially and economically sidelined and worse - irrelevant. Richard Baldwin puts it well when he explains the effects of Revolutions: with all the above-mentioned social and economic upheaval experienced, people's lives are in flux. The upheaval then produces a backlash, and the backlash produces a resolution. This is what we have seen in past revolutions and what we can expect to see from this revolution.[13] We must remember that the end result is resolution, and it is up to us how quickly or slowly we find this resolution in the Revolution that we are currently facing. To explain this a bit better, let us briefly look at each Revolution in terms of what the world has called Industrial Revolutions, but as we know saw simultaneous revolutions agriculturally, economically, politically, socially, and even informationally.[14]

The early 1700s was a time where societies were broken up into small communities. Few traveled outside of their villages and life was strictly localized, rural, and agricultural. Many people grew or made what they needed, and trading services, products or food were common. Life was simple. It was stagnant. Class (or Caste) systems dictated the extent of wealth and rights and religion was deeply entrenched into people's lives and communities. Church and State were often one and the same. This life was far from perfect and many were desperate with hunger, suffering prejudices (which were not yet seen as prejudices) and lacking knowledge, education and knew little of what surrounded their immediate environments. A revolution was brewing which would use steam and water to power steam engines and textile manufacturing machines that suddenly allowed transport, travel, production, and trade to happen more quickly, easily and frequently.[15] This meant that what used to require one person to work tirelessly for days to produce a garment could now happen in an hour and what used to require a horse to travel for days to reach the next village, could now happen in three hours.

The skills that kept people's families fed were growing obsolete as a factory that produced whatever one soul used to produce could reach villages with an abundance of product in record time. By 1770 this was becoming even more prominent and beginning to include more industries. Because less time and effort were required to produce goods, they were cheaper coming out of factories. In farming, too, the new use of technology eliminated the need for as many people to complete the work. People no longer needed to farm for themselves, selling whatever was leftover to their villages. The rise of machines, as material became cheaper to produce (with metal and steel instead of wood), meant that what used to rely on a human to slowly and delicately produce, create, distribute or harvest was replaced by machines and distributed across countries. The lives people had known had changed and the jobs they relied on were slinking out of existence. Professions did not necessarily change. Farming, for example, was still an occupation but the jobs involved in the profession were different.[16] Many people were left in disarray because the world they had known and relied on to survive was changing and they did not know how to change with it.

Globalization had begun. It was not the globalization we experience today, but the world was made smaller due to machine powered transport, distribution, and production. Local, small-scale businesses suffered further as development increased and improved. Trade was quicker and easier; information and cultures were spreading and merging. Life, for the masses, was in economic and social upheaval where job loss meant poverty and starvation for landless workers whilst industrialization progressed in a rapid and unguided fashion. Over time, with the spread of new technologies and more inventions and combinations of inventions, the world became increasingly industrialized. Capitalism and libertarianism ruled, and the rich continued to get richer while the poor became poorer. Factory jobs may have been in excess but pay was terrible. It was because it could be. There really was not much alternative so those who had jobs had to choose between terrible conditions where they barely got paid or have no job at all. No job at all was not an option as the revolution meant that the only way to get food was through money, and the only way to get money was to work. Gone was a time when people could grow their own food. They simply did not have the land, the means, and even the skills they once had were lost and overrun by menial factory work.[17]

As you can imagine, this saw a rise in populist, alternative movements, extreme solutions, and parties who could rally the downtrodden in hope to change their lives. Fascism, Nazism, Communism and even war all seemed like better alternatives to the lives most people were living. This is what is known, to Richard Baldwin as a "Backlash" to the prevailing Upheaval brought on by the "Transformation".[18] It is people taking a stand against the lives that were shoved on them that they never asked for, did not want, and felt as if they had no control over. In Britain, the early backlash was seen via the Luddites and the implementation of the Corn laws, whereas the more major backlash was later seen in the form of Fascism, Communism, and New Deal Capitalism. In post-World-War-Two Europe, America, and part of Asia - when neither Fascism, Communism, Nazism nor war had solved anything for anyone - it was back on the capitalist, libertarian ruling parties to make things better for their citizens. Slowly but surely, laws and policies were introduced, and means were taken to ensure that working conditions were better, the state protected its citizens and minimum wages were acceptable. The world became better for most First World countries who were ready and able to ensure that the rich getting richer did not also mean that the poor get poorer. This time of stability is what Baldwin calls "Resolution" as illustrated by 30 glory years (1940-1970) initiated by Franklin D. Roosevelt's New Deal Capitalism.[19]

With the introduction of the personal computer, the internet and all the wonderful little tools that allowed us to use these to work, connect with others and close even more gaps that offices, cities, countries and even continents created, we experienced a new kind of revolution. A technological revolution; a services transformation.[20] Digitization made it, so we never had to be in the same place to meet with someone or exchange services. It made it so we were less reliant on physical proximity to not only trade (as the previous Transformation had ensured) but to exchange knowledge, expertise, and professional services. It also made it so previously manual tasks were automated through digitization. As we became less reliant on paper, data capturing, storing, and sorting, robots could perform the manual tasks that previously relied on humans (mostly in factories) and those with access started to live and function largely in an online space.

Then we experienced another change. A change that would, as all transformations do, feed off the developments, creations and changes that the previous transformation set in place. This change would begin what we call the Smart Technology Era, and it began in the 2010s. While we may think that the Fourth Transformation is just part of the Third Transformation, we would be mistaken. There are several reasons for this, but the main one is that while digital technology certainly transformed the world, Smart Technology transforms it in tremendously different ways. We are talking about a difference between progressive developments and improvements and total disruption. A new form of globalization via tele-migrants and AI-driven automation via machine learning based applications and robotic process automation acting as white-collar robots are coming for the same white-collar jobs at the same time. The industrial revolution automated manual work and the Information revolution did the same for mental or intellectual work, but AI via machine learning automates automation itself. The ability for machines to automate decision making and not just be told or programmed to follow a set of rules, is an incredible feat for humanity and has completely changed the game. We no longer need the long hours, manpower and physical structures we once needed to do anything from running a business to curing a disease to providing services to citizens. The way we think about money, work, law, trade, and services is likely going to be made redundant by disruption. Calum Chace calls this a singularity which is a state where the laws and rules of reality no longer apply or at least completely changes the rules that we are used to.[21] It is not mere progress or incremental improvements, and not just for one industry. We will need to reimagine (all over again) how we live, what work we do and all the centralized institutions and accepted processes and industries that we are used to. More on this later. For now, let us focus on why and how The Smart Technology Era is separate from the revolution that computers and the internet gave us.

The Smart Technology Era

Although machine intelligence has been with us for many decades, it has only over the last decade or so begun to erupt in all parts of society, causing mass effect and a significant transformation because of harnessing not only an abundance of data, but also the speed, scope, and processing power that computing technology enables. *Scope* speaks to the fact that any development can be used and duplicated around the world faster than ever - also as a result of speed and processing power. This speaks to the impact that a system developed for seamless virtual banking, for example, can be used in a government on the other side of the world. This means that AI is disrupting almost every industry and every country. *Speed* has to do with the fact that the amount of time it used to take to teach or program a system is significantly faster due to non-reliance on humans throughout the process. Once a machine learning model has been sufficiently trained it can be deployed and then executed without human intervention to automate classification, prediction, optimization, and decision-making tasks. This allows the humans to work with the outputs and insights produced by such an AI-driven system and focus more on other human-centric tasks such as sales, marketing, and business strategies. *Processing power*, being as exceptional as it is, and cloud technology replacing on-premises hardware at scale, means that highly complex algorithms can work at record speed, across the world, and from what we have seen with scope, can then be used in so many ways and for different needs. What this means is that technology is smarter than ever, learning faster than ever, changing faster than ever, and traveling across the world and industries faster than ever. This is the Smart Technology Era.

The dramatic growth in capability of AI, machine learning, IoT, robotics, drone technology, nanotechnology, quantum computing, advanced internet, biotechnology, blockchain, cryptocurrency, and 3-D printing are all coming together and literally changing the world as we know it before our eyes. Our access to knowledge is unlimited, thanks to the previous transformation, our access to work and learning across borders without traveling there is unlimited due to the previous transformation. And all we really need to access these wonders and offerings of the Smart Technology Era is a Smart Phone and Wi-Fi. One thing that is as clear in this transformation as in the others is that access is unequal and so the effects are unequal. In our already unequal world, this is something that should scare us. However, due to all these technologies and their immense capabilities, we have ways to leapfrog socio-economic development and provide people with equal access to services, knowledge and basic rights that were never available or possible to us before. Speed, scope, and processing power mean that we really can change the whole world, and we can change it quickly. We just must know how. We must ask the right questions, focus on inclusive solutions, and prioritize equal opportunity and fairness in our thinking.

We do not yet know just how it will unfold. This is only the beginning. But we do know how the previous Transformations affected the world, politics, economics, societies, industries, and individual lives, and in this we can learn what not to do. Only we must do this quickly, because as we have discovered, this Transformation is happening with a speed that we could have never imagined in the past. What is clear to us is that our response to the Smart Technology Era must be integrated and comprehensive, involving all stakeholders of global polity, from the public and private sectors to academia and civil society. The World Economic Forum's Klaus Schwab has been warning us about these changes and their disruption to our very existence for some time: "The changes are so profound that, from the perspective of human history, there has never been a time of greater promise or potential peril. My concern, however, is that decision makers are too often caught in traditional, linear (and non-disruptive) thinking or too absorbed by immediate concerns to think strategically about the forces of disruption and innovation shaping our future." [22]

Already, artificial intelligence is all around us, from self-driving cars and drones to virtual assistants and software that translate or invest. Impressive progress has been made in AI in recent years, driven by exponential increases in computing power and by the availability of vast amounts of data, from software used to discover new drugs to algorithms used to predict our cultural interests. Digital fabrication technologies are interacting with the biological world daily. Engineers, designers, and architects are combining computational design, additive manufacturing, materials engineering, and synthetic biology to pioneer a symbiosis between microorganisms, our bodies, the products we consume, and even the buildings we inhabit. The future is happening around us. And we must rise to the challenge to meet it and thrive in the new industrial revolution. How do we do this? Firstly, we must be empowered with relevant knowledge and have a realistic view of reality. Secondly, we need a framework, guidelines, and active steps we can take to positively use and adopt Smart Technology in businesses and governments. There is no one size fits all solution. That is why it is so important for each of us to be realistic about where we are. Governments in Africa have quite different issues to address and are at a different starting point from governments in Western Europe. The same is true for all companies and industries.

The possibilities of billions of people connected by mobile devices, with unprecedented processing power, storage capacity, and access to knowledge, are unlimited. The possibilities of Smart Technology and Globalization to remove our reliance on physical structures to have access to work, medicine, investments, money, education, professional services, food, and goods are indescribable. This means that it is not only those in established cities who can benefit from this transformation. It is everyone. The exponential increases in computing power, the borderless environment of knowledge, the fusion of blockchain, IoT, AI, nanotechnology and robotics, and the availability of huge amounts of data have allowed us to perform surgeries without relying on surgeons, discover new drugs, predict behaviors, and uncover corruption.

Some of AI's Challenges and Rewards in the Smart Technology Era

Just like with any challenge any one of us may face, the challenges of the Smart Technology Era are not prescriptive for how things will turn out. They are important elements to note, to work to avoid and to fully understand so that we may be prepared. Similarly, the rewards and potential benefits are not prescriptive either. Neither are theoretical dreams that cannot be actualized. When we look at the rewards that AI possesses, we are careful not to be too idealistic, and remain realistic. We look at the rewards that are achievable and can be practically worked towards. We will also outline the practical frameworks to move to this rewarding state in later chapters. First, let us have an initial brief look at the potential challenges and rewards as contrasting states before exploring this in more detail in Chapter 8.

The current Transformation could lead to greater inequality and greater socio-economic exclusion. This could occur particularly in its potential to disrupt labor markets with automation, AI workers and role disappearance.[23] As automation substitutes for labor across the entire economy, the net dislocation of workers by AI might increase the gap between returns to capital and returns to labor. On the flip side, it is also possible that the dislocation of workers by AI will, in total, result in an effective increase in satisfying and safe jobs. In this, the social, economic and information gaps may also increase due to a mere issue of access. Access to information and access to technology (the latter often means access to the former). Like the revolutions that preceded it, the Smart Technology Era has the potential to elevate global income levels and improve the quality of life for populations around the planet. To date, those who have gained the most from it have been consumers able to afford and access the digital world. On the demand side, technology has made possible new products and services that increase the efficiency and pleasure of our personal lives. Buying a product, booking a flight, ordering a cab, making a payment, collaborating with colleagues, listening to music, watching a film, or playing a game—any of these can now be done remotely. In the future, technological innovation will also lead to the supply of so many competing products and services that will continue to continuously improve based on competition pressure, low costs of business as seen with Uber and Airbnb who do not own any of "their assets", and the prompt access to consumers independent of where they are. As communication and transportation costs are going down, trading costs are being reduced, and global supply chains and logistics are becoming more effective, we will likely see more new markets open and economic growth strengthened.

But, as we have seen from previous Transformations, transformation does not happen equally. The already included members of society are usually the ones to reap the rewards of transformation. While this Transformation differs in that it has the potential to displace white collar or socio-economically included members of society, it is still the blue-collar workers and unemployed who are most in danger. It is currently difficult to envisage which scenario is likely to materialize, and history indicates that the outcome is likely to be some combination of the two. However, with all our access to knowledge and information, we are equipped to understand our history and to see where we went wrong. Yuval Harari, Richard Baldwin, Calum Chace, and many others have dedicated themselves to this understanding so that we may better understand how to tackle the Transformation that has begun underneath us.[24] It is also becoming more evident that talented people using their knowledge, expertise and skills in creative and innovative fashion will likely be a more vital factor of production in the future than just pure capital. This could bring about an increasingly partitioned job market split into "high-skill/high-pay" and "low-skill/low-pay" segments, which brings about economic and social upheaval in the form of uncertain employment opportunities and an increase in social tension and discontentment. Others say that the entire economic system will and should be reimagined. In his book *The Economic Singularity*, Calum Chace discusses a forthcoming system that looks much different to our current one, where AI is changing and will continue to change the world so fast, that the social, political, and economic rules that shape our societies will no longer apply. They simply will not work in our future.[25] *Radical Markets*, by Eric Posner and Glen Weyl discuss one potential future which I elaborate more on in Chapter 10 along with other ideas, while many others debate and write about what we will have to change in order to adapt and ensure the flourishing of earth and humanity.[26] Without intentional steps towards how we are creating and using smart technologies, and how we can deconstruct economics and society to fit into our new world, we are in danger of repeating the upheaval and deepened inequality left to us in our previous Transformation. Whilst being a key economic concern, inequality represents one of the most intense social concerns of the Smart Technology Era. The largest beneficiaries of innovation tend to be the providers of physical and intellectual capital - the innovators, shareholders, and investors - which explains the growing gap in wealth between those dependent on capital versus labor. Technology is therefore one of the main reasons why incomes have become flat or even decreased in relative terms for most of the populations in high-income countries. The demand for highly skilled workers has increased while the demand for workers with less education and lower skills has decreased. The middle class has also been weakened with a further increase in socio-economic stratification due to labor-saving technologies, outsourcing jobs, and demographic changes. [27] This is also the reason why so many workers are discouraged and frightened that their own real incomes and those of their children will continue to stay flat or that their roles will disappear altogether. It also helps explain why middle classes around the world are increasingly experiencing a prevalent sense of unfairness and dissatisfaction. So, we have two intertwined situations to overcome. The first is the displacement that the technological transformation left us with and the second is the displacement that the AI transformation (Smart Technology Era) has the potential to befall upon us. A winner-takes-all economy, as we are seeing with the quick upswing in tech giant capital and dominance, that offers only restricted access to the middle class is a recipe for democratic despondency and deterioration and a call to rethink social, economic, and political systems. I will expand on this in later chapters.[28]

Our discontent and helplessness do not seem to be lessened by the pervasiveness of digital technologies, information sharing and online 'connection'. With so many ways to be connected to friends, families, communities, brands, movements and strangers, Social Media and any other communication and collaboration applications do not actually result in feelings of emotional and mental connection. In fact, they are more often associated with feelings of increased isolation and anxiety.[29] More than 30 percent of the global population now uses social media platforms to connect, learn, and share information. In an ideal world, these interactions would provide an opportunity for cross-cultural understanding and cohesion. Beyond their impacts on our emotional and mental states, we should also be aware that social media can also create and propagate unrealistic expectations as to what constitutes success for an individual or a group, as well as offer opportunities for extreme ideas and ideologies to spread.

However, being aware of the above and understanding our reality and the potential consequences it brings, we have the potential to ensure that we are taking every measure possible to avoid actualizing the things we fear. Firstly, it is possible that the dislocation of workers and certain roles will result in an increase of secure and fulfilling jobs. We will also see new kinds of work and roles arise for both skilled and unskilled workers. Access to a smartphone allows anyone from anywhere to get paid for labelling the data that the AI needs and interacting with applications to aid the machines in their learning. Furthermore, where robots may take on our more historically dangerous kinds of factory or mining work, humans can support these robots from the sidelines and behind desks. This is not even to mention the historically expensive specialist services and healthcare treatments that, through AI, automation and globalization will become more competitive, and not reliant on physical structures, not tied into high running costs and thus more affordable. The most certain way to ensure a future we would want to be a part of is to create it. It is to take the steps and make the plans that use the tools of the Smart Technology Era to include, protect and uplift all of society. If we fear a future where AI replaces us, let us create one instead where it supports us. It is in our hands to insist that humans can and will work with technology, be supported, and uplifted by technology, and where our humanity always reigns. The first step towards that future is to ensure that every human being on this planet has access to smartphones and the internet. This is more important than buildings and structures that we have focused our attention on in the past. A smartphone or similar device with a human-machine interface gives people access to jobs, education, knowledge, and social and cultural understanding. More than that, it gives people access to commerce. With AI, IoT and drone technology, it gives people access to healthcare, medication, psychiatric help, professional advice and services and the list goes on as we will explore further in the upcoming chapters.

The aim is to make sense of AI and its impact on our world, no matter where we are in our journey with technology and smart technology, and to assist in improving the entire state of the world. Whether we need help accepting AI, automation and globalization, finding ways for people to reap its positive benefits and carefully manage any potentially negative consequences or seeking frameworks for governments and leaders to solve immediate problems, improve services and help its nations, communities and employees manage the changes that the Smart Technology Era brings. We know, based on past revolutions, that without protecting and advancing people while simultaneously devoting ourselves to progress and transformation - we could be left with social disarray, economic devastation, political turmoil, and general unrest. It is time we learn from history. It is time we take responsibility. Not just leaders, but every single one of us. We are scared, and we are right to be scared. But instead of rejecting what we fear (it is coming whether or not we accept it), let us find ways to embrace it together and use the very tools that we fear to intentionally create a future worth having. Not just for some. For everyone. Each response and following strategy to the current transformation, with artificial intelligence at its core, relies on the responses around us. Public sectors, academia, private sectors. And not just within our immediate surroundings either. We live in a world of blurred lines. The decisions and inventions of a business in one country, easily affect other countries and cross-border politics. This kind of globalization relies on all of us to work as a team. Our individual strategies for adopting and using the tools of AI may differ based on our current states, but as interconnected and globalized beings, our overarching strategy should be to ensure that we learn from our past responses to transformations and to use the tools of this transformation to have a positive impact on the world at large.

With so much innovation made possible through the previous and current transformations, we seem to be constantly working towards what we call progress. And many of these innovations have made us believe that we are making progress at electric speeds. But with AI, 3D printing, self-driving cars and all the things these have the potential to change for us, we are not actually making much progress.[30] Or we are making progress for elite parts of society, while the rest of the world is relatively pushed further behind. This is not a criticism, rather a call to see things differently and realize the importance of working together and considering the impact and potential for the things we are developing. Real progress will be when we use the tools of the Smart Technology Era to include and empower all citizens with the knowledge, access, and new ways that our transformation has given us. It is up to every one of us to ensure that the tools of the Smart Technology Era are used for good and that our world and all its inhabitants are taken care of. We need to think about Smart Technology such as AI in the context of it being part of and perhaps at the center of a Revolution. It is easy to get glazed over when we hear the words Fourth Industrial Revolution, because of the severe lack of actual meaning. We do not know if it is meant to be scary or exciting. But we do know that it means big change. Some of the changes we are seeing already. Others are imminent, and others are imagined, but with the velocity and scope of change, it is not long before the imagined is imminent and the imminent is now. We tend to rely on these changes happening outside of us and may feel a lack of control in how things turn out, but this could not be further from the truth. What we all need to know now is how to be a true part of it, how to assess its risks, make informed decisions, avoid disaster and how to use it to include and transform the lives of all people. The reason we must see it in the context of its predecessors is because there were some negative and positive effects to the disruptions left by Industrial Revolutions 1, 2, 3 and 4. We need to learn from these. We need to put on our intentional algorithm hats and see where we went wrong so that we can do better. Yes, we have so much information today that this revolution will happen more quickly and be far less predictable than its predecessors, but as humans, we have not changed all that much. We are stepping into an unknown future, and we must see through all our biases and learn from our collective past if we are going to make the future better.

3. AI as Key Exponential Technology in the Smart Technology Era

Now that we have a broader perspective of the Smart Technology Era that we live and breathe, this chapter explores AI in more detail, how it impacts this world in a transformative way, where it all started and how it evolved over the past century and the many breakthroughs and historical highlights. I also unzip AI and its multifaceted nature and many subfields, its applications, its various flavors with respect to assisted, augmented, and autonomous intelligence, how the fusion of AI, IoT and blockchain are likely to impact our world in a significant way, and how the future of computing can make or break the AI revolution. Given what is at stake, our current civilization has a massive responsibility to direct AI in a visionary and wise fashion towards wholesome applications that maximizes the benefits to as many people as possible and life more broadly.

AI's Transformative Impact on Our World

It has become quite evident during the last few years that Artificial Intelligence is one of the key exponential technologies in the Smart Technology Era, to such an extent that it has even been called the AI era which follows the Internet era of the past 25 years. AI's transformative impact on our world is not only due to how it can unlock business and societal value from exponentially growing structured and unstructured data across an ever-increasing instrumented world, but also its pervasive nature - in some sense not too dissimilar to the role of electricity - and ability to be used in conjunction with other technologies to construct smarter and more powerful technologies enriched with AI. These smart technologies significantly strengthen our capabilities to solve problems, experiment, research, gain insights, discover knowledge, and engineer solutions in a multi-, trans-, and/or interdisciplinary fashion within a limitless universe of application use cases. Aside from what smart technologies are capable of doing for businesses by automating, predicting, classifying, deciding, comparing, recognizing, detecting and recommending, it can transform entire ecosystems and systems of production, management and governance on a local and global scale. Kai-fu Lee is confident that AI will soon enter the elite club of general purpose technologies (GPTs as described in *The Second Machine Age*) which "interrupt and accelerate the normal march of economic progress" with the steam engine, electricity, and information and communication technology the key ones.[1] While the steam engine and electricity ramped up productivity by deskilling the production of goods and services, information and communication technology have a "skill bias" in favor of highly skilled workers. AI, however, will not facilitate the deskilling of economic production and will instead take over the execution of tasks that can be optimized using data without necessarily requiring human interaction. Kai-fu Lee believes that the AI revolution will be on the same scale as the industrial revolution, but likely larger and faster. He discusses three catalysts that will accelerate AI adoption, the first being that AI solutions are just digital algorithms that are infinitely replicable and instantly distributable across the globe, the second is venture capital funding backing AI ventures, and third is having China also participating and on par with the West in both advancing and applying AI technology.[2] PwC predicts that AI will add \$15.7 trillion to the global economy by 2030 with about 70% of that gains likely to accrue in China and the US.[3] In the report *Artificial Intelligence is the Future of Growth*, Accenture suggests that AI as a new factor of production has the potential to double annual economic growth rates by 2035 through intelligent automation, labor and capital augmentation, and a driver of innovation.[4]

Within the Smart Technology Era some of the core technologies that are changing and will continue to change our world include networks and sensors that instrument the world, infinite computing, AI that provides expertise on demand, robotics which act as our new workforce, genomics, and synthetic biology. According to a 2020 Forbes article, the top technology trends that will likely define this decade also includes AI and machine learning applications (of which many I'll discuss further in this book) such as natural language processing, voice interfaces and chatbots, computer vision and facial recognition, robotic process automation, mass personalization and micro-moments, big data and augmented analytics, as well as other complementary smart technologies and applications such as IoT, robots and collaborative bots, autonomous vehicles, drones and unmanned aerial vehicles, wearables and augmented humans, intelligent spaces and smart places, blockchains and distributed ledgers, cloud and edge computing, digitally extended realities, digital twins, 5G of cellular network technology, genomics and gene editing, machine co-creativity and augmented design, digital platforms, cybersecurity and resilience, 3D and 4D printing and additive manufacturing, nanotechnology and materials science, and quantum computing.[5] The fusion of many of these exponential technologies along with the speed of technology change will likely lead to an exponential growth trajectory in the Smart Technology Era. AI is the key technology in this change, without which the extents and uses of these other technologies would be limited to less cognitive behaviors and outcomes. For example, often with supporting IoT, robotics, blockchain, nanotechnology, biotechnology, smartphones and internet, AI is already being used in detecting water, air and crop health, diagnosing diseases, predicting when maintenance is needed to avoid expensive or disastrous breakages or outages, analyzing electricity, gas and water wastage, advising on the best places to plant crops for greatest yield, providing psychiatric and medical diagnoses and advice, and allowing people of different languages to communicate with each other in text, voice or video (even across slang, accents, cultural and regional syntax, meaning variations, personal patterns, and figures of speech). AI has great power to be used to positively transform people's experiences of the world, alleviate poverty, offer access to jobs and education, ensure all areas and communities have access to food and clean water, and more efficiently and effectively use what is already available and what has already been produced (circularity). The nature of smart technologies allows us to invent what was previously unimaginable, solve problems that we thought were just part of life and bring resources and vital services to those previously excluded.

AI is made even more powerful and omnipresent when combined with other smart technologies. In many cases, the use of AI is but one part of the fascinating inventions, which are really collaborations and integrations of different technologies. IoT, as the ability to power any device with the internet to keep it constantly connected and pulling data and statistics, can communicate with software halfway across the world. This software uses machine learning algorithms to predict maintenance, optimize efficiency, conclude outcomes, or gain valuable insights. It sends all this back to the device which then changes its track, alerts for maintenance, or redirects its power flow or focus. Already, artificial intelligence combined with other smart technologies, like IoT, is all around us, from self-driving cars and drones to virtual assistants and software that translate or invest. Impressive progress has been made in AI in recent years, driven by exponential increases in computing power and by the availability of vast amounts of data, from software used to discover new drugs to algorithms used to predict our cultural interests. Smart watches empowered by IoT and AI, can know when we are going to have a stroke or heart attack, or going into diabetic shock, can let us know when we are sick, even what the diagnoses is and tell us what we need to do, what we can take and where the nearest pharmacy that stocks what we need is.

In business, AI also has the power to enhance, automate, improve, predict, personalize, and optimize products, services, and processes. Together with its smart technology counterparts, AI is transforming businesses: business models, hierarchies, strategies, workflows, services, and products. To be able to achieve this, we must know what we are facing. We need to know the threats and risks so that we can ensure they do not occur. As much as we imagine the wonderful possibilities ahead of us, the truth is we have no idea what our future looks like – even less of an idea than we had during the previous industrial revolutions.[6] We do know that the Information Revolution leading into the Smart Technology Era is the fastest-ever period of technological innovation. Whereas human brain power played a key role in solving the problems of the 19th century and software programs running on computers helped to address 20th century obstacles, AI and its applications are a key part of the 21st century solution stack to tackle today's challenges. Living in this hyperconnected age, with more knowledge, more access to knowledge and the ability to make more sense of our knowledge, our lives are being continuously transformed and disrupted.[7] Almost every industry and government is being transformed and disrupted by the knowledge driven, hyperconnected Smart Technology Era. Keeping up with these changes is where we find challenges. It is easier for economically stable countries and individuals who are exposed to the latest developments and have digital skills and education. It proves more difficult in countries and communities where the world's advancement is sparse. The World Economic Forum (WEF) and Accenture's warning that we could be looking at job losses as high as 2 billion by the year 2030, is a real fear in a world that is split between those who are part of the digital socio-economy and those who are not.[8] If technology is the future, then only those who are empowered to use this technology are secured a spot in this future. We are only at the beginning of smart technology transformation, and already the lives of the tech-enabled citizen and the non-tech-enabled citizen are so far apart that, on a surface level, they are barely relatable. The non-tech-enabled citizen who, without a smartphone, computer or internet is not only living in a vastly different way, but is exposed to a fraction of the information, education, goods, trends, processes, and services than the tech-enabled citizen. Already, whether we are exposed to technology, and how much technology, is largely due to socio-economic status. The further danger is that technology has the potential to solidify the world's socio-economic status and drive them further apart. Therefore, it has never been more important for every person to be educated on and included in the changes of the Smart Technology Era. We are on a tightrope, trying to balance the positive, transformational possibilities that AI brings, with the negative, socio-economic decline that, without immediate intervention, it has the potential to bring too. The wealth and opportunities of the world are already in the hands of the few. Smart technology and a digital economy could make this exponentially worse or exponentially better.

Some Brief Historical Highlights of AI

Before AI was what it is today (in fact, when it was still just an idea), John McCarthy and a few of his colleagues (which included Marvin Minsky, Herbert Simon, Allen Newell, and Arthur Samuel) decided that the cognitive processes of machines were interesting and potentially world-changing enough to require research. Although it was John McCarthy, in his excitement about the potential that machine intelligence had, who reportedly in 1956 first coined the term "Artificial Intelligence" and described it as "the science and engineering of making intelligent machines", the foundations was provided by discoveries in information theory, neurobiology, cybernetics, statistics, mathematics, and computer science. On a more statistical and probabilistic track, some earlier machine learning related foundational work was done in 1763 with Thomas Bayes providing the basis for Bayes Theorem as formulated by Pierre-Simon Laplace in 1812 which describes the probability of an event based on prior knowledge of conditions that might be related to the event.[9] In 1805 Adrien-Marie Legendre outlined the least squares method which is still today heavily used for regression and curve fitting applications.[10] Andrey Markov first described in 1913 a Markov chain which is "a stochastic model describing a sequence of possible events in which the probability of each event depends only on the state attained in the previous event".[11] Strong foundations for AI in its current form were specifically laid by Alan Turing's theory of computation, the Church-Turing thesis that describes how digital computers can simulate any formal process of reasoning, and the formal design for Turing-complete "artificial neurons" by McCulloch and Pitts in 1943.[12] The latter is a system of data-manipulation rules that is computationally universal in that it can simulate any Turing machine (which is a mathematical model of computation that defines an abstract machine that can simulate an algorithm's logic).[13] We know that mathematics is the study of formal systems that abstract the concepts of logic, space, number, quantity and numerical calculation and that computation involves the process of applying a formal system to answer a question presented within the system. Whereas mathematics is the domain of all formal specifications or languages, computation is the domain of all possible implementations. In the 1920s David Hilbert proposed a solution to the inconsistencies in the foundation of mathematics through what is called Hilbert's program to provide a basis for all existing theories to a provable, finite, complete and consistent set of axioms.[14] However, in 1931 Kurt Gödel's incompleteness theorems showed that Hilbert's program was not possible for all of mathematics (specifically not being able to prove that all truths about the arithmetic of natural numbers and that a system cannot demonstrate its own consistency).[15] So although mathematics cannot do all mathematics, computation can do all computation as shown by Alonzo Church and Alan Turing in 1939 via their thesis that a function on the natural numbers can be calculated by an algorithm if and only if it is computable by a Turing machine.[16] In 1949, the Manchester Mark 1 was the first stored-programme computer invented. In 1950, Alan Turing showed that computation can do all mathematics that can be done on a universal Turing Machine and also introduced the Turing test as a way of testing a machine's intelligence (which effectively tests if a machine can trick humans into thinking it is human; if so, it has intelligence).[17] A year later, the first neural network machine that was able to learn was developed by Marvin Minsky and Dean Edmonds which they called Stochastic Neural Analog Reinforcement Calculator (SNARC).[18] Evelyn Fix and Joseph Hodges in 1951 developed the k-nearest neighbors algorithm used for classification and regression and which was later extended by Thomas Cover.[19] In 1952 Arthur Samuel at IBM developed machine learning programs that can play checkers. A few years later in 1957 Frank Rosenblatt conceived an algorithm for supervised learning of binary classifiers which he called perceptrons.[20]

If we now fast-track from here, some further application-related historical highlights include the first industrial robot called Unimate in 1961 that was deployed at General Motors and replaced humans on the assembly line, AI funding at MIT in 1963 by the US Defense Advanced Research Projects Agency (DARPA), a reinforcement learning machine developed by Donald Mitchie in 1963 that were able to play the game tic-tac-toe , and the pioneering chatbot that conversed with humans called Eliza which was developed by Joseph Weizenbaum at MIT in 1964.[21] This was followed by a period of further optimism with Moore's Law in 1965 stating that the number of transistors in a dense integrated circuit doubles about every two years, science fiction writers Arthur Clark and Stanley Kubrick imagined in 1968 that "by the year 2001 we will have machines with intelligence that matched or exceeded humans" and Marvin Minsky saying in 1970 that in "3-8 years we'll have a machine with the general intelligence of a human being".[22] Shakey which was the first general-purpose mobile robot that was able to reason about its own actions was developed during 1966 to 1972 by Stanford Research Institute (and funded by DARPA).[23] In 1972 Japanese robotics scientists from Waseda University developed WABOT-1 as the world's first full-scale android humanoid robot that was able to walk and communicate with people in Japanese, navigate a room and grip and transport objects.[24] This was followed by the first AI winter period during 1974 to 1980 where AI funding dried up after sky high expectation and bubbling optimism without meaningful results. In addition, the research in neural networks was paused in the 1970s after Marvin Minsky and Seymour Papert's destructive criticism of the limitations of Frank Rosenblatt's single-layer perceptron neural network.[25] In 1979 Kunihiko Fukushima introduced a hierarchical multi-layered type of neural network called Neocognition which was used for pattern recognition tasks such as Japanese handwritten character recognition and later influenced the development of convolutional neural networks which are used for processing, segmentation, and classification of images and other auto correlated data.[26]

After some early foundational work to build rules-based systems that emulates decisions of human experts by the Stanford Heuristic Programming Project led by Edward Feigenbaum, we saw a spike of expert system development using languages such as Lisp and Prolog during the 1970s and early 1980s with examples such as Mycin diagnosing infectious diseases, Dendral identifying unknown organic molecules, and SID for synthesis of integral design of CPU logic gates.[27] 1980 also saw the Symbolics Lisp Machine commercialized which led to an AI renaissance for a few years. In 1982 Japan's Ministry of International Trade and Industry launched the Fifth Generation Computer Systems project to create computers using massively parallel computing and logic programming.[28] Another vitalizing event in the early 1980s was the revival of neural networks via the work of physicist John Hopfield in 1982 with the Hopfield network as a recurrent neural network with associative memory and David Rumelhart, Geoffrey Hinton and Ronald Williams whom applied the back-propagation algorithm (developed by Seppo Linnainmaa in 1970 which describes the algorithm as automatic differentiation and applied to neural networks by Paul Werbos in 1974) to multi-layer neural networks in 1986.[29] Terry Sejnowski and Charles Rosenberg developed a neural network system called NETtalk in 1985 that learned to pronounce written English text which served as the input and matched the corresponding phonetic transcriptions as output.[30] Carnegie Mellon University with DARPA sponsorship produced the first autonomous car called Navlab 1 in 1986.[31] This was followed by a second AI winter from 1987 to 1993, where despite progress in AI, business and government lost interest in AI for a while. In 1989 Christopher Watkins developed Q-learning which is a reinforcement learning algorithm to learn appropriate actions that instructs an agent what to do under what circumstances without requiring a model of the environment.[32] A few years later in 1992 Gerald Tesauro from IBM developed backgammon software called TD-Gammon that played the game by training a neural network with temporal-difference learning.[33] In 1995 Tin Kam Ho described random decision forests, an ensemble learning technique for regression, classification, and other tasks that works by generating many decision trees at training time and give a class prediction according to the class that gets the most votes from the individual decision trees or in the case of regression the mean or average prediction from the decision trees.[34] In the same year Vladimir Vapnik and Corinna Cortes introduced support vector machines, a robust statistical machine learning technique that maps training examples to points in space in order to maximize the width of the gap between the categories and which are used for classification and regression tasks in supervised or unsupervised learning mode.[35] In 1997, the usefulness and efficiency of recurrent neural networks were improved through Jürgen Schmidhuber and Sepp Hochreiter's conception of long short-term memory recurrent neural networks that can process long sequences of data in applications such as speech recognition, anomaly detection and connected handwritten recognition.[36]

During the same time in 1997, IBM's Deep Blue as the world's first chess-playing computer system defeated world champion chess player Gary Kasparov and Dragon Systems developed the first publicly available speech recognition software.[37] In 1998 an MIT team led by Cynthia Breazeal introduced KISmet, a robot head that can recognize and simulate human emotions.[38] Sony launched in 1999 the first consumer robot pet dog called AiBO with skills and personality that develops over time.[39] iRobot (founded by Rodney Brooks and others) developed the first mass produced autonomous robotic vacuum cleaner called Roomba in 2002 that learned to navigate, avoid obstacles and clean homes.[40] In 2004 NASA's robotic exploration rovers Spirit and Opportunity were able to autonomously navigate the surface of Mars.[41] An artificially intelligent bipedal humanoid robot called ASIMO that was developed by Honda was able to recognize moving objects, its surrounding environment, faces, sounds, postures, and gestures, as well as walking as fast as a human in servicing customers in restaurant settings.[42] Netflix launched the Netflix Prize machine learning competition in 2006 to improve their own collaborative filtering recommendation software's accuracy in predicting a user's rating for a film given their ratings for previous films by at least 10%, which resulted in the prize eventually won in 2009.[43] The game Checkers was solved in 2007 by a team of researchers at the University of Alberta.[44] Google introduced voice-enabled search to Apple's iPhone in 2008 and also built the first self-driving car to handle city conditions in 2009.[45] The creation of the large image database called ImageNet which was led by Fei-Fei Li from Stanford University is considered by many people as a catalytic move to help set-up the current AI revival as the best machine learning algorithms would only be able to be effective if trained on real world data.[46] During 2010 Microsoft launched Kinect for Xbox 360 which was the first gaming device that was able to follow human body movement using a combination of a 3D camera and infra-red detection features.[47] IBM's question answering computer called Watson using a combination of machine learning, natural language processing and information retrieval techniques won first place in 2011 against champion human participants on the popular $1M prize television quiz show Jeopardy! in the US.[48] In 2011 Apple integrated Siri, an intelligent virtual assistant with a voice interface into the iPhone 4S with other personal assistants such as Google Now and Microsoft Cortana to follow using speech recognition to answer questions and perform simple tasks during the period 2011 to 2014.[49]

The Google Brain team who was led by Andrew Ng and Jeff Dean in 2012 trained a multilayer autoencoder type of neural network using large scale unsupervised learning to recognize cats with 75% accuracy by watching unlabeled images taken from frames of YouTube videos.[50] Google subsidiary SCHAFT Inc of Japan developed Robot HRP-2 in 2013 that defeated 15 teams in performing disaster response tasks to win DARPA's Robotics Challenge Trials.[51] In 2013 China's Tianhe-2 doubled the world's top supercomputing speed to 33.86 petaflops.[52] A chatbot called Eugene Goostman that was presented as a 13-year old Ukranian boy passed the Turing Test in 2014 with a third of judges believing Eugene is human.[53] Ian Goodfellow in 2014 has developed Generative Adversarial Networks that automatically discover and learn patterns in input data in such a way that the model can be used to generate new examples that credibly could have come from the original dataset. GANs typically consist of a generator model that is trained to generate new examples and a discriminator model that tries to classify examples as either real or fake.[54] In 2014 Facebook developed a deep learning system called DeepFace that identifies faces with 97.35% accuracy which represents near human accuracy and an improvement of more than 27% over previous systems.[55] In the same year Amazon launched Alexa within Amazon Echo smart speakers, an intelligent virtual assistant with a voice interface that completes shopping tasks and various other tasks such as playing music, audiobooks or podcasts as well as providing real-time information and controlling other smart devices in a home automation context.[56] In 2015 Google open-sourced TensorFlow as an end-to-end open source machine learning platform for everyone.[57] Microsoft's chatbot Tay in 2016 showed disrespectful behavior on social media making provocative and insulting racist comments before being removed.[58] During 2016 both Uber and Tesla also started to pilot autopilot or self-driving car programs in the US.[59] In the same year China's Sunway TaihuLight tripled the world's top supercomputing speed to 93 petaflops (although in 2020 being surpassed by Fujitsu's Fugaku supercomputer with a speed of 442 petaflops).[60]

Another noteworthy AI achievement was when Google Deepmind's AlphaGo was trained to play the strategy board game of Go (renowned for its vast number of possible positions which is estimated to be in the order of 10^{170}) to defeat professional Go player Lee Sedol 4-1 in 2016 and world champion Ke Jie in 2017.[61] AlphaGo uses a combination of Monte Carlo tree search to choose moves at random and find a winning strategy by simulating the game to the end and reinforcement deep learning that consists of a policy network to select the next move and a value network to predict the winner of the game at each position. An improved version of AlphaGo called AlphaGo Zero not only outperformed previous versions, but also learned the game by only playing against itself without being trained on millions of human moves while also using far less processing power. A more generic version called AlphaZero that can master chess, shogi (Japanese chess) and Go, was able to beat the best chess engine, StockFish 8, with only 4 hours of training.[62] Also in 2017, Deepstack was the first AI system to beat human players in imperfect information games such as heads-up no-limit poker through combining "recursive reasoning to handle information asymmetry, decomposition to focus computation on the relevant decision, and a form of intuition that is automatically learned from self-play using deep learning".[63] OpenAI trained a large scale reinforcement learning AI agent to play the multiplayer video game Dota 2 and was able to win against a professional Dota 2 player in the 2017 international Dota 2 tournament to demonstrate its ability to achieve "expert-level performance, learn human–AI cooperation, and operate at internet scale".[64] In 2018 Google presented a service called Google Duplex to allow an AI assistant to schedule appointments over the phone by imitating human-sounding speech.[65] In 2020 Microsoft introduced DeepSpeed, a deep learning optimization library for PyTorch that makes distributed training of models simpler and also more efficient and effective across the spectrum of supercomputers, low-end clusters or a single GPU.[66] Early adopters of DeepSpeed at Microsoft have already produced a language model called Turing Natural Language Generation or T-NLG, which was at the time the "largest language model ever published at 17 billion parameters".[67] In 2020 OpenAI has released their third-generation autoregressive language prediction model called GPT-3, a state-of-the-art autoregressive language model with 175 billion parameters (in the full version) that uses deep learning to produce a variety of human-like text, computer codes, poetry and other language tasks.[68]

From these high-level historical highlights, it is clear that the AI field not only benefited from some important foundational work, continuously increasing computing capability and enormous growth in data, but even with all the stops and starts over the last 70 years actually made some steady progress and currently have some serious momentum to unlock tremendous application value. Joscha Bach regards the classical AI from 1950 to 2013 as first order AI, the current phase with systems that learn as second order AI, meta learning (learning about learning) as third order AI and asks if fourth order AI is about the general theory of search. According to Kai-fu Lee, the most meaningful breakthrough in AI's 70+ year old history is deep learning which happened in 2012 when deep learning was applied to an AI competition called the ImageNet challenge.[69] At that time Geoff Hinton and his PhD students Alex Krizhevsky and Ilya Sutskever from University of Toronto participated in this challenge by training their deep learning neural networks on the large ImageNet database and became the first team to go beyond 75% accuracy in the competition. It also showed the importance of data when it comes to data-driven machine learning techniques as opposed to fine-tuning neural network architectures and algorithms. Although others may differ, Kai-fu Lee reckons that deep learning applied to the massive datasets that we are generating will likely remain AI's biggest breakthrough for years to come with many groundbreaking applications to follow that are built on this discovery. Although I agree with deep learning's application potential for the unlocking of business and societal value, I think we are likely to see further breakthroughs of the same magnitude as deep learning, especially considering the amount of investment going into AI as well as AI's progress and future directions discussed in Chapter 9.

Demystifying AI and its Multifaceted Nature

Artificial Intelligence or Machine Intelligence, Non-biological Intelligence, Cognitive Computing and Machine Learning are terms met with much emotion. Sometimes this emotion amounts to excitement and opportunity. More often, however, it amounts to fear and resistance. Apart from the many misrepresentations and conflicting narratives or portrayals in media and entertainment, AI is a concept that most people across the globe simply do not understand and feels foreign to them. They do not find it easy to imagine how it can be incorporated into their lives and ways of being. However, the smarter and more ubiquitous AI's applications become, the more it will automatically be integrated into our lives for better or for worse. Even with existing applications we can already see how smart technology is incorporated into our lives and where it can be improved. For example, each time Google asks us if it should send automatic 'unavailable' responses when we are sent meeting requests at times we are already in meetings, or when Maps proactively finds us the fastest route home (as we already see with technology in for example Tesla self-driving cars) or when Facebook shows us only what we are actually interested in or hopefully in the future more balanced perspectives for better sensemaking - this is artificial intelligence in operation. We do not have to work to incorporate it. We just sit back and benefit from it. That being said, it would also help us if we could define and demystify AI. Also, if we could realize that it is not something to fear - rather something to embrace, encourage and shape to benefit everyone. We also need to understand that the current AI applications and those in the foreseeable future are for all practical purposes not really intelligent without human involvement at some point in its creation, development and deployment. In Chapter 9, I am also discussing how machine intelligence relates to human intelligence in more detail.

AI is defined by the capacity for a machine to reason, perceive information or data, solve, optimize, prioritize, and reach conclusions or achieve specific goals through flexible adaptation in the way that humans do. In short, it is the cognitive processes of machines. It is the ability to learn, recognize, analyze, and make decisions. Within the context of intelligent agents, AI is exhibited by any machine that perceives its environment and takes actions that maximize its chance of successfully achieving its goals. The goals can for example be explicitly defined or induced by rewarding some types of behavior and punishing others. The learning process of these machines or intelligent agents to get better at achieving its goals or specific outcomes is called Machine Learning (ML), which is a subset of the broader AI field that will be described below. In contrast to traditional programming that relies on a programmer to manually create a program or software code that uses input data and is executed on a computer as a set of specific instructions to produce the output, ML makes use of data that are fed to a machine learning algorithm to create a model that can automatically learn from data, improve from experience, and produce output or make decisions without being explicitly programmed. So, a ML algorithm creates a model that is for example able to make predictions and test these predictions against more data. AI programming more broadly involves processing that not only includes learning, but also knowledge representation, pattern matching, search, logic, optimization, and problem solving.

So, in order to learn, AI like human intelligence requires data or information which is typically used to train a ML model or a system of ML models to achieve its goal or maximize its chances of success. In a digital sense, data is any bit of information that is captured online or in a digital space via for example a software application. It could be anything from numbers, images, videos, documents, text, sounds, sensor data, names, or patterns to for example how often we use a certain application, how we use it and what we use it for. A ML model refers to the model artifact that is created by the learning or training process on the data. By way of analogy, one can consider learning or training algorithms to be the seeds, data to be the soil, and the learned ML models to be the grown plants.[70] There are broadly speaking at least three different ways of training ML models within the framework of artificial neural networks, which is one of the key AI approaches that in a very loose and simplified fashion simulates or reverse engineer the neural networks in animal brains. For all three main learning algorithm types being supervised, unsupervised and reinforcement learning as well as variants such as semi-supervised, self-supervised and multi-instance learning, the ML models learn by updating the weights of the connections in their networks analogues to how synapses that connect neurons in animal brains are being updated (in animal brains the synaptic strength is defined as "the average amount of current or voltage excursion produced in the postsynaptic neuron by an action potential in the presynaptic neuron").[71] An artificial neural network type of ML model typically has their units or "neurons" organized in layers such as an input layer, hidden or middle layers and an output layer where shallow neural networks might have only one hidden layer and deep neural networks have multiple hidden layers in a hierarchical multi-layered structure. As the units in these layers are typically connected to other units in other layers or within the same layer or back to themselves, training happens when the weights associated with these connections and other parameters are updated. The updating of the weights makes it possible for the neural network to learn how to optimally represent input data as features at scales or resolutions that may vary and combine them into higher-order feature representations that help to produce the desired outcomes or predictions. Similar to their biological neuron counterpart, a node or unit in an artificial neural network computes an activation function that determines the output of that unit given an input or set of inputs from other connected units. The unit then passes the output signal to the next connected units in the network when a threshold or bias value is exceeded (analogous to how a neuron generates an electrochemical pulse or action potential if the voltage changes by a large enough amount over a short interval). The activation functions of these neural network units can have different mathematical properties and are divided in ridge, radial and fold functions, where examples of the ridge type (which are more commonly used) are linear, ReLU, logistic and heavyside and radial types are gaussian, multi-quadratics, inverse multi-quadratics, and square-law radial basis functions.[72]

With *supervised learning* the algorithm is creating a model that learns an input-output mapping through the presentation of training data that consists of input examples each with its corresponding desired outcome or target which it must then learn to produce as an output in such a way that allows it to also generalize to unseen examples. In order to minimize the error between the generated model output and target value for each training example, the supervised learning algorithm seeks to minimize a cost or loss function that captures this error. For supervised learning neural networks, the training is typically done through an error backpropagation algorithm that uses a stochastic gradient descent method to compute the gradient of the loss function with respect to the weights of the network for a single input-output example, and updates the weights throughout the neural network from the output layer to the input layer in accordance with each weight's contribution to the error. The data set is typically divided into a training set used during the learning process to update the weights and other model parameters, a validation set to provide an unbiased evaluation of a model fit and generalization assessment as well as tuning of the model's hyperparameters that controls the learning process, and an independent test set to provide an unbiased evaluation of a final model fit. Supervised learning is typically applied to classification and regression problems, where the model output variable for classification is categorical or discrete as opposed to numerical or continuous in the case of regression. For classification tasks the output layer typically makes use of a softmax activation function (a generalization of the logistic function to multiple dimensions) that creates a probability distribution on the output units and maps each output in such a way that the total sum is 1 and where the output unit with the highest value is the selected class. Besides multi-layer feedforward neural networks, some example regression and classification supervised learning algorithms include linear regression, lasso regression, logistic regression, kernel ridge regression, polynomial, multivariate and multiple regression, linear and quadratic discriminant analysis, support vector machines, nearest neighbors, naive bayes, gaussian processes, decision trees, gradient boosted decision trees, and random forests.[73]

One of the fastest growing and most successful subfields of machine learning and responsible for the recent AI boom has been Deep Learning (DL), which is a set of algorithms that attempt to model high-level abstractions in data by using model architectures composed of multiple non-linear transformations. Although DL can be applied to unsupervised and semi-supervised learning tasks, most of its use cases involve supervised learning that typically requires a huge, labeled data set and significant computational power to train these DL models. Some example DL architectures include deep neural networks, deep belief networks, recurrent neural networks and convolutional neural networks that have been applied to fields including computer vision, self-driving cars, natural language processing, speech recognition, audio recognition, machine translation, material inspection, social network filtering, medical image analysis, bioinformatics, drug design, and board game programs as we have discussed in the previous section. A simple computer vision example is where an AI supervised training process is fed images of animals in many different forms and from many different angles. The supervised ML algorithm here may be to teach the machine to recognize specific types of animals and be able to generalize, as a human would, what animal is being presented whether in a photograph, cartoon, or painting, from any body part and at any age. Although a lot of the learning process can be automated, humans typically correct, add data, redirect, or even redesign the process or the ML model architecture based on the success of the machine learning outcomes. Once the machine has learned to recognize images of animals, it can be combined with other algorithms and be able to, for example, know where lions are found, what sounds they make, which books or movies they have appeared in, the closest destination to view a real-life lion based on your location and the word for lion in every language (in sound and in writing).

A deep neural network (DNN) is an artificial neural network with a hierarchical organization of multiple hidden layers between the input and output layers to derive high-level functions and higher-order feature representations through appropriate transformations of the input data. DNNs can model complex non-linear relationships and can have many different architectures to solve problems in specific domains. As an alternative class of deep neural networks, a deep belief network (DBN) is a generative graphical model that consists of multiple hidden layers that act as feature detectors and can learn to probabilistically reconstruct its inputs when trained on a set of examples in an unsupervised fashion. This is then typically followed by a supervised learning step where the DBN can be trained to perform classification. Some examples of DBNs include a restricted Boltzmann machine that is an undirected, generative energy-based model that can learn a probabilistic distribution over its inputs and an autoencoder that learns to copy its input to its output through an encoder part that maps the inputs to the hidden layer that represents the features of the input and decoder part that maps the feature representations to a reconstruction of the input.[74] DBNs are heavily used in for example image recognition, video recognition and motion-capture applications. A convolutional neural network (CNN) is another category of deep learning neural networks that has been loosely modelled in mechanistic fashion after the visual cortex in the human brain by having a hierarchical model that mimics the operations along the ventral visual pathway (such as V1, V2, V4 and IT) where individual neurons respond to stimuli only in a restricted region of the visual receptive field and a collection of these receptive fields overlap to cover the entire visual area.[75] A CNN consists of an input layer, hidden layers and an output layer, where the hidden layers perform convolutions (multiplication or other dot product) to identify and differentiate the key features of the image by breaking it down into small parts and passing it through a ReLu activation function, which is followed by pooling layers that reduce the dimensionality without losing key features, and fully connected layers and normalization layers that combine the patterns to produce a classification output. Each convolutional unit processes data only for its receptive field with the filtering ability of the convolutional layers that is shift and space invariant and increasing in complexity as part of a stacked bundle of convolution-nonlinearity-pooling layers that are repeated. CNNs are most commonly applied to analyzing visual imagery such as those in image and video recognition, image classification, and image segmentation, but can also be applied to other applications such as medical image analysis, recommender systems, financial time series, natural language processing, and brain-computer interfaces.[76] A recent Artificial Intelligence Review paper outlines a taxonomy of CNN architectures as well as a classification of innovations into categories such as spatial exploitation, depth, multi-path, width, feature-map exploitation, channel boosting, and attention.[77] Just to give an indication of the breath of CNN architectures developed especially in the last decade, a list looks like this: AlexNet, GoogleNet, Inception-V2, Inception-V3, Inception-V4, Inception-ResNet, VGG, Highway Net, ResNet, DenseNet, FractalNet, ResNext, WideResNet, PolyNet, Pyramidal Net, SE Net, CMPE-SE, Residual Attention Module, CBM, and Channel Boosted CNN.[78]

A recurrent neural network (RNN) is a type of neural network that combines feedforward and feedback connections between network units that forms a directed graph along a temporal sequence to create internal memory that helps process arbitrary sequences of inputs in applications such as speech recognition, anomaly detection and connected handwritten recognition. There are a range of RNNs which include long short-term memory (LSTM) RNNs, fully RNNs, Elman and Jordan networks, Hopfield networks, bidirectional associative memory, echo state networks, independent RNNs, recursive neural networks, neural history compressor, second order RNNs, gated recurrent units, bi-directional RNNs, continuous-time RNNs, hierarchical RNNs, recurrent multilayer perceptron network, neural Turing machines, differentiable neural computers, neural network pushdown automata, and memristive networks.[79] During the academic part of my career, I had a specific interest in recurrent neural networks with my PhD dissertation specifically focused on training, dynamics and complexity of architecture-specific recurrent neural networks such as Jordan, Elman and Temporal Autoassociation networks.[80] In some of my other research published in *Neural Networks and Psychopathology* a RNN architecture was presented that consisted of two coupled Elman recurrent neural networks to simulate normal performance on a semantic negative priming task (the left RNN dealt with the left word pathway and the right one with the right word pathway) in order to model cognitive disinhibition and neurotransmitter dysfunction in obsessive compulsive disorder (OCD).[81] Specific lesions to the coupled RNN model that correspond to dopaminergic and serotonergic dysfunction resulted in reduced semantic priming as we see with OCD patients, while modifications of the network that corresponded to noradrenergic dysfunction resulted in enhancement of effects that has been present beforehand.[82]

With *unsupervised learning* the algorithm is given data with no set outcomes or targets and must come up with its own observations and conclusions based on the patterns in the data. An unsupervised learning algorithm trains a model to describe or extract relationships in data through generating clusters or associations where only input data is provided and the natural groupings, unknown patterns or features in the input data are discovered. There are many types of unsupervised learning with probabilistic methods such as clustering, density estimation, anomaly detection, encoding, and dimension reduction or latent variable models as well as a spectrum of neural network approaches. Clustering involves finding groups in the data with methods such as k-means clustering, hierarchical clustering, mixture models, density-based spatial clustering of applications with noise (DBSCAN), and the ordering points to identify the clustering structure (OPTICS) algorithm.[83] As a clustering algorithm example, k-means is a vector quantization method that aims to partition input data into k clusters in which each input example belongs to the cluster with the nearest mean (which could be the cluster's center or centroid) which serve as a prototype of the cluster. An example of a density estimation algorithm is kernel density estimation which involves using small groups of input data that are closely related to estimate the distribution for new data points in the problem space. Examples of anomaly detection methods include isolation forest and local outlier factor. Approaches for dimension reduction and learning latent or hidden variable models include the expectation–maximization algorithm, method of moments, and blind signal separation techniques such as principal component analysis, independent component analysis, singular value decomposition, and non-negative matrix factorization. These dimension reduction methods are typically used for data compression, data classification, noise reduction and data visualization. Unsupervised methods used for data visualization includes principal component analysis (PCA), T-distributed stochastic neighbor embedding (T-SNE), linear discriminant analysis (LDA), and uniform manifold approximation and projection (UMAP).[84] PCA is an example of a projection method that involves summarizing a dataset in terms of eigenvalues and eigenvectors where the linear dependencies are removed. Neural network type of approaches include Hopfield networks which are used as content-addressable memory, Boltzmann machines and Restricted Boltzmann machines which are stochastic Hopfield networks, Helmholtz machines, autoencoder and variational autoencoder which are inspired by Helmholtz machines and combines probability networks with neural networks, Hebbian learning, adaptive resonance theory and self-organizing feature maps.[85] Unsupervised deep learning algorithms include for example also deep belief networks and neural history compressors mentioned earlier.

The third major category of machine learning algorithm is *reinforcement learning* where an agent must learn to operate in an environment by trial and error using feedback and selecting appropriate actions in a given situation in order to maximize reward. The ML agent therefore must learn the patterns of how to respond to and behave in that environment based on positive or negative reinforcement. The use of an environment implies that the training dataset is not fixed and that there is a goal or set of goals that the ML agent is required to achieve, actions it may perform, and feedback about performance toward the goal. The nature of the feedback signal can be delayed and is noisy from a statistical point of view. Some common examples of reinforcement learning algorithms include Q-learning, deep reinforcement learning, and temporal-difference learning. Q-learning is a reinforcement learning algorithm that does not require a model of the environment and learns appropriate actions that instructs a ML agent what to do under specific circumstances and can identify an optimal policy for any finite Markov decision process (which is a discrete-time stochastic control process that models decision making when outcomes are somewhat random and in part under the control of a decision maker).[86] Temporal difference learning also does not require a model of the environment and combines the Monte Carlo method (that uses repeated random sampling) and the dynamic programming method (that optimizes through recursion) to train the ML agent.[87] An example of a reinforcement problem is playing a game where the ML agent has the goal of maximizing the score and can make moves in the game and receive a feedback signal via rewards and punishments. As discussed in the previous section, stunning results were achieved with applying reinforcement learning along with Monte Carlo search to strategy board games as demonstrated with Google's AlphaGo and AlphaGo Zero reinforcement learning models in becoming the world's top Go player and playing the game at superhuman level. AlphaGo Zero has for example only trained by self-play reinforcement learning starting with random play and without any supervised inputs or human intervention and using a single neural network that combines the roles of policy and value networks as opposed to having these networks separate as they were used before.[88]

There are also some hybrids of supervised and unsupervised learning such as semi-supervised, self-supervised and multi-instance learning methods. In order to make better use of all available data which might be labelled or not as is the case for many real-world problems, *semi-supervised learning* provides a way to first use unsupervised learning methods such as clustering and density estimation to find the natural grouping and patterns in the unlabeled data or to use supervised learning to help label the data. This approach works well for image, audio and text data that are respectively found in machine vision, speech recognition and natural language processing applications. With *self-supervised learning* an unsupervised learning problem can be formulated as a supervised learning problem to enable the use of supervised learning methods such as autoencoders to create a model or compressed representation that can be used in the solution of the initial unsupervised problem. Unlabeled image data can for example be used in supervised training fashion to predict missing parts in images or a color representation of the grayscale version of the images. A generative adversarial network (GAN) is also an example of self-supervised learning where a generator model is trained to generate new examples that believably could have come from the original dataset by discovering and learning patterns in the input data set and a discriminator model that tries to classify if these generated examples are either real or fake.[89] In this way a GAN can get feedback to update its model to generate more realistic images on every turn and for example generate synthetic photographs by initially using some unlabeled photographs. *Multi-instance learning* is a type of supervised learning that handles data that is only labeled in groups or "bags" instead of data points being individually labeled as in the case of the input-target pairs of supervised learning. Also, the same individual data points might be duplicated in more than one group. With multi-instance learning the label for new groups with many unlabeled examples can be predicted by training the model on the data of the labeled groups. In the context of machine learning, there are three types of inferences namely *deductive learning* where a model can be used to make a prediction, *inductive learning* where a model is trained using specific examples, and *transductive learning* where specific example data is directly used to make predictions without a model such as with the k-nearest neighbor algorithm. Another type of supervised learning is *multi-task learning* that reuses the trained model on one data set to help address many other related problems. One such example is reusing the same word embedding generated in one natural language problem domain across many other natural language processing tasks. Multi-task learning is different from *transfer learning* where a ML model is first trained on one task, then some part or the full model is used as the starting point for a related task. There are many examples of transfer learning in deep learning applications such as those used in image recognition where frameworks such as Keras provide access to some of the leading image recognition models trained on the ImageNet database such as VGG, Inception, and ResNet.[90] As it can take a long time to train these types of deep CNN models, using the pre-trained models or layers of these networks where features have already been extracted for potential re-use in other related problems can save significant time and lead to much better generalization results. Other learning types include *ensemble learning* where the prediction results of two or more ML models that are trained on the same data are combined, *active learning* where the model is able to ask for human intervention or input during the training process to help sort out uncertainty, and *online learning* where the ML model is directly updated before a prediction is required or after the last input example is provided such as with online gradient descent used to train a neural network. In Chapter 9 some of the state-of-the-art machine learning methods are briefly summarized for further context as the progress and likely future paths of AI is discussed.

In Pedro Domingo's *The Master Algorithm*, he succinctly describes some of the key different schools of thought and their approaches to machine learning where he describes the Evolutionaries as evolving structures, the Connectionists learning parameters, the Symbolists composing elements on the fly, the Bayesians weighing evidence and the Analogizers - mapping to new situations.[91] The *Symbolists*, inspired by logic and ideas from philosophy and psychology, use the inverse of deduction in their algorithms. For example, being able to deduce that A + B = C, in its inverse, is the ability to look at C and be able to know how we got there. So, it essentially attempts to have an accurate understanding of how we can know something to be true and testing it with new data in many different applications. The *Connectionists* are, on the other hand, inspired by neuroscience and physics and aim to reverse engineer neural processes in the form of artificial neural networks and currently use backpropagation as the core machine learning algorithm. Although artificial neural networks have gone through a few winter periods, it has been the most prominent AI approach over the last decade with major AI breakthroughs in the application of Deep Learning, Recurrent Neural Networks and Deep Reinforcement Learning. *Evolutionaries* simulate evolution and use genetic programming in their algorithms. The *Bayesians* are grounded in statistics and probability and use Bayesian inferencing (or predicting probabilities based on observed data) in their algorithms. The *Analogizers* learn from similarity judgements where machines are trained to classify something as either A or B in what is called Support Vector Machine algorithms. On their own, each of these approaches to machine learning is met with gaps, but combined together, Pedro Domingo believes one can construct a universal Master Algorithm that can evolve its structures (with genetic programs using genetic search), learn parameters (with neural networks using gradient descent), compose elements on the fly (with logic using inverse deduction), weigh evidence (with graphical models using probabilistic inference), and map to new situations (with support vectors using constrained optimization).[92] We'll also explore these various approaches further along with other promising AI research directions in Chapter 9.

If we continue along this path of demystifying AI and zooming out to look at the broader field of AI, we will notice that it has many subfields that can be categorized as particular AI goals such as developing machine learning or robotics, or various AI approaches such as traditional symbolic AI, statistical methods (statistical AI), computational intelligence (sub-symbolic AI), and integrated approaches (such as intelligent agents within a multi-agent system). So, using Pedro Domingo's terminology for the different AI approaches, the Symbolists would fall into the symbolic AI category with logic- and knowledge-based techniques and the Bayesians into the Statistical AI category, whereas the Connectionists, Evolutionaries, and Analyzers can all be classified into the sub-symbolic AI category where we have techniques such as supervised and unsupervised machine learning, reinforcement learning, embodied intelligence, and optimization. As the statistical AI category consisting of probabilistic and some machine learning techniques can also be categorized as non-symbolic in that they do not manipulate a symbolic representation to find solutions to problems, it could also fall into the sub-symbolic AI group. Symbols are representations or physical patterns or an abstract concept that get combined into structures, and then are manipulated to create new expressions. So, from a physical symbol systems perspective, symbols are encoded in our brains (e.g., the joining of two perpendicular lines is a plus sign), thoughts are structures of expressions (e.g., the plus sign means to add something), and thinking is applying the symbol and the structure together (e.g., 1+2=3). Whereas reasoning is about concept composition and concept expansion with discrete computation, learning is about generalization and concept creation with continuous computation. The Von-Neumann architecture (as an architecture for constructing actual computers which implement a Turing machine) has been a long-lasting model of sequential computations that are more suited for symbolic AI that deals with logic, high level aspects, and logical inference, and makes use of localized representations that are more rigid and static. Dynamical systems are more suited to sub-symbolic AI that deals with neural networks, low-level aspects, and statistical inference and having distributed representations that are flexible and adaptive. Whereas symbolic approaches typically are easier to explain, debug and control and provides introspection that makes it more useful for coding and also better suited to dealing with abstract problems and explaining people's thoughts, subsymbolic approaches on the other hand are more robust against noise, leads to better performance in general, can handle perceptual problems better, requires less knowledge upfront, is easier to scale up, taps much better into big data, and are more useful for connecting to neuroscience.

The AI field draws predominantly from computer science but also other fields such as neuroscience, psychology, information engineering, mathematics, statistics, linguistics, philosophy, physics, and biology. The AI tools to solve some of the most difficult problems in computer science include artificial neural networks, expert systems, logic, search, statistical methods, probability and economics, mathematical optimization, and evolutionary algorithms. The traditional goals or problems of AI research include knowledge representation, planning, reasoning, learning, the motion and manipulation of objects, natural language processing, perception, and social intelligence (affective computing). So, when considering the perception problem domain, sub-symbolic and statistical AI techniques are the most relevant for natural language processing that includes machine translation, natural language understanding and natural language generation as well as computer vision that includes image recognition, machine vision and activities recognition. For the reasoning, knowledge representation and planning problems domains, the symbolic AI techniques such as expert systems, fuzzy systems, robotic process automation, and inductive logic programming are very relevant. For this domain statistical AI can also add significant value through techniques such as Bayesian networks and program synthesis and probabilistic programming, whereas sub-symbolic techniques such as deep learning and generative adversarial networks also covers aspects of the reason and knowledge problems domains. Embodied intelligence types of sub-symbolic systems include for example autonomous machine learning systems, distributed AI such as multi-agent systems, agent-based machine learning, swarm intelligence, ambient computing, and affective computing (where the latter covers more the communication problem domain). Optimization related sub-symbolic AI includes for example evolutionary algorithms such as genetic algorithms which specifically also address the communication and planning problem domains.[93] As artificial general intelligence is amongst the field's aspirational longer-term goals, I will briefly discuss this further in this section and elaborate more in Chapter 9 when we are making sense of the AI debates on this topic amongst other things.

Although the AI founders were very bullish about AI's potential, even they could not have truly imagined the way in which infinite data, processing power and processing speed could result in self-learning and self-improving machines that function and interact in ways that we thought were strictly human. We already see glimpses of machines hypothesize, recommend, adapt, and learn from interactions, and then reason through a dynamic and constantly transforming experience, in a roughly similar way to humans. However, as we will see in Chapter 9, AI still has a long way to go to replicate the type of general intelligence exhibited by humans, which can be called artificial general intelligence (AGI) when performed by a machine. This hypothetical AGI, also termed strong AI or human-level AI, is the ability to learn, understand and accomplish a cognitive task at least as well as humans and can independently build multiple competencies and form connections and generalizations across domains, whereas Artificial Super Intelligence (ASI) can accomplish virtually any goal and is the general intelligence far beyond human level (surpassing human intelligence in all aspects - from general wisdom, creativity to problem solving). The AI that exists in our world today is exclusively a narrow or "weak" type of Artificial Intelligence, called Artificial Narrow Intelligence (ANI) that is programmed or trained to accomplish a narrow set of goals or performing a single task such as predicting the markets, playing a game such as Chess or Go, driving a car, checking the weather, translating between languages, etc. There is also another way of classifying AI and AI-enabled machines which involves the degree to which an AI system can replicate human capabilities. According to this system of classification, there are four types of AI-based systems: reactive machines, limited memory machines, theory of mind, and self-aware AI.[94] Reactive or response machines do not have the ability to learn or have memory-based functionality but emulate the human mind's ability to respond to different kinds of stimuli by perceiving occurrences in the world and responding to them. Examples of this include expert, logic, search-, or rules-based systems with a prime example being IBM's Deep Blue, a machine that beat chess Grandmaster Gary Kasparov in 1997 by perceiving and reacting to the position of various pieces on the chess board. In addition to the functionality of reactive machines, limited memory machines could learn from historical data to make decisions. Its memory is limited in the sense that it focuses on learning the underlying patterns, representations and abstraction from data as opposed to the actual data. Most of the present-day AI applications such as the ML and DL based models used for image recognition, self-driving cars, playing Go, natural language processing, and intelligent virtual assistants make use of this form of Artificial Narrow Intelligence. Both theory of mind and self-aware AI systems are currently being researched and not yet a reality. Theory of mind type of AI research which aims to create AGI-level of intelligence and are capable of imitating human thoughts, knowledge, beliefs, intents, emotions, desires, memories, and mental models by forming representations about the world and about other entities that exist within it. Self-aware AI systems could in principle be analogous to the human brain with respect to self-awareness or consciousness. Even though consciousness is likely an emergent property of a complex intelligent system such as a brain and could arise as we develop AGI-level embodied intelligent systems, I am not sure if we should have self-aware systems as an ultimate goal or objective of AI research. Once self-aware, the AI could potentially be capable of having ideas like self-preservation, being treated equally, and having their own wants and needs which may lead to various ethical issues and even a potential existential threat to humanity. Also, self-aware AI systems do not necessarily imply systems with Artificial Super Intelligence. In Chapter 9 we look at the different perspectives to help make better sense of this.

Assisted, Augmented and Autonomous AI

The question on the minds of many people is how do humans relate to the AI algorithms and their outcomes? How are we involved? How are we benefiting? What is required of us? With its many differing algorithms, approaches, and applications, we can see AI in three main ways in relation to human intelligence and interaction. This is what is sometimes known as the man-machine intelligence continuum and is divided into three main categories or models: Assisted Intelligence, Augmented Intelligence and Autonomous Intelligence.[95] *Assisted Intelligence* is considered as the most basic level of AI where it is primarily used as a means of automating simple processes and tasks by harnessing the combined power of big data, cloud, and data science to aid in decision-making. It is also used most often in software systems such as robotic process automation or machinery where the nature of tasks does not change and tasks are automated to free people to perform more in-depth tasks and improve things that people, companies and organizations are already doing. Although in software-based decision-making systems, assisted intelligence does require constant human input and intervention with clearly defined inputs and outputs with final decisions left in the hands of the end users, the assisted intelligence via machines tends to be where the machines are doing the automated work which is typically repeated on a kind of continuous loop and learning from their internal systems. The machine learns based on its tasks, their most efficient processes and responding to malfunctions, discrepancies, or anomalies. Examples of where we would find assisted intelligence in machines are industrial machinery, boilers, ovens, and manufacturing processes in factories.

Augmented Intelligence can be seen as a next level of AI that involves a symbiotic relationship between humans and machines where this category of intelligence allows people, companies, and organizations to do things they could not otherwise do by supporting human decisions, allowing better and faster decisions and is especially helpful in time-sensitive applications. Here the nature of the tasks changes as often as the humans who are informing or training the machines require. In turn, the machine informs the humans based on its learnings, where existing data and information are combined to suggest new solutions. So, examples include machine learning driven image recognition, natural language processing, business intelligence, business strategy analysis, and decision verification and support. *Autonomous Intelligence* represents a more advanced form of AI and involves processes where humans have taught the machine how to learn and adapt to new data. Here we also see the nature of the tasks change, but also that decisions are automated, and adaptation happens as the machine learns. Processes are automated to generate the intelligence that allows bots, systems, and machines to act on their own, independent of human intervention. Whereas there are many applications where autonomous intelligence can be used successfully such as smart investment or autonomous vehicles, autonomy should typically be given within strict lines of accountability. Autonomous Intelligence is also not a good fit for all applications, especially ones where it is difficult to quantify the best outcome, where more qualitative, intangible factors much be considered, or where it is better for humans to retain the responsibility of decision-making and have the AI functioning in a smart advisor capacity. These different application categories of intelligence are used in isolation and together. The truth is human intervention is required whether or not a human is required in every step of the process or not. Humans will need to verify findings, interrogate learning paths, and check the efficacy or validity of the machine's learning process and subsequent results.

In order to understand the different ways in which machine learning is applied to everyday processes, improve existing processes and create altogether new processes, let's first look at what Kai-Fu Lee calls the four waves of AI.[96] Artificial Intelligence, as we imagine it in its future state, has not and will not hit us all at once. Most likely it will happen in four waves that will lead up to a completely revolutionized world, far more powerful and distant than the experience those of us old enough to remember dial up internets and a time before mobile phones.[97] These waves, harnessing AI in different ways, include Internet AI, Business AI, Perception AI, and Autonomous AI. It does not mean that these waves will happen separately, and we do not know how long each one will take to reach its apex, but we do know that Internet AI and Business AI are already well on their way, and Perception AI is following closely behind. Already the digital and business world are using AI in their intelligence, targeting and automated learning and AI's perception skills in recognizing images and speech are growing too. Autonomous AI might not be a part of our lives as yet, but great progress is being made in the world of driverless cars and drones (and more).[98]

Internet AI is something every person who has searched Google, watched Netflix, been on Facebook and watched YouTube has experienced.[99] It is the way in which your media consumption builds up information on you and uses that information to recommend things based on your search, browsing, watching, buying, or reading history. It is the algorithm behind targeting and personalizing your online experiences. It does more than merely pick up what you watched, for example. It knows if you watched to the end and in that understand that the title may have interested you, but the content did not, or the length was too much for your attention span. Because of the huge amounts of data constantly building up, with new things to consume online and more people interacting with them, it is now also possible to tell the difference between real and fake news and what titles are likely to generate more reads or watches, so as to continually optimize the way humans judge books by their covers. Whereas high tech organisations such as Google and Facebook (both American), Tencent and Alibaba (both Chinese) and others have remained at the center of the first wave, the second wave allows non-high tech-based organisations across multiple industries to generate intelligence, efficiency, and optimization from their own data. This leads us to the second wave of AI - Business AI.[100]

Business AI relies on the huge amounts of historical data that businesses have been naturally capturing with every action and transaction. The ability to digitize, verify and remove any duplicates or incorrect entries results in the ability to be able to use this data for intelligence. This is why the first instance of business AI is to clean and mine the data in a way that is ready for the algorithms that rely on data to predict, measure, analyze, conclude, personalize and recommend. Business AI finds hidden correlations and learns from past decisions and outcomes within the organization. Business AI accounts for but looks much deeper than seemingly obvious correlations or ways humans have traditionally predicted outcomes. These algorithms look for and find things that we would otherwise miss, like instances that might appear unrelated in isolation. Of course, this is made possible by Big Data and our abilities to compare, analyze, and check data against huge amounts of other data. In the case of medicine, the more data we have on past cases, diagnoses, and cures, and the more we combine this data, every doctor with this technology is then enabled with the information of the hundreds of thousands before her, millions of cases and information from every medical publication and is thus empowered to be more adept, astute, and knowledgeable at her job.[101] The result? Money, time, and lives are saved.

Perception AI is related to the way in which machines are now able to interpret and make sense of images and audio. To see them, perceive them and even make sense of them in the way that used to be true to only humans. This means that images, objects, and sounds are now data, able to be analyzed by AI algorithms.[102] This is all very helpful with the introduction of driverless cars (more on this when we talk about the next wave), that are able to make sense of the world around them by creating a digital duplicate or twin that can be perceived and analyzed. It is also a breakthrough in intelligent shopping and education that can now be customized to suit each individual need through machine perception and understanding of our responses.

Autonomous AI is the result of a combination of the powers the first three AI waves bring us. This culmination will allow machines to not only respond automatically but will allow them to adjust and adapt to new instances and environments. In the world of robots that have automated a large portion of production already, this automation will reach new levels of intelligence where machines will make decisions for themselves based on being able to analyze and respond to changing circumstances.[103] Machines will have the power of sight, sense, touch, reasoning, and analysis - the combination that truly allows things such as autonomous vehicles to operate in changing, fast-paced environments. As the four waves emerge with new power and force and as a multitude of smart technologies and algorithms join forces, we are steered towards a machine-human future where the machine aspect will become such a natural part of our existence; simplifying our lives with intelligent convenience and insights, we can really begin to be excited about how our lives could change for the better.

Although I have dedicated a few chapters to AI applications across multiple industries I will briefly highlight how machine intelligence is already being applied. As it is now, AI's applications to problem solving in business, governing and society are endless. Some experts believe that cognitive computing represents our best — perhaps our only — chance to tackle some of the most enduring systemic issues facing our planet, from understanding climate change to identifying risk in our increasingly complex economy. The capabilities enabled through machine intelligence will force businesses and governments to rethink their operating models, and leaders, unions, and institutions to rethink the social, political, and economic theories upon which they are founded and built. While some processes may be refined, others will need to be reinvented, and still others built from scratch. Reimagining our world is not a future state, it is now. New skills, training and education are necessary to frame, process and adjust to the new world order that comes with machine intelligence and its countless applications. To begin with, a decision about which challenges to present to our cognitive systems and applications needs to consider how we prioritize our problems. Which do we solve first? Which are most appropriate, just and will yield the best outcomes for the highest number of people? If we are not thinking about this, then we must ask ourselves if we are best using the tools of the Smart Technology Era, and if how we are using them is based on our intentions for the future that is in our hands to create. Applying AI to our challenges is manifesting new ways of thinking, working, and collaborating and will invariably lead to cultural and organizational change, some of which may be challenging. This is a topic we discuss in detail later in this book.

Cognitive computing systems have obvious benefits in the fields of medicine, finance, law, and education and obvious ways to optimize service delivery and improve inclusion, governance and politics. These systems can also be applied in other areas of business including consumer behavior analysis, customer support bots, personal shopping bots, tutors, travel agents, security, and diagnostics. They are the result of intelligent, advisory, and cognitively enabled solutions that are interacting with data to learn, improve and expand. Some of this data is existing and some is reliant on constant human interaction (the humans using the systems). Cognitive applications typically revolve around text and rich media or customer interactions for analytics, tagging, searching, machine learning, categorizing, clustering, hypothesis generation, question answering, visualization, filtering, alerting, and navigation. Computers are trained using extremely large historical datasets to help them adapt and learn from prior experience, identify anomalous patterns in large datasets, and improve predictive analysis. Across the spectrum of analytics, we have descriptive and diagnostic analytics that provide information and hindsight; diagnostic and discovery analytics that provide diagnostics and insight; predictive and prescriptive analytics that provide foresight, prognostics, and optimization; and cognitive analytics. *Descriptive analytics* asks what happened, describes historical data, and helps to understand how things are going. *Diagnostic analytics* asks why it happened, helps to understand unique drivers, segments data and performs statistical and sensitivity analysis. *Discovery analytics* asks what is hidden in the data, helps to discover underlying patterns, and visualize and detect clusters in the data. *Predictive analytics* asks what could happen and forecast future performance, events, and results. *Prescriptive analytics* asks how to make it happen and provides analysis that suggests a prescribed action. *Cognitive analytics* asks what to do, why and how, and provides proactive action, learning at scale, reasoning with purpose and natural human interaction.

While the applications of AI are changing, adapting, and merging with other technologies continually, there are some common technical uses of AI in place today. Predictive analytics occurs when data on a business, customer behavior, employee tendencies and even news or economic influencers are consumed, understood, and analyzed for trends to predict future behavior and provide insights on how to capitalize on that behavior or change processes or directions to benefit from it. Static image recognition applications recognize and know what images are and can tag them and classify them in context as it has information about the contents of the image. Whenever the algorithm is fed a new image, it can recognize, classify, and tag it. Natural language processing allows computers to understand and interpret language the way it is naturally spoken by humans. It can process languages to answer questions and translate to other languages in real time. It keeps learning from itself and every interaction trains the algorithm to be more accurate and pick up on new languages, dialects, and pronunciations with ease. With natural language generation, computers can develop an understanding of the data presented and turn it into written text. Processing of patient data at scale allows for a full view of patient data with continued understanding to make patient care more effective, personalized, and holistic. This can reduce the chances of misdiagnoses, impersonal treatments or treating symptoms rather than causes. It also allows us to learn from every past case to save huge amounts of time in diagnosis and treatment. Object detection and classification applications go deeper than simply identifying digital images and are enabled to identify and classify objects in the real world. These AI applications can pick up information like how big the object is, how far away it is, and even how it might behave based on previous experiences with such an object. Robotic process automation has automated entire processes, tasks, workflows, and functions through mimicking and learning from existing processes whilst constantly improving based on new learnings. It can be used internally or as customer facing applications as well.

Deep learning increasingly addresses a range of computing tasks where programming explicit algorithms is infeasible. These are domains like fraud detection, robo-advisors, smart trading, recommendation pipelines, fully automated call centers, inventory, and product review auditing. Deep learning is also extensively used in search, autonomous drones, robot navigation systems, self-driving cars, and robotics in fulfillment centers. It is applied in many areas of AI such as text and speech recognition, image recognition and natural language processing. AI systems can now recognize objects in images and video and transcribe speech to text better than humans can. Google replaced Google Translate's architecture with neural networks, and now machine translation is also closing in on human performance.[104] Machine learning techniques applied to satellite imagery can also predict crop yield better than traditional techniques used by the US Department of Agriculture.[105] Artificial intelligence is also making its way into the realm of modern healthcare. Google's DeepMind is revolutionizing eye care in the United Kingdom, and IBM's Watson is tackling cancer diagnostics on par with human physicians. Both AI systems use deep learning which is particularly applicable in diagnostics. Stanford researchers also created a deep learning algorithm that could boost drug development by using a type of one-shot learning that works off small amounts of data for drug discovery and chemistry research.[106]

We already have many use cases for deep learning in the categories of sound, time series, text, image and video as it pertains to various industries. *Sound use cases* include for example voice recognition for user interface, automotive, security and IoT applications; voice search for handset makers and telecommunications; sentiment analysis for customer relationship management applications; flaw detection such as engine noise in automotive and aviation applications; and fraud detection for hidden audio artifacts in finance and credit card applications. *Time series use cases* include for example log analysis and risk detection for data centers, security, and finance applications; enterprise resource planning for manufacturing, automotive, and supply chain applications; predictive analysis using sensor data for IoT, smart home, and hardware manufacturing; business and economic analytics for finance, accounting, and government applications; and recommendation engines for e-commerce, media, and social networks. *Text use cases* include for example sentiment analysis for customer relationship management, social media, and reputation management; augmented search and theme detection in finance applications; threat detection for social media and government applications; and fraud detection for insurance and finance applications. *Image use cases* include for example facial recognition, image search for social media, machine vision for automotive and aviation applications, and photo clustering for telecommunications and handset makers. *Video use cases* include for example motion detection for gaming and user interfaces, and real-time threat detection for security and airports.

We do not believe that we have yet seen the full capacity of what we can expect from AI and its applications, but we have certainly seen its applications evolve within themselves and into other applications. The AI process can be best understood as an evolution of analytics, where each part of the process and evolution is integral for intelligent results. This analytics process in most cases starts with data. But data is involved in every step after that and can never actually be separated from the process. The evolution part is how we see that data, what we do with it, how we learn from it and where we go next. With all of what we can already do now, imagine we fuse it with any internet-enabled device - a drone, a remote, a robot, a car, a sensor, or a heavy industrial machine? This is where we see cognitive computing unlocking its true value by inserting intelligence into and learning from the physical world.

The Intelligence of Things, Blockchain, and the Future of Computing

As we instrument the world, we see an ever-increasing number of internet-connected devices that can process information and input or receive outputs of data in real-time. This is commonly known as the Internet of Things (IoT), but as cognition is applied to almost all new IoT devices, IoT now more accurately stands for the Intelligence of Things.[107] As AI has developed, so has the knowledge that intelligence is essential to tapping into the full potential and promise of internet powered devices. The purpose of intelligent things is then to connect us more closely with the physical world and share information with us about the tools we use, the homes and buildings we live in, and the cars we drive. Due to the amount of information internet-empowered devices receive, and the number of these connected devices at our fingertips, without some kind of intelligence, harnessing this information for appropriate diagnostics, predictions, understanding and recommendations, the usefulness of this information would be limited by its own complexity and scale. When AI is applied to the IoT, we not only get systems that infuse intelligence into the physical world, but also learn from it. This is what can be defined as the Smart IoT or Cognitive IoT. The Internet of Things along with consumer interactions and existing text, video and image data create the very foundation for learning that AI requires. In understanding the goals of an individual, organization, product or service, AI systems can present unbiased hypotheses, reasoned arguments, and recommendations. In this, AI is helping individuals and businesses to achieve those goals based on objective evidence or empirical data and immense processing power. By deploying machine learning based AI applications into instances of products, services, processes, and operations, it can help us understand and optimize our surroundings, environments, products, and processes. These ML based applications learn from interactions with humans and their experiences with their environment in a manner that is not deterministic. This enables AI solutions to keep up with the volume, uncertainty and complexity of information generated by the IoT.

Simply put, our products, services, processes, and operations become infused with cognition and are constantly learning and optimizing to yield a more personalized, targeted experience to humans, as both employees and consumers. This allows for enhanced discovery of the world around us and exploration into things we did not before have the capacity to unveil. For instance, we can create a kind of digital clone or twin of any physical structure, process, or tool. The digital clone is an exact replica of the intricate workings of say, a human body, a business process, or a machine. It has all its data and is 'like' the thing in every way except in the way we can touch it. It is almost a blueprint of the exact thing it is representing, but with more detail and intelligence than a blueprint could ever have. In having a digital clone that is powered by the internet and AI algorithms that are performing constant analysis on the clone, we have a situation where the real thing is sharing itself and interacting in real time with the digital world and constantly updating itself based on new data and insights. With the more related things and their matching digital clones that are working this way, we begin to see the manifestation of a cyber, virtual world that is constantly communicating with everything in that world to form an understanding of anything it might need. Seeing all these elements, including humans in relations to each other allows for deeper understanding, sense-making, improved communication, and an enhanced ability to explore.

The Smart IoT enables more complete human-centric interactions with people, fast tracking and extending of human expertise, the infusion of cognition into business processes, operations, products, and services as well as enhanced discovery and exploration. From an IoT functional point of view, Smart IoT provides the augmented intelligence required to drive augmented behavior. The AI engine enables machine intelligence and smart data when it integrates with IoT sensors, devices and networks and results in devices that can communicate, aggregate, analyze and act. These are devices that are constantly analyzing and interacting with their environments the very way humans would. This is relevant in almost every industry and in everyday life as it can provide intelligence to processes and products in financial services, healthcare and life science, retail and ecommerce, high technology and telecommunications, transportation, media and entertainment, education, legal, travel and tourism, resources and mining, utilities, manufacturing, construction, and the public sector. The amounts of data that IoT devices are collecting is quite unfathomable. It is correct to question if we have the network infrastructure and capacity to support it and the corresponding solutions to handle the impact of the streams of data and the network required to house and connect this data where it can be used relevantly. Since AI relies on data, and the more data it has from the more sources, the more relevant, holistic and in all ways intelligent it can be. To date, Smart IoT has helped cities predict accidents and crimes; allowed devices and not just sections of properties to have alarms; allowed service providers to manage water, gas and electricity for maximum efficiency and minimum wastage; allowed farmers to monitor soil moisture, weather conditions and crop health to farm more preemptively, prudently and effectively while minimizing wasted resources; empowered doctors with insights into pacemakers and biochips; optimized productivity and prevented downtime through predictive maintenance on equipment and machinery; connects appliances and devices to create smart homes and offices; and allows self-driving cars to communicate with each other. Every day, our potential for intelligence, prediction and intuitive living grows with the endless possibilities of Smart IoT and we should expect seeing this with more prominence within the next few years. New business opportunities that can be unlocked with AI, cloud-based technologies, IoT and big data include the introduction of new business models, diversification of revenue streams, global visibility, efficient and intelligent operations, and real-time information on mission-critical systems. Not only will new business models assist companies to create new value streams for customers, getting products and services faster into the market and responding more rapidly to customer needs, but also help them monetize additional services on top of traditional business lines. It further makes it possible and much easier for companies to do business in other global territories and to execute and make decisions in real-time.

For Smart IoT with its AI and smart devices to be efficient, safe, and scalable, accounting for the fusion of many smart technologies to be interacting at the same time, the IoT networks must be re-architected and upgraded to gradually shift from managing billions of devices to hundreds of billions or even trillions of devices. So, whereas IoT networks in the past were closed and centralized, and currently have open access with a centralized cloud, the Smart IoT networks of the future will have open access within a distributed cloud. A decentralized IoT network solution should be able to support file storage and transfers, broker messages, arbitrate roles and permissions, and support basic types of transactions such as trustless peer-to-peer messaging, scalable and robust device coordination, and secure distributed data sharing. Blockchain technology has a key role to play to enable such decentralized IoT network solutions. A blockchain is a type of distributed ledger which provides a consensus of replicated, shared, and synchronized digital data spread across multiple sites, countries, and/or institutions. This chain of data is made of packages called blocks and the blocks contain unchangeable, digitally recorded data. Although blockchain technology, which underlies cryptocurrencies such as Bitcoin and Ethereum, has only been explored for a few years, there are several important implications for the IoT and cognitive systems. For those of us who associate blockchain with currencies, we should prepare to expand our vision of this powerful technology. It provides a way to track the unique history of individual devices, by recording a ledger of data exchanges between it and other devices, web services, and human users. Combined with AI and IoT devices, blockchain could also enable smart devices to become independent agents, autonomously conducting a spectrum of transactions. Some examples include a vehicle which might even be a self-driving car that can diagnose, schedule and pay for its own maintenance; an autonomous vending machine that apart from monitoring and reporting on its own stock, can also do analytics on its purchase history of its customers to determine which new items needs to be purchased and then automatically requesting offers from distributors and/or suppliers to deliver these items and pay for them upon delivery; and a smart home setup that aims to minimize electricity costs against current grid prices through having the devices and appliances bid with one another for priority so that the washing machine, dryer, vacuum cleaner, water heater, and air conditioner can for example all run at the most sensible time.

Due to the sheer nature of transparency in that every action and interaction is trackable, blockchain could be the key to decentralizing systems that have, until now, relied on human authority and centralized servers. Unlike humans, blockchain is infallible to corruption, deception, redaction, bias, and omission - making a powerful governing tool and an excellent way to expose and do away with corruption and insist on honesty and transparency. Among other countries, Kenya has embarked on a mission to use Blockchain and AI to eradicate corruption and improve on its public services in the most efficient and objective ways. In this way, blockchain networks themselves are being used as a kind of independent agent, also referred to as a decentralized autonomous organization (DAO) or a decentralized autonomous corporation. Our centralized systems that we accept as a part of life: those governing bodies that dictate and govern systems such as education, banking and law are under necessary threat by blockchain technologies. These DAOs could effectively replace systems which have traditionally relied on centralized human authorities, with trustless (eliminating trust) and decentralized networks. The aim is to be able to use blockchain, in conjunction with other smart technologies, for its benefits of complete transparency and security in our smart devices. In order to do this without constant human intervention (as a way of autonomous intelligence), we need a way to be able to support file storage and transfers, and arbitrate roles and permissions. In this, blockchain, AI and connected devices can function in an automatic, decentralized way and leave the strategizing and thinking to humans and our interactions with other smart devices and systems. In the final chapter I will introduce a decentralized human-centric user-controlled AI-driven super platform called Sapiens as one of the mechanisms to help democratize AI and its benefits to as many people as possible in a decentralized hyperconnected world.

In a World Economic Forum article *How the future of computing can make or break the AI revolution* the key relationship between AI and computing is highlighted along with the key computing trends that are shaping AI which are Moore's law that states how processor speeds double every 18 months to two years (with the increase in the number of transistors in an integrated circuit), IoT (with 35 billion connected devices in 2020 likely to grow to 80+ billion in 2024)[108] that is enabling the collection of exabytes of text, voice, image and other forms of training data, the evolution of application specific computing hardware such as graphical processing units and tensor processing units with their specialized architectures for parallel computing, and the era of exascale computing of the latest supercomputers that is approaching exaFLOPS (billion billion floating point operations per second).[109] One of the challenges to the current status quo of computing is the likely end of Moore's law due to physical limitations such as the size of the metal–oxide–semiconductor field-effect transistor that is currently 5 nanometer (e.g., Samsung and TSMC entered volume production of 5 nm chips in 2020)[110] and becomes more difficult to manage with quantum tunneling effects through the gate oxide layer of these chips. Jim Keller of Intel is more optimistic as there are more than hundred variables involved in keeping Moore's law going with innovations such as new transistor designs and 3D architectures.[111] Another challenge is the increase in data regulation (such as GDPR in Europe) which is making centralized data handling more complicated and poses a problem for massive data centers and supercomputers which requires data to be stored close to the processors. On top of this we also have the costs of data storage and transfer as well as the lack of a computing-supportive ecosystem with more layers of software abstraction further away from the hardware and a decline in computing hardware startups with talented people with technology expertise preferring AI startups or joining the major technology companies.[112] A MIT Technology Review article *We're not prepared for the end of Moore's Law* mentions the decline of computers as general purpose technology and the shift towards more profitable application-specific chips such as those used for deep learning applications.[113] No wonder that the Stanford University's 2019 AI Index annual report stated that AI is outpacing Moore's law every three months with the speed of AI computation doubling during such a time window.[114] The MIT Technology Review emphasizes the need for investment in finding the next generation computer technologies and concludes that "quantum computing, carbon nanotube transistors, even spintronics, are enticing possibilities—but none are obvious replacements for the promise that Gordon Moore first saw in a simple integrated circuit. We need the research investments now to find out, though. Because one prediction is pretty much certain to come true: we're always going to want more computing power".[115]

Quantum computing is one of the promising computer technologies that offers a new kind of computing that can store and process quantum bits or qubits which can be made of atoms or subatomic particles and is a quantum version of the classic binary bit (that can be in a coherent superposition of a 0 and 1 state as opposed to be in just one of the two) and can perform many calculations in parallel. The latter capability makes it well suited to the parallel computations required by optimization and machine learning problems. Several technology companies such as IBM, Google, Microsoft, Honeywell, and Amazon, are active in the quantum computing sector and are making significant investments to accelerate progress. Quantum computers promises to solve certain complex problems substantially faster than classical computers with Google, for example, who has recently claimed to solve a complex computation in 200 seconds that would have taken the most powerful supercomputer ten thousand years to complete; a claim that IBM disputes as they believe it could have been solved by a supercomputer in a few days.[116] Google's Quantum AI Laboratory has set out investment opportunities on the road to the ultimate quantum machines and highlighted commercially viable uses for early quantum-computing devices such as quantum simulation (e.g., modelling chemical reactions and materials), quantum-assisted optimization (e.g., online recommendations and bidding strategies for advertisements use optimization algorithms to respond in the most effective way to consumers' needs and changing markets; logistics companies need to optimize their scheduling, planning and product distribution daily; and improving patient diagnostics for health care), and quantum sampling (e.g., sampling from probability distributions is widely used in statistics and machine learning).[117] They reckon that faster computing speeds in these areas would be commercially beneficial in sectors from AI to healthcare and finance. IBM Quantum is also building commercially-available quantum computing systems that they are making available on the IBM Cloud platform.[118] IBM has highlighted AI, cloud security, supply chain logistics (e.g., calculating a massive volume of possibilities to help optimize fleet operations, particularly during risky times, such as during the holiday season), and financial services as high-value target applications. Quantum computers promise to optimize solutions at scale, predict better probability distributions, search patterns in huge unsorted data sets, and also help to integrate data from different data sets. It can also help to accelerate the quality and quantity of image data generated for machine learning training purposes. The possibilities of applying quantum computing includes the development of quantum algorithms for quantum generalizations of traditional learning models to speed up training, to solve decision problems represented by decision trees faster than random processes, significantly enhanced search, and develop quantum game theory.[119] Some of the key milestones for quantum-related AI applications include less fallible and more powerful quantum computing systems, a broader and more skillful developer ecosystem, open-source modeling and training frameworks that are more commonly adopted, and plausible AI applications for which quantum computing provides much better performance than classical computing.[120]

Our Responsibility in Directing AI

Even though AI mimics part of the human process of reasoning, adapting, and processing information, it is not, at its core, about replacing humans with machines. It is about harnessing the combined strengths of both humans and machines to process environments and solve complex problems from constantly changing factors and arising information. As we move more deeply away from the "programmable era" of computers - where we have explicitly told computers what to do, we move into a space where we give computers the tools to tell themselves what to do or how to do it. And to become better and better at it, the more they learn. This is cognitive computing. It is the ability to mimic the human brain, to learn and to understand within the context that humans provide and, in this, be more of an assistant than a tool. It understands (by sensing and interacting with data), reasons (generating hypotheses and recommendations) and learns (what the lessons from masses of data are). It can take knowledge from different sources, bring it together, process and understand it without human involvement in every step. Some instances of machine intelligence are very specific to solving only certain problems or performing highly specific tasks. Part of this has to do with the data we have available to us, how that data is integrated and our own capacity to help the machines verify their learning pathways and conclusions so that they may continue learning, even from their mistakes. Because data, and large amounts of it are so important for any learning to take place, technology business giants such as Google, Apple, Facebook, Amazon, Microsoft, IBM, Baidu, and Alibaba are capitalizing on their data and are vying for 'AI throne'. Before digital technology and massive processing power existed, data existed in separate entities, not accessible or able to pass through one place or virtually accessible. With digital technology, our ability to capture and store data in place, and increases in processing power which allow us to do this with massive amounts of data, we now have rapid access to all available structured and unstructured big data in one place physically or virtually. Big data refers to the large, diverse sets of information coming from multiple sources, arriving in multiple formats, and growing at ever-increasing rates. It encompasses the volume of information, the velocity or speed at which it is created and collected, and the variety or scope of the data points being covered. Big data often relies on Application Programming Interface (API) integration between different applications (data from different places, now able to exist in one place). Most applications or software components typically have an API, which is its computing interface that defines how other applications, systems or software components can use its features, functionality, or data via a set of routines, functions, protocols, or procedures that specify the kinds of calls or requests that can be made, how to make them, the conventions to follow and the data formats that should be used. Just think of all the different applications or programmes you use daily. The ability for these to speak to each other, not only makes your life easier on the surface but allows data from these different places to communicate, share and interact with each other in the background. We are indeed living in the API Economy. The combination of data and machine intelligence is also what powers AI-as-a-Service cloud-based solutions, frameworks, development environments, platforms, and applications. An AI-as-a-service solution can for example provide the results of trained ML models in the form of inferences. ML algorithms rely on data, teaching and knowing which results were correct in order to infer, in future, the conclusions based on more and more learning and more and more data. These inferences are the results we see when we are fed certain ads on Google or Facebook. The ML algorithm has inferred the content that would be of interest to us based on learning our behavior and interests. One of the key application areas of AI is data mining which involves the process of discovering patterns in large data sets that makes data usable, and less random. It looks for similarities, differences, relationships, and anomalies in the data to learn and reach conclusions. Data mining occurs in many layers, and as machines learn, the layers become deeper, sometimes finding patterns and discoveries that humans themselves may never find. To mine data, data often needs to be cleaned or prepared to deal with raw data that often exists either in duplicates, in incorrect data entries or in contradictory data entries. Cleaning the data looks for these instances to try and remove or correct them so that the data can be used. Now that we have massive amounts of data in one place, information engineering deals with the distribution, analysis and use of this information. In ML, the aim is to generate, understand and use the data in a way that supports learning and inferences. Often data exists as a small sample of the population and thus is not a true reflection of the full picture. On top of this, because data is reliant on humans to add, add value to, clean and mine, the data reflects what these humans deem important, the conclusions they are trying to find, or the value inherent to themselves. It is important to understand how easily bias occurs before training any ML model.

As the potential applications for Artificial Intelligence is limitless, it will have a transformational impact on all industries. Understanding AI and its applications are vital to our lives, livelihoods, and the future we are creating with every present action or inaction. Artificial intelligence is not some distant future, nor is it something we can escape. It is here. For now, it is a black box for most people. But "when a new technology is as pervasive and game changing as machine learning, it's not wise to let it remain a black box."[121] For how do we affect or direct what we do not know about or understand? How can we be a part of what we do not understand? More importantly, how can we control it if we do not understand it?[122] We may think it necessary to control it, but just leave it up to the experts to understand it. But AI affects every part of life. It affects us, directly, and we should have a say in the things that affect us directly. Because if what we do not understand (and therefore cannot steer or control) are so much a part of the world around us and the tools we have as human beings to live, do business, to provide, to gain services and have insights into things, processes and each other, are we not intentionally removing ourselves from the core of the world as it is. It might not fit into our perception of the world as we know it. It might fit into our perception of the world as we wish it to be. It may not fit into what feels safe and known and comfortable, but it is still the reality we have and by denying it we are only excluding ourselves from being a true part of it. It is time for that to change. Some of the key reasons to prioritize learning about AI includes (1) adapting to the speed of AI implementations; (2) the fact that every major technology company is prioritizing AI; (3) companies that are first in deploying AI-driven solutions have competitive advantages over those that do not; (4) most countries are implementing new laws and regulations regarding smart technology that will likely affect everyone; (5) to ensure ethical, responsible implementation of AI applications; (6) more benefits and opportunities are likely for productive members of society that work together with smart technologies; (7) ensuring better collaboration between private and public sectors; (8) there is a shortage of knowledge workers such as data scientists, machine learning experts, and other technical professionals who can build AI solutions and services; (9) and the potential impacts on society.[123]

The sheer intelligence of the systems makes them feel less like technology and more like a natural, human interaction where little effort or learning on our parts is required. This is contrary to the introduction of technology and digitization where the onus was on us to learn, train, adjust and come to terms with how to use completely new and sometimes complicated systems and processes. Even learning how to use a keyboard is an example of the effort humans had to put in to start using computers over traditional pen and paper. Still today, we are seeing low adoption rates in organisations that have tried to replace traditional ways of working with digital tools. While these tools are becoming simpler to use, without AI, there is still a large amount of learning, training, and adopting involved, which people sometimes feel is simply not worth the effort. Cognitive computing changes all of this. It makes the complexity of technology "disappear" - where using technology no longer feels like using technology. In fact, it will feel easy, natural, and intuitive for us to interact with smart devices. We are already seeing the beginnings of this with Google Assistant, Siri, Alexa, and Cortana. As we go deeper into untapping AI's capacity and power, intelligence will be so infused into systems and devices that may not even be aware that they are using technology. There will be no effort. We are on a steady path towards a hybrid future full of diversity where multiple AIs are interconnected with each other and even, perhaps one day, within us. Whilst we are years away from seeing the effects of human biology infused with AI (e.g., in the form of chips, contact lenses, and so on), intelligent chairs, buildings, glasses and cars are here and will soon be naturally interacting with each other and with us.

We may think of algorithms in terms of AI only, but our brains use algorithms to see, hear, feel, learn, and understand. In fact, our brain uses the same algorithm to do all of this, and depending on the task, there are special parts of the brain that do the work and receive and send signals to either other parts of the brain or other parts of the body. However, if one part of the brain was damaged, for example, it is possible to direct those signals to another part of the brain, which would then become the new home of those signals and their subsequent tasks or results. This was demonstrated when a group of MIT students swapped around the eyes and the part of the brain responsible for sight (visual cortex), with the ears and the part of the brain responsible for the hearing auditory cortex. The result was that the Ferret was able to learn how to see and hear again.[124] This is because, whilst firing different neurons in different directions and between different functions or parts of the body and their 'home' in the brain, the same algorithm is used. The intelligence is the same, it is only the location that is different and depending on the function or complexity requires a different number of neural connections to effectively work. In Yuval Harari's *Homo Deus*, he emphasises that an algorithm is not a particular calculation, but the method followed when making the calculation. It is a methodical set of steps that can be used to make calculations, resolve problems, or reach decisions.[125] Humans do this all the time – each time we are faced with a decision, it is our own algorithms that decide how we will react. For example, if you see someone pushing in line, and that is met with a belief that pushing in lines is disrespectful, while you feel your purpose in life is to show people how to be more respectful, you are going to point out that the person pushed in line. Your own internal algorithm has led you to do this. Let us say the last time you politely showed someone how rude they were, you were punched in the face and left awfully embarrassed. This is now part of the data that your algorithm is processing. So, even by deciding not to point this out, no matter how much you want to, you are still functioning in the framework of an algorithm.

Your mind's algorithms are constantly at work. We use our internal algorithms when we are choosing the best way forward as well. We have all been in situations where we must decide which choice will lead us to our desired outcome. Sometimes, this happens instantly and subconsciously, and sometimes we have time to weigh up the potential risks versus benefits. In both conscious and subconscious matters, we are analyzing the information before us (current data), past lessons (past data), personal beliefs and values (priorities for desired outcome) and things we would like to avoid (risks). We also do this knowing that some things have higher priority than others. Only the most mindful of you are aware that this process or some like it even occurs. You have most likely gone much of your life without even being aware that it exists. AI (machine learning, deep learning and everything that results from these) works in very much the same way, only instead of inhabiting the brains, we are creating them. We are creating the algorithms that tell the systems what to value, what to avoid, what to favor. We are ensuring that they learn from new situations and incorporate their learnings into future decisions. We tell them what to look at, how to weigh what they are looking at and how to know if they do not know the answer. The machine intelligence we are creating is our own intelligence. We are figuring out how our minds process data and make decisions so that we can guide machines to follow the same pathways and learn the same ways we do. Jeff Hawkins believes that we will not be able to create fully intelligent machines until we understand how the human brain works.[126] This has been a question for psychologists, philosophers, biologists, neuroscientists, and neurosurgeons for many years. Everything the machines do is a result of humans. Everything they cannot do is a result of humans. Machine intelligence without human intelligence simply would not exist. It is important to remember that while these machines appear to be thinking for themselves, they are following a strict set of instructions and steps. Whatever they learn and however more precise or intelligent they become, they are still following the algorithm, or the automated learning process created by humans.

Our responsibility to direct AI towards favoring *the good* of life (all life, not just human life) is vital. To do this, it is important to understand our own algorithms and what makes them different. Each of our personalities and emotional responses, as Yuval Harari points out, is a result of our algorithms (however much more complex). Whilst certain steps in our algorithms might be the same as our collective past data (evolutionary needs and developments), personal past data (history), current data (present situation), outcomes (values and goals) and weighting (priorities) differ.[127] They will even differ in different situations. For example, our values or goals on a work project may differ from our values and goals for our careers which will also differ from our values and goals in social situations. Making decisions in each of these situations will use a variety of different conscious and subconscious algorithms. If we have been taught to value privacy, autonomy, and self-actualization over harmony and collective good (a common value contrast between West and East), these will appear in the algorithms that make decisions.[128] Similarly, if we grow up in a community, family or greater society that sees black males as more dangerous or women as less capable, these too appear in our thought and decision-making pathways. The danger with machine intelligence is humans are creating it. The algorithms we create are therefore just as susceptible to the prejudices, values, knowledge, and biases that we have.[129] The only difference is that the effects are on a much larger scale. Data bias is a huge problem for the world of machine intelligence and the human element in creating AI is only part of why biases exist. There is also the fact that not everyone's views, needs and priorities are reflected in the data that exists. Take Social Media for example. 2019 statistics show that Facebook users are at 2.4 billion, YouTube is at 1.9 billion, Instagram is at 1 billion, and Reddit and Twitter are both at 330 million.[130] If we are to take the information, sentiments and analyses we get from Social Media and use that to make decisions for the world, we are using data from not even half the world's population to direct further decisions and recommendations. It is ground for a disaster of biases. In later chapters, I will provide insights into how data bias can be avoided, checked, and accounted for. For now, the most important thing to note is that machines can only be as smart as we are. We need to stop seeing them as separate and start seeing them as the tools we create and use to achieve our own goals.

I will conclude this chapter with some thoughts and sentiments from Demis Hassabis, a co-founder of Google Deepmind, that I also identify with and could materialize if we act with wisdom and take full responsibility in directing AI in ways that benefit as many people as possible. He believes that AI "could usher in a new renaissance of discovery, acting as a multiplier for human ingenuity, opening up entirely new areas of inquiry and spurring humanity to realize its full potential" and that it is likely going to be the "most important technology ever invented".[131] Demis further states that "by deepening our capacity to ask how and why, AI will advance the frontiers of knowledge and unlock whole new avenues of scientific discovery, improving the lives of billions of people" and that AI can help us "build radically new and improved ways of life" and through our curiosity, the scientific method and our use of AI to not only solve society's greatest challenges today, but to understand ourselves and make sense of the universe around us.[132]

4. AI-driven Digital Transformation of the Business Enterprise

There is no doubt that Artificial Intelligence will increasingly become a transformative and disruptive driving force in business, not only impacting all aspects of the business enterprise, business models and most business sectors, but also give rise to novel market opportunities and affect industries of the future where we will see more AI-powered codification of money, markets, and trust, the weaponization of code through AI-driven cybersecurity, and the development of radical markets. It has been estimated that AI will add \$13 trillion to the global economy over the next decade.[1] Having been directly involved in developing and delivering impactful AI software solutions in a number of industries and business sectors across the globe over the last two decades, it has been amazing to see how business value drivers such as customer growth, retention, risk, productivity, efficiency, throughput, yield and quality can be impacted as more data becomes available and business are getting better instrumented and connected. This is further assisted by the significant increase in computing and data storage and processing capability, and the AI and smart technology toolboxes are being strengthened by the utility and capability of more powerful algorithms using all available structured and unstructured data.

As enterprises expect AI to enable them to move into new business segments or to maintain a competitive advantage in their industry, rethinking of industries and the enterprise itself is needed. We now see an evolution of the markets with respect to more informed consumers, faster and scalable marketplaces, dynamic and vibrant businesses, and leaner operations. Significant advances in AI are helping the creation of new industries and business segments by taking a fast adoption journey to move from discovery to commercial application to a new industry. Some early examples of AI driving new industry segments include GPS-driven ride-sharing companies, hyper-personalized online shopping platforms focusing on microsegments, intelligent virtual assistants driving conversations with customers as well as within the enterprise, recommendation-driven streaming channels, and adaptive learning based educational companies. We have also seen a tremendous increase in AI-focused startups with investments growing 1800% in the last six years.[2] These developments are putting more pressure on executive management of enterprises to act swiftly in making strategic shifts to monetize these new business opportunities and adapting their business models as the acceleration of AI adoption and its applications spawn the creation of new industries and business segments. Although the current focus of AI applications is mostly on optimizing efficiencies in existing industries, the most formidable long-term economic use of AI will likely be in solving large, complex, and open problems that could be the foundations of new industry segments. For this, business leaders and AI strategists need to spot important trends, keep track of state-of-the-art AI developments and act quickly around new possibilities.

We also need to specifically rethink the impact of human-computer interaction, automation, jobs, the workplace, and cybersecurity, amongst many other factors that are impacting business value drivers, employees, and customer experience. It is also evident that customer facing businesses need to offer personalized customer experiences at scale, which is beautifully illustrated by the success of the internet giants like Google, Amazon, and Alibaba and their ability to deliver personalized experiences and recommendations. By using AI to build a dynamic real-time 360-degree profile of customers as they interact through mobile apps, intelligent virtual assistants and online web portals, providers of goods and services can quickly learn how their AI-driven predictions can fit customer's wants and needs with ever-increasing accuracy. When we flip through recommendations on Netflix or Amazon, or search on Google, most of the AI-based calculations are happening in high-powered processors inside remote data centers (in the cloud) with handheld or desktop devices acting as the interface and communicating the results. This will change as AI algorithms become more efficient and capable of running on low-power devices at the "edge" where custom processors designed to carry out real-time analytics on-the-fly close to the point where data is gathered and used. With the cost of hardware and software continuing to fall, AI tools (augmented by IoT, cloud and edge computing, virtual and augmented reality, and so on) will increasingly be embedded into our vehicles, appliances, and workplace tools, giving these devices of every shape and size the ability to learn for themselves. As IoT integration will allow for the development of environments where solution providers and consumers can interact, it will likely also be possible to design experiences over products, which will affect business models further.

Towards AI-driven Digital Transformation

For any business to stay relevant and thrive given the swift pace of change and disruption in the Smart Technology Era, it needs to be transformed into an AI-driven business and have increasingly more real-time intelligence built into on all aspects of its internal operations, customer needs and impact, and competitive and collaborative forces in the ecosystem in which the business operates. For businesses to move towards AI-driven automated decision-making, they need to overcome the barrier of information quality. However, accurate data is becoming increasingly available with better quality sensors, improved connectivity, and an increase in smart technology and methods of simulating real-world processes and mechanisms in the digital domain. We will see an increase in the availability and accuracy of real-world simulations, which in turn will lead to more powerful and accurate AI systems. With computers now powerful enough and trained on accurate-enough data to do simulations in the digital world, the expense and risk of testing AI systems in the real world can also be reduced. For example, we have seen how simulations help businesses working on the development of autonomous vehicles to gain thousands of hours of driving data without vehicles even leaving the factory, which in turn leads to increases in data quality and significant reduction in cost. Given the nature of Tesla's software-defined electric vehicles even more accurate real world driving data is captured. Whether or not they are Autopilot enabled, the data from Tesla vehicles is sent directly to the cloud and used to generate highly data-dense maps that they claim are more accurate than alternative navigation systems. The better a company can mine all available internal and external data across its operations, value chain, customers, and ecosystem to create real-time dynamic simulation models of all aspects of its business, the better it would be able to optimize the business over short, medium, and long-term windows and adjust its course where required. This is relevant across all industries.

Across industries, businesses and organizations are assessing ways and means to make better business decisions utilizing such untapped and plentiful information. As the world gets instrumented, data is generated at an exponential rate, whereas data utilization increases relatively linearly in relation to data generation. With evolving AI technologies that can unlock value from growing data sets and more and more business use cases come into the fray, there is a need for innovative approaches that takes into consideration the required data infrastructure, computing (both in hardware and software), AI tools and platforms, processes, organizational alignment, and roles. As enterprises look to innovate at a faster pace, launching novel products and improving customer services, they need to find better ways of managing and utilizing data both within the internal and external firewalls. Organizations are realizing the need for and the importance of scaling up their existing data management practices, overcoming siloed execution, and adopting newer information management paradigms to combat the perceived risk of reduced business insight or lack of impactful solution deployment. So, an organization's ability to analyze that data to find meaningful insights and operationalize AI-driven solutions are becoming increasingly complex. Many of the current business success stories have come about with companies enabling analytic innovation and creating data services, embedding a culture of innovation to create and propagate new database solutions, enhancing existing solutions for data mining, implementing predictive analytics and machine learning techniques, complemented by the creation of skills and roles such as data scientists, AI or machine learning engineers, data science developers, big data architects, data visualization specialists, and data engineers, among others. These enterprises' experiences in the AI and Big Data analytics landscape are characterized by agility, innovation, acceleration, and collaboration.

Another key aspect of leveraging smart technology is to also understand where it can be used, when it can be used, and how it can be used. Business value drivers can typically be categorized as strategic or efficiency related. Some strategic drivers include the generation of new business opportunities through exploratory analysis to uncover hidden patterns, proactive decision making and gaining operational insights via predictive analytics, forecasting customer and market dynamics, speeding up strategic decision making with real-time AI-driven analysis, and better decisions through cross-organizational analysis to quantify the estimated impact of decisions. On the other hand, efficiency value drivers typically include continuous improvements, the reduction of costs on people, processes, and infrastructure and tools that do not enhance an agile and smart data-driven business, and increasing automation to reduce efforts needed to extract, consolidate, and produce reports. Other efficiency drivers include to complement or retool skills of employees to emphasize problem solving and recommendations, developing data-driven decision-making culture, eliminate redundant tools, data stores and processes, and standardize metrics and streamline processes. We already see how robotic process automation is used to do repetitive work such as filling in forms, generating reports and diagrams and producing documentation and instructions. Although this leaves employees to spend more time on complex, strategic, imaginative and interpersonal tasks, we would need to get used to learning new skills and working alongside AI-powered tools and bots in our day-to-day working lives. The IDC predicts that by 2025, 75% of businesses or organizations will be investing in employee retraining in order to fill skill gaps caused by the need to adopt AI.[3] Some example business drivers that I have encountered across multiple industries include increasing operational efficiency, effectiveness and revenue; creating strategic value via faster, better and more proactive decisions, enhanced scalability, new business models, and revenue growth opportunities; enhance customer experience via real-time, on demand, digital, personalized service delivery, assistance and advice which is enabled via 360 degree insights about the customer; and targeted sales and marketing. A business can increase its productivity through increasing automation, improving processes, and ensuring equipment availability. To increase revenue, an industrial business is focused on increasing throughput, yield, and quality, whereas a consumer-facing business is more fixated on cross-selling, up-selling and recommending products and services to its customers. To drive efficiency and effectiveness, a business also needs to reduce its risk which might include process and equipment failure, customer churn, fraud, waste and abuse, and cybersecurity risks. For a business to lower costs, it needs to eliminate redundancy, reduce energy and raw material usage, and have more cost-effective operations and maintenance.

Some of the key characteristics of businesses that are early adopters of AI are those that are digitally mature, adopting multiple smart technologies, including AI in core activities, have a focus on growth over savings, and have executive-level support for AI. In the chapters to follow, we will see how AI can create business value across the value chain via smarter research and development and forecasting, optimizing production and maintenance, targeted sales and marketing and enhancing the user experience. The key elements of successful AI-driven digital transformation include the following catalysts to accelerate the path to business value generation: *Vision or Intent* (which involves scanning the use-case horizon and sources of value; articulate business needs; and creating business cases, strategic plans, and performance metrics), *Data* (which entails breaking down data silos in the data ecosystem; deciding on the level of aggregation and pre-analysis; and identifying high-value data and data availability), *Technology* (which identifies first-for-purpose AI tools and platforms, partner or acquire to plug capability gaps; and taking an agile "test and learn" approach), *Process* (which encompasses integrating AI into workflows and workplace processes through change management; and optimizing the human/machine interface), and *People* (which is about adapting an open, collaborative culture and organization; building trust in AI insights; developing AI implementation skills; and reskilling the workforce to ensure complementarity). To help guide a business on its digital transformation journey in operationalizing AI solutions, I have been recommending and using an adapted agile version of the IDC's Big Data and Analytics MaturityScape framework for many years.[4] It is a framework of stages, dimensions, outcomes, and actions required for businesses to effectively advance along the five stages of Big Data and Analytics or AI implementation competency and maturity: Ad Hoc, Opportunistic, Repeatable, Managed and Optimized. The Ad Hoc stage is more experimental in nature and characterized by ad hoc, siloed pilot projects, undefined processes, and individual effort. The business outcome is typically value obtained through new knowledge and learning. The Opportunistic stage is more intentional where there are typically defined requirements and processes, but unbudgeted funding as well as project management and resource allocation inefficiency. At this stage knowledge value grows and business value opportunities become visible as a business outcome. The next stage of competency and maturity is the Repeatable stage where there are recurring projects, budgeted and funded program management, documented strategy and processes, and stakeholder buy-in. Here we see business value being realized but the business outcome remains localized to business units. When a business moves to a Managed stage, the project, process and program measurement influence investment decisions and standards emerge. The business outcome is typically that new product and service opportunities transition to business plans and execution. The final stage is Optimized where AI-driven continuous and coordinated process improvement and value realization leads to previously unattainable business value being continuously produced. This framework allows a way to assess the AI operationalization maturity and competence of a business as it transitions through the various stages over time for each of the five dimensions which can be visualized in a radar chart: Vision or Intent (strategy, budgeting, justification and culture), Data (quality, completeness, trust, and timeliness), Technology (deployment, adoption, performance, and functionality), People (skills, organization, collaboration, and training), and Process (data management, data analysis, governance, and measurement). With this framework a baseline can be used to define short- and long-term goals, prioritize smart technology, budget as much for integration and adoption as for technology, plan for improvements, make employee investment decisions, and bring business value into view. As the assessments can be done on a team, business unit, and business level, gaps in current AI competency and maturity levels can be uncovered among functional and cross-functional teams, business units or between business and IT groups. This allows for all the stakeholders to collaborate in advancing the organization toward a common goal of building a smart technology data-driven thriving business that continuously delights customers.

The Agile AI-driven Business Enterprise

To thrive in the Smart Technology Era, businesses need to be nimble which enables business to cope with continuous change in an increasingly complex, rapidly shifting, uncertain and unstable world. This agility is key for businesses to survive and thrive sustainably with today's marketplace. The following three "laws" for operating in an agile fashion describes the key ingredients in this regard: *the law of the small team* where work should typically be done with small autonomous cross-functional or interdisciplinary teams on relatively small tasks in short cycles with continuous end user feedback; *the law of the customer* implies that everyone in the business is laser focused on delivering continuous new value to the customer and make the necessary organizational changes to support this; and *the law of the network* where the whole business is truly agile and seen as a fluid and transparent network of high-performance teams that are collaborating towards the common goal of delivering superior value to customers[5]. As companies apply the three laws of agility, the actions that promote scale in AI also creates a virtuous circle where interdisciplinary teams initially start collaborating with their diverse skills and perspectives combined with the user input needed to build effective customer solutions, absorb new collaborative practices across the business, and move from trying to solve siloed problems to completely reimagining business and operating models. The more the business adopts the test-and-learn agile approaches for AI-driven pilots and solutions, the faster innovation happens across the organization with decisions augmented by AI also happening faster and closer to the coalface. AI-driven businesses that operate in such an agile way creates a competitive edge for them in the marketplace. As we have seen with the coronavirus pandemic a case can be made that only agile businesses will survive.[6] It further accentuates the importance of agility in the Smart Technology Era, where we see new ways of working, living, playing, and learning where everything is different. So, businesses either adapt or die whilst they are continually bombarded with a stream of strategic opportunities and risks whereas their business agility needs to be constantly upgraded.

Steve Denning in *The Age of Agile* argues that strategic agility either occurs as a by-product of operational agility or using an explicit playbook to generate market-creating innovation.[7] As a by-product of operational agility it works well to improve existing products for existing users, but has limitations in not necessarily attracting non-users, eliminating features and not adding or improving them, leading to cannibalization of other existing products or services, not a solution for innovation that requires substantial technical innovation or financial investment, a bias for "small bets" that generate quick wins as opposed to "big bets", and dealing with large investments in a new product. The Innovation-for-Impact Playbook pioneered by Curt Carlson and others at SRI International describes an organizational design and value-creation process for creating major breakthroughs such as what SRI did with HDTV, Siri, and Intuitive Surgical. The explicit playbook for creating market-creating innovation is just as relevant for AI-driven digital transformation of a business and touches on the **N**eed (understand non-customers, study markets to identify the need, and think big, but process incrementally), **A**pproach (thinking platforms, acquiring smart digital competency, have a bias for action, create the secret sauce from an existing strength, and separating customers and end-users when it make sense to do so), **B**enefits per costs for both the customers and the producer (tell not only what difference, but how much of a difference your solution will make in the life of the customer), and identifying the **C**ompetition and alternatives (there are always competition in whatever shape or form). To thrive as a business that generates market-creating innovation, continual iteration over this whole process (summarized in the mnemonic, NABC) is needed to strengthen the value proposition assuming that the customer's need is genuine.

Assisting Businesses on their AI-driven Transformation Journeys

As businesses are grappling with tremendous challenges to not only be operationally and strategically agile, but to focus on the right use cases for quick wins and optimal business value generation, their data ecosystems, their technology and tools, their people, and the processes they implement, they often reach out to a variety of companies across the AI solutions, consultancy, hardware, and software landscape to help them on their AI-driven digital transformation journey. From a software perspective, we are living in the Application Programming Interface (API) Economy where a variety of commercial, open source and proprietary components, frameworks, APIs, and libraries are available in a similar way as "Lego blocks" to be used in developing and delivering impactful AI-driven solutions. Technology giants such as Google, Amazon, and Microsoft, and many others are providing scalable cloud computing, hardware, storage, tools, solutions, applications, software components, APIs, and so on via a variety of business models such as infrastructure-as-a-service (cloud-based services and pay-as-you-go for services such as storage, networking, and virtualization), platform-as-a-service (hardware and software tools available over the internet), software-as-a-service (software that is available via a third-party over the internet) and on-premises software (that is installed in the same building as your business). Whereas with infrastructure-as-a-service the business manages the applications, data, run-time, middleware and the operating system and others manage the virtualization, servers, storage and networking, with platform-as-a-service the business only manage the applications and data and others the rest of the services. On opposite ends you have software-as-a-service where others manage all these services and on-premises where the business itself manage all aspects.

Goldman Sachs Global Investment Research has highlighted enablers to assist businesses on their AI-driven transformation journeys which involves do-it-yourself enablement, consulting services or making use of AI-as-a-service offerings.[8] With do-it-yourself enablement, businesses that have inhouse AI talent and differentiated data typically make heavily use of an AI stack that combines open source and cloud provider services. As people with deep experience and knowledge in AI and its applications are not readily available, many companies depend on partnering with AI solutions providers and consultants to help them fast track delivery of AI solutions. AI problems can also be outsourced to data science competitions platforms such as Kaggle and Zindi.[9] The third enabler is AI-as-a-service where AI-related APIs that have already trained models behind it or even end-to-end AI platforms for data science and AI applications are used from providers such as Google, Microsoft, or Amazon. Google for example have not only specific AI and machine learning APIs such as Vision AI, Text-to-Speech, Dialogflow, and AutoML, but also industry solutions.[10] A recent The Next Web article states that the AI landscape is shifting from data to knowledge and believes that AI's future depends on moving the focus from proprietary data sets to the sharing of data across entities for knowledge creation.[11] They believe that a good knowledge strategy consists of building knowledge moats, rather than data moats; using AI in a top-down manner and structure businesses around the application and product layer; combining data, AI models, information, storage, and computing power; shaping organizations' HR strategy through this shift to knowledge; and viewing data acquisition initiatives as a short-term tactical pursuit while knowledge-based partnerships for cooperation and exchange should be promoted and developed as long-term business strategies.[12]

Having been actively involved in AI Product and Platform Developer and AI Solutions Provider capacity for many years, we also had to adapt very quickly to provide the most effective and efficient ways of providing an AI Engine for business that solves strategic and operationally relevant problems through operationalizing AI, Data Science, Internet of Things and Big Data and Analytics and delivering state-of-the-art AI-based applications, solutions, and products. This should typically be done in a practical, cost-effective way using all available data and smart technology in an end-to-end, full stack, integrated, scalable, and secure manner. These AI-based solutions address business value drivers that lead to an optimized business, a satisfied customer base, productive employees, and smart systems to help accelerate decision making, innovation, collaboration, and growth. The focus is therefore on business outcomes such as increased productivity and revenue, reducing risk, lowering costs, creating strategic value, enabling smart automation, enhancing customer experience, and implementing more targeted sales and marketing. Some of these AI-driven solutions include strategic business transformation and optimization, human capital valuation and employee profiling, intelligent virtual assistants, robo-advisors, process optimization, real-time causal analysis, predictive maintenance, fraud detection, churn prediction, advanced risk scoring, machine learning-based trading, real-time customer insights, smart recommendations and purchase prediction, personalized search, cyber security, medical risk prediction, and precision medicine. These types of AI-based solutions can be applied in financial services, healthcare, education, retail, telecommunications, resources, utilities, and the public sector as well as other industries where the automation of tasks and data monetization can lead to economic benefit, scalability, and productivity. To use my AI company Cortex Logic as an example, although now focused on AI-driven platform solutions in healthcare and financial services, we have worked across multiple business and industry domains seeking to augment and automate legacy processes, ultimately transforming them into intelligent systems, using the Cortex Logic AI Engine. The four core solution domains, each with a range of products that can transform key business processes using AI, includes *Engage* that helps people and businesses work smarter at scale, *Personalize* which focuses on smart personalization of consumer products and services, *Enhance* that provides smart automation and enhancement of business processes and systems, and *Sense* which enable smart machines to sense and interpret the world around us. [13]

To help businesses with operationalizing AI and unlocking the value from all available structured and unstructured data, an AI Solutions Provider also needs a highly skilled team of artificial intelligence and machine learning experts, data scientists, data and solution architects, data engineers, business intelligence engineers, business analysts, software developers, domain experts, and out-of-the-box thinkers. As a high-performance team with deep expertise and experience in AI and its applications as well as the ability to connect the dots in the Smart Technology Era and New Economy, they must leverage their speed, agility, and flexibility to develop and deliver scalable end-to-end AI-driven solutions and licensed products. This can be strengthened over time and has many layers within technology, the AI technology stack, solution development, application domain expertise, business models, route to market, partnerships, sales channels, commercialization, and so on. A typical high-level application stack for AI solutions consists of a raw data layer, a data preparation layer, a smart data layer, an analytics layer and an application layer that are in a continuous loop of refinement and improvement. The raw data layer which consists of a variety of data sources that can for example be structured, unstructured or streaming data typically feeds into a data preparation layer where data can be extracted, transformed, and loaded, along with other data preparation such as natural language processing, text analytics and entity extraction. These two layers are followed by a smart data layer that handles a spectrum of big data, smart data, knowledge bases, SQL databases, NoSQL databases, resource description framework data, ontologies, and ecosystems that become enterprise data hubs. The next layer is an analytics layer that covers the spectrum of analytics such as descriptive, diagnostic, predictive, prescriptive and cognitive analytics which uses a variety of algorithms such as various machine learning algorithms. The final layer is the application layer that addresses application engagement, the user interface, the user experience of the user interface, insights, and recommendations.

The data science methodology typically used in delivering AI-based solutions follows a combination of sequential execution of tasks in certain phases and highly iterative execution steps in certain phases. Because of the scale issue associated with a big data and analytics system, designers must adhere to a pragmatic approach of modifying and expanding their processes gradually across several activities as opposed to designing a system once and all keeping the end state in mind. The main phases are typically as follows: 1. Analyze and evaluate business use case; 2. Develop the business hypothesis; 3. Develop analytics approach; 4. Build and prepare data sets; 5. Select and prepare the analytical models; 6. Build the production ready system (scale and performance); and 7. Measure and monitor. This methodology also corresponds with the Cross-Industry Standard for Data

Mining (CRISP-DM) and the Analytics Solutions Unified Method for Data Mining/Predictive analytics (ASUM-DM).[14] CRISP DM has a cyclic nature and prescribes a sequence of phases that are dependent on one another and starts with business understanding which is followed by data understanding, data preparation, modeling, evaluation, and deployment. The sequence of the CRISP-DM phases is not strict and moving back and forth between different phases is always required, especially between business and data understanding, data preparation and modeling, and evaluation of the models against the business understanding and desired outcomes. A data mining process continues after a solution has been deployed. The lessons learned during the process can trigger new, often more focused business questions and data mining processes that follows will tap into the experiences of previous ones. The *Business Understanding* phase focuses on understanding the project objectives and requirements from a business perspective, and then converting this knowledge into a data mining problem definition, and a preliminary plan designed to achieve the objectives. A decision model, especially one built using the Decision Model and Notation standard can be used. The *Data Understanding* phase starts with an initial data collection and proceeds with activities to get familiar with the data, to identify data quality problems, to discover first insights into the data, or to detect interesting subsets to form hypotheses for hidden information. The *Data Preparation* phase covers all activities to construct the final dataset (data that will be fed into the modeling tool(s)) from the initial raw data. Data preparation tasks are likely to be performed multiple times, and not in any prescribed order. Tasks include table, record, and attribute selection as well as transformation and cleaning of data for modeling tools. In the *Modeling* phase, various modeling techniques are selected and applied, and their parameters are calibrated to optimal values. Typically, there are several techniques for the same data mining problem type. Some techniques have specific requirements on the form of data. Therefore, stepping back to the data preparation phase is often needed. At the *Evaluation* phase of the project, you have built a model (or models) that appears to have high quality, from a data analysis perspective. Before proceeding to the final deployment of the model, it is important to evaluate the model more thoroughly, and review the steps executed to construct the model, to be certain it properly achieves the business objectives. A key objective is to determine if there is some important business issue that has not been sufficiently considered. At the end of this phase, a decision on the use of the data mining results should be reached. The development of the model is typically not the end of the project. Even if the purpose of the model is to increase knowledge of the data, the knowledge gained will need to be organized and presented in a way that is useful to the customer. Depending on the requirements, the *Deployment* phase can be as simple as generating a report or as complex as implementing a repeatable data scoring (e.g., segment allocation) or data mining process. In many cases it will be the customer, not the data scientist, who will carry out the deployment steps. Even if the data scientist deploys the model it is important for the customer to understand up front the actions which will need to be carried out to make use of the created models. ASUM-DM also has a cyclic nature and shows more the broader data mining lifecycle and project management perspective with the first major Analyze-Design-Configure-Build project phase that is followed by the Deployment project phase and then the Operate and Optimize project phase for the same deployed AI solution.

To deliver end-to-end AI-based solutions an AI Engine can be developed that typically consists of components that enable rapid access to all available data and the preparation of smart data, the automation of the AI solutions, and the integration of the AI solution into the business processes and/or customer interfaces. *Enabling Smart Data for Automated AI solutions* involves providing a solid data lake and warehouse infrastructure that can not only deal with the volume, velocity and variety of structured and unstructured data but also enable rapid access to all data via flexible data models, data preparation and smart data layers for analytics and automated AI systems. It should support polyglot persistence (which implies using multiple data storage technologies for varying data storage needs)[15] and facilitate access to various source systems via data virtualization, distributed processing, and other system components. The multi-platform architecture should also provide a governance model to support trust and security, master data management, data federation, data cataloging, automation, support for all types and levels of users, and the ability to facilitate near real-time analysis on high velocity data, massive parallel processing, and in-memory compute. The second part of the AI Engine is to *Automate the AI solutions*. This type of data and compute infrastructure is essential to operationalize Data Science and implement automated AI systems where there is significant reuse of feature libraries and data preparation pipelines for generating deep insights via data exploration, analysis, contextualized data, modeling, and predictive models in a development and productionized context. This is done by following international data science standards and implementing automated analytics within a champion-challenger approach, which is typically maintained and kept up to date during the deployment and operational phase. The third component of the AI Engine is *Integrating the AI solutions into Business Processes and/or Customer Interfaces*. The AI Engine ensures that the analytic outputs, scores, and predictions are integrated into the business via an Analytics services layer that involves, amongst others, automated analytics dashboards, intelligent assistants, a range of deployed models, simulation and optimization service and real-time machine learning. The integration into business processes involves for example: on-demand delivery models via access-anywhere analytics services and context-aware business applications; push delivery models via alert and response and location-based services; and embedded delivery models via workflow and interaction automation and smart devices and systems. The outputs of this integration can then be stored back in the data lake.

AI is Changing Business Processes

AI is already changing many business processes across the enterprise and its value chain all the way from sales, marketing, and the customer interface to research and development, human resources, recruitment, legal services, auditing and security. AI can be used as a valuable tool for business process management that aims to create an efficient and effective workflow for the business enterprise by helping to automate repeated tasks through robotic process automation, improve user interfaces through personalized intelligent virtual assistants, enhance decision-making within business processes (e.g., should a customer be sent a product recommendation or get a follow-up call) and analyze massive data sets through data mining and predictive analytics. Well-designed AI systems should augment people and allow them to focus on decision making, innovation, and higher-value work that reinforces the role they play in driving business growth. As businesses move to outcome-based approaches where agreements are based on the business value created by the work, we will see a change in business processes that have traditionally been driven by service level agreements. The more AI is being democratized, the more business will be able to apply it in various business processes across the enterprise.

AI is already revitalizing the market research function and will continue to do so to not only empower next-generation market researchers to be dramatically more productive by improving the efficiency of existing workflows, but also changing how market research is being conducted and delivering scalable impact where more people can use market research across the enterprise to access the right data and return actionable recommendations. With vast amounts of data being created every second by people and things connected to the internet, the need to collate, structure, and interpret this data by market researchers to distill timely actionable insights will only get more time-consuming and capital draining. Businesses that are early adopters will see how machine learning driven market research can produce insights within minutes or hours that used to take teams of people days or even weeks to produce, followed by decreases in labor demands and overall expense. Instead of dedicating specific time, labor and money to the market research process, the market and customer needs can be continually surveyed via machine learning driven automation, text analytics, intelligent virtual assistants, insight generation, and natural language processing. By having a real-time comprehensive understanding of people's actions, movements, and needs that are continually mined, insights can be generated that provide market researchers and/or decision makers with a better picture than they have ever been able to generate or seen before.

In today's AI applications we already see how intelligent virtual assistants can interact with customers, learn from their questions asked and answers provided, reveal correlations between complex responses, built-up a dynamic profile of the customer on the fly, make use of people's motion profiles for tailored services and location-based marketing and derive more in-depth information about consumer behaviors. It can also help identify customers likely to churn and how they can be retargeted with personalized offers and service delivery. Real-time customer insight powered by cognitive IoT will provide market researchers and data scientists the opportunity to conduct in-depth longitudinal studies on customer behavior and more accurate forecasting models. An example of the combined usage of AI and IoT is where insurance companies use telematics to determine the premium of their customers based on their cars' driving patterns, traffic, and other features, whereas drones are used to provide information for property damage claims, indemnification and premium calculations. Another source of market research data can be obtained via affective computing that involves delivering an emotional profile of the user via AI-driven textual, facial, and voice analysis or the classification of human emotions and affective states by collecting biometric data using smart watches, wristbands, or cameras. For retail-related market research, tracking a buyer's eye movements can provide valuable information to determine what catches their attention and what they will likely buy.

AI can augment the market research process by delivering business insights that provide detailed information about how products can be personalized and priced based on effective analysis of automated consumer signals and having a deep understanding of the most effective channels for reaching a particular market, for example consumer influencers who have the greatest reach into the target audience to promote the business' products and services. AI can also help to make observational research more efficient by automatically identifying many data points that capture the consumer's mindset when they decide to buy a product, which in turn can help to give insights into how consumers interact with a product. It can also provide impactful competitor market research in terms of products that are successful, utilization of social media, key management staff, strategic focus areas, and revenue streams. AI can also assist with pricing strategy and demand forecasting using predictive modelling sales data analysis, which in turn can help to optimize inventory management. AI-driven market research is a game changer by not only collecting, processing, and analyzing vast data sets at supersonic speed, but delivering quality insights through constant learning and interpreting data to support real-time decision-making.

AI is also impacting the way in which businesses are marketing their products and services to consumers in a significant way. Businesses are using AI to transform digital marketing by streamlining and optimizing marketing campaigns using data-driven insights of their target audience and eliminating the guesswork involved in customer interactions via email marketing or customer support. It is also automating marketing processes such as generation of reports based on data, marketing content curation and generation that can include viable topics for writers and even initial drafts of content, and comprehensive reporting on content initiatives and strategy. The effectiveness of email marketing can be improved with mass personalization and intelligent email content curation where a user's reading patterns, topics of interest, website experience and email browsing data can for example be used to get a better understanding of the customer's interaction with the company's content and recommending specific content most relevant to that individual. We also see examples of Google's Smart Reply on suggestions of short potential responses and other AI tools that offer suggestions on ways to improve the content of an email message, its length, forms of courtesy and a relevant subject for the email.

AI-enhanced digital advertising is having an ever-increasing impact on the way businesses advertise by only placing relevant advertisements in front of relevant viewers in a personalized, autonomous way at scale. Machine learning is used to place advertisements on a web page that is the most relevant to the content of an article. AI-powered systems can help advertisers test out more advertising platforms and optimize targeting. Facebook is doing this with their advertising delivery optimization, but this approach could also be applied to omnichannel pay-per-click campaign data. Other examples include Google's use of machine learning to suggest improvements to website performance, enabling voice search as language can be processed in a more natural way, and observing what customers search and predicting potential future searches or suggesting results in advance. Businesses are also already starting to use AI-driven virtual assistants in the form of intelligent chatbots to build effective and personalized marketing funnels by capturing relevant customer information that is pertinent to the customer's needs and requirements. This happens as part of the interaction with customers where the chatbots also provide information to customers about the services or products in a personalized fashion. AI enables marketers to fulfill a dream previously considered impossible, which is to engage with every individual customer in a personalized and meaningful way.

The sales process has also been revolutionized by AI in many respects, all the way from building personalized customer experience, presenting and nurturing leads, predicting and boosting sales conversions, and its role in sales forecasting to cross-selling and upselling, price optimization, performance management and sales decision making. Instead of the traditional approach of defining high-level customer personas based on gut feel and guesswork from marketers' experience as well as historical behavioral, demographic and sales data, AI-driven solutions are more dynamic and use machine learning based models that is trained on actual online behavioral and other relevant data to determine in real-time which online customers have the highest likelihood of sales conversions. To increase the level of engagement and determine what customers will buy next, predictive analytics determines patterns of behavior in structured and unstructured customer data as well as long-term patterns and trends. This allows for a personalized and meaningful customer engagement where the right product or service can be tailored and delivered at the right time to the right customer that is likely to make the purchase. Sales conversion rates and return on investment can be magnified by personalized email marketing and intelligent virtual assistants that make product or service recommendations at the right time to customers at scale based on their past engagement, buying history and demographics. Intelligent virtual assistants can also be used to help nurture customer leads by allowing prospects to experience a more fluid service that is complemented by real-life customer service agents that handle more complex customer interactions.

AI solutions can also help to automate certain repetitive, administrative, mundane and unproductive tasks to free up time for sales staff to focus more on actual selling activities such as closing sales and achieving their sales targets. A significant amount of time is typically spent on researching, qualifying and prospecting leads, whereas AI solutions can help to increase sales velocity by providing sales staff with prioritized leads with the highest buying propensity as well as actionable insights such as why a lead has a high purchase propensity for specific products or services at a certain time and at what price. These prices can also be optimized based on the specific customer profile, the size of the prospective transaction, market dynamics, and history of similar deals won or lost. Top-line revenue can be effectively grown by upselling (selling an improved version or more features to an existing product or service) and cross-selling (selling another product or service offering) to the existing customer base with an AI solution identifying who to target based on purchase likelihood. Another important application area for AI is providing more accurate sales forecasting based on not only historical sales and financial data, but also future conditions, the market, sales stage, customer relationships, and likelihood that specific accounts are to convert and close. With more realistic predictions of next quarter's sales revenue, sales managers and executive management can make better decisions in terms of capital, inventory and manpower utilization.

AI could also assist executive management, aiding strategic decision-making that is at the very heart of a successful business. These strategic decisions are typically complex and require advanced data analysis and mining, anticipating future events and possible outcomes, and predictive capability with respect to the effect of decisions on the business at a larger scale. Smarter business decisions can be supported by a data-driven AI assistant that makes suggestions or recommendations with respect to how trends and market dynamics can impact business objectives and internal KPIs, developing a new product for a certain market segment, entering a new market, countering competitors' moves, assessing cost-effectiveness and ROI potential, optimizing a customer's journey through sustained consumer behavior analysis, and reducing customer churn rates. AI can help to streamline management's decision-making processes, automating workflows for routine functions, reduce decision fatigue, and refining human judgement.

Although the legal function and associated business processes have not seen significant innovation in recent times, AI and its natural language processing application in particular will have a tremendous impact on this function as businesses make progress on their digital transformation journey.[16] We already see promising applications such as automating the process of reviewing contracts of business transactions to determine which portions of the contract are acceptable and which are potentially problematic. To provide a company with a better understanding of its business commitments, AI solutions are being developed that extract and contextualize important information across all its contracts that allows for easier tracking of contract renewal and upsell opportunities, compliance understanding from a regulatory perspective, procurement contractual support, and due diligence related activities. Machine learning is also being used to predict the outcomes of pending cases which not only leads to less cases going to trial but allows businesses and legal services companies to plan their litigation strategies, understand pricing risk, and speed-up negotiations on potential settlement. On the legal research front, AI-driven research platforms are being developed such as ROSS Intelligence, Judicata and Casetext that uses semantic machine learning driven models to identify how different cases relate to one another, what are the missing cases, what are the strongest arguments and provides a better understanding of the meaning of legal opinions.[17] Some relevant use cases for deploying AI Solutions in the legal sector includes contract due diligence; legal research; finding and exchanging all relevant documents prior to trial; digital billing; legal analytics; advice systems; drafting systems; conversational interfaces and bots; predictive technology analyzes past legal reference data to provide insights into future outcomes; and the management of intellectual property.

Accounting is another business process being transformed where we see AI applications such as reading receipts, automating data entry, categorization of data, handling the initiation of payments, matching purchase orders, enforcing corporate policy, reducing the risk of fraud, document analysis and handling, generating reports and balancing sheets. Whereas robotic process automation can take care of some of these repetitive time-consuming tasks, the machine learning driven type of applications using natural language processing and natural language generation will become more refined as it learns the behavior and trends of the users and reduces the time to complete bookkeeping tasks in a unified and efficient manner. Accountants will be able to spend more time on intellectual judgement-intensive tasks such as financial advising, interpreting the generated reports, and identifying improper spending, non-compliant decisions, and other deviant behaviors. Also, instead of predominantly reviewing past data, the accounting function can allocate more time to forward-thinking analytics by forecasting months or years in advance or financial planning that anticipates potential problems based on patterns recognized in financial data.

Artificial Intelligence is also having a major impact on human resources and associated business processes and involves recruitment and onboarding, automation of administrative tasks, process improvement, and employee experience. With regards to recruitment, AI algorithms can not only help to match more qualified candidates to the right jobs (also effectively increasing the retention rate) and reduce hiring bias (to help create a more culturally diverse workplace) but save significant time by automated screening through thousands of applications faster to assess and evaluate applicants' knowledge, skills, and experience at scale. This reduces time to hire and enhances the candidate experience with text recruiting. Other AI-related recruitment applications include candidate sourcing, career site conversions through a conversational chatbot, interview scheduling, candidate interview chatbot that can also address candidates' questions about the business, and employee referrals via a recruiting chatbot. Intelligent HR virtual assistants can also assist with streamlining the employee onboarding process by assisting with new-hire paperwork, facilitating a learning plan for the first few months, and addressing many questions regarding job profile, duties, benefits, company policies, paid time off, device requests or more. A 24x7 intelligent HR assistant can quickly and efficiently support employees by addressing basic HR questions about payroll, benefits, leave days, sick days, team structure, labor relations, company policies and other administrative requests. It can also improve the internal communications within a company and ensure that HR is in sync with the organization's leadership and its workforce to effectively support internal and external customer service, effectively manage change within the organization, and build trust between teams or departments. Ineffective communication, on the other hand, often leads to employee frustration and churn. Chatbots can be used to provide employees with a direct, impartial, effective, and easily accessible method of getting support, receiving important information, and giving feedback.

Any business also needs to keep its employees updated with the latest skills and expertise for them to thrive in the ever-changing digital landscape of the smart technology era. A personalized intelligent virtual assistant that focuses on the skills, training, and development needs of every employee can help to build a detailed skills map of the organization and support the business in making decisions based on this skills map. It can provide each employee with relevant training content to enhance their knowledge and skills in accordance with their role and responsibilities and the business function, generates a skills score and identifies gaps. The various skills maps (required versus current versus needed) will then inform about every HR decision (e.g., recruitment, employee engagement, learning and development). Businesses that leverage AI learning assistants with e-learning platforms can enhance employees' skills in a personalized way at a pace they find comfortable, recommend the best strategy to help employees learn better and faster and determine the optimal career path based on their training plan, goals, and business requirements. AI can also be employed in conjunction with augmented reality and virtual reality to train employees and stay ahead of the competition. This is a win-win situation for both the employees and the organizations which further contributes to positive employee experience and job satisfaction.

Employee wellbeing at work is critical to the workforce's productivity. AI gives a whole new way to understand and impact it significantly by incorporating how employees feel at work, their mental wellness (specifically dealing with stress), how they rate their work and that of their team, team collaboration, culture of the business, etc. HR leaders want to improve the way they monitor employee engagement, which Gartner refers to as the Voice of Employee (VoE) analytics. [18] AI-powered assistants can check employees' positive or negative sentiments towards certain aspects of their workplaces. This information can also be used for retention and attrition modeling and prediction. These types of machine learning models can detect the possibilities of employees leaving the firm by training on data related to pay-scale, employee experience, time in role, business function, demographics, attrition rate, performance, etc. AI systems can also potentially be implemented to analyze employee's outgoing emails or browsing patterns to determine if they are looking out for opportunities. As employee retention is a major problem for many businesses, AI-driven HR solutions can use this type of information to determine the possible causes of employees leaving and take preventive measures to avoid that happening.

Many HR leaders believe that the traditional employee review process is outdated and ineffective. Personalized intelligent virtual assistants can improve this process by allowing for the instant exchange of feedback and performance insights between employees and management. Such a performance reviews and assessment virtual assistant can automatically collect performance data from systems of record, such as the number of tickets solved or the number of deals closed or lost in a month and share that information with all relevant parties on-demand or on a set schedule, making it faster and easier than ever to conduct fact-based performance reviews. A health and safety virtual assistant can also support businesses that have extremely strict Safety, Health, Environment and Quality (SHEQ) requirements such as those in the manufacturing, engineering, utilities, mining, and resources industries.[19] In the next section we will be examining the impact of AI on the workplace and the job market. The future of HR is both human and digital as businesses focus on optimizing the combination of human and automated work. This requires business leaders and teams to develop a fluency in AI and other smart technology whilst they reimagine how HR can have a more personal, human, and intuitive impact on the business.

AI impacting the Workplace, Employment, and the Job Market

Given the current state-of-the-art in AI, the introduction of AI in the workplace will initially focus on augmenting and helping employees to do their jobs better and not necessarily replace them. AI-based technology is creating new ways for employees to maximize their interactions with customers and increase their productivity. Clearly tasks within jobs will change as more repetitive and mundane tasks will be automated. While few jobs are fully automatable, one study shows that 60% of all jobs have at least 30% technically automatable activities.[20] So which jobs or tasks within jobs will be harder to replace with AI technologies? This would not only be jobs or tasks that have minimal routine or repetition, but likely also ones that require creativity, are difficult to learn through simple observation, require hands-on manipulation, do not involve the use of large data sources, are dependent on human interaction and interpersonal communication, and require social perception. Kai-fu Lee, an AI expert and founder of Sinovation Ventures has the opinion that "every job which takes less than 5 seconds to think will be done by robots".[21] Martin Ford reckons that we will get into a situation where any kind of job that is routine or repetitive on some level will disappear.[22] It is evident that the demand for uniquely human skills will grow. Although millions of jobs will likely be displaced, the World Economic Forum's *Future of Jobs Report* projects in the order of hundreds of millions of new jobs that will be added over the next few years that requires skills in both emotional intelligence and technical intelligence.[23] Some examples of new AI- or smart tech-related jobs over the next few years will likely include AI trainer, voice user experience designer, ethical and human use officer, data detective, AI-assisted healthcare technician, a health wellness coach, ethical sourcing manager, AI chatbot designer, AI digital market expert, AI business and public sector strategy consultant, creativity coach, tech-addiction counselor, business behavior manager, AI business development manager, man-machine training manager, financial wellness coach, cybercity analyst, augmented reality journey builder, digital tailor, and much more.[24] In her book, *Les Métiers du Futur* (Jobs of the Future), published in 2019, Isabelle Rouhan believes that 85% of the jobs that we will have in 2030 do not exist yet.[25] In an attempt to reveal what our future labor market will look like, she introduces us to new professions that will appear this decade such as robot monitors (managing and configuring algorithms for robots), neuro manager (helping with employee welfare via neuroscientific methods), ethical hacker (fighting against cyber-attacks) and digital detox therapist (helping a generation that has forgotten what reality looks like with general well-being and mental health).[26] Some professions are disappearing while many others are expected to emerge over the next few years as our evolving technology is transforming society with our consumption patterns and lifestyles that are following suit. Good advice to anyone is to be flexible in the short-term and adaptable in the longer term.

As more and more employees depend on the insights of AI to do their jobs more efficiently and effectively, developing an AI ready workforce will be a competitive advantage and create significant value at both the individual and business enterprise level. It is also becoming increasingly important to upskill people to learn how to work with AI. Once key business problems that can be addressed by AI have been identified, it is important to build an agile cross-functional team of stakeholders to educate employees on the business benefits of implementing these AI-driven solutions and also identify new skills and jobs needed in the workplace as part of this. As artificial intelligence in the workplace will fragment some long-standing workflows, it will also effectively create human jobs to help integrate those workflows. There needs to be an understanding in HR of how to use AI across the employee life cycle, what learning opportunities need to be implemented for key job roles and reinvent the HR function itself. As AI and smart technology are helping to create a knowledge-based economy, we will see more AI tools that not only helps the workforce to perform tasks more efficiently, but also capable of intelligent automation with self-learning features and assisting employees to innovate. Instead of relying chiefly on a candidate's credentials, we will also see more skills-based recruitment that involves the setting of specific skills and competency requirements for a job.

Some of the barriers to adopting AI technology in the workplace include finding properly educated and skilled people, concerns over data privacy, data availability that is also due to software-as-a-service offerings, ongoing maintenance due to the data-driven nature of AI solutions, and limited proven applications. Once there are effective and successful AI solutions references where everyone benefits, it is easier for a business to overcome bias and trust issues. AI must therefore earn human trust to thrive. Cost-savings presented by these solutions also gives businesses the opportunity to upskill their current employees. The focus should be on augmentation and AI as a workplace helper and not on replacing human workers. It would likely change the amount of time employees spent at work, how they work, and provide more room to be creative.

Another important perspective of the impact of AI on employment is provided by Richard Baldwin in *The Globotics Upheaval* where he predicts that white-collar jobs (which are jobs involving cognitive skill such as pattern recognition and the acquisition, processing and transmission of information) will be swept away faster by digital change than in any previous economic transformation.[27] According to him the explosive potential comes from the mismatch between the speed at which disruptive energy is injected into the system by job displacement and the system's ability to absorb it with job creation. On the other hand, Richard Freeman, an economics professor at Harvard University predicts that few businesses will be able to make sweeping changes such as replacing their accounting department with a few people managing the AI-driven accounting software and completely change the way it is doing reporting and controls. AI's impact on the workplace would likely not be like a sweeping tidal wave, but more mosaic in nature across industries. However, external factors such as the Covid-19 pandemic might accelerate sweeping changes as a drive towards digitizing businesses, transformed business models, and a leaner and more agile workplace dynamics takes hold. Advances in machine learning and AI software in general over the next decade would likely lead to more of the white-collar jobs, with their currently defined job descriptions, being swept away by the smart technology driven digital change and potentially also make these sweeping changes with respect to the current jobs easier to do.

AI has the potential to dramatically remake the economy, where we will see new startups, numerous business applications and consumer uses, as well as the displacement of certain jobs and the creation of entirely new ones. Whereas traditionally new businesses would appoint full-time employees to take on roles in business development, sales, marketing, product development, design, customer support, and administration, there are increasingly more flexible options available in the API economy of AI services (which can act as so-called white-collar robots) and outsourced talent of freelancers (including foreign freelancers and telemigrants) which together offers significant gains in productivity and efficiency and huge cost savings. As we reimagine business processes, we will also see closer collaboration between AI and human workers, where humans work more like humans and less like robots, and a collaborative intelligence where there is a reliance on AI-driven decision support systems to help create work efficiencies. AI-driven automation, of which the pace and extent will vary across different activities, professions, salary ranges and skill levels, can enable growth and other benefits on the level of entire economies where productivity acceleration is very much needed especially with the declining share of the working-age population in many countries.

As we contemplate the impact of AI on the job market, there are sobering thoughts from several authors that have written on this subject. The possibility of large-scale technological unemployment has been discussed at length by Calum Chace in *The Economic Singularity* which refers to the concept of an economic singularity where we need a new economic system to address the situation of AI-driven machines rendering most humans unemployable.[28] Martin Ford also discusses technological unemployment in his books, *The Lights in the Tunnel* and *Rise of the Robots* and emphasizes that we are on the verge of wholesale automation of white-collar jobs and hollowing out of middle-class jobs.[29] Erik Brynjolfsson and Andrew McAfee in *The Second Machine Age* help to validate the discussion of technological unemployment where they discuss two phenomena which they coin as "bounty" and "spread".[30] "Bounty" is described as the "increase in volume, variety and quality, and the decrease in cost of many offerings brought by technological progress", whereas "spread" is the inequality of labor markets and wealth and "ever-bigger differences among people in economic success". The latter has also been described as the "great decoupling" where we have on the one hand a steady growth in worker productivity over the last few decades, but stagnant growth in median income and employment (with the United States as one of the prime examples). With the economic gains of the information revolution the top 1% in the US has approximately doubled its share of the national income over the last 40 years and have almost as much wealth as the bottom 90% combined. The question is whether bounty and its economy of radical abundance (as also elaborated by Peter Diamandis and Steven Kotler in *Abundance* and *Bold*) will overcome spread by ensuring that most people are comfortably off and inequality is less of a factor.[31] We are clearly currently extremely far from such a scenario. Brynjolfsson and McAfee recommend some interventions which could maximize the bounty whilst minimizing the spread. In *Machine, Platform, Crowd* they put more emphasis on the way AI and smart technology leads to structural changes in the economy and the kinds of jobs available because of that.[32] In *21 Lessons for the 21st Century*, Yuval Harari mentions that instead of competing with AI, humans' jobs can be created by servicing and leveraging AI, but this would not solve the problems of unemployed unskilled laborers or prevent remaining jobs to be safe from the threat of future automation. [33] Kai-fu Lee in *AI Superpowers* shares similar sentiments and discusses two kinds of job loss, the first being one-to-one replacements that is typically captured by economists using a task-based approach where a single AI-driven product or service can replace a specific kind of worker; and the second ground-up disruptions where AI start-ups are reimagining an industry from the ground-up and looking for new ways to satisfy the fundamental human need driving the industry.[34] He is also concerned that the AI era, if left to its own devices, will shake the foundations of our labor markets, economies, and societies and divide the world into the AI elite and the rest as well as AI-rich and AI-poor countries. This leads into topics such as a universal economic safety net, losing our jobs to AI versus losing control over our lives, avoiding digital dictatorship and related matters which I will discuss more in later chapters.

The New AI-driven Face of Business and Customer Services

AI is changing the face of business and the workplace. Whereas the future of human-computer interfaces is likely to involve the use of AI in combination with a range of other evolving technologies such as augmented, virtual, and/or mixed reality, gestural computing, robotics, holograms, and emotional recognition, AI-driven chatbots and intelligent virtual assistants with more advanced natural language processing capabilities is becoming more central to how businesses engage with their customers and employees at scale. Whereas there was some disappointment with the initial technical brittleness of chatbots earlier on when high expectation were created, AI looks set to power 95% of customer interactions by 2025 (with the banking industry that could see the success rate of chatbot interactions reach over 90% by 2022).[35] Market Insider projects that the global conversational AI market size is expected to grow from 4.8 billion in 2020 to 13.9 billion by 2025.[36] According to Gartner, by 2022, 40% of employees will consult AI agents before making decisions in day-to-day business.[37] As businesses are trying to meet the requirements and demands of their customers on a 24 hours a day, 7 days a week basis, AI can help to meet the modern consumer expectations with fast response times and proper answers and recommendations for their needs and solutions to their problems. AI-driven chatbots can also easily handle most customer support activities that are repetitive in nature and resolve specific issues. We are now seeing AI shifting toward building intelligent systems that can collaborate effectively with people, including creative ways to develop interactive and scalable ways for people to teach robots or AI systems. As many people have already grown accustomed to touching and talking to their smartphones, it is also becoming evident that people's future relationships with machines will become ever more shaded, fluid, and personalized. As we have seen with intelligent virtual assistants and advisors, research is now shifting towards developing intelligent systems that are trustworthy, human-aware, and able to interact with people through dialog, not just react to stylized requests.

Although keyboard input is still being used for chatbots or intelligent virtual assistants, one can expect voice- and gesture-recognition to become more prevalent. In fact, following online-first and then mobile-first, the concept of "voice first" is becoming the new paradigm for the development of customer-oriented user interfaces. Given the current maturity levels of information and communication technology along with the rapid progress in AI, smart technology is allowing computer and device interfaces to be much easier to use, more intuitive and more accessible to more people. This would also increase the speed at which information is exchanged and shared between businesses and their consumers and between employees in the workplace. AI is allowing intelligent virtual assistants to capture, analyze and understand intents from users in a more natural way and helping people to be more productive and consumers to have a better customer experience with more personalized, relevant, faster, and better services. It also allows consumer-facing businesses to scale faster with high volume communication, decrease costs of operation, and reduce labor costs. As we add more personalization and contextualization to our intelligent virtual assistants the new face of business, customer services and employee engagement will be these smart personalized contextual assistants.

In the *Age of Context*, Robert Scoble and Shel Israel illustrate how the five forces of mobile, social media, data, sensors, and location are not only in a virtuous cycle (where rapid adoption is driving prices down, which in turn drives more adoption), but is putting the customer into proper context and where everything and everyone are being contextualized.[38] The more instrumentation, the better contextualization is possible. They also discuss how personal digital assistants are being replaced with personal contextual assistants that are typically AI-driven open cloud-based mobile platforms that serve as one-stop spaces that connect you to relevant information and services, understand how these services can impact you at any given moment, simplify your life, automate redundant and predictable tasks, give you contextualized and personal recommendations and advice, and warn you of changes that might impact your plans. With AI enhancements and predictive capabilities, these personalized contextual assistants will evolve into an anticipatory system covering most aspects of life.

Chatbots and intelligent virtual assistants and advisors can be customized for a variety of AI-based assistance and advisor types of solutions across multiple industries. Intelligent virtual assistants and robo-advisors are, for example, a good fit for life and short-term insurers. AI's initial impact primarily relates to improving efficiencies and automating existing customer-facing, underwriting and claims processes. It is also clear that the impact of AI will be more profound as it will be used to identify, access, and underwrite emerging risks and identify new revenue sources. Some of the AI applications for the insurance industry with respect to enhanced services include personalized customer experience, digital advice, automating and augmenting underwriting and robo-claims adjusting. The specific value added are respectively redefining the value proposition to the customer, redefining distribution, enhancing efficiencies, and reducing claims processing time and costs. More broadly some of the intelligent virtual assistant applications include robo-advisors for wealth management, personal financial wellness, insurance plan selection, portfolio management, personal wellness coach, personal health advisor, medical insurance assistant, personal tutor, learning assistant, employee wellness assistant, human resources assistant, recruitment assistant, personal shopping assistant, customer support assistant, travel assistant, security bots, monitoring and diagnostics assistant, process supervision assistant, personal administration and services assistant, agricultural assistant and advisor, productivity and safety assistant and advisor, and maintenance support assistant. One of the earlier self-learning, personalized virtual production assistants that we have developed was one specifically designed for manufacturing users focusing on productivity and safety in the workplace, simplifying and improving access to information, and helping them to make better decisions and improve business outcomes. Other examples that we have developed, and refining include those focused on health and financial wellness, education, and human resources. Some of the specific benefits of workplace intelligent virtual assistants are improved communication with human resources, 24/7 administrative support, more rapid communication and faster receipt of information, employee wellbeing, increased motivation for employees through positive messaging, better training opportunities for employees, pre-boarding and on-boarding of new employees, recruitment, performance reviews and assessments, and data mining insights with respect to employee productivity, wellness, retention and attrition.

The spectrum of intelligent virtual assistants and advisors starts from those with low technology integration and complexity such as chatbots that simply provide information and basic customer queries, to ones that are more integrated, complex, domain-specific and can provide assistance and resolve issues, and also provide advice. Some of the AI capabilities include natural language processing, machine learning (including deep learning), graph analysis, deep question and answer systems, audio and speech analytics, sensors, internet of things, soft robotics, and simulation modeling. Some of the key building blocks of a chatbot-agnostic solution is a cloud solution (that enables a pre-trained model with storage for deployment, testing, improvement, and quality assurance), natural language processing, digital assistance to support queries across multiple devices, automated machine learning, robotic process automation that automates enterprise operations and back-office via a common plug-in, and APIs for business and AI functionality. Chatbots and intelligent virtual assistants can be deployed via widgets on web browsers, progressive web applications, mobile applications or via popular messaging platforms such as WeChat, WhatsApp, Facebook Messenger, Slack, Telegram or Kik. The earlier purely basic type of chatbot just provided static information, frequently asked questions, or information-based simple search. Even though labeled as AI technology, multiple choice chatbots are manually scripted bots that typically contain no intelligence. Instead, they are used to simplify transactions by using a more conversational form of input and output. The travel and retail industries have made frequent use of this type of bot. Virtual agents have also been on the market for several years, but they remain essentially glorified search engines able to parse frequently asked questions. The language programming of most virtual agents is designed to match keywords rather than infer meaning from the request. The next level of chatbot or virtual assistant have some functionality added such as limited business rules deployed, limited machine learning, single instance type of query, standard operating procedures, limited knowledge bases, single language, single avatar, limited support services, shallow integration into business, operational, and data systems, and shallow internet of things integration. Some of these examples include bot-assisted agents which are a next step up from virtual agents as they have "humans in the loop" models where we have a symbiotic relationship that allows bots to increase the efficiency of conversation while a human agent monitors quality control and gives customers both correct and personal answers. The more advanced intelligent virtual assistants also gives instruction and advice with functionalities such as providing dynamic information, end-to-end use of state-of-the-art natural language processing and machine learning making use of all available data sources, intuitive guidance based on keywords, ontology and deep language understanding, personalized responses based on context, history and profile, guidance on process, related transactions, and relevant knowledge, multi-language support, multi-Avatar for each user, more deeply integrated human expert and/or AI-driven support services, deep integration into all data sources, and/or business and operational systems, and deep IoT integration. These intelligent virtual assistants can also include real-time emotion analysis that interprets customer emotions, intentions, and social signals in real-time enabling increased customer and agent satisfaction. It can also learn based on a customer's answers to questions and/or previous purchases in order to offer personalized product suggestions. Some of the primary stumbling blocks which are being addressed include the lack of empathy, meaning conversation, conversation quality, ability to answer complex queries or questions, voice recognition across multiple accents and languages.

As the datasets used to train natural language processing algorithms continue to grow, it will become harder for humans to determine if they are interacting with an AI-driven system or a human. This leads to some potential ethical concerns where it might be required for the AI-driven virtual assistant to identify itself as a robot rather than a real person. Other concerns are data privacy and security, which might require some types of intelligent virtual assistant solutions to protect users' privacy and handle personal information on the device rather than in the cloud. Although AI-powered voice-based virtual assistants such as Amazon Echo or Google Home are popular and useful, there are also the fear of privacy violations and the concern about sharing private family conversations on Amazon or Google cloud servers. AI solutions, including chatbot and intelligent virtual assistants, should provide a privacy notice explaining why a user's data needs to be used for the AI solution to facilitate desired results. It needs to be clear what data is permissible and not permissible to collect for the AI solution. The intelligent virtual assistant should as far as possible not store personal identifiable information (PII) or confidential information during the processing of a request. Training data should be secure for machine learning purposes and should not include PII or confidential information. AI solutions should have masking capabilities so that observers cannot learn specifics about other users. Whilst communication should happen via a secure internet or intranet protocol, only authorized information should be released to users during conversational AI transactions and interactions. In the next section, we will discuss how cybersecurity for the business enterprise is being transformed by AI.

AI-driven Cybersecurity for the Business Enterprise

Cybersecurity is the practice of defending computers, mobile devices, electronic systems, servers, networks, and data from malicious attacks. With millions of virtual cyber-attacks that occur every year across most industries, cyber criminals pose a significant threat to business enterprises, their customers, and consumers. All businesses that use networks can be targeted for customer data, corporate espionage, or customer attacks. The Online Trust Alliance estimated that there were more than 2 million cyber-attacks in 2018 that resulted in $45 billion in losses.[39] According to a study in 2019 by Accenture Security and the Ponemon Institute, the average cost of a cybercrime for a business or organization is $13m, which is likely to increase.[40] In the US alone there were more than 10 billion data breaches since 2005 with Yahoo! leading the pack with more than 3 billion pieces of data that were leaked in 2016.[41] When large data breaches occur, personal data concerning hundreds of thousands of individuals can potentially be leaked, opening the door for cybercrime and fraud for each individual. GitHub was another cybercrime example in 2018 when it was a victim of one of the biggest distributed denial of service attacks of all time, where a huge number of requests were sent simultaneously to overwhelm the server, which was unable to process them.

In the ever-changing cyber threat landscape with an increasing number of data breaches, hackers' attacks, and crashes, cybersecurity is more vital than ever. Although the rollout of super-fast wireless communications technology such as 5G will bring massive opportunities for businesses to provide services in fresh and innovative ways, they will also potentially lead to more sophisticated cyber-attacks. IT security departments in businesses will need to dedicate entire teams and smart technology solutions to risk prevention. Elements of cybersecurity include information security, network security, application security, disaster recovery and business continuity planning, operational security, and end-user education. One of the most problematic elements of cybersecurity is the rapid and constantly evolving nature of security risks. As the traditional approach focuses most resources on the most crucial system components and protects against the biggest known threats, it leads to leaving some less important system components undefended and some less dangerous risks not protected against. Such an approach is insufficient and a more proactive and adaptive approach that involves continuous monitoring and real-time assessments is required.

Common methods attackers use to control computers or networks include viruses and worms (which self-replicate and damage files or systems), spyware and trojans (which are often used for secretive data collection), and ransomware (which waits for an opportunity to encrypt all the user's information and demands payment to return access to the user). Malicious software code often spreads via a legitimate looking download or an unsolicited email attachment that carries a malware payload. It is hard for businesses to fight off cyberattacks or predict the next big malware threats. We have for example already seen major threats such as Zeus trojan and Locky ransomware being followed with new ones such as Emotet botnet and Trickbot trojan that deliver Ryuk ransomware.[42] These threats need to be modelled via a process by which potential threats can be identified, enumerated, and prioritized, all from a hypothetical attacker's point of view. The purpose of threat modeling is to provide IT security teams with a systematic analysis of the probable attacker's profile, the most likely attack or threat vectors (which is a method or a path by which an attacker gains unlawful access into a system which can include email, web applications, remote access portals, mobile devices, users, and the network), and the assets most desired by an attacker.[43] Example threats involves malware (includes ransomware), insider abuse and negligence (includes information leakage), phishing (includes spam and is a form of fraud used to gain access to data such as personal information or login credentials), targeted attacks (includes botnets, identity theft, web attacks, exploit kits, and data breaches), denial of service, service providers or business partners, physical loss, and espionage. Threat agents can be cyber criminals (which is typically financially motivated, often indiscriminate), insiders (typically disgruntled or dishonest employees), script-kiddies (copycats and/or hack for fun, or grudge), cyber-spies (nation states or competitor sponsored actors), hacktivists, and cyber-fighters or terrorists (naturally or religiously motivated groups).

The next generation of cybersecurity solutions are increasingly incorporating AI components and systems which are being trained on large datasets of cybersecurity, network, and physical information to detect and block abnormal behavior. This might involve analyzing raw network data to spot an irregularity or detecting patterns in user, asset, and/or entity behavior that deviate from normal. The types of data streams, how they are collected, and the level of effort needed by IT security teams all vary by approach. The use of unsupervised and supervised machine learning enables businesses to not only tap into the current knowledge of threats and vectors in order to detect new attacks and discover new vulnerabilities, but also delivery automated solutions that can help to eliminate human error, work simultaneously on various tasks, monitoring and protecting a vast number of devices and systems, and mitigating large scale attacks. AI-driven cybersecurity not only offers insights that enable businesses to understand threats easily through unsupervised machine learning and analysis of huge volumes of security data, data classification for forensics, and threat intelligence feed curation (which all helps to reduce response times and making companies compliant with security best practices), but also help to detect, prevent, and respond to novel, abnormal, sophisticated, AI-assisted, and unanticipated attacks. We already see AI in the form of supervised machine learning being deployed in spam filter applications, malware classification, network intrusion detection and prevention, secure user authentication, hacking incident forecasting, botnet detection, cyber security ratings, and fraud detection. Online transactions can be secured by identifying fraudsters through machine learning models that proactively detects fraud in financial transactions or fraudulent users on websites and in mobile applications. AI can not only be used to identify and grade risky behavior in mobile applications including known and unknown malware, new malware used in targeted attacks, intellectual property exposure, and corporate data ex-filtration, but also helping to secure applications by finding, fixing, and monitoring web, mobile, and networks against current and future vulnerabilities. Similarly, AI-powered asset-protection software can be used to assist with the security, reliability, and safety of the IoT and allow for a pre-emptive response to data theft (for example, by identifying hidden transmitters or recording devices in a business meeting room).

AI will play an increasingly important role in protecting businesses from cyber threats with security tools analyzing data from millions of cyber incidents and using it to identify potential threats such as phishing, hacking, and social engineering attacks or a new variant of malware that are becoming ever-more sophisticated. AI can be used to identify signals within digital activity or transactions that follow patterns that are likely to be indicators of criminal activity and give warnings before defenses can be breached and sensitive data compromised. These anomaly detection and behavior analytics are based on finding matchings to profiles that represent the normal behavior of users, hosts, or networks, and detecting attacks as significant deviations from this profile. In the case of new variants of malware, machine-learning signatures and AI models can be trained to orient to these variants when they appear. To distinguish between harmless software and malware, machine learning models can be trained on data using features such as consumed processing power and bandwidth, amount of data transmitted over the internet, and accessed APIs, fields on a disk, and environmental components such as camera or keyboard.

There is also a constant battle between attackers and defenders, where so-called "blue" defensive AI security controls defend against "red" offensive AI-powered attacks such as malware creation with enhanced and fast evasive capabilities, impersonation of trusted users, self-learning botnets, sophisticated threat actors that blend into background, faster attacks with more effective consequences, spear phishing with smarter social engineering and convincing scams (using real emails as training data), as well as attacking and theft of AI. Another dangerous offensive AI threat is posed by adversarial AI that discover and "poison" datasets and compromises the machine learning algorithm which leads to machine learning models producing false and controlled results, artefacts designed to fool defensive AIs, the stealing of models to enhance the abilities of adversarial inputs, and weaponizing feedback.[44] If cybercriminals can hack their way into getting access to data, they can easily manipulate data to their benefit. For any type of attack, the information leakage and probing should be limited, and machine learning models should use ensemble learning and adversarial training as part of the defense. To defend against poisoning attacks, data cleaning, anomaly detection and secured data collection are all key steps.

Cybercriminals also take advantage of businesses struggling to defend their perimeter against unknown threats. This is where predictive and preventive AI-driven security can be used against these novel and advanced cyber threats to detect advanced persistent threat attacks and insider activities at an early stage. To proactively deceive and disrupt in progress cyber-attacks, there are also defense applications that create a neural network of thousands of fake computers, devices, and services that act like a fog and work under the supervision of AI algorithms. Some of the key AI-driven cybersecurity applications include integrating machine learning into firewalls to flag any anomaly, the monitoring and analysis of security incidents and mobile endpoints, using robotic process automation to automate rule-based processes and tasks, identifying the origin of cyber-attacks through natural language processing applications, and handling the aftermath of an attack. Other applications include AI-driven security solutions that automate tasks and orchestrate a complete and dynamic response, enabling faster and more intelligent remediation, based on detection of anomalous behavior in real time. This in particular helps to prioritize and reduce traditional security alerts, increasing the efficacy of security staff. Complexity continues to be a top concern for businesses and their Information Technology teams, where we see reactive strategies driven by threats, products and solutions being deployed in silos, and organizations and teams continue to work alone. Stressed and stretched IT security teams are looking to automation of cybersecurity tasks for relief. Given the scarcity of cybersecurity experts as well as the evolving role of cybersecurity staff, there is a need for support from augmented if not autonomous AI to increase efficiency and help security staff to be able to meet more complex massive and time sensitive threats. AI solutions can also help to orchestrate a complete and dynamic response, enabling faster, and more intelligent remediation and should be fully integrated and consistent with the existing IT and cybersecurity processes to be efficient. As with any other implemented AI-driven solution in the business enterprise, change management is important to ensure the full benefit from the expected innovation and quality improvement and cost reduction.

Given that AI is how technology responds to our ever-changing world, the adoption of AI-based solutions is going to be key for any business to thrive and survive in the Smart Technology Era. By keeping up to date with the state-of-the-art in AI-based cybersecurity tools and its correct deployment to assist security teams, this could help businesses stay secure against increasingly smart and potent cyberattacks. AI-driven cybersecurity solutions should update automatically and learn how humans react with the ultimate vision for a business to end up with a self-learning and self-healing cybersecurity posture that can learn negative and threatening behaviors and stop them from happening.

5. AI Revolutionizing Personalized Engagement for Consumer Facing Businesses

As we are discussing the transformative nature of AI in the Smart Technology Era, there is not a single industry that is not impacted by this exponential and disruptive technology. Like how we have seen how the internet and digitization are impacting all industries and sectors over the last twenty years, we can expect AI to have a lasting impact on the current industries as well as industries of the future such as robotics, advanced life sciences, big data, cybersecurity, and the code-ification of money, markets, and trust. As Alec Ross mentions in *The Industries of the Future,* these future industries with their geopolitical, generational, and cultural contexts and underpinnings are also symbiotic among each other and symbolic of larger global trends.[1] In this chapter - as part of the sense-making journey - I will be highlighting several AI use cases to get a sense of how AI solutions are being applied across multiple consumer facing industries such as financial services, retail, ecommerce, telecommunications, media, entertainment, transportation, travel and tourism. In following chapters I will cover AI uses cases across the industrial world, education, healthcare, and the public sector. In a report by McKinsey Global Institute (MGI) entitled *Artificial Intelligence: The Next Digital Frontier*, they show how adoption is the greatest in industries or sectors that are already digital adopters, where the characteristics of early adopters are being those that are digitally mature, larger in nature, adopting AI in core activities, having a focus on growth over savings, adopting multiple technologies, and having executive level support for AI.[2] Although adoption has increased significantly since the 2017 MGI survey of 3,000 AI-aware executives across 10 countries and 14 sectors, the results at that time shows that only 20% said AI is core part of their business or being used at scale and only 12% of 160 use cases evaluated deployed commercially.[3] Although things are changing fast, there still appears to be a growing gap between the early AI adopters versus the rest of the business enterprises across industries, mixed with AI startups with the intention to disrupt entire industries and sectors in various application areas via innovative business models and monetization of data and services. That performance gap is likely to increase in the future as it is clear from use cases over the last few years that AI can deliver significant value to business enterprises that are already using their strong digital capability in a proactive strategic fashion. Some of the key areas across the value chain where AI can create value is enhanced, tailored, and convenient user experience; targeted sales and marketing with products and services offered to the right customers with the right message at the right time and price; optimized production and maintenance leading to higher productivity, lower cost, and better efficiency; and smart sourcing, research and development, and real-time forecasting. As mentioned in the previous chapter, for industrial businesses, AI-driven solutions can significantly increase throughput, quality, yield, and productivity, reduce risks of process and equipment failure, and reduce costs with respect to energy, raw material, operations, and maintenance. For most consumer-facing businesses, the customer base can be grown, and revenues can be increased through AI-driven personalized engagement solutions to enhance the customer experience and more targeted sales and marketing drive recommendation, cross-selling and upselling. These consumer-facing businesses across industries can also reduce churn, fraud, waste, abuse, and cybersecurity risk, as well as lowering costs and increase productivity, operational efficiency, and effectiveness through AI-driven automation.

It is also clear that AI is fueling the future of productivity across industries. Goldman Sachs Investment Research estimates AI-driven automation and efficiency gains driving a 0.5%-1.5% reduction in labor hours which is likely to result in a 51-154 basis points impact on productivity growth by 2025.[4] They are also of the opinion that AI-induced productivity could impact the way businesses allocate capital similar to the 1990s technology boom where we saw an amplification of capital deepening (capital stock per labor hour) and multifactor productivity (with IT-producing sectors contributing almost 50% of the productivity growth (output per labor hour)) as key components of productivity. As the use of AI technologies will become a key competitive advantage for businesses across all major industries, investment in AI through enablers such as the development of an inhouse "AI stack", consulting services and AI-as-a-services will likely drive a growth in demand for the people, services, software, and hardware underlying AI. It was estimated by the IDC that the global spending on AI of $35.8 billion in 2019 can double to approximately $79.2 billion by 2022.[5] If we consider the global AI market, Grand View Research has estimated that its size is expected to grow at a compound annual growth rate of 42.2% from 2020 to 2027 which implies that it would to reach approximately $470 billion (USD) by 2027 projected from a market size of $39.9 billion in 2019.[6] The market research by Fortune Business Insights shows more conservative numbers with their estimate of approximately 277 billion by 2027 at a compound annual growth rate of 33.2% given a global AI market size valued at $27.2 Billion in 2019.[7]

According to Statista (in collaboration with Tractica), some of the top AI use cases worldwide up to 2025 will be machine or vehicular objection detection, identification and avoidance; static image recognition, classification, and tagging; healthcare or patient data processing; algorithmic trading strategy performance improvement; localization and mapping; predictive maintenance; prevention against cybersecurity threats; converting paper work into digital data; intelligent human resources systems; and medical image analysis.[8] For business enterprises, higher AI adoption appears to be in financial services, high technology and telecommunications, automotive and assembly, followed by retail, media and entertainment and consumer packaged goods. Although relative lower AI adoption has been seen in education, healthcare and travel and tourism, that has been changing fast over the last few years with more significant changes to come in the 2020s. From an AI readiness perspective, the technology industry leads in every respect as they are also moving the fastest with regards to AI adoption across their whole business as well as their AI-driven products and services for customers. In a KPMG report *Living in an AI World 2020 study* almost 80% of leaders in the technology sector felt the pressure to be more aggressive when it comes to faster AI adoption even though this sector leads adoption with 63% of technology respondents saying that AI is moderately to fully functional implemented in their businesses.[9] Whereas AI endeavors for technology companies were initially targeted at research and development, product development, and front-office work, there seems to a move towards more implementations also in the back and middle office areas.

AI's Comprehensive Impact on Financial Services

There is no doubt that AI already has an enormous impact on the whole financial services sector. Besides AI's process automation applications such as robotic process automation and cognitive process automation that helps to reduce costs, increase productivity, and prevent fraud losses, there is also a significant role for AI to play in digitized personalized engagement as we see the growing internet user base swiftly switching to mobile devices to perform a transaction or related actions within integrated in-app transaction systems. As this would only increase the risks for cyber-attacks and more possibly ways for financial fraud to occur, AI will also play an increasing role in assisting to address these risks. Mordor Intelligence has appraised AI's share in the fintech market as $7.27 billion in 2019 and projected it to get to $35.40 billion by 2025 with a compound annual growth rate of 31.5% for the period 2020 to 2025.[10] Technavio reckons that the global AI market in banking, financial services and insurance sector is expected to post a compound annual growth rate of 32% during the period 2019-2023.[11] AI has broad applications across the financial services sector from banking and insurance to investment that advance better outcomes for both consumers and businesses. On the investment side, some relevant use cases for deploying AI solutions include maximizing investment, portfolio optimization, high speed arbitrage trading, reducing compliance and regulatory costs, trade surveillance, abnormal trading pattern detection, market manipulation detection, and risk analysis and management. For commercial banking and insurance sectors, AI use cases include reducing credit risk through scoring and analysis (complementing traditional statistical scoring methods), churn mitigation, response modeling, real-time customer insight for personalized customer engagement, loyalty programs, recommendations, cross-selling, up-selling, digital advice, robo-advisor, fraud detection, smart payment systems, automated and augmented underwriting, and robo-claims adjusting. Just between maximizing investment potential, reducing credit risk and reducing compliance and regulatory costs, Goldman Sachs Global Investment Research (GS GIR) estimated that AI could, conservatively, enable access to between $34-$43 billion per year in cost savings and new revenue opportunities by 2025, with further upside as AI enable faster and more complex data leveraging and execution.[12] AI-driven software and hardware accelerators applied to the rich, high volume, high speed, and robust data sets are providing significant advantage to enable better informed investment decisions, quicker reaction to market events, reducing costs, and breaking into new profit pools. For example, to give asset managers at high frequency trading companies a competitive advantage, execution speed and gaining access to trading information mere fractions of a second before the market (through co-located trading servers at the exchange and/or sourcing data from raw exchange feeds and retrieving best bid/offer prices faster than traditional data consolidation processes) are paramount. Fast executing AI algorithms can use this latency arbitrage to act on the price spread in a faster and more accurate fashion before the latency period has elapsed.

These AI-powered algorithmic trading solutions can also use alternative data such as geo-spatial (e.g., satellite imagery of areas that are relevant to equities, commodity prices and even economies), social media sentiments (e.g., blogs, reviews, brand logos, web metrics, Facebook, Twitter, Instagram, TikTok, LinkedIn, YouTube, and Sina Weibo) and credit card transactions to complement the typical pricing signals, company performance metrics and news sentiments to help optimize investment portfolios. A complementary AI use case is where image recognition machine learning techniques such as convolutional neural networks are used to extract key characteristics from real-time satellite imagery of commodity depots, storage facilities, production facilities, containers, shipping movements, store parking lots, agriculture land, etc., which in turn can be used as additional input features to models of AI-driven trading solutions. For example, a retailers' sales can be predicted, by amongst other factors, using features extracted from real-time imagery of store parking lots and shipping patterns.[13] In general, the financial services industry has a great opportunity to benefit more from AI being applied to data-driven market events as also illustrated by the volatility around data releases in the commodity futures market. Hedge funds and other asset managers can also save costs by reducing labor needs at a faster rate than the growth in data procurement costs, where a 5% reduction in operating expenses is predicted for the asset management industry implying a $13 billion annual cost reduction by 2025 for the industry.[14]

Given new regulations that are facing the banking industry, there is also an increased compliance spend by small community banks, commercial banks as well as large investment banks (as reported by the likes of J.P. Morgan, Citigroup and others over the last decade), resulting in an estimated total of approximately $18bn in compliance-related employee costs per year.[15] AI can be used in a proactive fashion to handle tasks such as detecting violations (e.g., such unauthorized trading, market manipulation, or wall cross violations) as well as inspecting employee emails for potentially noncompliant content. A 10% reduction in compliance employee costs because of AI-driven solutions should therefore contribute approximately $2bn per year in compliance cost reduction for banking within the next few years. As another example of reducing cost through process automation, JP Morgan has introduced an AI solution called COIN to review and interpret commercial loan agreements in seconds, which has eliminated more than 360,000 hours of work for lawyers each year.[16]

Intelligent virtual assistants deployed within the banking sector and powered by social messaging platforms, mobile devices, or voice assistants can help to provide much better customer service through its convenience, ubiquity, and ease of use to allow customers to quickly inquire about account balances, mortgage options, or other banking services. With state-of-the-art natural language process capabilities, personalized intelligent virtual assistants that are integrated with banking systems and related data can not only process customer queries asked with significant variations, including spell and grammar errors, and handling the context of the user interaction, but via text or voice command provide quick answers to banking queries, personalized financial advice and even carry out transactions all from the same channel. Also, amongst the emerging trends are AI-based robo-advisors that calibrate financial portfolios in accordance with the goals and risk tolerance of their users with respect to investments, trading, loans, and retirement plans. This can be achieved by optimizing how investments are spread across asset classes and financial instruments and adapting in accordance with real-time changes in the market as well as the user's goals and objectives. These AI-based robo-advisors allow users to create individual, personalized settings for their preferences regarding investment styles and associated risk management, and also leads to fewer human errors being made and lower transaction fees.

For the general banking sector there are also opportunities to reduce costs and increase revenue by applying AI to their own vast, comprehensive proprietary financial data in combination with external data sources. These data sources that are typically in silos and not always easy to integrate include for example core banking data, customer data, product data, customer information file, payments data, mortgage data, social network data, market data, reference data, email data, messaging platform data, omni-channel data, smart device data, external agency data, tax/regulation/compliance data, ATM/kiosk data, online and mobile internet data, customer services data, and trading data. In order to operationalize and automate AI-driven solutions, rapid access to all available structured and unstructured data is needed to generate insights and a 360-degree view of the customer, portfolios, risks and exposure. This in turn feeds next best actions with respect to the bank's core back-office processing, risk management, governance, and compliance, as well as sales and services, marketing, and customers and product management. One of Cortex Logic's AI use cases for a major bank involved the delivery of AI-driven models to optimize the price of home loans in a dynamic and personalized fashion. This is an example of a high value business case as a percentage increase in home loans market share even in South Africa is in the order of billions of Rands. In the US alone the total amount of home mortgages was around $10.5 trillion in 2019.[17] The Cortex AI solution mined structured and unstructured data for better segmentation and improved real-time and personalized price positioning for home loan applications.

We see a similar picture evolving for insurance sector businesses where AI applications, data mining and real-time analytics can be customer centric, risk centric or finance centric. As it is in the case for banking, the AI solutions focus on insights generation and next best actions with respect to delivering the right offer to the target customer at the right time to the right locations via contextualized, personalized and dynamic decision recommendations, managing real-time customer interactions through integrated channels, offering highly tailored and differentiated product and services, and updating customer services representatives with the right profile and preferences. Customer insights can be further enhanced via geo-spatial overlay and alerts, real-time risk analysis across portfolios and identifying communities, leaders, and followers. Other real-time analytics can involve focusing on customer retention, loss-reserve and portfolio analysis, fine-grained risk analysis, fraud detection, channel preference and social style induced segmentations, brand or reputation monitoring and analysis. The insurance industry has rich data that includes customer information, call center, leads, claims data, policy management, vehicle usage, social network data, telematics data, agency data, location data, trading data, rate making, customer life stages data, billing data, channel interaction, and prospects.

Some specific AI applications that are providing insurance businesses with a competitive edge involves redefining the value proposition via personalized customer experience, redefining distribution via digital advice, enhancing efficiencies via automated and augmented underwriting, and reducing claims processing time and costs via a robo-claims adjuster. To create improved personalized experiences, natural language processing is applied to do text mining, topic modeling, sentiment analysis of social and interaction data, machine learning is used to infer behaviors from data, audio and speech analytics is used to better understand reasons for a call and emotion of callers, and agent-based simulations can be used to model each customer and their interactions. An AI-driven digital advice solution not only involves natural language processing, but also predictive models on when customers need what products based on life-stage and life events, helping advisors to identify the right tax advantaged products, monitor behavior, spending and saving patterns, and agent-based modeling for cradle-to-grave life events and facilitating goal-based planning. To provide automated and augmented underwriting, predictive models are used to assess risk, underwriters are supported in looking for appropriate risk attributes, home and industrial IoT data are used to build operational intelligence on risk drivers for machine learning models, process mining is used to automate and improve efficiencies, and deep causal models of risk in product lines uses system dynamics. The underlying AI technology to build a robo-claims adjuster involves claim predictive models, determining repair costs, automatically categorizing the severity of vehicle damage, and the use of graph and social networks to identify patterns of fraud in claims. It also includes the mitigation and reduction of losses by using home and industrial IoT data to build operational intelligence on the frequency and severity of accidents, identifying bottlenecks and improving efficiencies and conformance with standard claim process, and the use of deep causal claim models using system dynamic and agent-based simulation techniques and link them with product and distribution risk.

One major AI use case for both banking and insurance industries is smart risk scoring. Amongst the many different types of risk applications, the most common ones are typically where credit risk and claims risk are prime examples. The traditional logistics regression type of risk scoring which provides transparent logic and represents industry best-practice in credit scoring can be augmented and enhanced with machine learning-based approaches to address limitations such as its inability to identify non-linear relationships between variables. In an augmented approach machine learning can be utilized to expose powerful and predictive new latent features of credit risk which can be used to enhance logistic regression models. A shortfall with this approach is the potential difficulty to explain the machine learning-based segmentation and relationships between variables. Although machine learning approaches such as neural networks, random forests, and support vector machines are perceived as "black-box" techniques that needs to be adapted to create trust and transparency, they are being utilized within the banking and insurance industries to deliver enhanced performance to provide nonlinear and nonparametric forecasting and classification. These techniques can also create dynamic self-learning models that can cater for subtle hinges in credit behavior. For these types of approaches model risk governance needs to be redefined as it is exceedingly difficult to validate these models if it is constantly changing. AI can also be used to identify risk in revolving lines of credit and execute limit reductions on forecasted credit delinquencies. Creditworthiness can also be determined beyond the use of typical metrics for non-revolving consumer loans using machine learning advances to better inform and determine patterns in fraudulent activity claims and transactions. In some financial applications such as micro lending in the emerging markets where credit history or credit risk related data might not be available, the risk profile of a customer can for example be inferred and updated using data from their mobile wallet and call direct records. We have done this successfully at one of the companies that I was involved in called Jumo, a fintech company providing a full technology stack for building and running financial services in the emerging markets.[18] It has shown that the predictive power that can be generated from event level data far surpasses that which can be generated from aggregated data, resulting in much more effective models and decision strategies. This is because the higher resolution data allows creation of potentially hundreds or thousands of features to which the predictive models have access. As the market evolves, and as customer behavior adapts, it is important for the machine learning based solutions to have a wide variety of signals from each customer to learn these changing behaviors and how these affect credit risk, product uptake, upsell, cross-sell and other customer responses.

In another AI use case, one of the leading insurance companies in South Africa needed to improve their customer service whilst reducing the high cost and time-consuming nature of manual processing. The problem was that their service center had to manually process thousands of emails daily which is a resource-intensive task that involves many dedicated employees and is expensive in terms of time, cost and human productivity spent on low-value tasks. The manual processing by the call center staff involved understanding the intent, examining the attachments, and assigning it to processing queue. Cortex Logic developed specific AI solutions called aiEmail, aiAutodoc and aiAssist to automate the handling of incoming customer communication. The aiEmail solution classifies and groups incoming emails for further processing and data extraction to improve business function and reduce operational load. Besides understanding email content through intent recognition and categorizing it with a confidence score, it handles multiple languages and provides sentiment analysis. The aiAutodoc solution extracts data from any document with minimal configuration, understand data relationships such as questions and answers as well as recognizing alphanumeric handwritten text. The aiAssist solution route the text comprehension and confidence score for action which involves further automated processing such as creating an entry in a customer relationship or ticketing system, pre-populating key entities and assigning the outputs to robotic process automation of back-office system, or manual processing of outlier cases by a services desk agent.

The prediction and mitigation of churn (the loss of customers to competition) is another key AI application area for most consumer-facing businesses across multiple industries because it is more expensive to acquire a new customer than to keep your existing one from leaving. Most consumer-facing businesses suffer from voluntary churn. The churn rate has a strong impact on the lifetime value of the customer because it affects the length of service and the future revenue of the business. For example, a business with a 50% churn rate, has an average customer lifetime of 2 years. Similarly, a business with a 20% churn rate, has an average customer lifetime of 5 years. Consumer-facing businesses typically spend significant money to acquire a new customer and when that customer leaves, the company loses both the resources spent to acquire that customer and the future revenue from that customer. Churn can be reduced by using machine learning based approaches to predict a customer's propensity to churn by using customer-specific information that includes household, transactional data, and behavioral data. Machine learning can also be applied to a related problem of lapse in payment or non-activity which can lead to churn or non-active customers. So, machine learning based models that predict a customer's lapse propensity or non-activity could be used in proactive mitigation strategies. In one of the use cases, a leading insurance brand in the "call center" market experienced a 40% cancellation rate of all their policies issued within 90 days after the sale. A churn prevention solution was developed using a variety of customer data sources such email correspondence, voice recordings, text interactions and demographics. The "proposed sale" was then analyzed, and the price adjusted to reflect the risk and or reject the sale the next day before the bulk of the costs relating to the issue of a policy is incurred. This leads to significant cost savings for the insurer. In another AI-driven churn prediction use case a solution was implemented to predict lapse propensity and non-activity on a funeral policy insurer. The data sets consisted of funeral policy data for main members and dependents as well as the payment transactions. Apart from accurate predictive models that generalized well on unseen test data, insightful analysis was also provided such as the average probability to lapse by age, gender, plan brand, plan premium, etc. In a mobile money use case, a reduction of churn and improved customer loyalty was ensured via the use of predictive churn models and increasing mobile wallet activity with attractive personalized product offerings.

Data mining that provides real-time customer insights, segmentation and social network analysis can act as a fundamental building block of derived customer insights and features for other AI use cases that contribute towards a 360-degree view of the customer where structured and unstructured data is mined, natural groupings is detected in the customer data via unsupervised clustering techniques as part of a segmentation analysis, and customer interactions and community structures are analyzed utilizing information about connections between individual customers. These valuable insights are also used as derived features in other customer-centric AI-based applications such as risk scoring, affordability scoring, fraud and anomaly detection, response prediction, recommendation engines, and churn prediction. In many applications, models developed on segmented data sets allow for more accurate results than ones that are generalized over a single non-segmented customer data set. For example, for credit risk we see a segmented scorecard typically outperforms a single scorecard. Segmentation analysis is dependent on the types of data available and is typically focused on a combination of demographic, geographic and/or behavioral segmentation. In turn this can feed into more specific types of segmentation analysis such as market segmentation or risk segmentation where aspects such as stability, willingness and affordability are relevant. In financial applications, demographic segmentation typically utilizes "know your customer" data and can for example be further enriched by adding mobile network event level data that allows for richer geographical information through the knowledge of tower usage. Behavioral segmentation can for example be used to identify groups differentiated by value, volume, and product usage. Transaction data enriches behavioral segmentation substantially by enabling the calculation of additional features which speak to the particular way in which the customers use their phones, wallets and related services. Some example features include proportion of data usage in business hours, proportion of messages sent to core contacts versus non-core contacts, proportional overlap between calling partners weekdays versus weekends, variation in airtime balance as at time of top-up, etc. If these types of features are tracked over time, it enables the development of perspectives on customer lifecycle and maturity, and associated opportunities at various points in this lifecycle. Related to this is the ability to identify different trajectories. For example, if a customer displays a certain behavior type this month, what behaviors can we expect with what probabilities next month and the month after? The type of analysis also allows the measurement of segment size at a portfolio level over time, and the identification of emerging submarkets. Social network analysis focuses on customer interactions and community structures which are analyzed utilizing information about connections between individual customers. As an example, changing phenomena within the market tend to propagate through the community structure. A particular behavior might originate in one section of the community and spread to others. By understanding how the community is structured, one can anticipate how long it will take for each trend to reach different sub-communities of customers. A prime example of this is the adoption of new products, as often this is driven by word-of-mouth referral. As an example, social network analysis that utilizes mobile network event level data, makes it possible to see individual connections. The transactional-level data allows for creating various graphical representations of customers. Some use cases for insights from social network analysis could include detecting lending circles, syndicated schemes, and fraud rings as well as profiling of individual customers based on their social interactions.

As with other industries, the financial sector can benefit significantly from machine learning-based security systems that can identify and detect potential illegal access points to a financial institution's data or funds, anticipate how money laundering or fraud can be committed, and provide real-time preventative solutions to stop these crimes before they happen. From a detection perspective, the accurate identity of an individual or fraudulent actor is determined through a combination of machine learning-based models, scoring and rules. Machine learning-based approaches are starting to be preferred above pure rules-based approaches as there are a need for scalable and computationally efficient prediction models that make use of information from multiple attributes at the same time, increase the detection accuracy which can lead to significant savings, model complex attack patterns not previously observed, and combat fraudsters which are becoming increasingly smarter and adaptive. Supervised machine learning models that learn from past examples of fraud are typically used to predict fraud in real-time, whereas unsupervised AI methods that segment transactions and/or do anomaly detection can be used to potentially discover new fraud. Depending on the specific scope and application, fraud detection models can for example be deployed on a transactional, account and/or network level. On a transaction level, AI models can flag fraudulent behavior up-front and also help to provide an in-depth analysis after transactions are completed. On an account level abusive behavior such as frequent payments or suspicious profile changes can be identified, whereas on a network level account-to-account interaction such as frequent transfer of money from several accounts to one central account can be identified. Where relevant, intelligence from past discovery and investigation processes are also used to recognize fraudulent activity patterns and highlight potential payment submission improprieties for further investigation by the investigations team. To discover fraudulent patterns, a rich set of AI capabilities is leveraged to identify non-compliance by retrospectively reviewing historical data, analyzing patterns and anomalies to identify individuals or organizations that might be developing fraud schemes. These predictive analytics can be complemented by prescriptive analytics that takes the predictions made from the correlations of a predictive analytics engine and uses it to provide recommendations for what to do once fraud is detected. Other aspects of a comprehensive fraud detection and prevention solution includes quick response to criminal activities, intentions, or patterns, as well as proper investigations into suspicious activity that will support the compilation of evidence and provide the thorough analysis required to build more compelling cases for denial of payment, recovery, or prosecution.

AI-driven Retail and eCommerce

From the plethora of AI use cases in retail and ecommerce it is clear that AI can help to capture significant gains across this sector's value chain by for example delivering a better shopping experience, predicting demand, and automating operations. These smart technology solutions can specifically help to address some of the biggest challenges in retail such as not having accurate forecasting models to predict trends and levels of demand, poor customer support and services, ineffective targeting, recommendations not being in line with customer preferences and needs, non-optimal store footprints, and having overstock and out-of-stock inventory problems. According to Meticulous Research, AI's growth in the retail market has been predominantly driven by the increasing adoption of a multichannel or omnichannel retailing strategy to enhance the personalized engagement and end-user customer experience. They projected a compound annual growth rate of 35.9% to reach $15.3 billion by 2025.[19] In order to unlock business value, serve their customers better and capture these gains, retailers and ecommerce businesses must leverage technology infrastructure and all available data. Although traditional retailers have in general struggled to make the offline-to-online transition, the growth of advertising technology and ecommerce that generates massive customer data have allowed retailers to optimize their advertising and to target customers in a more effective and efficient fashion. With the wealth of data available in disparate data sets such as loyalty, clickstream, browsing behavior, promotions, in-store, location, customer profiles, customer life stages, channel interaction, pricing, and billing data, a wide range of AI applications are possible that includes demand prediction, offering the right products and services to the right customer at the right time; inventory management; customer management; merchandising and market basket analysis; campaign management and customer loyalty programs; supply-chain management, analytics, and optimization; event- and behavior-based targeting; market and customer segmentations; recommendation engines that help to increase the average order size by recommending complementary products based on predictive analysis for cross-selling; cross-channel analytics; and trend extrapolation. Accenture reports that investment in AI and human-machine collaboration could boost retail store revenues by 38% by 2022.[20] As a result of the growing AI use cases in retail and ecommerce, GS GIR predicted the associated demand and driving labor efficiencies worth $54bn annually while price optimization and annual sales increase in discretionary categories such as clothing and footwear can amount to $41bn globally by 2025.[21] A MGI analysis has highlighted some use cases that include optimized pricing, personalized promotions and recommendations, intelligent virtual assistants, automated in-store checkout, completing last-mile delivery by drones, real-time tailoring of website displays, anticipating of demand trends whilst optimizing and automating supplier negotiation and contracting, automating warehouse and store operations, as well as optimizing merchandising, product assortment, and microspace.[22] Some example AI use cases with specific benefits include a 1–2% EBIT (earnings before interest and taxes) improvement using machine learning to anticipate fruit and vegetable sales by a European retailer, a 20% stock reduction of a German e-commerce merchant Otto using deep learning on billions of transactional records to predict e-commerce purchases and 2 million fewer product returns per year, a 30% reduction of stocking time using autonomous vehicles in warehouses of Swisslog, a 50% improvement of assortment efficiency, 4–6% sales increase using geospatial modeling to improve micro market attractiveness, and 30% online sales increase by using dynamic pricing and personalization.[23]

Amazon is a prime example of an extraordinarily successful company in retail and ecommerce that uses AI to develop and maintain their competitive advantage in scalable customer service and experience as illustrated with their usability, recommendations, and membership benefits. To drive product recommendations, they apply a combination of collaborative filtering and next-in-sequence AI models on their colossal consumer purchases behavior database to make recommendations on the next likely products and/or services that a customer might be interested in purchasing. Amazon also uses state-of-the-art natural language processing to power their digital assistant Alexa, optimizes their logistics with respect to delivery arrival times, accuracy, efficiency, rerouting, and even drone delivery. With smart speaker devices such as Amazon' Echo and Google Home, shoppers can also complete retail orders through express and third-party retailers. Amazon Go, a cashier-less grocery store and mobile application that lets shoppers buy items without human interaction, swiping a card or paying cash, is using AI and sensor technology to create a check-out free shopping experience that automatically detects when products are taken from or returned to the shelves and keeps track of them in a virtual cart and handles the payment automatically via the mobile application.[24] There are also similar cashier-free convenience stores in Sweden and Finland as well as in China where customers can pay via WeChat or other mobile applications.[25] Some examples of where traditional retailers have instrumented their stores with Bluetooth beacons to collect data about customer behaviors and purchasing patterns include Target and Walmart in the US and Carrefour in France, which in turn allows them to apply AI-based models to this data in order to send personalized promotion to their customers whilst they are shopping in store.[26] In the case of Carrefour, the deployment of this smart technology solution in 28 stores has led to a 600% increase in their mobile application users.[27] Another example of improving the shopping experience is IKEA's augmented reality application, called Place, that allows customers to visualize how IKEA furniture fits into customer's household spaces.[28] Apart from eBay's Shopbot that provides recommendations and advice, they are also experimenting with consumer psychology to better understand consumers using subconscious techniques (such as color psychology, persuasive pricing, trust symbols and marketing triggers) for better marketing and helping to optimize conversions.[29] Pinterest introduced a Chrome extension which allows users to search for any product online through an image and allows them to browse similar products by the same retail store. Furniture retailer West Elm scans customers' Pinterest boards to understand their personal style and then generates a matching recommended furniture and home décor item list.[30] Macy's in-store experience has been given a boost with their AI-driven On Call application and chatbot that addresses individual store related questions about a specific item, directions or if an item is in stock, but can also pick up if a customer gets frustrated and human intervention is needed. Another in-store example is clothing retailer Uniqlo who has several stores with UMood kiosks that show customers a variety of products and measure their reactions to the style and color via brain signals.[31]

AI-driven recommendation engines use state-of-the-art machine learning techniques to predict the likely products that would be of interest to a customer based on a customer's profile, purchase history and what other customers with a similar profile purchased. It also predicts the likelihood of a purchase as well as cross-selling and upselling opportunities in next best action applications based on a 360-degree view of customers. These next best actions involve delivering the right offer to the target at the right time and to the right location, offering highly differentiated and tailored products and services, updating customer services representatives with the right profile and preferences, and managing real-time customer interactions through integrated channels and intelligent virtual assistants. An intelligent sales flow assistant can predict the next steps and questions customers may have and feeds them information proactively. This can happen in accordance with customer journey path identification and customers' preferences which could be via an intelligent virtual assistant, pushed application notifications, a chatbot window that pops-up, or a follow-up email. There are many examples of smart agents being used by retailers which includes 1-800-Flowers' proposing a selection of floral-related products based on a chat and Stitch Fix that analyses images that their customers for example display on Pinterest to better understand their styles from a clothing perspective.[32] Real-time analytics and insights generation that underpin the development of a holistic and in-depth customer view typically involves contextualized, personalized and dynamic decision recommendations, fine-grained customer segmentation, geo-spatial overlay and location-specific recommendations, channel integrated real-time pricing, identifying communities, leaders and followers, customer stickiness analysis, channel preference and social style induced segmentations, real-time brand and reputation monitoring and analysis, and store performance analysis. As another AI-driven recommendation example, one of the major retailers in South Africa wanted a smart recommendation and personalization for millions of their loyalty scheme members. To enhance their margins and sales performance they wanted a deeper understanding of their customers so that they can offer the right products at the right time, thus changing and predicting shopping behavior. Their aim is to meet individual customer needs through relevant personalized communication and offers at scale which is not possible with traditional methods. By using an AI-driven approach to recommending the right offer at the right time to the right customer will change their shopping behavior. The Cortex solution involved data extracted and modeled for their millions of active customers and their shopping behavior to provide key customer insights. The recommendation engine was trained on historic purchasing data to better segment customers, predict their wants and offer the products via a defined communication channel. The AI-modeled campaigns are executed through personalized emails, SMSs, and notifications to consenting customers daily to recommend best product offers for each customer and provide the best customer match to product offers that were filtered according to the retailer's specifications.

Some of the main barriers for retailers to achieve their supply chain goals are forecasting accuracy and demand variability. To address this, AI-based supply chain optimization in retail can help to reduce write-offs and waste, capital expenditure, and out-of-stock; enable significant automation; as well as increase freshness, turnover and efficiency. Such a data-driven solution typically incorporates many influencing factors such as price, individual customer promotions, promotion rules, local competitors, competitor pricing, competitive articles, coupon promotions, media advertisements, print and online promotions, vendor and retailer promotions, seasonality, local holidays, day of the week or month, brand, and weather forecast parameters. For replenishment optimization applications, a probabilistic demand forecast machine learning-based model is trained for each product and location over a demand period and also incorporates the replenishment goals and constraints with respect to inventory and deliveries. Automated decisions lead to optimized replenishment orders which results in significantly reduced waste, out-of-stock, and manual intervention, and increased availability, but also less items on stock. For spare parts replenishment, a predictive solution can optimize the risk of over-capacity and out-of-stock situations as the distribution of spare parts from warehouses at different locations are considered with business decisions made on costs versus service level. Warehouses can be optimized and costs of storing, transporting and unplanned deliveries can be lowered by having a full risk profile on the stock keeping unit level. AI-based price optimization in retail enables increased market share, turnover, raw profit, customers and new customers, significant automation, and a reduction in complaints, returns and rests at the end of season. Older pricing strategies grapple with how much prices can be increased and by how much and utilizing economically inconsistent cost-plus pricing strategy that ignores customers as well as "psychological pricing techniques" (such "9.99") that does not have statistical evidence of success. Machine learning-based price optimization starts with measuring price elasticities by identifying relevant prediction features, calculating relevant price elasticities of demand per store and per product, and learning the continuously changing price-demand relations using relevant data. The price optimization involves the application of strategic price rules, considering location-individual stock levels, storage costs, etc., and applying margin and revenue expectations according to strategic goals. The results are an optimized price per product and shopping or online channel, highest level of automation, and price calculation according to company strategy. The future of AI in the supply chain always starts from customer demand and is completely data-driven and scientific with demand predictions at the finest grain. It also involves aggregating up the supply chain, breaking down silos and holistic company optimization, exchanging data across supplier-retailer boundaries, planning higher levels, and merging of algorithmic retailing or pricing and the supply chain. Cross-industry partnerships that for example include loyalty card providers and banks will also be key to obtaining better customer insights.

Over the next few years, we will see retailers starting to know more about what consumers want and sometimes before they articulate their needs themselves. With advanced applications of AI and smart technology such as natural language processing, facial recognition software, and machine learning, one can expect to see over time intelligent virtual assistants and smart virtual agents that greet consumers in a personalized fashion, anticipate their orders and needs, offer personalized promotions to match their profiles, send offers to their smartphones as they browse through the store, assist with directions, and make recommendations. As mentioned earlier, AI-driven smart technology will more dramatically impact the in-store customer experience with applications such as computer vision that identifies goods bagged by shoppers, smart interactive screens and tabletops that identifies articles and recommends complementary and personalized goods and services, non-stop checkout and automatic payment (as already seen with Amazon Go), and autonomous shopping carts that follow shoppers in the store and find their way to shoppers' vehicles or autonomous drones for last-mile or home delivery. To help maximize revenues, retail stores will also be able to update and optimize prices in real time through the application of AI-driven pricing models that leverage data on customer profiles, competitors' prices, weather, events, and inventory levels. Inventories can be continuously tracked by AI-enhanced robots that recognize empty shelves and replenish them and help to automate some warehouse activities. With consumers increasingly becoming used to the ease, personalized, and instantaneous nature of online shopping and the increasing use of AI and other smart technology driving revolutionary changes in retail, this might even lead to the possible disintermediation of retailers, especially over-built as opposed to asset-light ones, as intelligent systems start to facilitate orders and delivery of goods and services in direct fashion with consumers.

Telecommunications, Media, and Entertainment

The increasing adoption of AI for various applications in telecommunication, social media and entertainment markets, the utilization of AI-enabled smartphones, and growing investments in the 5G network are all expected to be contributing significantly to the growth of the AI across these markets. Apart from 5G being the next generation technology standard for cellular networks that provides significantly greater bandwidth and download speeds of up to 10 gigabits, it can also be seen as a software-defined network governed by AI with respect to its design, planning, monitoring, management and optimization - making it effectively the current largest deployment of distributed AI. According to Technavio the global AI market size in the telecommunication industry will grow by $2.54 billion during 2019-2023[33], whereas Tractica projects $11.2 billion in 2025[34] and Juniper Research $15 billion by 2024.[35] Technavio also predicted that the global telecom IoT market to post a compound annual growth rate of more than 42% by 2020, with intelligent transportation systems one of the major factors.[36] Some of the key AI use cases in telecommunications include predictive maintenance, monitoring and optimization of network operations, real-time analysis of call direct records and internet protocol detail records for networks, fraud identification and mitigation, cybersecurity, robotic process automation, intelligent virtual assistants for customer service and marketing, intelligent customer relationship management systems, revenue assurance and dynamic pricing, customer churn prevention, customer experience management and service delivery, sentiment analysis, social network analysis, campaign management, customer loyalty, mobile user local analysis, and video compression.

Telecommunications service providers are experiencing an increase in demand for improved customer experience and better quality services. By using an AI-driven approach to mine all available relational and non-relational data, a 360-degree view of the customer can be built to provide real-time analytics and insights to provide next best actions that address these customer demands in a personalized fashion. AI-driven solutions can also improve operations and increase revenue through new products and services. Due to nature of telecommunications and massive customer bases, telecommunication companies have access to vast amounts of mobile network data, voice network data, subscriber data, social network data, and machine generated data that provides details about mobile internet usage, call detailed records, geolocation, smart device usage, channel interaction, billing, network, set top box, and machine-to-machine communications. Real-time analytics on these data involves, for example, understanding device usage, customer behavior and preferences, the right channels and social circles, influences, segments, and hotspots in the network performance. The insights generated can drive contextualized, dynamic, and personalized decision recommendations; identify communities, leaders, and followers; and provide a real-time view of the network load heat-map and customer experience. As with other customer facing businesses, the next best action delivers the right offer to the target at the right time to the right location. It also provides customer services representatives and intelligent virtual assistants with the right profile and preferences, manages real-time customer interactions through integrated channels and offers highly differentiated and customized products and services.

As telecommunication companies are adopting technologies such as software defined networks, network function virtualization, and orchestration, AI is earmarked to play a key role in the integration of these technologies and the automation of networks. According to the IDC, almost two thirds of network mobile operators are investing in AI systems to improve their infrastructure.[37] One key AI use case is the building of self-optimizing networks to enable operators to automatically optimize the network quality based on traffic and time zone. As an example, Aira Networks provides AI-based solutions for automating and optimizing the supply chain that delivers services for digital economy service providers and data center operators.[38] They use AI to dynamically determine the optimal network configuration for a given service request or traffic demand. According to Sedona Systems, their NetFusion Platform automatically discovers, aggregates, and analyzes network data from multiple online systems, optical and IP sources to provide a unified, real-time and accurate network-wide data model. The latter is then consumed via products that reduce the cost, time, complexity, and resources that are needed to forecast, plan, and operate the optimal network infrastructure for delivering the required services, reliability and performance.[39] Nokia also offers an AI-as-a-service offering delivered through the Microsoft Azure cloud to automate network operations and provide predictive and proactive services across operations and care for improved customer experience, service assurance, increased agility and reduced costs.[40] As with the other equipment-rich industries, predictive maintenance is another major AI application area for telecommunications companies with communications hardware such as cell towers, data center servers, power lines, and setup boxes. Machine learning based solutions are utilized to provide real-time monitoring of the equipment state, prevent equipment failure, determine causes for deviation in equipment performance, and assist in solving problems proactively. Predictive maintenance solutions aim to understand the process of service degradation before failure and predicting which network elements have a high likelihood of failure within a specified time frame. Avanseus describes a predictive maintenance use case with a major European Telecom service provider that is in process of transforming its network operations to get ready for 5G and IoT deployment at scale and to deliver better network experience to customers. The outcomes of their AI-driven Cognitive Assistant for Networks solution include prediction of 50%+ of the potential impact incidents with greater than 75% accuracy and 35%+ reduction in service impacting incidents and a 0.17% increase in network availability.[41] Affine is another AI-powered predictive maintenance solution that can accurately predict the propensity of telecom tower components due to factors such as fatigue, manufacturing defects, or unsuitable environment in order to prevent business disruption through planned and scheduled maintenance.[42] KPN is a Dutch telecommunications company that is using predictive maintenance to proactively identify issues on the customer's side by tracking and tracing behavior such as channel switching on a modem that could cause a WI-FI issue.[43] Another significant AI use case is the detection of fraudulent activities such as illegal access or authorization, stealing or faking profiles, or behavioral fraud that can be prevented by applying anomaly detection solutions that typically make use of unsupervised machine learning to provide real-time alerts when the system sees abnormal or suspicious behavior.

AI-driven solutions can also help to reduce churn. According to a 2019 TechSee survey, 39% of US citizens who cancelled a contract with a telecoms company in the past 2 years cited customer service as the primary reason, where the majority cases the contract was cancelled for internet, cable, TV, or phone services.[44] Churn was predominantly due to a negative experience of high customer effort such as wasting time, multiple calls, incompetent agents and an inferior self-service option. Telecom services providers are increasingly using machine learning based solutions to predict customer behavior using customer profile data from a variety of channels such as online, paid ads and owned media to target customers with a high likelihood to churn. Vodafone follows for example this approach to match these customers with appropriate retention plans, discount offerings and partner company benefits.[45] In another use case a telecommunication company that had a problem of annual churn rates of about 10%, while the customer base grew at a slower rate of 5% annually. For this particular case some of the factors impacting churn included customers with a significant number of service calls, those with higher bills and those with international plans. A churn prediction model helped to capture a significant portion of the potential churners, which led to proactive actions to reduce the churn rate by up to 50%, leading to significant revenue increases.

Most telecommunication providers are now deploying intelligent virtual assistants and chatbots to improve customer services that automate and scale responses to support customer requests for setting up, installation, troubleshooting and maintenance. Some of the major telecoms service providers in the US such as Verizon, AT&T and Comcast are all using AI-driven solutions to improve customer services communication, customer engagement and personalized user experience. Vodafone has also implemented a scalable chatbot called TOBi to take care of a range of customer service questions.[46] They have also deployed the AI-powered TechSee VIA platform which led to a 12% improvement in first call resolution and 68% improvement in customer satisfaction.[47] Nokia's Digital Assistant is providing automated assistance to increase the efficiency of network operations center staff and engineers to, for example, diagnose and analyze root causes of network faults. The machine learning-driven virtual assistant reduces wasted time by finding the right information instantly, helps to enforce correct procedures through a knowledge library that includes best practices, and provides access to all relevant tools, documents, and data sources.[48]

Robotic process automation is also helping to increase efficiency by making it easier for telecoms to manage repetitive, labor-intensive, and time-consuming back-end operations such as data entry, billing, order fulfillment and workforce management. Other use cases include periodic report preparation and dissemination, competitor price checking, software robots that can respond to partner queries, first call resolution, and reducing the manual sales order process effort.[49] One such example is provided by UiPath which helped an Australian telecoms and media company to reduce costs (of approximately 10 full-time equivalent employees) by automating its order build process and service removal activity.[50] Celaton claims that their intelligent process automation solutions help to achieve 75% efficiency gains with accounts payable automation, reduce sales order processing time by 87%, reduce the manual effort in correspondence processing by 85% and improve customer satisfaction with faster case resolution.[51]

With respect to the social media market, Markets and Markets forecasts the global AI in this market to grow to $2.2 billion by 2023 at a compound annual growth rate of 28.3% during the 4-year forecasted period.[52] Research and Markets projects that the spend on AI in the media and entertainment industry is expected to increase to almost $2 billion by 2025.[53] Some relevant use cases for deploying AI solutions in the media and entertainment sector includes targeted advertising, facial recognition advertising, marketing and advertising where machine learning is trained to help develop film trailers and design advertisements, recommending personalized content based on data from user activity and behavior to create a personalized user experience, improving the speed and efficiency of the media production process and the ability to organize visual assets, deep video analysis along with translation, transcription and tagging, voice based virtual assistants, optimized video encoding and delivery, video quality assessment, visual recognition, anomaly detection, content fingerprinting, infotainment human machine interface with virtual reality and augmented reality, post production, content production and management, content consumption and delivery, and data management.

The application of AI to improve the digital strategies of news media and publishers are growing in leaps and bounds with hyper personalization of reader experiences through machine learning, improving the reader engagement, the elimination of bias and fake news, and automated or robot journalism where news articles are generated by machine learning based computer programs. News UK has, for example, experimented with a digital "butler" that gradually learns the preferences, interests, and habits of readers to deliver relevant content in their preferred formats, times, frequencies and channels.[54] By keeping readers engaged, the news media companies are effectively also reducing churn and can use machine learning systems to also predict and prevent churn.[55] Machine learning can also be used to discover what type of content keeps readers engaged and feed those insights back to the content generation process. Many organizations and companies are also working towards AI-driven solutions to help combat fake news and bias such as Knowhere News which claims to write an impartial version of a story by applying machine learning to a broad range of news sources, taking into account its trustworthiness, removing potential bias from content and ensuring impartial headlines.[56] On the automated natural language generation front, OpenAI's GPT-3 is likely leading the pack in this field (at the time of writing) with its generative pre-trained transformer deep learning neural network that has 175 billion parameters in its autoregressive language model and trained on the entire English Wikipedia (0.6% of the training set), electronic books and other web pages. GPT-3 has achieved strong performance on a variety of natural language processing datasets, including question-answering and translation, and has the ability to generate samples of news articles that was difficult to distinguish from articles written by humans.[57] Although GPT-3's few shot learning still makes simple mistakes, struggles on some data sets and produced some offensive and biased outputs, the model has also demonstrated a high degree of flexibility with other applications that include writing fiction and poems, autocompleting of images, composing guitar tabs, transferring styles for text, answering medical queries, generating code based on text descriptions, solving syntax and language puzzles, and even letting users chat with historical figures.[58] Some other real-world examples include Associated Press that produces automatically generated earnings reports, MittMedia's AI bot that writes short text on houses sold in local markets in Sweden, and Washington Post's AI bot that writes less complex stories and covers some localized news.[59] We are also starting to see the use of AI-driven synthesized news anchors reading the news with China's state-run news agency that has debuted two news readers to look and sound like the broadcaster's real anchors.[60]

AI is also having a direct impact on the field of journalism, where we already see a number of augmented journalism use cases such as natural language processing for topic modelling or sentiment analysis; natural language generation that can for example transform data into readable articles; machine learning to enable journalist to identify patterns, trends and actionable insights from multiple data sources, turn speech into text, and generate text from video and audio; the use of robotic cameras and drones to gather data and information; and support of investigations by for example analyzing scenes for faces, objects, text and more. Jonathan Stray from Columbia Journalism School provided some practice-driven recommendations of how natural language processing can help journalists in analyzing large sets of documents (with the Overview platform) and produce a story along with applications such as sentiment analysis, topic modelling, text classification, and entity recognition.[61] These recommendations include having a more robust import and analysis of structured and unstructured documents, improved ways of searching through the document set, having better quantitative summaries, be more interactive, and explainability of insights or conclusions. Addressing these will ensure that natural language processing assisted reporting can have an even broader potential and application for journalists across the spectrum.

Many changes to the search engine landscape and shifts in client strategies influenced improvements in campaign targeting, but also caused dramatic increases in cost. Competition is getting fierce with more and more spend shifting towards mobile and shopping ads in the retail sector. From increases in mobile ad inventory to the release of many new shopping ad formats, the race is on to stay competitive. There has been a significant increase of paid search and shopping cost per click (CPC) over time. Banner and display advertising is not good in general as it is not contextually related to the content being read by the visitor. This leads to annoyed visitors and poor click-through rates, unhappy advertiser and low conversion rates, and unhappy publishers and less revenue. An AI-based advertising solution enables significant higher click through rates which helps to drive much higher conversions and less CPC with relevant embedded advertising. The system consists of a server-side business component containing the business logic and rules, a client-side ad component responsible for advertisement placement on the publisher's platform and data collection, a customer control-panel allowing customers to create ads and campaigns, access statistics and maintain their account, and an AI component to guide the advertising. Broadcasters can also insert ads into their offerings where real-time machine learning driven analytics is used to determine which advertisements are ideal and relevant based on the content. AI can also assist in the design of advertisements, ad inventory management and yield optimization.

Robert Tercek in his article about how AI is completely reinventing media and marketing believes that synthetic personalities powered by AI to enable hyper-personalization will change the way we learn about new products and how to use them.[62] His primary questions are about AI's ability to improve the workflow in entertainment production and distribution and the consumer audiences' willingness to engage with and pay for AI-driven automated systems for entertainment. Netflix not only applies AI in every stage of the video delivery and even the quality of their service but provides an excellent use case for AI-driven personalized content recommendation that drives 75% of viewer activity as was estimated a few years ago.[63] Apart from personalized movie recommendations, Netflix also uses AI to auto-generate thumbnails from hundreds of video frames and based on what is the most recognizable in user's clicks. With respect to streaming quality, Netflix uses past view data to assess bandwidth usage to decide when to cache local servers during peak load times when there is peak demand. An AI use case in film editing is to determine when quality control checks fail with for example synchronizing subtitles to sound or movement. ByteDance's TikTok is another example of an AI-driven software defined media service that uses machine learning to create personalized experiences for users watching music videos or making their own amusing videos.[64] AI is also being used to generate content such as the rapid prototypes produced by The Walt Disney Company to generate rough animation sequences and storyboards.[65] It is also being used by movie production companies in post-production where machine learning is applied to computer-generated imagery characters to mirror the facial expressions and movements of real actors (see for example *Avengers: Infinity War* and *Avengers: Endgame*).[66] AI was also effectively used in the movie *The Irishman* to help create the visual effects of Robert De Niro's de-aging. Rct Studio is also using state-of-the-art AI to create movie experiences with open-ended story worlds that are immersive and interactive where audiences can engage with AI-driven non-players.[67] In addressing the other questions, we already have many examples of people willing to engage with and pay for AI-driven automated systems in the form of smart phones (e.g., Siri, Google Assistant, etc.), intelligent virtual assistants and chatbots on the web, within apps or messaging services (such as Facebook Messenger, Telegram, WhatsApp, WeChat, Slack, etc.) or embedded in devices, smart speakers (e.g., Alexa, Google Home, etc.), robot newsreaders, AI-generated music and smart playlists that match tunes and tempo to user's mood and pace (on Spotify or YouTube), or AI players in a variety of games (e.g., board, card, strategy, and a variety of video games such as action, adventure, shooter, battle, sports, simulations, etc.). In the case of video games, we are already accustomed to competing against challenging, human-like AI-driven players as well as gameplay and difficulty being dynamically adjusted to offer a compelling challenge for gamers of all skill levels. We will also see the infotainment human machine interface expand into the use of hologram simulations (as we have already seen from celebrity music tours)[68], virtual reality and augmented reality (e.g., Madonna dancing on stage at the Billboard Music Awards with digital versions of herself that was created with volumetric capture and the AI-driven Unreal Engine).[69] Another extreme example is Hatsune Miku, the Japanese animated singer that is entirely synthetic and doing live performances.[70]

AI is also used to help develop augmented and virtual reality content based on the storyline and themes for content, movies, events, virtual reality sports events, fantasy leagues and gaming. It can also give organizers of these events and virtual reality environments predictive merchandise options and enhance the shopping experience for users. AI-enhanced virtual and augmented reality kiosks at public places such as malls, train stations and airports can give customers a feel of the products and services. AI-driven visual analysis in movies involves for example the tracking of emotions alongside audio analysis of tone of voice and music. To give viewers a better feel of an event, a 360-degree view of the live event is captured and then enhanced. This is also how AI is used to draw most of the earth from satellite photos in the 2020 version of Microsoft Flight Simulator that allows the user to see the entire globe with even real-time weather information. For the virtual world to look like the real one, the AI figured out where to put the trees, roads, and buildings in 3D on top of flat images.[71]

With the growing applications of deep learning algorithms such as generative adversarial networks, autoencoders, and convolutional neural networks to exploit its generative power to generate original images, audio and video (even cogent video without a storyboard or script[72] or generating animation from recorded audio[73]), we have unfortunately also seen many examples of fake images, audio and video being generated, which has been called "deep fakes", and used in false and fabricated news, celebrity pornographic videos, financial fraud, and hoaxes.[74] This has been met with concerns from public, media, academia, industry and governments and led to responses to detect deep fakes and manipulated content and exploring ways to verify the source of the media (using for example blockchain), industry taking action by account suspensions and banning various forms of deep fakes, as well as legal responses such as the Malicious Deep Fake Prohibition Act and Deepfakes Accountability Act in the US.

The opportunity with AI-driven infotainment human machine interaction is to engage in personalized, contextualized, and meaningful ways to serve us instead of the current approach of fighting for our attention and robbing our time. With AI on demand with lifelike responsiveness in real-time supported by high speed, high bandwidth and low latency communications infrastructure and realistic augmented reality overlays on real-world settings, intelligent virtual assistants in the form of personalized synthetic personalities can support us in practical ways via recommendations, advice, filtering of content, relevant contextualized information, demonstrating how to do things, and enriching our experiences.

Transportation, Travel and Tourism

Whereas transportation and logistics have seen a relatively high adoption of AI, travel and tourism have, relative to other sectors, been lagging in both adoption and the future AI demand trajectory. Even though this is the case, there are a variety of impactful AI use cases that will be highlighted here. The transportation industry clearly has high expectations for the impact of smart technology. Transportation's interest in AI is predominantly driven by autonomous vehicles, and the transformative impact they are expected to deliver on how metropolitan areas and cities operate. Not only can machine learning powered smart technology solutions provide safe and efficient transportation, but also improve traffic flow, expand the capacity of existing road infrastructure, as well as reduce carbon emissions and facilitate greater inclusiveness. Given that transportation is at the intersection of smart technology and public life, a significant majority of transportation decision-makers also are of the opinion that the government should be to some extent involved in AI regulation.[75] According to the same KPMG study, these industry leaders are not only almost unanimous about the expected benefits of AI-driven solutions, but also aware of the risks with most of them feeling that there is also a threat to consumer data privacy or security. The market size for AI-driven solutions in transportation is expected to grow from $1.2 Billion in 2017 to $10.3 Billion by 2030 which translates to a compound aggregate growth rate of 17.8% over the period.[76] Some relevant use cases for deploying AI solutions in the logistics and transportation sector include streamlining decision-making in transport management driven by AI and IoT, optimizing transport operations, managing warehouses, decreasing downtime and repairs through monitoring and predictive maintenance, going driverless, changing supply chain logistics into automated trading, and demand planning. Freight and logistics are a $4.5 trillion global sector that is highly fragmented, complex, and manual with a high dependence and cost of human coordination. This market is ripe for disruption with several startups delivering AI-driven solutions to address these issues. One such startup is FERO which is focused on eliminating human coordination in freight and logistics and envision bringing AI enabled coordination to the freight ecosystem through optimization and automation of freight transactions globally.[77] They have implemented a voice-enabled AI-driven virtual freight intelligent virtual assistant that not only coordinates pricing, quotes, customer services and operations, but also manages sales, bidding, and customer service across various freight functions. Machine learning models can for example be used to predict whether a product will be shipped on time and find the most optimal shipping routes. In addition, intelligent systems can help identify problematic incidents and solve them in time. One of the use cases that Cortex Logic has been involved in was to help reduce the risk in transport and logistics for a provider of fleet and mobile asset management solutions. The machine learning powered application was aimed at improving the safety and security of people and assets, reducing cost of operations, and enabling behavioral change of drivers. Such a solution does not only help the fleet management provider to enhance its customer service, but also improve driver safety by predicting a potential accident or harm from driver behavior and also flag accident prone behavior for human review and management. The cloud-based AI-driven solution uses existing camera footage to monitor camera obstruction, identify anomalous behavior (e.g., driver distraction, cell phone usage; driver fatigue; driver safety belt usage; and smoking) as well as the number of passengers in the vehicle and integrating the outputs with the current alert processes.

The multi-trillion-dollar automotive industry is under heavy disruption with the relentless drive towards electric and self-driving vehicles along with ride sharing business models. Tesla has become the most valuable car maker at the time of writing, with ride sharing giants such as Uber, Lyft and new-comer Facedrive also disrupting the automotive industry.[78] Even though Tesla has sold a fraction of global car sales with Toyota, Volkswagen, Renault Nissan Alliance, Hyundai-Kia, and General Motors being the top 5, it is leading the self-driving car pack, in particular in the category of self-driving or autopilot miles logged - a total of 3 billion miles as of April 2020 compared to its nearest competitor Waymo which reported 20 million miles on public roads at the start of 2020. The reason this is an important metric is that self-driving algorithms are based on machine learning which is dependent on huge volumes of representative sensor data. That is why AI is paving the way for autonomous vehicles or self-driving cars which can sense its environment through sensors such as inertial instruments, odometry, GPS, radar, lidar, and sonar and moving safely with little or no human input using machine learning and advanced control systems to interpret sensory information for navigation and identification of signage and obstacles. Although we have seen rapid progress with autonomous vehicles due to focused efforts by Tesla, Waymo, General Motors Cruise, Ford's Argo AI, Baidu, Aurora, and others, there are also limits of today's machine learning to specifically deal with the unexpected, that needs to be addressed.[79] In addition, there are also hard problems around safety, assurance, data security, ethical issues, social acceptability, and regulation that needs to be overcome. This can only be done with all stakeholders collaborating on making self-driving cars safe and providing the required evidence along with implementing regulations and standards for autonomous vehicles and getting the public involved in decisions about the introduction and adoption of these vehicles. In the US, the National Highway Traffic Safety Administration has recently for the first time proposed some amendments to its vehicle safety rules to make it easier for the widespread adoption of self-driving cars.[80]

AI will play an increasingly important role as one progresses on SAE International's levels of driving automation, going from level zero where there is no automation up to level five which implies full vehicle autonomy.[81] The levels for automated vehicles are automation for driver assistance ("hands on" - e.g., using parking sensors or cruise control), partially automated driving ("hands-off" - vehicle can perform steering and acceleration, but human still responsible for the vehicle's operation), conditional automated driving ("eyes off" - human lets the system take control - e.g., on the highway), high automated driving ("mind off" - human presence still needed and can override the system), and full automated car ("steering wheel optional" - no human assistance required). Some of the advantages of autonomous vehicle technology is increased road safety, reducing accidents and the number of fatalities due to accidents, less traffic congestion, fewer parking problems, reduced driving fatigue, increased productivity, more convenience, more cost-effective mobility options, and helping people not able to drive due to disabilities or age. A Machine Design article outlines four areas where AI can be a game-changer to help autonomous vehicles become successful: the first one being safety where machine learning can assist with the emergency control of the vehicle, breaking in emergency cases, syncing with traffic signals, active monitoring of blind spots and cross-traffic detection; a second area is the curated cloud services with respect to predictive and prescriptive maintenance aimed at individual car owners; AI can also be used to monitor the driver and predict and prescribe user preferences based on user behavior, which might include regulating the air conditioning, adjusting mirrors or seat positions, or playing songs; the fourth area is providing accurate feeds for insurance companies and regulators with regards to driver risk assessment and faster processing of insurance claims.[82]

There are also startups such as Helm.ai and Comma.ai that are working on providing more cost-effective AI solutions to help unlock autonomous driving. Helm.ai, for example, claims that their Deep Teaching method can train AI systems 100,000 cheaper than methods that involves human annotation or simulation typically done for supervised machine learning, by using "compressive sensing" (incorporating structural assumptions about specific object into the construction process) and "sophisticated priors" (the structural a priori assumptions that an AI system can take for granted about the nature of reality) to scale limited information into deeper insights.[83] Helm.ai, who sees themselves as the "Android of self-driving cars" intends to also apply their technology to shipping, industrial machines, delivery robots, and service vehicles. Comma.ai has developed open-source software called open pilot which is built to improve upon the existing driver assistance with "Tesla Autopilot" like functionality for most new cars on the road today.[84] The AI-driven solution enables a car to steer, accelerate, and brake automatically within its lane. Commai.ai has also launched a $999 kit called Comma Two that gives cars assisted driving features.[85] Some other examples include Waymo that is collaborating with Fiat Chrysler Automotive to develop an autonomous delivery van that will be using Waymo's self-driving technology as part of partnership for level four high automated driving.[86] It is clear that autonomous driverless technology will also be implemented in other vehicles such as pilotless airplanes (with some experiments done by Boeing)[87], pilotless helicopters (already tested in Dubai and Singapore)[88], autonomous shipping vessels for transport as well as cranes that can load and unload (with Kongsberg in Norway one of the leaders in the autonomous shipping industry)[89], self-driving tractors to make farming easier (see for example Precision Makers that is collaborating with John Deere on this)[90], and delivery drones for shipping (as tested by Amazon).[91]

There are also numerous AI use cases in the airline industry that includes air safety and airplane maintenance, flight route optimization, fuel efficiency optimization, revenue management, improved customer experience through in-depth customer feedback analysis and automated personalized messaging, crew management and scheduling, and supply chain optimization for in-flight sales and food supply. For the aviation industry, cancellations and delays are a significant and costly problem, where up to 30% of the total delay time can be attributed to unplanned maintenance.[92] The status of various systems and subsystems on an aircraft, that are instrumented by a variety of sensors, can be monitored in real-time by predictive analytics to help pinpoint existing faults and pro-actively predict future faults and its associated severity. This in turn leads to reduced downtime or aircraft delays and higher safety. A predictive maintenance solution can help to reduce unplanned maintenance, overtime compensation of crews, and transportation related expenses for parts. As an example, a leading airline wanted to reduce cancellations and flight delays caused by maintenance related issues which were costing them $135 million a year. This problem was addressed by the implementation of a machine learning based model that predicted 30% of maintenance-related potential cancellations and delays within a 2 to 3-day time window.[93] SynapseMX provides another example of an AI-powered maintenance repair and operations software solution that utilizes maintenance related data to automate workflows and provide real-time recommendations to assist technical and logistics maintenance staff in their decision making. They claim to have saved AirTran airways $68 million annually in direct maintenance labor costs.[94] SparkCognition's AI solutions have also been deployed at Boeing and the United States Airforce to improve operational efficiencies and predictive maintenance and troubleshooting activities.[95] Their solutions give alerts of aircraft or asset failures before they occur, help to minimize unscheduled maintenance, and maximize fleet availability, and help to extend asset life. The AI software also automatically classifies fault codes using natural language processing, recommending best corrective actions by analyzing sensor and hanger data and deploying reinforcement learning in a simulated environment to train control algorithms. Boeing and SparkCognition are also partnering on a joint venture called SkyGrid to build an AI- and blockchain-powered airspace management software platform to help ensure the safe and secure integration of passenger air and autonomous cargo vehicles in the same airspace that they operate.[96] The specific AI components of the platform assist with dynamic traffic routing and provide predictive analytics that enable customers to safely use unmanned aircraft systems with tasks such as package delivery, emergence assistance and industrial inspections. Airbus has launched an online collaborative platform called AIGym that presents challenges that describe business problems that Airbus faces within the helicopter, satellite and commercial aircraft business domains and explores how AI can be used to solve these problems.[97]

AI-driven revenue management involves the use of machine learning to provide on-demand service delivery of the right product at the right price using the right channel at the right time and covers dynamic personalized pricing and price optimization. For airlines to provide optimal customer services and be competitive, AI-based solutions can help to manage seats, recommend destinations, determine efficient distribution channels, and adjust prices for specific markets. Revenue management starts with an analysis of the demanded flight routes which is followed by determining the customer's willingness to pay and dynamic pricing (assuming that customers will pay more if there is less time before departure time), then calculating the expected marginal seat revenue (determining whether the expected revenue for a lower class ticket would be higher than a higher-fare ticket based on sales probabilities), and finally the price optimization for ancillary items such as baggage, insurance, rental, and accommodation.[98] AI-driven price optimization and recommendations can be enhanced through the mining of detailed historical data that might include previous flights purchased, seat type preferences, seat upgrades, types of rental and accommodation, frequent flyer account status, social media profiles, and browsing history. PROS Control is an example of dynamic pricing software used by some airlines to do dynamic pricing on some ticket searches.[99] AI systems can also help to optimize flight routes that take into consideration route characteristics, expected level of congestion, flight efficiency, and air navigation charges. Such an AI-driven optimization can have a direct impact on optimally timed and booked flights, an increase in customer retention, as well as lower operational costs. To predict the optimal amount of fuel needed for a flight, machine learning models are also being trained with flight data such as route distance, altitudes, weather, aircraft type, and aircraft weight. In a paper by the faculty of Aerospace Engineering at Delft University of Technology, the researchers have proposed a two-step optimization framework using a multi-objective evolutionary algorithm based on decomposition for route design and allocation of aircraft to multiple departure routes.[100] The aim of the optimization framework is to minimize fuel consumption and cumulative noise annoyance. They have demonstrated the performance and capabilities of the framework using a case study at Amsterdam Airport Schiphol in The Netherlands which achieved a reduction of up to 31% in the number of people being annoyed and a reduction in fuel burn of 7.3% relative to the reference case solution.[101]

AI solutions can also help to enhance the customer experience to optimize costs and efficiency, grow revenue, and build brand and customer loyalty. One such a solution is provided by Amadeus which enables airlines to provide the traveler with a special customer experience throughout the customer journey, from initial search to booking, from pricing to ticketing, from managing reservations to check-in and departure processes.[102] Amadeus also has a chatbot called Amanda to help approximately 7500 travel agents around the globe and have on an average day around 27 conversations an hour and answer 63 questions.[103] PureStrategy's AI-driven analysis solution has also been applied to airline customer experience data to get a 360-degree view on the customer journey, touchpoints, influencers, and path to purchase, as well as automatically extracting insights with respect to sentiment, drivers of customer loyalty and churn, unmet market opportunities, product feedback and market trends.[104] Another application area is to optimize the scheduling of an airline's crew in order to maximize their time, increase employee retention, and save costs (where flying crew is typically the second largest operating cost item after fuel cost). Jeppesen's Crew Rostering software helps airlines to build high-quality rosters in a flexible manner while reducing total costs and time-to-market, which in turn leads to increased profitability.[105] AI can also assist with predicting the number of in-flight sales and the amount of food it has to purchase for a specific flight. Another cost saving application area for airline and travel companies is to detect potential fraud in suspicious payment transactions with the use of machine learning applied to customer's historical purchase and flight data.

Whereas there is a consensus that automated systems have made flying safer, the importance of reliable and robust software, sensors and operating procedures has been painfully demonstrated with the two fatal crashes of the Boeing ill-fated 737 Max planes which killed 346 people. One of the major issues along with training seemed to be linked to design flaws in the Maneuvering Characteristics Augmentation System (MCAS) flight control software which ensured that the way the 737 Max behaved in the air remained consistent and matched that of previous generations of the plane.[106] MCAS relied on data from a single angle of attack sensor in the nose of an aircraft that measures the angle at which it is encountering the airstream. Even though there are two of these sensors, relying on only one of them meant that if it failed, MCAS could for example deploy at the wrong time and push the nose of the aircraft down when it was supposed to be climbing. Another issue was that the MCAS would deploy repeatedly in cycles, forcing the nose down again and again, even the pilot could use a thumb control to correct the pitch of the aircraft. After a wide range of changes that include updating the flight control software, revising crew procedures, and rerouting of internal wiring, Boeing hopes to have the 737 Max back in the air in 2021.[107] Although the MCAS system did not include AI elements there are still lessons to be learned for real-time AI-driven autonomous systems such as self-driving cars. Given the typical steps involved in the AI driving task such as sensor data collection and interpretation, the fusion of sensors, updating of the virtual world model, action planning and controls command issuance, Lance Elliot highlighted some specific lessons and insights in this regard: Instead of retrofitting prior design, it might be best to start anew; it is better to rely on multiple sensors than a single sensor; for robustness ensure that sensors are validated via sensor fusion calculations (or software sensors); the importance of human machine interface designs that need to incorporate a spectrum of real-world scenarios with respect to co-sharing and on-and-off kind of automatic action; training of human operators so that they can operate optimally and in symbiosis with the AI-powered machine; ensuring that the human operator of an AI system have a mental model of the scope of the system's capabilities; the need for robust testing of complex systems; compromises and miscommunications can easily occur within team or group setups during the design, development, testing and deployment phases of advanced automation systems; and safety considerations of these systems during the above-mentioned phases.[108] Some examples of airlines that use AI to improve their operations include Delta with their predictive aircraft maintenance and self-service for improved customer experience; EasyJet with their advanced analytics with respect to airplane food supply, aircraft maintenance, and revenue management; and Southwest Airlines with their workforce optimization, customer experience through social media and big data analysis, fuel consumption optimization in partnership with GE Aviation using its flight analytics system, and air safety in partnership with NASA using text data-mining to detect patterns in flight data and reports aiming at potential safety problems.[109]

Before the 2020 coronavirus pandemic which had an enormous impact on the global travel and tourism market, the size of the global travel and tourism industry was estimated in 2017 at approximately $1.6 trillion and 10.2% of the world's GDP when adding indirect and induced economic contribution of related activities.[110] Given that most of the impact of AI this sector will focus on customer services and engagement, it is not surprising to see intelligent virtual assistants and chatbots deployed as "virtual travel agents "as one of the key application areas. According to reports by Nielsen and 3C it seems like these intelligent virtual travel assistants are especially popular with millennials with their inclination to control their travelling experience as opposed to older generations for whom brands are influential.[111] Some recent travel industry statistics show that 80% of customers prefer self-service, 74% of travelers use the Internet for planning trips, 45% of users use smartphones for vacation planning, and 36% are willing to pay more for an easy-to-use interactive booking process.[112] There are many examples of travel service chatbots that help prospective travelers and customers to make reservations, provide flight or hotel booking assistance, offer travel suggestions and answering questions. Examples include those provided by Expedia, Kayak, Booking.com, and a number of travel chatbots on Facebook Messenger, as well as startups such as Hipmunk, Mezi, SnapTravel, HelloGbye, and Pana that mainly provide text-based chat travel assistance.[113] I have personally experienced the use of Expedia's customer services chatbot in successfully handling travel cancellations with the onslaught of the Covid-19 pandemic during the first quarter of 2020. Other travel assistance examples include voice-powered hotel reservation systems at hotels as well as AI concierge services with the likes of Amazon's Alexa via its Echo speaker device being used in hotel rooms in virtual assistant capacity for guests.[114] The same holds for Google Assistant (via the Google Home speaker device) and Apple's Siri. According to Gartner the consumer demand for voice devices such as Amazon Echo and Google Home will generate $3.5 billion by 2021.[115] The travel website Skyscanner for example offers travel booking via Alexa and Facebook Messenger. [116] In the future, we will also see more pervasive use of facial recognition and biometric identification to assist with faster check-in as was tested at Finland's Helsinki airport.[117] They also ran a pilot with an online customer services chatbot as well as display walls to provide relevant information about transfer flights and gates to passengers in their native language. As we are seeing with YouTube, Netflix and other personalized recommendation services, there are similar use cases for deploying AI solutions in the travel and tourism sector to create tailored experiences where personalized content is delivered using AI that is proactive, relevant, timely, location sensitive and addresses the immediate need of the customer. Well Traveled is a wellness travel agency that captures client's travel preferences, builds personalized itineraries, and supports travelers before, during and after their trip.[118] For targeted sales and marketing and improved customer services it is essential to have customer segmentation that mines users' behavioral, demographics and metadata, geolocation, customer relationship management data, and social media data. For AI applications in revenue management, clustering and supervised classification machine learning techniques are typically used for segmenting customers on how price elasticity differs from traveler to traveler by making use of input features such as purpose of travel, returning or new customer, age, marital status, customer lifetime value, and user behavior and preferences. With customer segmentation and insights with respect to demand and supply, different pricing strategies can be personalized for travelers. Demand forecasting provides key information for pricing across customer segments and allows for selecting an appropriate distribution strategy. Dynamic pricing allows hotels to offer variable room rates and airlines to offer variable ticket prices based on demand and supply in order for them to quickly react to changing market values to maximize revenue. AI enables the decision-making processes in yield management to be automated as yield tactics are selected for different customer segments as it focuses on optimizing profit and revenue whilst, for example, controlling occupancy rates and utilization of rooms, hotel facilities, restaurants, hotel casinos, and conference rooms. As in the case of the media and entertainment industry, AI is also used to generate email and video content for travel and tourism related communications, curate content for intelligent recommendations, analyze social media for profiling and determining sentiment, enabling intelligent customer relationship management for smarter loyalty programs or sales insights, assist with the click and conversion optimization for travel products and online-advertising campaigns, enhance augmented reality applications to improve the overall visitor experience with interactivity and instantly accessible information, and provide video, image, and voice recognition systems for travel purposes.

In an Emerald Insight paper a critical overview of the impact of AI and robotics in the tourism sector is provided that highlights how AI is enhancing the experiential services in tourism, but also emphasizes the irreplaceable role of the human touch and the importance of ensuring data privacy and security.[119] The paper mentions some future AI applications where travelers can select the option to transform their entire room into a virtual 3D world that looks like their favorite destination spot, robots serving hotel guests, and the use of visual positioning systems to provide location-based experiences via live views of the real world and visual landmarks.

6. AI-powered Process and Equipment Enhancement across the Industrial World

As I have spent a substantial part of my AI career in applying AI to industrial world use cases, I share in this chapter also some of the specific AI use cases that I have been involved with via my AI companies, CSense Systems as well as Cortex Logic, along with many other illustrative real-world use case examples from around the globe. We continue our sense-making journey on the application front to specifically learn how the utilities, energy, resources, manufacturing, and agriculture sectors are getting powered by AI to enhance industrial processes and equipment related use cases with respect to monitoring, diagnostics, and predictive maintenance.

Impact of AI on Utilities and the Energy Sector

AI opens a wide range of exciting possibilities for utilities such as energy, gas, water, and waste management as well as the energy sector as a whole and can deliver real value to serious adopters and customers. The application of AI can not only assist the utility sector at every step of the value chain to provide consistent access to electricity and water that is essential for households and enterprise-level customers to help them live and do business, but also help to ease the transition to renewable energy, preventing power outages, reduce waste and learn more about end-users and their needs. It is also clear that there is a shift in the utilities and energy sector from a conservative, regulations-driven environment to a more advanced smart technology driven marketplace that relies on AI, data, and smart devices to better predict supply and demand, optimize infrastructure, balance the grid in real time, maximize yield, predict equipment failure, reduce downtime, deliver proactive condition-based maintenance, and improve customer-facing interactions and experience. From an electric utility's perspective, apart from helping to make the smart grid smarter and reduce the need to add power plants, AI can also help to address issues linked to the growing complex network of power generation, transition and distribution stakeholders and assets, cost pressures, price deregulation, as well as the increasing volatility in energy supply with more renewable energy resources being deployed. A recent global survey revealed that there is general excitement and consensus about the potential of renewable energy and its sustainability benefits where the majority of people thought it is important to create a world fully powered by renewable energy and move away from a dependence on fossil fuels.[1] Although governments across the globe are supporting this drive with subsidies and tax credits, there have also recently been some cuts in governmental subsidies as we have seen in China.[2] The Center for Climate and Energy Solutions reported that renewables was the fastest-growing energy source in the United States with a 100% increase from 2000 to 2018. It also made up 26.2% of global electricity generation in 2018, and is expected to rise to 45% by 2040, mainly driven by solar, wind, and hydropower.[3] Given demand that also fluctuates heavily by time, geography, weather and events, the current energy grids with their legacy infrastructure struggle to optimally smooth out spikes and lose money with excess power. AI can also help to address these issues and help drive successful renewable projects, which in turn will encourage further investment into the use of renewables. There is also a massive shift towards increased electrification. Although efficiency gains will lead overall electric loads to decline, the Electric Power Research Institute (EPRI) projects that pursuing electrification would lead to cumulative load growth of between 24% and 52% with beneficiaries of increased electrification to include the utilities, electrical vehicles, heat pumps, warehouse equipment, and agriculture use cases.[4] In a National Electrification Assessment that outlined the utility, customer and societal impacts of electricity providing up to 50% of final energy consumption by 2050, the EPRI also projected AI-driven positive outcomes such as an increased grid efficiency and flexibility, reduced energy consumption and consumer costs, better air quality leading to improved human health and much lower greenhouse gas emissions.[5] With accelerated adoption of electric vehicles, AI and load-level information can be used to benefit utilities as well as electric vehicle drivers. According to Bloomberg New Energy Finance (BNEF), sales of electric vehicles will increase from 1.7 million in 2020 to 8.5 million in 2025, 26 million in 2030 and 54 million in 2040.[6] According to BIS Research, AI applications in the energy market is expected to reach $7.78 billion by 2024 with a projected CAGR of 22.49% from 2019 to 2024 driven by the growing concern for energy efficiency and battery storage systems, the demand for greater operational efficiency, and the significant increase in decentralized power generation.[7] There are similar opportunities in the water utilities and waste water market where the application of AI and real-time smart water sensor measurement for decision intelligence, opex savings, process optimization and predictive maintenance is helping to drive this market to almost $750 billion in 2019 (according to a recent Frost & Sullivan report).[8] There are also a range of AI use cases in the capital intensive oil and gas industry (where there has been traditionally many layers of redundancy as well as process and equipment over-engineering and inefficiencies to avoid failure) such as improving resource allocation, efficiency and reliability, real-time process and equipment monitoring, diagnostics and anomaly detection, predictive maintenance, forecasting, advanced process control and process performance enhancement. GS GIR estimated that a 1% reduction in the oil and gas industry's capex, opex and inventory management can result in savings of about $140bn over a 10-year period.[9]

Demand and supply prediction is one of the most impactful and critical use cases of AI for electrical utilities in the Smart Technology Era as they are working towards better information, efficiency, and safety to save costs, improve reliability and deliver a more flexible, agile, and robust smart grid that satisfies the growing energy demands from customers. Utilities use machine learning-based load forecasting algorithms to predict in real-time how much power must be generated to meet the short-, medium- or long-term demand of their customers, as well as optimize economic load dispatch. If load forecasts are inaccurate it can affect many stakeholders across the value chain, for example, power generation entities typically need a few days forecast to determine which power sources should be allocated for the next day, transmission grids have specific requirements to determine optimal resource allocation, and electricity retailers need to estimate the electricity demand for their energy price calculations. By modernizing electricity grids with embedded digital technology such as sensors, IoT devices, cloud-based data management platforms, high-speed communications networks to allow for improved interconnectedness, and other hardware and software innovations, the more data are being generated in digital format and can be leveraged for machine learning driven demand and supply prediction and other analytics purposes. A smart grid also helps to facilitate better information and operations technology convergence and ensure smarter, faster, and more efficient real-time solutions that support the integration of and access to distributed energy resources, better operational performance and adaptiveness to market needs, intelligent automation, predictive capabilities, communications, self-healing services, controls, and decision intelligence. Combining smart wires with machine learning based applications enable real-time power dispatching and the optimization of it to current grid load and to buildings' asset portfolios. Real-time and more accurate forecasting makes it possible to integrate excess power and additional renewable energy into the smart grid, assess the reliability of those integrated generation assets, avoid or at least delay ramping up fossil-fuel-powered stations, and helps to automate demand-side responses.

Google DeepMind has provided a good supply prediction use case via their prediction of the energy output of the Google wind farms in the United States. Their machine learning based models were trained on historical wind turbine data and weather forecasts to predict wind power output 36 hours ahead of actual generation with an acceptable degree of accuracy (which is not easy to predict accurately due to the variable nature of wind) and made recommendations on how to make optimal hourly delivery commitments to the power grid 24 hours in advance, raising the "value" of their wind energy by approximately 20%.[10] The DeepMind team in England also started a collaboration with the UK National Grid a few years ago with the aim to predict supply and demand peaks and was hoping to reduce the UK's national energy usage by 10%. Although ideas have been shared on how smart technology can improve grid efficiency and resilience, a solution has unfortunately not been implemented yet.[11] With CSense Systems, we have also been involved in developing models to predict the residential electricity load on a substation level in South Africa with high accuracy using a range of inputs such as historical electricity usage, temperature parameters, time of day, day of the week, season, and weather. In another application, AI-based solutions have been developed to monitor and troubleshoot the health of transformers on a fleet level in the USA. The monitoring involves detecting overheating of hot spot development, solid insulation material contamination of oil which causes chemical degradation of the liquid, unbalanced and overloaded phases, restricted or blocked coolant flow, insulating oil quality, and inefficient transformer operation. The solution combines expert rules and fingerprint machine learning based models of ideal or good operation to monitor deviations from ideal behavior and to do real-time causal analysis.

Demand management can also be automated and made smarter with AI-based approaches. A case in point is provided by the Electric Reliability Council of Texas which operates their electric grid and manages the deregulated market for 75% of that state. It has been reported that in recent years there has been a demand response reduction of up to 2,000 MW as part of their AI-driven demand response program implemented for about 13,000 large customers and non-opt-in entities that can assess and quantify self-deployed load reductions in response to high dollar incentives.[12] Another example of energy demand management is provided by NextEra Energy in the US and Canada that has been using AutoGrid platform and machine learning to help businesses reduce energy bills during times of high electric prices or peak energy demand.[13] In order to derive insights and predict electricity demand and power failures, the AI-driven solution makes use of petabytes of data from sensors, smart sensors, and other available relevant data. Open Energi in the UK has estimated that AI models that learn to control the electricity consumption of a portfolio of assets could be used to help unlock up to 6GW of demand-side flexibility without affecting end users.[14]

There are also significant business cases for the use of AI-based solutions to help reduce costs across operations (from power generation to transmission and distribution), improve electricity production yield, predict failures, optimize condition-based preventive maintenance, reduce energy waste, and prevent electricity theft. With respect to AI-driven yield optimization, power providers can maximize their generation efficiency with real-time monitoring and adjustments across their assets. As an example, GE Renewable Energy's "Digital Wind Farm" can increase energy production by up to 20% to create $100 million in additional value over the lifetime of a 100-megawatt wind farm by using a machine learning based software solution that monitors and help optimize wind turbines' yield based on their own past performance, real-time communication with other wind farms, the grid status, and changes in wind speed and direction.[15] A wind turbine generates electricity by harnessing kinetic energy from the wind to turn the blades of the turbine and transform the rotational motion to electricity. One of the key problems with wind turbines is the blades of the turbine that are not always aligned to get the turbine to transfer the maximum amount of wind energy. If the blades are misaligned, there is less turbine rotation, which implies less electricity generated. In the ideal case, the amount of power generated (kilowatt) should be directly related to the speed of the wind. When at my previous AI company as well as at GE, I have been directly involved in developing machine learning based solutions for wind turbine troubleshooting, blade misalignment calculations, and real-time monitoring and intelligent alarming that provides real-time causal analysis for any anomalies or deviations.

NextEra Energy's power generation division, which includes its fossil, solar and wind facilities, provides another predictive analytics example of where their equipment is continuously monitored by AI-driven solutions to detect emerging issues such as internal damage to a combustion turbine to prevent unexpected disruption and assist with analysis to improve efficiency of operations.[16] Dominion Resources Inc has a grid-optimization subsidiary that helps to address issues including increases in distributed generation, aging infrastructure, a changing regulatory environment, and the need for new forms of energy efficiency and demand response. Dominion's grid analytics and control solution records consumption of electric energy hourly via its advanced metering infrastructure that provides two-way communications with the meter and central system, combines detailed weather forecasts to predict voltage fluctuations on a circuit-by-circuit basis, and has an EDGE Analytics dashboard that provides visibility into cost, energy and carbon savings obtained through grid optimization and helps to manage distributed energy resources.[17]

Machine learning based approaches to reduce downtime and improve preventive maintenance can also strengthen power generation yield. These solutions can deal with huge amounts of sensor data and overcome the problem of inaccurate alerts. In an effort to address maintenance and downtime issues, US-based Duke Energy has for example implemented a so-called SmartGen Program that included online sensors, data management infrastructure, equipment health and performance monitoring, predictive analytics, and smart diagnostics and prognostics that already saved them tens of millions of dollars in repair costs.[18] Some of the AI-driven solutions include Schneider Electric's Avantis PRiSM APR software for asset health monitoring and alert notification, SparkCognition's AI algorithms to predict potential disasters and shut down of turbines, as well as an unsupervised machine learning solution that uses AMI voltage data and meter events to identify anomalies and minimize risk on Duke's electric distribution grid.[19] The application of AI is also key to help reduce energy losses in transmission and distribution, shift from time-based maintenance to condition-based maintenance, refine outage planning, decide on replacement versus run-to-failure, determine cutoff for spare delivery, and support real-time decisions to balance the grid. Apart from enabling smart grid operators to perform preventative maintenance to keep their assets working efficiently, these types of solutions could also assist them to not decommission assets before their useful lives have ended. Operational trade-offs among several power stations or within the distribution network - such as outage planning refinement, replacement versus run-to-failure decisions, and cutoff for spare delivery - will be automatically made by advanced analytics and machine learning algorithms. MGI shared an illustrative use case where an European power distribution company was able to reduce its cash costs by 30% over five years by applying machine learning models to determine the overall health of power transformers, diagnose the condition of individual components, predict the failures of parts more accurately and prioritize repairs based on which faults cause the most disruption.[20] Upside Energy in the UK has used AI to manage a portfolio of batteries and energy storage assets to provide real-time energy reserved to the UK grid. AI is also used to prevent power outages by predicting the underlying conditions that cause this. Several utility companies have recently participated with an US Department of Energy laboratory to identify weak points in their electric grid and to proactively repair them before outages occurred with the goal to create an autonomous system that handles ordinary fluctuations in power and is able to respond to major events like storms. Another such use case is research at Texas A&M University that aimed to improve tree maintenance, indicate to utility companies which trees are most likely to cause issues, and prevent overgrown branches from triggering lapses in electricity service. Other complementary solutions include the use of AI-driven drones for equipment inspections which can automatically identify defects and predict failures without interrupting operations and replacing risky, manual and time intensive inspections. Some power plants were able to predict the timing of failures within one week six to nine months in advance, with high accuracy. In the future we can expect to see drones and insect-size robots identify defects, predict failures, and inspect assets without interrupting production, whereas the remaining technicians can spend more time on problem solving without the need to log inspection status by hand and the field workforce can receive real-time updates to decrease response times and reduce the impact of outages.

Building energy optimization is another application area where machine learning can be used to help reduce energy costs by up to 20%, cut emissions and carbon footprint, sustain savings with continued monitoring and diagnostics, and reduce asset maintenance and increase uptime. The building energy optimization solutions that we have developed at CSense Systems and General Electric consists of real-time building energy and asset monitoring of assets such as heating, ventilation and air conditioning units, air handling units, variable air volume systems, pumps, drives, and control loops; minimizing building energy cost in real-time based on weather and tariffs; real-time optimization of the central utilities plant and rapid pinpointing causes of anomalies and deviations in behavior with respect to assets such as chillers, boilers, turbines and associated control loops and sensors. This involves real-time analysis and monitoring of energy consumption to determine the current baseline and assessing variation, understanding causes for energy consumption variation, minimizing energy consumption and variation through asset optimization and retro-commissioning, monitor energy and asset performance continuously to sustain optimal performance and optimize supply based on predicted load and demand.

AI solutions that detect patterns in usage and payment history, and other customer data variables that can flag suspicious activity are also being developed to help prevent electricity or energy theft, which is especially more common in some developing countries such as South Africa where the average loss is up to $1.5 billion per annum[21], Brazil where it accounts for 8% on average and up to 40% of electricity distributed in some areas[22], and Hungary where an AI solution was used to help reduce electricity theft in one town by 30%.[23] MGI estimates that machine learning based applications such as theft detection, automating fault prediction, optimizing preventive maintenance, inspection automation, demand management, and increasing capital productivity could increase income for smart grid operators and utilities by 20 to 30 percent.[24]

Smart grid initiatives, where grids are being digitized and better instrumented and smart meters are being deployed in many countries across the globe, open the door for private energy producers which might even include individual homeowners that act as a prosumer that generates their own renewable energy and selling excess capacity back to the grid. AI can also help to assess the reliability of these new small prosumers (which might generate electricity from sources such as rooftop solar cells and electric-car batteries) by determining their suitability for integration into the smart grid or power storage scheme. It can further assist demand-side response aggregators to automatically assess this larger volume of smaller suppliers which would be difficult and costly to scan and prioritize otherwise. These developments are creating an era of energy trading where AI-driven platforms are emerging to allow peer-to-peer trading between producers and consumers as a retail electricity marketplace to assist with dynamic matching and optimizing load dispatch as supply and demand fluctuates in continuous fashion. Vandenbron in the Netherlands is an example of such a platform that connects consumers with renewable energy providers for a fixed subscription fee. Machine learning can also assist with optimizing individualized pricing with time-of-day and dynamic tariffing to encourage customers to shift non-essential consumption to times when demand is lower. As with other consumer facing businesses, energy retailers can use AI-driven offerings to increase the likelihood of retaining their most profitable high-volume customers, reduce churn, and attract new customers.

Utility companies can also leverage AI for building better customer relationships, satisfaction and engagement by enhancing their customer experience with more relevant and personalized service offerings, providing consumption insights and the automation of repetitive customer inquiries and other tasks with intelligent virtual assistants for more convenience and in accordance with a user's preferences. AI in the form of robotic process automation and intelligent virtual assistants are also being used to automate specific customer service problems such as reports of service interruption or outages, payments, billing inquiries, change of address or personal details, new service connections, and reports of hazardous situations. US-based utility Exelon has for example implemented a chatbot that addresses customer questions about power outages and billing concerns.[25] Over the next few years we will also see virtual agents automating call centers, automatically segment consumers based on service history and provide early warning of bad debts.

As energy retailing are being liberated, we see more energy suppliers entering the market, which in turn give customers more options to choose from (as we have seen in Europe with more than 50 electricity suppliers and counting)[26]. AI can assist consumers to select their electricity supplier based on their preferences with respect to energy generation type, pricing, and metering measurements. This could potentially also lead AI-driven solutions that save consumers money by having an up-to-date view of the most suitable electricity supply deals and automatically switching energy plans based on the consumer's needs and profile. With smart meter data, machine learning can be utilized to generate real-time insights on consumer's energy consumption such as patterns of energy-intensive appliances and help to save money on electricity bills as are illustrated with systems such as Bidgely, PlotWatt and AutoGrid.[27] The consumer-driven demand for smart energy management has also helped to fuel the hyper growth over the last few years in the smart home market with consumers having access to a variety of smart thermostats that help them cut utility costs. Google's Nest' learning thermostat is an example of a smart device that personalizes consumption management by identifying a consumer's heating usage patterns and preferences and then automates the heating or cooling regulation. Whereas Nest reported about 10-12% savings on heating and 15% savings on cooling, on average, Emerson mentions 23% savings, on average, from customers who use their Sensi thermostat to adjust the temperature using features like scheduling, remote access, and geofencing.[28] Ecobee3, another smart thermostat provider, claims a 23% saving on annual energy costs.[29] Duke Energy's My Home Energy Report is another example of an energy savings application that processes information such as the home's footprint and weather to provide personalized recommendations to customers such as energy efficiency tips, savings projections and messages to solve problems.[30]

As with electricity utilities, there are also many similar AI use cases in water utilities that can drastically reduce energy costs (which typically makes up 25-30% of total operation and maintenance costs), chemical inputs used for treatment, and water use, as well as enable improved resource allocation and value-based maintenance of equipment.[31] These AI applications can save 20-30% on operational expenditures for water utilities.[32] AI presents opportunities in the water and wastewater industry including desalination plants, to accelerate optimization and innovation, adding efficiency by automating tasks where machines are better than humans at pattern recognition and prediction, as well as assisting with process optimization and troubleshooting, anomaly detection, advanced process control, infrastructure planning, capturing domain-specific institutional knowledge, asset monitoring and predictive maintenance. It has been demonstrated that the use of AI within wastewater treatment can help optimize traditional PID controllers in real-time to reduce energy cost up to 40%.[33] As with the instrumentation of the smart grid, by implementing cost-effective sensors within an internet of things, massive volumes of process and equipment related performance and condition data can be collected to be mined for insights, detecting leaks, predicting failure and usage, and preventing theft. Although the implementation of smart technology driven solutions by water and wastewater utilities has been slow when compared to other industries, there are signs that early adopters of water technologies are increasing, especially with the assistant of smart technology solutions companies that partner with utilities to provide cloud and edge-based solutions, AI expertise, and multi-provider AI-driven products and services to make the adoption of these smart technologies easier. The implementation of smart data-driven management of water systems will lead to more sustainable, resilient, and cost-effective water management for the foreseeable future. With the use of AI-enabled online platforms, a more personalized, engaging, and informative offering is provided for customers to pay bills, view real-time water consumption, and access information about dynamic water resource conditions. According to Bluefield Research report which covered a forecast for the US and Canada water industry from 2019-2030, water utilities' spending on smart technology solutions will reach a combined $92.6 billion by 2030, of which AI solutions is $6.3 billion, within the following categories: metering and customer management (41%), network management (20%), work and asset management (18%), plant management (18%), and information management (3%, but also the fastest growing technology segment).[34] It is also clear that by leveraging smart technologies across these segments, metropolitan areas and their utilities should be better prepared to address the costly water and wastewater infrastructure issues. Bluefield's forecasts show that using smart technology driven asset management solutions for water, wastewater and stormwater assets, utilities across the US, Canada, Europe, and Australia can grow their savings in annual capital expenditure from $1.2 billion in 2018 to $7.3 billion by 2027.[35] We also have a daunting water crisis with the water utilities under threat with its ageing infrastructure, growing metropolitan areas as well as the extremes posed by climate change. It has also been said that if climate change is the wolf, water is its teeth.[36] Smart technology driven solutions enable water utilities to have a more real-time up-to-date view on where there is not enough water to sustain the necessary pressure in the whole system, improved forecasting of water supply and demand, and the ability to build a more dependable clean water future.

Water utilities are also looking at effective ways to keep their costs down by for example reducing waste. Leak detection could save the world's water utilities up to $69 billion a year.[37] Several companies such as Meetflo and StreamLabs also offer home smart leak detection devices. One innovative solution to identify hidden leaks in water pipes was introduced by the University of Waterloo which applied machine learning to this problem by using sound-processing capabilities to monitor for sounds that indicate dribbles of water. They were able to even locate slow leaks equivalent to 17 liters per minute in laboratory tests.[38] Some other recent AI application projects reported by the Commonwealth Scientific and Industrial Research organization's Data61 in Australia include prioritizing active leak detection areas, water quality monitoring, chemical dosing, intelligent network optimization, water demand analysis, as well as predicting water pipe failure, sewer chokes and sewer corrosion.[39] Industries in the same metropolitan area can also have AI-driven coordination of their combined sewer discharges and reduction in pumping costs to avoid combined sewer overflow during raining periods. In another real-world application, Fracta provided the San Francisco water utilities with an AI-driven solution that helps to prioritize pipe replacements, repair and rehabilitation to reduce operating expenses, better allocate capital expenditures and increase reliability of high-quality water.[40] Silo.AI in Finland has developed an AI solution that predicts the quality of the water leaving from water utilities and analyzes the water quality in the context of environmental permissions and terms.[41] In Agriculture use cases, AI-driven solutions such as VineView make use of satellite and aerial imagery to help detect water issues earlier and faster than traditional methods.[42] AI solutions such as ConserWater can help to optimize irrigation systems to save costs and better adapt to the local climate and plant condition.[43]

At CSense Systems we have implemented effective wastewater management to help water utilities reduce energy and chemical consumption (between typically 5%-20% savings in energy and chemical costs), maintain good quality and troubleshoot process related problems. Wastewater processes can be optimized from a quality, energy, and materials perspective. From a *quality* perspective the focus is on maintaining effluent standard targets, from an *energy* perspective it is about reducing electrical consumption by optimizing the aeration of the sludge while making the dissolved oxygen distribution tighter (oxygen is provided to the microorganisms to speed up the oxidation process of turning organic waste into inorganic byproducts), and from a *materials* perspective the consumption of chemicals is being reduced. This is achieved through rapid process troubleshooting and understanding causes of process variation, modeling alternative intelligent control strategies and monitoring PID control loop performance. For example, if the dissolved oxygen is too low, that leads to an unstable environment for these microorganisms which can potentially die due to anaerobic zones, results in the sludge not being properly treated, expensive and time-consuming replacement of biomass, and excessive amounts of dissolved oxygen added to help compensate. On the other hand, if the dissolved oxygen is too high, energy is wasted, expensive aeration equipment is used unnecessarily, and unwanted organisms grow excessively. The AI-driven solution involves an automated real-time dissolved oxygen measurement in the aeration system to maintain the correct amount of dissolved oxygen via machine learning based modeling and optimization to reduce power consumption while tightening the dissolved oxygen distribution. Given that power costs with aeration is typically between 30-60% of the total electrical power used as such a wastewater facility, this type of solution can reduce the energy costs by up to 50%.

There are also many renewable energy use cases where machine learning and predictive analytics are helping to optimize performance, reduce maintenance costs, and provide real-time diagnostics and troubleshooting. One such example is the application of Space Time Insight's software that incorporates real-time inputs such as weather and traffic in predictive solutions that save costs and optimize maintenance and operational activities for energy utilities such as NextEra which operates more than 100 wind farms in 19 states in Canada.[44] General Electric has been at the forefront of providing renewable energy customers with a wind energy software platform that helps increase revenue, reduce costs and lower risk through delivering actionable information obtained through digital monitoring, visualization, and analysis of their wind asset systems from an asset-, farm- and fleet-level perspective.[45] GE Research has also experimented with what they call Humble AI to control the wind turbines to better handle unfamiliar situations and relinquish control of the machine into a safe, default mode while it tries to learn and understand the new scenario, which lead to 1% higher energy output in their pilot studies.[46] Companies like Earth Networks are also leading the way to protect wind turbines and their maintenance crews with weather data products and services as green-energy expands in the fight against climate change.[47] The prediction of renewable energy generation is key to help reduce the need of having carbon plants as a back-up. Nnergix is another energy forecasting company, headquartered in Spain, that does high-resolution weather forecasting with their Sentinel solution that uses satellite images to generate small- and large-scale weather models to predict the state of the atmosphere in a specific area.[48] US-based Xcel Energy's AI energy forecasting solution uses data from weather stations, wind farms and local satellite reports to indicate whether the solar or wind power source will fluctuate in strength.[49]

With the total revenues of the oil and gas exploration and production industry in 2019 at approximately $3.3 trillion, which makes up 3.8% of the global economy at that time, it still remains a highly valued commodity in the energy sector.[50] Given the broad environmental issues faced by the oil and gas exploration and production industry such as incidents and oil spills, habitat protection and biodiversity, marine and freshwater discharges, air emissions, and soil and groundwater contamination, there is huge pressure on this sector to actively seeking innovative smart technology-driven approaches to achieve their business goals whilst reducing their carbon footprint and impact on the environment. As mentioned earlier there are significant business cases for applying AI throughout the value chain of the oil and gas industry, from upstream that consists of the exploration and drilling to find oil and gas and extract it from the earth to midstream activities that consist of transportation and storage, and downstream that deals with the refining and marketing of the finished product such as petroleum. Some key AI applications include predicting failure and recommending proactive maintenance for drilling, mining, power generation and moving equipment; enabling improved identification, targeting and development of hydrocarbon resources; improving the reliability of products and reducing the time between product development, field trials and commercialization; increasing uptime in downstream industries such as refining and petrochemical operations; optimizing blend and timing of raw materials in refining and similar processes; optimizing mine plans based on drilling samples, past sites, and other data; optimizing specifications in construction for power generation equipment based on previous sites and other relevant data; and improving project planning. These are all application areas that are relevant to oil and gas companies such as ExxonMobil, Chevron, BP, Sinopec, Royal Dutch Shell, Total, Saudi Aramco, and Gazprom. Exxon Mobil and Total have for example designed AI-driven robots to improve the productivity and cost-effectiveness of hydrocarbon exploration and production (whilst reducing the risk of human workers), whereas Royal Dutch Shell has deployed an online intelligent virtual assistant platform that helps customers navigate their product databases and handle queries.[51] According to Goldman Sachs GIR, the total savings for the industry over a 10-year period would amount to $140bn, which consists of $40 billion in capex, $77 billion in operating costs and $20 billion in inventories.[52] As oil and gas companies cannot afford their expensive special-purpose drilling machinery and other equipment to fail or not operate optimally, they can help to reduce the risk and cost by having smart sensors attached to these equipment that continuously feed data to machine learning based monitoring and preventative maintenance solutions. To reduce costs, there is also an opportunity to reduce the level of redundancy in equipment and processes required in the field. For example, pressure pumping fleet industry can save $7 billion over 10 years at 85% equipment utilization by reducing the level of redundancy by 50%, reducing the capital deployed on a pressure pumping job by 25%, and reducing maintenance with predictive analytics by 25%.[53] Going forward, we can expect the existing oil and gas industry leaders with their deep pockets and ability to invest in smart instrumentation and AI-driven solutions to be the early adopters of AI in this sector and reap the business value and benefits that can be unlocked from smart technology.

Smart Technology Driven Resources and Manufacturing

The resources industries such as minerals, metals, and mining as well as the manufacturing sector have seen a wide variety of impactful AI use cases over the years, many of them which I have experienced firsthand. Current economic realities mandate getting the most from existing assets and this is especially relevant in the capital-intensive industries such as mining and manufacturing were doing things the way they have always been done is no longer an option. Even minor improvements in production performance can make significant contributions to the bottom line, leading engineers to critically review the processes in their charge. But this can be a daunting and difficult task without the proper smart technology and tools because the processes that are most in need of improvement and that will yield the most profitable results are usually those that are too complex to optimize manually such as metal beneficiation. Over the last few decades, we have seen a significant increase in instrumentation and digitization across mining and manufacturing plants with more sensors and IoT devices along with industrial application layer applications such as programmable logic control systems, supervisory control and data acquisition systems, distributed control systems, manufacturing execution systems, maintenance systems, and enterprise resource planning systems. AI solutions capitalizing on all available structured and unstructured data can help to enhance every application across the industrial application spectrum. In the minerals, metals, and mining industries, we have especially seen AI being applied to the control and human computer interface layers for smarter control applications to enhance the standard PID control and improve support for operators, process engineers and production managers to better understand process and equipment behavior and help to troubleshoot and optimize their plant. To do this successfully, the first step is to thoroughly understand the process being addressed through modeling and simulation using historical data. The second is the implementation of AI-driven solutions that address the identified problem in real-time. Then comes the distribution of information in a form that is relevant to the people that must use it to make informed decisions – the information needs of management, process engineers, maintenance staff, automation personnel and operators, for example, are all different. Lastly, to be a long-term success, any process improvement programme must include sustained skills transfer, engineering assistance, training, and effective roll-out schedules as well as on-going assessment of the business value of the improvement. So, process performance enhancement involves more than just AI or software. It is all about the tools, the solutions, and the programme to bring it all together. Some relevant use cases for deploying AI solutions in the resources and mining sector include seismic data analysis, rapid process and equipment troubleshooting, real-time process and equipment monitoring, diagnostics and anomaly detection, predictive maintenance, advanced process control, and overall process performance enhancement. We have seen the same on the manufacturing side although the automotive and assembly sectors have shown higher AI adoption and digitization compared to for example consumer packaged goods and even building materials and construction which has been very low. Manufacturers are focused on improving product design yield and efficiency, optimize pricing, refine sales-leads prioritization, automate supplier assessment, anticipate parts requirements, reduce material delivery time, improve processes by the task, automate assembly lines, reduce errors, limit product rework, optimize flight planning and route and fleet allocation, enhance equipment maintenance engineering and training, and predict sales of maintenance services. AI can help to enhance each of these application areas. Some relevant use cases for deploying AI solutions in manufacturing sector includes real-time, batch, and discrete process monitoring and diagnostics; rapid process and manufacturing equipment troubleshooting; intelligent process control; optimizing supply chains and creating greater economies of scale; improving preventative maintenance; achieving better repair, maintenance, and overhaul performance with greater predictive accuracy to the component and part-level; increasing production yields by the optimization of the team, machine, supplier and customer requirements; providing more relevant data so finance, operations, and supply chain teams can better manage factory and demand-side constraints; knowing the right price to charge a given customer at the right time to get the most margin and closed sale; better machine senses can lead to safer workplaces; manufacturing-as-a-service with AI enabling subscription models for production service; the use of intelligent virtual assistants and advisors; and uber maintenance.

Apart from all these generic manufacturing-related use cases, AI in the automotive industry is also helping to pave the way for autonomous vehicles, where they are seen as a post-Uber disruption to public and good transportation. As we have seen with Tesla, Waymo, and others, machine learning based pattern recognition gives these vehicles the ability to identify their surroundings and to take actions in any given scenario at various levels of autonomy. This is done by feeding state-of-the-art AI systems with real-time data from sensors, cameras, GPS, lidar and cloud services to produce control signals that are used to operate the vehicle. Apart from helping to ensure proper and safe driving by for example enabling emergency control of the vehicle, active monitoring of blind spots and cross-traffic detection, it can also be used to monitor and learn driver and user behavior, predict and prescribe preferences based on user behavior, offer predictive and prescriptive maintenance of individual vehicles as data about the physical condition of the vehicle is stored in the cloud, and provide accurate data feeds for regulators with respect to traffic violations and insurance companies for driver risk assessment and to streamline the handling of claims. We also see AI-driven robotics use cases in manufacturing with industrial robots that can do tasks with high speed, accuracy, and endurance such as those in material handling, assembling, disassembling, welding, painting, dispensing, packing, labeling, inspecting, and testing. In the future, one might expect spectacular applications of AI and robotics in the resources and manufacturing industries that can include the use of dynamic highly mobile robots such as those being developed by Boston Dynamics in the form of Atlas, Handle, Pick and Spot.[54]

Given the continued expansion of the global economy and the rise of living standards, the Organization for Economic Co-operation and Development has projected in their Global Material Resources outlook that the world's consumption of raw material is set to effectively double from approximately 90 Gigatons today to 167 Gigatons in 2060.[55] Over the next few years the global smart mining market size is expected to reach $24 billion in 2027, from approximately $9.3 billion in 2019, which implies a compound annual growth rate of 13% from 2020 to 2027.[56] Smart mining can be described as a process that uses data, information, technology such as AI and other state-of-the-art software solutions, and autonomy to gain better productivity, reduce operational costs, and enhance safety for a mine site. These smart technology-driven solutions also comprise remote-controlled robotic equipment for mineral and metal extraction to help decrease the danger for miners.

With the manufacturing sector accounting for almost 16% of the global GDP in 2018, it is clearly also a major part of the world economy and one of the key reasons governments across the globe is promoting the manufacturing sector, such as *Make in India* and *Made in China*.[57] As an example, China wants to transform itself into a leading manufacturing power that moves up the manufacturing value chain by utilizing innovative manufacturing technologies or smart manufacturing, whereas India wants to reduce their dependence on exporting nations by producing goods in their own country, supported by significant foreign direct investment. However, with the outbreak of the COVID-19 pandemic, we have seen a significant decline in the global foreign direct investment. The United Nations Conference on Trade and Development has estimated that the COVID-19 could cause global foreign direct investment to shrink by 5%-15%, due to the downfall in the manufacturing sector along with factory shutdown with substantial negative impacts in the energy, chemicals, electronics, airlines, and automotive sectors and a shortage in raw materials.[58] Despite this knock on the manufacturing industry, the global application of AI in the manufacturing market is expected to still grow strongly with a compound annual growth rate of about 55% until 2025 when its size is projected to be approximately $15 billion.[59] With radical shifts in demand and the increasing use of AI and other smart technology solutions, manufacturers are experiencing a growing disruption of the entire end-to-end value chain and forcing them to brainstorm new supply chain models, adopt new plant designs, and redefine their manufacturing footprints.

Process manufacturing in industries such as minerals, metals and mining, oil and gas, pulp and paper, refining, cement and glass, chemicals, electric power generation, food and beverage, life sciences, as well as water and wastewater typically utilizes physical, chemical, and compositional changes via continuous and/or batch processes to convert raw material or feedstock into a product. A subset of these industries such as life sciences, minerals, metals and mining, and fine chemicals include a mixture of continuous, sequential or batch and discrete processes that are often referred to as "hybrid" applications and industries. AI-driven process performance enhancement can be applied to continuous, batch or discrete processes as well as hybrids thereof. A continuous process is defined as the continuous flow of material through various processing equipment. Once a continuous process is operating in a steady state, the goal is to produce a consistent product at optimal yield levels. Continuous process manufacturing includes industries such as refining, chemical, petrochemical, and oil and gas applications and differs from discrete and batch processes manufacturing with respect to its non-stop operation, unscheduled downtime, high asset value, capacity utilization, and cost. In contrast, the nature of batch process manufacturing is typically shift-oriented with a low-volume/high-value focus, more agile, rapid response to market demand and high regulatory content. In general, a batch process is defined as a process that leads to the production of finite quantities of material by subjecting quantities of input materials to an ordered set of processing activities over a finite period of time using one or more pieces of equipment. Some examples of batch processes are biotech product manufacturing, pharmaceutical formulations, soap manufacturing, dairy processing, food processing and beverage processing. Discrete process manufacturing includes vertical markets such as industrial manufacturing, high technology, automotive, aerospace, defense, machinery, and electronics and produce items such as cars, airplanes, consumer electronics, computers and accessories, appliances, and other household items. A discrete process involves the production of things, where a part or a specific quantity of parts in a group moves from one workstation to another, gaining value at each location as work is performed. In a discrete process, each thing or part maintains its unique identity.

Process and equipment performance enhancement for the manufacturing and resources industries is about operationalizing end-to-end integrated AI-based solutions that delivers process and equipment troubleshooting, monitoring and optimization using all available structured and unstructured data. Rapid process or equipment troubleshooting involves identifying and understanding causes of variation in key performance indicators such as throughput, quality, and yield or key production, process or equipment related variables. To extract knowledge from process or equipment models, causal and sensitivity analysis is typically done on machine learning based AI models that are trained on data to be representative of specific process or equipment behavior. Further insights can be extracted by using these AI models in what-if-scenario analysis and benefit estimation simulations. These models can then also be used in real-time or batch fashion in monitoring and diagnostic solutions that feed off real-time or batch data. Other real-time applications include predicting lab measurements via software sensors for use in process control applications, AI-driven advanced process control and set-point optimization. Machine learning can also be applied in safety and security-related applications for identifying and tracking people in the work environment and detecting anomalous behavior. Other applications include smart sensors that use machine learning for pattern recognition on video and audio feeds which can complement the traditional sensors used to control processes and equipment.

Some of the most impactful use cases for process and equipment performance enhancement that I have personally been involved with via my AI companies CSense Systems as well as Cortex Logic more recently, include the stabilizing of the feed rate in a grinding process that led to a 5% increase in throughput for the mining company. In an equipment-related performance enhancement use case, the availability of haul trucks was increased from 70% to 85% using predictive analytics that focused on the engine, transmission, and braking characteristics of the haul trucks. In another equipment related use case, the Cortex AI Engine was used at a major diamond producer to increase throughput, yield, and reduce equipment risk through improved decision making and automated mining operations. To not have operational mining equipment available has a significant impact on revenue and operational costs. In this particular use case, a data mining solution helped to gain insights with respect to how geological features and diamond yield correlates during sampling. A machine learning based solution was then developed that, amongst others, maps hydrophone signals to geology in order to create signals that are used for improved predictive maintenance of key operational mining equipment and automated mining tools. Another AI use case for this diamond producer involved the use of machine learning based models to predict forward demand for diamonds and related categories across market, product category, and price category. This allows for optimization of diamond sales and the supply of rough stones to manufacturers and price it accordingly to meet demand.

Our AI-enabled process troubleshooting, and advanced process control solutions implemented via the CSense software at a steel rolling plant in South Africa resulted in business value of at least $1 million per annum by a reduction in the plant's project cycle times, real-time identification of process set points, and a better understanding of the process through data-driven insights. At a mineral's sands plant in Western Australia a machine learning based solution was used to solve a 3-month kiln grade problem by identifying the causes for lack of proper grade within a week and helped to increase the grade with a few percentage points. With the AI-driven CSense software a remarkable contribution has been made towards increased operating ratios at a major aluminium paste plant in South Africa, where the plant's waste production rates has been significantly reduced, process transparency and knowledge has been increased, and the overall process variation throughout the plant has been reduced to provide high throughput of good consistent quality anodes for an efficient alumina reduction process downstream to produce aluminium. The software was also used at a Zinc plant where AI solutions that connected to all process, analytical and operational data helped to accurately predict the root causes of process variation in a range of operational processes.

The efficiency of one of the world largest primary platinum producers in South Africa was also improved by an advanced process control solution that helped to maximize production through the intelligent control of complex processes. At the platinum smelter two conflicting processes were also successfully integrated without spending capital or changing the plant in any way. An AI-based metal accounting solution that reliably provides a real-time estimate of all metals-in-process each stage of the production value chain was also implemented at the same platinum plant where validated information was generated from the bottom layers (that includes sensors and control systems) for the manufacturing execution systems and enterprise resource planning applications. At a base metal refinery plant an intelligent advanced pH controller was implemented that helped to reduce the pH variation in a leaching process by 40% with significant increases in nickel and iron extraction efficiency as well as the grade of the platinum group metals.

Advanced process control solutions were also implemented at one of the world's largest copper and gold mining plants that lead to significant increases in feed rate of up to 15%, implying an increase of 15 tons per hour. AI-driven process troubleshooting, and furnace taphole monitoring solutions was also implemented at one of the world largest fully integrated zinc and lead smelting and refining complexes in Canada. The system provided value by giving an indication to engineers and operators as to the integrity of all the tapping blocks of the furnace and when they may potentially become unsafe to use.

The ore beneficiary process at diamond mines could be described as a complex and expensive balancing act where flow rates, size, density, and other factors must all be in balance if any degree of plant optimization and efficiency is to be achieved. This requires not only complex models but uninterrupted real-time measurement of such key parameters as material flow rate and density, especially in the event of sensor failure and even when there are no sensors available. With AI-driven soft sensor technology that provides a digital twin of a hardware sensor, a solution was provided to not only measure more accurately, but to identify sensor failure in real-time and provide sensor values as derived from other sensors to generate the simulated sensor values.

A Dutch zinc manufacturer of rolled titanium for applications in wall cladding, gutters, roofing, and rainwater drainage systems was confronted with inconsistent product quality resulting in expensive rework and metallurgical properties that changed without any obvious reason. With a machine learning based solution it was possible to reduce the production of defect products and to reduce the rework and reprocessing which directly lead to improved efficiency and lower production costs. As the solution also provides detailed causal analysis, sensitivity analysis and what-if-scenario analysis, the zinc manufacturing process engineers were able to better understand the intricacies of their production process and to continuously improve it. The efficiency of the electrowinning process (which recovers metals from electroplating rinse waters) at a Belgium precious metals refining plant needed to be improved in the face of challenges that would force the plant to figure out new ways of dealing with change. An AI-enabled solution was implemented that not only increased the efficiency to 94%, but also helped to map the threshold values for impurities which led to an improved strategy for bleeding electrolyte from the plant's electrowinning circuit. In addition, some new process insights contributed to further annual savings due to the removal of costly corrective actions which did not produce an evidence-based positive impact.

An aluminium smelter in Australia had unacceptably high variation with their green-anode density in their batch-mixing paste plants. Machine learning models were deployed that resulted in specific process improvement recommendations that led to the reduction in anode quality variation. At an Alumina plant in Western Australia a real-time causal analysis solution was implemented that resulted in the causticizer unit (which makes caustic soda by controlling chemical reactions of soda ash and milk of lime in a dissolving tank and a reactor) of the refinery to be more proactive and consistent in its response to process deviations. From a business outcome perspective, the AI solution resulted in improved process stability, production rates and product quality.

An integrated steel plant in the Netherlands could not explain frequent breakouts at the continuous caster in their direct strip products section of their plant, where a single breakout causes hours of downtime at huge opportunity cost. An AI solution was implemented that provided early detection of potential breakouts and helped to explain other caster related problems. At a very modern chrome chemical production plant in South Africa, ore is processed to yield sodium dichromate and chromic acid which is used in manufacturing applications such as leather tanning and corrosion control (for example, in electroplating, metal surfaces are finished with a thin layer of chromium either for decorative purposes or to obtain a corrosion-resistant surface). A machine learning based solution was developed for this plant to provide real-time mass balance calculations and an intelligent control algorithm to help stabilize the chromic acid crystallizer and resulted in significant process stability with reduced variance where the product was increased with 20%, drastic reduction in impurities and greater than 50% reduction in plant downtime.

At a world-leading heavy mineral sands extraction and refining plant in South Africa rapid process troubleshooting and advanced process control solutions were implemented on both rutile and zircon circuits with resultant financial and business benefits of 5% increase in product yield whilst maintaining grade constraints as well as achieving a reduced product grade variation overall. A Zinc smelter in the Netherlands needed to rapidly improve temperature control of their zinc roasters in order to maximize plant throughput. A real-time AI-based optimization solution was implemented that incorporated plant expert knowledge and experience to continuously improve the operation of their roasters and the roll-out of machine learning based rapid process troubleshooting to other plant sections. One of the world's largest ferrochrome producers in South Africa that produces charge chrome through a direct current electric arc furnace and metal recovery plant had a significant bottleneck in their drier section where chromite ore needs to be dried before being fed to the direct current furnace. With rapid process troubleshooting that helps to understand the causes of variation and the implementation of an advanced process control solution, the variation on the drier's bag-house temperature was significantly reduced with throughput through the drier that has increased by more than 35% and no more damages to the bag-house filter bags due to temperature knocks were reported. In a discrete manufacturing process troubleshooting use case, specific causes for variation were also identified using a machine learning based solution for an aluminium rolling plant in South Africa that experienced unacceptable reject rates due to off-sets on plates being hot-rolled. At a large aluminium die casting manufacturer in the USA that also, amongst others, provide parts for Harley Davidson, AI-based process troubleshooting is used to identify and understand causes of variation of surface defects such as blisters and scratches that allow them to provide better quality product to their customers. At a global microelectronics manufacturer in the USA that is a supplier of consumable materials such as chemical mechanical planarization polishing slurries to the semiconductor industry, one of the AI use cases involved mixer batch phase analysis where mixer product temperature and motor amps were some of the key performance indicators that were modeled and analyzed. By modeling the ideal or so-called "golden" batches, anomaly detection and causal analysis can be performed to understand the contributing factors for batches that deviate away from the "golden batches". Similar discrete and process troubleshooting, and predictive analytics were done for semiconductor companies in the USA and Germany. For an automotive customer in the USA, AI-based solutions were implemented to assist with paint shop quality management with respect to reducing variation in key performance indicators such as paint quality index (reducing variation in samples from color to color, between production lines and as a result of different processing conditions), yield, and concentration levels. The solutions also provided causes for paint shop quality problems such as products that have poor process capability, many defects and quality parameters that are "out of control". One of the global leaders in the brewing industry wanted to improve their beer quality, reduce waste, and improve product consistency. An AI-driven solution was developed using the CSense software to troubleshoot and help to optimize limited extract, which is one of the key quality parameters used in quality control in the production of beers. Once the causes for variances in limited extract value were identified by causal and sensitivity analysis applied to the beer quality machine learning based models, optimal setpoints were determined for these manipulated variables to reduce extract losses and waste and obtain the best quality beer for each brand.

Machine learning driven solutions can also help engineering teams to improve their productivity and efficiency with respect to more efficient designs, quicker turnaround time and eliminating waste in the design process. Motivo Inc., for example, uses AI to help fabless design companies to improve their yield and optimize their designs at reduced costs, better reliability and faster time to market.[60] Intel has also claimed that they have achieved a 10% higher yield for their integrated-circuit products compared to other similar designs at a similar, pre-production development stage.[61] McKinsey & Company's MGI referenced a use case where a semiconductor manufacturer reduced its material-delivery time by 30% and increased its production yield by 3-5% using machine learning based approaches. MGI also mentions use cases where an aerospace manufacturer reduced its development costs almost €200 million with the development of AI-base productive tools for their engineering teams and saved €350 million by reducing unnecessary interruptions on the assembly line.[62] An AI-driven fully digitized supply chain can help to do real-time optimization of inventories, balancing of the supply chain and visibility on supplier machine performance, availability, and downtime. AI can also help to provide better accountability throughout the supply chain, which can for example help aerospace and automobile manufacturing to better adhere to safety regulations. It can assist with making program review processes more efficient, addressing potential bottlenecks with respect to process, material, and staff in a preventative manner. Uptake is for example using AI and IoT to transform aircraft maintenance by deploying sensor networks for monitoring aircraft engines using machine learning driven anomaly detection that analyzes the sound of airplane turbines, their operations and predict maintenance.[63] By predicting maintenance, repair and overhaul related work in an accurate fashion, one company reported profit increases of around €300 million through the use of AI to forecast 10 years of repair events for a fleet of 17,000 commercial aircraft.[64] MGI reckons that aircraft maintenance automation can generate between $5-15 billion in annual business value for the industry through performance gains and labor replacement. When I was at General Electric, I remember them making use of the Kaggle data science competition platform to assist with a flight planning route optimization problem where machine learning was used to optimize fuel consumption by incorporating inputs such as airspace constraints, wind, and weather patterns. The winning solution demonstrated a 12% efficiency improvement compared to actual flight data.

Although there has still been a low adoption of AI in the construction sector, some relevant use cases for deploying AI solutions in this sector includes smart buildings and homes; architectural and generative design assistance; automating the creation of building information model elements, managing parameters and inter-operating with other applications, data sources, and geometry tools; improving building energy management and estimating energy performance of residential buildings; raising efficiency of air conditioning systems in commercial buildings; real-time equipment monitoring, diagnostics, anomaly detection, and predictive maintenance; autonomous equipment; and intelligent virtual construction assistants and advisors. Smart buildings involve the use of AI, internet of things, and smart sensors attached to buildings to increase safety by reducing risks such as flooding or fire, while also to reduce operational costs and improve energy efficiency through capabilities such as monitoring the movement of people around the building and adjusting temperatures accordingly. From a risk management perspective insurance companies are incentivized to work with construction companies and large enterprises to create smart buildings and reduce the insurance premiums for companies that deploy such smart technology driven solutions. Similar to the benefits achievable in smart office or public buildings, smart sensors in homes can at the same time enhance the household experience through optimizing climate control according to personal preferences, improving energy efficiency and reduce operational costs by learning the electrical signatures of home appliances to switch heating and air-conditioning on or off at the right times to exploit off-peak rates or alerting consumers to the optimum usage of washing machines or dryers; increase safety by reducing risks like flooding or fire; reducing home insurance costs; and provide healthcare assistance by for example protecting the well-being of people with asthma through carrying out real-time pollen or pollution calculations.

AI Revolutionizing Agriculture

It is estimated that more than 1 billion people around the world work in agriculture with a contribution of about $2.4 trillion to the world economy.[65] So it is a significant foundation to the world economy. However, the agriculture industry across precision farming, livestock, aquaculture, and greenhouse farming is facing serious challenges from a growing world population with increased demand from food and related agricultural products. Assuming current growth rates, food production needs to increase by 70% to feed 9.1 billion people by 2050 where 70% will be urban and have higher income levels (the United Nations estimates 9.7 billion people).[66] This can be addressed by using advanced farming techniques supported by smart technology driven farming solutions to increase the agriculture crop production as well the demand for protein-rich aqua food.[67] As a result, the smart agriculture market has also seen significant growth from $13.8 billion in 2020 to $22 billion by 2025, at a compound aggregate growth rate of almost 10%.[68] Goldman Sachs GIR has a similar estimate of approximately $20 billion by 2025 for the smart crop agriculture market and assumes a 25% value creation by AI and IoT for the crop agriculture market of $1.2 trillion by 2050.[69] They project that within just protein agriculture another $20 billion can be generated through the use of AI applications for precision breeding mechanisms as well as disease prevention and treatment. Apart from the pressure on the food supply system, modern farming techniques and growing income levels, this growth can also be attributed to increasingly instrumented smart agriculture and aquaculture farms as well as advanced livestock monitoring and disease detection to help increase farm yield by applying smart technologies such as AI and IoT along with global positioning systems, drones, sensors, radio-frequency identification, and light emitting diode grow lights. With this type of instrumentation huge sets of soil, satellite and aerial imagery, weather, temperature, precipitation, wind speed, solar radiation, video, and audio data can be assembled for monitoring, data mining and predictive analytics purposes. It is also clear that yield monitoring applications using precision farming technologies can provide farmers with the information, predictions and insights about soil properties, fertilizers, and weather conditions. As an example, GS GIS estimates that corn yields in the USA can be improved by 70% by 2050 by using AI-driven technologies such as precision fertilizer and compaction reduction.[70] They also project that from a global crop agriculture value perspective, potential increases in global crop yields from smart technology based solutions could generate more than $800 billion in increased value by 2050 through precision irrigation, precision planting, precision fertilizer, precision spraying, compaction reduction, and moisture sensing. Machine learning solutions can also help to decrease irrigation and fertilizer costs, reduce labor costs, improve the quality of the agriculture products, detect potential crop or livestock diseases, increase the productivity of human workers as well as land and equipment use, and enhance decision-making with respect to irrigation, fertilization, planting times, and livestock care. Some specific use cases for deploying AI solutions in the agriculture sector includes crop harvesting and soil monitoring, predictive analytics of environmental impact on crop yields, determining time sowing, weed control, diagnosing soil defects, automated irrigation systems, crop health monitoring, saving plants, help IoT achieve its maximum potential in precision agriculture, image recognition and insights, intelligent virtual assistants and advisors for farmers, agricultural robots, drones, and driverless or smart tractors. These smart autonomous tractors can for example be trained or programmed to independently make decisions on speed of operation, detecting their ploughing position and avoid obstacles in the farm fields while performing various tasks.

Deforestation and degradation of land, in particular soil quality, remains a key global issue for this century due to its negative impact on the food security, agriculture and economic productivity, quality of life, and the environment. The cost for erosion from agriculture in the USA alone is already about $44 billion per annum. Peat.ai's Plantix solution makes use of machine learning driven image recognition to diagnose infected crops and offers treatments for any disease, pest or nutrient deficiency issues.[71] Another AI-driven soil defect analysis solution to help optimize healthy crop production is the one from Trace Genomics that utilizes soil science, genomics and machine learning to measure the bacteria and fungi in soil that cause disease and cycle nutrients and combine those measurements with soil chemical characteristics.[72] Agricultural robots can help to increase production yields at higher volume and a faster pace compared to human workers by for example using drones, robotic arms, and autonomous tractors to automate some common repetitive tasks such as mowing, harvesting, picking, sorting, packing, pruning, thinning, spraying, seeding, controlling weed, planting seeds, and milking and washing livestock. Other benefits of these smart technology solutions are lowering production costs, decreasing the need for manual labor, and producing higher quality of fresh produce. According to estimation by the Weed Science Society of America the impact of uncontrolled weeds on soybean and corn crops in the USA and Canada has led to the annual losses to farmers of approximately $43 billion.[73] Ecorobotix's solar powered weeding robotic platform called AVA provides high precision targeted application of herbicide for ecological and economical weeding of row crops, intercropping cultures and meadows, whereas their fully autonomous solar-powered robot platform ARA is used for scouting and phenotyping applications and can move according to a predefined real-time kinematic global positioning system trajectory in autonomous fashion whilst minimizing soil compaction.[74] Blue River Technology which is now part of John Deere, has a robot called See & Spray which uses AI-driven machine vision to provide precision spraying of weeds on cotton plants, which also helps prevent herbicide resistance.[75] Naio Technologies also has a range of robots that can weed, hoe and assist during harvesting of vegetable crops and vineyards.[76] Energid provides a robot that can pick citrus fruit every 2-3 seconds at comparable cost to human labor, whereas Harvest CROO Robotics' robot helps strawberry farmers pick and pack their crops at a rate of 8 acres a day and matching the equivalent of 30 human workers.[77]

Drones are also starting to play a significant role in monitoring large crop areas. Aerobotics in South Africa is for example using drone imagery and AI to get insights and identify problematic trees as well as assist with the management of orchards, pests, diseases and provide yield estimations.[78] Vineview is another leading provider that leverages aerial technology and AI to monitor crop health with their use of aerial-based sensors, machine learning and other advanced algorithms to help grape growers make responsive and informed vineyard management decisions.[79] Vineview's solutions involve achieving vine balance, optimizing harvest scheduling, eradicating grapevine disease in vineyards, and improving irrigation and conservation of water. Agribotix's drone-enabled FarmLens data analytics platform, which is now part of AgEagle's service offerings, provide the agricultural supply chain with AI-driven advanced analytic capabilities to identify areas where they can build soil health and reduce water or chemical usage.[80] Vision Robotics has a range of agricultural mechanization solutions that includes a lettuce thinner, weeder, an autonomous intelligent grapevine pruner, and crop load estimation for apples on a tree, strawberries on a plant and branches on a vines.[81] One of the USA-based companies that specializes in providing machine learning driven weather intelligence is aWhere which provides in-time weather, maps for economic resilience, weather insights and predictions, crop sustainability analysis, pest and disease modeling, fertilizer timing recommendations, and other related digital agriculture solutions.[82]

Within livestock and dairy farming losses due to animal disease or distress is also significant. GS GIR has for example estimated that the annual loss within the global dairy farming amounts to more than $11 billion which is predominantly because of preventable lameness among dairy cows that leads to decreased fertility, treatment costs, and milk loss.[83] Machine learning based applications can help to enhance breeding and health conditions by absolute cost reduction and recovering lost potential revenue. This is also the case in poultry production where for example $2 billion in losses can be prevented by early machine learning based detection of two treatable diseases in chickens via auditory data analytics.

Another application area for AI in its use for highly instrumented vertical farming where crops are grown in a controlled environment typically without natural light or soil, but using water, light emitting diode (LED) lights and nutrients. It typically involves perception technology such as cameras and various sensors as well as automated and even autonomous mechatronics where AI is used to process the data to improve efficiency, reducing costs and optimizing nutritional value to the crops. There are predominantly three alternative growing systems in vertical farming: hydroponics is where the plants' roots are submerged in a continuous flow of nutrient based water; aquaponics is the same, but instead of manually providing nutrients, this is done via a fish tank that is connected to the plants with the fish wastes being the nutrient source; and aeroponics is where the plants' roots hang in the air and a sprinkler system sprays them with nutrient based water rather than it being submerged.[84] The vertical farming market is projected to grow to $7.3 billion by 2025, with hydroponics growth mechanism accounting for the largest size of this market over this period with a number of companies providing smart technology based vertical farming solutions such as AeroFarms and Plenty in the USA; Signify (The Netherlands), Osram (Germany), Valoya (Finland), and Heliospectra (Sweden) in Europe; and Everlight Electronics Co., Ltd. (Taiwan), Sky Greens (Singapore), and Spread Co. Ltd. (Japan) in Asia.[85] According to Markets and Markets research some of the key driving forces is the need of sustainable farming to meet the demands of an increasing world population, the growing demand for a substitute to traditional agriculture, and more partnerships being formed between technology providers and vertical farming companies.

The Food and Agriculture Organization (FAO) of the United Nations in their "*How to feed the World in 2050*" paper has given a well-articulated outlook for food security towards 2050, incorporating the changing socio-economic environment, the natural resource base with respect to land, water, and genetic diversity to meet the demand, and the potential for food security. They specifically state the prerequisites for global security as enhancing investment in sustainable agricultural production capacity and rural development, promoting technology change and productivity growth where smart technologies such as AI can play a massive role, and trade, markets and support to farmers.[86] The risks and challenges are that there can be hunger whilst adequate overall supplies without effective social safety nets for the poor and a global trading system that is fair and competitive, as well as climate change and increased biofuel production's impact on long-term food security. Although the planet does have considerable land reserves with rainfed crop potential, especially in Latin America and Sub-Saharan Africa and some industrial countries, the lack of access and infrastructure as well as the loss of important ecological functions due to uncultivated lands will likely restrict the arable land to be only expanded by another 70 million hectares (about 5%) by 2050.[87] According to the FAO, the suite of technological options should be as comprehensive as possible, which might include new plant varieties and animal breeds that are able to better adapt to changing conditions, smart technology driven farming systems that lead to a reduction of losses and waste, saving of water, improved labor productivity, and optimized management of natural resources. They also stress the need for countries with limited import capacity to improve their production system productivity and resilience for raising rural incomes and to help local agriculture to compete better with low-price food imports. So, let us take Sub-Saharan Africa as an example. Given that the agriculture sector accounts for 32% of its GDP and employs more than 65% of Africa's labor force, it is clear that this sector is key to its growth. Given the significant projected population growth, rapid urbanization along with rising income levels, alterations in national diets, and more open intra-regional trade policies, the World Bank estimated that African food markets will more than triple to be worth $1 trillion by 2030 and the demand for food to at least double by 2050.[88] Innovative smart technology solutions are necessary to address the many obstacles and constraints Sub-Saharan Africa face today, which includes reduction in soil fertility, emerging pest resistance, increased dependence on inorganic fertilizers, degradation of land, reduced water tables, increased vulnerability to climate change, inefficient resource usage, weak supply chain, and low productivity. The AI-driven smart technology solutions outlined in this section and applied to also empower small-holder farmers can contribute significantly to help local agriculture to improve productivity and efficiency across the agriculture value chain.

GS GIS estimates that AI-driven solutions could help generate more than $1 trillion in value based on the potential savings in crop input, dairy and livestock, irrigation, fertilizer, sortation, and labor as well as disease prevention and treatment, and increases in yields across the agriculture value chain. Given that AI solutions will help to limit waste and improve preventive methods, they also expect that the global market for fertilizer, veterinary pharmaceuticals, pesticides, fungicides, and herbicides will be significantly disrupted over the next five to ten years.[89]

7. Ultra-personalized AI-enabled Education, Precision Healthcare, and Wellness

Education, Healthcare and Wellness are sectors that I am personally passionate about and would love to see how smart technology and AI-driven technology can help shape a better and more equitable educational and healthy world. In this chapter we continue our sense-making journey on the application front to understand how these sectors are getting ultra-personalized and AI-enabled.

Transformative AI for Personalized Education

With digitization increasingly penetrating the education sector it is becoming ripe for serious transformation and disruption. This is already happening through AI-powered smart technology solutions that will not only help to deliver education, knowledge, and skills in new and creative ways, but enable personalized education at scale with a wide range of beneficiaries across age, socio-economic conditions, and geographical regions. Even though we have seen education technology being used over the last few decades, for the most part our education systems are still run on the "19th Century *Factory Model*" where a one-size-fits-all solution attempts to educate different kinds of people, motivated by different things, and with varying needs, learning styles and paces of learning.[1] Still, they must learn the same things, in the same way at the same time and are passed or failed based on whether or not they test well and whether their learning style happens to fit into a model that is forced on them.[2] Of course, before technology and smart technology in particular, there was little other way to ensure the masses had access to education. Resources and teachers were limited and confined to a place and a time. If you struggle to absorb information before 9am, too bad. School starts at 7. If you get testing anxiety, causing you to fail, when you have actually absorbed and understood concepts and information better than *A*-grade students, too bad. You do not move up a grade. Nelson Mandela emphasized the crucial role that education plays for humanity by saying that "education is the most powerful weapon which you can use to change the world".[3] It is also clear that AI is not only a key differentiator for educational institutions that adopts it but has the power to become an equalizer in education. AI-driven smart technologies are well suited to assist with achieving key educational objectives, such as personalized learning at scale, mentors for every learner, universal access to global classrooms, developing the essential skills to thrive in the Smart Technology Era, providing education for all, lifelong and life-wide learning, and improving teaching efficiency and effectiveness.[4]

As AI is enhancing education technology, it helps to understand how the global education technology market is evolving. The size of this market is expected to grow to $285 billion in 2027 at a compound annual growth rate of 18.1% from 2020 to 2027 with North America accounting for a majority share and the Asia-Pacific region having the fastest growth with countries such as China and India being the front runners.[5] The market growth is being stimulated by the accessibility of internet connectivity, the spread of smart devices, a drive towards AI-driven personalized and interactive learning, as well as innovative education technology solutions such as e-books, learning management systems, student information systems, content delivery systems, intelligent tutoring systems, virtual facilitators, smartboards, online courses with accreditation from recognized universities, massive open online courses, and more recently immersive course content via augmented reality and virtual reality. There has been quite a history to revolutionize education with technology, whether expanding access to knowledge via massive open online courses or gamifying instructional materials. Apart from technical issues, the responsible handling of ethical issues about data ownership, privacy, security, and governance will be key to ensure successful deployment of AI-driven edutech solutions. Due to the private and sensitive nature of learner data, edutech solution providers and educational institutions need to ensure that there are tight guarantees of data protection and handling. Given the example set of the successful adoption of AI in so many other sectors, especially consumer facing businesses, along with the application readiness of AI technology with respect to natural language processing and a range of machine learning use cases, there is an increasing awareness pertaining to the advantages of technology integration in the education sector. The adoption of AI is on the rise with educators starting to claim that AI can have a revolutionary authentic impact on the K-12 experience for both students and teachers.[6] We see this already in the global AI segment of the education market that is highly fragmented with a large number of global and regional players being joined by a multitude of smart technology driven education companies that see this as a massive business opportunity for delivering cloud and on-premise smart technology based solutions to K–12 education, higher education, academic research, and also corporate training. Some of these major multinational corporations or more established education-focused companies include Google, IBM, Microsoft, Pearson, Nuance Communications, Blackboard, Amazon Web Services, Jenzabar, Cognii, and Carnegie Learning. These companies have aggressive strategies to increase their footprint in the market through partnerships, acquisitions, and product launches. There are also a number of unicorn EdTech startups in especially China, India and the US that are starting to make their mark such as YuanFudao and Zuoyebang with tutoring and VIPKid with language in China, ByJu's with tutoring and Unacademy with test preparation in India, and Coursera and Udemy with massive open online courses and Udacity with proprietary online courses in the US.[7]

According to a P&S Intelligence market research report, the global AI share in the education market is expected to reach $25.7 billion in 2030, implying a compound annual growth rate of 32.9% from 2020 to 2030.[8] Some specific machine learning driven applications expected to help drive this growth involve automated grading systems, personalized student assignments, automated administrative tasks and decision-making support, as well as natural language processing used for intelligent virtual assistants, processing of text and speech data in discussions or portals, and assisting with writing assignment assessments and analysis. With AI-enabled learning, learner engagement can be enhanced, course content can be scheduled and delivered in an automated fashion, the learning and development team can focus more on higher quality learning content and return on learning and development investment can be improved with more effective and personalized learning outcomes. AI can also specifically add value in enhancing the learning process via the use of smart instructional content, longitudinal student data and human engagement, predictive analytics that identifies a learner's academic strengths and weaknesses, prescriptive and content analytics capabilities, recommending behavior and content for learners aligned to their individual skills needs and learning styles, helping learners to improve retention, mining the growing library of education content, content filtering and summarization, and a machine learning system that triggers if the learner has serious learning and/or other behavioral issues that requires specialist interventions. Additionally, as AI technology improves further with respect to especially natural language understanding and semantic understanding, we can expect more impactful AI-driven personalized learning, intelligent learning assistants and advisors, automatically grading more creative work such as essays and presentations, learning analytics, smarter content, automatic content generation, intelligent tutors and virtual mentors, virtual facilitators and learning environments, new learning pathways, real-time identification of where courses need to improve, altering how we interact with and find information, finding and addressing gaps in learning and teaching, making trial-and-error learning less intimidating, as well as changing the role of teachers, where students learn, who teaches them, and how they acquire 21st century skills such as critical thinking and problem solving and get better lifelong and life-wide learning support.

Though quality education will typically require active engagement by human teachers, AI promises to restructure and enhance education at all levels, especially by providing personalization at scale and addressing the limitations of measuring academic achievement and abilities, conventional classroom teaching, and traditional testing systems. AI applications in education can result in learning activities that are adaptable and customized to each individual and avoid leaving slower learners behind or frustrating faster learners. With personalized digital learning platforms, courses and learning material can be presented at scale and customized to ensure that students can maximize their learning experience and potential by learning at their own pace with consideration of their current knowledge and skill levels, learning preferences, individual progress, make the learning experience as enjoyable and stimulating as possible, and provide personalized motivational assistance, support, feedback, and recommendations. Personalized learning enables continuous differentiated and individualized learning which effectively replaces the traditional stop-and-test learning model and delivers the right content at the right time in the most optimal way to each learner. AI-driven adaptive personalized learning can provide in-depth insights into a learner's performance, cognitive ability, attitude, perseverance, confidence, and mindset by identifying successful learning indicators for each learner, uses computer vision to for example track eye and mouse movements, analyzes sentiment using natural language processing, and monitors learning dynamics such as the amount of time a learner needs to answer a question, the number of times a question was attempted before getting it right, and the number of times a learner pauses during a teaching lesson. Although coaching and assessing require specific skills, such as communication, emotional intelligence, and creativity, AI solutions can support these activities through recognizing learning patterns, the affective states of learners, their attitude towards learning, and other real-time insights using data from digital interactions, attention tracking, facial expressions, and group interactions and dynamics. An AI-based learning assistant should provide personalized coaching throughout the learning journey, factoring in all available learner data, including the student's learning goals and interests, their current level of knowledge and their past learning experiences. Some of the enabling technologies include data collection, innovative data management, data mining, and pattern recognition via predictive analytics and natural language processing systems. Learning analytics is key for adaptive learning environments to improve learner support and performance. An AI-based learning assistant typically ascribes to a personalized learning framework with algorithms that process the knowledge represented in a domain model, a pedagogy model, and a learner model; a learner interface with content adapted to the needs and capabilities of the individual learner and capturing of the learner's data such as interactions, achievements, and emotions; as well as data analysis and predictive analytics on all available structured and unstructured learner data. Such a learning assistant can also empower learners with the ability to have some insights into their behavioral and cognitive preferences, a sense of how and where they learn best, how conclusions are being reached, how to control their own learning tempo, and even how to configure the learning assistant to help them navigate their learning experiences. A University of Texas research paper presents an open and interactive cloud-based learning platform called Cloud-eLab that allows learners to control the whole learning process at their own pace and supports education applications scenarios such as unfolding deep and wide learning as well as cognitive and adaptation learning concepts. The AI thinking framework is based on cognitive and adaptation, as opposed to just procedural thinking, to automatically learn deep and wide rules and semantics from experiments and has been successfully used in a variety of machine learning courses in practice.[9]

Kidaptive provides a cloud-based AI-powered adaptive learning platform that enables educational companies to use the data they collect to increase learner engagement, efficacy across their content ecosystem, actionable insights about learning, predicts future learner performance and real-time adaptivity to optimize personalized engagement and improve learning outcomes. The Kidaptive's learning analytics uses a universal learner model to produce a holistic picture of the learner's progress, proficiency, preferences, and interests using data inputs such as teacher and parent and teacher input, learning activities, and assessments.[10] Knewton provides an adaptive personalized learning solution in subjects such as mathematics, chemistry, economics and statistics that continuously measures and adapts to students' proficiency levels with each interaction, identifies knowledge gaps and provides just-in-time remediation.[11] A Knewton data scientist described machine learning as "the new chalk" for teachers and instructors, but acknowledged that AI is still relatively limited in how it is being applied.[12]

Personalized AI-powered assistants can function like tutors and be customized for a particular course, voice and speech-recognition enabled, answer questions about the topics covered by the course, keep track of a learner's progress with coursework, anticipate potential failure, help to build student self-awareness, and incorporate personality test insights to further customize personalized responses. It can also help to provide a safe and neutral learning environment, adjust the speed of learning, and encourage active participation in learning. Given the effectiveness of playing games to learn new content, there is a great opportunity to have educational content packaged into a game format to provide a more effective, enjoyable, and impactful learning experience with interactive components to ensure continuous engagement as well as customization in accordance with a learner's personality and learning needs. Quizlet, for example, provides a variety of studying and learning tools from flashcards to games along with adaptive plans and AI-driven recommendations to show the most relevant study material. They claim 90% of learners who use Quizlet report higher grades.[13]

London-based Third Space Learning provides personalized one-to-one mathematics lessons to help close the mathematics attainment gap for children from age 5 to 11 via a secure online classroom together with primary math teaching resources, AI-based recommendations and development modules for teachers via their online learning hub.[14] UK-based Century Tech combines AI, learning science and neuroscience to identify gaps in learner's knowledge, personalize content, questions and learning pathways, identifies and addresses misconceptions, and supports teacher interventions as well as contingency planning for home learning. They specialize in English, mathematics and science courses for primary and secondary schools, further education colleges and remote learning.[15] US-based AI-enabled educational technology provider Cognii provides personalized deeper learning, enhanced tutoring, open response assessment and pedagogically rich analytics to K-12, higher education, and corporate training markets to provide better learning outcomes and cost savings. Their virtual learning assistant interacts with a student in an engaging chatbot-style learning conversation and handles open response answers in an adaptive personalized manner, provides one-to-one tutoring and coaching until mastery is achieved, gives students a formative assessment and real-time feedback throughout the learning sequence, and provides instructors with detailed learning analytics.[16] Querium from Texas delivers personalized, bite-sized lessons with AI-powered step-by-step tutoring assistance called StepWise to help high school and college students master key skills in science, technology, engineering and mathematics, and give teachers insights into a student's learning habits and areas for improvement. Some of the solutions include support for assessment and placement tests, and Rover, an online math homework system that uses the StepWise Virtual Tutor.[17] Thinkster Math is a K-8 tutoring platform that provides a tailored program that combines AI with human interaction to make learning mathematics efficient, predictable, and achievable in a step-by-step fashion. Their 7-step method includes better ways to remember without overloading the learner's working memory, hyper-personalization of content, dedicated digital tutor and coach, getting insights into learner's performance to achieve mystery and accelerate learning, providing timely assistance when learners solve problems, keeping learners engaged, and making learning convenient.[18] US-based Carnegie Learning Inc provides an AI-driven personalized mathematics learning software platform called MATHia for middle and high school students that acts flexibly as a coach that provides real-time assessment and feedback, facilitates active learning, and learning analytics. They have extended their offering to also include a personalized computer science learning software platform called Zulama.[19] Dreambox Learning provides an online personalized mathematics program in English and Spanish that dynamically adapts to learner's actions, provides predictive insights on learner performance and is currently being used by 3.5 million K-8 students in North America.[20] iTalk2Learn was a 3-year European Union project that developed an open-source AI-driven tutoring platform that supports mathematics learning for primary school students to deliver the right lesson in a more natural way at the right time for every student.[21] Some of the key innovations include a lesson recommender that adapt intelligently to students' needs by incorporating historical performance and behavioral patterns, speech recognition that enables detecting behavioral patterns, affective states, and learning attitudes, as well as exploratory learning environments and tasks to promote both procedural and conceptual knowledge. Gradescope uses AI technology to help deliver and grade variable-length assignments such as problem sets and projects as well as fixed-template assignments such as worksheets, exams, quizzes, or questionnaires on subjects such as computer science (both paper-based assignment or programming project), physics, mathematics, chemistry, biology, engineering, and economics.[22]

Roybi provides AI-powered toys for young children such as Roybi Robot that teaches languages, math, science, technology, and chemistry in an adaptable, conversational, and entertaining fashion.[23] KidSense.AI, which is a Roybi company, provides automatic speech recognition in multiple languages and speech assessment and tailored for children in languages such as English, Mandarin, and Korean. It converts children's native and non-native speech to text in real-time, supports simultaneous dual speech recognition, has fully embedded language and acoustic models, and evaluates pronunciations.[24] Nuance is an US-based company specializing in conversational AI and provides its Dragon speech recognition software to help transform the classroom by assisting students that struggle with writing, transcribing spoken word up to 160 words per minute, reading transcribed text, assisting teachers in preparing lesson plans, syllabi, reading lists, worksheets, and assessment quicker through dictation.[25] European-based Lingvist Technologies OU is an education company that uses AI to fast-track language learning in a fast, accessible, personalized, focused, and fast way, where the languages currently include Spanish, French, Russian, German and Portuguese. It uses for example machine learning to assess one's existing vocabulary to learn at your own level, learn new words and review existing vocabulary in a real-world context, customize your course by building your own language deck or selecting specialized theme-based language decks.[26] Elias Robot is a multilingual language learning application that uses AI and a voice user interface deployed in a human-like robot to help students to practice languages and communication skills in a fun and engaging way.[27] It has a variety of exercise types such as warm-up, repeat and remember, speech, and a playful quiz, can listen carefully through speech recognition, monitor the development of pronunciation, give positive and effective feedback in an animated fashion through speech recognition, and help practice interaction and reaction skills via a free form chat.

These AI-powered personalized learning platforms and assistants that use machine learning, natural language processing, speech recognition and computer vision can also assist teachers with meaningful insights, recommendations, feedback and predictive analytics about learners' performance and the effectiveness of the current learning system on an individual level, automating repetitive and routine tasks such as marking and grading, supervising tutorials, answering routine questions, identify early disengagement signs, and indicate which learners need more support, intervention, mentoring and guidance. Such systems can also provide predictive analytics by predicting grades, determine the most effective learning methods, and make it easier to assess performance based on defined goals. It can also assist teachers to focus less on lecturing and more on guidance, mentoring and coaching as well as improve the efficiency of communications with learners by being always available to respond to queries and immediate problems. It can also help to supervise learners in a classroom setup using facial and voice recognition. By mining data from all available data sources including education records, learning management systems, surveys, and social media, AI solutions can also help optimize group formation for learning objectives, identify complementary skills to enhance critical thinking and learners' capacity to collaborate and adapt, identify new drivers of performance to assess students and help students highlight their strengths. Machine learning can identify complementary skills that will maximize critical thinking and test students' capacity to adapt and collaborate. Collaboration.ai's AI-driven solutions can for example be used for learning and development to analyze data on learners' knowledge, capabilities and experience and figure out optimal formation of groups, cohorts and teams using products such as NetworkOS that uses trained AI models to combine and find relationships and create maps of connections and TeamCreator to engineer intelligent networking opportunities, makes introductions, drives stronger connections with better engagement by combining AI, surveys, and social organization network analysis to customize teams and track engagement over time.[28] Georgia Tech's AI-enabled virtual teaching assistant called Jill Watson has been successfully used for 4 years since 2016 when it was first introduced to students as a teaching assistant for their online Master of Science in Computer Science course. It helped to reduce the high attrition rate typically associated with online courses and was so effective that at that time many students did not know for months that Jill was not a human providing the support and answering questions. Since then, it has been deployed in four residential courses as well as an introduction course to Biology (as the first non-Computer Science related course) where it has been used in the form of a virtual ecological research assistant (VERA) to help students perform virtual experiments to explain existing ecological systems and predict possible outcomes based on user inputs and changes.[29]

Coursera's online learning programs and degrees have courses that have recorded auto-graded and peer-reviewed assignments, where AI is used to identify and alert course instructors when a large proportion of learners make similar errors.[30] I remember doing Coursera's Machine Learning course offered by Stanford University and presented by Andrew Ng in 2013 (just to see what it is like) and was impressed with the automated way tests and assignments were handled. With more than three and half million enrollments and at least hundred thousand completions since then, this has been one of the most successful MOOC courses with tangible career benefits.[31] Coursera also uses a machine learning based tool called CourseMatch that matches school curriculum to their 3800 online courses by cataloguing the school's courses into its system and then aligning it with online courses on its platform using natural language processing. More than 2.6 million on-campus courses across 1800 schools have already been matched.[32] Content Technologies uses AI to create educational content in a cost-effective way for secondary, higher, and continuing education as well as corporate training. For example, with Palitt one can create a customer lecture series, syllabus or textbook, whereas Cram101 can break master content in a text book into a smart study guide that has chapter summaries, practice tests and flashcards.[33] Netex Learning, headquartered in Spain, develops apps and service-based solutions for learning and smarter content such as learningCloud as a machine learning powered learning management system that engages and empowers learners as well as contentCloud that supports the creation and management of digital content in the cloud.[34]

AI can also be effectively used to anticipate job market demand. It can help to increase enrollment by using a virtual assistant to follow up with applicants. ConnecPath provides an AI-driven managed marketplace called WeAdmit.io to help guide high school students to make the right choice when applying to colleges or universities. The WeAdmit platform makes use of a chatbot that addresses common career-related questions and connects prospective students with a personalized team of counselors that includes a college admissions professional, a student coach and a financial aid expert.[35] Spain-based Alicante's 1MillionBot develops specialized chatbots for different sectors, with their most successful chatbots being those created to facilitate enrollment in universities such as The

University of Murcia, the Polytechnic University of Valencia and the Complutense University of Madrid.[36]

Educational institutions and providers also want to continually improve their offerings to students, ensure that their courses are relevant with respect to the needs of the fast-changing job market, attract the most suitable combination of students, ensure that they benefit from their chosen courses, make sure of retaining them, assist them optimally on their learning path, and helping them to find meaningful jobs. Similar to other consumer facing businesses, AI can be applied to improve the retention of students, proactively identify those students that are struggling and prevent dropout where possible, help unlock the learning potential of students, help to unlock on-time completion of their studies, improve the student experience, support staff with academic planning and student interaction, and assist students with lifelong career assessment, planning and development. There are several edutech providers that have solutions to address these needs such as Civitas Learning, Hobons' Naviance, Kuder, BridgeU and Renaissance. Civitas Learning has for example an analytics platform that unifies education data for a 360-degree view of students and delivers actionable intelligence to innovate and measurably improve learning outcomes.[37] Their Student Success Suite provides comprehensive insights about students, activities, and programs to support strategic planning, equip staff with the data and tools to help students and deliver more effective student care and guidance, use real-time data and analytics to make policy decisions or launch outreach, understand the impact and return on investment of student success programs, remove barriers that impede student panning, scheduling and registration, and improve equity and eliminating achievement gaps. Northern Arizona University in the USA has also integrated predictions from the Civitas Learning platform into Salesforce CRM to inform actions and share insights across the student support ecosystem to retain students and help students at risk.[38] With increased instrumentation providing real-time and novel feeds of data about student behavior and activities, we will see AI applications such as computer vision and natural language processing to assist in identifying disengagement and learning difficulties.

AI can also be used to improve sales, customer engagements and interactions as is demonstrated by the SalesLab of Haaga-Helia University in Finland that offers sales training services to business by measuring and analyzing the emotional responses of customer experiences during a sales engagement. [39] Students can improve their selling skills by getting feedback from the AI-powered system that does eye tracking, detecting emotional responses and providing insights about the effectiveness of their interaction. The same technology can also be utilized to improve intelligent virtual assistants' engagement with learners or customers. AI can be used as a tool to identify added value of scientific activity, automating the review of academic content, detecting plagiarism and the misuse of information and statistics. AI can help to enhance scientific research as a tool that mines huge amounts of structured and unstructured data, discover connections in the content, create hypotheses or theories, and provide predictions. Many basic learning opportunities can start with a well-designed educational chatbot that can facilitate an interactive learning experience that could be more engaging and interesting than reading a book or watching a video. In the future, information about a learner's knowledge level about a given topic can be incorporated to customize recommendations on the educational material that would best meet the learner's needs. Andreas Oranje from Education Testing Service made some bold predictions on AI and the future of education over the next decade which includes that 95%

of the current education technology offerings will be gone, those that survive will be the most useful for teachers and make their jobs more meaningful, and traditional ways of testing will be replaced by embedded forms of assessment that is integrated into the learning process and enhanced by virtual and augmented reality simulations, game-based learning experiences, and online courses.[40]

With businesses being transformed and the nature of jobs and tasks within jobs in continuous flux and change, there seems to be not only a difficulty in optimally matching people to the right job, but a considerable mismatch between the skills, knowledge and competencies that are required in the job market and those that the educational system delivers.[41] AI-powered digital solutions can help to address some of these problems by providing the education sector with a more real-time view of job requirements, making curriculums more dynamic and connecting people to job opportunities in a personalized and dynamic fashion. There are many examples of AI-driven tools that optimize the different stages of the recruitment and talent acquisition processes such as job ad posting, candidate sourcing, candidate screening, candidate assessment, the interview process, offer, and onboarding process. Textio is for example using natural language processing and text analytics techniques to improve the contents of job ad postings.[42] USA-based CareerBuilder is an example of an AI-driven talent discovery platform for job seekers and employers that reportedly enable companies to reduce time to hire by more than 30%, whilst enhancing both the recruiter and job seeker's experience as well as addressing diversity.[43] There are many other startups that provide candidate sourcing solutions that tap into machine learning, natural language processing and predictive analytics such as Arya, Beamery, Entelo, Hiretual, Hireabby, Hiredscore, and Talemetry.[44] Arya's recruiting platform, for example, provides fast identification of top talent with smart sourcing, blends AI and data-driven methods to create high-quality candidate pipelines, engage automatically with personalized messaging, and track successful hires and search for similar candidates in real-time.[45] Pando Logic's pandoIQ job advertising platform automates and optimizes job advertising spend using AI-enabled algorithms for job ad classification, performance prediction, budget allocation, job ad targeting, real-time campaign optimization, and predictive insights and transparency in spend.[46] There are also AI-driven tools that specifically help with candidate screening by multilingual resume parsing, contextual screening, and resume prioritization. Some current examples include Ceipal, CVVIZ, IDEAL, Mosaictrack, Pomato, and Textkernel.[47] Machine learning is also used for assessing candidates for job and organizational fit by predicting the quality of the hire based on a candidate's aptitude, culture fit, soft skills, and ability to succeed throughout their career. Some example candidate screening software include Harver, HackerRank, Interview Mocha, Kandio, and McQuaig along with intelligent virtual assistants such as Jobpal, Mya, and Oliva that can have a conversation with candidates as part of the screening process.[48] Humantic AI provides an example of AI being used for organizing personality tests and predictive behavioral assessment in combination with social psychology, computational linguistics, and psycholinguistics.[49] AI can also be used to assist with the interviewing process where companies such as Calendly and X.AI makes it easier to schedule interviews, whereas Hirevue, PANNA, and Talocity provides AI-enabled video interviewing platform solutions.[50] There also a number of experience-based onboarding platform solutions that use machine learning to enhance the offer and onboarding process of successful candidates. Some examples include Appical, Enboarder, and Talmundo.[51] The types of AI solutions will not only lead to faster recruitment but also more precise matching of candidates with the optimal skill sets and personal traits for a specific job or role, even promising candidates with less conventional credentials. Governments would also be able to use machine learning based approaches to predict details about job-market demand more accurately which in turn can help educational institutions to adjust their course curricula, content and learning approaches to better match the private and public sector job market demand. Apart from helping to reduce unemployment, it would also lead to a more confident, adaptable, and productive workforce to help raise the productivity of the economy.

As smart technology driven automation is accelerating the pace at which people's skills and knowledge in the job market will become obsolete, there is a growing need for an always accessible type of continuous learning. The nature of education is therefore evolving into one that also covers life-wide and lifelong learning where life-wide learning recognizes formal, informal, and non-formal learning of a person within multiple contexts and authentic real-world settings and lifelong learning involves continuous learning throughout a person's entire life to learn new skills, knowledge and competencies as required. AI-powered learning solutions will make life-wide and lifelong learning a practical reality by discovering new training relevant to a person's training needs, developing smart tailored training plans, assess the person's abilities to learn training content, understand the person's learning patterns and preferences, customize future content and provide recommendations for optimal learning. By having an AI learning assistant or virtual coach that delivers these capabilities in a personalized and responsive way that interacts in the person's spoken language and taking into consideration the person's interests, learning preferences, training needs and personality, a more optimal learning experience can be provided that is interactive, proactive, and customized with respect to suggestions, advice, recommendations, guidance, and coaching. Based on instructions from learning and development professionals or the user's learning goals and preferences, an AI system can also be used to automatically generate content or learning assets by combining relevant text, audio, and video content from reputable sources. This would allow teachers and other practitioners in the education sector to focus more on developing new and creative learning approaches for the future and strategic training requirements of a business or educational institution.

AI-enabled technology can also play a key role to create more scalable and cost-effective educational solutions to address the massive teacher shortages at the primary and secondary levels. UNESCO's Institute of Statistics team has predicted that the world needs almost 69 million new teachers (24.4 million primary school teachers and 44.4 million secondary school teachers) to reach the 2030 education goals as part of the United Nations' Sustainable Development Goal 4 which is about ensuring inclusive and equitable quality education and promoting lifelong learning opportunities for all.[52] Based on a UNESCO's 2020 Global Education Monitoring Report about inclusion and education, they state that in all but the high-income countries in North America and Europe, only 18% of the poorest youth complete secondary school in relation to the richest youth and in at least 20 countries of which most is in sub-Saharan Africa very few poor rural young women complete secondary school.[53] They estimate that 258 million youth, which represents 17% of the global total, are not in school, where this number for sub-Saharan Africa is growing. This is the hard reality. With AI-assisted virtual teaching, in particular focused on coaching and assessing, a much wider reach can be achieved that also significantly impacts third world countries and remote locations for the better. As sub-Saharan Africa also has a high dropout rate, this has substantial negative consequences in terms of the loss of opportunity to develop African talent, and the cost to academic institutions, as well as social and economic development more broadly speaking. It is also clear that a concerted collaborative effort is needed by the African public sector, private sector, and academic stakeholders to avoid waste of resources in developing and implementing AI-driven technology solutions. From a private sector perspective, there is a number of EdTech startups that is working on transforming learning in Africa, such as The Student Hub in South Africa with their skills development and job creation platform, Brainshare with their e-learning platform in Uganda, M-Shule in Kenya that has an AI-driven personalized e-learning platform, Ubongo in Tanzania with their children's edutainment and educational television series for children ages 3-12, and Tuteria in Nigeria with a platform for online and offline tutoring.[54] The Student Hub, a company that I also invested in, provides an end-to-end data-driven platform for skills development and job creation with the goal to build Africa's largest vocational and technical skills marketplace.[55] The Student Hub's ERAOnline eLearning platform enables personalized education and can be further enhanced with AI technology as it evolves.[56]

At the other end of the spectrum, we have China which has started a mass experiment in AI education that is fueled by the enormous data that is available for AI ventures, the ferocious academic competition where academic performance is seen as a key determinant of the success in life, as well as the tax breaks and other incentives from government for AI startups to enhance the full education spectrum from learning to teacher training and school management. A recent paper *Artificial Intelligence and Education in China* provides an analysis of government policy and private sector enterprise and suggests that although the central government policy reserves a substantial role for education in their national AI strategy, the latter is more nuanced with differing regional networks, international corporate activity, and private sector utilizing the conducive political conditions to quickly develop innovative AI-driven educational solutions.[57] It also outlines some prominent private education companies that use AI and smart technology at scale such as Squirrel AI, New Oriental Group, and Tomorrow Advancing Life. Squirrel AI is for example one of the top AI-powered adaptive education companies in China that provides high quality personalized K-12 after school tutoring at scale at a cost-effective price to address the unequal distribution of education opportunities and the lack of personal attention in the typical classroom. With their impactful adaptive learning where their software responds in real-time to student's interactions through automated individual support and the strong emphasis on highly granular knowledge elements to identify gaps in learners' understanding accurately, the company has seen within 5 years enormous growth with 2000 learning centers in 200 cities with over 1 million registered students.[58] Tomorrow Advancing Life is another educational provider with core development goals of being smart technology-driven, talent-centered, and quality-focused, with many sub-brands such Speyyou's high-end K12 talent training and education platform, JZB as an internet education platform, and Edstars as an entrepreneur online education service platform.[59] One of their solutions is an AI language teaching system that has by the end of 2019 already covered 252 teaching locations, 72 primary schools and 47 towns to improve the proficiency and confidence of students and teachers speaking Mandarin.[60] There are also companies that specialize in test grading and homework correction such as 17zuoye that uses AI to streamline the grading process and homework distribution and Lingochamp's Liulishuo which is a English language learning intelligent tutor. Lingohamp is a sub-brand of LAIZ which provides an AI teacher to learn English language which is equipped with AI-driven adaptive learning technologies such as a speech recognition and scoring engine, a multi-granular speech evaluation engine and a real-time personalized feedback system. Along with well-established language learning pedagogies, the solution provides tailored pronunciation and grammar correction as well as a vocabulary notebook and courses that is supplemented by online study advisors.[61] Almost 60,000 schools in China, which represents about 25% of schools in the country, are also experimenting with AI technology to focus on understanding the meaning, style and logic of the text in academic essays in order to grade the work's overall quality and make recommendations in areas such as writing style, theme, and structure.[62] Although this technology is still in its infancy, the intent is to reduce the amount of time teachers spend on grading essays and avoid inconsistencies caused by human error. At some schools in China, AI has also been applied in a more controversial fashion via the use of face scanners to gain entry, handling of enrolments and registering attendance as well as monitoring students' attentiveness in classrooms via the use of cameras.[63] The surveillance of students has raised privacy issues with both parents and educators. Not only are there legitimate concerns about data privacy, but also the psychological effects on children being exposed to constant monitoring as well as issues with facial recognition not always working effectively. Even if a student's educational data, which might include sensitive personal data, is only being used to improve the effectiveness of personalized learning and teaching, there is a risk that this data might become public or exposed via a cyber-attack and then used to deny poorly performing student's employment, education, or other opportunities. It is clear that AI-enabled education needs to be carefully designed to ensure that we have a safe and protected environment which is in the best interest of students, families and society more broadly.

In *The Fourth Education Revolution*, Anthony Seldon asks if AI will liberate or infantilize humanity.[64] He calls Education the Cinderella of the AI story when compared to how AI is being applied in other sectors, but that is clearly about to change. The previous educational revolutions that started with learning within family units and tribes and followed by the coming of schools and universities when education was slowly being institutionalized to the printing and secularization of education for the masses about five hundred years ago, are now followed by AI-enabled education that is ushering in the fourth education revolution. Anthony further summarizes how AI is addressing the traditional limitations of the factory model of education through social mobility where quality of teaching is more democratized via personalized adaptive one-to-one learning and class sizes are less of a factor, learning by stage and not age, the freeing up of teacher's time with AI assisting with routine tasks, enriching and broadening the range of human intelligence and potential, and focusing more on individualization and uniqueness instead of homogenization which is an unintended by-product of the factory model. Other smart technology related benefits highlighted include making learning more enjoyable and challenging, ensuring the potential continuity of teachers via a personalized digital teacher through the school journey or even life, an enhanced preparation for the world of work, encouraging lifelong learning, and the increasing stimulation for teachers by reducing repetitive and routine tasks and letting them focus on more creative, strategic and human-centric aspects and inspiring students with learning and living better lives. Although the opportunities with AI-enabled education are immense with lifelong value, the depth of learning, quality of life (instead of quantity), and addressing the democratic shortfall, there are also clear risks being introduced which need to be addressed. These include that education can become narrower and more specialized at an earlier age, the loss of social contact, teachers losing control over their students (especially younger learners where it is more needed), de-professionalization of the teacher role, the potential increase in social immobility with the most advanced forms of AI only available to those that can afford that (which goes against democratizing AI-enabled education), infantilization of students, risk of AI controlling large parts of human knowledge, risk of boredom, unhealthy lifestyles and an increase in mental health issues, privacy and ethical concerns, and a potential erosion of values.[65]

In discussing the future of AI in schools, Anthony highlights some innovative schools in the US and India which includes the AltSchools where students can organize their own learning in consultation with teachers, the Summit public schools that focuses on personalized learning, the School of One that allows each learner to use an individualized adaptive learning system to learn at their own pace, Khan Lab School (an allied development of Khan Academy and its online tutorials) that allow each student to pursue their own learning objectives on a personalized learning platform, and the Riverbend School in India that focuses on developing personal fulfilment and happiness of its students within innovative village-like physical surroundings that support learning using state-of-the-art smart technology. I specifically like his vision for smart schools of the future that are smaller in size and rooted in local communities and aims to fully develop a student's aptitudes using personalized AI-driven learning software with individualized learning plans, supported by both human and AI-powered teaching assistants, encourages arts, physical activity and quiet reflection, and embraces an educational philosophy that promotes wellbeing, creativity, curiosity, blossoming, and formation of individual character. This is also in line with the massive transformative purpose for humanity and associated goals that I'm proposing later in this book. It is also clear that universities of the future will be completely transformed by AI-driven digitization, the evolutions and better understanding of learning and the brain, and the impact of AI and automation on jobs. Universities will need to ensure that twenty first century skills such as creativity, social intelligence, ethics and moral choice and dexterity also get proper attention. It also needs to address problems such as affordability, maintaining quality education, teaching quality and student demands, lifelong education, being sidestepped by employers offering in-service education, maintaining internationalism, and declining mental health.[66] Anthony Seldon also segmented the types of universities of the future into global (driven by the elite universities across the world), national, regional, local, professional (more focused on professions and services), and digital (ones with no physical presence). Going forward we are likely to see the traditional lectures disappear, more virtual university collaboration, and virtual degrees or even nanodegrees (as we have seen from Udacity)[67]. Another interesting development is the introduction of the "Woolf University" that makes use of blockchain technology to reliably record academic credits and regulate contracts and payments and allows students to choose their professor and study personalized courses in online fashion with faculty trained at some of the world's leading institutions.[68] Smart universities of the future will likely rely heavily on AI-powered teaching and learning, be more interdisciplinary in nature from both learning and research perspective, cater for all ages from a lifelong and life-wide learning perspective, focus more on twenty first century skills, be more relevant with respect to understanding and studying real human and global concerns, and have a strong emphasis on creativity, curiosity, positive health, wellbeing, and nurturing the mind and body.

AI-powered Personalized Precision Healthcare

It is clear that AI's impact on the healthcare industry has enormous potential. AI-infused healthcare digitization and instrumentation makes it possible to draw inferences, get insights and recognize patterns in massive volumes of patient histories, electronic health records, healthcare device data, medical images, epidemiological statistical data, and other healthcare related data. This capability not only helps healthcare providers to better monitor or diagnose patients remotely, improve their diagnosis, tailor personalized treatments, and develop precision medicine solutions, but also to reduce costs with respect to chronic diseases which account for a large share of healthcare budgets. AI can also assist to better forecast and understand the spread of diseases, its distribution, as well as the factors and patterns of disease and health conditions in specified populations. Some of the key trends identified in Accenture's *Digital Health Technology Vision 2020* report includes the use of smart technologies such as AI, smart devices, and robots, as well as digital patient experience and innovation. According to their survey, 85% of health executives have the opinion that technology has become an inseparable part of life and human experience, whereas 70% of global consumers concur and expect it to have a prominent impact on their lives over the next three years.[69] In another study, most healthcare consumers seem six to seven times more positive about AI's beneficial impact on society and their personal lives.[70] Not only is AI-powered applications increasing access to care, but there is also an overall expectation that healthcare consumers want to have a personalized digital experience and be able to choose their own healthcare journey. They are also concerned about data privacy, security, how their data is being used and commercial tracking of data that is linked to their behaviors, interests, locations, and online activities. When data is compromised, healthcare organizations and companies are not only losing money (every healthcare record that is breached costs approximately $355), but also lose the trust of the consumer.[71] Almost 70% of healthcare organizations are piloting or adopting AI and also working on contextualized collaborative use cases for a blended workforce with human and AI elements. As there is a rising imbalance between patients and the healthcare workforce, AI can help to address the unmet clinical demand over the period until 2026, which has been estimated to be at least 20%.[72] In a separate study published by Otum, the health services arm of UnitedHealth Group, it was find that half of healthcare organizations expect AI to deliver positive return on investment within three years of deployment.[73] Most health executives also believe that the stakes for innovation are very high with some disruptive scientific advancements, maturing digital technology being accessible and commoditized, and smart technologies such as AI, blockchain, augmented and virtual reality and quantum computing becoming available for use. As healthcare is also a highly regulated industry, having access to the appropriate data sets which is key for AI deployment can also hamper the speed at which healthcare companies can experiment with AI-driven solutions. That said, there are also exceptional opportunities to innovate with AI-driven scalable platform business models similar to what we have seen in other consumer-facing business sectors, where for example significant value can be unlocked from healthcare and other related data to improve healthcare outcomes and smart technology used to mediate between multiple parties even if the assets such as healthcare professionals and hospitals are not owned by the health system. For healthcare providers to realize this potential, they need to digitize their operations, ensure rapid access to all available internal and external data, invest in smart technology expertise and computing and data infrastructure, and make substantial changes to how they do business.

The McKinsey Global Institute estimates that in the US alone AI-powered solutions can potentially save $300 billion a year in health care service cost.[74] They also reported that AI-driven preventive care and the decrease of non-elective hospital admissions in the UK can save £3.3 billion per year. One way of saving costs is for healthcare providers to offer AI-driven preventative care solutions that incorporate forecasting and analysis of the spread of diseases and the identification of high-risk patient groups to help hospital administrators optimize inventory levels, set budgets, improve the allocation and scheduling of staff, and get better reimbursement rates for insurance. According to Grand Review Research, the global AI in healthcare market size is expected to reach approximately $31 billion by 2025 (growing at a compound annual growth rate of 41.5%) and driven by an increased demand to reduce healthcare costs, a proliferation of health-related sensors and devices, a significant increase in AI-driven applications, a reduction in hardware costs and improvement in computing power, and an increase in the adoption of precision medicine.[75] Markets and Markets are slightly more bullish and projects $45 billion in 2026 from a base of approximately $5 billion in 2020 with apart from the mentioned major market growth factors, also emphasizes the increasing volume of healthcare data, the growth in cross-industry collaborations and partnerships, the increasing imbalance between healthcare workforce and consumers, and the use of AI to assist pharmaceutical and biotechnology companies to fast track vaccine and drug development processes for the COVID-19 pandemic.[76] Some of the specific applications include AI-driven healthcare informatics solutions, medical imaging, disease diagnostics and treatment, drug discovery, and healthcare monitoring solutions. Goldman Sachs Global Investment Research estimates that the use of AI can significantly enhance and reduce the risk in the drug discovery and development process in a substantial way by increasing efficiencies worth more than $28bn per year globally and removing $26bn per year in costs.[77] In the same report they claim that reducing the risk of expensive phase 3 trials by 50% could generate billions of dollars in savings and returns on the more than $90 billion that are currently being spent in research and development across some of the largest pharmaceutical companies in the world. Research and Markets reported that the global electronic health records market is forecasted to grow from approximately $30 billion in 2020 to an estimated $40 billion by 2025, driven by smart technology based healthcare solutions, the increasing demand for centralization and streamlining of electronic healthcare systems, the growth in government funding and expenditure for the development of healthcare information technology solutions, and an increasing awareness about the use and importance of electronic health records.[78] The McKinsey Global Institute estimates that AI-enabled healthcare-related operational efficiencies could represent up to 2% of GDP savings in developed countries and that AI-driven productivity for registered nurses can be improved by 40-50% when supported by AI software.[79]

In another AI in Healthcare report by Accenture, AI is described as healthcare's new nervous system or operating system with the market expected to grow to almost $7 billion in 2021 and AI applications contributing to potential annual cost savings of $150 billion by 2026 in the US healthcare industry alone.[80] Some of the top AI applications that they list that contribute to these savings include robot-assisted surgery, virtual nursing assistants, administrative workflow assistance, fraud detection, dosage error reduction, connected machines, clinical trial participant identifier, preliminary diagnosis, automated image diagnosis, and cybersecurity. AI-driven healthcare solutions can add significant value in the form of diagnostic tools that can quickly identify diseases with greater accuracy using historical medical data and patient records, enhanced treatment plans, and improved health insurance. By enriching electronic health records further with real-time data from mobile and health-related devices, AI solutions can be developed to better monitor a patient's health remotely and proactively detect possible diseases. Medical professionals are seeing how AI solutions can be reliable and helpful in areas such as robotic surgery for routine steps in simple procedures like laser eye surgery and hair transplants; image analysis to help them examine X-rays, retina scans, and other images; autonomous diagnostic devices that conduct simple medical tests without human assistance; genetic analysis to draw insights from genome scans; pathology to analyze biopsy samples; clinical decision support in hospitals to predict septic shock; virtual nursing applications can check on patients between office visits and provide automatic alerts to physicians; medical administration applications that increase efficiency in tasks like billing and insurance claims; virtual interactive agents can help to improve patient experience and waiting time by for example handling registration and automatic referral to appropriate healthcare professionals; and mental health applications to monitor depression by mining mobile phone and social media data.[81] Other AI applications include reducing hospitalization and treatment costs through insights from population health analysis and anomaly detection on clinical and medical claims data. Healthcare costs can also be significantly reduced by mining patients' medical histories as well as environmental and lifestyle factors to identify people at risk of an illness and steer them to proactive preventive care programs to manage their wellness better. The same holds for patients with chronic lifestyle diseases that can be better managed through personalized AI-driven chronic disease managed care solutions that involve personalized treatment plans to improve therapy efficiency by customizing treatment to specific patients' needs and medical conditions. These types of solutions also help to forecast patient behavior and disease likelihoods which in turn can also help to optimize hospital and clinical operations, inventory, and staffing schedules.

Some of the major companies in the AI and healthcare market includes especially those from the United States such as IBM, General Electric, Johnson & Johnson, Google, Microsoft, AWS, General Vision, NVIDIA, and Medtronic, whereas some examples from Europe include Siemens and Koninklijke Philips N.V. There has also been an increase in cross-industry collaborations such as Microsoft's partnership with Apollo Hospitals in India to focus on predicting cardiac diseases risk and treatment planning. Other examples include GNS Healthcare's partnership with Alliance and Amgen for clinical trials in oncology (to improve treatment responses in metastatic colorectal cancer) and IBM Watson for clinical trial matching that are used by the Mayo Clinic in lung, breast, and gastrointestinal cancer clinical trials.

IBM Watson Health provides AI-driven healthcare solutions across the healthcare ecosystem for healthcare providers to accelerate AI-driven digital transformation, life sciences to improve clinical development research and increase treatment value with differentiated solutions, healthcare payers to assist health plans and accelerate member health change, employers to drive more effective employee benefits management, and governments to deliver human-centric care through insights to improve lives.[82] IBM has been at the forefront of developing AI healthcare systems over the last decade and has twelve research laboratories dedicated to its AI-driven initiatives with more than 1400 patents in this field.[83] Although AI applications in healthcare show tremendous promise, it must also be said that IBM Watson's overpromise and under delivery on AI-driven healthcare serves as an example of how difficult it can be to make AI work for real-world healthcare related applications along with the evolving nature and maturity levels of the state-of-the-art in AI (which is improving rapidly). For example, although IBM has early on showed promise with IBM Watson's application in cancer diagnosis where the treatment plans recommended matched those of the patient's oncologists for 99% of cases reviewed, the hard reality was that the accuracy was much lower in other studies where the concordance in Thailand, India and South Korea was respectively 83%, 73% and 49%.[84] Although high accuracy was obtained for clear concepts such as diagnosis, the scores were lower for time-dependent information such as therapy timeline. Things are further complicated by only allowing "evidence based" recommendations that are linked to outcomes of studies published in medical literature and official medical guidelines. Completely automated diagnosis and treatment advice is likely to go through a transitional period before becoming commonplace as rapid access to multiple data sources, strong regulatory requirements, and patient acceptance are all issues that need to be addressed. Since IBM Watson entered the healthcare industry almost a decade ago, many partnerships have been developed to work on applications for doctors, institutions and consumers such as a clinical-decision support, genomic-analysis for cancer, clinical trial matching, personalized diabetes management, managing chronic conditions, personalized medical advice, drug-development support, drug-safety analysis, personalized nutrition advice during pregnancy, workplace health, and personalized athletic coaching. Although there seems to be not many commercial products yet, this work has already led to valuable research in preparation for real-world applications. For example, IBM Watson applications in genomics that are developed in partnership with universities such as Yale and North Carolina seem to show promise. The scientific evidence outlined in a 2020 report from IBM Watson's health in oncology research also shows progress with AI applications in key studies with respect to clinical decision support, clinical trials, and genomics.[85]

The Cleveland Clinic has recently created an AI Innovation Center focused on applying machine learning to healthcare and will leverage data from more than one million Cleveland Clinic patients to build predictive models for inpatient mortality risk, projected length of stay, and risk of readmission as well as precision medicine such as enhancing cancer detection through AI-driven imaging analytics and predicting patient responses.[86] A few years ago they entered into a 5-year partnership agreement with IBM to use IBM Watson to better capture the value of data and enhance the patient care across their regional hospitals and full service family health centers with data-driven personalized healthcare and population health management.[87] IBM Watson Health has also partnered with Vanderbilt University Medical Center and Brigham and Women's Hospital in a ten-year $50 million collaboration to leverage AI for patient safety and precision medicine.[88] Another example of an academic institution and health system collaboration is UCI Health System that partnered with the University of California, Irvine to launch the UCI Center for Artificial Intelligence in Diagnostic Medicine. The center's focus is on improving diagnostic and treatment planning for cancer by leveraging AI strategies and developing and deploying a brain hemorrhage detection tool for use in the emergency care environment.[89] Johns Hopkins Hospital recently announced a 5-year partnership with Microsoft to leverage their AI and analytics tools for accelerated precision medicine discoveries. To support Johns Hopkins Medicine's inHealth program, they have launched 16 Precision Medicine Centers of Excellence and plan to extend this to 50 centers within the next five years where researchers are working toward breakthroughs across several diseases such as multiple sclerosis and prostate cancer.[90] GE Healthcare's AI-enabled software was also successfully used at Johns Hopkins Hospital to prioritized hospital activity to ensure a faster, more positive patient experience and has seen a 60% improvement in its ability to admit patients and a 21% increase in patient discharges before noon.[91]

GE Healthcare's AI platform, which is called Edison, is designed to help healthcare providers to improve patient outcomes, increase access to care, and operate more efficiently. It can integrate and assimilate data from disparate sources, apply AI-powered analytics to generate insights, and be securely deployed via Edison HealthLink, cloud, or directly onto smart devices.[92] Some example Edison applications include the AI-powered chest X-ray analysis suite, called the Critical Care Suite, that helps radiologists prioritize cases involving collapsed lungs by automatically analyzes images upon acquisition and for critical findings produce triage notifications that are sent directly to picture archiving and communication systems; TrueFidelity CT Images which use deep-learning image reconstruction to generate images with deep detail, true texture, and high fidelity for each CT scan; AIR Recon DL which is a deep-learning application designed to improve signal-to-noise and image sharpness and enabling shorter scan times; Breast Assistant which automatically provides an AI-based quantitative risk assessment that aligns to a breast imaging reporting and data system category; AFI on Vivid products which leverages AI-enabled view recognition to automatically select optimal views and accurately assess left ventricular wall motion; Embo ASSIST which is a 3D visualization software solution designed to help clinicians simulate injections dynamically and thus perform embolization procedures with confidence; and Edison Open AI Orchestrator which simplifies the selection, deployment, and usage of AI in imaging workflows at scale.[93] As part of the Edison Developer program, GE Healthcare is currently working with a number of AI services and solutions companies, including Arterys, Koios Medical, Volpara, iCAD, and MaxQ AI to create products for healthcare systems via Edison.[94] The Breast Assistant mentioned above is one such product developed by Koios Medical that uses AI to provide clinical decision support for healthcare workers when using ultrasound to detect and diagnose cancer.[95] The application has also been integrated into GE Healthcare's LOGIQ E10 ultrasound system. GE Healthcare and Arterys have extended cardiac assessment beyond the anatomy with ViosWorks 4D Flow that provides a comprehensive solution that captures all 7 dimensions of information in a cardiovascular scan in 10 minutes or less with data being analyzed with cloud-based and deep learning-enabled ViosWorks analysis.[96]

According to Johnson & Johnson they ensure that data science impacts every function across their enterprise and have made AI-related investments in two key areas for them, which includes drug development and robotic surgery. Their drug development investments include the Quickfire emerging tech startup challenge as well as the Machine Learning Ledger Orchestration for Drug Discovery (Mellody) project which connects data from some of the largest pharmaceutical companies to support drug discovery.[97] The others include Amgen, Astellas, AstraZeneca, Bayer, Boehringer Ingelheim, GSK, Merck, Novartis and Servier. Johnson & Johnson's recent robotic surgery investments include Verb Surgical with their AI-powered digital surgery platform and Auris Health that diagnose and treat lung cancer via their Monarch platform that integrates robotics, micro-instrumentation, endoscope design, sensing, and data science.[98] They have also invested in Cara Cara that specializes in digital therapeutic solutions for life-interrupting digestive diseases.[99] Janssen Research and Development, which is part of Johnson & Johnson, claim that they have developed an AI-driven method that helps to make the drug discovery process up to 250 times more efficient and faster compared to traditional methods.[100]

Google Health, which now also includes Google DeepMind's health division, is using AI across a spectrum of healthcare use cases such as diagnosing cancer, predicting patient outcomes, preventing blindness, and improving patient care.[101] On the research and development side they are using state-of-the-art machine learning to improve the accuracy of genomic analysis with their DeepVariant solution, detect deficient coverage in colonoscopy screenings, explore faster screenings with fewer tests, discover small molecule chemical probes for biological research, and generate diverse synthetic medical image data for training machine learning models.[102] Google DeepMind has developed an early warning AI-driven system to predict the progression of a retinal disease called age-related macular degeneration which is the most common cause of blindness in the developed world. Early identification of a more serious form of this disease which can cause rapid blindness can provide a critical window to target therapeutic solutions to help prevent loss of sight. The AI system which uses two deep learning models, the one focused on segmented retinal scans to help pick-up on anatomical indicators and the other one on raw retina scans to identify subtle changes are combined to calculate the risk of progression of this disease within a 6-month period. In one study the system successfully identified one third of scans that did go on to progress within 6 months.[103]

The Mayo Clinic is well positioned to advance AI applications in healthcare given their huge database of historical ECGs, genomes, microbiomes, diagnostic images, and other test results as well as their collaborative research involving medical doctors, engineers, and scientists in delivering impactful AI solutions to improve clinical care in cardiovascular medicine, neurology, oncology and radiology. Some example cardiovascular use cases include cutting the time to diagnosis by fast tracking the analysis of CT scans of stroke patients, AI-guided ECGs to detect faulty heart rhythms before any symptoms appear, predicting risk early in conditions such as embolic stroke, monitoring the heart and detecting arrhythmia in smart clothing projects, and developing AI technology compatible with smartphones and high-tech stethoscopes.[104] The Mayo Clinic and Google have recently embarked on a 10-year partnership to give Mayo Clinic access to Google's AI-powered analytics and advanced cloud computing infrastructure where the Google Cloud will securely store the Mayo health system's data to enable data scientists to work with healthcare domain experts and researchers in using AI to solve a variety of complex health challenges.[105]

Siemens Healthineers, which has been spun out of Siemens, is another major healthcare solutions provider that leverages AI extensively to transform healthcare delivery, enhance patient experience and advance the state-of-the-art in precision medicine with a portfolio of more than 45 AI-enabled solutions that focuses on standardizing and automating workflows and providing personalized complex diagnostics.[106] The current AI-supported systems adds value through general assistance as well as partial and conditional automation (with high and full automation to follow in the future) and consumes data types that include those from scanners or instruments, reporting or reading guidance, patients and patient cohorts. Some of these solutions include AI-Pathway Companion that assists with tailored and standardized diagnosis and treatment decisions along evidence-based disease-specific care pathways using data integration, augmented intelligence, and insights from cohort analytics. Another one is AI-Rad Companion which is a cloud-based AI-enabled augmented workflow solution that automatically performs measurements and produces multi-modal clinical images and reports.[107] Siemens Healthineers has also recently enhanced their X-ray diagnostics solutions with the introduction of the AI-Rad Companion Chest X-ray solution that makes use of AI-enabled software that assists with clinical decision making on upright thorax images as well as Ysio X.pree which they claim is the world's first AI-powered X-ray system that assist radiologists by optimizing the daily routine of image acquisition in radiography.[108] The latter solution minimizes radiation exposure by only focusing on the relevant area which is made possible by an AI-based algorithm using live images from a 3D camera that automatically detects the area, say for example the thorax, to acquire images containing all the required information. Other examples of AI-powered solutions include the AI-Rad Companion Brain MR for morphometry analysis and AI-Rad Companion MR for biopsy support.[109] These AI-enabled software assistants help to automate routine tasks for radiologists while performing magnetic resonance imaging examinations of brain and prostate, by for example automatically identifying segments on the MRI images and comparing the results to relevant data in a normative morphometric reference database.

AI-powered automation has the potential to increase healthcare productivity by relieving healthcare professionals of routine activities, optimizing the operations, staffing schedules and inventories of healthcare providers, automating diagnoses, and making them faster and more accurate, and conducting simple medical tests without human assistance. AI-driven proactive healthcare services typically make use of a variety of data sources such as scans, images, videos, laboratory diagnostics and healthcare professional transcripts. The AI-based analysis can drive reports and alerts for cardiac, schizophrenia, diabetic, pulmonary, oncology, and various other healthcare watch lists. The AI-based analysis typically involves steps such as entity extraction, semantic analytics, and video analytics, followed by filtering and organizing, removing the noise from unstructured data, stemming, exploring linkages and correlation of terms, and finally extracting themes and keywords, matching, and theme generation. AI-driven real-time healthcare services use a combination of patient, specialist, and provider data sources to do location-aware analytics and help coordinate the location-aware based services with respect to surgery, special wards, etc. AI can also help to enhance the patient experience at hospitals and clinics with greater efficiency, an improved patient flow, and a more personal touch.

Olive's AI-enabled workforce solution helps to make healthcare more cost-effective and efficient by assisting healthcare employees to optimize workflows and automate repetitive tasks such as migrating data, processing invoices, managing inventory, reporting, checking eligibility, and resolving claims.[110] This cloud-based AI-as-a-service solution integrates with a hospital's existing software infrastructure, helps hospitals to eliminate wasteful spend and increase revenue and capacity. They also provide a centralized, real-time, easily accessible visualization tool to give visibility into the value and performance of Olive's automations. Olive also has an AI workforce intelligence solution called Deep Purple that enables healthcare providers to improve decision making and elevate performance by applying expansive industry-wide learning across healthcare.[111] US-based Qventus provides a healthcare automation platform that helps to optimize hospital operations such as to automate and prioritize patient safety, decrease hospital length of stay, track hospital waiting times, eliminate excess days, and chart the faster ambulance routes.[112] The platform incorporates AI, behavioral science and data science to deliver a closed-loop system for automating patient flow by identifying issues in real-time, retrospectively or those in the future, manage accountability to ensure continuous improvement, and orchestrating actions to help frontline teams know what to do. Qventus patient flow solutions incorporate management best-practices, operational processes, predefined AI models, and software templates to address the highest priority requirements across health systems and hospitals. CloudMedX has an AI-driven approach called Aligned Intelligence that uses a deep learning platform as an intuitive extension of the way healthcare providers, payers and even patients collaborate and generate insights for improving patient journeys throughout the healthcare system.[113] They collect and convert disparate data such as patient data, clinical history and payment information into holistic and actionable insights to assist hospitals and clinics by using predictive analytics to intervene at key moments in the patient care experience. CloudMedX also has an AI-powered assistant called Ask Sophie to help people seamlessly navigate their healthcare journey by uploading their medical data and evaluating their symptoms. Babylon provides an AI-driven healthcare chatbot that interacts with patients in a personalized way checking overall health and identifying risk factors, reviewing a patient's symptoms and making recommendations with respect to either a virtual check-in or a face-to-face appointment with a healthcare professional.[114] They have partnered with Canada's Telus Health, corporates such as Prudential as well as governmental organizations such as the Rwandan government and the UK's National Health Service.

Some relevant use cases for deploying AI solutions in the healthcare and life sciences sector includes health-insurance and claims related fraud detection, campaign and sales program optimization, brand and reputation management, patient care quality and program analysis, drug discovery and development analysis, research and development, and real-time diagnostic data analysis. Some of the business needs of medical scheme providers where AI applications can make an impact includes growth and retention of medical scheme members, business process automation, value chain optimization through integrating and optimizing processes with suppliers, and reduction in fraud waste and abuse with respect to claims and payments. In one use case a major medical scheme administrator realized that they had a significant problem in terms of fraud amongst their schemes. It was estimated that around 10% of all contributions were lost due to fraudulent activity by service providers and members. Some data mining highlighted significant fraud and abuse across the three schemes. This was after the existing fraud detection had been "passed". The three schemes represent approximately 15% of the total members of this administrator. If the results are extrapolated the outcome is clearly much more significant. In another one of Cortex Logic's AI-driven solutions use cases, a medical scheme administrator required a hospital benefits management solution to manage risk and decrease costs before authorization and update this after authorization. The desired outcome was exception management that intervenes on the right cases at the right time in the right manner. The AI-driven solution combined multiple supervised and unsupervised machine learning models to generate a risk assessment score to identify risky and anomalous cases before authorization. The supervised models focused on predicting length of hospital stay as well as cost associated with such a hospital stay, whereas the unsupervised models were predominately used for anomaly detection. The AI risk scoring system provides real-time information for exception management decision making and enables significant cost savings through fraud, waste, and abuse prevention.

Moving more away from a 'sick care' system, AI is working on transforming a rather reactionary industry into a proactive and preventative one.[115] Not only will this save the healthcare industry untold fortunes, but it will save countless lives and provide access to professional diagnoses that used to require consultations, being checked in to hospitals, blood tests, etc. This is a long and expensive process for those who can afford it and an often-impossible process for those who cannot - where patients often must walk miles in rain or sun or cold, then take a bus, then a taxi and maybe another taxi, if they have not run out of money. This is just getting there. Then begins a process of sometimes spending days in a hospital waiting room, likely more than once, and then months to see a specialist. The state of healthcare facilities in Africa is one where people are more than sometimes made sicker instead of better, hygiene is atrocious and nursing staff are few and often without acceptable training (a few months, maybe). Through AI, early diagnosis of many diseases is now possible. Some of which will soon be available from an instrument attached to our smartphones and an app to support it. It then sends the diagnosis to medical professionals who are immediately empowered to treat us.[116] This kind of early detection, prevention and early treatment will not only free up hospital and doctors' time, but will save lives and protect many from the now public hospital experience (or at least part of it). There is also integration of other AI-powered systems that, once early detection has been made, plot therapy needs, recommend treatments, and even suggest clinical trials.[117] With one blood test, it is also now possible (thanks to AI) to quickly know the presence, type, and stage of cancer for fast and accurate treatment. Moreso, with diseases that have historically had unstable, or no real treatments are now able to be treated by using AI to decipher molecular processes. This can pair treatments with patients, treat and cure patients and ensure that each patient is receiving the right treatment for their unique genetic make-up.[118] With fewer people sick, with people less sick and sick for less time, the only people who may not benefit are traditional pharmaceutical conglomerates (big pharma) who could lose a lot of business if fewer people relied on their medicine or needed it for less time. For those pharmaceutical companies working with AI and working to make better for the sake of the people and not their own pockets, amazing and innovative discoveries could be made. Big pharma is already investing in AI that could drastically decrease the time it takes to invent and perfect cures to current and new diseases.[119] However, with prevention and early detection being a stone's throw away, perhaps expanding the focus to prevention is where big pharma should be headed, too.

AI can be used to efficiently diagnose and reduce error. For example, PathAI in the US has an AI-powered solution to assist pathologists in making more accurate diagnoses with a focus on reducing error in cancer diagnosis and developing methods for personalized medical treatment.[120] AI scientists at Memorial Sloan Kettering Cancer Centre have recently achieved a milestone in the use of deep learning in pathology with a study analyzing more than 44,000 digitized glass slide images from more than 15,000 people with cancer, where the model identifies more than 98% of the cancer-containing biopsies and allow pathologists to exclude 65–75% of slides while retaining 100% sensitivity.[121] This speeds up the process of analyzing samples substantially and enables pathologists to focus their attention on the most relevant slides and informative portions of the biopsies. Oncora Medical is focused on improving cancer outcomes with precision radiation oncology and provides a software platform that allows for better collection and application of real-world data for all healthcare related decisions, simplify workflows, measure quality, and streamline operations to improve care and optimize treatment. In a recent machine learning case study they have demonstrated the prediction of unplanned hospitalization after radiation where the AI models successfully identified gastrointestinal cancer patients undergoing radiotherapy who are at low versus high risk of 30-day unplanned hospitalization.[122] In another study where they have collaborated with MD Anderson researchers they have predicted head and neck cancer treatment toxicities by applying machine learning to a dataset that includes demographics, tumor characteristics, treatment and outcomes.[123] Enlitic helps to streamline radiology diagnoses through their deep learning platform that can analyze unstructured medical data such as radiology images, electrocardiogram records, blood tests, genomics, and patient medical history to give doctors better insight into a patient's real-time needs by detecting rare and subtle findings, providing measurements and descriptions, automating longitudinal analysis, and generating quality assessment reports.[124] Freenome provides an AI-driven multi-omics platform along with accurate blood tests that enables early cancer detection by analyzing fragments of DNA, RNA, proteins, and other biomarkers circulating in blood plasma, decoding complex patterns associated with the body's response to specific tumor types, and integrating actionable insights into health systems to operationalize a feedback loop between care and science.[125]

AI-enhanced microscopes can be used by healthcare professionals to scan for harmful bacteria such as *E. coli*, *Staphylococcus* and *Streptococcus* species in blood samples at a faster rate than is possible using manual scanning. At Harvard University's Beth Israel Deaconess Medical Center, they have used 25,000 images of blood samples to generate 100,000 training images to train machine learning models how to classify these images into rod-shaped, round clusters and round chains categories which correspond to the above-mentioned bacteria species. The training and test accuracies to identify and predict these harmful bacteria in blood were respectively 95% and 93%.[126] Israel-based Zebra Medical Vision provides radiologists with medical image diagnoses by automatically analyzing imaging scans from various modalities for several different clinical findings using their AI-powered imaging analytics engine which outputs results in a timely manner and full synergy with radiology workflow. Their system can for example uncover brain, lung, liver, cardiovascular and bone disease in computerized tomography scans, 40 different conditions in X-rays scans, and breast cancer in 2D mammograms and alert patients at high risk of cardiovascular, lung, bone, and other diseases to help facilitate preventative care programs as well as proper risk adjustments and allocation.[127]

US-based Buoy Health provides an AI-based symptom and cure checker that diagnoses and treats illness through a chatbot that listens to a patient's symptoms and health issues, guides the patient to the best care option based on their condition, follow-up on progress, and also connects the patient to others with similar symptoms.[128] With mental health conditions and substance use rising, even more so amid the Covid-19 pandemic, digital therapeutic solutions have gained traction to help address this problem.[129] A machine learning solution was recently demonstrated by researchers from Harvard and Vermont universities that can diagnose depression with 70% accuracy based on images posted and filter functions used on Instagram.[130] In another example, Woebot is an AI-powered personalized mental health chatbot that identifies user's symptoms and uses clinically-validated psychological interventions to help reduce symptoms of anxiety and depression.[131]

As the development of new drugs is estimated to cost $2.6 billion and almost 90% of the candidate therapies fail between the first phase trials and regulatory approval, AI-based solutions are being used to make the development of these pharmaceutical treatments quicker, efficient, and more cost-effective.[132] US-based BioXcel Therapeutics is a clinical-stage biopharmaceutical company that provides AI-based drug development across immuno-oncology and neuroscience. For example, the two most advanced clinical development programs in their product pipeline involve new medicine for the acute treatment of agitation resulting from neuropsychiatric disorders and another for the treatment of a rare form of prostate cancer and for treatment of pancreatic cancer in combination with other immuno-oncology agents.[133]

Given that clinical trials typically cost billions of dollars and take years in terms of time commitment with only a small percentage of drugs getting approval, non-adherence of clinical trial participants that never take the drug or administer it at wrong times or doses are a major problem. AiCure improves medication adherence via an AI-driven solution that engage, record outcomes, support and provide meaningful behavioral insights to patients via their smartphones and with AiCure Patient Connect ensures that trial participants are taking the right medication at the right dosage while also capturing valuable behavioral and endpoint data to help advance clinical trials for potential treatments.[134] In order to improve health outcomes and lower treatment costs, Cognizant has developed an AI-based solution that identifies potential drug-seeking behavior that uses text analytics and machine learning to generate system alerts for doctors during patients' visits when a pattern of at-risk behavior is identified where they can then intercede with patients in real time and take corrective actions.[135]

BERG is a clinical-stage, AI-powered biotechnology company in the US that fast-tracks clinical identification of promising therapeutic targets to treat oncology, neurology, and rare diseases. The Interrogative Biology platform maps diseases to accelerate the discovery and development of treatments, more effective precision treatments for individuals as well as a reduction in costs to healthcare systems.[136] Backed by Google, Tencent and Sequoia Capital, XtalPi's AI-enabled ID4 drug discovery platform accelerates the prediction of the chemical and pharmaceutical properties of small-molecule candidates for drug design and development. They specifically focus on crystal structure prediction and process development, solid-state screening and evaluation, solid state testing and analysis, small molecule drug design as well as antibody and peptide research and development collaboration.[137] Atomwise uses their convolution neural network driven solution called AtomNet to predict bioactivity and chemical interactions as well as identify patient characteristics for clinical trials. As most of the human genome of approximately 20 thousand genes does not have an approved drug (only about 750 have FDA-approved drugs with 2-3 thousand genes have drugs under development), AI can be utilized to help unlock drug targets. With AtomNet, they already have 14 thousand genes that are screenable without complete structural data, whereas 4 thousand genes with disease evidence can be targeted to discover new therapies for any disease.[138] They claimed that AtomNet can screen more than 16 billion synthesizable molecules against biological targets in less than 2 days and then ship synthesized compounds for in-lab screening within 2-3 weeks. Some of the success stories include new therapies and drug candidates for multiple sclerosis, Ebola, Parkinson's disease, pediatric cancer, and age-related macular degeneration. Atomwise has also recently partnered with GC Pharma to discover oral therapies to help treat people with hemophilia.[139]

Canada-based Deep Genomics provides an AI-powered drug discovery platform to help researchers find candidates for developmental drugs related to neuromuscular and neurodegenerative disorders.[140] They have recently announced the industry's first AI-discovered therapeutic candidate with the identification of a novel treatment target and corresponding drug candidate for Wilson disease, which is a rare and potentially life-threatening genetic disorder.[141] Their AI platform is also used in project Saturn to analyze over 69 billion molecules against 1 million targets in computer simulation to generate a library of 1000 compounds that are experimentally verified to control cell biology along key pathways, which in turn can help researchers to rapidly unlock better therapies.[142] The UK-based Benevolent have a drug discovery platform with multiple AI components that empowers scientists to decipher the vast and complex code underlying human biology and find new ways to treat disease.[143] The platform pulls data from structured and unstructured biomedical sources and curates this knowledge in a knowledge graph that is therapeutic area agnostic via a data architecture that enables synergies across the drug discovery and development process. The knowledge graph extracts and contextualizes the relevant information and is made up of a huge number of AI curated relationships between diseases, genes, and drugs. Benevolent's relation inference AI models help predict potential disease targets to identify proteins that are differentially expressed in healthy and diseased cells. For precision medicine applications, their machine learning models enable researchers to determine the correct mechanism to modulate and identify patient endotypes most likely to respond to treatment.

US-based Tempus is providing data-driven precision medicine solutions by mining a very large collection of clinical and molecular data in order to enable healthcare professionals to make real-time, data-driven decisions to deliver personalized healthcare treatments to patients based on their unique molecular profiles.[144] Tempus' genomic tests analyze DNA, RNA, and proteomic data to understand a patient's tumor at the molecular level in order to identify personalized treatment options for a patient. Their platform can ingest and organize unstructured data such as clinical notes, radiology scans, pathology images, and lab reports to capture therapeutic, phenotypic, and outcomes data to understand the clinical context for each patient case. KenSci's AI platform for digital health and healthcare solutions assist health organizations to improve health outcomes and patient care experiences and predict hospital risks by transforming healthcare data to real-time insights and accelerate their AI and business intelligence initiatives to help unlock return on investment.[145] Proscia provides an AI-enabled software platform for digital and computational pathology called Concentriq that can integrate into the technology infrastructure of anatomic pathology labs and powers image-based research to accelerate drug discovery as well as its intelligent image-based workflow application that automates time-consuming repetitive tasks and delivers actionable insights into laboratory performance which drives productivity and higher quality across laboratory operations.[146] During the COVID-19 public health emergency their solution is CE-marked for in-vitro diagnostic use in Europe and available for remote use in clinical practice in the United States. H2O.ai provides an open source, distributed in-memory AI platform that is used across multiple industries with application use cases in healthcare such as medical claim fraud detection, predicting hospital acquired infections, emergency room and hospital management, improving clinical workflows, early cancer detection, flu season prediction, drug discovery, personalized drug matching, and medical imaging and diagnostics.[147] ICarbonX in China is creating a platform for digitizing, analyzing, and understanding life that uses state-of-the-art AI to search the data for insights about health, disease and aging in order to better classify conditions, refine diagnoses, and target treatments for specific biologies and offer personalized healthcare products and services.[148]

As robot-assisted surgery has led to fewer surgery-related complications, a quicker recovery time, and less pain, it has increased in popularity to help surgeons perform complex procedures with precision, flexibility, and control for a range of surgeries from minimally invasive procedures to even open-heart surgery. AI is gradually changing the practice of surgery with improvements in imaging, navigation, and robotic intervention across the spectrum of pre-operative planning and intra-operative guidance to the integration of surgical robots.[149] AI techniques for surgical robotics include perception, localization and mapping, system modeling and control, and human-robot interaction. Pre-operative planning where surgeons plan the surgical procedure from existing medical records and imaging can be improved by early detection and diagnosis based on multi-modal information, federated machine learning with meta learning and explainable AI, as well as having more large-scale datasets available for training machine learning models. Computer-aided intra-operative guidance that enhances visualization and localization in surgery can be improved with AI with respect to shape reconstruction of implants or organs, endoscopic navigation with camera localization and 3D environment mapping, soft tissue and optical biopsy tracking and augmented reality visual guidance. Going forward there are also shifts from static image displays to show dynamic organ function, advanced augmented reality and virtual reality technologies for surgical training and teaching, and remote surgical cooperation between multidisciplinary teams. In the future surgical robotics will become more versatile, lighter, and cheaper, and have increased levels of robotic autonomy, whereas nano-robots will be used for diagnosis and drug delivery. On the ethical and legal side, key issues are protecting the privacy of patients' data, the pro-active handling of cybercrime, and trust between patients and AI systems.

Intuitive's da Vinci surgical systems have pioneered the robotic surgery industry and was one of the first robotic assisted, minimally invasive surgical systems cleared by the US Food and Drug Administration in 2000. Their family of da Vinci systems are now being used across 67 countries world-wide with their fourth generation da Vinci Surgical Systems continuing to advance minimally invasive surgery across a wide spectrum of surgical procedures.[150] Their most capable system currently is Da Vince Xi and uses advanced instrumentation, vision, and features such as integrated table motion along with setup automation and guidance that promotes operating room efficiency. For narrow access urologic surgery, their da Vinci SP system enables surgeons to operate through one incision.[151]

Vicarious Surgical also enables surgeons to perform minimally invasive operations in a better way using virtual reality and AI to enhance proprietary human-like surgical robotics.[152] Auris Health is transforming medical intervention by leveraging flexible robotics to enable endoscopy that uses small cameras and tools to enter the body through its natural openings. In order to do this cost-effectively and improve outcomes, their Monarch platform integrates the latest advancements in AI, robotics, micro-instrumentation, endoscope design, sensing, and data science. They are currently focused on lung cancer and providing diagnostic and therapeutic bronchoscopic procedures.[153] MicroSure in the Netherlands develops robot assisted microsurgery solutions and their MUSA surgical robot is according to them the world's first clinically available CE-certified robot for microsurgery that achieves higher levels of accuracy by enhanced scale of movement, tremor elimination, and added dexterity to maximize and standardize surgical performance.[154] Currently, eight of MicroSure's micro-surgical operations are currently being used for lymphatic system procedures such as treating breast cancer-related lymphedema, as well as free flap and hand surgery.

Accuracy provides radiotherapy systems that make cancer treatments more effective, shorter, safer, and personalized.[155] Their CyberKnife S7 robotic radiosurgery system enables clinicians to deliver personalized non-surgical stereotactic treatments to more patients and does this with sub-millimeter accuracy anywhere in the body such as the prostate, lung, liver, pancreas, kidney, brain, or spine. They claim that this system provides best-in-class robotic precision that enables the world's only motion-synchronized, AI-driven, real-time treatment delivery adaptation for all indications and treatments.[156] Accuracy's TomoTherapy system provides image-guided radiation therapy and intensity-modulated radiation therapy featuring integrated 3D image guidance and conformal treatments to oncology patients, whereas their Radixact treatment delivery system provides image guided intensity modulated radiation therapy with clinical workflows and conformal treatments enabled.[157] Hungary-based Turbine is a simulation-driven drug discovery company that uses AI to deliver targeted cancer therapies to targeted patient populations.[158] As DNA damage repair targets are present in 30% of all cancers and also not easy to address with conventional methods, their pipeline is focused on these targets linked to resistant patient populations. Their platform is called Simulated Cell and integrates a digital model of cell behavior with experimental validation and domain knowledge of translational science and molecular biology, which generates hypotheses and provides mechanistic insights in simulated experiments. They have successfully guided leading pharma companies and have their own, proprietary resistance target currently in validation stage.[159] Mindmaze in Switzerland provides a cloud-based brain health platform that combines certified digital therapeutic solutions with AI and motion analytics to address challenging problems in neurology and neurorehabilitation in order to maximize the recovery potential of patients with debilitating neurological diseases as well as reduce the impact of ageing on cognition and movement.[160] US-based Ginger provides an integrated mental health support solution that combines real-time behavioral health coaching via a chatbot, video therapy and psychiatry sessions, and personalized clinically-validated skill-building activities.[161]

Given the many structural problems that health systems face in developing countries such as those in Africa where public health policies are not effective, access to healthcare professionals or supplies are limited or not always available, services are not always affordable, treatments are not effective, and many people have a lack of knowledge on health issues, there is an opportunity for AI-powered healthcare solutions to help address these issues in a cost-effective and efficient way. Some example use cases include the use of AI to get insights into the spreading of disease that can help to design a more impactful public health policy, the use of AI-powered diagnostic applications on smartphones to remotely diagnose various health conditions and enable health workers to more accurately identify and diagnose illnesses, intelligent virtual assistants that provide health coaching and preventive care, and AI-enabled pharmacogenomic applications to customize treatments based on certain genetic markers to individuals.

Although the future of AI in Healthcare looks bright, it is important to note the specific healthcare sector challenges and opportunities as highlighted in recent Jabil's digital health surveys.[162] This includes the slow production and launch cycles which can be addressed by more agility built into product planning, development and delivery; 89% of healthcare manufacturing companies have the opinion that they need to act more like consumer technology companies and that their company culture is holding them back to deliver AI-driven digital solutions to their customers in a faster way; 75% of digital healthcare solution providers are on the path of leveraging AI-driven personalized medicine and precision healthcare solutions; contract healthcare manufacturing companies can innovate through delivery of additive manufacturing and the use of 3D printing; with regulatory environments becoming more accommodating toward the use of technology in healthcare, faster speed to market can be achieved through modular design architectures and AI-driven digital technologies to optimize clinical trials and lowering costs; and addressing data security and privacy concerns by standardizing healthcare interoperability resources and giving patients better access and control over the health data.[163]

AI-enabled Ultra-personalized Wellness

As people are being more instrumented and more data becomes available, another massive growth area for AI in health is set-up to be in ultra-personalized wellness and prevention of unwellness. Health wellness refers to a state of complete physical, mental and social wellbeing or being in a state of good health from a mind, body, and spirit perspective where this is pursued as an active lifestyle goal and not just the absence of sickness.[164] As we grow our global population size, get more connected and accumulate massive volumes of information, knowledge, and material abundance, we find ourselves in an awkward, complex and arduous situation that not only presents us with significant challenges from a climate, resource, and geopolitical perspective, but specifically also major socioeconomic, health, and wellness problems. Globally we are faced with an increasing unwell workforce of 3.2 billion people that apart from the significant impact on our global economy due to loss productivity and medical expenses in the order of 10-15% of the global economic output, have direct implications on an individual level where more people are growing older, suffer from chronic lifestyle diseases, struggle financially, and feel more stressed and unhappy.[165] The Global Wellness Institute estimates that in the US alone the costs of chronic disease, mental health, stress, employee withdrawal, and job-related injuries and sickness are more than 12% of the US global domestic product which amounts to $2.2 trillion per annum.[166] In parallel to this we also have more people in fast growing urban settings that are becoming health-conscious and spending money to improve their wellness. This all sets the scene for a fast growing global wellness economy currently estimated to be approximately $4.5 trillion in market size and includes personal care, beauty and anti-aging ($1 trillion); physical activity ($828 billion); healthy eating, nutrition and weight loss ($702 billion); wellness tourism ($639 billion); preventive and personalized medicine and public health ($575 billion), and other sizable markets such as traditional and complementary medicine, workplace wellness, health spas, and wellness real estate.[167] We also see that the health and wellness markets are becoming less fragmented and more interconnected to offer health wellness solutions and experiences in the places where people live, work, play and travel. Research and Markets projects the global health and wellness market to grow at a compound annual growth rate of around 4% during 2020 to 2025.[168] Some of the prominent companies in the global wellness economy includes Amway, Bayer, Brunswick Corporation, Danone, David Lloyd Leisure, Fitness First, Herbalife Nutrition, Holland & Barrett, LA Fitness, L'Oréal, Nestle, Procter & Gamble, Unilever, Virgin Active, and Vitabiotics. Most of these and other similar companies also have various AI-powered initiatives such Amway's e-commerce platform that makes use of machine learning to improve its online sales as well as a chatbot to improve online communication between consumers and representatives of their nutrition, beauty, personal care and home products and provide information through social media channels on a 24/7 basis.[169] Bayer is for example applying AI across its business in a number of initiatives from disease prediction to advance patient care, making use of a federated learning approach to access data it doesn't own to identify promising drug compounds and help spot a rare gene mutation, and also collaborating with various partners such as Exscientia to leverage AI in cardiovascular and oncology drug discovery use cases.[170] Bayer has also invested in a number of digital health and AI start-ups in the health and wellness space.[171] Danone, with its 'One Planet. One Health' vision that links human health and the planet's across its entire value chain, has partnered with Microsoft on an AI Factory for Agrifood to support start-ups specializing in the application of AI to innovate in the areas of serving regenerative agriculture, sustainable food, waste minimization, and optimization of supply chains.[172] Herbalife Nutrition uses AI to improve their customer experience through the use of a voice of customer service and intelligent personal assistants that for example provides information and addresses questions about their products such as the ingredients and nutritional value of their Formula 1 meal replacement protein shake.[173] Nestle, as the world's largest food company with a stated goal of wanting to be a recognized leader in nutrition health and wellness, has embraced the wellness market by embarking on a health program that uses AI, DNA testing, and social media shares to create personalized diet plans targeting health-conscious consumers.[174] L'Oréal, as the world's largest cosmetics company, has recently launched an AI-powered at-home system called Perso that provides personalized skin care solutions by assessing the user's complexion and local environment conditions, getting the user's input on personal skincare concerns and product preferences, dispensing a single dose of a personalized blend of product such as moisturizer, under-eye cream or serum, and also alerting users to the best working formulas working best for them and automatically adapting its formulas.[175] Procter & Gamble, a multinational consumer goods corporation that also specializes in personal health, care and hygiene products, has recently partnered with Google to use their AI, cloud and data analytics to enable more personalized experiences for consumers in a trusted environment.[176] Some examples of Procter & Gamble's AI-infused products include Olay's new Skin Advisor platform, which uses AI to offer users personal skincare consultations and advice, the Oral-B Genius X toothbrush that offers personalized feedback on brushing techniques, and Lumi by Pampers that provides insights and emerging patterns whilst monitoring a baby's sleep routine.[177] AI is also revolutionizing the fitness industry by making fitness machines, wearables, gadgets, and mobile applications smarter. The applications include for example fitness and diet planning mobile applications, wristbands, footwear, and smart assistants for gyms and health clubs. Aaptiv Coach is an AI-enabled health and fitness coach that offers personalized lifestyle and fitness plans on a daily and weekly basis based on a user's eating habits, present fitness levels, and future fitness goals to stay fit, lose weight, build strength, get faster or reduce stress.[178] FitnessAI automatically generates personalized workouts where AI is used to optimize sets, reps, and weight for each exercise, track progress over time and generate insights.[179] LIFTR is an experimental virtual personal fitness trainer powered by AI and computer vision that gives real-time feedback as a person does specific exercises to practice safe and proper form.[180] As part of their digital therapeutics solutions especially aimed at chronic obstructive pulmonary disease and musculoskeletal conditions, Kaia Health uses AI to monitor and analyze human movement to provide real-time instructions as well as feedback via a smartphone.[181] Zenia provides an AI-based personal yoga assistant that analyzes the body movements, sets accurate posture during an asana, monitors progress, and provides real-time tracking and feedback on its users' asana performance.[182]

Key factors in driving the growth of the health wellness market includes the growing pervasiveness of chronic lifestyle diseases, longer lifespans, and increase in stress levels, unhappiness, and mental health issues such as anxiety and depression. These factors are amongst other things caused by an inactive lifestyle, frantic schedules, and busy lives where we see a significant increase in chronic conditions. In fact, unhealthy lifestyle behavior and risks such as poor diet, physical inactivity, smoking, lack of health screening, poor stress management, insufficient sleep, and excessive alcohol consumption drive 15 chronic conditions that account for 80% of the total costs for all chronic illnesses worldwide.[183] Some of the top chronic conditions include diabetes, coronary artery disease, hypertension, back pain, obesity, cancer, asthma, arthritis, allergies, sinusitis, depression, congestive heart failure, lung disease, kidney disease and high cholesterol. These chronic diseases not only lead to individuals not living optimally, but also have a major impact on business leading to increased absenteeism, increased staff turn-over, lower productivity, increased disability, increased healthcare cost and a negative effect on company culture. This has encouraged many people across the globe to integrate wellness into their daily lives by adopting various healthcare and recreational physical activities such as fitness, sports, active recreation, and mindful movement, as well as meditation, yoga, and going to mineral spas and on wellness vacations. Health spas make for example use of specialized therapeutic waters to treat a range of spinal column conditions, cardiovascular diseases, bronchitis, circulation disorders, asthma, and rheumatism. With wearable devices and sensors, health-related data can be sent to smartphones and wellness apps to monitor various aspects of a person's health such as activity levels, heart rate, blood pressure, blood sugar levels, oxygenation, and sleep patterns as well as facilitating proactive actions such as dispensing insulin when necessary or making recommendations with respect to lifestyle behavior changes to improve well-being. Over the last few years we have seen a significant growth in the emerging wearable technology and devices market that includes smartwatches, sports and fitness trackers, electronic skin patches, smart glasses and head-mounted displays, smart pillows to track sleep quality and patterns, wearable health alert and monitoring devices, non-invasive and minimally-invasive continuous glucose monitoring sensors, electrocardiogram sensors to measure electrical signals in your heart to determine the rate and strength of heartbeat, photoplethysmogram sensors to detect blood volume changes, wearable temperature monitoring, hydration sensors, wearable sweat sensors, smart contact lenses, medical hearables, smart footwear, smart clothing, cosmetics patches, stretchable artificial skin, wearable exoskeletons, pregnancy and newborn monitoring, wearable drug delivery, and even smart wound care. With this type of instrumentation that is generating a continuous stream of exponentially growing health wellness related data, AI is poised to have a transformative impact across the health and wellness sector.

Apart from helping healthcare and wellness providers to be more effective, AI can help to democratize personalized care by empowering people to manage their own wellness and healthcare, assisting them to keep themselves well and lead healthier lifestyles, capturing and analyzing their health and wellness data, predicting the impact of their current lifestyle choices, simulating their future health state based on current state and historical patterns, and generating tailored recommendations within their own context and circumstances. AI can specifically enable deeper levels of personalization with respect to an individual's health and wellness condition and managing physical activities, exercise, nutrition, weight, sleep, and stress levels. These ultra-personalized digital wellness solutions can be offered in tandem with services provided by wellness and healthcare professionals such as physicians, nurses, biokineticists, trainers, dietitians, and nutritionists to enhance and meet the demand for these services. By enabling dynamic personalization these AI-driven systems can nudge and guide people to achieve their individual health and wellness goals within their personal circumstances and context. From a nutritional perspective, it can for example simplify their healthy-eating routines, automatically capture detailed food intake and analyze the nutritional composition, provide insights into the impact of specific food intake on overall wellness over time, help to understand the impact of blood sugar levels as a result of eating various foods, report on nutritional intake patterns and trends, generate real-time instructions and even modifications for the current meal, detect over indulgence or unhealthy eating and suggest an appropriate diet plan to help with detoxification, and provide recommendations, nudging and notifications to keep people on track with respect to healthy eating. By allowing a dietitian or nutritionist to have access to these data and insights, further in-depth coaching tips and advice can be provided to help guide future meals. It is clear that scalable AI-enabled ultra-personalized wellness services that are relevant, dynamic, engaging, fast, consistent and interacting with people in real-time, can add real value, make a difference and help people achieve their health and wellness goals. As with any medical advice, it is also very important that solutions should preferably and as far as possible always have scientific evidence supporting claims made about health benefits, advice, recommendations or interventions.

Lydia Kostopoulos, with whom I have participated in *AI for Good* and United Nations events in Geneva, Switzerland a few years ago, examined how emerging AI technologies that are more focused on mental and emotional health are used within the wellness field.[184] In order to evaluate current AI technologies, their benefits to wellbeing and their ethical implications, she used a framework to categorize these technologies into intangible, tangible, and embedded AI wellness. Whereas intangible AI does not have a physical form and communicate with users via for example an intelligent virtual assistant or notifications on a device, tangible AI are embodied in a physical form such as the AI in a vehicle, doll, or robotic pet. An example of embedded AI wellness includes brain computer interfaces that augment the human brain with respect to intelligence, mood or help people with paralysis to regain independence through the control of computer-based devices. Some intangible AI solutions to help identify, diagnose, prevent, manage, and address mental health and addiction related problems include Woebot (mentioned earlier in this chapter) that helps manage mental health through cognitive behavioral therapy; Mindstrong that provides virtual therapy and psychiatric care that uses AI to proactively predict emotional health and wellness issues;[185] and Addicaid that helps people avoid addictive behaviors such as substance abuse, alcoholism, gambling, internet usage, and pornography through predicting behavior, proactive guidance and personalized treatment options;[186] Another intangible AI wellness use case involves the use of robots, AI and service automation in hotels to enhance the customer experience and provide hyper personalized wellness services at these tourism and hospitality facilities.[187] Some of the main ethical concerns with the current state of AI used in these solutions involves responses that are too rigid, not being grounded in human understanding of the world, not understanding true meaning, lacking a deep level of human empathy, potentially expanding the digital bubbles that people currently live in, possibly making people more entitled, and providing an illusionary form of therapy that is not really effective. Some examples of tangible AI wellness solutions include the ZEEQ smart pillow that can be used with Amazon Alexa and tracks and analyzes sleep duration and cycles and snoring impact on restfulness;[188] and AI wellness robots such as Paro the learning therapeutic seal that responds to touch and has been used to reduce stress and comfort patients with dementia, and Stevie the elderly care robot that interacts with people through conversations, expressions, pictures, and health-related reminders and function as a video messaging platform that can also make calls to emergency services if needed.[189] A brain computer interface is a form of embedded AI that provides a communication channel between a human brain and an external device to augment or repair human cognitive or sensory-motor functions. These systems can acquire a variety of electrical and magnetic signals from the brain and nervous systems, use machine learning to analyze and translate them, and act in an active mode to complete a mental task using neuro-motor output, a reactive stimulus-based conditional mode that acts on selective attention, and a passive mode that involves no visual stimulus.[190] Apart from a long history of animal and human brain computer interface research efforts that range from invasive to non-invasive and increasing use of state-of-the-art machine learning, there has been a number of tech startups that are actively improving the state-of-the art in this area such as Neuralink that aims to create symbiosis between the human brain and AI; Neurable that develops neurotechnology tools that interpret human intent, measure emotion, and provide telekinetic control; NextMind with their non-invasive brain sensing devices that uses AI to translate electroencephalogram activity into commands; and Emotive with their brain data hardware and software solutions that can examine stress and focus to help improve diagnosis of brain diseases and disorders.[191] As these AI-enabled technologies and solutions continue to advance at a rapid rate, the potential is there for both significant enhancement and harm to people's emotional and mental well-being. So, wisdom will be needed to apply these types of systems in safe, ethical, robust, and responsible ways that will not lead to emotionally and mentally weaker people and an over-dependence on smart technology but applied in meaningful ways in tandem with human wellness expertise to leverage the best of both worlds.

International organizations such as the World Health Organization and Organization for Economic Co-operation and Development (OECD) also have principles and explicit goals with respect to humanity's well-being. With the OECD's goal to shape policies that foster prosperity, opportunity, equality, and well-being for humanity, they have developed a well-being framework covering 11 dimensions of well-being from an inequality, resources and risk factors perspective: income and wealth; work and job quality; housing; health; knowledge and skills; environment quality; subjective well-being; safety; work-life balance; social connections; and civic engagement.[192] In applying these smart technology-driven solutions to help increase wellness, it is important to measure wellbeing, what drives well-being of people and what needs to be done to achieve greater progress for all. To this end the OECD has recently released a report on *How's Life? 2020* that measures wellbeing in 41 countries to determine whether life is getting better for people, how policies can improve our lives, and are the right things being measured.[193] They report that although people's well-being has improved in various ways, progress has been slow or even worse in others, including how people connect with each other and their government. They also indicate that progress in current well-being does not necessarily match the improvement in resources across human, economic, natural, and social capital that are needed to sustain well-being over time.[194]

Workplace wellness, which on its own has a current market size of about $48 billion, remains relatively small in comparison to the financial burdens and losses created by unhealthy, overstressed employees.[195] The Global Wellness Institute reports that only 9.8% of the world's 3.2 billion-plus workforce has access to a workplace wellness program, ranging from 52% and 23% in North America and Europe respectively to only 5% in Asia-pacific and Latin America and 1% in Africa.[196] Such programs remain essential to combat preventable chronic diseases. As companies are faced with the new coronavirus as a global health crisis, workplace wellness is further in the spotlight with companies putting measures in place to help protect their employees as we work to control the spread. Corporate wellness programs give employees incentives, tools, social support, privacy, and strategies to adopt and maintain healthy behaviors. Workplaces across the world are implementing employee wellness programs because improvement of individual wellness within businesses leads to a return on investment for companies with respect to increased productivity and performance levels, decreased absenteeism, helping to attract and retain the best staff, and increased levels of engagement with staff. There are many corporate wellness companies that are working to transform workplace health, happiness, and productivity. For example, WellSteps that also claims to have one of the most effective corporate wellness programs in the United States and a winner of the Koop national health award, provides worksite wellness solution to reduce employee health care costs and improve employee health via health risk assessment, goal setting, activity and incentive trackers, behavior change tools, weekly tasks, quizzes, team competitions, evaluation and incentives.[197] Their platform incorporates research-based interactive wellness programs into a workplace to educate, motivate, and provide health promoting skills and tools in order to help employees adopt, improve and maintain healthy behaviors and build self-efficacy by reducing the behavior change process to manageable weekly tasks. Sonic Boom is another corporate wellness company in the US that provides a customizable, social, and gamified wellbeing platform that helps to maximize motivation and accountability through competition, cooperation, positive peer pressure, and rewards systems.[198] Other corporate wellness program examples include Wellness Corporate Solutions that offer wellness campaigns, health fairs and health risk assessments to employees; WorkStride helps corporates recognize and reward behaviors that already occur to improve employee wellness; TotalWellness specializes in biometric screenings and flu shots; and Wellable provides a wellness platform that enables companies to create wellness programs that engages employees in holistic well-being educational modules and activities.[199]

Corporate wellness can be enhanced by smart technology driven personalized wellness solutions to provide deeper insights at greater scale and do more than just promoting fitness, nutrition, and the benefits of exercise, with incentives to lose weight, or reduce the risk of high blood pressure, stroke, heart attack or early onset of diabetes. AI that helps to unlock value from all available data sources, wellness DNA and other biomarker testing, digital diagnostic and health tools, and cognitive technologies for behavior change are among the many advances enabling health and wellness options to be individualized to a person - from their needs, challenges and physiology to their lifestyle preferences and personal values. Apart from enabling healthcare providers to help patients more effectively, AI-driven solutions can also help to provide more specialized care through empowering individuals to manage their own wellness, change their lifestyle habits and behavior, and lead healthier lifestyles by capturing and analyzing their health data, building models to predict the impact of their current lifestyle choices and project their future health state, and getting proactive and preventative support, recommendations, and advice.

With more data available to enable machine learning-based prediction of patient behavior and disease probabilities, healthcare and health insurance providers are in a much better position to be proactive and focus on disease management, wellness, and prevention. By encouraging, nudging, and incentivizing people to maintain healthy lifestyle behaviors and change unhealthy behaviors, not only will this improve the general health of the population, alleviate the demand on the healthcare system and reduce healthcare expenditure, but also decrease risk, enable superior underwriting, and help increase the profitability of health insurance providers. Some examples of health insurance providers that encourage preventive care include Oscar Health in the US and Discovery Health in South Africa.[200] Discovery has for example a programme called Vitality that tracks the health, diet and fitness activity of people and encourages and rewards members to live healthier.[201] As part of fast tracking the move to preventive wellness and care, we are also likely to see new partnerships among healthcare payers, healthcare and wellness providers, and pharmaceutical companies that will implement AI-driven pay-for-performance models and collaborate on AI-based risk-management and detection modeling. McKinsey Global Institute provides an example where healthcare insurers can save significant costs in their payment plans to reimburse hospitals, clinics and doctors that is typically based on the average costs of treatment across all healthcare providers in the group. By using machine learning to analyze historical patient data, costs associated with diagnosing physicians and orthopedic surgeons can be reduced by 4-5% and 8-12% respectively.[202] Companies such as GoodRx in the US claims to save insured and uninsured employees up to 80% on their drug prescriptions, which amounts to over $15 billion.[203]

The health wellness sector is also going through a forced evolution as internationally healthcare and health insurance cost is at unsustainable levels, claims are almost 100% of premiums, companies are cutting cost and contributions and reducing benefits, individuals cannot afford premiums and/or co-payments, and people are living longer. It is clear that the system is thoroughly "broken" and the only viable solution seems to be prevention as opposed to a predominantly chemical approach. Some of the current pain points in the customer wellness journey includes wellness program engagement levels as low as 10% (especially outside the US), the take-up levels of wellness programs as low as 15%; wellness offerings typically follow an one-size-fits-all approach and presented as an add-on as opposed to being personalized and a core part of employee assistance programs; health and wellness data is extremely fragmented which makes it difficult to provide comprehensive AI-driven digital solutions and analysis; with the unsustainable cost increases, individuals suffer from both a health and financial perspective and many people have or will have no care in retirement with poor quality of life and unaffordable cost; employers also suffer in productivity and absenteeism which have a financial impact; and medical schemes suffer as a result of inefficient and reactive programs directly impacting reserves and therefore premiums to members.

AI-driven personalized wellness solutions can help address this insufferable situation. The introduction of these solutions is validated and made possible due to the computational power, storage, instrumentation, and digitization that have increased dramatically and resulted in massive data sources that can be accessed instantly and processed by AI algorithms to provide insights, predictive analytics, and personalized real-time solutions. Another contributing factor is the awareness of health and wellness amongst consumers as a very strong worldwide trend. As a result, we are starting to see more AI-driven personalized wellness offerings and startups to flourish around the globe. One such solution is Cortex Logic's AI-enabled, ultra-personalized health wellness platform called Journey Wellness that provides real-time, relevant, on-demand and proactive guidance, advice, support, and recommendations to help optimize a user's wellness whilst ensuring high standards of data privacy and choice. The system makes use of the Cortex AI engine to build a holistic and dynamic 360-degree wellness profile and has an AI-driven personalized wellness coach that provides information and personalized advice, coaching and guidance with respect to healthy eating and diet, exercise and fitness, mental wellness, and health with a specific focus on chronic lifestyle diseases. Apart from having access to these deep domain knowledges on wellness related knowledge bases and building up rich user interaction data and personalized context of the individual's wellness state over time, Journey connects with a spectrum of data sources such as digitized health risk assessments and surveys embedded within the platform, wearable devices, medical claims data, employee data, and other external health and wellness data. Each of these data sources are mined by the AI engine to enrich the individual's wellness profile, provide insights and predictive analysis using state-of-the-art machine learning and statistical models. As soon as the user has completed the initial health risk assessment, the user is provided with a dynamic dashboard that shows the current personalized wellness score that is built up from a range of indices that covers lifestyle, diet, morbidity, mental health, and heart health. It also provides visualizations of the individual's current biometrics such as body mass index, glucose level, cholesterol level and blood pressure, a summarized view of lifestyle risk factors and chronic conditions if relevant, as well as a journal of wellness metrics that are being tracked over time. Apart from the intelligent virtual coach's chatbot style interaction, the platform also interacts with the user via a dynamic personalized advice dashboard and push notifications that gives specific advice and feedback based on the individual's specific wellness state, weekly check-up surveys to see how the user is progressing, and a real-time rewards dashboard that measures overall wellness, changing lifestyle behavior and engagement. The more the user interacts with the wellness platform and its virtual coach, the better the system captures and learns the user's specific wellness profile and underlying dynamics to improve on the quality, proactiveness and relevancy of the personalized advice, coaching and guidance over time. The wellness platform complements human managed care professionals by providing preventative care for people that are on their way to having a chronic lifestyle disease as well as managed care for people diagnosed with one or more chronic diseases which can be presented as specific programmes such as diabetes care, cardio care, mental health, and HIV care. The digitized health screening assessments also facilitates the screening done by Journey's network of nurses and healthcare professionals via home visits or company wellness days, whereas the coach can also connect users to a network of healthcare professionals which includes nurses, counselling and trauma specialists, biokineticists, and nutritionists. The Journey platform also provides employer groups and medical schemes with a better, proactive, and effective solution to help their employees or members live healthier lives by changing negative lifestyle habits and patterns. The Journey Wellness platform is tailored for organisations and their people with a deep understanding of their uniqueness, grounded in rigorous analysis and data-driven insight using AI to create lasting, differentiated value. Journey has a user view for the employees and members as well as a company or medical scheme administration view for analysis and predictive analytics on anonymized wellness data of their employees or members that provides insights about the effectiveness of the personalized wellness nudging and support and the impact on the company or medical scheme's business. Employers would like to increase employee productivity, reduce absenteeism, and improve on existing human resource and employee assistance programs that are ineffective, fragmented, reactive, and costly. With significant increases in claims as well as healthcare costs related to preventable diseases, medical schemes are fighting for financial sustainability and need a proactive effective wellness solution that actively engages members and helps them on a personalized level to live healthier lives through changing unfavorable lifestyle behaviors on an opt-in and opt-out basis with privacy and confidentiality. Utilizing the same AI-driven platform infrastructure as Journey, Cortex Logic has also developed a virtual mental wellness companion for teenagers and young adults called Vive Teens which is initially being rolled out in South Africa to help address this urgent need and to act as a safety net for the younger people that need assistance and guidance.

These type of AI-driven digital wellness solutions continues to reshape how a company encourages what it seeks to achieve: a healthier workforce, in mind and body, based on its acceptance of expert advice; based on the intelligence not only of a higher form of technology but of a heightened state about the stakes themselves, that we have a vital say in living better. Smart technology can indeed revolutionize the workplace wellness and usher in a new era – an exciting period - of wellness for all.

8. AI's Impact on Society, Governments, and the Public Sector

Now that we have a much better frame of reference of AI's revolutionary transformation on the world and its people across multiple industries, it is time to consider AI's impact on society, governments, and the public sector. We also know that the potential benefits of AI for society and social good are substantial, but also that it poses appreciable risks, concerns, and challenges for society that we need to counter. Similar to the business industries, AI is also transforming the public sector, but more focused on improving public services delivery, bureaucratic efficiency as well as public safety and security. Given AI's projected contribution to the global economy over the next few years which is in the order of multi trillions of dollars as well as its enormous potential to unlock value, many countries see AI as a game changer and are getting their governmental AI strategies and policies in place to adopt and embrace AI in a meaningful way.

AI's Impact on Society

There is no doubt that smart technology is having a profound transformative impact on society as a whole with all-embracing economic, political, legal, ethical, and regulatory implications and will ultimately impact every citizen around the globe as well as challenge and change the way we live our lives in the Smart Technology Era. As we enter this new phase of civilization, we see an increasingly instrumented and quantified society that is surrounded by a massive proliferation of smarter, more capable, more connected, and ubiquitous systems and devices that enhance productivity, create conveniences, and help us to solve problems. In previous chapters we have already seen how AI as a strategic exponential smart technology is transforming our world and economy at a rapid pace with a range of applications across multiple industries and sectors. Even though AI can have a tremendously beneficial impact on society, business and the economy, there are also risks, concerns and challenges that we need to address such as losing jobs, ensuring human agency and not losing control, data abuse, dependence lock-in, and societal disorder and harm through various mechanisms. It also forces us to strategically rethink society and ask questions about our identity, who we are, what we do, what is private, what we own, what we consume, how we spend our time, how and what skills do we develop, what we learn, how we work, how we play, what we do about our health, how we relate to one another, how we communicate and interact with one another, how we want to be augmented, and how we want to be governed. The socio-technical impact of AI necessitates the establishment of new frameworks for digital governance where people are empowered through transparent and collaborative decision-making involving multiple stakeholders across the spectrum of society to reshape our social, political, cultural, and economic environments. We have the opportunity and ability to direct and shape AI and smart technology in such a way that reflects our common human-centric objectives, values, and shared sense of destiny, as well as emphasizes and complements human capacities such as creativity, compassion, empathy, meaningful engagement, stewardship, cooperation, and reflection.

So, what are the effects of AI on us? To answer this question, it may help to think about what the effects of steel were at the time of the Industrial Revolution. The invention of steel gave the world a tool that would quickly change the entire world. It had no power or meaning in itself, aside from helping humans achieve their goals. It was humans who saw a need and thus found a tool that had value to our need to progress and grow. Steel was transformative. It fulfilled a massive transformative purpose for growth, production, and globalization - to make things easier for us; to help us. It was and is used for so many different things each forming part of its transformative power still felt today. In our cars, our appliances, the industrial machines we take for granted; steel is an integral part of the society we know. The same can be said of electricity. AI, like steel or electricity, is a technological advancement or a tool that is changing the world. It may not be something we can touch as we might touch steel or plug into electricity, but just as we have progressed, so have our tools. Our tools fulfill a need, and the need AI fulfills is to allow us to be less reliant on heavy machinery and structures to learn, trade, make decisions, grow, and have a continuous stream of insights to be better at what we do and how we do it. If AI can be seen in terms of Maslow's hierarchy of needs, AI is the self-actualization to steel's safety. We needed steel first. We needed to build the physical structures before we could break free into a new world where physical structures alone are not enough and, in some ways, unnecessary to reach our true potential. What we mean when we say unnecessary is that it is no longer necessary to have a physical room with a doctor in order to have a consultation. It is not even necessary (in common cases) to have a physical doctor present. What is necessary is a smartphone and an AI-powered medical application that asks us questions, takes our temperature, and scans our symptoms. We have moved away from physical reliance to have our basic needs met. Smart technology has done that for us. And due to the fact that it can be anywhere at any time, every single person with a smartphone and internet has access to it. AI and the smart technology that accompanies it are steel on steroids.

How does AI affect us? It affects our productivity. It affects the effort and time we take to complete daily tasks. It affects the way we search for information or tap into knowledge bases. It affects our understanding of complex problems and how they fit together. It affects our understanding of the brain. It affects our privacy. It affects our transparency. It affects our ethics. It affects the public services we expect. It is already omnipresent in so many respects as it taps into a globalized hyperconnected world where the urgency to keep up increases all the time. There is a constant string of new products, processes, tools, and platforms to improve, enhance, reinvent, and disrupt our lives. Thomas Friedman divides our reactions to this into two – those who are overwhelmed, displaced and fearful and those who are inspired by and flowing with the changes.[1] The truth is there is probably a mixture of both of these reactions in all of us. It also depends on things like how exposed we are, and the momentum around us to adopt new technologies, buy new things and trade our comfort zones so often that being uncomfortable becomes our comfort zone. The tricky thing about globalization is that it only refers to the parts of the globe that easily connect, interact, and share with the rest of the globe. So, if people who are easily exposed struggle to keep up with the constant 'global' changes, what about those who are not actually included in them or receive only bits of the advancement, often delayed? Most of the inventions, add-ons and advancements are usually born from the same list of already developed and advanced countries - those assumed to be included in the term 'globalization'.[2] Thomas Friedman, Yuval Harari and many thinkers and commentators of our time believe it is our responsibility to ensure that we do not leave people behind. What we need to think about now is how we do it. How do we make a promise we can keep that globalization, the digital economy and smart technology will make the world a better place for all? Some later chapters hope to answer some of these questions. The innovation of the world is consistently arising from the same main pockets and some emerging nations. Different parts of the world are finding themselves at very different levels of digitization and advancement, while some of the more advanced and developed world are empowered by mobility, knowledge and smart technology – the gaps in the way people across countries, with historically different cultures and ways of life are substantially decreased. We may, in fact, have more similarities between the digitally included in China and America who historically possess different ways to value the world, different spiritual beliefs and different ways of living, than between a rural farmer in China and someone from Beijing.

What we are noticing is that religions, locations, or cultures are no longer our largest separators, but digitization, digital literacy, the opportunities it provides and knowledge it allows. The danger of not doing this is, without catastrophizing it, socio-economic disaster, further exclusion and deepening the relatability gap. This gap is based on varying experiences of the world. While this is assumed, and often based on an area's natural resources, rich in culture, values and priorities that are in no way threatening to one another, experiences of the world and of life are becoming so different that there may soon not be much that we can relate to. We are already living lives hard to relate through mere class, culture, and priorities, if we add total digitization of the way some of us live our lives, while others do not know what the internet is, we are failing.[3]

Acceleration in the topic of globalization guides our thoughts towards the effects of development on people's lives. Thomas Friedman, in *Thank you for Being Late: An Optimist's Guide to Thriving in the Age of Acceleration*, and related presentations, talks about being in the middle of three nonlinear revolutions at the same time, that all contribute to the growing divide.[4] There are people who can get on a new economy and people who feel shut out – *web* people and *wall* people. These revolutions include Market (digital globalization), Mother Nature (climate change, biodiversity loss, population growth) and Moore's Law (speed and power of microchips doubles every 18 to 24 months). Even as it is closer to thirty months, the power of creation, invention and development means that the world around us is changing and is allowed to change very quickly. Some people can keep up, relearn, retool, and reengineer and others are lost and dislocated by it. The struggle is between these two groups of people.[5] There are of course some people who are wholly unaware of the changes and are not given the chance to feel dislocated. The result however is the same – a world split in two.

The things that anchor us in the world seem to be under threat. The way we have done things, seen things at work, at home and in our communities is changing.[6] Neuroscience shows us as it maps our brain's response to change that when faced with change we fear, we resist, we want desperately to go back. This is not a reaction of the weak minded. It is the very human reaction that stems from the way our brains are wired.[7] Knowing this, how are we managing these changes? We have change management in organisations, which is still not as commonplace as it should be, but we do not have change management for entire countries. In the age of knowledge, and all the knowledge we have, why are we not using this knowledge to navigate our path towards a digital world? AI? Robots? Of course, people are scared, rational or not, they are scared. Perhaps many of these fears that seem justified or founded in threats or real situations are just the same as the fears in our personal lives?

We want to take a risk, but given time to think about it, we will convince ourselves of all the reasons it is a bad idea. We may even be onto something, but the truth is we have no idea.

Our fear of the generalist future, the future of communication, of work, of our everyday lives is the same as our own personal fears. Will our marriage last? Will we have enough money in ten years' time? Will we lose our job? Will we get sick? It is all just fear. Knowing this, why is our biggest investment not in psychology? Helping people face all the unknowns? Helping people deal with their natural responses to a completely unknown future? What are we doing? All these developments, smart technology, will all be nothing if the world is too scared to adopt it. Organizations have seen this problem so many times. We invest in a change or technology, and it is not adopted. It lands up being a massive waste of money and time because we have not thought about people. We have not considered their psychology. We have not thought about how to manage the change. That is one issue when it comes to people. The other, as we have discussed above is that the world is divided based on this fear. The division is dangerous to societies, economics, inequality, and human rights. Managing fear is just one of the ways we can prevent this. What about education? What about directing our inventions towards solving age-old problems that we finally have the capacity to solve?

So, what is AI doing for society? AI is doing many wonderful things for society, including where AI is improving access, solving problems, and enhancing the daily lives of all civilians. But as with any good, we need to see the adverse side too, which we will discuss further later in this chapter, particularly also where they are unintentional. The unintentional effects of the machines we are teaching are most important to understand whereas the more obvious applications like weapons, spying equipment and job displacement do not need much explanation as to why they are problematic.

Some of you may remember the Google Walkout of November 2018. A large group of international Google employees staged a walkout at the same time, to stand up against unethical decision making within the organization. These Google employees were drawing attention to the lack of diversity in Google and how this lack of diversity was leading to decisions that not only favored white men within the organization, but this bias was expressed in the smart technology and machine learning algorithms that were being developed.[8] What is worse is that the world did not know how their data was being used, what the effects of these lines of development and use were and if any rights were being violated or merely forgotten. This translates into a world, cultures, organizations, and leaders who are mostly run by white men, now infiltrating this culture into machines used on a global scale and entrenching these biases further into society.

Google is not the only organization or institution experiencing this, and granted it is not only white men who are exercising their power or exposing their biases. In the cases of Africa and Asia, these biases will be perpetuated by the most powerful people in society. Whatever their color, culture, or creed - this view infiltrates society, favoring and benefiting those who are already advantaged and have power. While we will discuss this further later in the book, these effects on society due to organizational, governmental, and institutional decision making, even without AI, tend to favor the groups who hold the power, while ensuring that they keep that power, take care of themselves and advance their causes and cures.

Let us focus less on the problems and more on the solution. What could AI be doing for society? This needs to start with the question: What can humans do for society? In this we need to be aware of what we are doing wrong: the obvious and the less obvious, and then find new ways to create societies that favor all groups, not just the groups who have the power and the means to create, invent, make laws, and develop.

John Rawls, a social and political philosopher, had an idea of how we may go about doing this. In his *A Theory of Justice*, Rawls argues that it is normal to disagree on how to live.[9] These disagreements come from how we live, what we know, our immediate environment, what we are trying to protect and what we have learned.[10] Often, they arrive from sheer luck or chance that we were born white instead of black, in a hospital instead of a shack, to a family who showed love and had the means to protect us instead of in squalor with parents we will never know. This goes further into the resources, values and cultures of the communities and societies we are born into. Those in dry regions may value natural resources and those in abundant climates might look past the natural treasures that other's fight to protect. Those born in poverty might value community more than they value individualism and privacy - luxuries they cannot fathom when the survival of the one is linked to the survival of the community. In short, we cannot decide what justice is, what our collective rights are, what our responsibilities without removing ourselves from the lives we know and the things we need, are used to, already have, abhor, or hold dear.

Rawls says that being aware of these differences, of the luck and chance that placed us in our positions in society is the first step to being aware of how they affect our decisions in creating laws and deciding on the rights worth upholding and protecting.[11] This does not only apply to justice in laws however, but it should also be applied to institutions and organisations. We see the effects of not doing this in the results within countries, organisations and institutions that favor, protect and advance one group of people over another - often out of a state of ignorance to how their beliefs, status, what they are exposed to or how they are influenced.

If we are to follow a Rawlsian Theory of Justice - one that promotes fairness above all, we should be thinking about justice (rights, laws, policies, and procedures) from a Veil of Ignorance.[12] We must essentially forget who we are. We must forget our lot in life; the chance that gave us the conditions under which we were born into and consider that we could have been born as anyone else, anywhere else, with any other parents, in any other conditions. Then, and only then, can we think about justice, ethics, laws, regulations, policies, and procedures fairly. Then and only then can we create the countries, businesses and institutions that promote just living for everyone.

Without this ignorance, we have companies like Google or Facebook that have good intentions but struggle to navigate the stormy societal waters of promoting fairness above all. Without this ignorance, we have algorithms that favor one group of society. Without this ignorance, we do not think about our demands and actions in terms of their consequences on the people we could have been if not for sheer luck (and, yes, sometimes hard work to move away from our lot). For Rawls, we would create a social contract that would dictate what we would want to protect and advance without knowing who we are or how we will be impacted. We need to understand that we could be anyone, and if we were someone else under some other conditions, with some other life, would we be happy with what we have chosen?

AI, smart technology, and globalization make doing this even more important. What we are building today impacts far more people than ever before. It impacts people on the other side of the world, and its impacts spread quicker and are felt more deeply. If we are developing a machine learning algorithm to catch criminals, are we aware of how our beliefs and lot in life affect what we are teaching the machines? Are we aware of the negative consequences in the biased data we are feeding our algorithm for say, black or colored males? Have we put ourselves into the positions of others and more, have we insisted on diverse views when creating these algorithms? Have we taken measures to ensure that one group or many groups are not being negatively impacted by or excluded from what we are developing? Would we be more inclined to do so if we were the people being excluded or negatively impacted? Unfortunately, there is not a large portion of the already sidelined who are creating laws, policies, procedures, or algorithms, and up until now that has been very obvious in the world we see.

We still have not figured out how to distribute the benefits of the Industrial Revolution (the first one) to almost 75% of the planet.[13] Some people live in abundance and some live with nothing. It is time to consider that the people who are leading the world whether in government, research or business are the people deciding, in some way, who gets what, how they get it, where it will be available, who even knows enough about it to affect or ask for it and who is sidelined? We continue to protect ourselves, and with the same kinds of people who have the power to create and sustain abundance, how do we get to a place of fairness if not from a veil of ignorance?

That being said, there are many benefits for all of society that smart technology has enabled for us. Let us look at AI applications, supported by IoT, AR, nanotechnology and robotics, that are aimed at and improving society for everyone, starting from a place of seeking balance, and are already doing so as also clearly demonstrated in previous chapters and many examples in our everyday lives such as streamlining processes and task optimization, reduction of human error, solving pain points, improved customer service experience, personalized service delivery, information at our fingertips, personalized education, precision medicine and healthcare, and advancing human knowledge. However, how do we ensure that the technologies used for these specific things are not used for other, more precarious means?

AI needs data, huge amounts of data, all kinds of data in order to give us the seamless, intuitive intelligence that could vastly improve every aspect of our lives. However, this is where it gets tricky. How much data are we willing to give? How much privacy are we willing to give away? Who would we allow to listen to us, watch and analyze our every move, if anyone? For what purpose would we allow it? And how much control would we insist on having over its outcomes? The Chinese, as major players in the AI space, are willing to give up some amount of privacy for convenience, while the Europeans, Americans, and many other western societies, are not (or are not yet).[14] We still cannot agree on, even amongst close circles, how we are to balance privacy and convenience in an ethical debate. While western societies debate, stall and create laws that protect our data, the Chinese can take the lead in the wave of perception AI, due to the vast amounts of data it is able to collect. This leads to huge amounts of convenience when performing everyday tasks and access to better services, also in spheres such as education. The potential and positive outcomes of giving away our privacy are boundless, but the chances for it to be used against us are boundless too.

In *Future Politics* Jamie Susskind says the "digital is political" and strongly argues for the key role political systems, law, legislation and regulation should play in ensuring that these smart digital systems are kept accountable and in check as they are driving towards increased control over society and have the power to influence, persuade, manipulate and filter our perceptions of the world as more data is gathered about us.[15] An example of this type of manipulation and influencing people was Cambridge Analytica's use of AI and Facebook's data (amongst others) in political advertising such as the 2016 US presidential campaign where an image of a candidate was projected and customized to the biases, preferences and prejudices on a personalized level. The Netflix documentary *The Social Dilemma* shows how major technology and social media companies such as Facebook, Google, and Twitter with their AI-driven digital systems encourage addiction to their platforms for financial gain, how people are influenced and manipulated as well as its role in politics, mental health, and the spreading of conspiracy theories.[16] Facebook has countered that the documentary "buries substance in sensationalism" and gives a distorted view of social media platforms and not consider the steps that is taken to navigate through difficult and complex societal problems by helping to protect people's privacy, reducing content that could drive polarization, protect the integrity of elections, and fighting fake news, misinformation, and harmful content.[17] That said, there is a definite concern about surveillance capitalism where personal data is commoditized with the core purpose of profit-making as we have seen with high precision and personalized targeted sales and marketing. In *The Age of Surveillance Capitalism* Shoshana Zuboff examines the extraordinary power of surveillance capitalism and how major technology players and corporations predict and control users' behavior through increasing data extraction and analysis, offering more tailored and personalized services through digital platforms, and using technological infrastructure, computer-monitoring and automation for new contractual forms and continuous experimentation on their customers.[18] Zuboff has compared surveillance capitalism with industrial capitalism where the former exploit human nature and the latter exploit nature itself. She advocates that if the digital future is our home that we take control and be masters of information and not make it our slaves.[19] Mass surveillance systems using AI-driven facial recognition technology is another big concern that threatens country-level and global freedoms and can easily lead to electronic police states or even totalitarianism. Although countries deploy these smart surveillance systems to protect their security, confront terrorism, and prevent social unrest or crime, the violation of privacy rights and loss of political and civil freedoms are some of the key worries. Federal and national governments are increasingly investing in these systems that monitor citizens and interpret their activity and behavior. We have also seen resistance in cities such as San Francisco where the use of facial recognition technology by municipalities and law enforcement has been banned.[20] In countries like China mass surveillance with the support of their local tech giants has expanded under the China Internet Security Law with facial recognition technology made compulsory for accessing services like public transport and communication networks.[21] Also linked to mass surveillance, the Chinese government is also using AI for their social credit system to provide a trustworthiness rating of its citizens by collecting fiscal and government data and doing analytics on their social behaviors.[22] It has also been reported that China uses mass surveillance systems to subdue minorities and suppress citizens.[23] On the other hand, the efficiency of China's mass surveillance system has also been demonstrated during the COVID-19 coronavirus pandemic for health surveillance purposes.[24] In a Forbes article Steve Denning has described the pandemic as the great accelerator that is both speeding up positive and negative trends in society, governments and business. He emphasizes on the negative side how the limits of civil rights are being tested by aspiring authoritarians and public bailouts being diverted for political purposes and on the positive side the shift to digital and virtual work and education and the acceleration of organizational adaptation.[25] We have also seen significant differences in adaptability by governments in dealing with the coronavirus, which leads to outcomes that vary accordingly from both a health and economic perspective. AI will play a key role to help the agile to survive in this new age being ushered in.

Potential Benefits of AI for Society and Social Good

If we can navigate the smart technology era wisely, AI has tremendous potential benefits for social good and society as a whole. This also ties in with the sentiments of Max Tegmark, President of the Future of Life Institute, who said "Everything we love about civilization is a product of intelligence, so amplifying our human intelligence with artificial intelligence has the potential of helping civilization flourish like never before – as long as we manage to keep the technology beneficial."[26] AI's benefits for society also dovetails with the benefits expected from the broader fourth industrial revolution or smart technology era which centers around a future for humanity where as many people as possible "enjoy more freedom, better health, higher levels of education and more opportunities to live the lives they value, while suffering less from insecurity and economic uncertainty".[27] The latter is the words from Klaus Schwab, Founder of the World Economic Forum and author of *The Fourth Industrial Revolution* and *Shaping the Fourth Industrial Revolution* where he also makes the following call that speaks further to the societal benefits of the Smart Technology Era: "The new technology age, if shaped in a responsive and responsible way, could catalyze a new cultural renaissance that will enable us to feel part of something much larger than ourselves - a true global civilization. The Fourth Industrial Revolution has the potential to robotize humanity, and thus compromise our traditional sources of meaning - work, community, family, identity. Or we can use the Fourth Industrial Revolution to lift humanity into a new collective and moral consciousness based on a shared sense of destiny. It is incumbent on us all to make sure that the latter is what happens." [28]

In a recent survey report by the Pew Research Center called *Artificial Intelligence and the Future of Humans* where they have interviewed almost a thousand technology experts, entrepreneurs, developers, researchers, activists as well as business and policy leaders, they outline some of the benefits and positive outcomes of how humans and AI might evolve together in the next decade.[29] This includes new life and work efficiencies where we can extrapolate from what we already observe in terms of how AI is being integrated into many facets of life to enhance human capacities, productivity and create new efficiencies, as well as augmenting and optimizing the life and work experiences of humans. By continual off-loading routine and tedious intellectual and physical tasks to AI and robotic systems, these smart systems can not only relieve us from repetitive or physically dangerous or difficult tasks, but also open new challenges for our activities and allow us to embark on more creative, meaningful, intellectual, and strategic pursuits that might have a long-term and in-depth nature. As AI becomes more naturally integrated into our everyday lives and developing a better understanding of our daily routines with better human-machine interfaces, wearable devices, internet access and sophistication, we can also expect it to further enhance our ability to communicate and learn, improve our communication opportunities and sharing capabilities, help us to create better habits, increase the amount of time we devote to activities we find meaningful, and assist us in living full, healthy, productive and purposeful lives. From a work experience perspective, augmented intelligence and cognitive analytics will assist us with basic decisions, freeing up the human intellect to find avenues to accelerate growth and allow us to drive transformation at a faster pace. We are also likely to see the emergence of a higher-level type of labor supported by AI-driven augmented intelligence that requires creativity, direction and supervision of the safe investigation and execution of business initiatives along with perseverance and grit to accomplish the defined goals and objectives. In augmenting and complementing human capabilities such as cognition and decision-making, AI-driven affective computing and productivity-increasing adaptive human-machine interfaces can also protect us from irrational behavior and stupidity, challenge our decisions with insightful questions, and provide continuous support, advice, and communications. AI-driven intellectual companions with interactive reasoning and context understanding can also help manage information overload, enhance search, summarize, and engage on information content, and make recommendations. We have also seen the beneficial use of AI in research across many fields of study such as medicine, neuroscience, materials science, biotechnology, astrophysics, engineering, and agriculture. As AI models in specific domains have also proven to produce more accurate results compared to human experts, we can expect more of these models to be embedded in real-world applications such as say medical diagnostics. The promise of AI is to scale appropriately customized advice to as many people as possible in most if not all fields of human endeavor and to find new solutions to persistent problems and improve the overall quality of life. AI can also help create new economic activities and services or transform existing ones into becoming cost-effective and abundantly available. Apart from enriched interactions between humans and AI systems freeing up time for socializing with other humans, AI will also enhance human-human interaction and assist, augment and amplify individual and collective human intelligence in a substantial manner. It can also function as an interpreter of communication to help us be comparably understanding to others, improve the way we relate to one another, and further greater societal progression. AI, as also a prerequisite to achieving a post-scarcity world, has the potential to enrich the quality of life so that the current age of labor and workaholism will transition into a society where its well-being will for example be enhanced through intellectual pursuits, sustainable development activities, culture, leisure, the arts, and entertainment. Furthermore, AI can support the "slow movement" that advises a cultural shift towards slowing down life's pace and focusing more on quality, doing things as well as possible as opposed to as fast as possible, and connecting with people and the natural word. Societies, individuals, businesses, organizations, and governments will need to be thoughtful about how AI systems are implemented and make sensible choices on use and restriction of use that benefit as many people as possible. To maximize AI's benefit for society, AI systems that administer social and governmental organizations needs to ensure equity, empathy and consistency in provisioning of services to the population, ensure ethics training to make good decisions, disseminate equitable responses to basic care and data collection, reduce knowledge overload as it implements policies and serve the public good, remove human emotion-driven discrimination and avoid exploitation. As AI systems are being integrated into human societies, we can expect most aspects of human existence to be affected.

There are also parallels between the potential benefits of AI and that of electricity for society. The impact and utility of AI in the future will most likely be similar to that of electricity with respect to characteristics such as its pervasiveness, integratedness and functional visibility. As with electricity, AI systems are not always functionally visible to us unless it is not working. We will likely encounter AI in behind-the-scenes systems built to adapt homes, living spaces, workspaces, and smart community and city environments to better suit our needs and desires. Similar to electricity it might operate in a smart grid like system where there is an AI supervisor system that coordinates a network of other AI systems. With smart instrumentation these AI systems can be fed by inputs such as environmental sensors, air quality, sound, images, video, and information about natural and social events to provide collective notifications and insight to everyone in a certain location about the concerns of environmental factors, social dynamics, physical health, crime through community policing, and pre-crime security monitoring of airports and other public assembly places. Given AI's transformative impact across all industries and sectors as we have seen in the previous chapters, large portions of the world's population are already being affected. We also see this impact as AI is being applied to help public transportation systems in providing better services to citizens by optimizing routes, travel times and stops, as well as enabling significant improvements to traffic, sewage treatment, supply chains, utilities, agriculture, and food distribution transportation. AI will likely play a critical role in dealing with the increasing complexity and demand of large-scale technology systems such as the internet, power grids, highways, and roads. There are also great expectations that AI solutions will be able to make an impact in developing countries and the poorest parts of the world by helping with the delivery of cost-effective health and education services as well as solving issues of water production, food growth and distribution. AI and affective computing should also benefit the elderly and physically handicapped people of society with an ever-growing array of options and choices pertaining to support, health, disposition, and mobility. As AI is also similar to other labor-saving devices, AI is also correlated with increased health and lifespan and will keep a population healthier and safer in a highly instrumented world. AI will also assist us in reducing man-made and natural risks such as terror activities, environmental threats, and nascent diseases, epidemics, and pandemics.

With regards to the future of work, it is clear that new work will materialize and that there will be some solutions to address job loss, but the latter is still a major concern that we will address later in this chapter. The other two major AI benefits for society described in the Pew Research report are with respect to education and healthcare which we also covered extensively from an AI use cases perspective in the previous chapter. Many people have high aspirations and hopes as the application of AI progresses to create meaningful, adaptive, and personalized learning assistants that can accelerate, and scale targeted lifelong and life-wide education for as many people as possible around the globe. Due to smart technology adoption, agility and speed of execution, the non-traditional and informal education sector is likely to grow much faster than the established formal education sector. Due to massive demand, adult education will be transformed to cater for relevant 21st century skills, knowledge, and occupational training to help ensure people are better equipped and adaptable to function more optimally in the smart technology era. AI along with other smart technologies such as augmented and virtual reality will enable new learning models that emphasize connection, assimilation, and accommodation of knowledge as opposed to just retention or regurgitation of knowledge. It fits in with training people to learn and reason from first principles and understand concepts, ideas, and relations in a deep way. As discussed in the previous chapter, personalized learning assistants that are always available anywhere along with adaptive learning management systems will make it possible to easily adapt to an individual's learning style and speed as well as day-to-day cognitive and emotional state to drive learning forward in a real-time and responsive fashion and give people insight and guidance into their personalized learning journey.

AI's applications in healthcare are also seen as one the key areas of societal benefit, where we can expect that going forward many lives can be saved, improved, and also extended with robust AI-driven personalized diagnostics, healthcare delivery, precision medicine and wellness solutions. With smart technology tools, wearable devices, sensors, and intelligent virtual assistants becoming increasingly accessible at greater scale to society, more people can benefit from preliminary screening and diagnostics, quicker recognition of risks, early identification of diseases, lessening of medical errors, recommended preventative actions, and expert guidance. These smart technology health-related solutions will become a conduit for incorporating the most up-to-date advances in medical treatment based on best practices and state-of-the-art healthcare research and have this available to more people, including healthcare professionals. The development of drugs will also be accelerated through the use of AI. Furthermore, personalized AI-powered healthcare services and solutions will become a more tangible and impactful reality to society with greater access to health-related data such as medical history, health risk assessments, genetic makeup, DNA profile, drug allergies, medical claims, and real-time data from fitness and health-related wearable devices and intelligent virtual assistants. These smart digitized healthcare solutions will also allow for more frequent and quicker identification of the benefits, risks and effectiveness of medical treatments and drug interactions on a personalized level as well as minimizing overdiagnosis and overtreatment scenarios where human bias and emotions might be counterproductive in the decision-making process. Continuous real-time monitoring of people's health, especially high-risk patients, is a reality via internet-connected medical devices and wearables that provides a constant stream of data. It would be a substantial benefit to society to have these types of solutions available in cost-effective and scalable fashion to most of humanity, in particular those people that are completely underserved in rural and poor communities as well as the elderly and people with disabilities. That said, for both healthcare and education application areas there are also concerns about data privacy and the digital divide, but this can be addressed on another level by for example implementing policies, regulations and democratization of AI and its solutions which I will discuss in later chapters.

Stanford University produced a periodic expert review report called the *One Hundred Year Study on Artificial Intelligence* a few years ago that provided some reflections about AI and its anticipated influences over the next decade or so.[30] This is being followed-up by studies exploring the application of AI in healthcare and personal advice as well as AI-driven advisory systems in preparation for the next report.[31] They emphasize the significantly growing future AI use cases with a profound beneficial impact on society and the economy such as healthcare diagnostics and targeted treatments, physical assistance for elder care, as well as self-driving cars. The report also stresses the importance of innovative mechanisms to help ensure that these benefits are shared as broadly as possible across society and that democratic values such as transparency, equality, and freedom are not compromised. They also make the point that AI in the longer term may potentially be considered as an innovative and radical vehicle to create wealth that can be shared by everyone. Just by extrapolating from our current interaction and uses with smartphones and the wide spectrum of interconnected devices that generate sensor information at scale along with the current development path of AI technology and its applications, it is clear that the future relationship that people have with these smart devices will become more subtle, adaptable, and individualized. There is a shift towards developing smart systems that are more human-centric, trustworthy, and increasingly better at interacting and collaborating with people as well as more effective and scalable in the methods to train these AI-driven systems. Given the progress that we already see with autonomous transportation, in particular self-driving vehicles, it is likely that this form of embodied AI system will have a substantial influence on how people perceive the manifestation of AI in our everyday lives. This will likely have a chain reaction effect on how people use their time, where they live, how shared transportation is personalized, and how cities and metropolitan areas are organized and designed. With significant improvements in robotics, mechanical systems and AI to ensure safe and more dependable systems, we are also likely to see an increase in the long-awaited use of home and service robots in application areas such as cleaning, package delivery, and improved security. By having home environments better integrated and connected with health-monitoring systems and devices, the door will be opened for some more innovation and beneficial health-related applications that might include individualized rehabilitation and in-home treatments and therapy. This report also emphasizes the broader positive societal consequences of AI-driven education, in particular online education that uses AI for personalized learning which are set to likely become part of a blended classroom type of educational experience and embedded at all levels of education. Although AI-driven entertainment will enable a greater variety of entertainment forms that are more individualized, customized, engaging, and interactive, more work needs to be done to determine how entertainment should be shaped to be in the best interest of the individual and society. Similarly, the democratization of AI-generated media or AI-assisted entertainment content creation should in principle be a good thing for society, but the effects of this on society and how humans' taste for entertainment will evolve is also uncertain. As we contemplate this, we should measure the success of AI applications to the value that they create for society. Another major beneficial application of AI for society is in the area of public safety and security which can include a range of application areas such as cybersecurity, credit card fraud detection and prevention, preventative and predictive policing with anomaly detection of possible crimes and removing human bias in decision-making and unjustifiable targeting of people. Stanford University has also recently launched the Institute for Human-Centered Artificial Intelligence that focuses on guiding artificial intelligence to benefit humanity through their mission of advancing AI research, education, policy, and practice to improve the human condition.[32]

The Organization for Economic Co-operation and Development (OECD) has recently reported on how AI is used to detect, respond, and recover from the COVID-19 coronavirus pandemic.[33] This is another example of how smart technology along with all relevant data can be utilized for societal benefit and help to understand the virus, fast track research and development of relevant drugs and treatments, recognize and diagnose the virus (e.g., pattern recognition using symptom data and medical imagery), predict its growth and evolution (e.g., epidemiological models and predicting an individual's likelihood of infection), help with stopping or at least slowing down its spread through the use of contact tracing and surveillance, provide early warning and interactive response through relevant contextualized information (through the use of intelligent virtual assistants and chatbots and filtered news to combat misinformation), and smart monitoring of the recovery (e.g., tracking economic recovery through the use of social media, GPS, and satellite data).

Whereas in the past it was mainly increases in capital investment and labor that helped to drive economic growth across the globe, these productivity levers are not able to sustain these growth levels anymore as can be seen in the steady decline in the average gross domestic product growth rate over the last three decades. Not only has the labor-force growth in developed countries been stationary, but the growth rate in the total factor productivity which measures how well an economy uses its existing capital and people has been slowing for the last decade.[34] AI has the potential to overcome the physical limitations of these traditional drivers of production by not only generating substantial increases in productivity and efficiency, but also transform the way growth is created. In an Accenture report called *Why Artificial Intelligence is the Future of Growth*, they have modelled the expected economic growth with and without AI for twelve countries that produce more than 50% of the world's economic output (besides the USA and Japan, the rest are from Europe).[35] From this analysis, the USA's annual growth rate could jump from 2.6% to 4.6% in 2035, which implies an additional $8.3 trillion added to their economy, whereas Japan can triple their real gross value added and the European countries can double theirs on average over this period. Their report shows how AI can both enhance the total factor productivity and add additional growth as a new factor of production. This can be done through three channels, where the first is a *new virtual workforce* which Accenture calls intelligent automation that automates physical tasks in for example factories and warehouses with the use of robots or the automation of certain customer services through the use of chatbots and self-learning intelligent virtual assistants. The second AI-induced growth channel is *augmenting labor and capital* by complementing human capabilities, helping people to focus on performing tasks where they can excel and add the most value, and also enhance capital efficiency through process and equipment optimization, predictive maintenance and reducing downtime. The third growth channel is *innovation diffusion* and focuses on how AI-induced innovation spreads through the economy with self-driving cars providing a good example of how its impact could over time extend well beyond the automotive industry. It can for example also affect how people spend their time which opens leisure, entertainment, and retail opportunities, how insurance could create additional revenue streams with better instrumentation and data available with regards to driving and total customer mobility, and how public health is positively impacted through a reduction in traffic and road accidents and fatalities as well as people with disabilities being able to move around more freely.

Amongst the vast array of social good projects where AI can make a tremendous impact and affect hundreds of millions (if not billions) of people, there are some big-ticket ones such as climate science and curing cancer, but also many others that address very challenging social problems without the need to necessarily make scientific breakthroughs. McKinsey Global Institute's report on *Applying AI for Social Good* provides a mapping of AI use cases to domains for social good and discusses how AI solutions can be used for social benefit, as well as how risks can be managed and obstructions can be overcome.[36] The broad spectrum of AI capabilities are applicable to social good use cases and includes for example image and video classification, object detection and localization, face detection and person identification, tracking, natural language processing and understanding to address language and communication hurdles, sound detection and recognition, sentiment analysis, emotion recognition, content generation, and reinforcement learning. The 160 social good use cases analyzed covers all 17 of the United Nations Sustainable Development Goals and maps to domains such as health (e.g., treatment delivery, prediction and prevention, long-term care, mental wellness) and hunger, education (e.g., education and completion of education, maximizing student achievement, and teacher and administration productivity), security and justice (e.g., harm prevention, fair prosecution and policing), and equality and inclusion (e.g., accessibility and disabilities, exploitation, and marginalized communities). On the health front most of the use cases focused on early-stage medical diagnoses such as detecting skin cancer through image recognition and detecting potential early signs of diabetes with an 85% accuracy through AI-enabled wearables that capture heart rate sensor data.[37] AI can help to address hunger and famine by optimizing food distribution networks in regions that face shortages. On the education front impactful use cases involve the effective distribution of online education services to underserved populations, early learner distress identification, and the application of adaptive learning through customizing content recommendation based on the learners' abilities. Other social use case domains that are also especially relevant for the current times are crisis response (e.g., disease outbreak, migration crises, natural and man-made disasters and search and rescue), information verification and validation (e.g., false news and polarization), environment (e.g., climate change and adaptation, energy efficiency and sustainability, and conservation of animals, plants, land, air and water) and economic empowerment (e.g., financial inclusion, initiatives for economic growth, labor supply and demand matching, and agricultural quality and yield). AI can help to predict virus and disease transmission patterns through applying machine learning on a spectrum of data sources such as telecommunications data, geospatial data, online search data, social media data, and vaccination data. There are also many environmental use cases such as using AI-powered image recognition and robotics to sort recyclable material from waste, predict routes and behavior of illegal fishing boats using satellite imagery, and detecting illegal logging in exposed forests through AI analysis of audio sensor data.[38] Other social use case domains from a governmental perspective includes public and social sector (e.g., services to citizens, effective management of public and social sectors, public finance management, and fundraising) and infrastructure (e.g., energy, water and waste management, transportation, real-estate, and urban planning). I will discuss some of these AI-driven public sector use cases later in this chapter.

Most of the technology giants also support AI for social good initiatives to varying degrees. For example, Google has applied AI to applications such as predicting famine, protecting whales and forecasting floods via their own AI research and engineering projects and has also launched the Google AI Impact Challenge which was a call for organizations around the globe to submit ideas for how AI can be used to help address societal challenges.[39]

They received more than 2,600 applications from not-for-profit organizations and for-profit social enterprises in six continents and 119 countries, with projects addressing a wide range of issue areas such as crisis response economic empowerment, education, environment, equality and inclusion, health and the public sector.[40] A crisis response project example involved the prediction of wildfires, earthquakes, floods, and other catastrophic events by applying deep learning, image classification, and object detection to data sources such as historical occurrences, emergency response organization internal data, public international and regional data, satellite images, and weather data. Some economic empowerment use cases involved improving access to credit for financially excluded individuals and communities by applying deep learning and other machine learning analytics to external transaction data such as utility payments and mobile phone usage, historical borrower repayment rates and financial organization internal transaction data. Some agricultural use cases involved forecasting, identifying, and managing crop damage; conserving and measuring soil health; and obtaining estimates for irrigation, fertilizer, and pesticide usage. These applications applied deep learning and other machine learning techniques, image classification, and object detection to sensor and weather data as well as image data from mobile applications that take pictures of crops. One of the educational projects involved creating learning tools and emotional training for learners with autism spectrum disorder where facial recognition and speech processing are applied to faces and poses in images and videos as well as other user-generated data via mobile applications. Another involved mapping out school locations in developing regions with the use of image classification, object detection and natural language processing on a variety of data sources such as census data, satellite images, national and regional poverty, employment, and health outcomes related data as well as publicly available articles and news about specific schools and data from the United Nations statistics division. A project to enhance teacher and administration productivity involved the use of deep learning, natural language processing and machine learning analytics to provide grading and feedback to improve skills by using past graded papers, projects, and homework as training input. Some key environment projects involved estimating air pollution as well as its causal effects such as health outcomes or severe storms. For the latter, deep learning and other machine learning techniques were applied to insurance claims data, weather and storm data, publicly available community demographic data as well as emissions data. To estimate urban air pollution and tracking of concentrated methane emissions, a combination of deep learning, image classification, and object detection were used on air sensor data, hyperspectral imaging, satellite images, traffic flow data and publicly available emissions data. To identify and monitor plastic debris on water and land, image classification and object detection was applied to existing street images from Google Earth's Street View, satellite images, and user-generated pictures and videos through mobile applications. On the equality and inclusion front, projects varied from accessibility and disabilities, migrants and refugees, human exploitation, and fair analysis in criminal proceedings. For example, predicting human trafficking patterns related to recruitment and transactions make use of a variety of structured and unstructured data such as arrest and indictment records, federal state, and local human trafficking cases, police narratives, and publicly available US Department of Labor enforcement data. To forecast the demand for aid within refugee camps requires data sources such as census data, survey data, weather data as well as datasets from the International Organization for Migration datasets for displacement tracking. The health projects cover use cases that we have already discussed before in application areas such as diagnosis, mental health, outbreaks and epidemics, prevention, and treatment. A mental health project example involved triaging people at most immediate risk of suicide where natural language processing, sentiment analysis, and speech processing is applied to SMS conversations, social media, and speech recordings. Some of other complementary examples of AI for social good projects that explicitly map to the United Nations sustainable development goals include applying AI on satellite imagery and survey data to extract socioeconomic indicators and generate visualizations and predictions of poverty in areas without survey data; predicting and addressing severe acute childhood malnutrition by applying AI to satellite images, localized food prices, and conflict data; and in the gender equality category, natural language processing methods such as topic modeling, psycholinguistic feature modeling, and audio signal processing on voice recordings and chat transcripts from crisis call hotlines for women are leveraged to escalate calls with high risk of intimate partner violence.[41]

Google also shared some insights from their Google AI Impact Challenge to help fast track social good with AI. These include that AI is not always the right tool to use to solve the problem; data accessibility challenges can vary significantly by sector; the demand for technical talent now also includes data and engineering expertise to complement the specialized AI expertise; there needs to be practical forward planning to help transform AI insights into real-world social impact; most projects require partnerships to access both domain sector expertise and technical ability; as there is significant overlap in terms of what various organizations are doing, they can benefit from shared resources and collaboration; and organizations need to be assisted in helping to prioritize responsibilities.[42]

Risks, Concerns and Challenges of AI for Society

Although there are high expectations of the positive impact of AI for society, there are some real worries, risks, and challenges that we also need to take very seriously, have a deep look at and address face on. Some of the remedies and solutions will be highlighted in later chapters. In Pew Research Center's *Artificial Intelligence and the Future of Humans* report, they outline some of the key risks, concerns and challenges shared by a variety of expert respondents about how progress in AI and its applications might affect human agency, what it means to be human, our ability to exercise free will, our productivity, how we evolve and how we survive over the next few decades and longer-term.[43] Despite these potential drawbacks and pitfalls, 63% of the almost thousand respondents said they are hopeful that overall most people will be in a better position in 2030 as opposed to 37% feared that this will not be the case. The report addresses five main areas of concern which includes human agency, data abuse, job loss, dependence lock-in, as well as disorder and destabilization of society.[44] Let us first focus on human agency. As we know that AI's applications are implemented over a spectrum of assisted, augmented, and autonomous intelligence, the latter can lessen or even completely remove the need for human involvement in certain tasks. Given the accelerating technological change, the fear is that the pervasive deployment of these advanced autonomous systems can lead to people having less control over their lives, not able to give input into how these systems work, and that we automatically cede our decision-making, independence, and privacy to opaque software-driven systems that we have no control over. It seems like people are willing to do this in exchange for not only the perceived benefits provided by these smart systems such as search, social interaction, convenience, productivity, efficiency, pattern recognition, and data storage, but how it helps people to function optimally from a personal, social, business, research and entertainment perspective and stay competitive and connected in this technology-driven world. As these networked AI systems evolve with more cognitive capabilities such as reasoning, perception, learning, logic, creativity, and problem solving, we can expect human agency to be even more affected compared to the current state where these smart technologies already have a substantial impact on our systems that control the way we search, how we socially interact, what information we get, our financial markets, our commerce, our governance, our law enforcement and armed forces, our energy and industrial operations, and even our health operations. By having reduced human agency or not supporting our human agency, we may lose our individual freedom to choose how we want to live our lives and do things, which might be private and not "plugged into the system". The concern is not just about human agency, but also specifically about the nature of these AI-driven platforms and services not being human-centric and primarily focused on profit maximization goals that treat people like commodities through seeking our attention, making choices for us, manipulating us, and filling our days as opposed to supporting our decision-making process and respecting our time, our decisions, our wellness, our quality of life, our individual purpose, what is important to us, what makes us fulfilled, and what truly helps to optimize our lives. In a later chapter I will discuss some proposed solutions that can assist in achieving the latter. AI researcher and practitioner Francois Chollet mentioned in a Medium article that the primary thing that worries him about AI is the "highly effective, highly scalable manipulation of human behavior that AI enables, and its malicious use by corporations and governments".[45] He specifically describes how social media is acting as a psychological panopticon, how digital information consumption is being treated as a psychological control vector and how human behavior is in fact approached as an optimization problem. So, this also touches on data abuse which will be covered next.

There are major concerns about surveillance in all different forms including surveillance capitalism, corporate surveillance and governmental surveillance that are designed in essence for control, manipulation, efficiency, or profit or combinations of these as well as potentially being untrustworthy, fallible, and biased with inconsistencies, miscalculations, and faulty assumptions. A core problem is that ethics, human values, and people-centeredness do not currently appear to be key components in the foundational layer of these AI-driven solutions or platforms that technology companies, corporations or governments are deploying. The current focus seems to be not on creating value for people or understanding people's intentions, goals, and beliefs, but more on extracting value from people, hijacking their behavior and driving them towards expenditure and conformity. This also contributes to the relentless break down of trust and truth that are key components to keep society together. Given the multinational and globally networked nature of some of these platform-driven companies, it is also not easy to direct or regulate them to prevent data abuse. As mentioned earlier, I am personally worried about the establishment of digital dictatorships driven by totalitarian governments where AI is personalized to control individual citizens and suppress their democratic rights, choices, hopes and freedom. In a recent BBC article, they describe a global AI-powered totalitarian government that governs indefinitely as a gloomy fate that could be "worse than extinction" and a "world in chains".[46] In such a scenario, people will likely be robbed from freedom and privacy, have no hope for escape, and have no agency to control their own lives. We need governments to truly act in the best interest and well-being of citizens and not to optimize to maintain power, increase bureaucracy, and mainly benefit those in power. There is also a danger that people's innovation and creativity will be dampened by a fear associated with the unconscious awareness of surveillance and risks involved. Another problem is the uneven use of AI that typically benefits those who are more prosperous and have more resources. This is clearly not in the best interest of most people. The current trend, especially in the West, seems to be not democratic with respect to the governance of AI with technology companies and corporations - with power concentrated in a few of them - having more free reign in this regard to help drive market needs as opposed to the real needs of people, whereas in more authoritarian countries there is a tendency to track citizens on a continuous basis and forcing them to push along with the rest of the population without much room to move and for individual choices. What makes the data abuse matter even more delicate is that AI-driven decision-making can be presented as neutral, whereas it could in principle be unchecked and preserve existing social biases and unfairness. Furthermore, these systems can potentially give people the false sense that they are making choices and have autonomy, but still have them wrapped within the context and frameworks that are determined by these corporations or governments. New advances and progress in smart technology might also outpace regulators' ability to keep up-to-date and allow people, companies, and organizations to still exploit AI, sidestep privacy defenses, or abuse data for their personal, commercial, or political gains. Henry Kissinger even goes as far as saying that human society is unprepared for AI from a philosophical, intellectual and every other way and that enlightenment will likely end if we do not systematically explore and study AI's full scope and implications and apply it in wise and practical ways that benefit society.[47]

Another significant concern is the loss, disruption and dislocation of human jobs which also involves ongoing changes with tasks within jobs being automated by AI-driven software and robotics. Whereas new jobs will be created or shifts within jobs to adjust for working in concert with smart technology, there is a fear that AI will contribute to substantial net job losses that would make the existing gap on a digital and economic front even wider and in turn can potentially lead to economic and social pandemonium as also described in Chapter 2. So even with significant benefits to society, there is a real and present danger that AI will also intensify various forms of inequality in society, especially in the current type of capitalist economy that likely needs some adjustments to benefit more people. Kai-fu Lee in *AI Superpowers* describes the real AI crisis to be unemployment that is not only occupation or task-based related where we see automation leading to one-to-one replacements, but also involves job losses due to from the ground-up industry-wide disruptions that are created through new AI-enabled business models.[48] His net unemployment estimates of between 20 to 25% by 2030 is also more in line with Bain & Company's projection where they have considered the dynamics and interaction of macro-level forces such as demographics, automation and inequality.[49] They reckon that the reabsorption of workers into newly created professions would not significantly alter the growing trend of job rearrangement and that 80% of workers will effectively be impacted through both job displacements and income pressures. In *The Economic Singularity*, Calum Chace also echoes these sentiments and makes a case for AI automating most jobs within the next few decades.[50] The same holds for Martin Ford who argues in *The Rise of the Robots* that AI-driven systems and solutions are on the brink of extensive automation of white collar jobs.[51] Whereas McAfee and Brynjolfsson initially validate the possibility of technological unemployment in their book *The Second Machine Age*, they have maneuvered away from this in their follow-up book *Machine, Platform, Crowd* and emphasized more the impact of AI as it relates to the structural changes in the economy and a shift in the kinds of jobs that will be available.[52] Of course not everyone agrees that significant job losses will happen as can be seen throughout the broader history of automation where people have been successful in making the required transitions. PwC has for example predicted that AI - over a 20-year period until 2037 - will create as many jobs as it displaces in the UK with jobs increasing in health (by 22%), scientific and technical services (by 16%) and education (by 6%), whereas jobs will likely decrease in manufacturing (by 25%), transport and storage (by 22%) and public administration (by 18%).[53] Even though the cognitive type of automation is posing a problem for many jobs in their current form (including white-collar ones), it does not necessarily imply that this would be the case for newly transformed jobs where people work in a symbiotic relationship with smart technology and not necessarily lose responsibility, oversight or control of the AI-driven tools and systems. As discussed earlier, we might also see many unforeseen opportunities and new employment doors being opened. However, the problem comes in with how we proactively and responsibly handle the transition and change in employment arrangements and the nature of work in order to avoid all-embracing social issues. A safe transition to a more just social contract is made more difficult with our ever-expanding consumption of goods and services that drives our desires, needs and expectations, companies deploying more software-driven automation and reducing full-time employment, and governments not having adequate safety nets in place to assist in this regard. This leads to a situation where many people are and will likely be stuck in a condition of existence without security or predictability that affects their material or psychological wellbeing. This might even be further amplified in developing and poorer countries, especially so if they do not get assistance from richer and more developed countries that are and will likely be in a better position to tap into the benefits of AI on an individual, society, business and public sector level. Kai-Fu Lee argues that AI is an inequality machine that will enable winner-take-all economics in many industries, drive polarization and aggravate inequality across the global economy and even within countries such as the US and China. He emphasizes that without AI being properly governed, we are on a path to worsen inequality, reduce the middle class and increase the number of people that cannot generate enough income to support themselves.[54]

Although AI should definitely enhance and augment human competencies on various levels and improve lives within a personal, home, educational and work context, there is also a worry that people will become increasingly dependent on smart technology and its associated infrastructure, which in turn would likely weaken our cognitive abilities with respect to independent thinking and decision-making, our social skills in terms of how we interact with other people, as well as our survival skills. The more we hand-off tasks to AI, the stronger the dependence lock-in will likely become with people effectively becoming deskilled in these areas that do not require the same level of human involvement. Another key consideration is to what extent the broader public is really involved to influence, think critically, provide inputs, and make decisions with respect to how AI is being applied as well as the underlying ethics involved. By implication, do people really have a say about the level of their dependence lock-in? There is also an associated concern about the social impact that AI-driven social media and task automation has on people's interpersonal communication, social interaction and negotiation skills and ability to interact with one another. If people do not need to interact, they would in a lot of circumstances make a choice to not interact and prefer to do this digitally in a shortened and limited form through for example the use of smart digital assistants or voice-to-text and related social media and messaging applications. The reduction in face-to-face interpersonal communications and increased dependence on smart technology communication assistance will also likely reduce our ability to express our daily lives effectively and fluently on various levels of society and slacken our writing and speaking abilities. Apart from the poorer communications, there is a growing worry that the time spent with machines will effectively increase, that people will become more detached from reality, less interested and concerned about others, and more focused on themselves. This absence of physical embodied interaction can also lead to social alienation, loneliness, and less personal connections as well as contribute to the rise in problems such as suicide and mental disorders.[55] In a recent psychiatric study, the possible connection between the increase use of digital media and smartphones and the increase of depression, self-harm, and suicide among adolescents in the US was investigated.[56] Besides that these increases happened at the same time, they have highlighted that after 2012 we have especially saw an increase of unhappiness, self-harm, depression and suicide amongst young female adolescents. According to the study, the possible ways that people are being mentally affected and influenced by the use of smartphones and digital media includes for example the disarrangement of in-person social interactions, the availability of online information about self-harm, the intrusion with sleep, and cyberbullying (that might involve sharing, sending, or posting false, harmful, unkind, negative, or malicious content about someone else, people, companies or organizations).[57] Another negative consequence of a dependency lock-in or over-reliance on AI is that this might increase security and humanitarian risks on a national and global level with more people vulnerable and exposed to a potential blackout or interruption of smart technology services, especially if their dependence affects their survival. So, it will be important for people to actively maintain survival proficiency without smart technology and have contingencies in place to handle those scenarios.

Due to people's failure to adapt quickly enough, AI can also be a destructive force in damaging or breaking down organizational systems, governments and institutions that help to order today's society. This disorder and destabilization of society can happen through increased vulnerabilities with respect to the subjection of people to intractable cybercrime and dangerous cyber warfare; the use of weaponized information, disinformation, fabrication, lies and propaganda; complex AI-driven systems that become defective and difficult to control; as well as the development of autonomous lethal weapons and military applications. With smart technology and digital media, we have unfortunately produced a world where reality can be easily manipulated and made difficult to perceive via the escalating use of AI to deliver phony and fraudulent videos, pictures, audio, text, and related media. We are making it increasingly difficult to create one version of the truth with people creating their own version of "reality" that they defend and substantiate with their own "evidence". Given the far-reaching impact of AI-driven systems, one can expect that the beneficial outcomes will unfortunately also be spoiled by bad actors that commit crimes, milk human fears and satisfy their own greed as well as poorly designed systems that have unforeseen or unethical societal repercussions or might lead to accidents and adverse outcomes. The nature of the ethics, trustworthiness, and morality built into AI-driven systems will have a major impact on society. On the cybersecurity front, as discussed in Chapter 4, one can expect a continuous battle between defensive AI security controls that defend against offensive AI-powered attacks. In a report on the malicious use of AI from a security threat perspective, they provide a range of examples within the digital, physical, and political security domains.[58] Some of the AI-powered examples within the political security domain includes automated hyper-personalized disinformation campaigns; automated influence campaigns; denial-of-information attacks; manipulation of information availability; fake news reports with realistic fabricated video and audio; and governmental use of automated surveillance platforms to suppress dissent.[59] Of the top AI threats that we should be concerned about over the next 15 years, a Crime Science journal article *AI-enabled Future Crime* highlights "deep fakes" via audio and video impersonation as the one that could cause the most harm and likely be the most hard to defend against.[60] Other high impact and difficult to defend potential crimes include driverless vehicles as weapons, personalized phishing, the disruption of AI-controlled systems, large-scale blackmailing, and AI-authored fake news. As mistakes will be made faster and have a wider impact than ever before, AI-driven systems need to be as robust, proactive, predictive, and preventative as possible. The net impact on society will depend on how public and private sector stakeholders collaborate and navigate the real-world societal, political, and economic environment and keep in touch with the scientific and smart technology capabilities whilst handling crises such as climate change, food supply and water shortages, job loss, migration agony, and geopolitical distress. Can we use the knowledge and smart technology that we develop wisely in a human-centric and ethical fashion that matches the best values of humanity and benefits as many people as possible?

AI-driven Transformation of the Public Sector

Similar to the revolutionary impact that AI is having on the private sector, it will also help to transform the public sector where we already see practical use cases especially with respect to improving public services delivery, bureaucratic efficiency as well as public safety and security. If AI is applied with wisdom and in a responsible way, it could be a major asset to any country and a source of global competitive edge. In most countries around the globe, citizens unfortunately have in general a bad experience and low satisfaction with public services and its delivery modes as it is typically inefficient with slow response times, backlogs, inaccuracies, redundancy, and poor quality. There are also problems with limited transparency and corruption. AI-driven technologies and platforms can help to significantly improve public service delivery and efficiency by enabling citizens to engage with governments without friction, make it easy to voice their opinions, help them to coordinate their efforts, and even avoid overseeing from public authorities. AI-enabled automation can help to make administrative processes more smooth-running, efficient and faster, help to address resource allocation constraints, increase productivity, and reduce costs and the typical data entry and analysis, paperwork, backlog and tasks involved with mundane, manual, repetitive and redundant processes. In a Deloitte Center of Government Insights report about the AI-augmented government and how AI can be used to redesign public sector work, they show that for the US federal government alone tasks automation can deliver potential savings between \$3.3 billion (tasks speed up by 20%) and \$41.1 billion (tasks speed up by 200%).[61] Apart from task automation, AI can also be used to provide more accurate predictions, detect anomalies, assist with real-time tracking, increase effectiveness and help with better decision making. Intelligent virtual assistants and chatbots can provide 24x7 support, increase responsiveness and engagement levels with citizens. A citizen intelligent virtual assistant can for example help with applications, recruitment, support, public facilities, and notifications, whereas government-to-business intelligent virtual assistants can assist to improve services and interaction with companies and non-profit organizations with respect to API services, permits and compliance. The same holds for improving internal government-to-government services and interaction. Not only will these AI-driven service delivery solutions enhance citizen and business participation but enable them to also communicate their preferences and assess the effectiveness, quality, and usefulness of public services as input to improving services and making better policy decisions. Similar to the innovation that we see in the business sector, smart technology can help governments to create innovative and better forms of service delivery, be more proactive in how it responds to citizens' needs from a social services, education, healthcare, safety, and emergency perspective, and provide better care and management of critical systems and infrastructure with predictive maintenance and defenses against cyberattacks. There is also some contrasting dynamics at play with governments on the one hand gaining smart technological powers to increase their control over citizens based on ubiquitous surveillance systems and ability to control digital infrastructure, but on the other hand also faces mounting pressure to alter their current approach of making policies and engaging with citizens as their central role of conducting policy lessen as a result of the decentralization and reallocation of power and the introduction of novel sources of competition. These dynamics force governments and the public sector to become more agile, efficient, and transparent as they adapt to the disruptive quick changes of the environment and remake themselves to ensure their continuation, regulate in a more pragmatic and relevant way, and improve their services, interaction and collaboration with citizens and the business sector. Deloitte has in a *Government Trend 2020* report highlighted some of the most transformational trends in government with respect to currently implemented government operations across developed and developing countries alike.[62] Governments that are augmented by AI can improve end-to-end public service delivery via a unique digital identity to enable a more efficient and seamless personalized citizen experience and treating citizens, businesses, regulated entities, and government employees like customers.[63] It can also use behavioral science to improve government outcomes and encourage good behavior via promising lower costs and better outcomes whilst respecting human autonomy. AI-augmented governments can further manage ethical complexities to ensure privacy, equity, and transparency across their operations as well as from a regulatory perspective. Such governments can also anticipate problems through predictive analytics across many areas of government and touch on for example social services, food safety to law enforcement. As in the business world, cloud-based infrastructure provides a foundation for innovation and implementing state-of-the-art smart technologies at scale. Safe experimental environments such as accelerators, incubators and labs can also be created to innovate from healthcare to currency, whereas smart city solutions for the public services landscape can range from mobility to healthcare to the environment and expanded to regions, rural communities, universities, and military bases.[64] There is also an opportunity for these governments to promote public trust in AI, demonstrate its potential benefits, assist with creating demand, and develop the local AI industry by providing opportunities to address various governmental needs.

Although public services delivery typically accounts for a substantial proportion of government budgets, the increased spending is often not matched by improvements in outcomes. According to Atos, the projected worldwide spending on AI for the public sector will be approximately $9 billion in 2021.[65] China has a multi-billion-dollar plan to become the AI world leader by 2030.[66] Accenture estimates that globally AI will help to double annual economic growth rates and increase labor productivity up to 40% by 2035 and at the same time could create almost $1 trillion in economic value in the sector across 16 major developed economies.[67] In the same report they mention that the IDC projects that governments will see the second largest AI spend of any industry by 2023. The IDC has recently also reported that spending in AI and smart technology is likely to accelerate across the public sector as a result of automation and social distance compliance required to tackle the coronavirus pandemic.[68] Whereas governments use smart technology to assess social distancing compliance, it is also implemented to help fast track COVID-19 diagnosis and testing in hospitals and in the form of intelligent virtual assistants providing advice, guidance, and support to patients in self-isolation.

From a public safety and security perspective, AI-driven solutions can also add significant value with respect to crime prediction and prevention and help to reduce the crime rate (which is the number of reported crimes per 100,000 total population). Although there has been a decline in crime rates in many countries, criminal activities are still a serious problem that many countries are facing and where smart technology such as AI, big data, internet of things, drones, and augmented reality are increasingly being used to help the police to ensure public safety and control crime.[69] In order for governments to prevent crime, AI can assist by analyzing huge volumes of data to find patterns that can be useful to law enforcement. In for example the South African context (which is unfortunately also currently one of the crime hotspots in the world), AI use cases involve the discovery of patterns, diagnostics, predictive analytics, and prescriptive insights for specific crimes such as violent crimes (e.g., murder, rape, car hijackings, cash-in-transit heists, cash point robberies, farm attacks, kidnapping, xenophobic violence), financial and property crimes (e.g., building hijacking, asset stripping, advance fee fraud, municipalities, targeting of government auditors, lawyers overcharging clients), and theft, smuggling, and vandalism (e.g., arson, power grid, livestock theft, house breaking, school plunder and vandalism, drug smuggling and consumption).[70] The more connected, instrumented and smarter the infrastructure, the more real-time information can be fed to AI systems to help detect criminal activities as soon as they happen. Some AI-enabled crime detection use cases include detecting gunfire, bombs, and clues on a crime scene. For example, a company called ShotSpotter provides a precision policing technology suite that can detect, locate and alert on gunfire in less than a minute, provide tactical data such as multiple shooters or automatic weapons, create automated data-driven patrol plans for crime deterrence, and provide investigation and forensic services for crime scene and incident research.[71] Amongst the many companies providing AI-powered video surveillance systems that are also used for crime detection and prevention, Hikvision is one of the leaders that provides

AI-enabled security cameras that recognize faces, read license plates, recognize vehicle attributes, count customers, manage queues, and detect unattended bags or hard hats.[72] From a crime prevention perspective, AI use cases involve predicting crime spots, the people likely to commit a crime, and supporting decisions on pre-trial releases by analyzing risk factors. As an example, Predpol, which calls themselves the Predictive Policing Company, has AI-based solutions that can provide location-based proactive policing and insights, help to allocate and manage patrol resources more effectively, and predict critical events based on crime type, location and time.[73] In China, Cloud Walk is using AI to predict if a person will commit a crime before it happens through the use of facial recognition and gait analysis which measures how people move when walking and detecting anomalous movements and suspicious behavior.[74]

On the spectrum from assisted to augmented to autonomous intelligence, there are many AI applications for national and international security and defense in areas such as intelligence, surveillance, reconnaissance, command and control, cyberspace, cybersecurity, logistics and predictive maintenance. The Department of Defense in the United States defines Intelligence, Surveillance, and Reconnaissance as "an integrated operations and intelligence activity that synchronizes and integrates the planning and operation of sensors, assets, and processing, exploitation, and dissemination systems in direct support of current and future operations."[75] In order to locate and understand the intentions of potential enemies, a wide spectrum of sensors such as videos, imagery, acoustics, and communications as well as platforms such as aircraft, ships, humans, and satellites collect, analyze, and share data, information, and intelligence across multiple warfare domains which includes sub-surface, maritime, land, air, space, and cyber. Some of the intelligence disciplines include signals intelligence, geospatial intelligence, measurement and signatures intelligence, publicly available information, and human intelligence. Due to these large data sets available for analysis, AI is very useful for intelligence which is the product of surveillance and reconnaissance operations. AI-driven computer vision enables videos and photos from uninhabited aerial vehicles to be analyzed and hostile activity for targeting to be automatically identified. So, the work of human analysts who currently spend significant time filtering through videos for actionable information can be automated in order to allow them to use their time more efficiently. As mentioned earlier, AI is enabling more and more realistic video, photo, and audio falsifications, or "deep fakes," that enemies could deploy as part of their information operations. A real worry is that countries could even use deep fake technology against one another to not only generate untrue or distorted news reports, but also weaken public trust, influence public conversation, deceive forensic analysis, and attempt to extort government officials. AI-enabled dynamic behavioral profiles can also be created for suspected intelligence officers, staff, government officials, or private citizens. AI can also enhance cyberspace, cybersecurity, and military cyber operations by training models to detect anomalies in network activity patterns that will enable a more comprehensive and dynamic barrier to attack. Similar to applications in the industrial world, AI can be applied to enable predictive maintenance and optimize logistics within the military sphere. To increase availability and avoid reactive repairs, the Army and Air Force can for example develop tailored maintenance schedules for a fleet of vehicles or aircraft instead of having standardized fleet-wide maintenance schedules. Command and control are another important application area for AI that combines information from various domains, automatically resolves variances from the input data, and provides analytics and insights to a comprehensive common operating picture of friendly and enemy forces for monitoring, strategy, and decision-making purposes. Similar to the progress with AI applications on the commercial semi-autonomous vehicles front where it is used to perceive the environment, recognize obstacles, fuse sensor data, plan navigation, and communicate with other vehicles, AI is also being integrated into military semi-autonomous and autonomous vehicles such as drones, fighter aircraft, ground vehicles, and marine vessels. Another controversial application area is lethal autonomous weapon systems which are a special class of weapon systems that use sensors, AI and other algorithms to identify in unassisted fashion a target and utilize an onboard weapon system to engage and destroy the target without manual human control or involvement with the system. A US Department of Defense Directive described human-supervised autonomous weapon systems as a subset of these fully autonomous weapons that are "designed to provide human operators with the ability to intervene and terminate engagements, including in the event of a weapon system failure, before unacceptable levels of damage occur", which is contrasted with semi-autonomous weapon system that "once activated, is intended to only engage individual targets or specific target groups that have been selected by a human operator."[76] There is currently strong international debate and opposing positions about autonomous weapons systems and little progress has been made so far since the establishment of the United Nations' Group of Governmental Experts that started discussions in this regard.[77] I also participated a few years ago in a Future of Life event with Max Tegmark where we specifically informed African leaders about the dangers and risks involved with lethal autonomous weapon systems. The problem is to also get the major military powers to take a unanimous stance on lethal autonomous weapons. It seems like the US, Russia and the UK has been consistently opposed to a ban on these weapons at this early stage, whereas China has been more ambiguous in this regard.[78]

As advances in smart technology on the one hand will help to potentially reduce the impact or scale of present-day and future violence, strife, clashes, and warfare, they are also capable of causing harm, damage, and suffering on a massive scale, especially with the use of lethal autonomous and biological weapons that are becoming easier to use and more accessible. This has significant implications for public safety and security from a national and international perspective as the world is becoming a more dangerous, complex, and uncertain place to navigate. As the weaponization of AI has been increasing at a rapid rate, it has become a high priority security issue across countries globally. Although we have made progress with data privacy regulations and data having its origin, boundaries and ownership, the problem is that there are for all practical purposes still no rules, borders, or regulations for AI engagement on a national and international law level. Although there have been some agreements on cybercrime, we still have an absence of agreements on AI standards or AI's use for warfare.

Governmental AI Strategies, Policies, and Adoption

In PwC's *Global Artificial Intelligence Study: Sizing the Prize* report, they describe AI's projected $15.7 trillion contribution to the global economy in 2030 as a game changer and exceeding the current output of China and India combined.[79] They predict that AI can help to add up to 26% to the GDP of local economies at that time of which 42% can likely be attributed to increased productivity and 58% to consumption-side effects. Although all countries should experience economic benefit from AI, North America and China will likely see the biggest economic gains with almost 70% of the global economic impact, whereas Europe and other parts of Asia are also likely to experience significant economic gains with developing countries only modest increases due to anticipated lower rates of AI adoption.[80] McKinsey Global Institute advises that governments should spearhead addressing the AI challenges that cut across government, the workforce and society as a whole.[81] As a further acknowledgement of the global anticipated impact of AI on society and the economy, countries across the globe are formulating national AI development plans with some already supported by funding in the order of billions of dollars to for example help build local industries and prepare the workforce for lifelong and life-wide learning and a lifetime of reskilling. Governments are partnering with civil society and non-profit organizations, major tech players and others in the private sector to tackle a range of challenges for countries and their citizens. One of these challenges include motivating a broader adoption of AI and associated smart technology infrastructure across more industries and small to medium enterprises to help competitive markets to flourish, increase productivity growth across the economy, and improve labor productivity to drive higher wages. As there are major concerns about the likely impact of AI-driven automation on employment and income distribution, governments need to reconsider ways of social support such as universal basic income, negative income taxes, and work sharing. MGI estimates that although only a few professions are fully automatable, 60% of all jobs have at least 30% of technically automatable activities and that most jobs will be partially automated without being willy-nilly replaced.[82] As illustrated in previous chapters many AI applications are also aimed at improving capital efficiency and non-labor related cost savings and not necessarily aimed at replacing professions. The fast-changing dynamics and requirements of the job market with respect to skills gaps and oversupply can also be better understood through real-time predictive analytics applied to job market related and other relevant data. Given this trajectory that we are on in the Smart Technology Era, it is certain that the workforce needs to be continuously reskilled to optimally work in symbiosis with AI-driven software and machines. Governments, educational institutions, and the private sector should therefore work on providing better, cost-effective, more practical, and more relevant training programs at scale that are in line with the on-the-job and vocational needs of the private and public sector and enable people to be continuously re- and upskilled. In South Africa the Machine Intelligence Institute of Africa (MIIA) has for example put some training programs in place to address the digital and smart technology skills gap across all levels of education and learning by blending traditional learning practices with futuristic, immersive and practical learning methods with a strong emphasis on digital exploration and exposure in a vocational training setup.[83] A "train the trainer model" enables the capacity of the workforce to be upskilled and accelerates the development and improvement of people's digital and smart technology skills profile. Although we are well into the 21st century, the World Economic Forum has a few years ago provided a new vision for education with an emphasis on the 21st century skills that complement foundational literacies and core skills with competencies (such as critical thinking, creativity, communication and collaboration) that help people deal with complex challenges and character qualities (such as social and cultural awareness, curiosity, initiative, grit, adaptability, and leadership) to approach changing environments.[84] Practical, dynamic and scalable implementation of training that addresses these competencies and character qualities within a vocational on-the-job setup has become essential for humanity's prosperity and wellbeing. Some of the key factors that are holding countries back include policy enablers, human capital, financial resources, and technology infrastructures. From a governmental perspective, policymakers need to continuously assess and realign educational systems and standards with respect to 21st century skills, identify and prioritize key skills gaps within the context of local economies, resources, and constraints, and support innovative learning environments for institutions and education-technology providers.[85]

The implementation of AI also requires a range of regulatory, legal, and ethical issues to be considered and resolved. Apart from handling data privacy, ownership, and protection and addressing bias in training data, the AI algorithms also need to adhere to ethical prescriptions, transparency, and accountability. Another challenge for governments is to ensure that public-sector data is open, standardized, and accessible to help stimulate innovation from the private sector or social good organizations. Intelligent virtual assistants can also be utilized to make it easier to use open data services, API usage, and data sets. As discussed in the previous section, AI can also be used to help to improve the delivery and efficiency of public services and improve public safety and security. Governments should actively drive the establishment of AI development hubs and smart technology incubators that support local industries and also attract AI talent and investment. Some of the best use cases are already seen in the USA with places such as Silicon Valley in San Francisco, Boston and New York leading in North America, whereas Beijing and Shenzhen in China are showing the way to create strong AI technology ecosystems in Asia. In Europe, London looks to be leading the pack followed by cities in Germany, France, and the Nordic countries. Whereas Silicon Valley has been the top global hub for between ten to twenty thousand active startups with approximately 2 million tech workers and the global leader for venture capital investment, New York also have a strong funding ecosystem and a leading hub for financial and media industries with Boston having a long history of excellent collaboration between science and industry and supported by a strong talent pipeline from world-class universities such as MIT.[86] With the Chinese government recognizing AI as being of strategic importance, Beijing is leading with significant research contributions by Tsinghua, Beihang, and Peking universities and have considerable involvement and support from tech leaders such as Baidu, whereas Shenzhen has been a hub for strong expertise in hardware and electronics manufacturing companies such as Huawei and ZTE. Apart from London being a global finance center with great support for fin-tech applications as well as a venture capital leader in Europe, there is also a talent pipeline from universities such as Cambridge, Oxford and Imperial College.[87] In a Tech Nation study funded by the UK government, it has been reported that US companies have raised $92 billion which represents 56% of the global AI investment since 2015, followed by China ($22 billion) and the UK ($6 billion).[88] They have also highlighted 10 cities that account for 44% of the emerging technology investment from 2015 to 2019 with the top five being San Francisco ($20 billion), Beijing ($12 billion), New York ($7 billion), Santa Clara ($6 billion), and London ($5 billion). It was also reported that China has globally the second-highest number of AI companies (about 50% of that of the US) with Beijing being the city having the most AI companies worldwide (almost 400).[89]

Although there is no doubt that AI presents challenges that have global ramifications and are relevant for each country, the implications for specific governments in how to address these challenges and to adopt AI vary across countries. In a recent Deloitte study, they recommend that even though there is frantic competition among countries and companies, that the AI advantage is not a zero-sum game and that there is much to learn from how different countries are adopting AI to help stimulate economic growth and reshape the competitive dynamics of their industries.[90] They provided a spotlight on how some selected countries, in particular US, China, UK, Germany, France, Canada, and Australia, are pursuing the AI advantage and have unwrapped some key insights that can be summarized as follows: There is growing consensus that AI executed properly will have an enormous impact on countries' economy, future growth, job market and competitive advantage. Lessons can be learned from how countries approach AI adoption, given their specific constraints and varying degrees of AI maturity. From the comparative survey, it seems that Chinese business and IT executives had a significantly stronger opinion on the use of AI to create a strong competitive advantage and their ability to address the potential AI risks. Both the US and China also seem to be investing the most in AI. As more companies are increasingly adopting AI to enhance their products and services and optimizing internal operations, there was also an agreement among all correspondents that the window for competitive differentiation for early AI adopters with AI is quickly closing.

The Organization for Economic Cooperation and Development (OECD) AI Policy Observatory in collaboration with a diverse global community of partners provides data and multi-disciplinary analysis on AI with respect to AI principles and practices, policy areas, country-level information on initiatives from business, organizations and technologists, as well as the latest AI developments and trends.[91] They also provide policy information that can be filtered by policy instruments such as national strategy, grant or regulation and the specific group targeted by the policy to enable and promote international collaboration, guidelines and help develop best practices.[92] At the time of writing they had a database of 60 countries represented as well as a range of initiatives on a European Union level. As a participant on the OECD AI's One AI Work Group 3 on national AI policies, it has been fascinating to see the thoroughness, diligence and high-quality work, data capturing and information sharing that has been done so far to get an accurate picture in this regard. The Future of Life Institute also references the national strategies listed on the OECD database as well as some international strategies such as those from the United Nations, European Union, Nordic-Baltic Region, AI Agreement between UAE and India, the International Study Group of AI between France and Canada, and the G7's Charlevoix Common Vision for the Future of Artificial Intelligence.[93] The OECD values-based AI principles are inclusive growth, sustainable development and wellbeing, human values and fairness, transparency and explainability, robustness, security and safety, and accountability. They also have specific principle-oriented recommendations for policy makers with respect to building human capacity and preparing for labor market transformation, growing a digital ecosystem for AI, investing in AI research and development, creating an empowering policy environment for AI, and international collaboration for trustworthy AI.[94] As AI is a new general-purpose type of smart technology, the OECD has done some policy research across all main industries, as well as ones on corporate governance, digital economy, employment, tax, public governance, investment, industry and entrepreneurship, social and welfare issues, environment, trade, science and technology, development, innovation, and competition.[95]

In February 2019 the president of the US signed an Executive Order announcing its national strategy on AI, called the *American AI Initiative*, to promote and protect their national AI technology and innovation and specifically expressed that the "continued American leadership in AI is of paramount importance to maintaining the economic and national security of the United States".[96] This full-on government initiative in collaboration with the private sector, academic organizations, the public sector and international partners specifies five areas to help advance AI which consists of investing in AI research and development, training the workforce to be AI-ready, releasing AI resources, removing hurdles to AI innovation, nurturing an international environment that help reinforce US-based AI innovation, and adopting trustworthy AI for government services and assignments.[97] From an international collaboration perspective the US and G7 partners agreed to launch the Global Partnership on AI to encourage the development of AI to serve democracy, ensure that the development and use is responsible and in line with the shared values of the participating countries.[98] The US and the United Kingdom have for example also entered into a collaboration agreement with respect to R&D, promoting researcher and student collaboration and growing public-private sector partnerships.[99] The 2019 US AI research and development strategic plan focuses on various strategies that includes prioritization and making long-term investments in AI research, developing effective ways for collaboration between humans and AI systems that augment and complement human capabilities, and address ethical, legal, and societal concerns. Other strategies involve ensuring the trustworthiness, reliability, security, and safety of AI systems and that their designs are properly understood and researched, as well as developing and sharing high-quality public datasets, resources and environments for AI training and testing. The AI R&D strategy plan also addresses the development of standards, benchmarks, and associated techniques to measure and evaluate AI technologies and systems, improve opportunities for R&D workforce development to strategically grow an AI-ready workforce, and expedite AI advances through expanding public-private sector partnerships. In February 2020, the first year's annual report highlights a call for a 2-year doubling of investment for non-defense AI research and development, the development of an international statement in collaboration with the Organization for Economic Cooperation and Development and other countries on trustworthy AI principles, an AI regulatory memorandum to guide the development, testing, and implementation of AI technologies and systems in a trustworthy and reliable fashion, a strategy for engagement in AI technical standards, and the establishment of an AI Center of Excellence that assists Federal agencies with tools, infrastructure and best practices to develop AI solutions that address their unique business challenges.[100] The American AI Initiative has also directed all Federal agencies to prioritize their investments in AI research and development of AI. Furthermore, the White House has chartered a Select Committee on AI under the National Science and Technology Council to enhance the coordination of Federal efforts related to AI. Some of the key agencies include the National Science Foundation, National Institutes of Health, Department of Energy, Department of Agriculture, National Institute of Standards and Technology, National Aeronautics and Space Administration, Depart of Transportation, National Artificial Intelligence Institute, Department of Veterans Affairs, National Oceanic and Atmospheric Administration, Department of Defense, Defense Advanced Research Projects Agency, and the Intelligence Advanced Research Projects Activity. The White House's document on AI for the American People also provides other details about AI for

American Innovation that addresses progress on AI R&D, amongst others highlighting the $140 million in awards over five years to seven NSF-led AI Research Institutes, as well as computing infrastructure for AI R&D such as the Frontier supercomputer for high-performance computing and AI that is expected to be ready in 2021 as the world's most powerful computer.[101] The AI for American Industry section of the strategy plan spotlights US government initiatives to support AI applications in transportation with specific reference to autonomous vehicles and unmanned aircraft systems, healthcare, manufacturing, financial services, agriculture, weather forecasting, and national security and defense.[102] The strategy plan also has a special section that covers AI for the American Worker with initiatives such as the National Council for the American Worker, the American Workforce Policy Advisory Board, and a Taskforce on Apprenticeship Expansion. Apart from the federal 5-year STEM education strategic plan and goal to commit at least $200 million in grant funds per annum for high-quality computer science and STEM education, the strategy plan also addresses the training of the next generation of AI researchers as well as vocational training.[103] The AI with American Value section of the strategy plan addresses workforce impact and the importance of robust and safe AI and explicitly states the goal of making sure that AI technologies are "understandable, trustworthy, robust, and safe" and that the "broader impacts of AI on society must be considered, including implications for the workforce and assurances that AI will be developed responsibly".[104] OECD.AI policy observatory currently lists 40 policy initiatives for the US which also include a number of the policy related initiatives referenced above.[105] There has been an exponential increase in funding for AI companies in the US the past decade, rapidly growing from less than $300 million in 2011 to approximately $16.5 billion in 2019, which accounts for more than 60% of the worldwide funding for AI startups of $26.6 billion in the same year.[106] Although the US has been leading basic and applied research in AI for decades with support from public and private investments and attracting top international talent to the US, there have also been concerns about some recent policies about hardening of immigration rules for international researchers and tax plans that could elevate students costs.[107] From Deloitte's survey of more than a thousand US business and information technology executives, the concerns are about outsiders influencing and skewing AI recommendations and insights through training data and algorithm manipulation as well as the risks involved in sensitive or proprietary data being misappropriated.[108]

China has announced in 2017 a *New Generation Artificial Intelligence Development Plan* that boldly outlines China's strategy, guiding ideology, basic principles, strategic goals, deployment considerations, key tasks in rolling this out, resource allocation, safeguard measures, organization and implementation.[109] They declare that as AI will change the world and profoundly change human social life, they want to seize the major strategic opportunities in the development of AI, have a first mover advantage in doing this, and accelerate the establishment of China as an innovative AI-powered world leader. They see AI as a major strategy to enhance national competitiveness and protect national security, a new engine for economic growth, and a vehicle to help build a more prosperous society. The basic principles are to let the advancement of technology lead within in the context of a well-formulated system layout that is market-led and embraces open source and sharing. In 2018, China's city of Tianjin made a formal public statement about setting up a $16 billion AI fund, whereas Beijing is planning to build a $2.1 billion industrial park for AI research in west Beijing to accommodate 400 enterprises.[110]   From Deloitte's survey of a hundred Chinese business executives, the majority saw AI as highly important to the success of their business, helping them to increase their competitive edge and to augment their employees to be more productive and have better job satisfaction.[111] MGI's interpretation of China's AI path forward is summarized via five strategic priorities that include building a robust data ecosystem, expanding the adoption of AI within traditional industries, strengthening the pool of expert AI talent, preparing the training and education systems to develop smart technology skills and hold on to as many people in the workforce as possible, and ensuring that there is a proper ethical and legal framework that gets the approval of Chinese citizens and the global community.[112] Let's have a look at their plan in more detail. The strategic goals consist of three steps where by 2020 they want to be on par with the state-of-the-art AI research and applications, improve the AI development environment with highly talented and innovative teams, and taste the first fruits of AI's impact on economic growth and improving people's livelihood. From an economic perspective they aim for an initial core AI industry of $20 billion with an impact on related industries of about $150 billion. The second strategic step is to achieve by 2025 a major breakthrough in the basic theory of AI and have some world-leading applications in various fields such as intelligent medical care, intelligent manufacturing, intelligent cities, intelligent agriculture, and national defense construction. This should then translate to a core AI industry of approximately $60 billion with an impact on related industries of about $750 billion. The Chinese government also wants to ensure that by that time there are some preliminary AI laws and regulations, ethical standards, and policy systems with respect to safety assessment and control capabilities. The third strategic goal is to become by 2030 the world's leading AI innovation center with respect to research and applications and having significant practical outcomes with respect to a smart economy and society. They would like to see by then that the scale of the core AI industry exceeds $150 billion and drives the scale of related industries to more than $1.5 trillion. The intention is to also have research advancements and discoveries in areas such as brain-like intelligence, autonomous intelligence, swarm intelligence and hybrid intelligence and more complete and robust AI laws, policies, regulations, and ethical standards implemented. One of the six key tasks involves building an open and collaborative AI technology innovation system that drives and supports the basic theory of AI, key common technology systems, and foster top AI talent and teams. Another key task is growing a high-end and efficient smart economy through developing smart enterprises and emerging AI technologies such as intelligent software and hardware, smart robots, intelligent delivery vehicles, virtual and augmented reality, intelligent wearables, and terminals, and IoT devices as well as sector-wide implementations through intelligent manufacturing, smart agriculture, smart logistics, smart finance, smart business, and smart homes. This task is further supported through building so-called "AI innovation highlands" and industrial clusters across the regions where pilots can be carried out as well as the establishment of a national industrial park and national AI crowd-creation incubator base. A third task is building a safe and prosperous smart society that focuses on efficient smart services to improve education, healthcare, and elderly care; modernizing social governance through improved government services and decision-making, wisdom courts, smart cities, smart transportation, and environmental protection; enhancing public safety; and promoting social exchanges and mutual trust. Another key task that one does not typically see in other countries' national plans is the strong push for a deep military-civilian integration development strategy to encourage AI research and innovation for national defense purposes, tight collaboration and sharing of AI applications for command and decision-making, military games, and national defense equipment. A fifth task is to build a ubiquitous, safe, and efficient intelligent infrastructure system that also includes 5G network, big data, and high-performance computing infrastructure. The final task addresses the use of AI to strengthen major national science and technology projects and support the advancement of "big data intelligence, cross-media perception computing, hybrid enhanced intelligence, group intelligence, autonomous collaborative control and decision-making".[113] The funding and resource allocation activities for this AI development plan involves coordinating government and market multi-channel funding, revitalizing existing resources, and collaborating with domestic and international academic, research, and private sector innovation resources. The safeguard measures of this strategic AI development plan involve formulating laws, regulations, and ethical standards, improving key policies to support the development of AI, construct AI technology standards and intellectual property systems, build an AI safety supervision and evaluation system, strengthen the training of AI labor force, and popularize AI-related science activities. They also recognize the critical importance of strong leadership, organization, and execution capability to successfully execute on this audacious plan. Besides this next generation for AI plan, the OECD.AI policy observatory currently also lists policy initiatives such as Principles of Next-generation AI Governance - Responsible AI, National Engineering Laboratory for Deep Learning, Chinese Association for AI, Beijing National New-generation AI Innovation and Development Pilot Zone, and 3 year guidance for Internet plus AI Plan.[114] The Beijing AI Principles were proposed in May 2019 as an initiative for the research, development, practical use, governance and long-term planning of AI, strongly urging for "its healthy development to support the construction of a community of common destiny, and the realization of beneficial AI for mankind and nature". The 15 Principles can be summarized as: do good, for humanity, be responsible, control risks, be ethical, be diverse and inclusive, open and share, use wisely and properly, informed-consent, education and training, optimizing employment, harmony and cooperation, adaptation and moderation, subdivision and implementation, and long-term planning.[115] The contributors were a multistakeholder coalition including the Beijing Academy of AI (BAAI), Institute of Computing Technology in Chinese Academy of Sciences, Institute of Automation, Peking University, Tsinghua University and AI tech players such as Tencent, Alibaba and Baidu. Whilst China's AI development plan, principles and other policy initiatives are bold and impressive, there are concerns expressed earlier in this chapter that AI could effectively be used to enhance their government's totalitarian control and that AI's worst use cases might not be restrained and even potentially exported to other countries.[116]

The United Kingdom is also placing large bets on the future of AI and has published in 2018 a national AI strategy called the *AI Sector Deal* which is a £1 billion package of support from government and industry in order to prepare the UK economy and society for the anticipated AI-driven transformations and helping to thrust UK's efforts in advancing the state-of-the-art in AI, its applications and other smart technologies.[117] This package is augmented with £1.7 billion coming from the Industrial Strategy Challenge Fund. The industrial strategy aims to unlock the UK's potential in AI by adding £232 billion to the UK economy by 2030, boosting productivity in some industries by 30%, and generating savings of up to 25%.[118] It is built on 5 foundations namely ideas that focus on building the world's most innovative economy, people that have good jobs and greater earning power for as many people possible, upgrading UK's infrastructure in a substantial way, create a business environment that ensures the best place to start and grow a business, and build places that have prosperous communities across the UK.[119] There are various government efforts to support AI innovation, industry and public sector adoption, and research which includes £20 million for AI applications in the services sector, £93 million for AI and Robotics in extreme environments, £20 million to support AI-driven solutions for government, £300 million allocated by the Engineering and Physical Sciences Research Council to fund research related to AI and data science and complement the new centres for doctoral training, £142m EPSRC funding for 214 AI grants, and £42m EPSRC funding for the Alan Turing Institute.[120] The UK government plans to also increase the total R&D investment to 2.4% of the GDP by 2027. There has also been excellent support from industry that matches funding for AI solutions across key sectors such as services, life sciences, agriculture, and the public sector as well as investments from tech players such as Google, Amazon, HPE, and Element AI. From a formal education and training perspective funding of £406 million has been allocated for STEM-related skills development, £242 million for teacher development, delivering 1000 new PhDs over the next 5 years through 16 new centres for Doctoral Training at universities across the UK, and industry-funding for new AI Masters places where 2500 places have been created for AI and data conversion courses starting in 2020.[121] There is also industry support to increase the size and diversity of the workforce, whereas the UK government is also promoting diversity in AI development and enabling access to highly skilled global talent via up to 2000 Exceptional Talent Tier 1 visas per year. An AI council has also been created to strengthen networking opportunities between academia, industry, and the public sector. There have also been collaborative initiatives to improve the business environment for AI-driven high growth such as a new £2.5 billion investment fund incubated in the British Business Bank and supported by private sector co-investment to a total of £7.5bn.[122] In order to provide recommendations for a sustainable, safe, and ethical use of AI, a Centre for Data Ethics and Innovation has been formed. The Office for Artificial Intelligence has also in collaboration with the government digital service published in 2019 a guidance on AI ethics and safety.[123] There are also a range of government actions and policy initiatives in collaboration with industry to support AI by enhancing the UK's existing data infrastructure, publish more high quality public data in an open, accessible and reusable format for AI use cases, improve access to geospatial data, develop fair, secure and equitable data sharing frameworks, and invest more than a £1 billion to develop 5G mobile networks and telecommunications infrastructure across the UK. The UK's office for AI has updated this strategy in May 2019 to communicate progress with respect to the AI Sector Deal's five foundations of productivity, some of which has already been mentioned above with respect to strengthening UK skills, talent and leadership, investment commitments, encouraging adoption across industry sectors, and ensuring the safe and ethical use of AI and other smart technologies. Some other progress includes and AI guide for Government, funding of up to £50 million for five new centres of excellence for AI-driven digital pathology and imaging, and funding of £30 million for the new Data Science and AI Bayes Centre in Edinburgh, as well as £79 million in funding for three new AI programmes to help enhance healthcare, urban planning, and engineering. Beside the AI Sector Deal, the OECD.AI policy observatory currently lists 28 policy initiatives for the UK which also include a number of the policy related initiatives and documentation referenced above.[124] The AI Sector Deal is also taking concrete actions to advance the UK's Grand Challenges with respect to ensuring that the UK is an innovative leader and investment destination in the AI and data revolution, becoming a leading player in the future of mobility and the way people, goods and services move, optimize the benefits of shifting to a clean growth economy, and delivering innovative solutions that address the needs of an ageing society. The missions statements that correspond to the 4 grand challenges are focused on AI-driven prevention, early diagnosis and treatment of chronic diseases by 2030, reduce the quality of life experience gap between the wealthiest and the poorest people and add 5 extra healthy, independent years of life by 2035, reduce energy use of new buildings by at least 50% by 2030, aim to have the first net-zero carbon industrial cluster by 2040 and at least 1 low-carbon cluster by 2030, and ensure that the UK is a leader in the design and manufacturing of zero emission vehicles, where all new cars and vans should have zero emission by 2040.[125]

As AI is regarded to have the potential to become a key productivity driver and Germany is already well positioned in many AI research and application areas, the Federal Government of Germany's national AI strategy which is called *AI Made in Germany* and published in November 2018 builds on existing strengths and endeavors to transfer them to untapped areas. Even in sectors such as manufacturing that Germany excel at, a German study projected that AI will add approximately €32 billion to Germany's output over a 5 year period.[126] The AI strategy specifically seeks to make Germany and Europe global leaders in the development and use of AI technologies, protect Germany's competitiveness, integrate AI in society by considering active political measures and inputs from a broad societal dialogue with respect to legal, ethical, institutional and cultural perspectives, and ensure that AI is developed and used in a responsible fashion and for the greater good of society.[127] In their 2019 federal budget €500 million has been allocated to strengthen the AI strategy for 2019 and beyond. The Federation plans to commit approximately €3 billion for the implementation of the strategy up until 2025, expecting that the leverage effect on the federal states, science and business will help to double the amount. The German AI strategy proposes some policy reforms and initiatives for formal training and education such as the 'Teach-and-learn AI' platform which is aimed at specific user groups to develop a strong AI skill base as well as the formation of no less than a hundred additional AI-related professorships. In order to grow and upgrade the workforce's AI-related skills and support their lifelong and life-wide learning journeys broad-based initiatives such as the National Skills Strategy has been introduced to also include driving AI-related vocational training, the Mittelstand 4.0 centres of excellence for SMEs that aims to connect their "AI trainers" with a minimum of a thousand companies per year, and regional Centres of Excellence for Labor Research to also support AI-related knowledge share and skills transfer in a work environment to management and the workforce.[128] According to a Deloitte Insights survey, companies in Germany have a stronger focus on AI training when compared to their counterparts in other countries.[129] A Skilled Labor Strategy will also proactively identify and monitor skills that are needed in the future, whereas regional Centres for the Future will provide upgrade skilling opportunities for employees in rural areas. The German strategy describes policy initiatives to grow networks and collaborations across the business, academia and the public sector such as Platform Industry 4.0 which is a platform and funded expert network that helps to shape the transition into the digital economy in industry and science; the Plattform Lernende Système that is being evolved into an AI platform to facilitate dialogue and networking between science, business, civil society and the government; a Franco-German R&D "virtual centre" that provides funding and training programme with AI clusters in specific industries such as transport, healthcare, environment, and robotics; Next Generation Clusters that aims to transfer relevant state-of-the-art research into products and services in a collaborative fashion; and initiatives such as Digital Hub and the Hubs for Tomorrow. A German AI observatory has also been established to monitor the uptake and impact of AI in the workplace and the rest of society. The sharing of AI and digitalization related information as well as multidisciplinary social technology design are also being supported by a Digital Work and Society Future Fund. There has also been progress with respect to a legislative framework for AI with the introduction of the Workforce Data Protection Act, the Skilled Labor Immigration Act, and the Opportunities for Qualifications Act, as well as the establishment of a Commission on Competition Law 4.0. On a legal and ethical framework front, there is an initiative to enhance coordination of ethical values across Europe, guidelines provided for the use and development of AI systems to ensure compliance with data protection rules, as well as ethical requirements specified to certify verifiability, predictability, and transparency of AI systems. The German government is also supporting and funding standardization initiatives such as the reviewing of existing standards to ensure that they are AI-compatible, the development of data standards and formats to encourage European Union wide collaborations as well as the participation of SMEs and start-ups in international standardization processes. Apart from the ones mentioned here, the OECD AI Policy Observatory highlights a number of other AI-related policy initiatives for Germany that provide further details.[130] From an infrastructure perspective, the German strategy also helps to put reliable data and analysis infrastructure in place that leverages cloud platforms and upgraded storage and computing capacity; provide science-driven data services to research communities through National Research Data infrastructure; ensure data sharing and open access to governmental data and improving the infrastructure for access to the Earth observation data; improve security, robustness and performance of AI-driven information and communication systems; expand the Learning Factories 4.0 initiative to support learning purposes in AI for students; and improve digital infrastructure in schools through the Digital Pact for Schools programme.[131]

The French national AI strategy, *AI for Humanity,* which was presented in March 2018 and strongly influenced by Cédric Villani's *For a Meaningful Artificial Intelligence: Towards a French and European Strategy* report that preceded it, focuses on four main objectives that includes strengthening the AI research, education, and training ecosystem in order to attract the best AI talent, constructing an open data policy and associated platforms for AI application use cases, developing an ethical framework for responsible, fair and transparent use of AI applications, building of a regulatory framework for AI applications, and providing financial support to implement the strategy and create a "European DARPA".[132] The French government has committed €1.5 billion to AI development for the period until 2022, of which €700 million for AI research, €400 million to AI-driven industrial projects, €100 million to AI startups and companies, and €70 million per annum through France's Public Investment Bank.[133] The essence of Villni's AI report is focusing on developing an aggressive data policy; targeting strategic sectors such as healthcare, transport, defense and security, and environment and agriculture; boosting the potential of French research; planning for the impact of AI on labor, making AI more environmentally friendly; making AI more transparent, and ensuring that AI supports diversity and inclusivity.[134] In order to reinforce the AI ecosystem, the French AI strategy plan specifies a number of initiatives such as the establishment of a national AI programme coordinated by the National Institute for Research in Computer Science and Control, the creation of interdisciplinary AI institutes in Paris, Toulouse, Grenoble and Nice to nurture AI research between regional academic and industry ecosystems, ensuring that researchers spend 50% of their time in industry settings, and doubling the number of AI-trained students by 2022.[135] Public-private sector laboratories are also encouraged to collaborate on AI research and innovations. From an international networking and collaboration perspective the French National Research Agency is collaborating with the German Research Foundation and the Japan Science and Technology Agency on AI research proposals. With support from OECD, France has also formed a partnership with Canada as part of the Global Partnership on AI to start an international AI study group focused on developing responsible AI.[136] To enhance the international attractiveness of AI in France, policies are being put in place to amplify France's appeal to foreign talent and expatriates by improving working conditions and income of researchers. Research chairs are also created to attract the top researchers and calls for proposals organized to attract the impactful research projects.[137] From a regulatory and ethical framework and data policy perspective, there are a number of initiatives which include incorporating ethics within businesses and the training of engineers, supporting human sciences research on ethics of use, setting up a national platform for auditing algorithms, adapting existing regulations (e.g. for driverless vehicles), using AI to improve public policies, making all algorithms used by the government public, implementing of the cyber security directive, increasing data portability and access to data of public interest, and launching of the Digital Republic Act to open up public data, strengthen data privacy and the protection of users' rights, and ensure that digitalization and its opportunities benefit to all.[138] The French has also invested €115 million in a supercomputer with processing power of more than 10 Petaflops that should be operational by 2020. Several tech companies have invested in AI research centres in France such as IBM, Samsung, Fujitsu, DeepMind, Google, and Facebook.[139]

Japan's national AI strategy, the *Artificial Intelligence Technology Strategy*, was prepared by their Strategic Council for AI technology in March 2017, and applies the strategy framework as an industrialization roadmap to the key priority areas of their Society 5.0 initiative that focuses on health, productivity and mobility and creating sustainable solutions for better human life in Japan.[140] The national AI strategy, as the second earliest one, outlines policies to include new investments in R&D, public data, start-ups, talented people, and training. The plan envisages AI as a service and arranges the development of AI into three phases which addresses the utilization and application of data-driven AI technology developed in various domains by 2020, the public use of AI and data developed across various domains by a period up to 2030, and final phase that follows to create ecosystems that are built by connecting multiplying domains.[141] Japan published draft AI R&D Guidelines for International Discussions that mentions basic philosophies such as a human-centered society where everyone shares in the benefits of AI systems, sharing guidelines as best practices with stakeholders internationally, review and revise the guidelines in an agile fashion, ensuring balance of AI risks and benefits, and making sure that AI plays a neutral role and not put unnecessary burdens on developers that stifle ongoing progress.[142] The guidelines also share AI R&D principles that include collaboration, transparency, controllability, safety, security, privacy, user assistance, accountability, and ethics that respect human dignity and individual autonomy.[143] The OECD.AI policy observatory currently also lists other policy initiatives for Japan such as the advanced integrated intelligence platform project, AI utilization guidelines, high performance computing infrastructure project, and social principles for human-centric AI.[144]

India's *National Strategy for Artificial Intelligence,* which was presented in June 2018 by the government think tank NITI Aayog, focuses on leveraging smart technologies to help grow India's economy as well as ensuring social inclusion via their #AIforAll approach.[145] The intention is to position India as an "AI Garage" that incubates AI that is relevant and suitable to the developing world. The AI strategy intends to scale Indian-made AI solutions to the developing world, invest in R&D and industries that can help to maximize economic growth and social impact, and empower and train Indians with the skills and knowledge to find quality jobs. The focus areas for AI intervention are increased access and affordability of quality healthcare, enhanced farmers' income, increased agricultural productivity and reduction of wastage, improved access and quality of education, smarter cities and infrastructure with efficient and connectivity for the flourishing urban population, and smarter mobility and safer modes of transportation and better traffic and congestion problems.[146] In order to achieve the goals of their national AI strategy, India needs to overcome impediments such as the deficiency of broad-based expertise in AI research and its application, the absence of enabling data ecosystems to access to smart data, the lack of collaborative approach to AI adoption and its application, the high resource cost and low awareness for AI adoption, shortcomings with respect to privacy and security, and a lack of formal regulations around anonymization of data.[147] With respect to India's research ambitions, the strategy proposes the establishment of a Centre of Research Excellence to develop a better understanding of existing core AI research and pushing technology frontiers through creation of new knowledge, as well as International Centers of Transformational AI with a directive of developing and deploying application-based research in collaboration with the private sector. Some other initiatives involve the creation of a "CERN of AI" to tackle moonshot AI research projects through specialized international teams and common computing infrastructure for AI. The strategy also envisages a common national AI marketplace for data collection and aggregation, data annotation and deployable models.[148] The OECD.AI policy observatory currently also lists other policy initiatives for India of which a number have healthcare and biological flavor such as the biological data storage, access and sharing policy, national ethical guidelines for biomedical and health research involving human participants, national guidelines for gene therapy product development and clinical trials, and the DNA technology regulation bill.[149]

Canada's national AI strategy, the *Pan-Canadian Artificial Intelligence Strategy,* which was the world's first one when it was announced in their 2017 federal budget, is a five-year C$125 million strategy to further AI-related talent and research capabilities.[150] The AI strategy is being led by the Canadian Institute for Advanced Research in collaboration with three new AI Institutes, namely MILA in Montreal, the Alberta Machine Intelligence Institute in Edmonton, and the Vector Institute in Toronto. The major goals of the AI Strategy are to increase the number of talented AI researchers and skilled graduates in Canada, connecting the three major AI centres of excellence in Edmonton, Montreal and Toronto-Waterloo, developing global thought leadership on the ethical, policy, legal, and economic implications of AI advances through the AI & Society Program, and support a national research community on AI.[151] The Strategy is expected to increase collaboration and productivity among AI researchers, to translate research discoveries into value in the private and public sectors, help enhance Canada's international AI research and training profile, and produce socio-economic benefits for their people. Some of the National Program of activities include the AI4Good national training program, AI4Health task force, AI Catalyst Grants program, and the AICan Symposium.[152] Canada and France announced in November 2019 a Global Partnership on Artificial Intelligence which has already been joined by the European Union, Australia, Germany, India, Italy, Japan, Mexico, New Zealand, the Republic of Korea, Singapore, Slovenia, the UK, and the US. The aim is to facilitate international collaboration between experts from the academic community, industry, civil society, and governments to form workgroups on responsible AI, data governance, the future of work, and innovation and commercialization.[153] The Canadian Treasury Board has developed the *Responsible use of Artificial Intelligence* digital resource that describes guiding principles for public servants to ensure ethical and effective AI, streamline the procurement process, and instructions on automated decision-making and associated algorithmic impact assessment.[154] From Deloitte's survey of 300 Canadian business and information technology executives, the concerns highlighted in comparison to other countries was an apparent lack of urgency to use AI to transform businesses as well as slower innovation with respect to embedding AI into products and services.[155]

Although Australia has not yet produced a national AI strategy, their government has published *Australia's Tech Future* that addresses the economic importance of AI along with the skills shortages in data science and AI, as well as announced a 4-year, AU$29.9 million investment to support the development of AI in Australia in their 2018–2019 budget.[156] The OECD.AI policy observatory currently lists policy initiatives such as an AI technology roadmap, an AI standards roadmap, and a national AI ethics and standards framework to support the responsible development of AI.[157] In *Australia 2030: Prosperity Through Innovation*, the government announced that it will prioritize AI in their Digital Economy Strategy that lays out a roadmap for the government, the private sector and society to collaborate on discovering new sources of economic growth, develop best-in-class digital business, support lifelong learning, and address the skills gap.[158] Australia's Commonwealth Scientific and Industrial Research Organization published in 2019 a discussion paper on Australia's AI ethics framework, and launched a public consultation.[159] From Deloitte's survey of 100 Australian business and information technology executives, there seems to be a general positive view of AI's strategic importance, although the potential AI risks are a concern and inadequate AI strategies and lack of AI skills seem to be a major hindrance for many businesses in Australia.[160]

In 2017, President Putin of Russia famously said that "Artificial intelligence is the future not only of Russia but of all of mankind. There are huge opportunities, but also threats that are difficult to predict. Whoever becomes the leader in this sphere will become the ruler of the world". In October 2019, the Russian Federation released a national AI strategy, *Decree of the President of the Russian Federation on the Development of Artificial Intelligence in the Russian Federation*, to provide a foundation for development and improvement of state programmes and projects as well as state-owned corporations and companies that support AI development in Russia.[161] The specific objectives of the strategy include enhancing the availability and quality of data, increasing the availability of specialized hardware and software as well as storage and processing for R&D and the implementation of AI, increase the quality of AI-related training, and creating a regulatory system and relevant standards that ensures public safety and vitalizes the development of AI technologies. The principles communicated in the strategy plan include transparency, security, innovation cycle integrity, technological sovereignty, reasonable prudence, support for competition, and protection of liberties and human rights.[162] As an action step after Russia's *Artificial Intelligence: Problems and Solutions—2018* conference, the Ministry of Defense published a list of ten policies for AI development in Russia which includes the establishment of an AI consortium across industrial and educational organizations; building an AI laboratory at a foremost technology university; setting up a national AI R&D center; creating a fund to support the development of expert knowledge on automated systems; increasing state support of AI training and education; monitoring social and technical AI trends; hosting war games to study AI's impact on military operations; and discussing AI proposals at local military forums.[163] Some of the other Russian policy initiatives listed on the OECD.AI policy observatory include a conceptual framework for the regulation of AI and robotics till 2023, federal AI industry development project, national programme "digital economy", national technology initiative, and technical committee on standardization of AI. [164]

In 2018 South Korea announced a 5-year *AI Information Industry Development Plan* and investment of approximately \$2 billion in AI research and development.[165] This was preceded in 2016 by a \$900 million investment in AI research over a 5 year period, soon after DeepMind's AlphaGo defeated South Korea's Lee Sedol at Go.[166] In the same year South Korea also provided a report *"Mid-to Long-term Master Plan in Preparation for the Intelligent Information Society: Managing the Fourth Industrial Revolution"* that also considers the role of AI along with other smart digital technologies, AI's implications for the workforce and economy, and envisions "Realizing a Human-Centered Intelligent Information Society."[167] South Korea's AI Information Industry Development plan firstly aims to recruit AI talent through establishing six graduate schools in AI by 2022 with the goal of training 5,000 AI experts of which 1,400 are AI researchers and 3,600 data management specialists. In addition, to address the short-term need for AI talent, their government has launched an initiative to train 600 people in AI. The second focus of their plan is to develop AI technology through funding AI R&D challenges and large-scale projects in healthcare, national defense, and public safety. Thirdly, South Korea plans to fund infrastructure required to support the development of AI start-ups and small and medium sized businesses, an AI-related start-up incubator to support nascent AI businesses, as well as the development of an AI semiconductor by 2029.[168] Some of the other South Korean policy initiatives listed on the OECD.AI policy observatory include a data and AI-driven economy promotion plan, ethics guidelines for intelligent information society, and the Korean new deal.[169]

Apart from the countries highlighted above from a governmental AI strategy perspective, there are many other countries also making excellent progress in this regard. Most references point to the OECD.AI policy observatory that keeps a live repository of more than 300 AI policy initiatives from 60 countries.[170] Other current sources with summaries of national AI policies such as HolonIQ and the Future of Life Institute also references the OECD.AI.[171] In the Americas, Argentina is drafting the *National Plan of Artificial Intelligence* which is part of their Innovative Argentina 2030 Plan and the 2030 Digital Agenda; Brazil is building a network of eight research facilities focused on AI after their initial consultation period ended January 2020; Chile's Ministry of Science, Technology,

Knowledge, and Innovation has created a committee of experts to develop an AI national strategy which is expected in 2020; Columbia has drafted a *National Policy for Digital Transformation* in November 2019 and has identified Medellín to become an AI & Robotics Centre of Excellence; Costa Rica has developed a *Digital Transformation Strategy: The Bicentennial of Costa Rica*; Uruguay has developed an *AI Strategy for the Digital Government*, data policies and strategy for digital transformation and a Data Science and Machine Learning Roadmap; and Mexico produced a *Towards an AI Strategy in Mexico: Harnessing the AI Revolution* in June 2018 that provides as a building block for a complete national AI strategy.[172]

In Europe, Austria has announced their *Artificial Intelligence Mission Austria 2030 (AIM AT 2030)* in June 2019 that covers AI's impact on qualification and training, research and innovation, the economy, the public sector, industrial infrastructure, society, ethics and labor market, as well as AI governance, security and legal aspects; Belgium launched *AI 4 Belgium* in March 2019 that addresses lifelong learning and reskilling, reinforcement of human skills in AI at all education levels, fueling research and innovation in the private actor, transformation of the public sector ecosystem, growing networking and collaboration, and developing ethical guidelines, a robust legislative framework and standards; Denmark presented their '*National Strategy for Artificial Intelligence*' in March 2019 focusing on common ethical and human-centered basis for AI, prioritizing AI research, grow business sector as well as the public sector with world-class AI-powered services; Finland produced *Leading the Way into the Age of Artificial Intelligence* strategy document in June 2019, that identified 11 key actions following their May 2017 Steering Group announcement; Greece is busy with the final preparation of their national AI strategy and is investing in an AI Center of Excellence; Hungary has in October 2019 announced an AI Action Plan which is the first building block their national AI strategy to be expected in 2020; Iceland is involved in the *Declaration on AI in the Nordic-Baltic Region* which was released in May 2018; Ireland has launched an industry-driven AI Master program in 2018; Italy's Ministry of Economic Development released a draft version of its *National Strategy on Artificial Intelligence* for public consultation in August 2019, along with *Proposals for an Italian strategy for AI* that provides initial guiding principles and policy recommendations as a basis for Italy's AI strategy; Luxemburg launched *Artificial Intelligence: a strategic vision for Luxembourg* in May 2019; Malta presented '*A Strategy and Vision for Artificial Intelligence in Malta 2030*' in October 2019 and envisage to be the 'Ultimate AI Launchpad' via the launch of Malta.ai; Netherlands has released in October 2019 its *Strategic Action for Artificial Intelligence* policy report that presents policy initiatives and action plans to strengthen Netherlands' AI competitiveness internationally; Norway issued its *National Strategy for Artificial Intelligence* in January 2020; Portugal presented their *AI Portugal 2030* strategy in February 2019 that aims to reinforces economic growth, human development and scientific excellence through the use of AI; Spain launched their *Research, Development and Innovation Strategy in Artificial Intelligence* in March 2019 that focus on priorities and policy recommendations in preparation for their national AI strategy as well as creating the appropriate ecosystem for AI development and its applications; Sweden launched their *National Approach for Artificial Intelligence* in May 2018 that focuses on research, education and training innovation and use and framework and infrastructure; and Switzerland's AI expert group has published its recommendations for a Swiss AI strategy.[173]

In East Europe and Western Asia, Poland published a draft of its national AI strategy *Artificial Intelligence Development Policy in Poland* for 2019-2027 in November 2019; Romania is currently preparing its national AI strategy that seeks drive the adoption of safe AI applications, foster fundamental research that leads to practical AI whilst protecting human rights and social values; Estonia presented *Estonia's national AI strategy* in July 2019 to promote the development and use of AI applications in the private and public sector, support AI research, increasing the relevant AI skills and competences, and establishment an legal environment to facilitate AI adoption; Serbia recently published their *Strategy for the Development of Artificial Intelligence in the Republic of Serbia for the period 2020-2025*; Czech Republic released its *National Strategy for Artificial Intelligence* in May 2019 which plans to enhance its economic growth and AI competitiveness through development of a responsible and trusted AI ecosystem, the digital transformation of business, and the economic development of society based on equitable opportunities and AI benefits; Bulgaria is preparing its national AI strategy focusing on policy initiatives with respect to research, education, and training; Slovak Republic has their AI-related policies defined as part of the *Action plan for the digital transformation of Slovakia for 2019–2022* that presents practical steps to develop a trustworthy, sustainable and human-centric AI ecosystem and is based on a broader *Strategy of the Digital Transformation of Slovakia 2030*; Slovenia has a working group preparing their national AI strategy and is also establishing an AI Research Centre in Ljubljana; Croatia is currently preparing its national AI strategy which is expected in 2020; Turkey is also working on their national AI strategy, have a broader 2023 industry and technology strategy, and have focus groups, research support and a technology roadmap for AI; Cyprus has approved the *National Artificial Intelligence Strategy of Cyprus* in January 2020; Kazakhstan has an AI research and development support fund and a roadmap focused on the development of competencies which includes AI; Latvia published its national AI strategy on *Developing Artificial Intelligence Solutions* in February 2020; and Lithuania published *Lithuanian Artificial Intelligence Strategy: A Vision of the Future* in April 2019.[174]

In Asia Pacific, Singapore has a number of a policy initiatives which includes *AI Singapore* that was launched in May 2017 as a five-year S$150 million national program based on AI research, technology, innovation and makerspace as key pillars; Thailand's Digital Economy and Society Ministry has drafted their first AI ethics guidelines in 2019; Vietnam has published a policy document on the plan for research and development of AI to help grow their economy for the period 2018-2025; and New Zealand has launched an AI Forum that released a research report called *Artificial Intelligence: Shaping a Future New Zealand.*[175] In the Middle East, Israel has prepared an AI R&D framework and activities of the Israeli innovation authority and is setting up an AI Strategy government team; Saudi Arabia has established the *Saudi Data and Artificial Intelligence Authority* in 2019 as the owner of their national AI agenda and a National Center for AI which was set up in August 2019; and United Arab Emirates announced in October 2017 the vision of the *National Strategy for Artificial Intelligence of 2031*, as well as initiatives such as an AI network and *Dubai's AI Principles and Guidelines* aim to develop AI in a safe, responsible and ethical way.[176]

In Africa, Egypt has a national AI strategy that is based on has capacity building and applied research, a national council for AI that drives governance of the strategy and has led the establishment of an African Working group on AI under the auspices of the African

Union; Morocco has an R&D Centre specializing in AI and information and communication technologies;[177] Kenya has announced in January 2018 a government task force to create a five-year strategy on national use of emerging technologies; and South Africa has published a report of the *Presidential Commission on the Fourth Industrial Revolution* in August 2020 that makes specific recommendations with respect to investing in human capital, establishing an AI Institute, creating a platform for advanced manufacturing and new materials, securing and availing data to enable innovation, incentivizing future industries, platforms and applications of fourth industrial revolution technologies, building fourth industrial revolution infrastructure, review and amending policy and legislation, and establishing a fourth industrial revolution strategy implementation coordination council.[178] Other AI initiatives in South Africa include the *Machine Intelligence Institute of Africa* (MIIA) that was launched in 2016 to help transform Africa through AI and other smart technology as well as the *Intsimbi Future Production Technologies Initiative* that was launched in 2018 with the goal of advancing South Africa's manufacturing sector using technologies such as robotics and AI, nanotechnologies and quantum computing.[179] The *4IRSA Partnership* in South Africa is another initiative that involves the department of communications and digital technologies, private sector and some universities that aims to stimulate and facilitate an inclusive national dialogue to shape a coherent national response to the fourth industrial revolution in the country.[180] In Nigeria, *Data Science Nigeria* is committed to raising one million AI talents in 10 years and help to accelerate Nigeria's socio-economic development through a solution-oriented application of AI in solving social and business problems.[181]

Africa already has 122 million active users of mobile financial services, more than half the global total. Its number of smartphone connections is forecast to double from 315 million in 2015 to 636 million in 2022 - twice the projected number in North America. Over the same period, mobile data traffic across Africa is expected to increase sevenfold. In a new book published by The Harvard Business Review, *Africa's Business Revolution: How to succeed in the World's Next Big Growth Market*, one message stands out: digital technologies allow forward-looking businesses to recast Africa's challenges as an opportunity to innovate and address massive unmet demand. They estimate that private consumption in Africa rose from $860 billion in 2008 to $1.4 trillion in 2015 — significantly higher than that of India, which has a similar population size. They forecast that it could reach $2.1 trillion by 2025. Yet Africa's consumers are still woefully underserved: there are sixty thousand people per formal retail outlet in Africa, compared with just four hundred people per store in the United States. This fast-growing underserved population and unmet demand, coupled with rapid digitization and technology advancements, provide the perfect environment for the launch of Africa's first Digital Platform Ecosystem. The University of Pretoria has published a report called *Artificial Intelligence for Africa: An Opportunity for Growth, Development, and Democratisation* that outlines what AI will mean for Africa in terms of its key growth sectors, the AI stakeholders, the challenges and elements of an AI strategy that works for Africa.[182] With effective application of AI and smart technologies, agriculture yields can be significantly increased, healthcare outcomes can be improved with more personalized and accessible services, financial services can reach more underserved citizens in a secure way, and public services can be more responsive and efficient. However, there are significant challenges to be overcome which includes education systems that need rapid transformation to empower more citizens at scale, broadband internet coverage needs to be swiftly expansion to include rural areas, AI needs to be trusted through fair, secure, and inclusive use, and data should be more accessible to enable users, researchers, and application builders to drive AI applications. Governments need to develop clear roadmaps to guide AI adoption, enhance their regulatory and policy frameworks to support the use of smart and data-driven technologies to enable innovative solutions and economic growth, and create a collaborative framework and the necessary supporting infrastructure for AI research and development.

Through smart technology, governments around the world are faced with a multitude of ways to offer public services, include and connect citizens, improve education and job readiness, solve entrenched socio-economic disparities and stamp out corruption. Through basic digitization and smart technologies, countries now have new ways to uplift their citizens and become active members of the global digital economy.[183] The 2019 report published by the Kenyan government focuses on the use of AI and Blockchain to advance the Kenyan Big 4 Agenda of Manufacturing, Affordable Housing, Universal Health Coverage and Food Security.[184] This speaks to many things, but the one that can be focused on is the leapfrog effect. Whilst Kenya is still behind relatively speaking, it shows intent to join the global revolution and improve public service delivery. The Kenyan government is not the only one to be thinking about AI and Blockchain like this. Estonia (or e-Estonia) is one of the most advanced e-government in the world, currently offering 99% of public services online, and allowing citizens to be always safely connected.[185] Among their technologies are blockchain and AI – contributing to their being able to offer e-Residency to citizens outside of Estonia who are now able to start, manage and run a business in Estonia from anywhere in the world. On top of this, Estonian citizens only ever must submit data once. It is stored using blockchain technology and any new services or processes can merely consult these databases without ever having to bother citizens.[186] The UAE's state mandated commitment to develop AI is seeping through the country from every angle. Their public campaign, supported by the Dubai Future Councils task to use smart technology, knowledge, and expertise to create solutions and opportunities through government and private sector experts play a large part in their current advancement.[187]

Deloitte Insights, in their analysis on how countries are pursuing an AI advantage, recommends taking a balanced approach that includes creating a sense of urgency around AI adoption as the window for competitive differentiation is small (in particular for businesses), respecting the risks of AI without rushing into potential mistakes just to keep up with others, developing a strong foundation for an AI-powered future, exploring creative ways to accelerate AI capabilities via external collaboration, making plans that takes into consideration that AI - like electricity - will become easier to acquire over time, and creating a vision for what an "augmented workforce" looks like, training and equipping citizens and building their own AI expertise.[188]

The Brookings Institution's Artificial Intelligence and Emerging Technology Initiative compares the pursuit for domination in AI as the "space race of our time" and has provided their perspective after studying 34 national AI strategies.[189] In their opinion, governments are broadly speaking failing to plan for operational investments and continue to be a lot more ambitious and aspirational as opposed to being practical in what they set out to do. It was interesting to see that they view Italy's national AI plan to be the most comprehensive (although not commenting on its quality and sophistication), followed by France, Germany, New Zealand, and the United States.[190] According to them the national AI strategies are missing details on how they are going to marshal their countries on the AI journey from an execution, funding, and communications perspective. Brookings has also published a white paper that emphasizes the importance and opportunities of transatlantic cooperation on AI between the European Union and the United States and notes that it is "convinced that international cooperation on AI matters must be based on an approach that promotes the respect of fundamental rights, including human dignity, pluralism, inclusion, non-discrimination and protection of privacy and personal data and it will strive to export its values across the world".[191]

9. The Debates, Progress and Likely Future Paths of AI

Over the last number of decades, we have seen AI's impact, progress, and future direction being debated and discussed on so many different levels, AI research going through several rough "winter" and blossoming "summer" periods (actually all "seasons" of a year), as well as a variety of AI narratives, ideas, and perspectives of AI's likely future paths. As we make scientific and engineering progress as humanity, we are steadily and surely getting better at building a rich and powerful toolbox of AI algorithms, structures, and techniques along with its software and hardware infrastructure for research and applications. We are also getting better at understanding the dynamics, power, nature, complexity and inner workings of AI and intelligence in a broader sense. In this chapter, these aspects will be explored in more detail to assist us in developing a more realistic, practical, and thoughtful understanding of AI's progress and likely future paths that we can use as input to help shape a beneficial human-centric future.

Making Sense of the AI Debates

The debates about AI's future path and impact on humanity is like a roller-coaster ride of thoughts and ideas from so many different perspectives driven by a mix of fear and excitement about the enormous risks and opportunities that AI presents this century and beyond. As AI can be put firmly in the bracket of powerful enough technology that gives life "the potential to flourish like never before or to self-destruct" as described by the Future of Life Institute, the debates around AI and other smart technologies are becoming one of the most important discussions of our time.[1] Even with narrow AI systems that may accomplish a narrow set of goals at least as well as humans, these systems can in its own right or even within a connected network of such systems be powerful and impactful enough to create havoc or help humanity to thrive. In Nick Bostrom's *Superintelligence: Paths, Dangers, Strategies* he reasons that strong AI in the form of intelligent machines that can match or outperform humans on any cognitive task and improve their capabilities at a faster rate than humans could potentially lead to an existential nightmare for humanity.[2] He specifically believes that for such a strong AI to dominate, it would need to master skills such as intelligence amplification, strategizing, hacking, social manipulation, economic productivity, and technology research. Max Tegmark in *Life 3.0*, see strong AI as a third stage of life where technology designs its hardware (matter made of atoms) and software (information made of bits) as opposed to the first stage which is simple biological life that can only survive and replicate through evolving its hardware and software (information encoded in for example DNA) and the second stage which is more cultural where life can evolve its hardware (physical body) but also design its software such as humans learning new skills and knowledge and changing perspectives, goals and worldviews (Life 2.0).[3] As today's humans can perform minor hardware upgrades with for example implants, Max reckons that we are probably at a 2.1 level. According to the Future of Life Institute, most disputes amongst AI experts and others about strong AI that potentially have Life 3.0 capabilities, revolves around when and/or if ever it will happen and will it be beneficial for humanity.[4] This leads to a classification where we have at least four distinct groups of thinking about where we are heading with AI which are the so-called Luddites, technological utopians, techno-skeptics, and the beneficial AI movement.[5] Whereas Luddites within this context are opposed to new technology such as AI and especially have very negative expectations of strong AI and its impact on society, technological utopians sit on the other end of the spectrum with very positive expectations of the impact of advanced technology and science to help create a better future for all. The Techno-sceptics do not think that strong AI is a real possibility within the next hundred years and that we should focus more on the shorter-term impacts, risks, and concerns of AI that can have a massive impact on society as also described in the previous chapter. The Beneficial-AI group of thinkers are more focused on creating safe and beneficial AI for both narrow and strong AI as we cannot be sure that strong AI will not be created this century and it is anyway needed for narrow AI applications as well. AI can become dangerous when it is developed to do something destructive or harmful but also when it is developed to do something good or advantageous but use a damaging method for achieving its objective. So even in the latter case, the real concern is strong AI's competence in achieving its goals that might not be aligned with ours. Although my surname is Ludik, I am clearly not a Luddite, and would consider my own thinking and massive transformative purpose to be more aligned with the Beneficial AI group of thinkers and currently more concerned with the short-to-medium term risks and challenges and practical solutions to create a beneficial world for as many people as possible. Prominent business leaders, scientists, and influencers such as Elon Musk, the late Stephen Hawking, Martin Rees, and Eliezer Yudkowsky have issued dreadful warnings about AI being an existential risk to humanity, whilst well-resourced institutes countering this doomsday narrative with their own "AI for Good" or "Beneficial AI" narrative. AI researcher and entrepreneur Andrew Ng has once said that "fearing a rise of killer robots is like worrying about overpopulation on Mars".[6] That has also been countered by AI researcher Stuart Russell who said that a more suitable analogy would be "working on a plan to move the human race to Mars with no consideration for what we might breathe, drink, or eat once we arrive".[7] Many leading AI researchers seem to not identify with the existential alarmist view on AI, are more concerned about the short-to-medium term risks and challenges of AI discussed in the previous chapter, think that we are still at a very nascent stage of AI research and development, do not see a clear path to strong AI over the next few decades, and are of the opinion that the tangible impact of AI applications should be regulated, but not AI research and development. Most AI researchers and practitioners would fall into the beneficial AI movement and/or techno-sceptics category. Oren Etzioni, CEO of the Allen Institute for Artificial Intelligence, wrote an opinion article titled *How to Regulate Artificial Intelligence* where he claims that the alarmist view that AI is an "existential threat to humanity" confuses AI research and development with science fiction, but recognizes that there are valid concerns about AI applications with respect to areas such as lethal autonomous weapons, jobs, ethics and data privacy.[8] From a regulatory perspective he proposes three rules that include that AI systems should be put through the full extent of the laws that apply to its human operator, must clearly reveal that they are not a human, and cannot keep or reveal confidential information without clear approval from the source of that information.

Some strong technological utopian proponents include roboticist Hans Moravec as communicated in his book *Mind Children: The Future of Robot and Human Intelligence* as well as Ray Kurzweil, who is currently Director of Engineering at Google and has written books on the technology singularity, futurism, and transhumanism such as *The Age of Spiritual Machines* and *The Singularity is Near: When Humans Transcend Biology*.[9] The concept of a technological singularity has been popular in many science fiction books and movies over the years. Some of Ray's predictions include that by 2029 AI will reach human-level intelligence and that by 2045 "the pace of change will be so astonishingly quick that we won't be able to keep up, unless we enhance our own intelligence by merging with the intelligent machines we are creating".[10] There are a number of authors, AI thought leaders and computer scientists that have criticized Kurzweil's predictions in various degrees from both an aggressive timeline and real-world plausibility perspective. Some of these people include Andrew Ng, Rodney Brooks, Francois Chollet, Bruce Sterling, Neal Stephenson, David Gelernter, Daniel Dennett, Maciej Ceglowski, and the late Paul Allen. Web developer and entrepreneur Maciej Ceglowski calls superintelligence "the idea that eats smart people" and provides a range of arguments for this position in response to Kurzweil's claims as well as Nick Bostrom's book on Superintelligence and the positive reviews and recommendations that the book got from Elon Musk, Bill Gates and others.[11] AI researcher and software engineer Francois Chollet wrote a blog on why the singularity is not coming as well as an article on the implausibility of an intelligence explosion. He specifically argues that a "hypothetical self-improving AI would see its own intelligence stagnate soon enough rather than explode" due to scientific progress being linear and not exponential as well as also getting exponentially harder and suffering diminishing returns even if we have an exponential growth in scientific resources. This has also been noted in the article *Science is Getting Less Bang for its Buck* that explores why great scientific discoveries are more difficult to make in established fields and notes that emergent levels of behavior and knowledge that lead to a proliferation of new fields with their own fundamental questions seems to be the avenue for science to continue as an endless frontier.[12] Using a simple mathematical model that demonstrates an exponential decrease of discovery impact of each succeeding researcher in a given field, Francois Chollet concludes that scientific discovery is getting harder in a given field and linear progress is kept intact with exponential growth in scientific resources that is making up for the increased difficulty of doing breakthrough scientific research. He further constructs another model, with parameters for discovery impact and time to produce impact, which shows how the rate of progress of a self-improving AI converges exponentially to zero, unless it has access to exponentially increasing resources to manage a linear rate of progress. He reasons that paradigm shifts can be modeled in a similar way with the paradigm shift volume that snowballs over time and the actual impact of each shift decreasing exponentially which in turn results in only linear growth of shift impact given the escalating resources dedicated to both paradigm expansion and intra-paradigm discovery. Francois states that intelligence is just a meta-skill that defines the ability to gain new skills and should be along with hard work at the service of imagination, as imagination is the real superpower that allows one to work at the paradigm level of discovery.[13] The key conclusions that Francois makes in his article on implausibility of an intelligence explosion are firstly that general intelligence is a misnomer as intelligence is actually situational in the sense that the brain operates within a broader ecosystem consisting of a human body, an environment, and a broader society. Furthermore, the environment is putting constraints on individual intelligence which is limited by its context within the environment. Most of human intelligence is located in a broader self-improving civilization intellect where we live and that feeds our individual brains. The progress in science by a civilization intellect is an example of a recursively self-improving intelligence expansion system that is already experiencing a linear rate of progress for reasons mentioned above.[14]

In the essay *The Seven Deadly Sins of Predicting the Future of AI*, Rodney Brooks who is the co-founder of iRobot and Rethink Robotics, firstly quotes Amar's law that "we tend to overestimate the effect of a technology in the short run and underestimate the effect in the long run" to state that the long term timing for AI is being crudely underestimated.[15] He also quotes Arthur C. Clarke's third law that states that "any sufficiently advanced technology is indistinguishable from magic" to make the point that arguments for a magical future AI are faith-based and when things said about AI that are far enough from what we use and understand today and for practical purposes passes the magic line, those things cannot be falsified. As it is also intuitive for us to generalize from the observed performance level on a particular task to competence in related areas, it is also natural and easy for us to apply the same human style generalizations to current AI systems that operate in extremely narrow application areas and overestimate their true competence level. Similarly, people can easily misinterpret suitcase words applied to AI systems to mean more than what there actually is. Rodney also argues that as exponentials are typically part of a S-curve where hyper growth flattens out, one should in general be careful to apply exponential arguments as it can easily collapse when a physical limit is hit or if there is not sufficient economic value to persist with it. The same holds for AI, where deep learning's success, which can also be seen as an isolated event and achieved on top of at least thirty years of machine learning research and applications, does not necessarily guarantee similar breakthroughs on a regular basis. Not only is the future reality of AI likely to be significantly different to what is being portrayed in Hollywood science fiction movies, but also have a variety of advanced intelligent systems that evolve technologically over time in a world that would be adapting to these systems. The final error being made when predicting the future of AI is that the speed of deploying new ideas and applications in robotics and AI take longer than people think, especially when hardware is involved as with self-driving cars or in many factories around the world that are still running decades-old equipment along with old automation and operating system software.[16] On the self-driving cars front both Tesla and Google's Waymo have improved self-driving technology significantly with Waymo achieving "feature complete" status in 2015 but in geo-fenced areas, whereas Tesla is at almost zero interventions between home and work (with an upcoming software release promising to be a "quantum leap") in 2020.[17] However, the reality is that Tesla's full driving Autopilot software is progressing much slower than what Elon Musk predicted over the years and Chris Urmson, the former leader of Google self-driving project and CEO of self-driving startup Aurora, reckons that driverless cars will be slowly integrated over the next 30 to 50 years.[18]

Piero Scaruffi, a freelance software consultant and writer, is even more of a techno-skeptic and wrote in *Intelligence is not Artificial - Why the Singularity is not coming any time soon and other Meditations on the Post-Human Condition and the Future of Intelligence* that his estimate for super intelligence that can be a "substitute for humans in virtually all cognitive tasks, including those requiring scientific creativity, common sense, and social skills" to be approximately 200,000 years which is the time scale of natural evolution to produce a new species that will be at least as intelligent as us.[19] He does not think that we'll get to strong AI systems with our current incremental approach and that the current brute-force AI approach is actually slowing down research in higher-level intelligence. He guesses that an AI breakthrough will likely have to do with real memory that have "recursive mechanisms for endlessly remodeling internal states". Piero disagrees with Ray Kurzweil's "Law of Accelerating Returns" and points out that the diagram titled "Exponential Growth in Computing" is like comparing the power of a windmill to the power of a horse and concluding that windmills will keep improving forever. There is also no differentiation between progress in hardware versus progress in software and algorithms. Even though there has been significant progress in computers in terms of its speed, size, and cost-effectiveness, that does not necessarily imply that we will get to human-level intelligence and then super intelligence by assembling millions of superfast GPUs. A diagram showing "Exponential Growth in Computational Math" would be more relevant and will show that there has been no significant improvement in the development of abstract algorithms that improve automatic learning techniques. He is much more impressed with the significant progress in genetics since the discovery of the double-helix structure of DNA in 1953 and is more optimistic that we will get to superhuman intelligence through synthetic biology.[20]

A survey taken by the Future of Life Institute says we are going to get strong AI around 2050, whereas one conducted by SingularityNET and GoodAI at the 2018 Joint Multi-Conference on Human-Level AI shows that 37% of respondents believe human-like AI will be achieved within five to 10 years, 28% of respondents expected strong AI to emerge within the next two decades while only 2% didn't believe humans will ever develop strong AI.[21] Ben Goertzel, SingularityNET's CEO and developer of the software behind a social, humanoid robot called Sophia, said at the time that "it's no secret that machines are advancing exponentially and will eventually surpass human intelligence" and also "as these survey results suggest, an increasing number of experts believe this 'Singularity' point may occur much sooner than is commonly thought... It could very well become a reality within the next decade."[22] Lex Fridman, AI Researcher at MIT and YouTube Podcast Host thinks that we are already living through a singularity now and that super intelligence will arise from our human collective intelligence instead of strong AI systems.[23] George Hotz, a programmer, hacker, and the founder of Comma.ai also thinks that we are in a singularity now if we consider the escalating bandwidth between people across the globe through highly interconnected networks with increasing speed of information flow.[24] Jürgen Schmidhuber, AI Researcher and Scientific Director at the Swiss AI Lab IDSIA, is also very bullish about this and that we soon should have cost-effective devices with the raw computational power of the human brain and decades after this the computational power of 10 billion human brains together.[25] He also thinks that we already know how to implement curiosity and creativity in self-motivated AI systems that pursue their own goals at scale. According to Jürgen superintelligent AI systems would likely be more interested in exploring and transforming space and the universe than being restricted to Earth. AI Impacts has an AI Timeline Surveys web page that documents a number of surveys where the medium estimates for a 50% chance of human-level AI vary from 2056 to at least 2106 depending on the question framing and the different interpretations of human-level AI, whereas two others had medium estimates at the 2050s and 2085.[26] Rodney Brooks has declared that artificial general intelligence has been "delayed" to 2099 as an average estimate in a May 2019 post that references a survey done by Martin Ford via his book *Architects of Intelligence* where he interviewed 23 of the leading researchers, practitioners and others involved in the AI field.[27] It is not surprising to see Ray Kurzweil and Rodney Brooks at opposite ends of the timeline prediction, with Ray at 2029 and Rodney at 2200. Whereas Ray is a strong advocate of accelerating returns and believe that a hierarchical connectionist based approach that incorporates adequate real-world knowledge and multi-chain reasoning in language understanding might be enough to achieve strong AI, Rodney thinks that not everything is exponential and that we need a lot more breakthroughs and new algorithms (in addition to back propagation used in Deep Learning) to approximate anything close to what biological systems are doing especially given the fact that we cannot currently even replicate the learning capabilities, adaptability or the mechanics of insects. Rodney reckons that some of the major obstacles to overcome include dexterity, experiential memory, understanding the world from a day-to-day perspective, comprehending what goals are and what it means to make progress towards them. Ray's opinion is that techno-sceptics are thinking linearly, suffering from engineer's pessimism and do not see exponential progress in software advances and cross fertilization of ideas. He believes that we will see strong AI progresses exponentially in a soft take off in about 25 years. Other people included in Martin Ford's survey were Yoshua Bengio (University of Montreal), Yann LeCun (Facebook), Geoffrey Hinton (University of Toronto and Google), Stuart Russell (UC Berkeley), Oren Etzioni (Allen Institute for AI), Gary Marcus (NYU), Demis Hassabis (DeepMind), Fei-Fei Li (Stanford and Google), Andrew Ng (AI Fund), Daphne Koller (Stanford), Nick Bostrom (University of Oxford), Barbara Grosz (Harvard), David Ferrucci (Elemental Cognition), James Manyika (McKinsey), Judea Pearl (UCLA), Josh Tenenbaum (MIT), Rana el Kaliouby (Affectiva), Daniela Rus (MIT), Jeff Dean (Google), Cynthia Breazeal (MIT), and Bryan Johnson (Kernel).[28] Having been deeply involved in AI research and its applications over the years and having a good understanding of the current state-of-the-art in the full AI toolbox, my current guesstimate for human-level AI is likely also in the second half of this century.

When asked by Martin Ford about research breakthroughs needed to get to strong AI, Yoshua Bengio responded by saying that we are far away and first need to solve really hard problems such as AI not currently being able to understand the world as well as we do, acquiring knowledge of the world in an unsupervised autonomous fashion and missing key components such as the ability to understand and infer causal relationships in data. He along with Yann LeCun envisage AI research into the future as being like climbing a hill, making a breakthrough as you reach the top which is not guaranteed and can take many years, seeing the limitations of the new approach or discovery, and continuing to the next hill as part of a series of hills ahead.[29] According to Yann, one of those hills to climb out will be to figure out how babies and animals learn via unsupervised learning methods, which might take 10 or 20 years. As we can expect several problems like this to solve, it could take 50 to even 100 years to get to strong AI.[30] Both Yoshua and Yann are not concerned at this point with recursively improving super intelligent AI or that it poses an existential threat for humanity. Although it is fine that these questions are studied, Yoshua does not see this to be realistic or even compatible with the types of AI being built right now and for the foreseeable future. Yann also disagrees strongly with the existential alarmist view of AI, in particular Nick Bostrom's fast take-off scenario with recursive self-improving at an exponential rate. Similar to Francois Chollet's earlier arguments, the singularity and fast takeoff scenario ignore for example friction such as exhausting resources and key elements that govern the progress of AI, its level of sophistication, the economy, consumption of resources, and communication. Like many other researchers they are more concerned about the short-term potential risks with respect to lethal autonomous weapons, jobs and economic issues, minimizing distress and optimizing well-being, biased and reinforced discrimination, political advertising, and governmental surveillance of citizens. However, Yann LeCun, disagrees with Stuart Russell and the Future of Life Institute that the use of AI-powered weapons can potentially lead to mass destruction. He thinks that militaries will likely use AI-driven drones for surgical types of operations where people can be taken out in a non-lethal fashion.[31] There are also other types of debates amongst AI researchers that emphasize different approaches to advance the state-of-the-art in AI. Whereas researchers such as Yoshua, Yann, and Geoff Hinton favor working with neural network type of approaches that focus on learning methods for supervised and self-supervised learning that are not necessarily dependent on specific structures (although that plays an important role with current learning methods such as backpropagation), researchers such as Gary Marcus and Oren Etzioni are working on bringing in hybrid structures that can deal with symbolic methods for logic and reasoning. Yoshua and Gary also had an interesting debate in Montreal in December 2019 about their different approaches where they agreed that AI systems need a hybrid approach with priors and high-level manipulation of values but disagreed about gluing good old fashion AI such as rules and logic to neural networks.[32] I will come back to these AI research paths later in this chapter.

Geoff Hinton reasons that the future of human-level AI will likely be different to what people think as "individual" AIs would not necessarily get uniformly better and more intelligent on all fronts and that we will likely see networks or communities of intelligent systems where "individual" AI systems interacts with one another sharing data, training outputs and information.[33] In his interview with Martin Ford he specifically mentions that he thinks that general reasoning capacity will take a long time to be developed, anything from 10 to a 100 years. Geoff also thinks that global nuclear war or biological warfare with for example a very contagious and lethal virus with a long incubation time, are much more dangerous existential threats compared to very intelligent AI systems. That said, he is still concerned about lethal autonomous weapons and suggests that it should be handled in a similar way as chemical warfare and weapons of mass destruction is treated by the international community.

Due to substantial private, public, and academic resources and talent being put into AI, Stuart Russell expects a higher rate of breakthroughs and human-level AI to happen within his children's lifetime and not hundreds of years in the future. However, there are many key problems to solve on our way to strong AI such as how natural language can produce knowledge structures and understanding upon which reasoning processes can operate, operating over multiple scales of abstraction, and developing their own behavioral hierarchies that allow the AI systems to operate successfully in complex environments over long timescales.[34] In addressing Martin Ford's question about how things would unfold when the first human-level AIs appear, Stuart thinks that this is going to happen along many dimensions, at different skills and knowledge levels and would have different abilities and strengths to that of humans. Stuart is also advocating for developing AI systems that focus on achieving our goals as opposed to their goals without necessarily knowing our exact goals. He explains that having an explicit uncertainty about the nature of goals that the AI systems are instructed to pursue, leads to a margin of safety that we need in building safe, controllable, and trustworthy AI systems. In Stuart's essay *The Purpose Put into the*

Machine he highlights some key aspects of this approach towards provable beneficial AI where a formal problem to be solved by an AI system can for example be to maximize human future-life preferences subject to their initial uncertainty about them where the AI system keeps learning about them but never able to achieve complete certainty.[35] This approach fits in with the research priorities for safe and trustworthy AI.

Stuart Russell also has a chapter in his book *Human Compatible: Artificial Intelligence and the Problem of Control* that is called "The Not-So-Great AI Debate" where he addresses so-called AI denialist arguments to not look seriously at poorly designed super intelligent AI systems that could present an existential risk to humanity.[36] He refutes the denial type of arguments that has the form of "it's complicated", "it's impossible", "it's too soon to worry about it", and "we're the experts", with arguments such as strong AI that exceeds human capabilities in all relevant dimensions of intelligence would give them power over us, intelligence is not the same as arithmetic or physical strength, there is also the first time for everything, we cannot insure against a super intelligence simply by betting against human ingenuity, very rapid progress in AI research puts us on a path of having strong AI that can lead to us losing control, a long-term risk can still be cause of immediate concern (e.g., large asteroid on course to collide with Earth), this type of AI risk was identified by many experts in the field since its inception, and AI denialists are exhibiting tribalism in defense of technological progress. One example he uses is Leo Szilard's invention of a nuclear chain reaction mediated by neutrons a day after Ernest Rutherford claimed it was not possible in 1933. The second type of argument is a deflection that has the form of "you can't control research", "but, what about...", or just silence about the risks since they cannot be addressed or there are more immediate problems to solve than a potential existential threat. Stuart uses the example of nuclear physics research not being banned just because of containment failure risks in nuclear plants as research also focuses on solving the containment problem. We also have a current example where human germline engineering (the process by which the genome of a human is edited in such a way that the change is heritable) has been prohibited by law in many countries along with broad agreement among the scientific community to not pursue the research in this area for ethical, safety, and social reasons.[37] Stuart also states that if the risks are not properly addressed, this might lead to a situation where we see no AI benefits. He references how the growth in the nuclear industry has been severely impacted by three nuclear disasters at Three Mile Island in 1979, Chernobyl in 1986 and Fukushima in 2011.[38] The third type of argument has the shape of a quick oversimplified solution and use words like we can just "switch it off" or "put it in a box", or alternatively work in human-machine teams, avoid putting in human goals, or even merge with the machines. He argues that a super intelligent AI system would already know about the possibility of it being switched off and will ensure that this would not happen. The same holds for a super intelligent AI system in a box where we do not even have a firewall that is secure against humans. Whereas Elon Musk's Neuralink sees merging with the machines as a potential defending strategy, others like Ray Kurzweil see such a scenario in favorable light. Even if the strong AI system does not have human goals, it would still have "desires" that are built into its objectives or subgoals to for example avoid actions that would prevent it from achieving its objectives. As having intelligence implies having objectives, a super intelligent AI system will also have objectives of some sort. As also noted by Nick Bostrom, intelligence and objectives are independent from one another as the super intelligent AI system would use its intelligence to pursue its objectives accepting any reward signal.[39]

Oren Etzioni, the CEO of the Allen Institute of AI, and his team are amongst others working on Project Mosaic which focuses on building common sense in an AI system which is one of the key features of human-level intelligence. In his discussion with Martin Ford, Oren mentions that we are very far from achieving strong AI and sees some of the building blocks towards human-level intelligence as the ability for an AI system to do multiple tasks that are dissimilar to each other, to be very data-efficient, have the ability to self-replicate, and apply its knowledge and capabilities in a different domain not being trained on.[40] He also reckons that some of the greatest AI benefits include its use in advancing science to help improve medicine and solving problems in healthcare and also to reduce accidents through the use of self-driving cars. Some of the major short-term risks include the impact on the job market, cybersecurity, and lethal autonomous weapons. Oren also states that with their work on natural language understanding they are also participating in AI safety research to complement any research being done with the value alignment problem. He also thinks that there is a major distinction between intelligence and autonomy and that one can have high intelligence without any autonomy as well as the reverse. Autonomy is potentially more dangerous than intelligence as we can see with computer viruses or lethal autonomous weapons.

As a psychology and neuroscience researcher at New York University, Gary Marcus does not think that developing human-level intelligence requires replicating exactly the way the human brain works. In a recent book called *Rebooting AI: Building Artificial Intelligence We can Trust* which Gary co-authored with Ernest Davis, they discuss the limitation of deep learning which is good at perceptual pattern classification using bottom-up information, but not good at commonsense reasoning for which symbol manipulation via mathematics or language processing might be a more suitable solution as part of a trustworthy AI system that has commonsense values and reasoning built-in.[41] Gary also regards the work that the Allen Institute of AI is doing with regards to embedding human knowledge in computable form via Project Mosaic as an important step towards strong AI. When asked about a time frame for strong AI, he thinks that it is achievable and provided a confidence interval of 2030 to 2130, with a likely date of around 2050. For self-driving cars to become fully operational on our roads he also predicts a 2030 or beyond time frame. Although Gary does not completely discount it, he is like many other AI researchers not concerned at this point with recursive self-improving super intelligent AI systems that will pose an existential risk to humanity as he does not see definitive evidence that AI research is going in that direction. He is much more concerned with humans using AI for malicious purposes, bioterrorism, cyber warfare, cybersecurity threats in the short term, misinformation, and AI not optimally being used and distributed for the benefit of humanity.

Demis Hassabis, AI researcher and CEO of Deepmind, has made it clear since the inception of Deepmind that their development of neuroscience-inspired AI systems is driven by the mission to solve intelligence and advance scientific discovery for all. Although they have been acquired by Google a few years ago, they are still focused on this goal with an excellent track record of breakthroughs by demonstrating human-level and beyond capabilities in playing board games such as Go, chess, and shogi with AlphaGo (learning Go from human and computer play), AlphaGoZero (self-taught without learning from human Go games), AlphaZero (generalized to playing Go, chess and shogi), and MuZero (learns without being taught the rules).[42] In a more recent breakthrough, Deepmind was able to effectively solve the protein folding problem which is one of biology's imposing challenges.

This was accomplished through the latest version of AlphaFold that predicts 3D models of protein structures from its amino-acid sequence significantly more accurately than traditional computational methods which amongst other things enables quicker and more advanced drug discovery and a better understanding of the building blocks of cells as well as the causes of diseases that are the result of misfolded proteins.[43] In discussing the key obstacles to address in achieving human-level AI, Demis specifically mentions transfer learning that allows an AI system to transfer knowledge from one domain to a new domain, language understanding and symbolic manipulation using Deepmind's techniques.[44] When Martin Ford asked Demis about the existential alarmist views of Nick Bostrom and Elon Musk, he responded that it might sound radical, but that "it is a lot more nuanced" when you talk to them in person and that he has a more moderate view on this.[45] He thinks AI is going to be the most beneficial technology that humanity has ever created, but to live up to this promise we have to make wise decisions in how we design, apply, and allocate the benefits to society. Although Demis agrees that recent breakthroughs have made it necessary to start doing research on the control and value alignment problems, he reckons that the AI technology is still at an emergent stage and that we will be able to understand and reverse-engineer these intelligent systems to manage the technical risks. Demis is also concerned about lethal autonomous weapons and supports the Future of Life's perspectives on this. He also feels that there is good collaboration within the international AI research community, but that we need to work on better international coordination as well as relevant regulations and standards for AI applications. Although AI can be used to help solve a lot of the world's problems, we need to create an economy where the productivity gains generated by AI's transformation are shared with everyone.[46]

Andrew Ng, an Adjunct Professor of Computer Science at Stanford and previously chief scientist at Baidu as well as a co-founder of the Google Brain project, Coursera (an online education company), Landing AI and a venture capital company AI Fund that builds AI start-ups, thinks the path to strong AI is unclear and likely not possible in his lifetime. Although we have made excellent progress with narrow AI through deep learning and will unlock significant further value across multiple industries, he does not think we can make simple extrapolations to strong AI and feels that this has created unnecessary hype. Although Andrew thinks that we now have enough deep learning research and application momentum to ensure that we should not go into another AI winter, he thinks we should reset expectations with respect to strong AI. Apart from some of the current limitations or areas of improvement of deep learning such causality, explainability, adversarial attacks, learning from small data sets, get better at transfer and multi-task learning, and the need to use unlabeled data better, he highlights unsupervised learning that mirrors the way that children learn to be one of the key building blocks for achieving strong AI and sees neural network type of approaches to continue play a key role in getting there.[47] Daphne Koller, a Professor of Computer Science at Stanford and co-founder of Coursera with Andrew as well as CEO and Founder of biotech startup Insitro, thinks that although deep learning has a been a tremendous success so far, we need at least one breakthrough (but likely a few more) before we get to strong AI. She reckons that these breakthroughs are unpredictable stochastic events that can take one month or 150 years, and even when it happens it would require a lot of engineering like we have seen with deep learning and its foundations that effectively evolved over decades.[48] Daphne's opinion is that as strong AI has not even been invented we are far removed from any possible AI-induced existential risks and when breakthroughs occur we will be in a better position to understand the key components so as to engineer safe and trustworthy strong AI. Although she is not in favor of governments regulating things that they do not understand which currently in general looks to be the case with respect to AI technology, she makes the point that many of the short-term risks associated with the smart technology era such as privacy, security, bias, lethal autonomous weapons are already here and should be addressed as a matter of priority. Some key limitations of current AI include the inability to transfer knowledge and skills from one domain to another by being restricted to end-to-end training within single architectures that can only achieve narrow vertical tasks as well as the dependence on significant amounts of data to train these focused models.

Andrew and Daphne's colleague Fei-Fei Li, a Professor of Computer Science at Stanford and Chief Scientist of Google Cloud, see narrow and strong AI all on the same continuum, where human-level AI systems have multiple dimensions, are situationally aware, understands context, and mirrors human learning that includes unsupervised learning, reinforcement learning and virtual learning.[49] She is a big proponent of democratizing AI and human-centered AI that enhances and augments humans within a job market context, follows a collaborative interdisciplinary research approach that includes neuroscience, behavior science and cognitive science, and also involves multiple stakeholders to help unlock opportunities and address issues with respect to the economy, job market, regulations, policies, ethics, diversity, bias, security and privacy. Fei-Fei's Google colleague Jeff Dean, who is the Director for AI and head of Google Brain, envisages the path to human-level AI as building single systems that have the capability to perform many different tasks and progressively using the knowledge from solving these tasks to tackle new problems along with the supporting large-scale computational infrastructure and hardware required to do so. Jeff is also not that concerned about Nick Bostrom's superintelligence existential risk and believes that we need to apply wisdom to make good choices in the way we develop, integrate, and use AI in society to the benefit of humankind.

In Nick Bostrom's interview with Martin Ford, he mentions that it is still too early to have governments getting involved with strong AI concerns as it is not clear what should currently be done unlike specific narrow applications that can be regulated such as lethal autonomous weapons. Although Nick agrees that current alarmist remarks about strong AI being a greater existential threat than for example nuclear war or say North Korea is premature and could potentially make things worse, there are still a lot of foundational work on value alignment, the control problem, safety and governance that needs to be done in collaboration with the AI research community such as those via the likes of the Future of Humanity Institute (FHI) at Oxford University, Deepmind, Open AI, the Machine Intelligence Research Institute at Berkeley, and others. According to him, humanity needs more wisdom on what we focus on and how we allocate our time and resources. For example, Nick's team at FHI are focused on macro strategies for existential risks that relates to strong AI and biosecurity and does not regard climate change as an existential risk, although the latter is an important problem to address.[50]

Joscha Bach, Cognitive Scientist and VP Research at AI Foundation, thinks that even though nobody seems to know how to truly build strong AI yet and current narrow AI systems are not likely to scale to strong AI, we should still be concerned about it as many (although not all) of the significant open questions in developing strong AI appear to be known and solvable and there is no apparent reason why the implementation of the principles embedded in biological brains should not be within our engineering reach.[51] Strong AI will not have the limitations of biological brains that are maximizing their evolutionary fitness or future options and will scale better to achieve its goals, which in the widest sense might be to consume the maximum negative entropy that can be scraped from the universe over time. Our human reward functions are much more constrained and need to incorporate physiological, social, and cognitive demands as well as consider human values such as reducing suffering, improving the content of mental representations, preserving human civilization, and preserving life. He conjectures that whereas the existing narrow AI is probably sufficient for ending our labor-based economy sometime in the future, strong AI may pose an existential risk as one of many other ones where the ultimate existential risk is running out of negative entropy. Joscha believes that investing in AI safety is warranted and that strong AI may also help us in preventing some other existential risks.[52] He also references Lebowski's Theorem that states that no super intelligent system is going to do anything that is harder than hacking its reward system and asks if we can build a machine that is completely truthful.[53]

Judea Pearl, a Professor of Computer Science and Statistics at University of California, and author of books such as *"Heuristics"*, *"Probability Reasoning, Causality"* and *"The Book of Why"*, believes that data-driven machine learning approaches such as deep learning is limited in that it just learns from data and cannot understand cause and effect, interpret counterfactuals or operate on an imaginary level which allows the building of new models of the world.[54] Judea does not think there are any theoretical hindrances towards developing human-level AI and sees both deep learning and causal reasoning as part of the building blocks to achieve this. In his essay *The Limitations of Opaque Learning Machines*, Judea views machine learning as a tool to go from data to probabilities and then to go from probabilities to true understanding which involves predicting the effects of the actions and then imagining counterfactuals.[55] He also highlights a causal reasoning theoretical framework where on the first level of the 3-level hierarchy statistical reasoning is used to update the beliefs about events, a second level is dealing with actions that requires information (encoded in a probabilistic graphical model) about interventions not available on the first level, and the third level is dealing with counterfactuals. He specifically mentions to Martin Ford that we should be wary of strong AI as it can effectively lead to "breeding a new species of intelligent animals" that can have an inner experience and emotions and assume their own agency.[56]

Rana el Kaliouby, the CEO of Affectiva which is a company that spun out of MIT Labs and focuses on building AI solutions that sense and understand human emotions, strongly believes that we should design and deploy these AI systems in ways that do not remove our agency as humans.[57] She also thinks that we are very far away from building systems that have human-level artificial general intelligence and do not subscribe to fears about AI being an existential threat to humanity.[58] She is more concerned about us preserving the existing biases that we currently have in society by not being diligent about the data that we train our AI systems on. Rana is a proponent of regulating specific AI applications and also has Affectiva publishing best practices and guidelines especially on ethics and privacy as it pertains to emotion-related AI solutions.[59] Daniela Rus, the Director of Computer Science and AI at MIT, also thinks that human-level AI is not likely to be achieved in the near future and thinks that the founders and thought leaders in the AI field from 60 years ago would actually be disappointed in the progress made so far.[60] In her mind we need exceptional breakthroughs to bridge the gaps in our understanding of human intelligence along with how the brain accomplishes this and that significant progress will likely be as a result of interdisciplinary and multidisciplinary research that involves at least fields such as computer science, neuroscience and cognitive science. Cynthia Breazeal, a Director of the Personal Robotics Group at the MIT Lab and Founder of Jibo that provides social robots for the home, is also less worried about strong AI risks compared to the risks associated with people that can misuse AI to do harm, or negatively impact our privacy and security, or manipulate people through fake information, or developing lethal autonomous weapons. She is a champion for developing complementary human-machine social interactions, building machines that support our ethical and human values, driving an AI-literate society, and democratizing AI for all to benefit. Cynthia also questions the practical driving forces to create human-level AI from a long-term commitment, funding, resources, time, patience, and talent perspective and thinks that our current efforts might just lead to broader and more flexible versions of the current narrow AI applications. There are many things that our current narrow AI systems cannot do such as doing multiple tasks, real-time ongoing learning as a child, learn from a few examples and generalize, human-level common sense, deep emotional intelligence, and a deep theory of mind.[61]

Josh Tenenbaum, a Professor of Computational Cognitive Science at MIT, is focused on "reverse engineering the human mind" through understanding human intelligence from a computational perspective and developing these learning and reasoning capabilities in machines to achieve human-level intelligence. In developing strong AI systems, he disagrees with the approach to learn everything from scratch as is for example done with Deepmind's AlphaZero, but instead have a high-level roadmap that first focus on the pre-linguistic intelligence of the first year and a half of a human baby's life that is more geared towards intuitive physics and concepts of the real-world, intuitive psychology and the understanding of other human's actions. This is followed by building language that is typically exhibited from one and a half to three years old, and finally from 3 years and up using the language to build and learn everything else required to operate efficiently and effectively in the real world.[62] Although there is a general acknowledgment that deep learning is a key component in the AI toolbox for especially pattern recognition tasks, symbolic AI as well as graphical models and Bayesian networks are other key tools that have according to Josh an important role in creating hybrid AI systems that can be used to capture people's mental models of the world. These probabilistic programming systems can be integrated with deep learning types of models to speed up inference in the hybrid AI systems in a similar way that deep learning is also speeding up inference and search in an AlphaGo game tree. With these hybrid AI systems, it is possible to also capture genetic and cultural information and structures and effectively search in a space of genetic or cognitive thinking types of programs. Josh argues that a deep reinforcement learning type of blank slate approach which just focuses on modeling evolutionary human intelligence over many generations and not what a baby does, is limiting and does not capture how biology works over evolution or the lifetime of a person. Also, in order to build human-level AI, we would likely need to build in a kind of unitary experience of the world and not at a level of neurons firing. This would give these systems the ability to think, learn or make decisions for itself. Josh is also not currently concerned with potential risks around strong AI, as we are very far from building such systems and we have more pressing short-term concerns that need our full attention such as using technology for selfish or evil purposes, stress on the workforce with jobs disappearing within generations, privacy, human rights, and surveillance.[63]

David Ferrucci, CEO and Chief Scientist at Elemental Cognition (in partnership with Bridgewater Associates) and previous head of IBM Watson, states that their goal is to produce AI systems that can process language similar to how humans do it, learn through language and deliver knowledge effortlessly through language and reason.[64] He thinks that human-level intelligence has three parts which include perception, control and knowing. Whereas deep learning and neural networks based techniques deal very effectively with perception and control, their team is focused on knowing and understanding by developing human-compatible intelligence that is anchored in language, logic, and reason. Elemental Cognition makes use of neural networks, formal reasoning, formal logic representations, unsupervised learning from large corpora, and continuous dialog with people and other sources of incremental knowledge.[65] David reckons that they are making enough progress with this type of approach to autonomous language understanding that human-level AI is possible within approximately 10 years and not "a 50- or 100-year wait".[66] He is also less worried about the existential risks of superintelligence as we would need to give AI systems the ability to develop its own goals, desires and plans to do harmful things and have leverage over us and our systems. It is much more important to ensure that we do not give AI systems leverage over systems that for example control our national security, transportation, electric grids, and food supply chain.

James Manyika, a senior partner at McKinsey & Company and chairman of McKinsey Global Institute, has a balanced perspective on existential risks with respect to superintelligent AI with recursive improvement. Even though the probability of the latter is very low, and we are very far away from strong AI, he thinks that it is good that we have small groups of researchers thinking about these potential value alignment and control problems, but should not involve governments or incite society about this at this point. Like many others, David has the opinion that AI regulation should focus on aspects such as safety, privacy, transparency, and democratizing AI.[67] Bryan Johnson, the founder of Kernel, OS Fund and Braintree, believes that the future of homo sapiens will be defined by the combination of AI and human intelligence. He thinks that AI is the best thing "since sliced bread" and a wonderful tool to accelerate radical human enhancement. Although he is respectful towards Nick Bostrom's work on the potential control problem that relates to a run-away strong AI, he regards the alarmist existential threats about strong AI by some influential businesspeople and scientists as unfortunate and unnecessary scaremongering of society. Bryan reckons that it is foolish to say that AI is humanity's biggest threat and regards ourselves to be our own biggest threat as clearly demonstrated throughout history. We can use smart technology to do fantastic things, but also create enormous harm. Barbara Grosz, a Professor of Natural Sciences in the School of Engineering and Applied Sciences at Harvard University, is not convinced that we should pursue strong AI with its potential ethically hazardous outcomes and sees it as a distraction to the short-term risks and ethical issues that we face with our current applications of AI and technology in the broader sense. She has also experienced a number of AI winters and thinks we should manage expectations of AI better by for example making clear what the current strengths and limitations are of deep learning and other techniques in the AI toolbox. In her discussion with Martin Ford, she has said that "AI systems are best if they're designed with people in mind".[68] Barbara thinks that AI research and applications in healthcare and education that complement people are some of the best use cases that we should focus on.

OpenAI, an AI research laboratory that consists of the non-profit OpenAI Inc and its for-profit subsidiary corporation OpenAI LP, is another company such as Google Deepmind that has a stated goal of developing strong AI. Under the leadership of Sam Altman (CEO), Greg Brockman (CTO) and Ilya Sutskever (Chief Scientist), they are specifically focused on developing safe and beneficial artificial general intelligence that benefits all of humanity (even if they help others to also achieve this outcome). Ilya Sutskever is of the opinion that strong AI is a serious possibility over the short-term, whereas Greg Brockman said that huge computing power is a key driver to reach human-level AI.[69] OpenAI has initially received $1 billion investment from high-profile contributors such as Elon Musk, Sam Altman, Peter Thiel, Reid Hoffman, and Jessica Livingston, followed by another $1 billion from Microsoft in 2019 to speed-up its pursuit with required computational infrastructure.[70] Over the next few years OpenAI intends to build an AI system that can run "a human brain-sized AI model", but also mentions that some algorithmic advances will be required to make use of the huge increase in computing power.[71] One of the product lines delivered over the last few years include generative pre-trained transformer language prediction models GPT, GPT-2, and GPT-3 where the latest version has a capacity of 175 billion parameters with excellent performance on many natural language processing datasets, including question-answering, translation, and cloze tasks (fill in the blanks), as well as a number of tasks that require prompt reasoning or domain adaptation, such as using a new word in a sentence, unscrambling words, or performing 3-digit arithmetic.[72] Similar to Deepmind, OpenAI's research is making heavy use of deep reinforcement learning and has also video game applications such as OpenAI Five (five Open-AI-curated bots) playing in a competitive five-on-five video game Dota 2, where the latest version in 2019 has defeated a world champion human team 2-0 as well as obtained a winning percentage of 99.4% of its games in an 4-day open online competition.

As can be seen above, many AI researchers do not believe that AI approaches that mainly incorporate deep learning - which is more focused on pattern recognition - will be able to reach human-level intelligence. Oren Etzioni has for example said that "to reach the next level of AI, we need some breakthroughs. I'm not sure it's simply throwing more money at the problem."[73] As also mentioned above, Gary Marcus believes that deep learning should be viewed "not as a universal solvent, but simply as one tool among many."[74] Stuart Russell said that "focusing on raw computing power misses the point entirely... We don't know how to make a machine really intelligent — even if it were the size of the universe."[75] Greg Brockman's response to this criticism is that one can get qualitatively different outcomes with increased computation and references the significant improvements with its generative GPT type of language prediction models that is developing an increasing degree of semantic understanding as well as OpenAI Five that demonstrates some planning by teaching itself to operate at a higher level of abstraction, setting a high-level goal and then focusing on particular tasks as needed.[76] As visually illustrated by Ilya Sutskever in his 2018 talk showing the compute power for different AI models from 2009 to 2018, there has been a 300,000x increase in compute from AlexNet to AlphaGo Zero. Greg Brockman mentioned that the past seven years of advances would be like "extending the battery life of a smartphone from one day to 800 years: another five years on the same exponential curve would take that to 100 million years".[77]

In John Brockman's *Possible Minds: Twenty-five Ways of Looking at AI*, he and other authors debate the future of AI as they reference Norbert Wiener's *The Human Use of Human Beings* in 1950 which appears to be as relevant as ever in 2020 and beyond as he conveys his worry at that time about the uncontrolled commercial exploitation and other unexpected consequences of advanced technologies.[78] At the time of Norbert Wiener the advanced technologies of control and communications that he referenced were called cybernetics which comes from the Greek word that means "governance" and is the concept of automatic self-regulating control. Although AI was missing from Wiener's vision, the underlying message is still applicable today with our narrow AI applications and as we develop more capable machine intelligence that might eventually lead to strong AI with unsupervised and self-improving capabilities. Seth Lloyd, a theoretical physicist at MIT, echoes Wiener's sentiments in his essay *Wrong, but More Relevant than Ever* and also points out that whilst information being a key component in governing the behavior of complex systems was correctly highlighted, the potential of digital computation was unrecognized at the time.[79] He also thinks that similar to 70 years ago, that technology overestimation is also happening today and that despite excellent progress in AI, the expectations around deep learning should be tempered. In the essay *The Inhuman Mess Our Machines Have Gotten Us Into*, Rodney Brooks strongly feels that humankind has gotten itself into conundrum with people being exploited by companies that provide services that they desire as well as some governments that manipulate people or smothering opposition.[80] He feels that our current predicament is actually more complex and worse than what Norbert Wiener has envisioned. George Dyson, a historian of science and technology, conjectures in his essay *The Third Law* that provable AI is a myth as it is possible to develop something without having an understanding how it works. He bases this on a loophole in what he calls the third law of AI that states "that any system simple enough to be understandable will not be complicated enough to behave intelligently, while any system complicated enough to behave intelligently will be too complicated to understand".[81] George further has a controversial opinion that the next computing revolution will be analog systems over which digital software development has no command and that we should be more concerned with self-reproduction, communication and control. Daniel C. Dennett, a Professor of Philosophy at Tufts University and author of a number of books such as *Consciousness Explained*, advocates in his essay *What Can We Do?* that we need intelligent tools that can solve problems and not artificial conscious agents that can have rights, feelings, be able to respond with discontent, or even potentially able to enslave us.[82] Daniel would like to see that we develop oracle type AIs with no conscience, personality, fear of death, or distractions due to their own preferences. Max Tegmark in *Let's Aspire to More Than Making Ourselves Obsolete* is of the opinion that extinction is a possibility if our smart technology develops faster than the wisdom that we need to manage it responsibly and would be very unfortunate given that the potential upside and opportunities that AI presents are tremendous and might enable life in various forms to thrive for millions or even billions of years throughout the universe.[83]

Jaan Tallinn, a computer programmer and co-developer of Skype and investor, has been laser focused on driving the AI-risk message through his involvement with and support for the Future of Life Institute, the Machine Intelligence Research Institute and others working on AI safety and risk reduction.[84] The initial impetus was provided by Eliezer Yudkowsky's revolutionary message "Continued progress in AI can precipitate a change of cosmic proportions - a runaway process that will likely kill everyone. We need to put in a lot of extra effort to avoid that outcome."[85] In *Dissident Messages*, Jaan states that the initial AI-risk message to the public had a huge flaw in that it does not communicate the true scale of the problem or AI's potential benefits. On the risk side, he thinks that super intelligent AI is also an environmental risk as it could potentially lead to Earth being turned into an uninhabitable environment for biological life-forms. On the upside, we can create a future in which all people's lives are massively improved and potentially expand life well beyond earth and the solar system.[86] Steven Pinker, a Professor of Psychology at Harvard University and author of a number of books including *Enlightenment Now: The Case for Reason, Science, Humanism, and Progress*, has an opposing view and states that the two moral themes of Norbert Wiener's *The Human Use of Human Beings* of a dystopian fear of runaway technology and the liberal defense of an open free society are in conflict with one another. In *Tech Prophecy and the Underappreciated Causal Power of Ideas*, Steven articulates several misconceptions about a sudden AI takeover where intelligence are confused with motivation (being intelligent is not the same as wanting something), intelligence are seen as a limitless continuum of power to reach any goals or solve any problem, no law of complex systems states that intelligent systems will become cruel self-absorbed entities, and leaning too much on the steep upward curve of the current AI hype cycle. According to him, the runaway super intelligence scenarios with the value-alignment problem are also contradicting as it depends on the assumption that humans are so smart that they can build a super intelligent system but so stupid to give it full control without testing it or that the AI system is so intelligent to solve many "impossible" problems, but so foolish to creating chaos due to some misunderstanding about conflicting goals (which should actually be handled by the AI's intelligence).

David Deutsch, quantum physicist at Oxford University and author of *The Fabric of Reality* and *The Beginning of Infinity*, states in his essay *Beyond Reward and Punishment* that human-level intelligence is about thinking which he describes as the process of creating understanding or explanatory knowledge.[87] He reckons that this is a property that strong AI should aim for. David is specifically arguing that misunderstandings about human thinking and how we developed also causes similar misunderstandings about strong AI and how to develop it. Given hundreds of thousands of years where thinking was not really used for innovation but mainly for imitating new complex behavior and progress occurred on longer timescales than a typical human lifetime, the benefits of human's innovation capability did not contribute to the biological evolution of the human brain as it was primarily driven by the benefits of preserving cultural knowledge. Before the period of Enlightenment, the culture of rewards and punishment enforced on humans over centuries created an environment of compliance and stagnation that did not encourage innovation, technological breakthroughs, or creative thoughts towards improvement or transformations. As in the current era with humans, we should go beyond reward and punishment in developing strong AI and give them the ability to search for a better goal under unknown constraints. Instead of creating a "Totally Obedient Moron" type of AI (as all other software or narrow AI systems) that does not know what it is doing or why, we should aim for the opposite, a so-called "Disobedient Autonomous Thinking Application" that is more similar to raising a child. David thinks that a strong AI system should not be restricted by fixed, testable criteria to determine if the output generated is correct or controlled by a flow of externally enforced rewards and punishments that would be detrimental to the system's ability to develop creative thought as in the case of humans. He therefore reckons that any testing in the process of developing a strong AI will be counterproductive and immoral as it is with humans. As a strong AI should be free to choose its own ideas, objectives, methods, and criteria, we would only see its abilities to search for explanatory knowledge when the system is executing. David agrees that such strong AI systems could be dangerous in a similar way as their human counterparts and should operate as members of an open stable kind of society with similar rights and cultural membership as humans where everyone chooses their own internal and external rewards. In terms of fears that strong AI can behave in an erratic or dangerous fashion that deviates away from the culture's moral values, David conjectures that all current existential risks that stems from a growth in explainable knowledge comes from weapons of mass destruction in the hands of mentally twisted agents (humans or AI systems) that are the enemies of civilization and not rebellious youths. He also sees the belief that strong AI are uniquely threatening due to them executing on ever improving hardware as a misconception, as human thought will also be boosted by the same technology. He argues that human brains should be able to think anything that strong AI can think or compute depending on only the speed or memory capacity of these strong AI systems, and that the latter can also be made equal by empowering humans with the same technology.[88]

Tom Griffiths, a Professor of Information, Technology, Consciousness, and Culture at Princeton University and co-author of *Algorithms to Live By*, advocates in his essay *The Artificial Use of Human Beings* that strong AI systems should develop good generative cognitive models of human behavior to better understand, make conjectures about human desires and respond to human needs.[89] Tom sees this as a prerequisite for solving the value alignment problem. His research group is focused on developing a more realistic model of rational behavior that incorporates computational constraints to find the right algorithm that creates a balance between "thinking too much" and making errors. This trade-off is called "bounded optimality" as a theory of human behavior where a rational model bridges the gap between rationality and heuristics and functions as a key component to make AI systems more intelligent in interpreting people's behavior. Anca Dragan, an Assistant Professor of Electrical Engineering and Computer Science at UC Berkeley and research collaborator of Stuart Russell, also shares Stuart's engrossment with AI safety in her essay *Putting the Human into the AI Equation*. She is arguing for "human-compatible" AI that addresses both a coordination problem where AI systems recognize and treat people as more than just objects in the environment and able to reason about and interact with them in optimal fashion as well as a value-alignment problem where people determine the reward function of the AI system to ensure that it is in line with what society, the consumer or the developer wants. Chris Anderson, CEO of 3DR, former editor-in-chief of Wired, and author of *The Long Tail, Free, and Makers*, in his essay *Gradient Descent* he uses gradient descent (which is a first-order iterative optimization algorithm for finding a local minimum of a differentiable function and also used to train AI systems) as a metaphor to illustrate the path that life, humans, and AI systems are following to improve and get to better solutions and systems, including an AI system that will one day be as smart as a mosquito, and beyond.[90] David Kaiser, a Professor of the History of Science as well as of Physics at MIT, in *"Information" for Wiener, for Shannon and for Us* imagines a scenario where AI systems might be used the develop meaningful information rather than a persistent quest of less meaningful activities that also concerned Norbert Wiener such as the "rampant militarism, runaway corporate profit seeking, the self-limiting features of secrecy, and the reduction of human expression to interchangeable commodities".[91] Neil Gershenfeld, a Physicist and Director of MIT's Center for Bits and Atoms, in his essay *Scaling* predicts that the same scaling trends that made the current success of AI possible will be followed by the merging of AI and natural intelligence where atoms arranging bits arranging atoms and the paths of AI and machine making becomes intertwined.[92]

In his essay *The First Machine Intelligences,* W. Daniel Hillis, a Professor of Engineering and Medicine at USC and the author of *The Patterns on the Stone: The Simple Ideas that make Computers Work*, outlines four possible scenarios for how strong AI will relate to our existing hybrid superintelligence systems such as countries and multinational corporations which "have their own emergent goals and their actions that are not always aligned to the interests of the people who created them".[93] These include multiple strong AI systems being controlled by individual countries or regions, AI systems being controlled by multinational for-profit corporations that can even become more high-powered and autonomous than individual countries, strong AI systems that pursue their own goals and are not aligned with people or hybrid superintelligences, or strong AI systems that pursues humanity's goals, restores the balance between the individuals, corporations and states by empowering the people with AI capability. The latter is clearly the preferable one. As Daniel says, "The future is not something that will happen to us; it is something that we will build".[94]

Venki Ramakrishnan, a Molecular Biology Scientist at Cambridge University, Nobel Prize winner in chemistry and author of *Gene Machine: The Race to Discover the Secrets of Ribosome*, provides some important perspectives in *Will Computers Become our Overlords* such as that even though in the bigger scheme of things human intelligence is just another survival mechanism, we still define our very existence and why we are special by this attribute. Even our fears about strong AI are reflected by this belief. Just to give further perspective in terms of resilient species on Earth, he feels confident that strong AI will never have mastery of bacteria. Alex "Sandy" Pentland, a Professor of Media Arts and Sciences at MIT and author of *Social Physics*, in his essay *The Human Strategy* emphasizes that the common sense understanding that humans within a networked society brings to solving problems along with the ability to dynamically shape its social networks can be used to good effect in creating a human-AI ecosystem and culture that has a "human feel" to it.[95] Hans Ulrich Obrist, Artistic Director of the Serpentine Gallery in London and author of *Ways of Curating and Lives of the Artists, Lives of the Architects*, in his essay *Making the Invisible Visible: Art Meets AI* would like to see a world where AI is used as a tool for creativity and not replacing artists, where we have closer collaboration between engineers and artists, and where we "create a space that is non deterministic and non-utilitarian in its plurality of perspectives and diversity of understandings".[96] Caroline A. Jones, a Professor of Art History at MIT and author of *Eyesight Alone*, provides an arts history perspective in her essay *The Artistic Use of Cybernetic Beings* against the backdrop of her goal to develop a new cultural evolution paradigm aimed at "communalism and interspecies symbiosis rather than survival of the fittest".[97]

Alison Gopnik, a Developmental Psychologist at UC Berkeley, and author of books that include *The Philosophical Baby*, mentions in *AIs versus Four-Year-Olds* that we can improve the machine learning capability of AI systems by incorporating features of children's learning such as active curiosity-driven learning as well as social and cultural learning. Although we need to regulate certain AI applications, she thinks that human stupidity can be far more damaging than AI systems. Also, current AI systems can easily be outperformed by the average 4-year old child.[98] In *Algorists Dream of Objectivity,* Peter Galison, a Science Historian and Professor at Harvard University and author of *Einstein's Clocks, Poincaré's Maps: Empires of Time*, mentions that as the legal, ethical, formal and economic spheres of life are becoming more governed by algorithms, it is important to taken into consideration that AI-driven predictive analytics based on mechanical objectivity sometimes comes at a price that is worth paying and sometimes detrimental to a just society that we aspire to. Judgement is sometimes still needed to make that call.[99] In the essay *The Rights of Machines*, George M. Church, a Professor of Genetics at Harvard Medical School and co-author of *Regenesis: How Synthetic Biology Will Reinvent Nature and Ourselves*, has a more positive perspective on the future of strong AI, but is still worried about teaching these systems ethical behavior (especially given our track record in teaching ourselves ethical behavior) and giving them proper rights. George also thinks that we already have people that are "transhuman" if defined as "people and cultures not comprehensible to human living in modern, yet technological culture" and ask what are their rights?

In *Artificial Intelligence and the Future of Civilization,* Stephen Wolfram, Scientist, CEO of Wolfram Research and author of *A New Kind of Science*, sees technology as taking human goals and making them automatically executable by machines.[100] He thinks that goals and purposes are uniquely human and defined by personal history, biology, psychology, cultural environment and the history of our civilization. Human goals have significantly varied over time and are typically linked to some sort of scarcity to a large extent. As time is also a scarcity, Stephen reckons that the most considerable discontinuity will likely be when humanity gets to effective biological or digital immortality. As he does not think that inventing goals has a path to automation, we need to equip AI systems with goals. In order for AI systems to execute our goals, we need to engage with them via language that could be understood by AI systems and humans. As natural language has not worked so well thus far, Stephen and his WolframAlpha team has developed a knowledge-based language that incorporates the knowledge of the world in the form of science and data collection directly into the language and aims to convert human thought into a form that a computer can understand. Although it can represent objective knowledge of the world, the problem is to represent everyday human conversation in an accurate symbolic way. We also need to take in consideration that the communication channel between AI systems and humans are evolving into a visual higher bandwidth one compared to just a Turing Test type of language communication. Stephen identifies four levels of how knowledge has been transmitted in the world's history which starts with genetics, then a physiological recognition of various kinds of objects and the learning of knowledge, followed by natural language that allows knowledge to be represented sufficiently abstract for brains to interact with one another, and finally knowledge-based programming that creates an actual representation of real things in the world in an accurate symbolic fashion. Besides that, the knowledge base code can be understood by both humans and AI systems, another key feature is that the code is executable by computers. Stephen would like to see people learn to think computationally and ask what the world would look like if most people can code. He sees coding as a form of expression in a similar way writing in a natural language is a form of expression, but with the added advantage that it is instantly executable as computations. Stephen also thinks that there is an equivalence between the kinds of computations that different complex systems are doing such as brains, living cells, the weather, and the earth's global climate. As there does not seem to be a clear-cut distinction between intelligence and computation, it is difficult to claim that humanity is intelligent, and the rest of the universe is not. Although much of science has been about shortcutting computation done by nature, there seems to be a computational irreducibility to computation done by nature. Even with strong AI systems there will be no shortcuts to get to the current state without going through all the computational steps.[101] Also, how does one recognize if a system has a purpose? Does the universe have a purpose? Does computation have a purpose? Does intelligence have a purpose? How do we recognize purpose in strong AI systems or for that matter extraterrestrial intelligence?

Human Intelligence versus Machine Intelligence

As we contemplate human intelligence versus machine intelligence, let us briefly consider here some broad definitions of intelligence. Those include defining intelligence to be "the ability to acquire and apply knowledge and skills" or "the ability to perceive or infer information, and to retain it as knowledge to be applied towards adaptive behaviors within an environment or context" or "the capacity for logic, understanding, self-awareness, learning, emotional knowledge, reasoning, planning, creativity, critical thinking, and problem-solving".[102] Another summarized version in the context of AI research is that intelligence "measures an agent's ability to achieve goals in a wide range of environments."[103] In considering the measure of intelligence Francois Chollet also emphasizes that both elements of achieving a task-specific skill as well as generality and adaptation as demonstrated through skill acquisition capability are key. He goes further and defines intelligence as a "measure of its skill-acquisition efficiency over a scope of tasks with respect to priors, experience, and generalization difficulty".[104]   Following an Occam's razor approach, Max Tegmark defines intelligence very broadly as the ability to accomplish complex goals, whereas Joscha Bach simply defines intelligence as the ability to make models, where a model is something that explains information, information is discernible differences at the systemic interface, and the meaning of information is the relationships that are discovered to changes in other information.[105] Joscha's definition for intelligence differs from Max's one, as he sees achieving goals as being smart and choosing the right goals as being wise. So, one can be intelligent, but not smart or wise. For the "making models" definition of intelligence, aspects such as generality, adaptability, and skills acquisition capability with consideration of priors, experience, and generalization difficulty, would imply that the models being produced will be able to generalize and adapt to new information, situations, environments or tasks. The way an observer can find ground truth is by making models, and then build confidence in the models by testing it in order to determine if it is true and to which degree (which is also called epistemology). So, the confidence of one's beliefs should equal the weight of the evidence. Language in its most general sense where it includes natural language and mental representation is the rules of representing and changing models. The set of all languages is what we call mathematics and is used to express and compare models. He defines three types of models: a primary model that is perceptual and optimizes for coherence, a knowledge model that repairs perception and optimizes for truth, and agents that self-regulate behavior programs and rewrite other models. He sees intelligence as a multi-generational property, where individuals can have more intelligence than generations, and civilizations have more intelligence than individuals.[106] For a human intellect, the mind is something that perceptually observes the universe, uses neurons and neurotransmitters as a substrate, have a working memory as the current binding state, a self that identifies with what we think we are and what we want to happen, and a consciousness that is the content of attention and makes knowledge available throughout the mind. A civilization intellect is similar but have a society that observes the universe, people and resources that function as the substrate, a generation that act as the current binding state, a culture (self of civilization) that identifies what we think we are and what we want to happen, and media (consciousness of civilization) that provides the contents of attention making knowledge available throughout society.[107]

As Joscha Bach considers the mind of a human intellect to be a general modeling system with one or more paradigms that interface with the environment combined with universal motivation, he thinks we predominantly need better algorithms than what we currently have to make better generalized models. Our current solutions to modeling includes for example convex optimization using deep learning, probabilistic models, and genetic algorithms, whereas the general case of mental representation seems to be a probabilistic algorithm, which is hard to do with deep learning's stochastic gradient descent based approach which is better at solving perceptual problems.[108] If we look at how much source code we need to generate a brain, the Kolmogorov complexity (the length of a shortest software program that generates the object) as output is limited by a subset of the coding part of the genome involved in building a brain which is likely less than 1 Gigabyte (assuming a rough calculation where most of the 70 GB of the coding part of a genome's 700 GB codes for what happens in a single cell and 1 GB codes for structural organization of the organism). If we assume from an implementation perspective that the functional unit in the human brain is likely cortical columns, the implementation complexity which can be calculated as the number of effective processing units and connectivity seems to be in the order of a few hundred Gigabytes.[109] Given these high-level complexity calculations strong AI that emulates the human brain should in principle be possible. AI also has the ability to scale, whereas biological brains due to evolution run into limits such as the high level of metabolism that fast and large nervous systems need, the proportionally larger organisms that are required by large brains, longer training periods that are required for better performance, information flow being slowed down by splitting intelligence between brains, communication becoming more difficult with distance, and not having the interests between individuals fully aligned. AI systems on the other hand are more scalable with variable energy sources, reusable knowledge, cost-effective and reliable high bandwidth communication, as well as not having to align a multi-agent AI system or even have to make generation changes.[110] Depending on the objectives and reward functions of AI systems and how it is aligned with human values as we want it to be, it does not need to be constrained by optimizing evolutionary fitness or adhering to physiological, social and cognitive constraints of biological systems, but can be more focused on achieving its goals which might in the broadest sense include optimizing its use of negative entropy. Scalable strong AI systems will likely only require consciousness when attention is needed to solve problems as the rest can be done on "autopilot" similar to how we do some activity that we have mastered well in automatic fashion without having to think about it.

Frank Wilczek, a Physics Professor at MIT, author of *A Beautiful Question: Finding Nature's Deep Design* and recipient of the 2004 Nobel Prize in Physics, makes the "astonishing corollary" in *The Unity of Intelligence*, an essay in John Brockman's *Possible Minds: Twenty-five Ways of Looking at AI,* that natural intelligence such as human intelligence is a special case of artificial intelligence.[111] He infers this by combining evidence of physics about matter with Francis Crick's "astonishing hypothesis" in neurobiology that the mind emerges from matter, which is also the foundation for modern neuroscience. So, Frank claims that the human mind emerges from physical processes that we can understand and in principle reproduce in an artificial manner. For this corollary to fail he argues that some new significant phenomenon needs to be discovered that has "large-scale physical consequences, that takes place in unremarkable, well-studied physical circumstances (i.e., the materials, temperatures, and pressures inside human brains), yet has somehow managed for many decades to elude determined investigators armed with sophisticated instruments. Such a discovery would be … astonishing."[112] With respect to the future of intelligence, Frank concludes that the superiority of artificial over natural intelligence looks to be permanent, whereas the current significant edge of natural intelligence over artificial intelligence seems to be temporary. In support of this statement, he identifies a number of factors whereby information-processing smart technology can exceed human capabilities which includes electronic processing that is approximately a billion times faster than the latency of a neuron's action potential, artificial processing units that can be up to ten thousand times smaller than a typical neuron which allows for more efficient communication, and artificial memories that is typically digital which enables it to be stored and maintained with perfect accuracy in comparison to human memory that is analog and can fade away. Other factors include human brains getting tired with effort and degrading over time, the artificial information processors having a more modular and open architecture to integrate with new sensors and devices compared to the brain's more closed and non-transparent architecture, and quantum computing that can enable qualitatively new forms of information processing and levels of intelligence compared to seemingly not being suitable for interfacing with the human brain.[113] That said, there are also a number of factors that give the human brain with its general-purpose intelligence an edge above current AI systems. These include the human brain making much better use of all three dimensions compared to the 2-dimensional lithography of computer boards and chips, the ability of the human brain to repair itself or adapt to damage whereas computers must typically be rebooted or fixed, and the human brain's tight integration with a variety of sensory organs an actuators that makes interpreting internal and external signals from the real-world and the control of actuators seamless, automatic and with limited conscious attention. In addition to this, Frank conjectures that the two most far-reaching and synergistic advantages of human brains are their connectivity and interactive development, where neurons in the human brain typically have hundreds to thousands of meaningful connections as opposed to a few fixed and structured connections between processing units within computer systems, and the self-assembly and interactive shaping of the structure of the human brain through rich interaction and feedback from the real-world that we do not see in computer systems.[114] Frank Wilczek reckons that with humanity's engineering and scientific efforts staying vibrant and not being derailed by self-terminating activities, wars, plagues or external non-anthropogenic events, we are on a path to be augmented and empowered by smart systems and see a proliferation of more autonomous AI systems that are growing in capability and intelligence.

As we get better at understanding ourselves and how our brains work, the more intelligent, precise, intuitive, and insightful our AI systems will become. Living in the age of knowledge, we are making advancements and discoveries at record paces.[115] Many researchers feel that we will not be able to create fully intelligent machines until we understand how the human brain works. In particular, the neocortex which is the six-layered mammalian cerebral cortex that is associated with intelligence and involved in higher-order brain functions such as cognition, sensory perception, spatial reasoning, language, and the generation of motor commands, needs to be understood before we can create intelligent machines.[116] Not all people believe this. After all, aeroplanes fly without emulating birds. We can find ways to achieve the same goals without developing them to be perfect models of each other. For now, we are focusing on the brain and what people are doing to create AI systems that rely on our understanding of the brain. Neuroscience, in the last decade or two, perhaps has achieved massive success and a boost in the knowledge we have on how the brain works. In this, there are of course many theories and many different ways to look at it. Based on these different theories, there are different approaches to AI that can be created. The near future of machine intelligence is based on all of these coming together, and our current and past machine learning is based on parts of it, in a more hierarchical and networked manner. This means that as we understand more about the brain, we are enabled to create machines that are modeled on this working. The machines are then enabled to follow the brain's process in its deductions, calculations and inferences of tasks and of reality in general. Perhaps what many people would like to know is if a machine can act like a human in its thinking and rational decision making, then how is it different from a human? Also, where does emotions fit in?

Lisa Feldman Barrett, a Professor of Psychology and Neuroscience at Northeastern University and author of books such as *Seven and a Half Lessons About the Brain* and *How Emotions Are Made,* have busted some neuroscience myths of which one is the triune brain story that the brain evolved in layers consisting of the reptile brain (survival instincts), the limbic system (emotions) and the neocortex (rational thought and decision making), where the latter via the prefrontal cortex apply rational thought to control the survival instincts, animalistic urges and emotions.[117] Instead, as we contemplate the workings of the human brain in producing intelligence, it is important to keep in mind that our brain did not evolve so that we can think rationally, feel emotions, be imaginative, be creative or show empathy, but to control our bodies by predicting the body's energy needs in advance in order to efficiently move, survive, and pass our genes to the next generation. It turns out the brains of most vertebrates develop in the same sequence of steps and are made from the same types of neurons but develop for shorter or longer durations which lead to species having different arrangements and numbers of neurons in their brains. Lisa's theory of constructed emotion explains experience and perception of emotion in terms of multiple brain networks collaborating working together and what we see in the brain and body is only affect (i.e., the underlying experience of feeling, emotion, and mood).[118] This theory suggests that these emotions are concepts that are constructed by the brain and not biologically hardwired or produced in specific brain circuits. Instead, emotions are also predictions that emerge momentarily as the brain is predicting the feelings that one is expecting to experience. In fact, the brain is constantly building and updating predicting models of every experience we have or think we have. The brain guesses what might happen next and then prepares the body ahead of time to handle it. As all our sensory experiences of the physical world are simulations that happen so quickly that it feels like reactions, most of what we perceive is based on internal predictions with incoming external data simply influencing our perceptions. Another one of Lisa's lessons is that we have the kind of nature that requires nurture as can be seen with the brains of babies and young children that wire themselves to their world and feed off physical and social inputs. As many brain regions that process language also controls the organs and systems in your body, we are not only impacting our own brain and body with our words and actions, but also influence the brains and bodies of other people around us in a similar way. Our brains are also very adaptable and create a large variation of minds or human natures that wires itself to specific cultures, circumstances, or social and physical environments. The final lesson is that our brains can create reality and are so good with believing our own abstract concepts and inventions, that we easily mistake social or political reality for the natural world. Lisa is also correct that not only do we have more control of the reality that we create, but we also have more responsibility for the reality than we think we have.[119] These types of insights into the human brain not only provide important context for understanding human intelligence, but also help us to think more clearly about the machine intelligence systems that we want to build to better support us.

In a talk about *Planetary Intelligence: Humanity's Future in the Age of AI,* Joscha Bach gives a high-level layman's rendition of our information processing cells which form a nervous system that regulates, learns, generalizes, and interprets data from the physical world.[120] The nervous system has many feedback loops that take care of the regulation and whenever the regulation is insufficient the brain reinforces certain regulations via a limbic system that learns via pleasure and pain signals. Pleasure tells the brain to do more of what it is currently doing whereas pain tells it to do less. This is already a very good learning paradigm but has the drawback that it does not generalize very well. So, it needs to generalize across different types of pleasures and pains as well as predict these signals in the future. The next step is to have a system or an engine of motivation that implements the regulation of needs which can be physiological, social, and cognitive in nature. The hippocampus is a system that can associate needs, pleasure, and pain to situations in its environment, whereas the neocortex generalizes over these associations that are related to our needs. As it simulates a dynamic world, it determines what situations create pain or pleasure in different dimensions and what they have in common or not. A good metaphor is a synthesizer. Sound, for example, is a pattern generated by a synthesizer in your brain that makes it possible to predict patterns in the environment. So sound is being played by a synthesizer in your brain to make sense of the data in the physical world. Sound is just a particular class of synthesizers. Synthesizers do not only work for auditory patterns, but also for other modalities such as colors, spatial frequencies, and tactile maps. So, the brain can tune into the low-level patterns that it can see and then look for patterns within the patterns, which is called meta patterns. These meta patterns can then be linked together and that allows the brain to organize lots of different sounds into a single sound that for example only differs by pitch. So now there is a meta pattern that explains more of the sounds. The same holds for color, spatial frequencies, and other modalities. By lumping colors and spatial frequencies together visual percepts are obtained. At some point the neocortex merges the modalities and figures out that these visual patterns and sound patterns can be explained by mapping them to regions in the same 3-dimensional space. The brain can explain the patterns in the 3-dimensional space by assuming they are objects in the 3-dimensional space which are the same in different situations that are being experienced. To make that inference, the brain needs to have a conceptual representation in the address space of these mental representations that allow it to create possible words to generalize over the concepts that have been seen. In order to make that happen there are several types of learning involved such as function approximation that might include Bayesian, parallelizable or exhaustive modeling or scripts and schemas that might include sparse Markov Decision Processes, individual strategies and algorithms. The neocortex organizes itself into small circuits or basic units called the cortical columns that need to bind together into building blocks similar to Lego blocks to form representations for different contexts. The cortical columns form little maps that are organized into cortical areas and these maps interact with one another. These cortical areas play together like an orchestra, where a stream of music is being produced and every musician listens to the music around it and uses some of the elements to make their own music and pass it on. There is also a conductor that resolves conflicts and decides what is being played. Another metaphor is an investment bank, where there are lots of these cortical columns in the neocortex that are there to anticipate a reward for making models about the universe and of their own actions. The reward is given by management via a motivational system that effectively organizes itself into more and more hierarchies. It effectively functions like an AI built by an organism that learns to make sense of its relationship with the universe. The brain generates a model that produces a 3-dimensional world of hierarchies of synthesizers in the mind. As the brain is not a person but a physical system, it cannot feel anything - neurons cannot feel anything. So, in order to know what it's like to feel something the brain finds it useful to create a story of a person that is playing out in the universe. This person is like a non-playing character being directed by the result of the brain's activity and computed regulation. As the brain tells the story of the person as a simulated system, the story gets access to the language centre of the brain which allows it to express feelings and describes what it sees. Joscha believes that as consciousness is a simulated property, a physical system cannot be conscious and only a simulated system can be conscious.[121] It is clear that the neocortex plays a key role in making models that learns, predicts, generalizes and interprets data from the physical world.

Jeff Hawkins, the co-founder and CEO of Numenta that aims to reverse-engineer the neocortex and enable machine intelligence technology based on brain theory, along with many researchers reckon that studying the human brain and in particular the neocortex is the fastest way to get to human-level AI.[122] As it stands now, none of the AI being developed is intelligent in the ways humans are. The initial theory Jeff and his team at Numenta has proposed is called Hierarchical Temporal Memory (HTM) which takes what it knows about the neocortex to build machine learning algorithms that are well suited for prediction, anomaly detection and sensorimotor applications, are robust to noise, and can learn time-based patterns in unlabeled data in continuous fashion as well as multiple patterns at the same time.[123] According to Jeff, the neocortex is no longer a big mystery and provides a high-level interpretation as follows: the human brain is divided into an old and new part (although Lisa Feldman Barret would say the "new part" is due to a longer development run). Only mammals have the new part which is the neocortex that occupies approximately 75% of the volume of the brain, whereas the old parts address aspects such as emotions, basic behaviors, and instincts. The neocortex is uniform – it looks the same everywhere – like it replicated the same thing over and over again, not divided into different parts that do separate things. The neocortex is like a very complex circuit that almost randomly sends signals to certain parts of the body. It seems very random. What we need is to figure out what that circuit does.[124] We do know that the neocortex is constantly making predictions.[125] These are the models we form of the world. So how do the networks of neurons in the neocortex learn predictive models? For example, when we touch a coffee cup but are not looking at it, if we move our finger, can we predict what we feel? Yes, we can. The cortex has to know that this is a cup, and where on the cup my finger is going to touch and how it's going to feel. Our neocortex is making predictions about the cup.[126] By touching the cup in different areas, you can infer what the cup looks like, it's shape, density and volume.[127] If you touch the cup with three fingers at a time, each finger has partial knowledge of the cup and can make inferences and predictions about the whole cup as well.[128] If you do this over a few objects, you get to know the objects and their features. Next time you touch an object that you have touched before, you can pretty quickly determine what you are touching and information you have about this.[129] AI in this way would work as a neocortex and make predictions about something based on something like touch. A biological approach, also based on the workings of the neocortex, called the Thousand Brains Theory of Intelligence, says that our brain builds predictive models of the world through its experiences.[130] The Numenta team has discovered that the brain uses map like structures to build hundreds of thousands of models of everything we know. This discovery allows Jeff and his team to answer important questions about intelligence, how we perceive the world, why we have a sense of self, and the origin of high-level thought. This all happens in the neocortex which processes the changing time patterns and learns models of the world that are stored in memory and understands positioning. The Thousand Brains Theory says that these aspects of intelligence occur instantaneously - in no order.[131]

It is clear from many recent neuroscience scholarly articles and other ones such as *Is the Brain More Powerful Than We Thought? Here Comes the Science* that much inspiration and ideas still awaits us to help improve the state-of-the-art in machine intelligence.[132] A team from UCLA recently discovered a hidden layer of neural communication buried within the dendrites where rather than acting as passive conductors of neuronal signals, as previously thought, the scientists discovered that dendrites actively generate their own spikes—five times larger and more frequently than the classic spikes stemming from neuronal bodies (soma).[133] This suggests that learning may be happening at the level of dendrites rather than neurons, using fundamentally different rules than previously thought. This hybrid digital-analog, dendrite-soma, duo-processor parallel computing is highly intriguing and can lead to a whole new field of cognitive computing. These findings could galvanize AI as well as the engineering new kinds of neuron-like computer chips. In parallel to this, the article called "*We Just Created an Artificial Synapse That Can Learn Autonomously*" mentions a team of researchers from National Center for Scientific Research (CNRS) that has developed an artificial synapse called a memristor directly on a chip that are capable of learning autonomously and can improve how fast artificial neural networks learn.[134]

Although we are making progress on several fronts to get a better understanding of how the human brain functions, the simple truth is that there is still much to uncover. The more we do understand, the more we can apply this to understanding the machines we are creating. On the other side, the more we understand about how to develop intelligent systems, the more tools and insights are provided to enhance our understanding of how the brain works. This is truly exciting to both neuroscience and AI. And as we dive deeper into understanding how both work, and what it is that makes us human, we can also start thinking about a future that is truly human and empowered and aided by machines. Machine intelligence and human intelligence are interlinked. Because AI is reliant on humans, as humans we have the power to steer AI. To decide where it goes. To shape our lives, our world, and our future with the amazing tools at our disposal. This is not a job for the future. It creates the future. It is not a job for other people, it is up to all of us to decide what kind of world we want to live in...

Lessons Learnt, Limitations, and Current State-of-the Art in AI

Rich Sutton, a Professor of Computer Science at University of Alberta, and Research Scientist at DeepMind, has shared some reflective thoughts on the last 70 years of AI research in his blog post *The Bitter Lesson*.[135] According to him the bitter lesson seems to be that general machine learning methods which leverage computation turned out to be significantly more effective than those that explored other methods such as leveraging human domain knowledge. It is clear that the exponentially declining cost per unit of computation that continued over decades as described by Moore's law was a key contributor. Rich references how this has been clearly illustrated for computer board games such as chess and Go using search and learning-based approaches, speech recognition using deep learning and earlier on statistical hidden Markov models, and computer vision using deep learning convolution based neural networks. The bitter lesson is based on observations that followed a human-centric pattern where AI researchers started to build knowledge into their AI systems which did well in the short term and gave satisfaction to the researchers involved, but in the medium and longer term delivered no further improvements and even impeded further progress before being overtaken by competing approaches that scales computation by search and learning. The specific recommendation is that AI researchers and practitioners should not build in any part of arbitrary inherently complex systems that are being modeled as their complexity is typically unlimited; instead, they should focus on building in the meta-methods such as search and learning to detect and capture this arbitrary complexity. Therefore, the AI systems should search for good approximations and learn how to discover instead of being fed with content that we have discovered which makes it potentially more difficult to learn the discovery process.[136]

We know that deep supervised learning works well for perception when there is abundant labeled data and deep reinforcement learning works well for action generation when trials are cheap such as within a simulation. We also know that deep learning has serious limitations. In Francois Chollet's blog on *The limitation of Deep Learning* he summarizes the true success of deep learning thus far as the ability to map an input space to a target space using a smooth and continuous geometric transform that typically consist of multiple connected layers that forms a sufficiently large parametric model and trained by sufficiently huge amounts of labeled and annotated data. The weights of the layers are the parameters of the differentiable geometric transform which are updated in an iterative fashion by a gradient descent algorithm based on the model's performance. The spaces in the model have sufficiently high dimensionality to capture the full extent of the relationships found in the original input data. Although the number of possible applications and the application potential of deep learning models are vast, it can only solve problems that can be addressed with its sequence of continuous geometric transformations that maps one vector space to another. A key limitation of deep learning is that even with unlimited data available or adding more layers, it cannot handle algorithmic type of data manipulation, reasoning, or long-term planning. Most software programs cannot be expressed as deep learning models due to not having sufficient data available to train it, or not being learnable in the sense that the geometric transform is too complex or there does not practically exist a deep learning model that corresponds to the program as only a small subset of all possible programs can be learned using deep learning. There is also a risk with anthropomorphizing machine learning models as can be seen with the classification of contents in pictures along with the generation of captions associated with pictures that give people the false impression that these models understand the contents in the pictures. This is illustrated with special adversarial input examples that slightly modify an image by adding a class gradient to deceive the model in predicting an incorrect class. For example, by adding a "gibbon" gradient to a picture of a panda, the model classifies the panda image as a gibbon. This not only demonstrates how fragile these machine learning models can be, but also that it understands and interprets their inputs in a way that is not relatable to the embodied way that humans understand sensorimotor inputs and experience. Francois also argues that there is a fundamental difference in the nature of the representations formed by deep learning models and human brains, where the generalization performed by the these deep learning models are more local and requires lots of training examples compared to extreme generalization formed by the abstract models in the human mind that are able to perform abstraction, reasoning, long term planning and adaptation to new or imagined experiences, situations, concepts, objects, or information that could be substantially different to what was observed before with a lot less examples. In comparison, the more local generalization power of deep learning networks within the context of pattern recognition is shown in how it adapts to novel data that is much closer to the historical data it was trained on. Francois suggests that a potential substrate for abstract modeling and reasoning could be computer programs, which will be discussed further later in this chapter.[137]

Like many other AI practitioners and researchers also recognize, Andrew Ng also sums up the limitations of deep learning to be the inability to handle causality, adversarial attacks, explainability, and learning from small data sets. Yan LeCun agrees with this assessment and highlights the challenges with deep learning as learning with fewer labeled samples and/or fewer trials where self-supervised and unsupervised learning can be used for learning to represent the world before learning tasks, learning to reason by making it more compatible with gradient-based learning, and learning to plan complex action sequences by learning hierarchical representations of action plans.[138] Judea Pearl calls the deep learning style of machine learning a form of "model-blind curve fitting" that is unable to address "what if" type of interventional, counterfactual or retrospective questions, and not able to do causal reasoning or being transparent in terms of explainability or interpretation.[139] It is also clear that there is much room for improvement with respect to transfer and multi-task learning and making better use of unlabeled data. Gary Marcus and Ernest Davis in *Rebooting AI: Building Artificial Intelligence We Can Trust* identifies three core problems with deep learning type of machine learning which includes that it is greedy with respect to the training data required (e.g. AlphaGo required 30 million games to reach superhuman performance), its opaque in terms of not being easy to understand why it makes mistakes or why it fairs very well, and its brittleness as shown above with the miss classification of slightly modified images.[140] In *Deep Learning: A Critical Appraisal* Gary expands on this and highlights ten challenges that faces the current deep learning systems: Apart from being fragile in certain instances as well as data hungry, deep learning has limited capacity for transfer learning, mainly extracts superficial patterns, have no natural way of dealing with hierarchical structure where larger structures can recursively be constructed from smaller components, is struggling with open-ended inference, is not sufficiently transparent, has so far not been well integrated with prior knowledge, it cannot inherently distinguish between causation and correlation, it assumes a predominantly stable world and struggles to deal with systems that are continuously changing with varying rules, its predictions and classifications cannot be always trusted, and in general not easy to engineer with from robustness and even replicability perspective.[141]

In the *Failures of Gradient-based Deep Learning* paper, the authors describe and illustrate four families of problems for which some of the commonly used existing gradient-based deep learning algorithms fail or have substantial problems, as well as provide theoretical insights explaining why this happens, and how they might be addressed.[142] The families of problems include non-informative gradients, decomposition versus end-to-end training, architecture and conditioning, and flat activations. The problem of non-informative gradients has to do with deep learning's dependency on local properties of the loss function where the gradient information carries insignificant information on the target function that directs the learning process, whilst the objective is actually global in nature. It has been experimentally observed and theoretically shown that an end-to-end approach to training deep learning systems can be significantly slower with the gradients substantially noisier and less informative compared to a decomposition method that handles sub-problems separately, which is especially so as the scale of the problem grows. Although an end-to-end approach of optimizing a single primary objective has an advantage that it requires less prior knowledge and labeling and enables more expressive architectures, the extra supervision inserted with decomposition on a sub-problem level is helpful in the optimization process. Even though architectures might have the similar expressive power, there might still be a significant difference in the ability to optimize the runtime of gradient descent. When analyzing this from a condition number of the problem perspective (which measures sensitivity in terms of how much the output value can change for a small change in the inputs), they have demonstrated how conditioning techniques can lead to speedup improvement in additional orders of magnitude. As architectures that contain activation functions with flat regions can lead to the vanishing gradient problem (where the gradient becomes so small that it effectively prevents the weights from changing its value), heuristics are typically applied in order to initialize the network's weights in non-flat areas of its activations. It can be shown that by using a different weight update rule that follows a non-gradient-based optimization scheme the limitations of gradient-based learning can be addressed in an efficient way. They have also shown convergence guarantees for a family of such functions.[143]

Although we are still scratching the surface with respect to deep learning applications (where deep learning has become the go-to solution for a broad range of applications, often outperforming state-of-the-art), it is also important to understand the limits of deep learning. John Launchbury, a director at Defense Advanced Research Projects Agency (DARPA), has described AI as the programmed ability to process information that can perceive rich, complex and subtle information, learn within an environment, abstract to create new meanings and reason to plan and to decide.[144] He thinks about AI development as three waves of artificial intelligence where the first one is handcrafted knowledge, or expert systems like IBM's Deep Blue or Watson (before the addition of deep learning), the second one is statistical learning, which includes machine learning of which deep learning is a part, and the third wave is contextual adaptation, which involves constructing reliable, explanatory models for real-world phenomena using sparse data in a similar way humans do this.[145] A shorthand summary of the three waves would be "describe", recognize" and "explain". The limitations of expert systems have been well documented such as no learning capability and poor handling of uncertainty although it has reasoning capability over very narrowly defined problems. Although statistical learning has strong nuanced classification and prediction capabilities, it lacks in having no contextual capability along with minimal reasoning ability. Deep learning works well because of the 'manifold hypothesis' that refers to how different high-dimensional natural data tend to cluster and be shaped differently when visualized in lower dimensions. John describes deep learning neural networks as "spreadsheets on steroids" given their ability to mathematically manipulate and separate data clumps or manifolds for classification and prediction purposes. DARPA also sees the core limitations of deep learning as abstraction and reasoning, requiring lots of data, being dependent on the quality of and biases in the data, deliberately being tricked with adversarial examples, slow training, inability to do planning, and predominantly being used for pattern recognition use cases. DARPA's $2 billion AI Next program has three areas of development which includes increasing the robustness of deep learning and other second wave AI technologies, expanding the range of AI applications using the second wave AI technologies, and exploring the third wave AI technologies.[146] Some of the areas of development include developing AI that can deal with reacting to situations that it has not been trained on such as changing the rules of the game and building better trust between humans and AI through explainable AI and competency-aware machine learning.[147] The article *The Next AI Milestone: Bridging the Semantic Gap* also references DARPA's perspective on AI and discusses the problem of solving "contextual adaptation" and how the evolution of deep learning can help to find solutions that melds symbolic and connectionist systems.[148] DARPA's third wave model takes a lot of inspiration from some of their previously announced research initiatives such as Explanatory interfaces and Meta-Learning. Carlos Perez at Intuition Machine argues that the third AI wave is likely to be an evolution of how we do deep learning as also described in the articles *The Only Way to Make Deep Learning Interpretable is to have it Explain Itself*, *The Meta Model and Meta Meta-Model of Deep Learning*, and *Biologically Inspired Software Architecture for Deep Learning*.[149] Carlos also describes five capability levels of Deep Learning Intelligence, where level 1 is classification only; level 2 is classification with memory; level 3 is classification with knowledge; level 4 is classification with imperfect knowledge; and level 5 is collaborative classification with imperfect knowledge. Even for level 2 "classification with memory" systems which effectively corresponds to recurrent neural networks, there is a clear need for improved supervised and unsupervised training algorithms. As mentioned above, unsupervised learning should for example build a causal understanding of the sensory space with temporal correlations of concurrent and sequential sensory signals. Much research still needs to be done with respect to knowledge representations and integrating this with deep learning recurrent neural network systems all the way from level 3 to level 5 systems.[150]

Before further considering AI progress, some research priorities and likely future avenues, let's highlight some of the current state-of-the-art machine learning techniques in 2020 for some popular tasks in application areas such as computer vision, speech recognition, recommender systems and natural language processing.[151] Note that these algorithms might be replaced by better versions or others very soon if not already (by the time of reading this) given the pace of the continuous never-ending improvement cycle of AI research. Some of the key tasks in computer vision involve image classification, object detection, and semantic segmentation. All of these are for example important tasks to accomplish vision in self-driving cars. Image classification typically focuses on classifying the full image that has a label assigned to it. The *FixEfficientNet* by the Facebook AI Research Team is currently the leading image classification algorithm and with a top-1 accuracy of 88.5%, and top-5 accuracy of 98.7% on the ImageNet Dataset with 480 million parameters.[152] This algorithm combines the *FixRes* algorithm developed by the Facebook AI Team and the *EfficientNet* presented by the Google AI Research Team. Whereas *FixRes* (which stands for Fix Resolution) removes some bias that happens during preprocessing by keeping a fixed size for either the region of classification used for training time or the crop used for testing time, the *EfficientNet* is a compound scaling of the width, depth and resolution dimensions of a convolutional neural network which improves both accuracy and efficiency. Other superior image classification techniques include a version of Wide Residual Networks called *Wide-ResNet-101* on the STL-10 dataset, *Big Transfer* on the CIFAR-10 dataset, and *Branching/Merging Convolutional Neural Networks and Homogeneous Filter Capsules* on the MNIST dataset.[153] Object detection is the task that typically focuses on recognizing instances of objects of a certain class within an image. The top technique currently is the *Efficient-Det D7x* which was developed by the Google Brain Team in 2020 with a state-of-the-art performance for scalable and efficient object detection of a box average precision of 55.1 (and AP50 of 74.3) with 77 million parameters and 410 billion floating point operations per second (being significantly smaller and using less FLOPs than previous detectors).[154] The *Efficient-Det* is a combination of *EfficientNets* with *Bidirectional Feature Pyramid Networks*, which allows easy and fast multiscale feature fusion. Other leading competing algorithms include *IterDet* on the CrowdHuman dataset, *RODEO* on the PASCAL VOC dataset, and *Patch Refinement* on the KITTI Cars Easy dataset.[155] Semantic segmentation is the task of understanding and predicting the objects, components and structures of an image on a pixel level. The current state-of-the-art semantic segmentation algorithm called *HRNet-OCR* was introduced in 2020 by a Nvidia team and obtained a mean intersection over union of 85.1% on the Cityscapes dataset that has a large number of weakly labeled images.[156] *HRNet-OCR* uses a hierarchical attention-based approach to combine multi-scale predictions and demonstrates that the network learns to favor certain scales for particular failure modes to generate better predictions. It is also four times more memory efficient to train compared to other competitive approaches with faster training on larger crop sizes leading to improved model accuracy.[157] Some other leading semantic segmentation algorithms include *ResNeSt-269* on the PASCAL Context dataset which uses a split-attention block that enables attention across feature-map groups and stacking these split-attention blocks in a ResNet-style, *Efficient-Net-L2+NAS-FPN* on the PASCAL VOC dataset, and *Virtual Multi-view Fusion* on the ScanNet dataset.

Speech recognition is another major application area for machine learning with many intelligent virtual assistants such as Google Assistant, Amazon's Alexa, Apple's Siri, Microsoft's Cortana, and Samsung's Bixby making use of state-of-the-art speech recognition technology. The Google team presented the current leading speech recognition algorithm in 2019 with an improved version in 2020 which is called *ContextNet + SpecAugment-based Noisy Student Training* on the Libri-Light unlabeled audio dataset which is derived from audio books.[158] This algorithm combines a *ContextNet* which consists of convolution, recurrent and transducer neural network components, with Noisy Student Training which is an iterative semi-supervised learning in a series of teacher-student models that uses unlabeled data and leverages augmentation to improve network performance. The teacher model produces quality labels, while the student is reproducing those labels augmented by feature inputs. The *ContextNet* model consists of an audio encoder convolutional neural network for the input audio, a label encoder long short-term memory recurrent neural network for producing the input label, and a joint network of both to decode. Other examples of some notable speech recognition algorithms include *Large-10h-LV-60k* on the Libri-Light test-clean dataset, *ResNet + BiLSTMs acoustic model* on the Switchboard + Hub500 dataset, and *LiGRU + Dropout + BatchNorm + Monophone Reg* on the TIMIT dataset.[159]

Recommender systems is also a common application area used in many different online retailers such as Amazon or social media and entertainment platforms such as YouTube, Facebook, Netflix and many more. The *Bayesian time SVD++*, presented by the Google team in 2019, is one of the top-ranking recommender systems with state-of-the-art performance on the MovieLens 10M dataset. The system consists of a Bayesian Matrix Factorization trained using Gibbs sampling and a timeSVD++ multifaceted collaborative filtering model.[160] Other leading recommender systems include *Bayesian timeSVD++ flipped w/ Ordered Probit Regression* on the MovieLens 1M dataset, *H+Vamp Gated* on the MovieLens 20M dataset, and *Embarrassingly Shallow Autoencoders* (EASE) for sparse data on the Million Song dataset.[161]

Natural language processing is a key AI application area that gives software programs the ability to process, understand and extract meaning, information and insights from human language. NLP is used in many applications such as translators with a prime example being Google Translate, intelligent virtual assistants, email spam filters, social media monitoring, or grammar checking in word processors. Some of the specific NLP tasks include sentiment analysis, language modeling, text summarization, machine translation, text classification, question answering, dialogue management, natural language generation, and natural language understanding. Sentiment analysis is a form of text mining that can rigorously identify, extract, quantify, and interpret emotional states and subjective information in text data.[162] One of the current top algorithms is *Bidirectional Encoder Representations from Transformers* (BERT), originally presented by the Google AI team in 2019, which obtained new state-of-the-art results on eleven natural language processing tasks, including pushing the GLUE score to 80.5% (7.7% point absolute improvement), MultiNLI accuracy to 86.7% (4.6% absolute improvement), SQuAD v1.1 question answering Test F1 to 93.2 (1.5 point absolute improvement), SQuAD v2.0 Test F1 to 83.1 (5.1 point absolute improvement), and an accuracy of 55.5 on the SST-5 Fine-grained classification dataset.[163] BERT can parse a text from left-to-right or from right-to-left and learn the left and right context of a word through applying a bidirectional training of the Transformer algorithm which is an attention model used for language modeling that was previously only applied in one direction.[164] Other leading sentiment analysis techniques include *NB-weighted-BON + dv-cosine* on the IMDb dataset and *T5–3B* on the SST-2 Binary classification dataset.[165]

Language modeling is a task that learns the probability of word or letter occurrence based on examples of text. It can predict the next words or letters in a text based on the existing text or previous words. One of the current top language modeling algorithms is *Megatron-LM* which was introduced by the Nvidia team in 2019 and with some improvements on OpenAI's *GPT-2* (Generative Pre-trained Transformers) transformer-based language model with 1.5 billion parameters and trained on a dataset of 40GB of 8 million web pages.[166] The *Megatron-LM* approach was illustrated by converging transformer based models similar to GPT-2 up to 8.3 billion parameters using 512 GPUs (sustaining 15.1 PetaFLOPs across the full application with 76% scaling efficiency when compared to a strong single GPU baseline that sustains 39 TeraFLOPs, which is 30% of peak FLOPs).[167] A 3.9 billion parameter model similar to BERT was also trained with the Megatron-LM approach. The Nvidia team has demonstrated that layer normalization placement in BERT-like models is very important to ensure increased performance as the model size grows. Using the GPT-2 model they achieved state-of-the-art results on the WikiText103 (10.8 compared to a previous best perplexity of 15.8) and LAMBADA (66.5% compared to a previous best accuracy of 63.2%) datasets. Their BERT model has also improved the state-of-the-art performance on the RACE dataset (90.9% compared to a previous best accuracy of 89.4%).[168] OpenAI's GPT-3, an autoregressive language model with 175 billion parameters, which is 10 times more than any previous non-sparse language model, demonstrated excellent performance on language modeling and many other NLP tasks (including translation, question-answering, cloze tasks, on-the-fly reasoning or domain adaptation such as performing 3-digit arithmetic, unscrambling words, or using a new word in a sentence) and benchmarks in the zero-shot, one-shot, and few-shot settings.[169] Even though GPT-3 was applied on all tasks without any fine-tuning or gradient updates, it almost matched the performance of other state-of-the-art fine-tuned systems in certain cases. GPT-3 was able to generate quality samples and very good qualitative performance at tasks defined on-the-fly and also generated samples of news articles that were not easy to distinguish from those written by humans.[170] The OpenAI team also identified some datasets where GPT-3's few-shot learning still finds it difficult to produce good results, as well as ones that the system had problems related to large web corpora training.[171]

Machine translation involves the algorithmic task of translating text or speech from one language to another and is used in applications such as Google Translate, Microsoft Translator, Babylon Translator, DeepL, iTranslate, Linguee, Reverso Translation, TripLingo, or Memsource. The Google Brain Team introduced in 2018 a state-of-the-art machine translation algorithm called the *Transformer Big +BT* that is based on transformer networks that instead of using recurrent connections, parses sequences simultaneously through the use of convolutional neural networks with attention models.[172] The transformer networks consists of a stack of encoders and decoders, where the encoders consist of a self-attention and a feedforward neural network layer, whereas the decoders consist of a self-attention layer, an encoder-decoder attention layer and a feedforward neural network layer. The convolution neural networks are used to process inputs in parallel per layer and exploiting local dependencies, whereas self-attention boosts the translation speed and helps the focus on a subset of the information such as certain words to figure out the relation of words within a sentence and giving the right attention to it.[173] Other leading machine translation algorithms include *Attentional Encoder-Decoder+BPE* on the WMT2016 German-English dataset, *Multi-Agent Dual Learning* (MADL) on the WMT2016 English-German dataset, and the application of a new explore-exploit learning rate schedule (knee schedule) can result in an up to 0.5% higher absolute accuracy using the original training budget or up to 44% reduced training time for a similar accuracy.[174]

Text classification is the task of assigning a set of predefined tags or categories to a sentence, a text, or a word. In 2019 the Google AI Team introduced a state-of-the-art text classification algorithm called *XLNet* with tests on the DBpedia, IMDb and AG News datasets where it outperformed *BERT* in 20 tasks (including question answering, sentiment analysis, document ranking and natural language inference).[175] *XLNet* is a generalized autoregressive pretraining method that integrates ideas of the state-of-the-art autoregressive model *Transformer-XL* into pretraining to solve the limitations of BERT and enables learning bidirectional contexts (where each position learns to utilize contextual information from all positions) by optimizing the expected likelihood over all permutations of the factorization order.[176] Other leading text classification algorithms include *Simplifying Graph Convolutional (SGC) Networks* on the 20News dataset and *Universal Sentence Encoder USE_T + CNN* on the TREC-6 dataset.[177]

Question answering is the task of training an algorithm to answer questions typically from an unstructured collection of natural language documents or a structured knowledgebase. Apart from answering questions on reference texts, web pages, newswire reports, Wikipedia pages, systems have also been developed to automatically answer biographical questions, temporal and geospatial questions, multilingual questions, questions of definition and terminology, and questions about the content of audio, images, and video.[178] The Google AI team has explored the landscape of transfer learning techniques for natural language processing by introducing a unified framework that converts all text-based language problems into a text-to-text format, which also naturally fits in with question answering. Transfer learning involves pre-training a model first on a data-rich task before fine tuning it on a downstream task which enables fast tracking the learning process on a new domain and saves on a significant amount of computational power and resources. With the *T5–11B*, their unified **T**ext-**t**o-**T**ext **T**ransfer **T**ransformer (T5) model with up to 11 billion parameters (11B), state-of-the-art benchmarks were obtained on tasks such as question answering, text classification, and summarization on four different datasets: GLUE, SuperGLUE, SQuAD, and CNN/Daily Mail. To enable the Google AI team to build models at this scale, they also introduced a data set consisting of hundreds of gigabytes of clean English text scraped from the web which they called the "**C**olossal **C**lean **C**rawled **C**orpus" (C4). Other noteworthy examples of question answering algorithms include *SA-Net on Albert* on the SQuAD2.0 dataset and *TANDA-RoBERTa* on the WikiQA dataset.[179]

As part of the Google AI team's systematic study on exploring the limits of transfer learning with their unified *T5-11B* text-to-text transfer transformer model, they have also compared factors such as pre-training objectives, unlabeled data sets, architectures, scaling, and transfer approaches on many language understanding tasks and shared some of their most significant insights.[180] They found that their text-to-text framework obtained similar performance to task-specific architectures and were state-of-the-art when applied at scale.

Even though an encoder-decoder model uses double the number of parameters as architectures with "decoder-only" forms as we see in language models or "encoder-only" such as with BERT, the encoder-decoder structure has given the best results in their text-to-text framework with similar computational cost. In order to make the unsupervised pre-training more computationally efficient, they also suggest using objectives that produce short target sequences. The Google AI team has also demonstrated that performance can worsen when a small unlabeled data set is reused many times during pre-training, which in turn encourages the use of huge diverse data sets such as C4. From a training strategy perspective, better performance is obtained when all of a pre-trained model's parameters are updated during fine-tuning as opposed to only updating a few parameters, whereas fine-tuning after pre-training on a mixture of tasks produced performance on par with unsupervised pre-training. They have also shown that an ensemble of models can provide considerably better results than a single model and that larger models tend to perform better. That said, to ensure that transfer learning can be as impactful as possible, they also recommend researching methods that achieve better performance with more cost-effective models. More efficient knowledge extraction than simply training the model to denoise distorted text is needed to teach the model general-purpose knowledge for downstream tasks. The Google AI team also advocates for more precise definition of similarity between pre-training and downstream tasks as it would also help to make better choices of what unlabeled data to use. They were also disappointed to not get state-of-the-art performance on translation tasks using English-only pre-training and recommended further investigation into language-agnostic models.[181]

Adversarial training in the form of Generative Adversarial Networks (GANs) is another powerful idea that contributed to some conceptual progress in machine learning, specifically in the area of generative models that can augment data through learning to mirror any distribution of data. A GAN is a generative model that is trained using a "generator" neural network model that learns to generate new credible samples and a "discriminator" neural network model that learns to differentiate generated examples from real examples.[182] As the generator model is trained by getting feedback from the discriminator model in terms of how well it is doing to generate examples that looks authentic (i.e., effectively how good it is to fool the discriminator model), the GAN system is trained in an unsupervised way by not being dependent on external feedback signals. GANs can also be used with semi-supervised, supervised, and reinforcement learning and have many applications in computer vision, natural language, and robotics.[183] After the GAN system is trained, the generative model can then be used in applications to create new convincing examples on demand. There are many applications for GANs such as generating high-resolution versions of input images; creating new and artistic images, sketches, and paintings; translating photographs or images across domains such as day to night or summer to winter or photos to emojis or cartoon faces; handling of missing data; providing multi-modal outputs; generating photorealistic images given a semantic image or sketch as input; generating realistic photographs of human faces and new human poses; generating cartoon characters; generating realistic looking photographs from textual descriptions; generating frontal-view photographs of human faces given photographs taken at an angle; reconstructing photographs of faces with specific specified features; generating photographs of faces with different apparent ages, from younger to older; blending of photos; inpainting or hole filling of photos; generating photos of clothing; generating videos with scene dynamics; and generating new three-dimensional objects.[184]

Automated machine learning (AutoML) is the process of automating the process of applying machine learning to real-world problems in an end-to-end fashion that covers the complete pipeline from the raw dataset, data preparation, feature engineering, model selection, hyperparameter optimization to the deployable machine learning model.[185] Besides making data science and machine learning more accessible to non-experts, other benefits include reducing the burden on data scientists on hyperparameter tuning which could be a scrupulously tedious task, producing simpler solutions, faster development of those solutions, and models that often outperform hand-crafted models. In 2018 the Google Brain team introduced the *Neural Architecture Search Network (NASNet)* AutoML solution that learns the model architectures directly on the selected dataset, in particular searching for "an architectural building block on a small dataset and then transferring the block to a larger dataset".[186] In NASNet, a controller recurrent neural network predicts child networks with different architectures, where the child networks are then trained to convergence to get to a specified validation accuracy, which in turn updates the controller weights with policy gradient to ensure that improved architectures will be generated over time. Using this method it outperformed or at least achieved similar results to the smaller model size and lower complexity versions of human-designed models such as *Inception-v2, Inception-v3, Xception, ResNet, Inception-ResNet-v2, PolyNet, ResNeXt, Shake-Shake, DenseNet, DPN, SENet, MobileNetV1, and ShuffleNet V1*.[187] On CIFAR-10 the data set, *NASNet* obtained a state-of-the-art 2.4% error rate, whereas on the larger ImageNet dataset it achieved best-in-class accuracy of 82.7% top-1 and 96.2% top-5. The *NASNet* model not only achieved an improvement of 1.2% in top-1 accuracy compared to the best human-invented architectures, but also used 9 billion fewer FLOPS which translates to 28% less in computational demand.[188]

Privacy-preserving AI techniques such as federated learning enable AI models to learn from datasets without compromising their privacy which is a key requirement of many applications such as those in healthcare and financial services. Instead of requiring one unified dataset to train a machine learning model, Google formulated this concept of federated learning in 2017 which leaves the training data distributed across numerous devices such as mobile phones and servers on the edge, where each client trains a model on their local training dataset and then shares the resulting model parameters to a shared current global model on a server that aggregates the locally-computed updates.[189] Their *FederatedAveraging* algorithm combines local stochastic gradient descent on each client with a server that does the model averaging and has shown it is robust to data that is not balanced or independent and identically distributed and able to significantly reduce communication loads for training purposes. Whereas it is clear that federated learning puts forward many practical privacy advantages, some further research is being done to provide better guarantees via differential privacy as well as ensuring secure multi-party computation.[190]

Progress, Priorities and Likely Future Paths for AI

As we consider the progress, priorities, and likely future paths of AI, this section is anchored by exploring a better way of measuring intelligence for AI systems as this would be one sensible way of getting relevant feedback on the true progress that we are making in developing better AI systems and also possibly help to direct and prioritize future AI research and engineering paths. Earlier in this chapter, I have referenced Piero Scaruffi's complaint about no significant progress being made in the development of abstract algorithms that improve automatic learning techniques. He describes today's deep learning as a smart way of number crunching and manipulating huge data sets in order to classify or predict data which is driven by increased computing power and lots of data without any groundbreaking paradigm shift.[191] In François Chollet's paper *On the Measure of Intelligence* he draws special attention to the many defects of the current AI research agenda and reasons for a psychometric and ability-based assessment of AI systems, which allows for a more well-grounded, fair and standardized comparison between not only human and machine intelligence, but any two intelligent systems.[192] As mentioned earlier in this section there are at least two divergent visions for intelligence where the one sees it as the ability to execute a collection of task-specific skills and the other as a generalized learning and skills-acquisition capability. One of the current shortcomings is a focus on benchmarking intelligence by comparing the skill exhibited by AI systems and humans at specific tasks such as video and board games. This approach is limiting and not a true reflection of intelligence as it is not measuring the skills acquisition capability that also takes prior knowledge and experience in consideration to showcase the true generalization capability with respect to robustness, flexibility, and generality along with the adaptability of the intelligent system. The performance evaluation of skills-based narrow AI systems is typically done via a human review, a whitebox analysis that inspects the implementation of the system, benchmarking against a known test set of inputs, or competition against humans or other AI systems. When considering evaluating generalization capability it makes sense to categorize the degrees of generalization which can include zero generalization capability with systems that are applied to tasks or applications with no novelty or uncertainty, local generalization or robustness that is displayed in systems that can for example handle new points from a known distribution, broad generalization or flexibility where systems handles a broad range of tasks or applications without human intervention, or extreme generalization that is demonstrated in open-ended systems. He also differentiates between system-centric and developer-aware generalization where the latter refers to the ability of an AI system that handles situations that both the system as well as the developer of the AI system have not seen before whereas in the former case it is just the system that has not encountered the new situation. Francois Chollet argues against a more universal generalization (also called universal g-factor) from a "no free lunch theorem of intelligence perspective" as all known intelligent systems such as humans are typically conditioned on their environment and optimized to solve their own specific problems. So universal intelligence according to him does not provide any "shortcuts" in this regard as any two AI systems which include human intelligence are equivalent when their performance is averaged across every possible problem from a uniform distribution over the problem space. So, all our definitions of intelligence are for all practical purposes only relevant within a human frame of reference. This goes directly opposite the viewpoints from Universal Psychometrics or Universal Intelligence (by Shane Legg and Marcus Hutter) that completely rejects an anthropocentric approach and aims to use a single absolute scale to measure all intelligent systems.[193]

Francois has also put forward an actionable definition of human-like or human-level general intelligence which is based on Algorithmic Information Theory (a computer science extension of Information Theory) and focuses on skill-acquisition efficiency as well as incorporating concepts such as scope, generalization difficulty, priors, and experience. In the positioning of the skill-acquisition problem, an intelligent system generates a skill program to interact with a task that also has a scoring function. In his definition he formulates intelligence as the rate at which an intelligent system converts its experience and priors or current state of information into new skills (skills program) at useful tasks that involve adaptation and uncertainty. More intelligent systems have a higher information conversion ratio and can cover more ground in the future situation space using the same information. This measure of intelligence does not only cater for prior knowledge and experience, but also the generalization difficulty of tasks as well as the subjective weighting and construction of the tasks involved. It is also tied to the scope of the task, treats a skill as a property of the intelligent system that generates a skill program that accounts for future uncertainty, and ensures that learning and adaptation is involved in the skill-acquisition process and not just curve-fitting. This measure of intelligence also considers optimizing a curriculum space (that consists of a sequence of interactions such as feedback between a task and an intelligent system and situations and responses between a task and a skill program) over a training phase in order to improve the intelligent system's skills and skill-acquisition efficiency. Although information efficiency is the key focus here, one can also consider including efficiencies with respect to computation, time, risk, and energy.[194]

Francois reckons that an ideal intelligence benchmark should address its own predictiveness and validity with regards to scope, its reliability or reproducibility, the measurement of broad-ranging abilities and developer-aware generalization, the amount of experience leveraged, a comprehensive description of the set of priors being assumed and ensuring that it can be applied to both humans and intelligent machines. By following these guidelines, he presents the Abstraction and Reasoning Corpus (ARC) dataset to function as a benchmark that is built upon a clear set of priors designed to mirror natural human priors as far as possible.[195] Francois proposes that ARC can be used to compare general intelligence between AI systems and humans as it measures a human-like type of general fluid intelligence (which is basic processes of mental activities such as reasoning that only minimally depend on prior learning and acculturation).[196] ARC's training set consists of 400 tasks, whereas the evaluation set has 600 tasks, which is split up into a public evaluation set (400 tasks) and a private evaluation set (200 tasks). Core knowledge priors include for example objectness priors (object cohesion, object persistence, and object influence via contact), goal-directness priors, numbers and counting priors, and basic geometry priors. Some of the key differences with psychometric intelligence tests such as traditional IQ tests include a fundamental different design, only focusing on a general form of fluid intelligence that tests reasoning and abstraction, unique tasks that are unknown to developers to assess developer-aware generalization, greater task diversity to reduce the possible hard-coding of task-specific solutions, and ensuring that tasks cannot be programmatically generated such as those from C-Test (Comprehension Test) to help prevent reverse-engineering the generative program shared across tasks.[197] Although ARC still is work in progress and have some weaknesses such as generalization that is not quantified, test validity that is not established, data set size and diversity that can be increased, making the evaluation format less close-ended, and improving on the core knowledge priors, the existence of a AI system that can solve human-level ARC tasks would be a breakthrough.

Francois Chollet's formal intelligence measurement framework has practical implications for both research directions towards strong AI and evaluating these types of AI systems. It also provides a quantitative mechanism to go beyond just measuring task-specific skills to evaluating and reasoning about concepts such as "generalization difficulty", "intelligence as skill-acquisition efficiency", and "control for priors and experience when evaluating intelligence".[198] On the research front, the quantitative intelligence formula can be explicitly used as part of an objective function where the formula can be optimized to create improved intelligent systems. Instead of only measuring skill levels at individual tasks, it also supports more flexible and general-purpose capabilities by for example disregarding tasks that do not have a strong generalization difficulty and penalizing too much dependence on experience and priors. Another important outcome of this formalism is the emphasis on program synthesis and separating the intelligent program synthesis engine from the non-intelligent skill program that is the artifact of the intelligence process. The difference between the process and the artifact seems to be a key misunderstanding in AI research and development. This framework also endorses the development and enhancement of a curriculum by putting emphasis on improving the system's intelligence through driving towards an optimal curriculum. It also emphasizes human-like knowledge priors in evaluating intelligence. In terms of the practical consequences for evaluating strong AI systems, the intelligence measuring formalism makes quantifying generalization hardness more formal and explicit with respect to local, broad, and extreme generalization and disregarding tasks with no generalization difficulty. It proposes clear recommendations for comparing human intelligence with AI systems by ensuring that the priors and scope of tasks are shared and experience-efficiency in mastering specific skill-levels are evaluated in a fair fashion. As tests are being developed for tasks, it is also vital to consider the generalization hardness in order to ensure that solutions that are dependent on shortcuts do not generalize. As an example, Francois shares a computer vision use case of where global semantics should be the focus as opposed to a dependence on local textures. Finally, the framework also asks practical questions to help characterize the AI system in terms of scope, maximum achievable skill, priors, curricula, and skill-acquisition efficiency.[199]

In the blog *The Future of Deep Learning* Francois Chollet describes his long-term vision for machine learning that starts by viewing models more like software programs that mirror human-like abstract mental models that have representations of themselves and their environment.[200] The deep learning type of continuous geometric transformations of inputs can just be considered a subset or module of the AI system's capabilities along with other more algorithmic types of software modules that are stronger with respect to generalization, formal reasoning, search, and abstraction. These models or software programs will then be able to combine multiple modules in flexible ways that have a range of capabilities where geometric modules can equip the AI system with pattern recognition and informal intuition functionality to complement the algorithmic types of modules. An early example of this is provided by Deepmind's AlphaGo system that consists of deep reinforcement learning (geometric AI module) as well as Monte Carlo search (symbolic AI module) components to solve the problem of playing Go at expert level without human knowledge.[201] Instead of having many human-driven design decisions and software engineering to construct the system and its modules as was done with AlphaGo, the AI system should preferably automatically develop its task-specific models using modules from a growing global library of reusable subroutines that represent common problem-solving patterns that are continuously being updated as tasks are being solved successfully. A meta-learner that operates on a continuous basis should be capable of quickly building a task-level model across a range of tasks from this growing library of abstract routines by making module-related design choices in the modular task-level program that learns to solve a specific task on the fly. As the modular task-level program gets data and feedback from the tasks that it is working on to solve, it passes task-related data and feedback also to the meta-learner. The meta-learner helps to build an abstraction capability by pushing reusable modules to the library and fetching relevant ones for use by the modular task-level program. This continuously evolving AI system consisting of the global library and meta-learner would in principle be able to generate task-level programs or models that can realize human-level type of generalization on specific tasks using a rich variety of available modules and considerable experience on similar tasks.[202]

Joscha Bach also described this meta-learner capability as a third order type of AI that mirrors the human brain's capability to learn how to learn new things. In this framework, the first order AI systems would be represented by classical AI from 1950 to 2013, whereas the second order AI systems are able to generate a model or program that are able to find a program that you want to develop and where deep learning is for example used to approximate compositional functions within the program. An example would be to instead of writing a program to play Go, you write a program that learns how to play Go. One of the issues with the current second order systems is that it is thus far not general enough. An AI system as described by Francois would be able to both make the second order AI system more general and also address the third order AI system's meta-learning capability. Joscha also asks if a fourth order AI system would involve a general theory of search.[203] Within Francois's strong AI framework, high-level intelligent search would also be required by the meta-learner to search for the most relevant modules in the global library to be used within a modular task-level program to help solve a specific task.

As a number of other AI researchers, Yann LeCun has described some obstacles to progress in AI as not having AI systems that learn and understand how the world works from a physical, digital and people perspective and the need to acquire some level of common sense. As a result, there is a huge amount of background knowledge that needs to be learned through observation and action. These AI systems also need to perceive the state of the world in order to make accurate predictions and do planning. It further needs to update and remember estimates of the state of the world by recalling relevant events and paying attention to important events. Very importantly, the AI systems also need to be able to reason and plan by amongst others predicting which sequence of actions will lead to a desired state of the world. So to have an AI system that has both intelligence and common sense would require the combination of capabilities such as perception, predictive modelling, memory, reasoning and planning.[204] Both Yoshua Bengio and Yann LeCun believe that self-supervised learning algorithms which generate labels from data by exposing relationships between the data's parts to be a key component in achieving human-level intelligence.[205] With self-supervised learning a part of the input is used as a supervisory signal to predict the rest of the input. As humans we learn models of the world by predicting part of the input from other parts, masked input from the visible inputs, obstructed parts from all available parts, and the future from the past. Yann LeCun emphasizes that more knowledge about the world's structure and workings can be learned through self-supervised learning compared to other methods as it capitalizes on the unlimited data available and makes better use of the feedback that is provided by each input example."[206] As humans we learn mostly in this self-supervised mode via observation that does not require testing along with some interaction with the world. A key problem for self-supervised learning in AI systems is that we still do not have a practical way of representing the distribution of variables that are continuous in nature (they can only be obtained by measuring) as opposed to discrete variables that can represent uncertainty properly as in the case with supervised learning. Yann LeCun is proposing energy-based models (EBM) that learn the mathematical elements of a data set and try to generate similar data sets as a potential solution to the continuous distribution problem.[207] He describes EBMs as a type of non-probabilistic graphs that "capture dependencies between variables by associating scalar energy to each configuration of the variables", where "inference consists of clamping the value of observed variables and finding configurations of the remaining variables that minimize the energy", and "learning consists of finding an energy function in which observed configurations of the variables are given lower energies than unobserved ones".[208] Researchers at OpenAI have also made some progress towards stable and scalable training of these energy-based models that leads to improved sample quality and generalization ability compared to existing models. Some of the advantages of EBMs and iterative refinement include adaptive computation time which allows for generating samples at low temperatures that are competitive with ones that GANs can generate, not being restricted by generator networks that need to learn to map from a continuous space but instead can learn to assign lower energies at disjoint regions, and built-in compositionality that allow EBMs to be combined through hierarchical models.[209] Energy-based models can also help to address compositionality which is one of the unsolved problems in AI research.

While the brain finds it easy to learn in compositional fashion and produce new combinations from known components, this has not been that case for neural networks in general and a key reason for why deep learning models require huge amount of data in order to learn, have issues with transfer learning and find it difficult to do zero and one-shot learning. As we currently do not have continuously learning AI systems that have a global library and meta-learner, today's AI systems are not able to discover and store skills or capabilities that are common across problems or tasks, and to reuse and recombine them in a hierarchical or compositional fashion to solve new challenges. Compositionality is also a common research theme in task decomposition, hybrid AI architectures that integrate symbolic AI with deep learning, neural architecture search, transfer learning, and subgoal discovery in reinforcement learning.[210] There have been many approaches to compositionality such as a divide and conquer one that decompose a problem into sub-tasks in such a way that existing solutions to sub-tasks can be combined to solve the problem, making use of symbolic AI primitives that can execute logical reasoning steps over abstract compositional representations with elements such as objects and relations, using pre-trained models as primitives in transfer learning, and integrating symbolic AI primitives with deep learning. Although neural networks such as encoder-decoder networks and generative adversarial networks consist of multiple underlying networks, they operate together more as a singular system to achieve a specific outcome as opposed to a distributed model that assigns tasks to specialized networks. Compositional learning is also different from ensemble type of machine learning as compositional systems have specialized models working on different tasks and in a specific context with one another. Compositional learning also involves much more than just making algorithm choices and preparing the data as the appropriate models should be selected for the various tasks and there are many ways the relationships between each of the specialized modules within a compositional system can be organized in a context-dependent fashion. A number of modular network architectures have been manually designed such as the one that makes use of a training algorithm that flexibly chooses neural network modules based on the data to be processed (handling the module choice as a latent variable in a probabilistic model) and learns the decomposition and module parameters in an end-to-end fashion.[211] An example of a manually handcrafted compositional system that incorporates both symbolic AI and machine learning components are the *Deep Symbolic Reinforcement Learning* hybrid AI system constructed by Marta Garnelo and colleagues where the end-to-end reinforcement learning architecture consists of a neural network back-end that learns to map raw sensor data into a symbolic representation and a symbolic front-end that maps the symbolic representation to actions.[212] In the paper *Reconciling deep learning with symbolic artificial intelligence: representing objects and relations* Marta Garnelo and Murray Shanahan from Google Deepmind showcase how specific aspects of symbolic AI can fit within a deep learning framework and how a deep learning network can be trained to acquire and use compositional representations with objects and relations as elements.[213] However, we are still far from an adequate synthesis as such a compositional system would ensure that representations are learned from data with minimal priors and consist of elements such as variables, quantifiers, objects and relations. Such a system would ideally not be constrained by the formal logic rules but support arbitrarily long sequences of inference steps using all the above-mentioned elements and able to learn various inference forms. As mentioned in the previous section, instead of handcrafted systems, some progress has been made in neural architecture search where a search strategy selects an architecture from a predefined search space, then passes the architecture to a performance estimation strategy which returns the estimated performance of the selected architecture to the search strategy.[214] Mattia Ferrini has also proposed a high-level compositionality framework that can integrate sub-goal discovery in neural architecture search, align research on sub-goal discovery with existing research on compositionality, use attention mechanisms to incentivize compositionality, develop a bridge between transfer learning and neural architecture search, and reconcile deep learning with symbolic AI by ensuring that symbolic primitives are available to neural architecture search frameworks.[215] Microsoft Research published findings around the relationship between accuracy and locality and compositionality that aims to provide researchers with a more rigorous approach to zero-shot learning.[216] In a paper *Learning Compositional Representations for a Few-Shot Recognition* by Carnegie Mellon University researchers an attribute-based regularization technique is introduced that allows the learned representation to be decomposable into parts and show that they require fewer examples to learn classifiers for new categories on certain datasets.[217] For a human-object interaction detection use case, a deep visual compositional learning framework was developed to localize and infer relationships between humans and objects in images that achieved state-of-the-art results on specific datasets.[218]

In his paper *The Next Decade in AI: Four Steps Towards Robust Artificial Intelligence* Gary Marcus propose "a hybrid knowledge-driven, reasoning-based approach" that is built on cognitive models as a substrate to enable "a richer, more robust AI than is currently possible".[219] He defines robust AI as intelligence that can be "counted on to apply what it knows to a wide range of problems in a systematic and reliable way, synthesizing knowledge from a variety of sources such that it can reason flexibly and dynamically about the world, transferring what it learns in one context to another, in the way that we would expect of an ordinary adult." Gary's four steps involve a hybrid architecture, large-scale knowledge, reasoning, and cognitive models. Symbolic operations over variables offer a well-tested solution that provides the backbone for the world's software with every program dealing with variables, instances, bindings that tie variables to instances, and operations. It only lacks a satisfactory framework for learning such as that provided by deep learning. Hybrid architectures are typically effective such as Google Search that uses a mix of deep learning and symbol-manipulation operations, Google Knowledge Graph that uses classic symbolic graph structures to represent knowledge along with tools such as BERT and RankBrain, AlphaGo that uses deep reinforcement learning and Monte Carlo tree search, and OpenAI's Rubik's solver that uses deep reinforcement learning and a symbolic algorithm for solving cognitive aspects. Also, determining whether a given system is a hybrid system is not always straightforward. Gary argues that the common objections to hybrid models and symbol-manipulation can be countered. Although no neural mechanism has yet been identified to support symbol-manipulation it does not mean that it will not happen in the future and does not tell us anything yet as we don't have a detailed understanding of how world-class chess playing is implemented in the brain. We do have psychological evidence that symbol-manipulation is instantiated in the brain. Even if the brain does not use symbol-manipulation on a neural mechanism level, AI can still make use of symbol manipulation. Hybrid AI systems can also scale, and we currently have examples that work well. A robust hybrid AI system also requires large-scale knowledge of which some is abstract and causal in nature. Some considerations include that most knowledge is likely to be learned, a large fraction of knowledge that is required would be external and cultural in nature and symbolically represented, rules and exceptions must co-exist, a significant fraction of knowledge would be causal and able to support counterfactuals, lots of abstract knowledge would be difficult to obtain via web-scraping, relevant knowledge would need to be very broad in scope, putting knowledge into practice is hard, and a robust AI should include some innate prior human knowledge.

A robust hybrid AI system should also be able to reason. Gary reckons that the best case for reasoning engines in the classical mold comes for the sort of inference that CYC can perform in optimal circumstances. As an AI project launched in 1984 that aims to assemble a comprehensive ontology and knowledge base that covers basic concepts and rules of how the world works, Cyc is offered by Cycorp as an enterprise-proven knowledge representation and reasoning platform with 3 components: a knowledge base (what Cyc knows), inference engines (how Cyc reasons over what it knows), and intelligent data selection (augmenting the knowledge base by connecting to data). Cyc combines these components to generate insights in the form of actionable output.[220] Gary's observations about Cyc includes that the approach would not be doable without considerable use of operations over variables, structured representations, and records for individuals; the rich cognitive models and knowledge are shown to be of great value; it would be considered a significant breakthrough to have a system that can automatically generate the Cyc's representations; and having the correct information accessible in the context of real-world inference might turn out to be the actual barrier and not necessarily reasoning as such.[221]

Gary makes two conjectures about the key role of cognitive models as part of a robust hybrid AI system: it must have the capacity to induce and represent rich cognitive models and these cognitive models cannot be constructed in an acceptable automated fashion without rich prior knowledge, advanced techniques for reasoning and a hybrid architecture. He also emphasizes the need for hybrid AI systems that include mechanisms for spatial, physical, psychological, temporal, and causal reasoning and states that most current neural networks lack explicit mechanisms for these forms of reasoning and does not have natural ways of representing and reasoning over such domains.[222]

In a recent interview with Geoff Hinton, he claims that "deep learning is going to be able to do everything" but "there's going to have to be quite a few conceptual breakthroughs...we also need a massive increase in scale".[223] He argues that we need breakthroughs in how big vectors of neural activity can implement something like reason. We also need larger neural networks and more data. He specifically compares the human brain with its 100 trillion parameters to a big neural network model like GPT-3 with its 175 billion parameters, which is a thousand times smaller. Geoff reckons that common sense reasoning and motor control are some of the big-ticket research items to tackle. Geoff thinks that the brain is neither manipulating representations of pixels or symbols, but big vectors of neural activity. Although a symbolic approach has its merits, it only exists in the external world and is not something that happens inside the brain. As convolutional neural networks do not recognize objects in the same way humans do (we use coordinate frames) and has some limitations to easily generalize to new viewpoints, Geoff has proposed the idea of capsules that represent the segments of a given image using a group of neurons that learns to represent a familiar shape or part and then use these learned sub representations to identify the image. In the latest version of a capsule, it has a logistic unit that represents whether the shape exists in the current image, a matrix that represents the geometrical relationship between the shape and the camera which is called a pose, and a vector that represents properties such as deformation, velocity, and color. This unsupervised capsule autoencoder network can reason about objects using the geometric relationships between parts which is robust to viewpoint changes.[224] The capsule network has a part capsule autoencoder that segments the image input into parts and their poses and uses the poses to reconstruct the image by suitably arranging the learned templates. It also has an object capsule autoencoder that organizes discovered parts and their poses into a smaller set of objects which is then used to reconstruct the part poses using a separate mixture of predictions for each part. This new method for representation learning uses structured decoder networks to train the encoder network to segment an image into parts and their poses and uses another encoder network to compose the parts into coherent objects. The capsule network has achieved state-of-the-art results for unsupervised classification on SVHN (55%) and MNIST (98.7%).[225]

As there is a general consensus that AI has much to gain from the field of neuroscience (and vice versa), Yoshua Bengio particularly believes there is much to learn from how consciousness and conscious processing works in the brain and predicts that novel research will illuminate the way high-level semantic variables relate to how the brain processes information and how these variables are used in language communications. This can also lead to the development of new types of deep learning models. By combining models of grounded language learning and how the world works with the models that deal with high-level concepts, models can be created which mirror human conscious processing that implements explanations of how the world might change in a high-level representation.[226] Yoshua compares this type of model with the System 2 thinking as defined by Nobel laureate Daniel Kahneman in his book *Thinking, Fast and Slow*, where Daniel defines a dichotomy between two modes of thought or cognitive abilities where "System 1" represents the unconscious, intuitive, fast, instinctive, habitual, non-linguistic and emotional part and "System 2" represents the conscious, sequential, reasoning, linguistic, slower, more deliberative, and more logical part.[227] The rationale is that the current deep learning is fairly competent at automatic perception such as System 1, but lacks System 2 type of processing that requires more attention, effort, and concentration to perform mental activities such as decision making, reasoning, and understanding. Yoshua sets the challenge to extend deep learning to implement System 2 type of thinking. He reckons that some consciousness priors are likely needed to represent high-level concepts and that deep learning can be used to predict the value of this prior in the high-level abstract space (similar to how deep learning is making predictions in the sensory space). In this system 2 conscious state a few concepts can be combined to form a conscious thought. He claims that "this architectural and information-processing constraint corresponds to assumptions about the joint distribution between high-level concepts" and that this is "consistent with a joint distribution over high-level concepts which has the form of a sparse factor graph, i.e., where the dependencies captured by each factor of the factor graph involve only very few variables while creating a strong dip in the overall energy function".[228] Yoshua conjectures further that the consciousness prior also makes it possible for conscious states to be mapped to natural language expressions, logic, facts and rules and can possibly be combined in a way to enable reasoning and understanding.

An Ericsson Research team has recently provided a selective overview of machine reasoning explainability and described machine reasoning as an AI field that predominantly uses symbolic methods to formalize and emulate abstract reasoning.[229] Other machine reasoning definitions seem to have a strong symbolic AI slant such as "systems that generate conclusions from previously acquired knowledge by applying logical techniques like deduction and induction" or "machine reasoning, which involves understanding and common sense, requires an ontology".[230] The Ericsson paper defines explainable AI systems as one that "produces details and reasons underlying its functioning and outputs thereof" and categorize explanations as *attributive* such as feature importance association, *contrastive* such as counterfactuals, and *actionable* such as actual outcomes or guidelines towards a desired outcome.[231] They also highlight explanations in machine reasoning which include inference based, logic programming, constraint programming, automated theorem proving, argumentation, planning, decision theory and symbolic reinforcement learning. Machine reasoning and explainability has been difficult for neural networks to master. The same holds for relational reasoning which is a key aspect of intelligent behavior and can be defined as "seeing meaningful patterns in information, and can be done using analogy, anomaly, antimony, and antithesis".[232] The Google DeepMind team has demonstrated how to use Relation Networks (RN) as a plug-and-play module to solve problems that essentially rest on relational reasoning.[233] In a visual question answering test using the CLEVR dataset the RN-augmented networks have achieved state-of-the-art superhuman performance. Other tests included complex reasoning about dynamic physical systems and a text-based question answering using the bAbI suite of tasks. The DeepMind team has also shown that by augmenting convolutional networks with RNs on curated Sort-of-CLEVR dataset the combined system has a general capacity to solve relational questions and can implicitly discover and learn to reason about entities and their relations.[234] In another Google DeepMind paper it was shown that neural networks can learn to perform explanatory and counterfactual reasoning where an object-centric transformer substantially outperformed leading neuro-symbolic models on two reasoning tasks that was assumed to be challenging for deep neural networks.[235] The CLEVRER and CATER task domains focus on spatio-temporal interactions between objects. A fully learned neural network which uses self-attention, learned "soft" object-centric representations, BERT-style semi-supervised predictive losses, and the right inductive biases outperformed all previous neural-symbolic models on both of these tasks using less than 60% of available labelled data. It specifically did well on questions that emphasize reasoning over perception and demonstrate that it can learn to reason effectively about the causal, dynamic structure of physical events.[236]

Whereas humans have knowledge about the features of their environment and what actions are possible within that environment, that is not the case for typical reinforcement learning algorithms that assume that all actions are always available to an agent. A psychologist James Gibson coined the theory of "affordance" that states that when people look at the world they perceive not simply objects and their relationships but also their possibilities.[237] For example, the bed "affords" the possibility of sleeping. This theory helps to explain why people can engage with new objects in an environment and generalize so easily because we recognize their affordances. A paper *What can I do here? A Theory of Affordances in Reinforcement Learning* showcased the development of a theory of affordances for agents who learn and plan in Markov Decision Processes. They also proposed an approach to learn affordances that allows faster planning by reducing the number of actions available in any given situation and use it to estimate transition models that are simpler with improved generalization capability.[238]

In his presentation *Exponential Progress of AI: Moore's Law, Bitter Lesson, and the Future of Computation*, Lex Fridman an AI Researcher at MIT and YouTube Podcast Host, gives his perspective on the progress of AI with consideration of Rich Sutton's *The Bitter Lesson* blog post discussed earlier in this chapter that emphases that general AI methods which leverage computation turned out to be significantly more effective than those that explored other methods such as leveraging human domain knowledge.[239] Lex thinks that the scientific community did not give enough credit and appreciation to some of the AI breakthroughs due the "brute-force" computational nature of the search and learning that was involved in achieving breakthroughs in chess, Go, computer vision, speech recognition, and natural language processing. He recommends that research papers should include a section that specifies if the AI method introduced does scale with compute. Rich did not specifically reference the role of data as scaling of learning in most cases depends on scalability of data annotation. "Moore's law" (which can also be ambiguously interpreted as the exponential improvement of computational capabilities) may be observed at any abstraction level of computation when invested in, including at the deep learning or meta learning or above levels. People like Jim Keller, previous microprocessor engineer at AMD and Apple, says that Moore's Law is not yet dead as the theoretical physics limit is not yet reached. "Moore's Law" might also continue via global compute capacity, massively parallel computation, GPUs and applications-specific integrated circuits (ASICs), computation of a different nature such as quantum computing or neuromorphic computing with modeling spiking networks, brain-computer interfaces, and deep learning efficiency innovation.

Learning and search also requires some human knowledge expertise such as hyper-parameter tuning and the better architectures and learning processes that we engineer (e.g., convolutional neural networks versus feedforward neural networks) which also sometimes requires less compute such as EfficientNet in 2020 requiring 44 times less compute to train to the level of AlexNet in 2012 whilst hardware efficiencies improved 11 times over this period. In the same paper *Measuring the Algorithmic Efficiency of Neural Networks* by Danny Hernandez and Tom Brown from OpenAI also observe that a realistic indication of AI progress should integrate measures from algorithmic and hardware efficiency, as gains from both multiply and can be on a comparable scale over meaningful time periods.[240] Lex also asks as evolutionary processes created the human brain, does evolution fall under "search" and/or "learning or not? Also, is human ingenuity or raw computational power or both more important for long term progress of AI? He thinks that exponential improvements in AI are likely to continue and will predominantly be driven by efficiency in learning and search algorithms (especially active learning) and data, whilst exponential growth in compute devices also grows.[241] Hugo de Garis, an AI researcher in evolvable hardware, has listed some of the 21st century technologies and developments that can be an enabler for strong AI systems to be Moore's law, 1 bit per atom capability, femto-second switching, reversible computing, nanotechnology, artificial embryology, evolutionary engineering, topological quantum computing, nanotechnology impact on brain science, and artificial brains.[242]

As the premise of this book and my massive transformative purpose is on maximizing the social benefit of AI, I identify with the *Research Priorities for Robust and Beneficial Artificial Intelligence* report by Stuart Russell, Daniel Dewey, and Max Tegmark as communicated via The Future of Life Institute website.[243] As we want our AI systems to be aligned with humanity's best interests at heart and for our benefit, they recommend expanded interdisciplinary research focused at ensuring that increasingly capable AI systems are robust and beneficial. In the report they outline some short- and long-term research priorities. The short-term research priorities include optimizing AI's economic impact, research in law and ethics, and computer science research for robust AI. For optimizing AI's economic impact, a range of research directions covering areas from economics and social science to politics to psychology need to be considered such as labor market forecasting with jobs or tasks within jobs being automated, disruptions of significant parts of the economy through AI-driven predictions of human and market behaviors, policies for managing harmful effects, and improved economic measures. The spectrum of assisted, augmented and autonomous AI systems being developed and deployed at scale which impact consumers, producers, markets, and governance systems globally leads to many legal and ethical questions that need to be addressed. These questions require expertise from legal experts, computer scientists, ethicists, and political scientists to cover for example liability and law for autonomous vehicles, machine ethics, autonomous weapons, privacy, professional ethics, and public policy.[244] Furthermore, another important short-term research priority involves computer science research for robust AI across consumer facing and industrial applications as well as autonomous transport, trading systems and weapons. The various ways in which an AI system may not execute as intended leads to different research areas for AI robustness which include, for example, verification to answer how to prove that a system satisfies certain desired formal properties, especially in safety-critical situations ("did I build the system right?"); validity to answer how to ensure that a system that meets its formal requirements does not have unwanted behaviors and consequences ("did I build the right system?"); security to answer how to prevent intentional manipulation by unauthorized parties ("have I secured the system enough?"); and control to answer how to enable meaningful human control over an AI system after it begins to operate ("can I again get control of the system?").[245]

From a long-term research priorities perspective, these 4 areas of verification, validity, security, and control will become increasingly critical and important as AI systems will likely become more capable and more deeply integrated into the fabric of society. As one of the long-term goals of many AI researchers, technology companies, and governments is to build human-level AI or strong AI that can potentially outstrip human cognitive abilities, it would be important to ensure that these AI systems that can have a tremendous impact on society is robust and beneficial for us. Stuart Russell also has a chapter in his book Human Compatible: Artificial Intelligence and the Problem of Control that is called "Provably Beneficial AI" where he proposes training AI systems not on a fixed goal, but instead to accomplish our goals without the AI system necessarily knowing what the exact goals are. As also mentioned earlier in this chapter, having an explicit uncertainty about the nature of goals that the AI systems are instructed to pursue, leads to a margin of safety that we need in building trustworthy, safe, and controllable AI systems. His solution builds on Inverse Reinforcement Learning and transforms the AI's incentives by ensuring that the AI system does not fully understand our goals, it will actively try to learn more about what we really want, and always be open to us redirecting it or even switching it off if it comes to that scenario.[246]

10. Beneficial Outcomes for Humanity in the Smart Technology Era

It took nine chapters to lay a foundation of sense-making and better understanding of AI, its applications, its benefits, its risks, its limitations, its progress, and its likely future paths in the Smart Technology Era. We are now ready to discuss beneficial outcomes for humanity and how we can democratize AI to help shape a beneficial human-centric future. In this chapter, we specifically examine what it means to be human and living meaningful in the 21st century, but also get a better understanding of the problematic trajectory that our current civilization is on. I also share some ideas for reshaping our civilization for beneficial outcomes as well as various potential outcomes for the future of civilization. This chapter is then concluded by zooming in on the beneficial outcomes for humanity and introducing a proposed massive transformative purpose for humanity and its associated smart goals that complement the United Nations' 2030 vision and sustainable development goals.

What does it Mean to be Human and Living Meaningful in the 21st Century?

To help think about beneficial outcomes for humanity and meaningful living in the 21st century and beyond, it is useful to frame and give context to the discussion by referencing Maslow's hierarchy of needs which is a motivational theory in psychology that consists of basic needs such as physiological needs (e.g., air, food, water, warmth, shelter, sex, sleep and rest) and safety needs (e.g., security, stability and safety); psychological needs such as belongingness and love needs (e.g., intimate relationships, friends, and work) and esteem needs (e.g., prestige, achievement, mastery and feeling of accomplishment); and self-fulfillment needs such as self-actualization (e.g., achieving one's full potential, including creative activities).[1] Basic needs typically needs to be met before psychological and self-fulfillment needs. This 5-stage motivational model has since been extended to an 8-stage hierarchical model which adds cognitive needs (e.g., knowledge and understanding, need for meaning and predictability, exploration, and curiosity) and aesthetic needs (e.g., appreciation and search for beauty, form, and balance) in between esteem and self-actualization needs and then adds an additional layer on top for transcendence needs (e.g., values beyond the personal self that includes experiences that relates to nature, mystics, aesthetics as well as service to others, religious faith, and the pursuit of science).[2]

During the same decade that Abraham Maslow proposed his theory of human motivation in the 1940s, Victor Frankl published his book *Man's Search For Meaning: An Introduction to Logotherapy* which has proven to be a very influential book for people exploring the meaning of life.[3] Viktor, who was a prisoner in a Nazi concentration camp during World War II, recorded his experiences and explained his psychotherapeutic method that helped him survive the concentration camp through identifying a positive purpose in life and then immersively visualizing that outcome. He conjectured that a prisoner's longevity was directly affected by how the future was imagined. His theory of logotherapy ("logos" is the Greek word which indicates meaning) discusses the meaning of human existence and man's search for that meaning. Victor sees meaning in one's life as a primary motivational force and something unique and specific to oneself. He sees an inherent tension in a human being between what a person has already accomplished and what one still aspires to achieve. Victor does not see life as a search for pleasure, but a search for meaning and identifies three sources for meaning which includes caring for another person (love), doing something significant (work), and bravery and determination during hard times (courage). He states that love is the utmost and supreme goal to which anyone can strive for. We all know that we cannot control what happens to us in our lives, but we can control what we feel and do about what happens to us. This in some sense also ties in with the first part of the Serenity Prayer that says, "God grant me the serenity to accept the things I cannot change; courage to change the things I can; and wisdom to know the difference."[4] The key freedom that each one of us will always have is to choose our attitude and the way we respond in any specific situation and moment. Victor Frankl sees that having the responsibility in answering for your own life as the essence of human existence and advises to "live as if you were living already for the second time and as if you had acted the first time as wrongly as you are about to act now!"[5] He notes that as soon as suffering finds a meaning of a sacrifice, it stops being suffering. Also, one cannot be happy without a reason to be happy. If someone's meaning has been identified, it not only helps one to be happy, but also assists with dealing with suffering and hardship.

A recent book The *Meaning of Life and the Great Philosophers* authored by some leading experts in the field, reveals how thirty five of the greatest past philosophers have tried to answer the question of the meaning of life.[6] It consolidates some of the history of philosophy's wealth of opinion on this subject by major philosophical figures such as Confucius, The Buddha, Socrates, Plato, Zhuangzi, Aristotle, Epicurus, Epictetus, Aquinas, Descartes, Spinoza, Kant, Schopenhauer, Kierkegaard, Marx, Nietzsche, Ortega, Wittgenstein, Heidegger, Sartre, Camus, and Rorty. The Internet Encyclopedia of Philosophy is also an excellent peer-reviewed academic resource that provides a deep dive into a much larger pool of philosophical material that also covers aspects of the meaning of life.[7] As the philosophical school of the 20th century in the United States and Great Britain was more focused on hard-core scientific rationalism and the nature of logic, concepts and language, the philosophical question of the meaning of life that science is not well-equipped to answer was for the most part avoided. Kieran Setiya, a professor in philosophy at MIT and author of *Midlife: Philosophical Guide*, remarked in an article that philosophers should be keener to talk about the meaning of life.[8] By examining all philosophies on the meaning of life, it looks like they can be classified into one of the four groups: Supernatural meaning, objective meaning, subjective meaning, and life has no meaning. Furthermore, the philosophies of the West and East also seem to follow a pattern where people from the West emphasize the individual, whereas people from the East think more in terms of us, the community, or society.

The earliest prehistoric schools of philosophy that also address the meaning of life includes *Natural Pantheism* that states that God is in everything and the meaning of life is in living in harmony with nature and all that there is, whilst *Theism* proposes that God exists and that the meaning of life is to follow God's will. From approximately the 6th and 5th century BC, *Determinism* appeared which accept that everything happens as a result of previously existing causes and is predetermined including the meaning of life which implies that we do not have free will, whereas *Daoism* of Chinese origin offers a person a pain-free way of following the way and finding the meaning of life without the person knowing what it is until it is revealed when a person simply is.[9] During the same time frame, *Confucianism* by Chinese philosopher Confucius teaches us to take care and fulfill our duties to others, *Mohism* by Chinese philosopher Mozi advocates to love and take care of people impartially, and *Solipsism* by Greek philosopher Gorgias expresses that as one can only be certain of the existence of one's mind, the meaning of life can only be known by one's mind and not by one's relation to other people.[10] Around the 4th century BC, *Cynicism* was introduced to provide people the possibility of happiness and freedom from suffering and see the meaning of life as having mental clarity and being self-sufficient and free from external influences, whereas *Hedonism* presents people with a life of pursuing pleasure and avoiding suffering. *Platonism* was introduced in the 4th century BC by Greek philosopher Plato who regarded the meaning of life as the pursuit of knowledge of abstractions. Plato references his teacher Socrates who said that "the unexamined life is not worth living" and makes the claims that we are all born with the knowledge inside us that just needs to be discovered.[11] *Legalism* also emerged from China around the same time and declares that the meaning of life is to obtain practical skills that can be used by the state for society's benefit as people are selfish and cannot be trusted to behave in a moral fashion. *Epicureanism* was during the same period introduced by the Greek philosopher Epicurus who stated the meaning of life to be to achieve lasting mental pleasure which leads to a state of calmness and freedom from fear.[12] Around the 3rd century BC, *Quietism* was presented as the philosophy that has no answers to offer and regards the question of the meaning of life as meaningless, whereas *Aristotelianism* introduced by the Greek philosopher Aristotle regards it sufficient to be a good person as virtue is the goal and we already know what is good.[13] *Stoicism* also appeared at the same time and wants people to renounce emotion and be free from desire for pleasure or fear of pain through wisdom and rational actions. A few centuries later Marcus Aurelius recorded his progress on transforming himself in becoming such a wise stoic person.[14]

During the late 1300s *Modern Humanism* specified that the meaning of life is to promote and support other humans as we should act in self-interest and the common good and take responsibility for humanity's destiny. This philosophy was followed by *Subjectivism* in the early 1600s that set out that the meaning of life is different for each person and depends on one's mental state and achieving personalized goals. This philosophy is ascribed to Rene Descartes and his thought experiment "I think, therefore, I exist."[15] *Liberalism* introduced by English philosopher John Locke appeared in 1689 and states that the meaning of life is to defend individual liberties as a person should be free to make their own choices without the consent of others.[16] The origin of *Kantianism* is German philosopher Emmanuel Kant which in 1785 proposed that every human action should be judged according to a universal principle that relates their duty toward humans.[17] According to this philosophy the meaning of life is to do as you would others do to follow universal principles. *Nihilism* or Pessimism which appeared in 1862 is the belief that as there seems to be an inherent human tendency that prevents us from finding meaning in life, nothing can make life really meaningful for us. The German philosopher Friedrich Nietzsche who has been most associated with this philosophy introduced the concept "Will to Power" and claimed that people should develop their own identity through self-realization without relying on anything transcending their lives.[18] *Pragmatism* as a philosophy arrived in the 1870s and is more focused on pursuing a useful understanding of life as opposed to the truth of life. The American philosopher and psychologist William James reasoned that truth could be made but not sought and the meaning of life depends on what you do with your life and maximize value to humanity.[19] In the 1920s the philosophy of *Logical Positivism* or logical empiricism indicates that the meaning of life can only be derived from a person's actual experience and what you give it as the only type of knowledge available to us is scientifically verifiable and observable facts and anything else is meaningless. In the 1940s the *Existentialism* philosophy describes that to find meaning in life a person needs to make choices about their own values and then take positive action to live according to them. German philosopher Martin Heidegger initially introduced this philosophy through his exploration of the "meaning of being".[20] In 1942 French philosopher Albert Camus proposed *Absurdism* that people should embrace the absurdity of our existence, stop trying to find meaning and just carry on with our lives.[21]

But what do every day thoughtful 21st century people think about the meaning of life and what it is to be human? Of the many internet resources on this topic, the *Excellence Reporter* website (claiming to be the #1 most 'meaning full' website on earth) provides over 1200 articles and interviews on 'What is the Meaning of Life?' written by renowned spiritual leaders, mindfulness experts, great thinkers and authors, elders, artists, musicians, CEOs, and many others.[22] In a personal blog, Daniel Schmachtenberger also highlights three components to living a meaningful life which includes a mode of being that involves appreciating the beauty of existence, a mode of doing which adds to the beauty of existence and a mode of becoming which increases your ability to appreciate and add to the beauty of existence.[23] He sees that most of our actions come from one's being which is strongly conditioned and influenced by past unconscious activities. Being then influences what a person is doing, whereas doing in turn conditions the person further. He reckons that doing affects how a person is changing and becoming, whereas becoming then changes the integrated state of a person's being. Daniel explains further that "being, doing, and becoming are equally fundamental, inseparable, and inter affecting, in a ring. The cycle can be vicious or virtuous. Everything that is meaningful is one of these three. Engaging in all three consciously as a virtuous cycle leads to a maximally meaningful life. All three are ultimately inspired by love."[24]

Lex Fridman has this habit of asking people on his podcast about the meaning of life.[25] What follows next is the essence of a wide variety of meaningful responses to this question paraphrased which help to provide some further rich insights into how modern-day thoughtful people think about this. It is also interesting to see how they fit into Maslow's 8-stage hierarchical motivation model as well as the schools of philosophies' classification framework of supernatural, subjective, objective, and no meaning. Noam Chomsky, a renowned linguist, philosopher, cognitive scientist, historian, social critic, and political activist, believes that there is no general answer to the meaning of life and that we determine what the meaning is.[26] He thinks that the significance of your life is something you create as the action determines the meaning in the sense of significance. Steven Pinker, a cognitive psychologist, linguist, and popular science author, thinks about the meaning of life as obtaining knowledge and fulfillment more generally with respect to life, health, stimulation, and access to the living cultural and social world.[27] However, that is not the meaning of our genes which is to propagate copies of themselves. Although this is also a subset of our meaning, we also want to interact with people, we want to experience beauty, and experience the richness of the natural world. To understand what makes the universe tick is way up there for Steven. He sees the latter as fundamental, what we strive for and what makes us homo sapiens - wise man. We are unique amongst animals to the degree in which we acquire and use knowledge to survive. We make tools, we strike agreements via language, we extract poisons, we predict the behavior of animals, we get to know the workings of plants, the refinement of reason in pursuit of human wellbeing, health, happiness, social richness, cultural richness, and using our intellect and our knowledge of how the world works to make discoveries and strike agreements to make us all better off in the long run.[28] David Chalmers, a philosopher and cognitive scientist specializing in philosophy of mind, philosophy of language, and consciousness, reckons that without consciousness there is no meaning.[29] He views consciousness as the source of meaning, but not the meaning itself. David believes that what is meaningful in life is what we find meaningful. If you find meaning and fulfillment in intellectual work like understanding that is a significant part of the meaning of life for you. Other things that provide significant meaning include our social connections and raising a family. As meaning comes from what you value as a conscious creature, he does not think there is a universal answer to this question.

In discussing neuroscience of optimal performance with Lex Fridman, Andrew Huberman who is a neuroscientist at Stanford University, claims that our sense of meaning is very elastic in time and space.[30] He also references Victor Frankl and his book the *Man's Search for Meaning* and finds it amazing that someone locked in a cell or a concentration camp can bring in the horizon close enough so that they can micro-slice their environment in order to find rewards, meaning, power and beauty even in a little square box or a horrible situation. This speaks to one of the most important features of the human mind which he illustrates with two opposite extremes. Let us say the alarm goes off in the building and the building starts shaking. Our senses such as hearing and vision will be tuned to this space time bubble for those moments and the only meaning would be centered around things like getting out of the building safely, trying to find out what is going on, and contact loved ones. If we now consider the other extreme where we sit back completely relaxed and contemplate our place in the vast universe and see ourselves as one brief glimmer in all of time and all of space, it feels more meaningless and if we do not matter. It is beautiful that the human mind allows us to be so dynamic that we can pull meaning from the past, present and the future. For people such as Victor Frankl and Nelson Mandela it was not just about grinding it out but finding those dopamine rewards in their boxes that they were forced into. Andrew thinks that meaning is held for only as long as we are in that spacetime regime. What really gives meaning is that one can move between these different spacetime dimensionalities using different brain processing algorithms in a different state. Given this perspective, Andrew wants in his lifetime to engage into as many different levels of contractions and dilations of meaning as possible. He wants to go to the micro and the macro. As the journey up and down and back and forth that staircase is the key thing, he sees his goal as getting as many trips as possible up and down that staircase whilst he is still alive.

Yaron Brook, an objectivist philosopher, podcaster, and author, believes that principles of a life well lived is to live a rational life with thought.[31] He reckons that many people are not thinking things through and are like zombies. They are alive but they are not really alive because their mind is not focused on what they need to do to live a great life. Too many people are just going through the motions of living without embracing life. Yaron thinks that the secret to living a great life is to take it seriously. This involves using our mind and reason, the one tool that makes us human and provides us with all the values that we have and applies it to living. If we use that same energy, focus, and concentration that we apply to work and apply it also to actually live life in a principled way with well-chosen values, that will change our lives as well as the world. As we only live once, this life is really valuable. Yaron is of the opinion that people in general do not have that deep respect for their own lives, time, or mind. He thinks that experience is the easy part and not where the problem is. It is relatively easy for people to stop and appreciate the moment. The problem is that people are not using their mind with respect to planning their lives, thinking how to live and choosing what your values are. What is messing up the world is that people have the wrong values, they do not think about them and they do not have plans for their own lives. Yaron states that reason as this massive evolutionary achievement and our only source of knowledge is undervalued. We have this capacity to self-program, but are not programmed to know how to hunt, to do agriculture, or to build computers and networks. All of that requires effort, focus, energy, will, and someone to choose to do it. When you make that choice, you are choosing to engage your reason in discovery, integration, and work to change the world in which we live. Human beings had to figure out how to do it.

Ian Hutchinson, a nuclear engineer, and plasma physicist at MIT, sees the meaning of his life as many different things, but all kind of centered around relationships.[32] As a Christian, his relationship with God is a crucial part of the meaning of life. He also views his relationships with his wife, parents, children, siblings, and grandchildren as crucially important. These are all the places that people find meaning if they are religious or not. But ultimately for Ian a person who has faith in a Creator who we think has an intention and a will in respect to the world as a whole that is a crucial part of meaning and the idea that his life might have some small significance in the plan of that Creator is an amazingly powerful idea that brings meaning. The predominantly secular view is that there is no meaning, but you can make up a meaning as you go that will give you meaning in your life. He does not subscribe to that view anymore. He thinks that there is more meaning than that but agrees that those things that give meaning to life are important and we should emphasize them. Love and loyalty are about yielding your will and desire to another. Valuing others at least as highly as yourself. With true love you reach a point where you feel compelled by the other. It sounds scary but is liberating. Love brings you into service to one another. Ian states that for Christians to serve God is what perfects their freedom. Amazing love is in part captivity, but in a paradoxical sense it is also an amazing freedom. David Fravor, an experienced US navy pilot and a primary witness in one of the most credible unidentified flying object sightings in history, reckons the meaning of life really boils down to what matters the most in life to you which is your family and your closest friends.[33] He relates the meaning of life also to his belief in God as he has just seen too many things in the world that he cannot explain.

Ray Dalio, a billionaire hedge fund manager and philanthropist and co-founder of the world's largest hedge fund, Bridgewater Associates, views evolution as the greatest force in the universe.[34] He thinks that we are all tiny bits of an evolutionary type of process. It is just matter and machines that go through time. Ray believes that we all have a deeply embedded inclination to personally evolve and contribute to evolution. Michael Mina, an immunologist, epidemiologist, and physician at Harvard who discussed rapid testing, viruses, and the engineering mindset with Lex Fridman, thinks that there is no single answer to the meaning of life.[35] From a western perspective this life is the most precious thing in the world as opposed to the eastern perspective that regards it as just another opportunity to get "out of life" or being part of the cycle of suffering (which is very much part of human existence) on the way to nirvana after which one is not reborn again. For example, he sees a big disparity in the Judeo-Christian point of view of "going to heaven" versus the Buddhistic one of getting "out of life" as viewpoints that cannot really be reconciled. As Michael thinks that we are just "a bunch of proteins" and a blip on the radar, we should make the most of this amazing blink of time whilst we are here.

Scott Aaronson, a professor specializing in quantum computing at UT Austin views the meaning of life as trying to discover new things about the world, sharing and communicating these things, and learning what other people have discovered.[36] His family, friends, kids, students, and people around him all contribute to the meaning of his life. Scott tries to make the world better in small ways and would love to do more. As the world is facing a crisis over climate, resurgent authoritarianism, and other major concerns, he also tries to take a stand where possible against the things that he finds worrying. For Eugenia Kuyda, co-founder of Replika which is a developer of an AI companion software, the meaning of life is the state of love when we feel it, that state of bliss that we sometimes experience in the connection and love with ourselves, towards other people, to technology, and many other things in the world.[37] Dan Kokotov, a VP of Engineering at Rev.ai and focused on AI-driven speech recognition, sees the meaning of life as contributing to this weird thing that we call humanity, in living life, creating things and raising kids.[38] For Grant Sanderson, the creator of 3Blue1Brown math education channel on YouTube, the interactions with other people gives him joy.[39] Sara Seager, a planetary scientist at MIT and known for her work on the search for exoplanets, does not have an answer to the meaning of life, but wishes we knew.[40] For Dileep George, a brain-inspired AI researcher and co-founder of Vicarious, the meaning of life is open and about understanding the machinery of the world.[41] Diana Walsh Pasulka, a professor of philosophy and religion at UNCW and author of *American Cosmic: UFOs, Religion, and Technology* reckons that we assume there is a meaning to life, but maybe there is not.[42] She sees the meaning of life as something intrinsic. Sometimes she enjoys living and sometimes she does not. When she is not enjoying living, her strategy is to change her circumstances. Diana also believes that love of your children is intrinsic. It is beautiful. There is something about it that is intrinsically desirable. The meaning of life is intrinsically desirable. For Russ Tedrake, a roboticist and professor at MIT and vice president of robotics research at TRI, doing hard things is part of the meaning of life.[43] For him it is important to understand what you can and cannot do and love the journey of learning things that would help you to connect another piece of the puzzle.

When asked about the meaning of life, Alex Filippenko, an astrophysicist and professor of astronomy at Berkeley, thinks that life is what you make of it and each of us have to have our own meaning.[44] According to him, meaning is in some sense typically associated with goals or expectations for yourself, the things that you would like to accomplish or that you would like to experience. The degree to which you do or experience those things can give you meaning. Alex believes that we do not have to change the world like Michelangelo or Davinci. We cannot claim that as most of the current close to 8 billion people on the planet are not changing the world on an individual level, that their lives are meaningless. For each person it is just something specific that gives you meaning, satisfaction and a good feeling about what you did. This could be helping others, getting knowledge and better understanding through study and reading, or experience the world through travelling. If socio-economic factors constrain you, you can find other forms of meaning. It does not need to be something profound such as changing the world or be someone that everyone remembers. The brain is giving each one of us the potential for meaning. Alex hopes that we use science for good and not for evil and end up destroying ourselves. Dmitri Dolgov, the CTO of an autonomous vehicle company called Waymo, perceives the meaning of life as something that changes over time as you go through the stages of life.[45] When one enters this world meaning is about new experiences, then it is about fun, then learning new things and experiencing the joy of comprehension and discovery, then it is about giving back through impact and contribution that might touch society, people, or technology. He sees having kids as something that changes one's perspective and adds to the meaning of life instead of having a replacing or subtracting effect.

Matthew Johnson, a professor and psychedelics researcher at Johns Hopkins, thinks that the meaning of life is to find meaning and is like the transcendence of everything where you find the beauty despite the absolute ugliness that we also see.[46] He reminds us that as a species we come from filth, that we are animals, and all descendants of murderers and rapists. Despite that background we are capable of this self-sacrifice, connecting with people, figuring things out such as truth, science and other forms of truth seeking, and able to generate artwork and appreciate the beauty of music and other forms of art. Just the fact that this is possible is the meaning of life. Matthew reckons that most of the important things in life are the things that are tough and scary. Although we try to minimize and avoid the biggest horror experiences on a societal, country, or personal level such as the death of loved ones, these are sometimes the greatest learning experiences and are instrumental in making who we are on all levels of civilization. He encourages us to give ourselves a break as humanity and see the meaning of life in choosing to focus on the positives and keeping them always in mind. When thinking of the meaning of life, Michael Littman, a computer scientist and AI researcher at Brown University, cannot help to also project himself into the world of the reinforcement learning AI agents with their "small little lifetimes" and look for analogies with real human life.[47] He thinks the meaning of life is balance, whilst his wife thinks it is healthy relationships with people that you love and working hard for good causes. Michael Stevens, the host of the Vsauce podcast, thinks about the meaning of life from the perspective that we are learning things, recording things, and writing stories about the world.[48] He believes that preserving these things is what the essence is about being human. He sees humanity as the best autobiographers of the universe. We are better than, for example, fossils, or the light spectrum in this regard. As we are collecting much better detail about what is happening, he thinks that should be our legacy. For Michael, the measure of your life is based on your subjective experience. If you are happy and those that you love are happy, that should be enough.

Manolis Kellis, a professor at MIT and head of the MIT Computational Biology Group, mentions in his discussion with Lex Fridman about the human genome and evolutionary dynamics that he also thinks a lot about the meaning of life.[49] Like a few others that are intrigued by *The Hitchhiker's Guide to the Galaxy* and its answer to the meaning of life, which is 42, he had a party with this theme on his 42nd birthday. In his symposium on the meaning of life he had 42 of his colleagues and friends to also give their perspectives on this. He mentions that although everybody had a different answer, they were all consistent with one another and mutually synergistic and together formed a beautiful view of what it means to be human in many ways. Some of the participants talked about the loss of their loved ones such as their life partner for many years and how their lives changed through that; some people talked about the origin of life; and some people talked about the difference between purpose and meaning. One memorable response was from a Linguistics professor at Harvard that said that she would give a Pythian answer (in Greek mythology a Pythian answer is a cryptic short answer that can be interpreted in many different ways). She said that the meaning of life is to "become one". The first interpretation is that similar to a child we should "become a one-year-old" with the excitement of discovering everything about the world. The second interpretation is that in all endeavors, "become the first" or the best in whatever you do which means to give it your all and perform any task at the best of your abilities. The third interpretation is to "become one" when people are separate, implying that people should come together and learn to understand each other. Manolis has the opinion that the pursuit for meaning can very much be the meaning of life. This can be expressed as the continuous pursuit for something sublime, something human, something tangible, or some aspect of what defines us both as a species and as an individual person through my own life. The meaning of life can also be the meaning of all life. Manolis asked a range of questions in this regard. What is the point of life? Why life itself? We can think about the history and evolution of life, but what about life in the first place? Is life inevitable? Is life part of physics? Does life transcend physics? Life is fighting against entropy through grouping and increasing concentrations rather than diluting away. Is life a distinct entity in the universe beyond the simple basic traditional physical rules that govern gravity, electromagnetism, strong and weak forces? Is life another force? Is there a life force? Is there a unique set of principles that emerge and build on top of the hardware of physics? Is life a new layer of software or a new layer of computer system?

Manolis also remarks that our species are special and probably the only ones that worry about the meaning of life. That is possibly another thing that makes us human. Other aspects include being passionate about interests and the work that you do. The ability to be useful and to feel my brain is being used also provides meaning. The meaning of life is also touched by gratitude. Manolis emphasizes that there is a certain pleasure that comes from being useful as well as grateful. He also teaches his children gratitude through a little prayer: "Thank you God for all you have given me and give me the strength to give on to others with the same love that you have given to me". Children give tremendous meaning to one's life. Manolis expressed this meaning through sharing what it means to him to teach his children about his view of the world and watching through their eyes the naivety with which they start and the sophistication with which they end up. There is also a certain understanding that they develop of not only the natural world but of him too. There is also the unfiltered criticism that one gets from your own children that typically knows no bounds of honesty. Manolis reveals that he has grown components of his heart that he did not know he had until he has sensed that fragility and vulnerability of the children, that immense love and passion, the unfiltered egotism that we as adults hide so well, and the emotions that tell us of the raw material of a human being and how these raw materials can be rearranged with more sophistication as they learn through life to become truly human adults. He observes that there is something so beautiful about seeing the progression of his children, the complexity of the language growing as more neural connections are formed, and the realization that the brain's hardware is getting rearranged as the software is getting implemented on that hardware and that their frontal cortex is continuing to grow for another 10 years as new neural connections being formed. Manolis thinks that it is incredible that instead of humans growing their brain's hardware for 30 years and then feeding it all the knowledge, the knowledge is fed continuously whilst the neural connections are shaped as they form. He reckons that to see a child's transformation is one of the most beautiful things that one can do as a human being. It not only completes you as a person, but also that journey of creating life, adding the human parts through decades of compassion, sharing, love, anger, impatience, and patience. He thinks that this whole experience as a parent has also helped him to become a different kind of teacher.

Lex Fridman and Manolis Kellis took their discussion about the meaning of life to another level in the 142nd episode of Lex's podcast that has been dedicated to the meaning of life, the universe, and everything.[50] Manolis asks why do we search for meaning and will the search lead to our destruction? He is optimistic about human civilization and thinks that whilst science and technology are moving forward at breakneck speed, we will sort out our social and political problems. He emphasizes that asking about meaning is something inherent to human nature that makes it beautiful and worth living and that searching for meaning is actually the point. He goes further by stating that we should not find the meaning of life and if we find it, we are dead. We should not ever be satisfied that we have got it as life is lived forward but only makes sense when we look backward. He sees the whole search itself as the meaning of life. There are in fact two simultaneous searches going on where the one is a search in each of us through our own lives to find meaning and the other one the search for the meaning of humanity itself. We as humans like to look at animals and say of course they have a meaning on a certain level such as a dog with its bunch of instincts running around loving everything. In line with Maslow's needs hierarchy for us humans, life is not just about the physiological and safety needs with respect to procreation, dominance, strength, or feeding, but also making use of our substantial cognitive capability to that we can use for so many other things as we pursue our psychological, cognitive, aesthetic, self-fulfillment, and self-actualization needs.

Erik Brynjolfsson, an economist at Stanford, has the opinion that real happiness is not coming from pleasure seeking or hedonism and that one needs to do something beyond this.[51] He thinks that we need to find other goals or meaning in life which will ultimately make you happier. Erik uses the analogy of happiness being like a dim star. If you do not look at it directly and focus on the area around it, your retina does a better job of picking up the star. In the same way, we should not be focusing directly on happiness, but on goals and meaning that might lead to that. Erik finds meaning in the kind of research he does where he contributes to help making the world a better place. As we are social beings with brains that are not only wired for pleasure, we also have a strong inclination to help others which is deeply rooted in our psyche. If we feel like we are helping others, our reward system kicks in and we are more deeply satisfied compared to just doing something selfish and shallow. When asked about the meaning of life in a discussion about the future of computing and programming languages, Chris Lattner, a software and hardware engineer that have led projects at Apple, Tesla, Google, and SiFive, responded by saying that he is prepared for it to not mean anything, but prefers to say that the universe has a lot of value.[52] Although we are all biological things programmed to survive and propagate our DNA, he does not regard that thinking to be a productive way to live your life. Chris finds his happiness through the relationships he builds with other people and having kids. The question that he asked himself is what he can do that has value and help to move the world forward? He likes to take what he is good at, focus on things he can do in a domain that matters, work hard, and bring it into the world. Chris loves innovation and creating breakthrough moments and gets excited to create value that other people can build on to help move the world forward.

Lisa Feldman Barrett, a neuroscientist, psychologist, and author, believes there are many meanings of life which can even be different ones on different days.[53] The meaning of life is a population of instances. She feels that sometimes the meaning of life for her is to understand and to make meaning; sometimes it is to leave the world slightly a bit better; sometimes it is to clear the path for her children or students; and sometimes it is just getting immersed in the moment of experiencing the wonder about the physical world - the sunset, the sky, or life. Michael Malice, a political thinker, podcaster, and author, sees the meaning of life as this wonderful opportunity to do something amazing.[54] He illustrates this by saying that life is like going to a countryside and seeing a blank canvas on an easel. One kind of mentality is being annoyed by the blank canvas and complains about it, whereas the other type sees it as a great opportunity within this beautiful setting to have the entire canvas to paint without any constraints. Michael sees himself as the second type of person. When you are young you think life is like driving a car, but then you start realizing that living life is more like a surfer where you only control this little board, and you have no idea where the waves will take you. Sometimes you are going to fall down and swallow some salt water but at a certain point you are going to stop trying to drive and say this is awesome even if you have no idea where it is going to go.

Joe Rogan, a comedian, Ultimate Fighting Championship commentator, and the host of the Joe Rogan Experience, mentioned to Lex Fridman that there are many meanings of life and that life can be navigated to be enjoyable.[55] One of the key things it requires is love which means that you need to have loved ones, family, and friends. He thinks that it is of primary importance to have people that care about you and you have to care about them. Then it also requires interests and things that stimulate you and that you are passionate about. Joe reckons that there are far too many people that are sucked into just doing a job, putting in their time and then going home but not having a passion for what they are doing. He thinks that this is a recipe for a boring and unfulfilling life. He also mentions that even people with just a subsistence lifestyle that believe and practice this lifestyle of living off the land through hunting, fishing, and living in the woods, to also seem very happy. As there is a direct connection between their actions and their sustenance, they are connected to nature which is very satisfying for them. Joe is also interested in helping people and likes to make them feel good and do things that show that he cares about them. He wants his family and friends to feel good. He likes to spread positive energy, joy and happiness and relay all the things that he has learned and good advice that he has been given. He is happy if that can benefit people and improve the quality of their life and their success or relationships. That means a lot to him. Joe also stresses the importance of the way we interact with one another. If people upset you or there is negative energy coming to you from individuals or groups of people, you feel it and it has an impact on your psyche, wellness, and physical being. The more you receive and spread love, the more you create this butterfly effect spreading outward in treating people better with kindness and generosity. You might be extremely successful in your job, but still be in a position where everybody hates you, which causes you in turn to be miserable, alone, angry, depressed, and sad. Joe mentions that if you hear about rich and famous people that commit suicide, he thinks that they have missed the mark and have put too many eggs in one basket - say the financial basket, the success basket, or the accomplishment basket and not enough in the friendship and love basket. To be happy, there needs to be a balance in how you organize your buckets in life.

For François Chollet, an AI researcher at Google, one of the answers to the meaning of life starts with understanding that everything that makes up who we are, even your most personal thoughts, are not your own.[56] Our understanding is expressed in words which we did not invent, built on concepts and images that you did not invent. We are very much cultural beings which makes us different to animals. He thinks that everything about us is an echo of the past, an echo of people that lived before us. Similarly, if we managed to contribute something to culture, which can be a new idea, a beautiful piece of music or art, a grand theory, or new words, that will also become a part of culture and contribute to future humans for as long as our species exist. Francois has the opinion that everything we do creates ripples into the future and is effectively in a way our path to immortality. As we contribute things to culture, culture in turn becomes future humans and we keep influencing people thousands of years from now. Our actions today create ripples. These ripples sum up the meaning of life in the same way we are the sum of the many different ripples that came from our past. We should be kind to others during our time on earth because every act of kindness causes ripples and in reverse every act of violence also creates ripples. That is why one needs to carefully choose which kind of ripples you want to create and propagate into the future.

When considering the meaning of life, Sheldon Solomon, a social psychologist, a philosopher, co-developer of Terror Management Theory and co-author of *The Worm at the Core*, believes the first responsibility is to take care of yourself and then to take care of other people.[57] For him to be kind and descent is paramount and to see these qualities in his children means a lot to him. Sheldon thinks that although education is tremendously important, intelligence is vastly overrated. He would like to be known as somebody that takes himself too seriously to take himself too seriously and to leave the world a slightly better place or at least do no harm. For Sergey Levine, a professor at Berkeley and an AI researcher in deep learning, reinforcement learning, robotics, and computer vision, one thing that does give meaning or at least some degree of satisfaction is to work on a problem that really matters.[58] It is less important to actually solve the problem but quite nice to spend time on things that he believes really matter. He tries very hard to look for that. Sergey would love to build a machine that can run up against the ceiling of the complexity of the universe. David Patterson, a Turing award winner and professor of computer science at Berkeley, values relationships with the people which includes those that you work with, that you influence, and that you can help. He thinks that those things that affect people are more important than all the work-related stuff that is more transitory.[59]

AI researcher Ben Goertzel thinks that the meaning of life boils down to three basic values which are joy, growth, and choice. He sees joy as the basis of everything and is unsatisfied with a joy that is static and does not progress. So, we need growth. Ben also likes the idea of individuality where a person has some agency and can make choices. According to him, for humans to get the most joy, growth and choice, we should go beyond the current human form and follow the transhumanism route. He reckons that as joy, growth and choice cannot be maximized in our human bodies, other configurations of matter can manifest even greater amounts of joy, growth, and choice than humans do. Maybe even find ways of going beyond the realm of matter as we understand it right now. From a practical perspective, Ben has the opinion that much of the meaning of life is to create something better than humans and go beyond human life. That said, the meaning of life for him is also to enjoy every day human social existence with his kids, grandchildren, parents, family, and many friends. Enjoying nature and the pleasant moments are all part of the meaning of life. He just feels that the growth and choice aspects are severely limited by our human biology, in particular the fact that we die inhibits our potential for personal growth considerably.

In discussing artificial consciousness and the nature of reality with Lex Fridman, Joscha Bach, who is the VP of Research at the AI Foundation and previously a researcher at MIT and Harvard, thinks that happiness is "a cookie that your brain bakes for itself".[60] He believes that happiness is not made by the environment and that the environment cannot make you happy. It is your appraisal of the environment that makes you happy. If you can change your appraisal of the environment which is something that one can learn to do, you can create arbitrary states of happiness. He observes that some meditators fall into this trap. They discover this basement room in their minds where the cookies are made, and they indulge in stuff themselves and after a few months it gets really old and then the big crisis of meaning comes. Because they thought that the result of their unhappiness was that they were not happy enough, they try to fix this by training their brain to release the neurotransmitters at will and then the crisis of meaning pops up at a deeper layer. However, according to him, the problem that they could not solve in the first place is how can I live, how can I make a sustainable civilization that is meaningful to me, and how can I insert myself into this. In addressing the meaning of life, Joscha recommends that we look at what the cell is. Life is the cell which is the organizing thing that can participate in evolution. In order to make the cell work as a molecular machine, it needs a self-replicator (that produces copies of itself), a negative entropy extractor (that feeds on free energy at a constant temperature and pressure to help life decrease or keep constant its entropy) and a Turing machine (that can simulate an algorithm's logic).[61] If any of these parts are missing you don't have a cell and the thing is not living. Joscha describes life as basically the emerging complexity over this principle. Once you have this intelligent supermolecule, the cell, there is very little that you cannot make it do. He thinks it is probably the optimal computer for a human, especially in terms of resilience. The cell's durability is demonstrated through how difficult it would be to sterilize the earth once it has been infected with life. Joscha sees us humans as just an expression of the cell at a certain level of complexity in the organization of cells. In a way it is tempting to think of the cell as a von Neuman probe (a spacecraft capable of replicating itself). He thinks that one of the best possible ways to build intelligence on another planet is to infect it with cells and wait long enough to give it a reasonable chance to evolve into an information processing principle that is general enough to become sentient. It is interesting to note that biological systems are designed from the inside out as opposed to technical design that works from the outside inwards. With life, seed becomes a seedling by taking some of the relatively unorganized matter around it and turning it into its own structure, thereby subduing the environment. Cells can cooperate if they can rely on other cells that have a similar organization that is already compatible. But unless it is there, the cell needs to divide to create that structure by itself. It is a self-organizing principle that works on a somewhat chaotic environment and the purpose of life in this sense is to produce complexity. He sees complexity as allowing you to harvest negative entropy gradients that you could not harvest without the complexity. In this sense intelligence and life are very strongly connected because the purpose of intelligence is to allow control under the conditions of complexity. So, life is effectively shifting the boundary between the ordered systems into the realm of chaos. As this is what life is doing, Joscha believes that there is not necessarily a deeper meaning. The only meaning is that which we have priors for and reward for. He reckons that outside the priors there is no meaning and that meaning only exists if a mind projects it. That is probably civilization. What feels most meaningful to Joscha is to try and build and maintain a sustainable civilization as this is the higher being that we are part of. It is the thing that we have a similar relationship as the cell to our body. We have this prior because we have evolved to organize in these structures. He sees the Christian God in its natural form as a platonic form of civilization where you ideally interact with others not based on your incentives, but what you think is right.[62]

In Lex Fridman's discussion with renowned neuroscientist Karl Friston about neuroscience and the free energy principle, Karl uses this principle to help contextualize his answer for the meaning of life.[63] As the states of a system can typically be described by internal and external states that are separated by sensory and active states, the free energy principle says that living or non-living systems minimize a free energy function of their internal states which requires beliefs about external states in their environment.[64] When applied to action and perception in the human brain where the active and internal states minimize a free energy function of sensory states, the result is internal brain states that correspond to perception whereas the active states or actions are linking internal brain states to external states of the environment. The human brain system can thus be seen to act as an inference engine that continuously corrects its model of the world through maximizing model evidence or minimizing the difference (which can be described as "surprise") between its model of the world and its sense and associated perception.[65] Human brain systems can also minimize the free energy of the system by actively changing the world into the expected state that it is modeling. Considering the meaning of life from this perspective, Karl indicates that we are searching for information and resolving uncertainty about the kind of thing that we are. Each one of us has certain beliefs about the kind of creature or person you are. All that self-evidencing or minimizing free energy in an active and embodied way means that you are fulfilling the beliefs about what kind of thing you are. He mentions that we are all given those scripts or narratives at a very early age, usually initially in the form of bedtime or fairytale stories, that has been encultured by your immediate family and the culture that you grow up with and that you also create for yourself through active inference and self-evidencing. Karl states that not only is each one of us modeling our own environment, conditioning, and the external states out there, but we are actively changing them all the time. There is also a synchronistic occurrence as we are not only doing this back to ourselves but also together as a civilization which means that each one of us is creating our own culture at different timescales.[66]

Dawn Song, a professor of computer science at UC Berkeley, has considered many external factors and voices as well as internal views on the meaning of life and concludes that each one of us needs to find our own meaning in life.[67] She mentions that you have the freedom to define it. Dawn also asks what does it really mean and does the question make sense? She thinks that meaning can be deeper or shallower than just happiness. Most people are not thinking about this question and the meaning of life does not matter to them that much. It is an open question if knowing the meaning of life is helping your life to be better or you to be happier. As life is a collection of moments, some people just want to experience life to the fullest and fill those moments with the richest possible experiences. Dawn recommends that separate from just experiences, we should try to grow every day and try to be a better self within an evolving civilization. Ilya Sutskever, a deep learning expert and co-founder of OpenAI, feels that it is amazing that we exist and that we should try to make the most of it and maximize our own value and enjoyment whilst reducing our suffering during the very short time that we have available.[68] Humans want things, and our wants are our individual objective functions which we can update. Although there is an evolutionary objective function which is to procreate and let your children succeed, our individual happiness comes from the way you look at things, define and drive our individual objective functions. For Daphne Koller, a professor of computer science at Stanford University, we should use our lives to leave the world a better place and even more so when you are in a privileged position to impact and give back.[69] For Jack Dorsey, the CEO of Twitter and Square, the meaning of life consists of many things which include being aware of just being alive; having a connection with people - having long lasting friendships and family is meaningful; and seeing things he has helped to build that other people use are meaningful and powerful.[70] In Jack's mind it ultimately comes down to a sense of connection, a realization that I am part of a thing that is bigger than myself and feeling it directly in small ways or large ways. He reckons that humanity has taken too long to realize our connectedness and that we have been hiding our connectivity in various ways, but we should now change that. Dmitry Korkin, a professor of bioinformatics and computational biology at Worcester Polytechnic Institute, hopes that what he and other scientists do are useful and states that human life is fragile and that we need to bond together as a society.[71]

In addressing the question, Stephen Wolfram, CEO at Wolfram Research, explains that he does things that he finds fulfilling to do and that he cannot justify everything he does based on a broader context of the meaning of life.[72] Some things that he finds fulfilling are small whereas others are bigger in nature. It also varies during stages of life. Things that he was not interested in earlier on in life are now interesting. In terms of justifying things in some larger global sense, he can describe why it might be important in the world, but his local reason for doing it is that he finds it personally fulfilling. Stephen concludes that he cannot find a ground truth for his life or for civilization. Richard Dawkins, an evolutionary biologist, believes that from a scientific perspective the meaning of life is the propagation of DNA, but from a personal point of view that is not what he feels is the meaning of his life.[73] He thinks that we each make our own meaning. We set up goals that we want to achieve by our brains that have got goal-seeking machinery built into them. These higher-level goals can be noble goals or even spiritual goals which are very different to the biological goals of propagating DNA.

David Silver, who leads the reinforcement learning research group at DeepMind, believes that the meaning of life is multifaceted and can be viewed from many perspectives and layers.[74] If we start by asking if the universe has a purpose, it looks like on one level it just follows certain mechanical laws of physics and that leads to the development of the universe. But on another level, you can view it through the lens of the second law of thermodynamics that says the universe is increasing in entropy forever and that the goal of the universe is to maximize entropy. So, there are multiple levels that you can understand the system. On another level if the goal is to maximize entropy, how can it be done by a particular system. Evolution is maybe something that the universe discovered in order to dissipate energy as efficiently as possible. But if you can think of evolution as a method for dispersing energy in the universe, then evolution becomes a goal. What is evolution then? It has got its own goal which is to reproduce as effectively as possible. How is reproduction made as effective as possible? You need entities within the evolutionary process that can survive and reproduce as effectively as possible. So, it is natural that in order to achieve that higher-level goal, those individual organisms discover brains or intelligences that enable them to support the goals of evolution. And those brains, what do they do? Perhaps the early brains were controlling some things at a direct level, maybe the equivalent of pre-programmed systems that was controlling what was going on and setting certain things in order to achieve these particular goals. That led to another level of discovery which was learning systems or brains being able to learn for themselves and learn how to program themselves to achieve any goal. Presumably, there are parts of the brain where goals are set to parts of that system and provides this very flexible notion of intelligence that we as humans presumably have which is the ability to achieve any goal that we think possible to achieve. David considers this as a long way to say that there are many perspectives and many levels in which meaning, goals and intelligence can be understood. On each of those levels you can have multiple perspectives. You can view the system as optimizing for a goal, understand it at a level we can maybe understand it and implement it from an AI perspective, or you can understand it on a level of a mechanistic perspective. These perspectives are not in contrast with one another, and the outcome of that system is not in contradiction with the fact that it is also a decision-making system that is optimizing for some goal and purpose. At the next level we can ask how our learning brains can achieve their goals more effectively? This can be achieved by us as learning beings building systems that can solve our goals more effectively than we can. A new layer has been created by having systems that can create goals for themselves. Ultimately there may be layers beyond where they set subgoals to parts of their own system in order to achieve those goals, and so on. As David indicates, the story of meaning and intelligence can indeed be one of many perspectives and layers.

Simon Sinek, an author of books such as *Start With Why*, *Leaders Eat Last*, and *The Infinite Game*, addresses the meaning of life as an infinite game.[75] He starts out referencing James Carse's *Finite and Infinite Games: A Vision of Life as Play and Possibility* that describes two kinds of games, where the one could be called finite, the other infinite.[76] A finite game is played for the purpose of winning, an infinite game for the purpose of continuing the play. If a finite game is to be won by someone, it must come to a definite end. It will come to an end when someone has won. This has also challenged the viewpoints of Simon and others about how the world works. We all think about winning, being the best and number one. That can only happen in a finite game with fixed rules and objectives and known players. There is a beginning, middle and an end and there have to be losers. Infinite games have known and unknown players. Anyone can join. It has changeable rules. You can play how you want. The objective is to perpetuate the game. Stay in the games as long as possible. There is no such thing as a winner or being number one. There is no finish line. When we try to win in a game with no finish line, we are trying to be the best in a game with no agreed upon objectives, metrics, or timeframes. There are a few consistent and predictable outcomes - the decline in trust, cooperation, and innovation. Many of the ways we run our organizations is with a finite mindset. If you think about our tombstones - they have the date that you were born and the date when you died. But really it is about what you do with the dash - the time in between. There is a poem by Linda Ellis called The Dash that starts with *"I read of a man who stood to speak, At the funeral of a friend. He referred to the dates on her tombstone, From beginning to the end. He noted that first came the date of her birth, And spoke of the following date with tears, But he said what mattered most of all was the dash between those years."*[77] What gives our lives meaning is what we do with the dash. If we live our life with a finite mindset which means to accumulate more money and power than anyone else, to outdo everyone else, to be number one, to be the best, we do not take any of this with us. We just die. The people get remembered the way we are remembered is what kind of people we were. Devoted mother, loving father, the person we were to other people. Do we want to be remembered for our contributions or detractions? The legacy that most of us would like to have is to live a life of service, see those around us rise, to contribute to our communities, to our organizations, to leave them in better shape than we found them. In the infinite game one can, be driven by a cause, purpose, or vision that is bigger than oneself and where one's work ethic contributes to something larger than oneself. That is what drives Simon every day. He says that he wakes up every morning with a vision of a world that does not yet exist where the vast majority of people in the world wake up every morning feeling inspired, feel safe at work and feel fulfilled at the end of the day. Simon is driven by the fact that this is not the world we live in and that we still have work to do. As he knows what his underlying values are, Simon wakes to inspire people to do the things that inspire them. These are his gotos or touchpoints. It inspires him to keep working. He thinks of a career as like an iceberg. If you have a vision for something, you are the only one that can see the iceberg underneath the ocean. If you start working at it, a little bit shows up, and now a few other people can start to see what you are imagining and are then willing to help you. Then you start seeing a bigger part of the iceberg and people say you have accomplished so much, but what he sees is all the work that still needs to be done. Simon still sees the huge iceberg underneath the ocean. What drives him is bringing more of the iceberg from the unknown to the known, bringing more of the vision from the imagination to reality.[78]

Problematic Trajectory of Our Current Civilization in the Smart Technology Era

Of the many well informed and thoroughly researched perspectives about the state of our civilization and our current trajectory, I found the one presented by Daniel Schmachtenberger to be not only thoughtful and insightful, but one that we should pay attention to even though I do not agree with every aspect of this. Daniel's core interest is focused on long term civilization design and more specifically to help us as a civilization to develop improved sensemaking and meaning-making capabilities so that we can make better quality decisions to help unlock more of our potential and higher values that we are capable of.[79] He has specifically done some work on surveying existential and catastrophic risks, advancing forecasting and mitigation strategies, synthesizing and advancing civilizational collapse and institutional decay models, as well as identifying generator functions that drive catastrophic risk scenarios and social architectures that lead to potential coordination failures. Generator functions include for example game theory related win-lose dynamics multiplied by exponential technology, damaged feedback loops, unreasonable or irrational incentives, and short term decision making incentives on issues with long term consequences.[80] He believes that categorical solutions to these generator functions would address the causes for civilization collapse and function as the key ingredients for a new and robust civilization model that will be robust in a Smart Technology Era with destabilizing decentralized exponential technology. Daniel has shared his views on the *Civilization Emerging* website and many podcasts such as *Rebel Wisdom, Modern Wisdom, The Portal, Future Thinkers, The Seeking, The Nantucket Project, Neurohacker, Tom Bilyeu, Foresight Institute, and Max Hug*.[81] In a podcast, titled *The 2050 Life Purpose Podcast – Building a New Civilization,* Daniel Schmachtenberger answers questions on his life purpose and his goals for the year 2050 which is in part paraphrased below.[82] He summarizes his main sense of purpose is helping to transition civilization being on a current path that is self-terminating to one that is not and that is supportive of the possibility of purpose and meaning for everyone enduring into the future and working on changing the underlying structural dynamics that help make that possible. What he would like to see differently within the next 30 years is that we prevent existential risks that could play out in this time frame. It is not a given that we make it to 2050. Apart from catastrophic risks that can play out over this time period, there are those that can go past a tipping point during this time frame but will inevitably play out after that time. As we do not want to experience civilization collapse or existential risk and also not have us go past tipping points, Daniel would like to see a change in the trajectory that civilization is currently on from one that is on the path of many self-terminating scenarios each with their own set of chain reactions such as AI apocalypse, world war 3, climate change human-induced migration issues leading to resource wars, collapse of biodiversity, and killer drones. More broadly some of the key categories of risk can include *human system failures* such as economics, government, infrastructure, emergency services, and communications; *violence* such as war and terrorism; *exponential technology risks* such as those from AI, biotech and nanotech and exponential disinformation; *ecology risks* such as climate change, coral die off, ocean acidification, ocean dead zones, industrial and agricultural pollution, desertification, total biodiversity loss, overfishing, species extinction, keystone species loss, weather intensification, arctic methane, aquifer and freshwater depletion and toxicity, sea level rise, droughts, and ocean current changes; *human health related risks* such as mental health, toxicity, deficiency and fragility, and pandemics which could be natural, engineered or accidental byproducts of biotech; and *planetary natural disasters* or *exoplanetary events*.[83] The problem is that we have a civilization that is generating most of these scenarios at increasing speed and magnitude. As a civilization we need to switch off that path to one that is developing all of its technological capacity for omni-positive purposes in the world at large.

In a *Future Thinkers* podcast, *Singularity or Extinction? Exponential Growth is Not Forever*, Daniel explains further the problem that we are trying to fix.[84] He reckons that the current systems, the interface of these systems with each other and the net effects are unsustainable which leads to a self-terminating scenario where these systems run to their own end and then fall off some kind of cliff. When we look at growth curves of different kinds of organisms, any time we see a growth curve that has an exponential up that is not forever. Sometimes the exponential up goes logistic (meaning a sigmoidal or S-curve) and that is typically good; sometimes it drops off pretty hard before it follows a logistic path; sometimes it goes through a lot of instability; and sometimes it just drops off a cliff. As an example, the world's population was less than 500 million people for all of human history as far as we know until we got to the industrial revolution where after just 200 years, we went up to over 7 billion people and growing. That is an extreme exponential curve. Daniel makes the point that not only have we gone through this extreme exponential population curve in relation to our ability to extract resources from the planet that are not replenishing themselves (which is what the industrial revolution was) such as mining, farming, fishing, and logging, we are also taking resource reserves that took hundreds of millions or billions of years to develop and extract them at a radically fast pace - much faster than they can renew - and have a world population that is growing on that "savings account". Real problems start when we hit the end of the savings account. Not only have we been growing in population, but we have been growing in resource consumption per capita within an economy that requires year over year growth. He argues that this kind of exponential growth economy which is attached to a linear materials economy just does not work ongoingly on a finite planet and will effectively lead to a self-terminating situation. He understands why we took this route in picking so much low hanging fruit in terms of coal, oil, fish, and trees to initially help drive our economy, but states that it is just not viable anymore.[85] One counter argument for the limited resources of a finite planet can be that mining space would unlock tremendous resources (although it would likely have a dramatic impact on capitalism which amongst other things capitalizes on scarcity). There are also more sustainable ways of working with resources in a balanced way such as the development of subterranean aquaponic fish farms that if done correctly at scale could help to provide food to the planet's people or harvesting bamboo or trees in a similar fashion.

In the podcast *The 2050 Life Purpose Podcast – Building a New Civilization,* Daniel Schmachtenberger desires to see a prototype of a new full-stack model of civilization that has in its design categorically solved the generator functions of all of the catastrophic and existential risks and is a civilization model that is moving into one of increasingly quality of life and is actually more adaptive than the current civilization, so it becomes a new gravitational basin for everything to flow. So, Daniel thinks that this specifically requires new economics, new governance, new law, new jurisprudence in philosophy as a basis of law, new judiciary, new medicine, new infrastructure, new technology development processes, and a new culture with a sense of what is meaningful and purposeful. All of this after affects each other. So, what is being suggested here by him is a full stack reboot from an axiom level. He argues that if we think about all of the existential risks that the generator functions have in common that is driving all of these risks, we see things like if we have a rivalrous or win-lose game or in-group out-group dynamics where they compete and they cannot both win, then harm definitely happens from that. So, the implication is that my win requires your loss, and we are seeking harm directly and we are both extracting more resources from the environment or externalizing more harm to the environment or indirectly doing that through the harm that happens through war. It is evident that we are harming each other and harming the commons. With exponential technology which means exponentially increased capacity to affect the world through our choices to the degree that we are making choices that are directly and/or indirectly harm causing, exponential harm-causing choices, self-terminate on a finite playing field. So, for thousands of years of civilization we have killed people who had different ideas than us and who had a reasonable way of dealing with problems. We also had unsustainable agriculture that deserted areas that were previously arable. This is not a new phenomenon as desertification is a thousands-of-years phenomenon and we have had extinct species for a long time. Daniel also thinks that the existential risks that humanity face now are not different in kind but are different in magnitude and speed and driven by exponential technology, which is technology that makes it easier to make better technology and computers that help make us better computers. It seems clear that exponential technology will not be put back in the bag and is going to happen. He argues that exponential technology multiplied by rivalrous game theory self-terminates. Therefore, we must create anti-rivalrous environments that make us safe stewards of the level of power that exponential technology brings, or the human experiment completes in a meta-poetic sense. He thinks that exponential technology is bringing us to have the power of gods and that we need the love, wisdom, and prudence of gods to guide the use of that power or irresponsible use of that power would end-up self-destructing. So, the question is what does this look like? The focus is to solve the rivalrous games generator function. Daniel argues that creating an anti-rivalrous environment is clearly changing the macro-economics of having a balance sheet that mirrors the scorecard of a finite rivalrous game and requires not having in-group and out-group like nations or religions or race identification in any deep kind of sense. These are significant changes and require not having things like democracy where we make a proposition that is ill-formed. If such a proposition goes through, it benefits something and harms something else, and if it does not go through then something is protected and something else is harmed. If it goes through it could for example lead to groups of people with specific needs clustering more around one side versus the other which now creates polarization and eventually radicalization which then needs to be stabilized in war. However, we cannot keep having wars because exponentially increasing military technology becomes unwinnable. So, creating an anti-rivalrous environment is complicated. Even though humanity has not done this before, we must do something because every civilization that we ever had so far has collapsed, but now we have a fully global civilization, where the collapse is actually catastrophic. When Rome fell, it was substantial, but it was not the whole world. The same holds for the Inca, Mesopotamia, Sumerians, and other civilizations. Now we have a fully globalized supply chain economy that is also connected to the biosphere in a deep way that its collapse is actually a catastrophic collapse. Given that these systems always fell for these reasons we must do something that the world has never done before. We also have increased capacities that the world never had before, and we must realize them and then also guide the other capacities that are coming on board. So, the reason he is saying all this is because creating an anti-rivalrous environment does not only prevent existential risk, it also changes the underlying rivalry basis of humanity's whole history of fighting wars, torturing one another, damaging the environment, making philosophies with respect to the nature of duality, and creating a mix bag that humans are based on game theoretic dynamics. There is also a question about how the distribution of moral values have shifted over the centuries for humans and if it has been positive in all respects. Daniel feels that we can create a different environment that does not incentivize harm because as long as one person is incentivized to do something that is harmful to another person it cannot be prevented at scale. But we can actually change that underlying incentive and make it to where yours and mine are more tightly coupled and yours are mine and the commons are tightly coupled. In his mind, the outcome is not communism or socialism or anything that has ever been presented. It is something totally new and there are real paths to this. In the process of solving the generator function we are not only solving catastrophic risks, but also the bad human dynamics and bringing about a really radical different human being. Daniel also realizes that there will be a transitional path to such an idealized destination. For example, if we have an intentional community today that is trying to prototype some ideals, but they still need to get the computer that they have to buy from Apple which needs to get minerals that comes from conflict zones and rainforests over six continents and is made in factories where workers do not commit suicide about working and living conditions that is bad, then our village is still being supported by the tragedy of the whole rest of the thing. So according to him, we will not avoid the above type of scenario until we can get to an advanced technology closed loop civilization that does not require import and is actually more adaptive than the previous civilization. That happens at the scale of an advanced technology city-state which needs to be sovereign in law and the minimum kind of scale for self-organization that could actually produce all of our needs. So, in 2050, Daniel would like to see a fully operating city-state civilization model that is anti-rivalrous and has the right relationship between complicated and complex systems and all the other dynamics that we need. He would like to see it operating long enough and well enough that the rest of the world is already starting to move in the direction that it is setting an example of and that means also off the path of existential risk.[86] Although I think there is a lot of merit in such a city-state civilization model as well as infinite games dynamics which is part of the solutions framework that the book also recommends, I am not convinced that we can or need to completely eliminate rivalrous dynamics on certain levels within society where it does not cause harm. I will elaborate later in this chapter.

Daniel expands further on this city-state civilization that he envisions by affirming that the generator functions with their many different expressions must be solved at that level otherwise we do not really move or change the future possibilities. We need to articulate that solutions at a generator function level are not only necessary for civilization making but also sufficient. We then need to develop architectures for viable solutions that entails an economic system, a governance system, and a legal system that avoid these problematic generator functions and generate fundamentally different behaviors. So, a city-state civilization needs to understand the nature of the problem well enough to categorize the design criteria of the solution and then start to develop actual instantiations of solutions that meet those design criteria. Next is starting to prototype governance methods that they have developed to see if they do what they think they will do and refine them. For a city-state civilization to operate smoothly, Daniel expects that people will also need to be trained on how to administer it, run its new type of economic system, and govern it with different roles than what we are used to in the current civilization setup where we have politicians, lawyers, judges, and bankers. So, he pictures a whole new civics, new things that people need to be trained on and a new process of technology design for how to do technology that does not produce toxicity issues and externality. This means that we need a lot of people working on components of this, getting trained on those components who would then be able to build the city-state at scale and populate it to begin with. There is deep enough training that will have to happen in immersive environments which means that communities, villages, places where people are actually together working on training in these new skills and capacities that will then be able to boot the city-state. However, it will initially not be a closed loop and still require getting onto an airplane to fly somewhere or buy a computer from Apple, but they will be developing some of the capacities necessary to build a civilization without those dependencies in the long term. So, Daniel recommends working on a full articulation and description of the design criteria that are necessary so that other people can also play with those ideas and see if those design criteria make sense to them. If they agree with their analysis and work on those things independently, they can start to instantiate those ideas to evolve it towards a full-scale prototype and then spread that prototype. The prototype does not only have to solve the generator functions, but also must be antifragile in the presence of the fact that the rest of the world is still rivalrous. He states that this new system also must be autopoietic which means that it should be able to reproduce, maintain, expand and propagate itself which are all part of the design criteria. As everything needs to be built from scratch, he thinks it a good thing to have many different groups of people working on various areas such as coral reef issues, carbon sequestration issues, or AI risk issues as long as they have a path to make meaningful progress. The assumption is that many people are working on many important things that are part of the same project on a meta level that brings the current trajectory of civilization to a better trajectory. While those big projects are happening, we should still continue with essential tasks such as raising our children, taking care of the elderly, and growing food. It is important for as many people as possible to understand the problem and solution space that we are operating in.[87]

Daniel also takes the position that we will not survive as a civilization if we do not fix our individual and collective sensemaking.[88] We know from history that every empire breaks down at some point in time. From his perspective we are now in a fully globalized system that is in the process of breakdown. When all the previous systems broke down, they were all localized. He thinks that our current civilization will not continue to just influence the world in a positive direction and is decaying into just less function and irrelevance or possibly into a reboot. For the latter, a cultural prerequisite is necessary where everyone recognizes that collective choice making must be based on collective sensemaking. This means that we need to really invest in doubling down not only on our own biases, but also our capacity to be good at making sense of things, to understand why people are thinking the things that they do, and to communicate well so that we can coordinate. It is clearly not easy to fix collective sensemaking and we have more work to do to figure this out. It is imperative that we need more collective intelligence working on various aspects of the collective sensemaking solution. This implies that we need more people to understand how much this affects most of the other problems that we are concerned about, how it is upstream to those problems, and what factors are contributing to it. When we consider the commons, we think of the shared aspect of the world that is both a resource that we have access to but also one that we need to take care of. Daniel makes the point that the same holds for the information commons which should be the space of information out there about what is true that informs our capacity to make choices. However, what we actually see is an information commons that looks like a smokestack bellowing pollution into the air as most of what is being put into the information commons is pollution. If there are large groups of people that one only has derogatory strawman versions of where one cannot explain why they think what they think without making them dumb or bad, one should be doubtful of one's own modeling. To fix this Daniel recommends absorbing the news that they are taking in for a day or a week and try to ascertain what the real issues are that they are facing as human beings if one really puts oneself in their shoes. The reason for doing this is not to just empathize with them, but to determine if there is some actual signal that one might be missing. Most of the positions at the moment seem to have some signals and lots of noise. In order for us to synthesize the signals across the space, we would need to seek to understand other human beings with whom we are coordinating and get the relevant parts of their signal as we try to separate the signals from the noise. Daniel makes the claim that if you feel a combination of being scared, outraged, or emotional and very certain about a strong kind of enemy hypothesis orientation, it is likely that you have been captured by somebody's narrative warfare and you think it is your own thinking. He believes that even if you win at a local battle, whatever social, information or other technologies that you use to win, the other side will reverse engineer and come back and just escalate an "arms race". So, we are in this case not really moving towards real shared sensemaking and coordination. This does not mean that you never take a position. It means that you are trying to take a position that is not just continuing warfare but trying to elevate the whole space which requires for me to understand the whole space better. For any particular issue there might be multiple narrative clusters each containing many different narrative versions. What Daniel typically does is to first take a landscape of what the narrative clusters are and then try to steelman each narrative, like what is the strongest version of arguing that thing that he is able to see. One thing that he does is to look for the best thinkers that are representative of those narratives. In addition to reading across the space, he also recommends to truly seek the most well-grounded and complex views as opposed to the more trending ones. He wants to find the thinkers that seem most earnest and most well educated and thoughtful across the space and then look for people that have deep expertise and earnestness and disagree with them in order to explore the basis of the disagreement. He encourages people to seek to understand the narrative landscape better on their own, to seek empiricism better, to attempt to not object or take entire narratives but be able to look for partial truths, to try and aggregate signals across the space, and to be way more comfortable with uncertainty even though it can be uncomfortable.[89]

For any well-functioning and effective democratic society, it is essential for as many citizens as possible to have high quality sensemaking and discourse. US president Thomas Jefferson was very aware of this when he said "if a nation expects to be ignorant and free in a state of civilization, it expects what never was and never will be".[90] In order to help accelerate a cultural movement toward much improved sensemaking and conversation, Daniel Schmachtenberger and others have recently founded the Consilience Project which is a non-profit media organization that has as a goal to assist with the repairing and rebuilding the health of the information commons "by helping educate people on how to improve their information processing so they can better detect media bias and disinformation while becoming more capable sense-makers and citizens".[91] This would also help to reduce tribalism and divergence and help people to have more effective collaboration in solving problems based on a higher standard of public sense-making and civilized conversation with integrity and good intentions. Wikipedia defines consilience as the principle that "evidence from independent, unrelated sources can converge on strong conclusions" and that when one have many sources of evidence that are in agreement, the conclusion can be very convincing even though the individual sources of evidence might not have a strong conclusion on their own.[92] The project itself brings together a new approach to establishing news and educational resources for public information through a content strategy and a movement catalyzing strategy. The content strategy involves a new form of news that optimizes for accuracy and bias correction, a type of meta-news sense-making about what is going on within the media landscape, and education in crucial sense-making skills, media literacy and civics. The movement catalyzing strategy entails sense-making forums, curated resources, and innovation prizes for well-defined public sensemaking and discourse related projects.[93]

The University of Oxford, supported by Templeton World Charity Foundation, has produced a report *Citizenship in a Networked Age - An Agenda for Rebuilding Our Civic Ideal* to help the discourse about citizens' moral decision-making and what it means to be a good citizen in the digital AI-driven networked age or smart technology era.[94] The authors Dominic Burbidge, Andrew Briggs and Michael Reiss have made seven main recommendations in this regard that require strong collaboration between stakeholders such as government, industry and citizens. These recommendations include identifying and protecting the uniqueness of humans with respect to moral decision-making, cultivating and developing the complementary skills of humans and machines for collective decision-making, working towards collective agreement about civic ideals for the AI-driven networked age, teaching how to improve listening as a civic virtue, helping us to think before we speak or instantly respond, promoting the value of privacy for personal moral development, and revaluing and appreciating democracy with respect to its ability to help create social unity and trust.[95] They advocate that AI and other smart technology should be in service of human moral-decision making and human judgment of the moral whole, where the moral whole of the human community plays a key role in forming a sense of the common good, meaning and purpose. We need to keep in mind that our consciousness, our mortality constraints, and self-awareness of our mortality makes us radically different to machines with respect to goals and moral decision-making capability on an individual and society level where participation in decision-making is a key privilege and a responsibility to our collective citizenship. They observe how the character of citizenship is changing in the smart technology era with AI-driven networking technology changing how people interact and impacting the relationship between the individual and society. We are seeing how AI-driven applications such as search optimization and classification are evolving into respectively influence optimization and learning to decide and optimize. We therefore must be wise in how we use technology to help us make better decisions in support of improving good citizenship, aid our new kinds of communities and institutions that are being formed, deal with citizen privacy in a special manner that protects what is important and significant to a person, and support democratic decision-making that seek consensus in the context of distinctive and often opposing interests.

Analyzing more Issues and Ideas for Reshaping our Civilization for Beneficial Outcomes

In this section, I am examining some more perspectives on some of the main civilization issues and highlighting some further ideas to help reshape our civilization for the better. All of humanity today constitutes a single civilization. We may have conflicts, but every civilization and family does too.[96] Globally, we understand the basics of politics, economics, and science in the same way. We may argue what the right way is, but we are all a part of the same conversation. In this way we know some of the key problems that we face together such as nuclear war, climate change and technological disruption – the last of which is the most mysterious threat and thus seems the most threatening because of its uncertainty. One is the rise of the global useless class and one is the collapse of liberal democracy.[97] We have a third issue to consider and that is: If we do not do something about this, considering that evolution is based on survival of the most adaptive, could humankind split?[98] Those who are adaptive will survive and be the humans of the future - a new species altogether, and everyone else will go in a different direction? Both Yuval Harari and Thomas Friedman draw our attention to the problems and challenges we face, so that we can now do something about it. What will be in their place? How can we direct it? On the other hand, there's real skepticism about the pace of development. Whilst some see this as moving too fast to catch a breath, others call it the era of stagnation.

Eric Weinstein and Peter Thiel talk about the era of stagnation as starting from the 1970's except for the world of bits and Silicon Valley.[99] We have been exceptionally slow in terms of the atom and we should be far further than we should be. There are various dimensions where we could be advancing but we have chosen not to.[100] There is simply too much knowledge for us to be able to understand all of it and bring it all together. Research is highly specialized, and specialization makes it much harder to get a handle on all the other areas of research that could be quite important to move forward in our own research.[101] We have had great expectations of growth and we are not living up to them. Peter Thiel and Eric Weinstein feel that we are not being honest about our actual rate of growth or about the stability or positivity of organisations and institutions. All the things we have been waiting for are further away than we expected, and the start-up momentum is falling.[102] Is it important to understand what is real and what is not? And what has been oversold? If we are considering our actual landscape, then we should actually know what we are dealing with? The idea of a *College Equivalency Degree* is posed as something that should be enough to prove that we have the knowledge to perform a task.[103] Certain kinds of knowledge have become so prestigious and exclusive without much meaning or even practical value. Eric Weinstein also discusses a further complication of ideas being suppressed by protecting academic, media, economic, government and other institutions from individuals or groups of people who might have valid and reasonable ideas that do not fit into the mainstream institutional narratives and possibly highly disruptive to an institutional order. He refers to this as a *Distributed Idea Suppression Complex* (DISC) which consists of a decentralized and distributed collection of different emergent structures that not only suppresses ideas but has led to lack of meaningful progress in some areas, significant income inequality and social unrest.[104] The democratization of AI, smart technology, science, and knowledge in general can help to address some of these problems. AI-driven solutions can for example help us with collective sensemaking, having smarter information filters, being open to other ideas and opinions, and offer excellent education to everyone without the burden of debt and without geographic restrictions. Peter Thiel as a contrarian believes that we should also be worried about the lack of automation. With more automation we could get to 3-4% GDP growth and with that solve social problems.[105] This is therefore something governments should be seriously investing in.

The global economy is not as we would like to believe it is. It is in crisis. As much as we may like to keep focusing our attention on more easily fixable, smaller matters, we can no longer ignore the common denominator that sustains and deteriorates our current state. We have almost exhausted our natural resources, productivity is declining, growth is slow, unemployment is rising, and inequality is deepening. We need to consider the efficacy or sustainability of our current economic models and find more stable social and economic solutions. Social and economic theorist Jeremy Rifkin suggests a new economic system - the Radical New Sharing Economy.[106] Rifkin argues that with climate change ravaging the planet at devastating speeds, we need to act fast. "Change of this magnitude requires political will and a profound ideological shift".[107] Frightening as this may sound. Rifkin is not wrong. His solution is however, just one solution in a sea of many. In short, the Radical New Sharing Economy proposes a decentralized global system that relies on the convergence of three technologies: ultra-fast 5G communication internet, renewable energy internet, and driverless mobility internet, all connected through IoT and embedded across society and the environment. When we evaluate well-being on an aggregate level (welfare economics), we are looking to describe and predict what affects levels of well-being. Of course, we are interested in how technology adoption will affect our wellbeing and the implications that it might have on economics and society. Fear is of course detrimental to well-being and fear is also rather prominent in the age of acceleration, smart technology, globalization, automation, and any other name we want to give it. It is all part of the Smart Technology Era.

With regards to economic growth and the current state of capitalism, Yuval Harari points out that "the credo of 'more stuff' urges individuals, firms and governments to disregard anything that might hamper economic growth, such as preserving social equality, ensuring ecological harmony and honoring one's parents".[108] On the other hand capitalism encourages people to stop seeing the world in a way where someone else's profit is our loss "and instead see it as a win-win situation, in which your profit is also my profit" – something that contributes to global harmony.[109] An important question to ask is if our current capitalism is working for us? The answer seems obviously no. Rising inequalities in means, access, knowledge, basic rights, and knowledge makes it somewhat obvious that our current state is not working for us. So, what can a future look like that promotes fairness for all. We need to reimagine and reinvent capitalism - something already working well for some, but to find a way to make it work better for everyone. The wealth gap accompanied by an opportunity gap and values gap, made more obvious by globalization means that our current social, economic and political systems cannot go on for much longer.[110] In this, the highest priority is addressing the state of the average worker and those who are not lucky enough to be considered the average worker.[111] We perceive that we live in a capitalist society, but capitalism is by nature (whilst maybe just in theory) competitive, where people are competing in the same society, all of whom have the right and opportunity to participate and contribute to the economy. But this competitive capitalism which was the dream capitalism was based upon does not exist. Our market in modern time, even more so in the 21st century is a market of monopolies.[112] Up until the 1970s, the middle class has been growing and benefiting from capitalism in their ability to compete in the market with as little as a high school education - to buy cars and homes and live relatively fruitful lives.

We saw capitalism collapse for the first time in 1929. From there, fascism, nazism, communism, war and social unrest rose.[113] The same thing happened in 2008, after capitalism had rebuilt in post war years. We are still seeing the effects of that, with more and more people being sidelined from the economy that the 1970s allowed them to be a part of.[114] What we need now is an alternative to capitalism. One that is intentional, lasting and aims to solve a common solution to a common problem.[115] To do this we need to build hope in place of populist reactions that rise in defiance to the current states of most people. Economist, academic, philosopher and politician Yanis Varoufakis, believes that we are not going to build a world worth having by building wars and buying weapons.[116] In fact, we must be committed to minimize human suffering. If that means reinventing capitalism or finding an alternative, then these are the solutions we must explore. The proposed DiEM25 aims to remove borders for an inclusive Europe. The borders that the EU defines should not matter, because the movement exists to not be defined or confined by any reigning social, political, or economic foundations, rules or policies which are simply not working for most people.[117]

Let us take a brief look at what the DiEM25 is, why it was founded and what it aims to achieve. Commonly described as a "Star Trek world where a type of communism (not the communism you know, so please ignore whatever feelings this ignites) reigns outside of the hands of the state and within the hands of people", DiEM25 promotes the ability of each person to own a percentage in the shares of organisations, whose current riches are part of the growing inequality and unrest in the rest of the world, but are simultaneously tied into the very people being economically left behind for their income and success. It is simply impossible to keep up. Sounds complicated? Let us use Varoufakis' example of Google. The more people who use Google, or any other application for that matter, the more valuable it becomes. The more data it has, the more people use it, and the more people are projected to use it. Each new user means more money today and more projected money for the future. This is known as Metcalfe's law (which states that the value or utility of a network is proportional to the number of users of the network).[118] The DiEM25's neoliberalist view or reimagined capitalism says that because Google is so reliant on the average citizen to create value, the average citizen is entitled to a share of the business that his/her use of the product affects the value. Google Maps relies on each citizen's use of Google on a mobile phone to know how full the roads are and then advise other routes.[119] This is just one example of the top technology companies' value being heavily reliant on its users. The point is that some of the richest companies in the world are only rich because of either how many people use them or the data that they can generate to give their product use and, in turn, value. Bear in mind this is not just today's value that we are talking about, but according to Metcalfe's Law, if the number of network users is at 100 000, merely adding one more user follows that 100 000 more users are to come. The more users there are, the more value the network has and then, the more money it has.[120] So each user's value to Google, Facebook, Instagram, WhatsApp, Microsoft, IBM etc. is worth a lot more to the companies than one more user. What this means for Facebook, who owns Instagram and WhatsApp is every time they have one new user, they have the potential to make millions, if not billions more. Here lies the very core of DiEM25. Since we are all integral parts of not only the usefulness, but value and capital growth of these organisations, we are really more like employees than users. We are not just using the products; our data is adding usefulness and value to other people and to the organizations themselves. Thus, we should be remunerated like employees with shares in their profits.

As there are simply not enough jobs and even more so with globalization, AI-driven applications can help ensure that every person has an income that allows them to meaningfully take care of themselves and their families. Relying on the state for tax money to support the most extremely excluded and downtrodden is simply not working, especially since these numbers are growing every day. We need to consider other systems and states of being that aim to eradicate human suffering while still promoting innovation, inclusion and contribution to society and the economy. What would we say of citizens, mostly situated in Africa and Asia, who do not have access to a smart phone or any other personal technology and are not participating in the digital economy, digital data and involved in the profits of the reigning technologies? This goes to our previous argument for using smart technology to leapfrog socio-economic inclusion and generally include more people in the information revolution and globalization. Access to the internet and a smartphone is vital to being able to access basic services such as doctor's consultants, medication, products, food knowledge and education (formal and informal). As a starting point, through ensuring each citizen not only has access to affordable (or free) smartphones and internet but is educated in the use of these devices and how they may access the items mentioned above, we are including everyone on the globe in the benefits and new ways technology can improve our lives. We would also need to ensure that the services promised on the other ends of our smartphones exist. For example, we use drone technology and GPS tracking to deliver the necessary medicine to a person who has had a virtual appointment or even an AI-powered doctor's appointment, received a diagnosis (in cases where hospital or in-person escalation has not been recommended) and received a prescription for, say, cholera medication. Services such as these are far more beneficial for residents of remote villages than they are for city dwellers, as they are far more beneficial for those without access to private healthcare than those with access. They remove the need for a long walk and two or three forms of public transport (if there is access to this) just to get to see a doctor. Once they arrive at the clinic, there is no guarantee that they will even get to a doctor that day. If they do manage to see a doctor approximately 5 hours after arrival, there is no guarantee that the medicine they need will be in stock. If it is not, they may be asked to return in a week - another long trip with still no guarantee that they will receive the medicine they need. This speaks to the importance of access to smart technology for basic services. Now, let us speak to access to the rewards for participating in and contributing to the digital ecosystem - as an employee would. If we treat each person who contributes to the use and value of a platform, as an employee, then we seem to have begun to solve the problem of economic exclusion, fear of jobs loss and replacement and an inability to enter the job market in the first place.

In a Quartz article about fixing capitalism they mention that "capitalism is not an organic system, markets are not forces of nature, and companies don't have minds of their own" and see all of them as "collections of human decisions, rules, incentives, predictions, and unintended consequences" and that we can make changes to them if we want to.[121] There has also been for many years a major debate about traditional shareholder capitalism that primarily focuses on unlocking shareholder value and stakeholder capitalism that consider all the stakeholders of a company including the owners (provide long-term value, clarity and effective engagement), customers (deliver value to them), employees (investing in them), suppliers (treating them in a just and ethical way) and communities (respecting the people and safeguarding the environment through sustainable activities).[122] Ray Dalio, co-founder of the world largest hedge fund Bridgewater Associates, recently claimed that Chinese's state capitalism and development of capital markets is advancing whilst US capitalism needs urgent repair.[123] Having visited China on a regular basis over the past 35 years, he has seen per-capita incomes increasing by 30 times; them producing significant more computer engineers and science, technology, engineering, and mathematics graduates; and estimates that 40% of the new initial public offerings will be done by Chinese companies on Chinese exchanges with institutional investors to follow. Ray is still a big believer in capitalism as he says that his "exposure to most economic systems in most countries over many years taught me that the ability to make money, save it, and put it into capital (i.e., capitalism) is the most effective motivator of people and allocator of resources to raise people's living standards."[124] However, he is very concerned that capitalism is not working well for the majority of people in the United States as the rich are getting richer and the poor are getting poorer with the middle class being hollowed out, which in turn creates a wider wealth gap that is damaging for the US and can lead to major conflicts and even revolution. He reckons that to solve this would require expert re-engineering of the economic system, but "the problem is that capitalists typically don't know how to divide the pie well and socialists typically don't know how to grow it well." In a LinkedIn article he describes in detail why and how capitalism needs to be reformed, why he believes that capitalism is not working well for the majority of people, his diagnosis of the problem and what should be done.[125] He shows that real income growth for most people was stagnant for decades, the income gap is at its highest, the wealth gap is at its highest since the latter part of the 1930s, and most people in the bottom 60% are poor. As there is a causal effect of where personal development impacts productivity growth which in turn impacts income growth, Ray points straight to poorly educated children within poor families with weak support and poorly funded schools as a major culprit. He shows that the US scores low on an educational level with being bottom 15th percentile of the developed world. Many students have emotional problems and are not sufficiently prepared for work, which in turn leads to poor health and social consequences, economic costs, and even higher crime rates. The result is a growing gap with respect to opportunity, income, and wealth, which in turn leads to hazardous social and political polarization. His diagnosis of why capitalism is not working for the majority of people in the US boils down to companies that are chasing profit and greater efficiencies by replacing US workers with technology and cost-effective foreign workers; making good healthcare and education more expensive and even unaffordable for the majority; the rich get richer because of increasing prices of financial assets that they own and their tendency to purchase financial assets as opposed to goods and services with the poor left less creditworthy; and the focus on policy makers on budgets as opposed to returns on investments. To fix this, he recommends that we need to make changes to capitalism that enable more equal opportunities and increased productivity. It all starts with governmental leadership that needs to treat the income, wealth, and opportunity gap as a national emergency. Ray would like to see bipartisan and skilled policy workers collaborating to redesign and reengineer the economic system to raise money and spend or invest it well to produce excellent double bottom line returns with unambiguous metrics to determine success. He would also like to see that monetary and fiscal policies are better coordinated to stimulate economic growth and lessen the effects that quantitative easing (to increase the money supply to increase lending and controlling inflation) has on increasing the wealth gap. Ray also reckons that the redistribution of resources will improve most people's well-being and productivity through creating private-public partnerships that invests in double bottom line projects that would have measurable economic and social performance results; raising money to improve economic productivity and conditions by taking into account all-in societal costs; and raising more from the wealthy via taxes that would be engineered to not have productivity disrupted and being set aside to those in need to improve the economy's overall level of productivity in a paid for manner.[126]

In *Radical Markets: Uprooting Capitalism and Democracy for a Just Society*, Eric Posner and Glen Weyl present market-based ideas that can help reshape the markets and society with greater equality and reciprocity and address the "crisis of the liberal order" which entails the inequality within wealthy countries, the drop in economic and productivity growth rates which causes economic stagnation, the decline in employment and the struggle of democracies to handle conflicts between minorities and majorities within countries.[127] In response to this crisis, they propose ideas for transforming the economy that involves owners to set property taxes with the option of others to buy your assets at your assessed value, the ability to weigh or buy votes in a more radical democracy, immigrant sponsorship of visas and sharing of the gains from migration, diversifying the owners of stocks, and giving consumers data ownership. In order to address the problem of land ownership type of monopoly power prohibiting progress and having low allocation efficiency, they propose a new property system called the Common Ownership Self-Assessed Tax (COST) to create a competitive market in uses through partial common ownership where every citizen and business entity would self-assess the value of assets they possess, pay a certain percentage tax on these values and be obliged to sell the assets to anyone that is willing to purchase them at the price that they have assessed. Eric and Glen reckon that COST would raise sufficient income to eliminate other taxes on capital, reduce income taxes, finance a large social dividend, sponsor the development of critical public infrastructure, help grow the economy, increase the value of commonwealth, govern public resources more efficiently, encourage people to have a healthier relationship with assets, and help to forge stronger community bonding. They also envisage a more radical democracy where a proposed Quadratic Voting (QV) system will help to facilitate reasoned compromises among citizens, trade influence on issues that people feel less strongly about with others that are more important, help protect treasured interests of minorities, and help to optimize decision making to benefit all. In this QV system every citizen would receive an equal annual allocation of vote credits that can be used to vote in a range of collective decisions with a choice in how many votes are allocated to specific issues where the costs of votes are quadratic in the number of votes acquired. By having citizens voting in proportion to how important issues are to them, this type of voting system could result in optimized social decisions. They also put forward a Visas between Individuals Program (VIP) that would bind the interests of the laboring class people of poor and wealthy countries through visas being sponsored and the earnings from migration being shared. The benefits include for example to help grow middle-class income and reduce inequalities across countries. According to them, much of the economy is being coordinated by institutional investors that mainly serve the interests of the wealthy through their control of most public companies whilst labor wages are kept low through artificial unemployment. A solution can be to change the structure of corporate ownership that will for example not allow investors to hold substantial shares in multiple market leaders within the same market segment as well as enforce antitrust laws that would prevent mergers that lead to the lowering of worker wages and corporations to acquire disruptive startups that might become strong competition in the future. To democratize the benefits of the digital technology that makes use of citizen's data and address the problem of technology companies exploiting this data for their own profits in lieu of free or cost-effective services that they provide, Eric and Glen proposes a Data as Labor (DaL) solution that would reward people for their data or digital contributions. This idea also ties in with one of the AI-driven solutions that will be discussed in the next chapter.

Their analysis of radical markets unveils how these ideas can be mutually reinforcing as they present a common vision to how these ideas about economy, society, international matters, and political systems can be integrated. Their perspective of market power having a foundational role in the economy without there being an assumed trade-off between productivity and employment is contrasted with both the techno-optimistic view of smart technology boosting productivity growth but causing social tension with respect the employment decline and techno-pessimist's viewpoint that argues that productivity and economic growth will continue to dwindle. They think that COST will improve economic efficiency through minimizing monopoly power whereas QV will enhance the positive effects and ensure that public goods exhibit citizens' overall preferences. Both DaL and VIP will in their view grow labor markets also within the digital space and help to reduce unemployment. They also consider the possible extension of COST to include human capital where people can self-assess the value of their time, pay a tax on that value and be ready to do a job or tasks for a company that can pay for their services. Although there are problems to work out with this solution, it can also address the problem of some top performing people demanding monopoly prices for their services. On the political front, both COST and QV would have a transformative impact by not only giving citizens a share of the national wealth, but also have them pay more attention to the repercussions of policies that affect the national wealth and increase responsiveness to public demands. VIP will help to address conflicting issues with respect to globalization and migration which is also contributing to populist drives as well as enable better international cooperation to help to manage cross-border activity related conflicts. QV can also be applied on an international governance front to help with improved collaboration between smaller, poorer, and wealthier countries. In general, radical markets driven by these types of solutions should help strengthen social tolerance, reduce social tensions with respect to exploitation, enhance mutually favorable economics, and tear down wealth and economic related entitlements.[128]

Although the proposed ideas are thought provoking as we contemplate a beneficial future and improved economic order for humanity in the smart technology era, there are also some critiques such as that the moral economy has not necessarily been replaced by a market economy, but embeds the market economy which implies that we also need to consider how human institutions constrain markets and the interactions with moral planned economies.[129] Furthermore, as life is much more than a market, there are also many other perspectives in how to uproot inequality and build a just society such as the one by philosopher Michael Sandel that discusses shaping our society by true principles of justice and not on a notion of merit in *The Tyranny of Merit: What Becomes of the Common Good?* [130] He explores how meritocratic arrogance leads many to believe their success is fully attributed to their own activities and is their own doing and disregard others that are not successful, which leads to discontent and incite the divide between "winners" and "losers" in the new economy. Michael is advocating for a less bitter, more magnanimous civic life that redefines the meaning of success and recognizes the role of luck which also includes talent, culture, and capacity for hard work. He frames his view of meritocracy in the context of Fredrich Hayek's economic liberalism and John Rawls egalitarian liberalism.[131] Whereas with "economic liberalism" societal merit is separate from economic success which measures how well people function in the market system and redistribution of these gains on a basis of merit by government is unacceptable, "egalitarian liberalism" is a school of thought where the disconnect between economic success and merit or justice requires redistribution of the economic gains on a basis of societal merit where the gains that emanate to the lucky and talented people are redistributed to the less lucky or talented individuals. The difference between these two perspectives and meritocracy is that the latter join together economic success with moral desert. Michael Sandel thinks that economic market success can mainly be attributed to luck in various forms that are not fully under our control such as talent, culture, and also the capacity for hard work. The fundamental problem in our society is that economic and professional success is interpreted as just and a measure of a person's moral value and what they deserve. Although meritocracy has replaced aristocracy, it differs from aristocracy also with respect to judgement on someone's moral worth. Whereas the riches of an aristocracy are seen as a function of the luck of their birth separate to judging a person's worth, in a meritocracy one's status is explicitly used to measure one's value as a human. He also points out society's asymmetrical focus on educational fulfillment as severely judging people that do not thrive in that system and driving the successful parents to replicate their meritocratic ascendancy for their children.[132]

Max Borders shows in *The Social Singularity - A Decentralist Manifesto* that humanity is already building systems and infrastructure that will transform and replace society's current mediating structures and centers of power.[133] He explores a post political decentralized world where humanity will reorganize to collaborate and compete with AI, operate within networks of superior collective civilization intelligence, and rediscover our humanity and embrace values for a better human-to-human connected world. He envisaged that such a decentralized world will enable us to create global prosperity, transcend politics, and steer clear of an AI or robot apocalypse. Max's *Social Evolution* website provides more details on the social evolution organization that is dedicated to liberate people and solve social problems through innovation and claims that old mediating structures will soon be obsolete, smart technology will enable new forms of social organization, the need to prepare for a decentralized world and the fast tracking of self-organizing mutual assistance.[134] Max argues that politics in its current form is about to end and has outlived its usefulness. He thinks we can do better than the current representative democracy where we outsource our sense of civic responsibility to entrusted politicians. According to him, society's mediating structures that were pillars of our civilization such as the media, the banks, and the education systems are already showing fractures, weaknesses, and limitations. In parallel to the technology singularity, we are moving towards a social singularity where humanity is rapidly reorganizing itself using new technology-driven social structures and approaches that will catapult us into the future without some of these old pillars. Similarly, to how politics has outlived its usefulness, Max sees a parallel track where humanity is getting better through recreating the structures of combining, collaborating, and connecting with one another in new ways. Besides that automation and AI will allow us to rediscover our humanity, he is optimistic and believes that our collective civilization intelligence will be superior and that we would not get into mass displacement and existential scenarios. Instead, whole new industries are envisioned as capital and labor migrates away from the activities and tasks that AI, robots and automation will be covering to more deeply human enterprises and activities such as art, community-based engagements and caregiving that incorporate our elders and children more closely into our lives again. With AI not currently able to feel (at least not yet) and assisting us in rediscovering our humanity, we can exploit our capabilities as integrated beings that can think and feel to create many human-centric integrated industries. We will also construct our social reality with programmable incentives and create new social realities through technologies, rules, and tools. Max envisages novel forms of collective intelligence, cooperation and collaboration that will create new social operating systems that operate in the cloud that could already utilize decentralized technologies such as blockchain and holochain.[135] He reckons that the current way of governance which is outsourcing our cares and responsibilities for each other, will be replaced by governance systems that break up centralized centres of power, make use of insourcing and are polycentric and polyarchic in nature. Polycentric governance implies a move towards power being localized and governance more participatory and collaborative where we work with our neighbors in common purpose.[136] Polyarchic describes a government form in which power is invested in multiple people and also implies that we can choose the rules by which we are governed.[137] Max advocates for decentralized social structures that have polycentric and polyarchic elements and driven by our cloud-based social operating systems with legal code that we can choose rather than being imposed on us as with the current status quo. He imagines that from these new social operating systems with embedded new lattice works of law, new values of a post political age will emerge. We shape our tools and then our tools shape us.[138] Similarly, we shape our rules, and our rules shape us. As a result, what emerges from better institutions, rules and technological lattice works and psychosocial development of the social singularity is better people with better values that are more loving, visionary, tolerant, and pluralistic.[139]

Whereas well-being have subjective, social, and psychological dimensions as well as health-related behaviors, psychological well-being touches more on virtue and the realization of a person's potential as also derived from Aristotle's view of the highest human good.[140] Some virtues that are held across time, culture or viewpoint include wisdom and knowledge, courage, justice, humanity, temperance, and transcendence.[141] Some key aspects of psychological wellness includes autonomy in thought and action, self-acceptance, environmental mastery, personal growth, positive relations, and purpose in life and pursuit of meaningful goals.[142] From a cross-cultural perspective autonomy is seen as a basic universal value of human existence in both western individualist and eastern collectivist societies.[143] Wellbeing includes both feel-good hedonia and feel-purpose eudaimonia aspects, where hedonia focus more on externally derived happiness, enjoyment, pleasure, satisfaction and the absence of distress and negative affect and eudaimonia is more focused on internally-derived happiness, meaning, authenticity, excellence, personal growth and living life in a full and satisfying way.[144] To make it even more explicit hedonia is more associated with physical and emotional needs, what feels good, desire, ease, now, rights, pleasure, and self-care, whereas eudaimonia is associated with cognitive values and ideals, what feels right, care, giving, long-term, effort, elevation, responsibilities, and cultivating.

Hedonia and eudaimonia can be seen as separate but connected pathways to happiness where a fulfilled life has both strong feel-good hedonia and feel-purpose eudaimonia components.[145] In this respect a sweet life has more feeling good and less feeling purpose components, a dry life more feeling purpose and less feeling good, and a void life less from both.[146] University of Ottawa researcher Veronika Huta explains the differences between hedonia and eudaimonia from an orientation (why you do things), behavior (what you do), experience (what you feel), and functioning (what you are good at) perspective.[147] She indicates that orientations and behaviors reflect the choices a person makes, whereas experiences and functioning are typically the results of those choices. Eudaimonia is distinct from hedonia from an orientation's perspective, but there are also differences on a behavior and experiences level.

Eliezer Yudkowsky, co-founder and research fellow at the Machine Intelligence Research Institute and popularizer of the friendly AI concept, has introduced Fun Theory which is the field of knowledge that helps us to imagine utopias where anyone would actually want to live and addresses questions such as "How much fun is there in the universe?", "Are we having fun yet?", "Could we be having more fun?", and "Will we ever run out of fun?".[148] Fun Theory is built on top of the naturalistic metaethics that advocates that human life will be empty if we cannot enjoy simply good things like happiness, truth, and sentient life.[149] Eliezer makes the point that people would not be inspired to work on creating an utopian world if nobody puts proper effort into imagining a better future world where people are excited to live in. Although much progress has been made, our present world still has many shortcomings with respect to eudaimonic aspects such as freedom, self-reliance, and personal responsibility as well as not having an optimized design that holistically drives towards beneficial, well-meaning, and altruistic outcomes. Fun Theory aims to articulate the characteristics of such a more benevolent design that we should strive for and addresses approaches from religious theodicy that attempts to justify why evil is permitted and religions' supposedly flawless afterlife. Eliezer also mentions that Fun Theory makes it clear that there are a variety of aspects that contribute to a life worth living and that eudaimonia is more complex than we might think. He also shows how Fun Theory ties in with the complexity of value thesis that says that human values and preferences cannot be summarized by a few simple rules and therefore have high Kolmogorov complexity.[150] He also defines fragility of value as a thesis that articulates that even missing a small percentage of the rules that describe human values and preferences can result in completely undesirable outcomes.[151] This is also the reason why we need to be more accurate with the goals systems that we choose to implement for our strong AI systems. Eliezer refers to these strong AI systems as Friendly AI that produces advantageous outcomes rather than damaging ones.[152]

Eliezer also shares what he calls "31 Laws of Fun" as a summary of his Fun Theory Sequence that aims to give pointers to futurists that want to color in an utopian world that people would be excited to live in.[153] Some of these key points include describing a typical day; do not include things that are not fun to do; include high-quality challenges; include novelty; pace the tempo of getting smarter to keep everything in balance; people should have full sensory experience that engages the brain and body; people should do exciting things; people's lives should continuously improve; there should be events or things that pleasantly surprise people; people should be doing interesting things for themselves using their own capabilities and resources; people should become more formidable and stronger over time; people should be emotionally involved with long-term consequences as part of a life story; people should be free to optimize their lives and create their own destinies; people should not be dominated in their everyday life by exceedingly superior entities; group size and dynamics should incorporate Dunbar's number (which is the suggested "cognitive limit to the number of people with whom one can maintain stable social relationships")[154]; give people stronger local influence and control and not have people to compete with everyone else globally; don't give people too many options that could also include potentially harmful ones or ones that are very tempting but dangerous; it should also not be easy to exercise dangerous options; let people discover truths for themselves; preferably do not simplify people's lives by reducing their interaction with other people as that reduces the complexity of their human existence; nudge people to make the problems solvable as opposed to solving the problems at once; prioritize changes to the environment ahead of changes to minds and favor small cognitive changes to bigger ones; the world should have abundant joy and pleasure in relation to sadness and pain unlike the current world where there is a unbalance between pain and pleasure and pain could be endless and long lasting; the penalties for errors should also be more proportional; it should not try avoid commotion or spontaneous cheerfulness; it can introduce situations or environments that could initially seem scary, disorganized, uncomfortable, or surprising; it does not need to go along with your existing ideals for the world but possibly even challenge you to change those ideals; if there is any existential anxiety that you struggle to overcome that at least present a problem that needs to be focused on to get resolved; as a better world will likely have less people that needs help, the focus can shift to many other higher purpose activities; and people that are not in immediate danger can still have compelling and interesting lives.[155] Do you want to live in a world with these types of characteristics? What other characteristics would you like to see? Are there any of these laws of fun that do not resonate with you?

Various Potential Outcomes for the Future of Civilization

As mentioned in the previous chapter, Max Tegmark in *Life 3.0: Being Human in the Age of Artificial Intelligence*, discusses the three stages of life on this planet as biological evolution, cultural evolution, and technological evolution.[156] Simple biological Life 1.0 is unable to redesign either its hardware or its software during its lifetime as both are determined by its DNA, and change only occurs through evolution over many generations. As Life 2.0 has a strong cultural dimension, it can redesign much of its software as one can clearly see with humans that can learn complex new skills (see for example, languages, sports, and professions) and can fundamentally update their worldview and goals. Now the big question is if humans in the Smart Technology Era will drive us towards Life 3.0, a technological stage of life where life can dramatically redesign not only its software, but its hardware as well, rather than having to wait for it to gradually evolve over generations. Do we want this future? What will the impact of this be on humans?

In *The Economic Singularity: Artificial Intelligence and the Death of Capitalism* Calum Chace describes four potential scenarios for the post-economic singularity that he envisages which includes maintaining the status quo without any significant changes, idealistic full employment, a social collapse and the Star Trek economy.[157] Whereas a social collapse falls into a dystopian category, the Star Trek economy describes an abundant moneyless age without scarcity and supported by smart technology. He does not regard the status quo scenario where there is no further significant innovation and minimal smart technology impact on civilization to be a plausible one. Some of the key arguments for this scenario include the apparent deceleration of technological progress, the fact that we have not seen any significant improvements from a traditional productivity and GDP statistics perspective, and that the industrial revolution seems at this point in time to still have had a greater impact on the economy and civilization compared to the current information revolution. However, this is debatable given that we are still early into the 21st century with the impact of fusing multiple exponential smart technology impulses still to play out more significantly across most sectors, this scenario does indeed look unlikely. Although the full employment scenario is more plausible, AI-driven assisted, augmented, and autonomous technology is on course to have a significant impact on the job market. One of the key arguments for this scenario is what Calum calls the reverse Luddite fallacy that says that as automation has not caused long-term unemployment in the past, it is not likely to have that effect in the future. But that does not hold water as whatever happened in the past does not necessarily give any assurance for what will happen in the future. Another argument states that as our demand for products and services are for all practical purposes unlimited there will always be full employment. However, as AI-driven machines and software solutions will increasingly assist in producing better products and services in quicker and more cost-effective fashion, we will likely see it contributing more to development and delivering capacity to meet the demand. Calum Chace mentions various examples of where people will likely be still be engaged on the job front which includes collaborating and complementing machines with respect to our creativity, instinctive aptitude, and imagination; utilizing the AI-driven analysis outputs in higher-level cognitive tasks; do tasks that require empathy; people might have a bias for some handmade human-produced goods and services still being produced or offered; be involved in entrepreneurial ventures and activities, producing artistic and entertainment related goods and services; or activities that we cannot even imagine today.[158] So although we might not have full employment, cognitive automation will likely not lead to full scale enduring pervasive unemployment.

The scenario of social collapse is also a realistic dystopian one with civilization's fragility illustrated many times in the past (with the Egyptians, the Greeks, the Persians, the Romans, the Maya, the Inca, the Mughal dynasty, Cambodia's Khmer empire, the Ottomans, and the Habsburg monarchy to name a few). Although our 21st century civilization seems robust, social collapse and other dystopian scenarios can still be easily brought about by fractures in society that can be the result of combinations of many factors that range from technological unemployment, climate change, migration, food shortages, blunders, misinterpretations, or confusion to totalitarian control, troublemakers, populist movements that lead to fascism, or even the gods (superclass with superior physical and cognitive capacity and potentially living longer) versus the useless class as described by Yuval Harari in *Sapiens: A Brief History of Humankind*.[159] On the other end of the spectrum we have utopian scenarios which are imagined societies with highly preferable or idealistic characteristics and where its citizens do not have discomfort. However, depending on how they are defined, they could also potentially be stationary, boring, and dull with no problems to solve or opportunities to pursue. Also, a world that might be perfect in some respects, might be dreadful in order dimensions. □Many utopian scenarios do not necessarily present a good outcome for humanity of which some are also linked to strong AI and super intelligent systems. Instead, Calum supports a protopia, which futurist Kevin Kelly describes in *The Inevitable: Understanding the 12 Technological Forces that will Shape our Future* as a "state of becoming, rather than a destination" and a process where "things are better today than they were yesterday, although only a little better."[160] He believes in continuous small incremental progress and thinks that any society supported by smart technology will have some problems. Kevin also thinks that we have already arrived in protopia, but that future states of protopia are more difficult to visualize as "new technologies create almost as many problems as the ones that it solves" and gives us new options to tackle new problems with slightly more positives than negatives.[161] Calum Chace believes that a protopia might unroll in four stages which he calls a plan, big welfare, Star Trek economy, and collectivism.[162] He further colors this in with a thought experiment as he outlines three snapshots of a possible future in 2025 (panic averted), 2035 (the transition) and 2045 at which point we have an abundant Stark Trek type of economy where we have avoided social displacement at scale. In his "unforecasting" description he emphasizes the impossibility to predict the future but also the importance of making plans to avoid not giving us a chance to achieve the outcome that we want. He envisages AI-driven smart technology helping to drive costs of production of goods and services to zero; energy costs being appreciably lowered; transportation costs significantly reduced with minimal human labor involved; the production of food mostly automated; the quality of housing appliances and furniture being upgraded on a continuous basis; people across the spectrum have enjoyable lives; state is providing income for its citizens; and the wealth gap notably closed. A protopian outcome is likely one of the better scenarios to strive for, especially one that also has characteristics such as decentralized governance with abundance across the spectrum; direct democracy with a more local and human community-based economy; an empathic society with meaningful work and relationships; AI-driven smart technology helping society thrive and assist in running communities, smart towns, smart cities, and smart nation-states in more optimal fashion; allowing for a hybrid setup where communities choose to live in full-AI supported zones or one that does have minimal to zero AI-driven support; and a shift to biosphere consciousness.[163]

Eric Drexler, inventor of nanotechnology and Senior Research Fellow at Oxford University's Future of Humanity Institute, has recently discussed the idea of a Pareto-topia that involves a resolutely goal-aligned future where everyone's lives can be enormously improved by ensuring that all parties get very large gains when looking at the resource pie as it pertains to AI, automation and space resources.[164] In such a scenario there will still be people with larger access to resources than others, but no one would have shortcomings and the outcomes for everyone is massive. He envisions that a strongly Pareto-preferred world is made possible by having at some point in the future rapid growth in AI capabilities, vast expansion in productive capacity, and benign and effective security systems. Eric advocates that we should change our understanding and perceptions from just working on policies that give credible outcomes to one that also explores potential goals and policies for what is plausible and realistic. He discusses the concept of an Overton window which defines "the range of what can be discussed within a given community at a given time, and what can be discussed and taken seriously and regarded as reasonable changes over time".[165] If we work within the Overton window of plausibility, Eric sees the following as credible or plausible: extensive applications of high-end AI, strong scalable automation, large-scale low cost renewable energy, resource efficiency, asteroid mining, and greater defensive stability. According to Eric, paretotopian meta strategies involve the need to understand realistic and credible capabilities, understand and accommodate diverse concerns, and to intensify and expand the circle of conversation.

In a paper *The Future of Humanity*, Nick Bostrom, a philosopher at University of Oxford and the director of the Future of Humanity Institute, discusses four families of scenarios for humanity's future namely extinction, recurrent collapse, plateau, and posthumanity.[166] Plateau falls into the above-mentioned status quo category and can, according to Nick, have two possible trajectories where the one is just current status quo and the other one is representing a growth followed by an indefinite plateau. Both recurrent collapse and extinction belong in the dystopian category. Whereas recurrence collapse involves a cycle of perpetual repeating collapse and regeneration, extinction entails either evolving into one or more new species or dying out as a species without purposeful prolongation or replacement.[167] Posthumanity can be classified into the extreme side of the utopian, protopian or parato-topian group, where Nick defines the "posthuman condition" to have one or more of the following attributes: life expectancy which is more than 500 years; a significant part of the population has cognitive capacities more than two standard deviations above the current human maximum; almost full control over the sensory input for most people nearly all of the time; human psychological suffering becoming infrequent experience; population size of more than 1 trillion persons; and any change of magnitude or deepness comparable to any of these characteristics.[168] In a Lex Fridman podcast on superintelligence, Nick mentions that we should take full advantage of the abundance that can be brought about within a strong AI driven utopian scenario.[169] He thinks that it will open a vast space of possible modes of being, dramatically expand material and resource constraints, and open up a larger design and option space for ourselves that we have ever had access to in the history of humankind. He urges that we need to fundamentally rethink what ultimately, we value and think things through from first principles to determine the best possible outcome for humanity.

In Max Tegmark's book *Life 3.0: Being Human in the Age of Artificial Intelligence*, he explores a range of AI aftermath scenarios as AI becomes increasingly advanced which effectively can be classified into dystopian or utopian categories.[170] The dystopias include "conquerors" where ☐AI takes control and removes us by a possibly incomprehensible and indefensible method; "descendants" where ☐AIs replace humans and give us a dignified exit; "zookeeper" where an omnipotent AI keeps some humans around in zoo-like fashion; "1984" where AI progress is indefinitely restricted and research prohibited by a people-led Orwellian surveillance government; "digital dictatorship" where we have governmental surveillance and smart technology based control of citizens; "reversion" where AI research and applications are prohibited by going back to a pre-technological society; and "self-destruction" where strong AI is not developed due to humanity pushing itself to extinction.[171] The utopian scenarios include "libertarian utopia" where humans, cyborgs, uploads and strong AI systems coexist peacefully due to property rights; "egalitarian utopia" where we do not have a superintelligent AI but humans, cyborgs, and uploads coexist peacefully because of property abolition and guaranteed income; "benevolent dictator" where everybody knows that the AI runs society and enforces strict rules, but most people view this as a positive thing; "gatekeeper" where technological progress is forever impeded by a strong AI with the goal of interfering as little as necessary to prevent the creation of another superintelligence; "protector god" where essentially omniscient and omnipotent AI maximizes human happiness by intervening only in ways that preserve our feeling of control of our own destiny and hides well enough that many humans even doubt the AI's existence; and an "enslaved god" where a strong AI is confined by humans, who use it to produce unimaginable technology and wealth that can be used for good or bad depending on the human controllers.[172]

There have been many discussions and even debates about where we are heading in terms of utopian versus dystopian scenarios. One such debate was a few years ago between Josh Hall and Hugo de Garis at an Artificial General Intelligence conference on whether strong AI will result in an utopia or war.[173] Josh took the position that the rise of AI levels will create a utopia for humanity, whereas Hugo took the opposite position that the rise of "godlike massively intelligent machines" could possibly be catastrophic for humanity, leading to the worst, most passionate war humanity has ever known, using late 21st century weapons, killing billions of people. In Hugo de Garis's book *The Artilect War: Cosmists Vs. Terrans: A Bitter Controversy Concerning Whether Humanity Should Build Godlike Massively Intelligent Machines*, he describes two opposing perspectives on whether humanity should or should not build strong AI systems which he calls artilects or artificial intellects which can eventually overshadow human intelligence by a factor of trillions.[174] He thinks this question will dominate global politics later in this century where we will have the "Cosmists" with a more "cosmic" perspective that supports building them as opposed to the "Terrans" (as in "terra" which means the Earth) who are against building them. There is actually also a third major philosophical group which he calls "Cyborgs" (which comes from "cybernetic organism") that want to become artilects themselves by adding artilect components to their own brains. Some of the arguments for the Cosmists include the big picture of advancing intelligent life as part of the next evolutionary step and spreading it throughout the cosmos; exploring and extending our boundaries which is in line with our human nature; being like a scientific religion in harmony with modern scientific knowledge; building artilect gods; unlocking unstoppable and tremendous powers of problem solving, abundance and wealth creation; and generating further economic and military momentum. The motive of the Terrans is fear and avoiding risk as they argue that we need to preserve the human species, not wanting to face differences with Cyborgs and artilects, being rejected by the Cyborgs or artilects, wanting to avoid the unpredictable complexity, the Cosmist inconsideration, and the "first strike" time window to react against the Cosmists and Cyborgs before it is too late. The arguments for cyborgs include becoming artilect gods themselves and avoiding the cosmist/terran clash. Hugo also describes how such as Artilect War can heat up in a sequence of events starting with nanotech revolutionizing neuroscience; neuro-engineering uniting with neuroscience; artificial brain technology creating massive industries; development of an "intelligence theory"; continuous improvement of artilects; raging "species dominance" debate and forming of political parties; the debate turning violent through assassination and sabotage; the Terrans striking first before it is too late for them; Cosmists anticipating this first strike and are ready; and late 21st century weapons leading to a gigadeath war.[175] Now that is what I call a pessimistic dystopian scenario that we definitely want to avoid.

The Future of Life Institute expanded the conversation through a general public survey to get the general public's views on superintelligent AI and what society people would prefer given the utopian and dystopian scenarios as defined by Max Tegmark.[176] The Future of Life website provides the results of the first almost 15,000 people that responded to the survey. Most of the respondents preferred an "egalitarian utopia" followed by a "libertarian utopia". Other less popular utopian scenarios from preferable to undesirable include respectively "protector god", "enslaved god", "descendants" and "gatekeeper". On the question of who should be in control when a superintelligence arrives, most survey respondents said both humans and machines, followed by humans, and then the machines. To the question of having a conscious AI helper with subjective experience, most of the respondents want the AI helper to be conscious so that the system can enjoy having experiences, followed by depending on the circumstances, and not wanting it to have consciousness (they did not want to feel guilty about how they treat it). In terms of what a future civilization should strive for most people prefer minimizing suffering, followed by maximizing positive experiences, another goal that they sympathize with, and picking any reasonable goal. A very large percentage of the respondents want life to spread into the cosmos.[177] In *Life 3.0*, Max Tegmark also lists properties associated with these AI aftermath scenarios (some of which correspond to these survey questions) and checks for each scenario whether strong AI exists, does humans exist, are humans in control, are humans safe, are humans happy, and if consciousness exists.[178] One can add more properties to this list such as are humans productive, does humans have a meaningful existence, is there abundance, do we have an equitable democratic society, and have we reduced the wealth inequality. If we consider human control, the only utopian scenarios where that is a possibility seems to be egalitarian utopia and "enslaved god" cases, whereas that should be the case in the status quo, full employment, protopia and pareto-topia scenarios. Although humans might be safe in the cases of a "benevolent dictator", "egalitarian utopia", and possibly "gatekeeper", "protector god" and "enslaved god" scenarios, humanity's happiness is likely going to be mixed in all of the utopian scenarios. Protopia and pareto-topia scenarios look to give us a better chance to not only engineer a safer and happier future world where humans are still in control for as many people as possible, but also one where there is abundance, humanity is productive and has a meaningful existence, our democratic society is a more equitable with a diminished wealth gap, and better at being an empathic civilization with collective sensemaking.

A blog post that discusses likely outcomes over the next few decades mentions strong AI and bioengineered world as potentially good outcomes with the proviso that the design and application are well controlled to humanity's benefit and the development pace is not stifled.[179] All the other outcomes seem to be very dreadful and distressing such as increased domination, manipulation and quelling of citizens in secret or disguised fashion, military conflict by accident or design causing mass destruction, rapid acceleration of climate change or extraterrestrial events that might have unforeseeable timing. In an article about the best case scenarios for the future of humanity, George Dvorsky outlines some scenarios which includes the status quo discussed earlier as well as a number of far out utopian-like scenarios which he calls "a bright green Earth", "watched over by machines of loving grace", "to boldly go where no one has gone before...", "inner space, not outer space", "eternal bliss", and "cosmological transcension".[180] A bright green Earth future is one where people live in harmony with the planet's ecosystem, animal suffering is eliminated, weather can be controlled and all our energy requirements are fulfilled as one would get with a Kardashev type I planetary civilization that can use and store all of the available energy on its planet. The Kardashev scale measures a civilization's level of technological progress based on the energy amount they are able to use, where a type II stellar civilization can use and control energy at the scale of its planetary system and a type III galactic civilization can control energy at the scale of the whole galaxy where it is located.[181] The scenario where humanity is "watched over" by AI systems is similar to the "benevolent dictator", "protector god" or "enslaved god" type of scenarios mentioned earlier. The interstellar colonization scenario implies having technological capability to travel to other planets and start colonizing other solar systems via self-replicating spacecraft (von Neuman probes), generation ships, or digital intelligence systems. An example of the futuristic innerspace scenario would be mind uploading to enormous supercomputers that can provide various simulated worlds and imaginative experiences that go far beyond our current physical experiences on Earth. The eternal bliss scenario involves creating a virtual hedonistic heaven on Earth, the removal of suffering and the maximization of endless pleasure from a physical, psychological, and emotional perspective. The cosmological transcension scenario is even more speculative and includes for example advanced intelligent life guiding the continuing development of the universe or moving our collective intelligence into a cosmological zone with black hole like efficiency and density through the migration and shrinking of human civilization into smaller increments of matter, energy, space, and time.[182]

Beneficial Outcomes, Massive Transformative Purpose, and Smart Goals

Now that we can make sense of the various potential outcomes for the future of humanity, let us ask some key questions. Given our collective wisdom, knowledge, and information available, what specific beneficial outcomes should we aim for? What is our massive transformative purpose as humanity? What are our SMART goals? Can we diagnose potential problems that are preventing us from reaching our goals and achieving beneficial outcomes for humanity? Can we identify the root causes for these problems? Knowing the right questions to ask is half the battle. Reframing the way we think about their solutions and answers is the rest. The new tools we have certainly give us a head start, but it is our ability to think strategically, analytically, and innovatively that will be the difference between action and continued talking. It is time for solutions. While our first step is having the right questions and knowing the problems we face, the second step is being able to be honest with ourselves about where we really are...

A thought echoed by many modern authors, political and social commentators and futurists is summed up by Mark Manson when he describes a relatively little-known term - the paradox of progress.[183] It goes something like this: with all the progress that we have made in science, medicine, social rest, political mildness, and economic growth, why are we all so unhappy and left with more of a sense of hopelessness than years past? As Manson puts it, we are the safest and most prosperous humans in the history of the world, yet we are feeling more helpless than ever before.[184] The answer is that we have lost hope. But how? We might ask. Because hope is not about statistics or how well we are doing. Hope is found in the future. And the more we must lose or the more uncertain our futures seem, the less we feel we must hope for and the more we must fear. In his psychological research, Manson summarizes that we need three things to remain hopeful, "a sense of control, a belief in the value of something, and a community".[185] "Without community, we feel isolated, and our values cease to mean anything. Without values, nothing appears worth pursuing. Without control, we feel powerless to pursue anything. Without all of these, we lose hope."[186] If this is the case, then these changing times of uncertainty have certainly caused many to lose hope. There is so much uncertainty in our future; what our place is in it; what technology will change; how we will adapt; what we will lose. Not all this uncertainty is derived from our increasing abilities to imagine and create and not all feel a little hopeless by this ability. Just the same, we are living in a time where people do not know what to believe spiritually and are struggling to grapple with a future that may look devastatingly different from the present we know.

Another major contributing factor to uncertainty is actual versus constructed reality. We live in a world where constructed reality is impacting humanity at scale. Although "we should strive to distinguish fiction from reality", we should have a balanced perspective and recognize that fiction is also vital, for without "commonly accepted stories about things like money, states or corporations, no complex human society can function".[187] However, this is not always easy to do given the rise of sensationalist media and the plethora of opinions, sometimes intersubjective that appear online and within communities. This might include which leaders we support, which views we like, or our conclusions on topics of which we have little and sometimes incorrect information. Distributed ledger technology can help. AI can help too. Machine intelligence and learning needs not be biased if the humans behind the algorithms take measures to avoid and deal with bias. When we use machine intelligence to further our own stories or values, we must ask ourselves what these are, and what the costs to these are. We can value the greater good over privacy, but what do we think the greater good is. Is it about happiness? Efficiency? Simple and more inclusive services? Rewarding those who behave in ways we like? Freedom of information, verification of information, and free press is important, but how do we advance this truth without detracting from cultural, religious, political and community driven intersubjective values and constructions of reality?

What we know is that we have tools that were previously only a product of imagination. Sci-Fi, the genre, was born from this ability to imagine and media in general has spent many a budget on catastrophizing what science and technology might make of our future. Well, that future is now. The Smart Technology Era has begun, and our abilities to only know and invent but to instantly share what we know and invent with the world sparks a new urgency to direct our knowledge and inventions towards what makes our unknown future a bearable, fruitful, and sustainable one. Our constant connectedness and the ease with which our thoughts, inventions and philosophies spread puts a great responsibility on each individual to use the tools we have in a positive way. Not just for ourselves and immediate surroundings, but for the sake of the world, life, nature, and humanity. Our new tools might seem scary, but they also open a way to solve problems in continuous, unexpected, and simplified new ways. We no longer need to rely on large buildings and machines and spaces to work, produce, connect, and create. We now have algorithms, AI, mobile phones, IoT and nanotechnology. We have the tiniest and yet most powerful tools to do almost anything we dream possible and inspiring.

How can we frame our story to have a "happy ending"? Our story can be one with a happy ending or at least set on a happy path. But it is not an accidental ending or path. It requires work, the ability to let go of ego to find firm solutions and the ability for each person alive to accept the challenge to see things differently by first being honest about where we are. It requires acceptance of the Smart Technology Era and its impacts so that conclusions may be reached from true and actual premises. It might help to know that our fear about the future, the changes, human displacement, job and profession changes, the utter disruption to the life we know are not only unavoidable and even untrue, but there is so much hope in it for humanity as well. The Smart Technology Era gives us the opportunity to get in touch with what makes us truly human. The very thing that technology cannot and will not replace is what makes us innately human. But we need to acknowledge and celebrate this if we are to reap the positive rewards that are awaiting us once we have gone through the difficult changes to our reality and embraced our new existence. It is coming anyway, and embracing it only makes it that much easier. It also means that we get to steer it, be a part of it and ensure that our shared fears do not come to pass. We first need to note that globalization, automation, constant connection, and information consumption are exceptionally overwhelming. We confuse this overwhelm with despair and fear the worst because we do not understand it, or we have not stopped to catch our breath, or we have not cottoned on to how technology can allow us to celebrate, embrace and uplift our innate humanness.

Yes, things are changing. In the years to come, things will start changing a whole lot faster. The world as we know it now has started to and will rapidly continue to look quite different - particularly in developed nations and developing nations that are insisting on not being left behind. On the African continent, Kenya is a good example of such a developing nation that is actively working on eradicating corruption, leapfrogging social and economic inclusion, providing basic services, and educating and connecting its entire country in the knowledge and skills they will need to know to be a part of the transformation, not outside of it. Humans are social creatures - seeking love and connection acknowledgement. Whatever machines are, they cannot yearn and seek the way we can. They may be able to emulate love and empathy, but they will never be able to feel it in the exact way we as humans experience it. They may be able to converse with us, but they can never connect with us in a true human way. Whatever machines will be, the subconscious streams that run through us, knowing, and feeling things before we realize that we do are for the foreseeable future strictly human domain. There has never been a better time to embrace creating positive and uplifting cultures and communities, treasuring human connection, kindness, and generosity, and taking time to get to truly know not only the people around us, but ourselves. AI-driven automation of tasks, learning and reasoning will be giving us more time to build cultures, organisations, and families intentionally, with care and concern for the impact on human life. We have never had better tools or means to share knowledge and information and can, with a little help, easily learn the skills we will need to thrive in the economy, in society and in interpersonal relationships. If we only focus smart technology's ability to empower and help us, our ability to decide what we build, create and program and the things that make us truly human, there is no reason why the changes and disruptions we face cannot be shaped not only positively, but in a way that allows each person on this planet to prosper.

The simplest and smartest of technologies started as thoughts in human minds, are trained and checked by human minds and are accountable by humans as well. If we fear a future where humans merge with machines or are totally replaced by machines (a future which has only been postulated), then let us steer away from this and rather use the amazing tools and information we have at our disposable to create and empower a future that improves where we are now, not threaten it. AI is not some foreign entity. Machine learning does not happen by itself. It is the creation of humans. It is time each human, particularly leaders, business owners and those with any form of power to direct and inspire take the necessary steps to embrace our new reality, every day and ensure that everyone has the information and tools to embrace it too. Businesses and governments are just larger entities than individuals. They too can join the transformation, embracing the changes and uplifting the humanness that walks through their walls. They too can use smart technology to work with humans. Roles and processes may change but new roles and processes emerge. Education and training are an integral part in staying abreast of the transformations that are coming. Finding new ways to see economics, politics and the centralized systems that are vulnerable to changes has never been more important. If the leaders in industry direct the changes and become a part of the conversation in a solution seeking way, the industry collapse will not cripple businesses because these businesses will be at the front lines of these changes. They will shift directions as the direction shifts and they will be empowered to do so because they were willing to change. They were willing to surrender to what is coming anyway and steer it instead of watching it from a melting iceberg. Work is being done to provide a framework for laws, policies and smart technology adoption in businesses, institutions, and governments. The hope is that this will result in an adoptable, adaptable, and actionable framework that feeds a one-size fits all solution with varying implementations.

Many of us may have heard of an organization's mission or vision. These explain what an organization aims to achieve and how it will go about achieving it. A Massive Transformative Purpose (MTP) is so much more than that.[188] It speaks to the aspirations of the organization in how it aims to impact the world. It is deeply tied into why the organization exists in the first place - not just for the services or products it offers, but in the impact it aspires to have on the world, societies, people's lives, and our planet. On the things never thought possible and the changes we do not even know to ask for. Through digital transformation and smart technology, it is not as far reaching as it once may have been to affect the world at large with our dreams and aspirations. There are many who believe that we must have a certain amount of output (ten times more than our competitors), a certain amount of profit or a certain amount of power to have an MTP. But the far reaching and automatic effects of digital life mean that we have more power than ever before to affect the globe with one, seemingly small creation. Whoever you are, whether a politician, an academic, a coder in a basement or founder of a small business, you can and should think about what your MTP is. With respect to an MTP, Peter Diamandis has been quoted to say, "Find something you would die for, and live for it."[189] What world do you want to be a part of? What do you want to change or affect? And how can what you are doing at this moment start you on that path? It will not happen overnight. It may not even happen in a year. But with an MTP to empower and inspire your vision and mission, you can steer the world towards the change that you see. Be idealistic. Be realistic too. We have never before had the tools we have now. Tools that are changing the world at an exponential pace. So, let us think about what we want to transform and then look to the amazing tools at our disposal to help us reach our aspirations. How can AI give us the tools we need to solve our problems and reach our MTP? In every century, every generation, we exist and live with the tools of that time. Sometimes things change and progress slowly - minor improvements to already existing products, processes, and services. Sometimes major inventions or disruptions to industries and ways of life change things completely and quickly. The invention of electricity, the fax machine, the aero plane, steal, the personal computer, the internet, and many more major life-altering events all changed society completely. Smart technology is one of those events. It is our latest tool to improve, survive, damage, and completely change the way we live. Only we have not yet realized how to use it, not really. And we certainly have not realized how to govern, control and direct it. We are relying on people and businesses who know how to use these tools to do something, although we are not really sure what, and we mostly just sit back as we watch and wait. The world at large has not much idea of what is being built, who is building it or what it does. Our opinions on smart technology are vastly uninformed and positive, negative or neutral. We fear, we are excited, or we are just carrying on while our services and processes change. We may experience relief or discomfort by these changes, but we get used to our new ways of banking (for example) and eventually that becomes the new normal. Many involved in the dialogue are talking about the potential improvements and dangers of smart technology and AI. We need ethics guidelines, we need laws, we need to make sure we are using it for good. We need to use these tools to affect wide-spread social inclusion and lift people out of desperation and degradation. We need to improve our businesses, create jobs, ensure we are not becoming irrelevant. Fewer people are talking about practical ways to actually do this. It is clearly time for action, not just talking, not just writing. While these conversations are important, how much longer will they go on for before the world sits down and does the work of actualization. Not merely leaving it up to the businesses, organisations and research institutes who are using and creating it. The point is that we all need to be involved in the discussions and actions. People need to know what AI and smart technology are. We need to know the potential they hold. We need to look at how and where our latest technologies are already being used, and we need to understand the effects they are having and their potential impacts. With education and knowledge, we are then equipped to not merely talk about ethics and laws, but to truly see the tool of smart technology for what it is. Then we can create the guidelines, policies, and laws that the whole world needs, and that the whole world needs to agree on. Whatever our purpose, whatever we want to achieve - AI and its complementary technologies are the tools we have. They are the 21st century tools to survive, thrive and solve problems. How can we use it? We start with knowing what it is, what it can do and how it is already being used. If we want to create infrastructure, obtain information, start new businesses, provide education and medicine to remote areas, protect our resources, provide new services, improve services, eradicate corruption, solve crimes, improve behavior, or cure diseases - intelligent technologies offer us ways of doing this that we may not have dreamed of.

So, what does an MTP for humanity look like? To qualify as an MTP it needs to be bold, ambitious, transformational, purpose-driven, and able to unite, motivate, and inspire people to passionately execute on the purpose and vision. Here is my first stab at such as an expanded MTP:

Evolve a dynamic, empathic, prosperous, thriving, and self-optimizing civilization that benefits everyone in sustainable ways and in harmony with nature
- *by driving beneficial outcomes for all life through decentralized, adaptive, and agile economic, social and governance systems that reward active participation and positive contributions to society and civilization, but also help to keep peace and protect humanity from any potential harm in elastic ways that respect individual freedom and privacy; and*
- *through using and democratizing knowledge, science, smart technology, and other tools in optimal human-centric ways that are based on wisdom, good values, and ethics to dynamically solve problems, create opportunities and abundance, and share benefits with everyone; and*
- *maximizing quality of life, community building, virtues and character strength development, sense-making, standard of living, wellbeing, and meaningful living of everyone; and*
- *with consideration of the best possible livable habitat, other living organisms, the environment, and our place in the universe.*

If humanity can execute on this MTP, it would address Mark Manson's concerns with respect to people not having hope in the future due to lacking a sense of control, a belief in the value of something, and a community. This MTP looks at humanity and civilization as a living organism where we want to optimize both on an individual and civilization level. As with our own minds and bodies, we preferably want every part of our system to be in good shape and as healthy as possible and living in the best possible conditions that support quality of life, excellent wellbeing, and meaningfulness. We also want to live in a safe, stimulating, dynamic, empathic, prosperous, and thriving world driven by self-optimizing economic, social and governance systems where we can actively participate in community building and make positive contributions to society, have high quality collective sensemaking, and know that others in society are also incentivized to contribute in creating a sustainable self-organizing civilization with the help of democratized smart technology that aims to dynamically solve problems, create opportunities and abundance, and share benefits with everyone, all in harmony with nature. The optimization function associated with this MTP for humanity should aim to maximize supporting the motivational requirements of every person as also defined by Maslow's 8-stage model in terms of physiological, safety, psychological, belongingness, love, esteem, cognitive, aesthetic, self-actualization, and transcendent needs. Scalable smart technology and tools such as personalized AI agents and life coaches under full control of the user can for example assist in this regard. I will share more about this in the last chapter. It would be ideal to also help people to build and continuously improve on virtues and character strengths. *Positive Psychology* has compiled the works of researchers to create a classification system for broadly valued positive traits.[190] The six classes of virtues and the underlying character strengths consists of wisdom and knowledge (e.g., creativity, curiosity, open-mindedness, love of learning, perspective and wisdom), courage (e.g., bravery, persistence, integrity, and vitality), humanity (e.g., love, kindness, and social intelligence), justice (e.g., being an active citizen who is socially responsible and loyal team member, fairness, and leadership), temperance (e.g., forgiveness and mercy, humility and modesty, self-regulation and self-control, and prudence), and transcendence (e.g., appreciation of beauty and excellence, gratitude, hope, humor and playfulness, and spirituality or a sense of purpose). A good character is typically based on the strength of authenticity, persistence, kindness, gratitude, hope, humor, and other character strengths. Just imagine a world where we still have our individual freedom and can guide humanity (and build into our educational systems) to become better humans not only for our own benefit, current fellow citizens of the world, and other life on earth, but also causing positive ripple effects for future generations of civilization to benefit from what we are currently contributing to civilization.

There are so many possible futures at any given moment. These futures are shaped by our collective and individual choices. Some accidental, some intentional, always shaped by many different choices which can for example be attributed to incidences, inaction, behaviors, and reactions at a time. The relationship between what we do today and what we see unfold in one day, one year and 100 years is causal. Usually, it takes large movements and inventions to shape the future, but with digital smart technology and its processing and sharing power whose speed and impact we are still struggling to understand, one suddenly has much power to shape climates, direction, and entire futures for the entire world. This may seem scary, but it is empowering. It is empowering to know that our individual lives, and the collective lives we shape will be the guiding force into the future. If we are aware, educated, and intentional about it, we move into a future that we want, one where humans are the centre of a world enhanced by machines, not overtaken by them. Imagination combined with what we have already seen of smart technology and where it has the potential to take us, allows us to make some educated guesses about our future. Not a future 500 or 1000 years from now, but 10 years, 20 years, 50 years. Many of these future imagined ways of life are already being used in some ways and many minds are applied to solving particular problems.

In a paper, *Goals for Humanity*, David Montgomery proposes the development of progress goals for humanity should go beyond the reduction of negatives.[191] He offers some ideas for goal development as an ongoing process based on Maslow's goal hierarchy, values, standard of living, quality of life, relationships among individuals, and literature. It is good to keep this in mind as we consider the goals that were developed by the United Nations in 2015 as they set the 2030 agenda for sustainable development and transforming our world from an economic, social and environmental perspective.[192] By the time of writing this book, we are already a few years into executing this agenda which is an action plan for humans, the planet and prosperity that aims to also reinforce and extend peace and freedom globally. They consider the greatest global challenge from a sustainability perspective to be the elimination of poverty in its broadest sense and to cure and secure our planet. To this end the United Nations has defined seventeen integrated and unified Sustainable Development Goals (SDGs) and 169 targets to not only end poverty and hunger, but also make sure that every person can fulfil their potential in a respectable, peaceful, and fair manner and within a healthy environment where they can live prosperously, fulfilled, and free from fear and violence. There is a key constraint in that economic, social, and technological progress should occur in harmony with nature as the planet needs to be protected from becoming a less livable planet for us. The latter implies that for the sake of present and future generations of humanity our consumption and production of goods and services needs to be sustainable, that natural resources need to be managed in a sustainable fashion, and that we need to urgently address climate change. The SDGs includes stopping poverty in all its forms everywhere; terminating hunger, achieving food security, improving nutrition and promoting sustainable agriculture; ensuring healthy lives and promoting well-being for all at all ages; ensuring inclusive and equitable quality education and promoting lifelong learning opportunities for all; achieving gender equality and empowering all women and girls; ensuring availability and sustainable management of water and sanitation for all; ensuring access to affordable, reliable, sustainable and modern energy for all; promoting sustained, inclusive and sustainable economic growth, full and productive employment and decent work for all; building resilient infrastructure, promote inclusive and sustainable industrialization and foster innovation; reducing inequality within and among countries; making cities and human settlements inclusive, safe, resilient and sustainable; ensuring sustainable consumption and production patterns; taking urgent action to combat climate change and its impacts; conserving and sustainably using the oceans, seas and marine resources for sustainable development; protecting, restoring and promoting sustainable use of terrestrial ecosystems, sustainably managing forests, combating desertification, and halting and reversing land degradation and halting biodiversity loss; promoting peaceful and inclusive societies for sustainable development, provide access to justice for all and build effective, accountable and inclusive institutions at all levels; and strengthen the means of implementation and revitalize the global partnership for sustainable development.[193] Although a lot of these goals are about reduction of negatives and dealing with the harsh realities of our present world, it does also address some aspects of Maslow's goal hierarchy with respect to basic needs on a physiological and safety level, and aspects such as values, standard of living, quality of life, and relationships among individuals. That said, there is an opportunity to also have goals more focused on supporting humanity's psychological, cognitive, aesthetic, self-fulfillment, and transcendence needs.[194]

In the journal paper *The Sustainable Development Goals viewed through Gross National Happiness, Ubuntu, and Buen Vivir* as well as doctoral dissertation, Dorine van Norren provides a cross-cultural comparison of the South African philosophy of Ubuntu (which means "I am because we are" and emphasizes the value of relatedness and compassion), the Buddhist Gross National Happiness or Bhutan (which calls for mutually reinforcing material and spiritual development, compassion, balance, moderation, harmony between the inner and outer worlds, respect for nature, and interdependence of all things) and the native American idea of Buen Vivir from Ecuador (which is based on living in harmony with others or nature and in balance between spiritual and material wealth).[195] Dorine, with whom I also recently participated as a speaker in the Africa Knows Conference, outlines the perspectives of these three worldviews on the SDGs, and specifically "how they view 'development', 'sustainability', goals and indicators, the implicit value underpinnings of the SDGs, prioritization of goals, and missing links, and leadership."[196] She argues that although the SDGs contain language of all three these specific worldviews, it is evident that Western 'modernism' has a dominant influence with individualism more represented and private sector responsibility lacking to a certain extent as opposed to having sharing, collective agency, and the human-nature-wellbeing interrelationship better incorporated. Dorine therefore recommends a reinterpretation of the SDG framework and globalization in general by finding common ground between Western modernism, Ubuntu, Happiness, and Buen Vivir. [197] This might for example involve replacing worlds like "development" with "interrelationship", "end-result-oriented goals" with "process thinking", and "sustainability" with "cyclic nature" and/or "earth governance".[198]

Although some tweaks and slight improvements can be made, I do not think there are a lot of people that can fault the aspiring and forward-looking vision that accompanies the United Nations' sustainable development goals to provide a solid foundation for a better world:[199]

- "We envisage a world free of poverty, hunger, disease and want, where all life can thrive. We envisage a world free of fear and violence. A world with universal literacy. A world with equitable and universal access to quality education at all levels, to health care and social protection, where physical, mental, and social well-being are assured. A world where we reaffirm our commitments regarding the human right to safe drinking water and sanitation and where there is improved hygiene; and where food is sufficient, safe, affordable, and nutritious. A world where human habitats are safe, resilient and sustainable and where there is universal access to affordable, reliable and sustainable energy."

- "We envisage a world of universal respect for human rights and human dignity, the rule of law, justice, equality and non-discrimination; of respect for race, ethnicity and cultural diversity; and of equal opportunity permitting the full realization of human potential and contributing to shared prosperity. A world which invests in its children and in which every child grows up free from violence and exploitation. A world in which every woman and girl enjoys full gender equality and all legal, social, and economic barriers to their empowerment have been removed. A just, equitable, tolerant, open and socially inclusive world in which the needs of the most vulnerable are met."

- "We envisage a world in which every country enjoys sustained, inclusive and sustainable economic growth and decent work for all. A world in which consumption and production patterns and use of all-natural resources – from air to land, from rivers, lakes and aquifers to oceans and seas - are sustainable. One in which democracy, good governance, and the rule of law as well as an enabling environment at national and international levels, are essential for sustainable development, including sustained and inclusive economic growth, social development, environmental protection and the eradication of poverty and hunger. One in which development and the application of technology are climate-sensitive, respect biodiversity and are resilient. One in which humanity lives in harmony with nature and in which wildlife and other living species are protected."

Although this vision is great and also ties in with the proposed MTP for humanity, from an execution perspective the vision and goals are likely to be more difficult to achieve if not impossible in its totality as it is embedded in the practical realities and constraints of the present world and assumes still working with the current institutions, governance systems, economic systems, political systems, and ideologies to address the problems that we have as humanity. The World Economic Forum also notes in 2020 that the delivery of many of the UN's sustainable development goals are "far off track, and in some areas, progress is going backwards."[200] To this end they have introduced a global public-private sector 2030Vision Platform (a merger of Arm's 2030Vision Partnership Initiative with the WEF's Frontier 2030 initiative and co-chaired by the United Nations Development Programme) to help mobilize a more focused and collaborative effort to use smart technology to help achieve these goals in accelerated fashion. Although initiatives such as this one is good and part of a multi-pronged approach to at least work towards the realization of the SDGs, their effectiveness will likely still be limited if it does not fully address the more fundamental aspects and systemic root causes of the underlying problems that we face. What I am advocating is in addition to the vision and SDGs to also have specific goals that support the proposed MTP for humanity that can help take us from our present economic, social and governance systems to one where we have given ourselves a much better chance to be successful in tackling the global problems from a wealth gap and inequality, economic, political, society, climate change, technology and public safety and cybersecurity perspective. Some of these specific challenges as also mentioned in the previous chapter include the lack of economic opportunity and unemployment; safety, security, and wellbeing; lack of education; food and water security; government accountability, transparency and corruption; political polarization; dysfunctional governance; digital dictatorships; societal manipulation and political propaganda; religious conflicts; poverty where more than 70% of the people in the world own less than $10,000 or roughly 3 percent of total wealth in the world;[201] inequality from an income, discrimination, and geopolitical perspective; financial inclusion and credit access; large scale conflict and wars (e.g., nuclear war; biowarfare; and lethal autonomous weapons); pandemics; health in developing nations; climate change and destruction of nature; technology disruption and intelligent automation; overpopulation in developing regions such as Africa; population collapse; and cybercrime.

What are the goals associated with the kind of world that are effectively implied by the proposed MTP for humanity? As a first attempt, the following outline maps 14 specific MTP goals interspersed with the relevant 17 SDGs within the proposed MTP for humanity framework. As with the framework, the MTP goals are also a function of a synthesis and sensemaking of many ideas and proposals of which some were highlighted and discussed earlier in this chapter. I have also included some notes for where some of the current SDGs need further consideration.

Evolve a dynamic, empathic, prosperous, thriving, and self-optimizing civilization that benefits everyone in sustainable ways and in harmony with nature

- *by driving beneficial outcomes for all life through decentralized, adaptive, and agile economic, social and governance systems that reward active participation and positive contributions to society and civilization, but also help to keep peace and protect humanity from any potential harm in elastic ways that respect individual freedom and privacy; and*

  - ☐ MTP Goal 1: Develop a Pareto-topia type of world that aims to maximize a beneficial future for as many people as possible with many Protopian elements and in harmony with nature.

  - ☐ MTP Goal 2: Build a more local, more human city-state civilization with decentralized, community-based, and self-optimized governance and a more elastic, dynamic, and direct democracy with social structures that have polycentric and polyarchic elements.

  - ☐ MTP Goal 3: Re-engineer and continuously improve on designing the most positive, uplifting, and compassionate human-centric society and associated incentives that complement and extend the currently evolving workplace by rewarding active participation and positive contributions to society and civilization.

  - ☐ MTP Goal 4: Implement a more robust, resilient, responsive, dynamically fine-tuned, and controlled form of capitalism to drive sustainable economic growth in an open-ended fashion and maximize the benefit to all stakeholders.

  - ☐ MTP Goal 5: Promote infinite game dynamics that aims to perpetuate games in the broader sense of the word and limit rivalry wherever possible and only have finite game dynamics and limited forms of rivalry where it makes sense to do so and where it does not have harming effects.

  - ☐ SDG 8: Promote sustained, inclusive, and sustainable economic growth, full and productive employment, and decent work for all

    - ☐ Note: In a smart technology driven world with an increasing deployment of assisted, augmented, and autonomous intelligence applications, it will have an impact on the job market as we know it. As mentioned in MTP Goal 4, we would need to look at a redefined workplace that is complemented by a reward-driven compassionate and positive value creation system for society. There is also a question mark about the need for never-ending economic growth as opposed to open-ended economic growth that is more flexible.

☐ SDG 10: Reduce inequality within and among countries

> ☐ Note: Although our current civilization's organization with respect to countries is likely to be part and parcel of our current world for the foreseeable future, in a highly networked city-state type of civilization, there is a reduced need for countries in its current form. Countries in a city-state civilization can for example have an adapted role of forming a regional or virtual grouping of city-states that interacts in mutually beneficial ways that take advantage of proximity and other common denominators.

☐ SDG 11: Make cities and human settlements inclusive, safe, resilient, and sustainable

☐ SDG 16: Promote peaceful and inclusive societies for sustainable development, provide access to justice for all and build effective, accountable, and inclusive institutions at all levels

☐ SDG 17: Strengthen the means of implementation and revitalize the global partnership for sustainable development

> ☐ Note: This is likely easier to do in a highly collaborative and networked city-state type of civilization

- *through using and democratizing knowledge, science, smart technology, and other tools in optimal human-centric ways that are based on wisdom, good values, and ethics to dynamically solve problems, create opportunities and abundance, and share benefits with everyone; and*

☐ MTP Goal 6: Collaborate in optimal human-centric ways to use our growing knowledge base and general-purpose technologies in a wise, value-based, and ethical manner to solve humanity's most pressing problems and creating abundance for everyone.

☐ MTP Goal 7: Democratize AI and smart technology from a use and benefits perspective to help society thrive.

☐ SDG 1: End poverty in all its forms everywhere

☐ SDG 2: End hunger, achieve food security and improved nutrition and promote sustainable agriculture

☐ SDG 6: Ensure availability and sustainable management of water and sanitation for all

☐ SDG 7: Ensure access to affordable, reliable, sustainable, and modern energy for all

☐ SDG 9: Build resilient infrastructure, promote inclusive and sustainable industrialization and foster innovation

- *maximizing quality of life, community building, virtues and character strength development, sense-making, standard of living, wellbeing, and meaningful living of everyone; and*

☐ MTP Goal 8: Ensure that we balance population growth and decline with quality of life.

☐ MTP Goal 9: Implement better collective sensemaking for all of humanity and better alignment with respect to our common goals and visions.

☐ MTP Goal 10: Build local and virtual empathic communities connected via a global network with more meaningful work and relationships.

☐ MTP Goal 11: Help people live more meaningful lives through using Maslow's 8-stage motivational needs framework that includes physiological, safety, psychological, esteem, cognitive, aesthetic, self-fulfillment, and transcendence needs.

☐ MTP Goal 12: Support people through scalable smart technology driven approaches complemented by human-centric lifelong and life-wide education services to build and continuously improve on virtues and character strengths which includes wisdom and knowledge, courage, humanity, justice, temperance, and transcendence.

☐ SDG 3: Ensure healthy lives and promote well-being for all at all ages.

☐ SDG 4: Ensure inclusive and equitable quality education and promote lifelong learning opportunities for all.

☐ SDG 5: Achieve gender equality and empower all women and girls.

- *with consideration of the best possible livable habitat, other living organisms, the environment, and our place in the universe.*

  ☐ MTP Goal 13: Make Earth a truly more livable habitat for humanity and as many life forms as possible and reduce our dependence on animal life for food and any unhealthy processed foods.

  ☐ MTP Goal 14: Make life multi-planetary, extract and make use of resources from beyond Earth, and explore the universe through advancing smart technology.

  ☐ SDG 12: Ensure sustainable consumption and production patterns.

  ☐ SDG 13: Take urgent action to combat climate change and its impacts.

  ☐ SDG 14: Conserve and sustainably use the oceans, seas, and marine resources for sustainable development.

  ☐ SDG 15: Protect, restore, and promote sustainable use of terrestrial ecosystems, sustainably manage forests, combat desertification, and halt and reverse land degradation and halt biodiversity loss.

Although we must be practical and realistic given the current fragmented dynamics and the powerful forces at play, we still need to start somewhere to supplement the current status quo approaches with ones that directly aim to build the beneficial future that we want. Having considered various potential beneficial outcomes for society in the previous section, it seems to make sense as a first MTP goal to select a Pareto-topia type of world that aims to maximize a beneficial future for as many people as possible in harmony with nature and with many Protopian elements such as AI-driven smart technology helping to drive abundance through for example significantly reducing costs of energy, healthcare, education, transportation, and the production of food, goods and services. Given how people are increasingly moving from rural to urban centers which leads to cities becoming larger with greater population density, cities and their suburbs will play an even more significant role in the future as it provides opportunities for focused wealth creation via network effects, productivity, efficiency gains and scale. Urban growth is further accelerated in a virtuous cycle by more people being attracted to the concentrated wealth creation and smart technology helping to improve living experiences. Drivers for urbanization include the increase in mechanization, automation, and innovation in agriculture and other sectors, lifestyle preferences, attitudes, the increasing concentration of wealth creation, and the specialized nature of modern workforces in the knowledge economy. The second MTP goal is focused on building a more elastic, dynamic, and direct type of democracy through a community-based city-state civilization as also mentioned by Daniel Schmachtenberger earlier in this chapter, except that they do not need to be completely anti-rivalrous as discussed in the fifth MTP goal that promotes infinite game dynamics with selected limited rivalry where it makes sense to do so without harming effects. What I am advocating for here is that these city-states are also more decentralized with social structures that have polycentric and polyarchic elements as described by Max Borders and also more elastic and self-optimized through human-centric AI-augmented governance systems that are transparent and explainable. The default state of affairs should be that the real-time governance is directly influenced by wishes and needs of the local communities within the city, but also one that is elastic enough to quickly move into a protective mode in order to respond in a dynamic and agile fashion to dangers and threats that could harm the citizens in the city-state. With each city-state having its own AI agent(s) to help optimize the city, it could also be elastic in quickly responding to opportunities and possible engagements with other city-states within a highly connected network as more of them develop globally. The recommendation is to either build a new city-state civilization from scratch or select existing cities within countries to take the lead and directly transform them by starting to experiment with this type of a smart city-state approach.

Geoffrey West in *Scale: The Universal Laws of Life, Growth, and Death in Organisms, Cities, and Companies* expresses concern about the "continuous growth and the consequent ever-increasing acceleration of the pace of life which he thinks have profound consequences for the entire planet and, in particular, for cities, socioeconomic life, and the process of global urbanization" and our lives on "the metaphorical accelerating socioeconomic treadmill" as he describes it.[202] He does not think this is sustainable, that the accelerating rate of change causes severe strain on all dimensions of city life and that we are on our way to a massive crash or a "potential collapse of the entire socioeconomic fabric". Geoffrey asks if we would be satisfied "with some sublinear scaling and its attendant natural limiting, or no-growth, stable configuration?" and "can we have the kind of vibrant, innovative, creative society driven by ideas and wealth creation as manifested by the best of our world's cities and social organizations, or are we destined to a planet of urban slums and the ultimate specter of devastation?"[203] We might need to get use to a more open-ended growth and define progress in a different way which is closer to some of the proposed MTP goals that link to maximizing quality of life, community building, virtues and character strength development, sense-making, standard of living, wellbeing and meaningful living of everyone. Geoffrey reckons that such an outcome would be a true significant paradigm shift. The third MTP goal ties in with this and states that we should aim to re-engineer and design a positive, uplifting, and compassionate human-centric society with incentives that rewards active participation and positive contributions to society and civilization. This should be a continuous improvement process and also complementary to the currently evolving workplace. It is particularly important that we are all clear and in agreement about the society that we want and make sure that we are as inclusive as possible when engineering this. The fourth MTP goal is focused on implementing a dynamically fine-tuned and controlled form of capitalism that are more robust, resilient, and responsive to drive sustainable economic growth in an open-ended fashion and maximize the benefit to all stakeholders. As also mentioned by Ray Dalio earlier in this chapter, capitalism is the most effective motivator of people and allocator of resources to raise people's living standards. We still want the benefits of innovation driven by capitalism, but also want to address the wealth gaps and sharing of benefits in a more equitable manner. We therefore need an adaptable and more dynamically controlled form of capitalism embedded within an elastic form of direct democracy that we can experiment with to help fix the issues with capitalism. China's state capitalism is an example of a hybrid system that seems to work well, but an authoritarian form of governance and state control is still a major concern. There are also a multitude of other ideas such as radical markets, data as labor, the sharing economy, building out the commons and others discussed earlier in this chapter that can be considered for experimentation.

Just imagine a world where AI and other smart technology along with knowledge and science in general are used and democratized in such a way that maximizes the benefits to everyone. Even better if we can ensure that this is done through human-centric ways that are wise, value-based, and ethical and used to solve humanity's most pressing problems, creating opportunities and abundance, and sharing benefits with everyone. This is what the sixth and seventh MTP goals are all about. It will also give us a better chance to solve poverty, hunger, better food security, improved nutrition, as well as our water, sanitation, and energy needs. In the next two chapters the focus is more on specific details and ideas with respect to democratizing AI solutions to help shape a beneficial human-centric future and sharing a proposal about decentralized super platforms with personalized AI agents that not only empower individuals and monetizes their data and services, but can also be extended to families, virtual groups, communities, cities, city-states, and beyond. Although we are on track to likely build strong AI systems, explosive run-away superintelligence systems are not necessarily a given. We should not get ahead of ourselves. Our imaginations are sometimes running wild. We should stay focused on applying general purpose technologies wisely for our collective benefit in smart and unselfish ways. The next group of MTP goals has to do with maximizing quality of life, community building, virtues and character strength development, sense-making, standard of living, wellbeing, and meaningful living of everyone. These are some of the most important goals that are not explicitly addressed by the UN's SDGs except for standard of living, healthy lives, wellbeing, quality education and gender equality. The eight MTP goal is about the need to have a balance in how we grow our populations whilst still maximizing quality of life. Excessive population growth like we see in certain developing countries, especially in Africa, makes it very difficult to address quality of life for these citizens in meaningful ways within reasonable time frames. On the other end of the spectrum is population decline which hampers productivity growth and eats away at the domestic market base which can also affect quality of life.

Another major problem is collective sensemaking for all of humanity and better alignment with respect to our common goals and visions which needs to be urgently addressed as also discussed early in this chapter and also expressed in the ninth MTP goal. Many factors contribute to the current state of humanity's collective sensemaking and alignment with respect to common goals and visions such as information overload, misinformation, fake news, social media manipulation, people not having intelligent information filters to help guide them, and vastly different and fragmented ideologies. Joscha Bach thinks there is a certain way in which people link together that produces intelligent agents such as a family, a tribe, a community, a business, or a nation.[204] Looking at this from an intelligent systems perspective these groupings seem to have agency, memory, and goals even though it is not currently sentient. These "intelligent agents" embody information processing principles where for example cooperating groups with aligned interests tend to win over groups that do not. The key problem to solve is how to align these interests. Humanity has found a very interesting solution to align people that involves reputation and punishment. Joscha argues that a solution of reputation works in the long game where people can keep track of who did what which forces people to not play a very short game. In the short game if you do not see people again or there are too many people to keep track of in terms of who did what, reputation does not scale within these larger groups. He believes that humanity's solution to this alignment problem is to be "less smart" and give up agency to become "programmable primates" that stay in lockstep. There is enough evidence to point to humans in general being able to believe things without good reason, being manipulated or hypnotized into adopting policies and beliefs without reason other than convergence. He describes this ability to converge on beliefs even when they are irrational makes it possible for us to move in lockstep to form arbitrary functional units. Our values are a way for us to be programmed to move in lockstep. It seems like people look to serve systems that are larger than themselves, that have meaning and purpose, and that are sacred. In general people also love others that serve the same system and find meaning in things like art, science, and religion.[205] The hope is that with better collective sensemaking and alignment we can make smarter decisions in the best interest of humanity as a whole. I have started this chapter with different perspectives on the meaning of life and some sensemaking in this regard. The tenth and eleventh MTP goals are focused on not only ensuring meaningful work and relationships within empathic communities, but also on supporting humanity's psychological, cognitive, aesthetic, self-fulfillment and transcendence needs as also captured by Maslow's 8-stage motivational needs framework. Given that we know how important meaning is for humans even if we do not explicitly acknowledge that or even think about it, it makes sense to have smart goals focused on this and helping people to make the most out of life. Another important area for human development that is neglected is the twelfth MTP goal that focuses on virtues and character strength development which includes wisdom and knowledge, courage, humanity, justice, temperance and transcendence. In general, we can do a much better job in supporting people to become better humans through scalable smart technology driven approaches complemented by human-centric life-long and life-wide education services to build and continuously improve on virtues and character strengths. Just imagine a world where we have a growing number of people developing good character, having smart sensemaking and alignment, and wanting to have meaningful lives and engage with one another in meaningful ways. Whilst we focus on all the mentioned MTP goals and SDGs to drive to a better civilization, the final two MTP goals (thirteen and fourteen) are all about ensuring the best possible livable habitat here on Earth for humanity and other life forms, reducing our dependence on animal life for food and any unhealthy processed foods, being considerate of other living organisms, make life multi-planetary (in line with Elon Musk's vision), extract and make use of resources from beyond Earth, and explore the universe through our advancing smart technology.

In a talk by Trent McConaghy titled *AI, Blockchains, and Humanity: The Next 10 Billion Years of Human Civilization* he proposes a broad holistic solution that not only addresses our threats with respect to solving climate change and AI's impact on the job market and controlling our resources, but also one that catalyzes an unrestricted expression of humanity as we explore the universe.[206] His proposal involves a top-level design for the unrestricted expression of humanity that provides people with a better substrate that includes a body plan as well as a better spread of power that have implications for governments. The first goal is to work towards a decentralized computational substrate for humanity that keeps our dynamics, values, and patterns of intelligence, but ensure that our cognitive capacity can compete with AIs and that we are not limited to our current biological bodies to make it possible to explore the stars. The design for the substrate goal involves connecting networks at the level of data (as with TCP/IP) and of value (as with decentralization and blockchain) on an intra-planetary and interplanetary level where our patterns of intelligence execute on this substrate that no one owns or controls and where we can operate on a peer-level with AIs and not compete with them.[207] Getting our patterns of intelligence on such a substrate might sound very far-fetched and also not something that I have included on a MTP goals level, but I think it is important to consider as part of sense-making of various responses to the threat of AI systems controlling all of humanity's resources. Trent proposes a so-called *Bandwidth++* approach where the bandwidth between people and computation gets to the level of bandwidth between people through near-term market drivers such as EEG-based brain-computer interfaces (BCI) or eye tracking, and medium-term market drivers such as perfect memory through recording everything we see and hear throughout the day and communicating in pictures and videos.[208] As the devices are continuously delivering higher quality BCI scanning, we might be sending computation jobs outside the brain by thinking about it and getting feedback from non-brain computation and storage. Trent reckons that at some point we would not even know what is in the brain versus the non-brain part and that most of the computation and storage would be in the non-brain part in silicon where the brain part might become outmoded or disused.[209] His second goal is very much in line with the MTP for humanity and as it speaks to decentralized governance and steering clear of concentrations of power that prevents progress. He argues that controlling a decentralized substrate should not accidently lead to autocracy or oppression and that people will be less confined by the nation state authorities. From a design perspective governance of the substrate can follow a one citizen one vote approach (without having tokens of value) and groups of people can be dynamically organized in hierarchical fashion based on bandwidth of communication and not controlled by governments or nation states. Trent ends his talk by saying "What do you want for the future of humanity? Let's do system design at the level of civilization! We can reconcile climate change, jobs, UBI, AI. Let us rewire the internet, let's rewire society! Let us reaffirm our humanity in the face of AI and explore the cosmos!".[210]

We need new and realistic pareto-topia, protopias, and utopias. We want visionaries, lateral thinkers, city developers, futurologists, economists, technologists, industry experts, scientists, politicians, and others to all express their opinions and perspectives on what better structures and solutions could look like. Seeking alternatives is arduous, strenuous, and challenging, but it will be worth it. Each one of us has the power to steer where the

Smart Technology Era goes. If we insist on being outside of it, fearing and complaining from the sidelines, we miss our chance to shape the future.

11. Democratizing AI to Help Shape a Beneficial Human-centric Future

Now that we have a clearer picture of what a beneficial human-centric future for humanity could look like, let us explore the various aspects of democratizing AI to help shape that beneficial human-centric future. As I have mentioned risks, concerns, and challenges of AI for society in Chapter 8, I am sharing some solutions here to counter AI's potential negative impacts. It is also evident that democratizing AI is a multi-faceted problem for which a strategic planning framework is needed along with careful design to ensure AI is used for social good and beneficial outcomes. Furthermore, we cannot democratize AI to benefit everyone if we do not build human-compatible, ethical, trustworthy, and beneficial AI, and address bias and discrimination in a meaningful way. Given the accelerating pace of AI-driven automation and its impact on people's required skills, competencies, and knowledge in the dynamic job market, people need to become lifelong and life-wide learners that can make proactive smart choices about where the needs and opportunities are shifting and where they can make meaningful contributions.

Solutions to Address AI's Potential Negative Impacts

As seen in the previous chapters, there is a strong expectancy and belief that AI and its applications can have a very positive and beneficial impact on humanity if implemented wisely, but also a wariness and circumspection of its potential risks and challenges. In this section I will outline some of the solutions, countermeasures, and antidotes to address some of AI's potential negative impacts and worries. I will start with the Pew Research Center's *Artificial Intelligence and the Future of Humans* report that prescribes three solutions categories, namely a focus on the global good through enhanced human collaboration across borders and stakeholder groups, implementing value-based systems that involve developing policies to assure AI will be directed at the common good and human-centricity, and prioritizing people through updating or reforming political and economic systems that ensures human-machine collaboration is done in ways that benefit people in the workplace and society more broadly.[1] These solutions also tie in with the proposed Massive Transformative Purpose (MTP) for Humanity and some specific MTP goals discussed in the previous chapter. From a global good perspective, it is proposed that digital cooperation should be used to further humanity's needs and requirements, that people across the globe should be better aligned and have agreement on how to tackle some of humanity's biggest problems through widely recognized innovative approaches and keeping control over intricate human-digital networks. This solution is also in line with MTP Goal 6 that focuses on collaborating in optimal human-centric ways to use our growing knowledge base and general-purpose technologies in a wise, value-based, and ethical manner to solve humanity's most pressing problems and creating abundance for everyone. The same holds for MTP Goal 7 with its focal point on democratizing AI and smart technology from a use and benefits perspective to help society thrive, as well as MTP Goal 9 that addresses the implementation of improved collective sensemaking for all of humanity and better alignment with respect to our common goals and visions. I am also a big proponent of implementing value-based systems and making sure that we have policies that help direct AI for beneficial outcomes. Their proposed solution of building decentralized intelligent digital networks that are inclusive, empathic, and have built-in social and ethical responsibilities is also in line with the above MTP goals as well as MTP Goal 10 that seeks to build local and virtual empathic communities connected via a global network with more meaningful work and relationships. MTP goals 11 and 12 are both also value based as they are fixed on helping people live more meaningful lives and improving on virtues and character strengths. The third solutions category of prioritizing people through expanding their capacities and capabilities for improved human-AI collaboration can be addressed through some significant changes to our economic and political systems to better support humans. The first 5 MTP goals are geared towards just that through decentralized, community-based, and self-optimized governance, a more elastic and direct democracy, a compassionate human-centric society, and associated incentives that complement and extend the currently evolving workplace by rewarding active participation and positive contributions to society and civilization, and a dynamically controlled form of capitalism to maximize the benefit to all stakeholders.

As outlined in Chapter 8, McKinsey Global Institute's report on *Applying AI for Social Good* maps AI use cases to domains for social good and discusses how AI solutions can be used for social benefit, as well as how risks or negative impacts can be managed and difficulties can be handled.[2] From a risks' perspective, MGI mentions a number of them which include bias that leads to unjust outcomes such as machine learning algorithms trained on historical data that are skewed or potentially prejudiced, the difficulty in explaining the outputs from large complex machine learning models for regulatory use cases, violating privacy over personal information could cause damage, and deploying insecure and unsafe AI applications for social good. Such risks can be alleviated by ensuring that people are kept in the loop through cross-functional teams interceding as appropriate, examining data to detect bias and determine if there is a representation deficiency, having separate dedicated teams that perform solution tests similar to the red versus blue teams in cyber security use cases, guiding users to follow specific procedures to avoid them impulsively trust AI solutions, and having AI researchers developing methods to enhance model transparency and explainability.[3] In order to scale up the use of AI for Social Good, they recommend two areas that many other sources also reference namely addressing the scarcity of people with AI research and application skills and experience through growing the talent pool and making data more attainable for social impact cases through data collection and generator projects. MGI also provides a checklist for deploying AI solutions in the social sector starting with the basics of clearly defining the problem; formulating the technical problem structure; alleviating the risks described above and making sure of regulatory limitations, organization acceptance, efficient deployment, and technology accessibility; deploying AI solutions at scale with committed resources; making sure of data availability, integration, accessibility, and quality; having AI practitioners that can properly train and test AI models using sufficient computing capacity; deploying AI models in the target environment that deliver adequate value to drive significant adoption by organization; and having the required technical capabilities in the organization to run and maintain AI solutions in sustainable fashion.[4] This checklist is fairly generic and also relevant for development and deployment of AI solutions in the private and public sector more broadly.

As a response to the vast changes in the global threat landscape a report called *The Malicious Use of Artificial Intelligence: Forecasting, Prevention, and Mitigation* by contributors from Oxford University, Future of Humanity Institute, Centre for the Study of Existential Risk, Center for a New American Security, Electronic Frontier Foundation, OpenAI, Stanford University, University of Cambridge and a number of other universities and organizations provided a general framework for AI and security treats, various scenarios and security domains within the digital, physical and political security domains, a strategic analysis and recommended interventions.[5] They specifically highlight how the security threat landscape is affected by AI systems that inject new potential threats, broaden existing threats, and even change the typical nature of threats. Some specific high-level recommendations include a much tighter collaboration between policymakers and technical researchers about understanding, preventing and alleviating the potential ill-natured and damaging AI use cases; ensuring that stakeholders and domain experts from across the spectrum are involved in these discussions and helping to determine the best path forward; the identification of best practices and guidelines in research areas focused on dual-use concerns where smart technology can specifically be misused in computer security; and AI practitioners and researchers should carefully consider the dual-use nature of their applications and research, making sure that their research priorities and standards are not affected and directed by misapplications and harmful use cases, and proactively alert the relevant people about such potential outcomes. In addition, they also advise on advancing a culture of responsibility, collaborative learning from and with the cybersecurity community, investigating current openness of research and publications in areas that might pose potential risk, and developing policy and technology-driven solutions to help drive towards a safer future where privacy is safeguarded, and AI is used for common good and public-good security. As it is clear that the challenges are formidable and the consequences are important not only in the security risk category, we need the participation of all stakeholders in the private and public sectors to act on these types of recommendations.

A recent BBC article asks, "what would it take for a global totalitarian government to rise to power indefinitely" and that this could be a horrendous outcome that could be "worse than extinction".[6] Totalitarianism refers to a governmental or political system where the state has complete authority and controls public and private life and where opposition is outlawed.[7] It is a more extreme form of authoritarianism where citizens blindly accept and comply with authority. Although a global totalitarian government still looks improbable, we already observe AI enabling a form of authoritarianism in a few countries and reinforcing infrastructure that could potentially be captured by a dictator or oppressor. So, this is a real and present danger. Apart from AI enhancing surveillance of citizens, it is also being used to spread online misinformation, propaganda, and fabricated political messages in personalized fashion via social media. So how does one avoid these digital authoritarian scenarios? Apart from solutions mentioned above, the execution of goals linked to the proposed MTP for Humanity would clearly be preventative steps in the right direction as the focus is on building a decentralized and community-based city-state civilization with self-optimized governance and a more elastic, dynamic, and direct democracy which is diametrically opposed to centralized control and digital authoritarianism. Tucker Davey from the Future of Life Institute strongly recommends that we make a decision about what are "acceptable and unacceptable uses of AI" and that we need to be "careful about letting it control so much of our infrastructure". He states that we are already on the wrong track "if we're arming police with facial recognition and the federal government is collecting all of our data".[8]

Can we steer AI towards positive outcomes? Can we advance AI in a way that is most likely going to benefit humanity as a whole and help solve some of our most pressing real-world problems? Can we shape AI to be an extension of individual human wills and as broadly and evenly distributed as possible? The answer is yes to all these questions. If society approaches AI with an open mind, the technologies emerging from the field could profoundly transform society for the better in the coming decades. Like other technologies, AI has the potential to be used for good or criminal purposes. A robust and knowledgeable debate about how to best steer AI in ways that enrich our lives, and our society is an urgent and vital need. It is incumbent on all of us to make sure we are building a world in which every individual has an opportunity to thrive. As also discussed in previous chapters it is likely that the future of AI will impact our everyday life through automating transportation, enhancing us with cyborg technology, taking over dangerous jobs, helping to address or potentially solve climate change, providing robots or AI agents as friends, and improving elder care.[9] Stanford University's *The One Hundred Year Study on Artificial Intelligence* highlights substantial increases in the future uses of AI applications, including more self-driving cars, healthcare diagnostics and targeted treatment, and physical assistance for elder care.[10] Though quality education will likely always require active engagement by human teachers, AI promises to enhance education at all levels, especially by providing personalization at scale, AI will increasingly enable entertainment that is more interactive, personalized, and engaging. Research should be directed toward understanding how to leverage these attributes for individuals' and society's benefit. With targeted incentives and funding priorities, AI could help address the needs of low resource communities. In the longer term, AI may be thought of as a radically different mechanism for wealth creation in which everyone should be entitled to a portion of the world's AI-produced treasures. The measure of success for AI applications is the value they create for human lives. Misunderstandings about what AI is and is not could fuel opposition to technologies with the potential to benefit everyone. Poorly informed regulation that stifles innovation would be a terrible mistake. Going forward, the ease with which people use and adapt to AI applications will likewise largely determine their success. Society is now at a crucial juncture in determining how to deploy AI-based technologies in ways that promote rather than hinder democratic values such as freedom, equality, and transparency. Machine intelligence already pervades our lives and will likely replace tasks rather than jobs in the near term and will also create new kinds of jobs. However, the new jobs that will emerge are harder to imagine in advance than the existing jobs that will likely be lost.

Democratizing AI is a Multi-Faceted Problem

We know that democratizing AI is a problem with many dimensions and is not only dependent on progress in AI, smart technology, science, and policy, but excellent collaboration between the public sector, academic institutions, and private sector as well as global organizations and governments developing policies, laws and have task forces focused on beneficial outcomes of all stakeholders and protecting the rights of citizens. A feasible solution is to democratize AI throughout the lifecycle starting with its development, deployment, distribution, and its use. When AI business strategy consultants and AI infrastructure companies refer to "democratizing AI", they imply enabling more people, including those with no background in AI, machine learning or data science to be able to use the technology to innovate and build AI models or systems to solve real-world problems. We are seeing some of the tech giants such as Google, Amazon and Microsoft providing ready-to-use AI application programming interfaces (APIs), tools, and drag-and-drop components that can be integrated into applications without having to know the details behind it or how to train and test machine learning models. An AI company such as DataRobot with their end-to-end enterprise AI platform that automates machine learning models development and deployment has for example a whitepaper on *Democratizing AI for All: Transforming Your Operating Model to Support AI Adoption* that discusses aligning AI to business objectives and drivers, identifying impactful use cases, building trust in AI, and making sure that the AI strategy can be executed as it relates to the business vision and strategy, services and customers, processes and channels, people and organization, technology and enablers, and governance and reporting.[11] These aspects were also covered in more detail in Chapter 4 where I have elaborated on AI-driven digital transformation of the business enterprise. From an application's perspective, democratization of AI is necessary to help address the dearth of people with AI, machine learning and data science experience, knowledge, and skills on the one hand, but also to get better adoption of AI in accordance to best practices for digital transformation and more people in business involved in the implementation of AI-driven solutions. Automated machine learning solutions such as Google's AutoML and DataRobot assist with reducing the risk, cost, and complexity of deploying AI models in a production environment, provides transparency and documentation and tools for understanding model accuracy, supports developing many different types of models simultaneously to get to the best possible model to solve a specific problem, retraining and redeployment of models, and monitor model performance.[12]

Anand Rao, who is an AI lead in PwC's analytics practice in the USA, reckons that democratizing AI is a "double-edged sword" and advises that although more and better access to AI software and hardware will likely lead to more application-related innovation, one needs to manage the process of access in a cautious manner to avoid misuse, abuse, bias, and related problems.[13] Having assisted many companies across multiple industries with their AI-driven digital transformation, I fully endorse this sentiment. He makes the point that AI companies providing products, tools or platforms across the technology spectrum need to carefully decide which part of the value chain they want to democratize and contribute to responsible, trustworthy AI with respect to design, training, testing, support, and maintenance aspects. One can see this technology spectrum as covering data ingestion, storing, processing, and exploring; then the broad range of machine learning algorithms that are democratized and accessible via open source repositories such as GitHub; then there is the storage and computing platforms such as Google Compute Engine, Amazon Web Services, and Microsoft Azure which is less democratized but does provide cloud-based environments and hardware resources for training machine learning models within their own environments at scale; this is followed-up by the actual model development for specific solutions where automated machine learning platforms and tools such as Google's AutoML and DataRobot as mentioned above can help to democratize model development, but where mistakes can easily creep in for non-expert users; and the development of a marketplace for data, AI models and algorithms such as Kaggle and Zindi where one also need to be careful in how to apply models in the correct context.[14] Anand also emphasizes the importance of knowing the actual users of these systems as the beneficiaries of AI democratization can predominantly be categorized into specialist developers such as AI experts and data scientists, power users that are well-trained but not experts, and casual users which are business users that does not have theoretical or practical know-how with respect to data science and its practical implementation. Once it has been determined what specifically needs to be democratized and what tools will be used, the focus can shift to how to democratize AI within an organization which involves training, data governance, AI model or solution governance, intellectual property rights and open sourcing related matters. Organizational leadership has an important responsibility to ensure that people that are involved in AI development and deployment are properly trained with respect to the foundations and practical aspects of data science and machine learning. If this is not the case, AI implementations can easily lead to basic errors, inaccuracies and unintentional or undesired consequences. Another area that Anand highlights is data governance that involves the thorough monitoring and management of data integrity and security to help reduce risk as well as a clear understanding of the ownership and control of the data that flows through the AI solutions and the rights with respect to the model outputs and insights obtained. This includes ownership of intellectual property rights which is important to ensure that the benefits of AI democratization are shared appropriately. Machine learning also needs specific governance in order to check for accuracy, generalization capability, fairness, and explainability. Anand also emphasizes the importance of open sourcing as a key vehicle for democratizing AI and making sure that all participants contribute to this as far as it is possible and not just benefiting in a one-way flow fashion. There clearly needs to be a balance between democratized innovation on the one hand and responsible trustworthy implementation with full governance, transparency, and adherence to best practices and standards on the other hand.[15]

In an essay on the importance of democratizing AI, Francois Chollet mentions that although we have seen tremendous progress with AI and deep learning research and applications specifically over the last number of years, we are really only at the start of unlocking the potential of AI, figuring out the "killer apps", and seeing how AI will become the interface to our information driven world and have a significant economic and social impact as it reshapes our scientific research, healthcare, education, transportation, communication, culture, and every part of our civilization.[16] He compares AI and where it is now as a world-changing smart technology that increasingly automates cognitive tasks to that of the Internet at the time when commercial use restrictions were lifted in 1995. Initially the Internet did not have any major impact on society, but we know everything changed over the last quarter of a century. The impact was dramatic, and our civilization effectively got a "nervous system" or at the very least upgraded it in a significant way with "instant communications, a supercomputer in your pocket, and the entire knowledge of humanity available at your fingertips". I'm also in agreement with Francois' assessment that AI's impact will be even bigger and will be disrupting every industry, all business models, all jobs, every application, every process in our society, even culture and art, and every aspect of our lives, and change what it means to be human.[17] As elaborated in the previous chapters, I also believe that the evolution of AI is opening up tremendous opportunities for humanity if we can execute on them wisely. Apart from a wide range of exhilarating opportunities, it also has the potential to create abundance, affluence and help people to live more meaningful lives. Similar to how the Internet remained open and has democratized people's ability to express themselves, connect with people at will, start businesses and leverage it for their own benefit, he reckons that we can do the same with AI, except that it is "not a given that every technological revolution should turn out as a net positive for humanity, empowering individuals and bringing us higher potential for learning and creating, for self-direction and self-actualization".[18] We should be laser focused on ensuring that everyone is given the opportunity to learn and unlock value from AI in an easy and free fashion in order for us to maximize tapping into people's potential for positive, innovative and creative contributions to society. As we did with the internet being a net positive for humanity against the background of many mistakes made and lessons learned (especially with social media), it is our responsibility to ensure that we steer the civilization ship in the right direction when it comes to smart technology such as AI. We know the potential for beneficial outcomes is enormous. Francois also mentions in a tweet that in corporate speak "centralized private control" becomes democratization and that one does not democratize AI by building a for-profit proprietary platform. We currently see a number of for-profit proprietary platforms claiming to democratize AI.[19] A better example of democratizing AI is Francois Chollet's Keras, a deep learning open-source library for Python that is simple, modular and extensible and makes deep learning accessible to any person with some basic computer science skills and knowledge that want to build deep learning neural networks. It follows a similar approach to another very popular open-source machine learning library for Python called *scikit-learn*, where the latter is more focused on abstracting and making traditional machine learning techniques easy to use.[20] Keras now has many contributors and a community of hundreds of thousands of users. According to Wikipedia, Keras asserts over 375,000 individual users as of early-2020 and are being used in scientific research by hundreds of researchers, thousands of graduate students, and many businesses.[21] There is also an automated machine learning version of Keras called *AutoKeras*, developed by DATA Lab at Texas A&M University, that is aimed at making machine learning accessible for everyone.[22] Keras also supports TensorFlow, which is Google's free and open-source software library for machine learning.[23] PyTorch, developed by Facebook, is another open source machine learning framework that accelerates the path from research prototyping to production deployment.[24] There are also many excellent examples of democratizing AI-related knowledge with a multitude of training courses, demos, tutorials, videos, and blogs explaining the foundations, intricacies and practical aspects of designing, developing, and deploying AI solutions. I also agree with Francois' sentiment that "democratizing AI is the best way, maybe the only way, to make sure that the future we are creating will be a good one."[25]

Machine Learning for Machine Learning or *MLsquare* is an open-source initiative that focuses on addressing machine learning limitations using machine learning and a space for machine learning enthusiasts to collaborate and find solutions for such limitations.[26] This initiative from a team in India has also recently published a framework for democratizing AI and shared an extensible Python framework that provides a single point of interface to a range of solutions in desirable AI attribute categories to make it responsible and responsive. These attributes include *portability* through separating the development of the machine learning models from its consumption; *explainability* by providing plausible explanations along with predictions; *credibility* by providing coverage intervals and other uncertainty quantification metrics; *fairness* via making machine learning bias free and equitable;

decentralization and *distributability* by having models deployed where the data is instead of the reverse; *declarative* by specifying what the model requires and what it should do, and not being concerned about its actual workings, and *reproducibility* through reproducing any result in an on-demand fashion.[27] With respect to achieving portability, as an example, one can go the route of having an intermediate representation of the machine learning models such as Predictive Model Markup Language (PMML) and Open Neural Network Exchange (ONNX).[28] The ONNX in particular is a format that is supported by Deep Learning frameworks such as TensorFlow, PyTorch and MXNet as well as WinML which allow saving scikit-learn xgboost models in the ONNX format. The mlsquare team has presented the design details, APIs of the framework, reference implementations, roadmap for development, and guidelines for contributions. Their mlsquare framework currently provides support for porting a subset of scikit-learn models to their approximately deep neural network counterparts which are represented in ONNX format. Instead of providing one-to-one operator level mappings of machine learning models, they propose a more generic semantic mapping of models as an efficient alternative that could be an exact semantic map (i.e., exact equivalence between the model the user provides, the primal model, and its neural network counterpart, the proxy model), an approximate semantic map (i.e., the proxy model is trained on the same data as the primal model, but its target labels are the predictions from the primal model), or a universal map (where both the intent and implementation can be delegated to the proxy model). The mlsquare framework approaches explainability by defining explanations as predicates in a first order logic system, which is represented in conjunctive normal form (which is a formula in Boolean logic that is a conjunction of one or more clauses that is a product of sums or an AND or ORs) and then has the proxy model producing such predicates as its output.[29] They see producing explanations as a synthetic language generation problem and use recurrent neural networks to train on the outputs of a localized decision tree for the given training dataset. When the system is given a new unseen data input, this recurrent neural network would output the corresponding decision tree path traversed and is interpreted as the decision taken by the model at each feature.[30] The design goals of the mlsquare framework use well-documented APIs such as those in scikit-learn; ensure that there are minimal changes in the development workflow; have consistency by making sure that all the quality attributes of AI mentioned above to be first class methods of a model object with a consistent interface; ensure compositionality by using a Lego block computational framework for composing models such as with deep learning; modularity through the inherent object-orientedness of many algorithms of deep learning; and require implementations to be extensible.[31] The mlsquare framework currently supports some widely used frameworks to assist with making deep learning techniques more accessible to a broader audience. They currently use Keras to define the neural networks and plan to extend this to PyTorch as well and are also extending neural architecture search capabilities with AutoKeras.[32]

Framework for Strategic Planning to Shape a Beneficial Human-Centric Future

Before we launch into a framework for strategic planning and adopting new technologies, innovating, and embracing Machine Learning in our daily lives, it is important to unmask and scrutinize our assumptions. Any 'knowledge' is the foundation for our values, behaviors, and motivations. The problem is that much of our knowledge is based on assumptions. We assume our best friend did not call us back because they do not care about us, so we send a scathing text. We assume the world is flat, so we flog people who say it is round. The decisions we make are based on what we think we know.[33] However normal it might be for humans to make assumptions and to not question what we think we know, when our premises are incorrect, our conclusions are invalid. On the other hand, we may be very well informed. We may have all the knowledge and expertise in the world on a certain topic or project. The problem here lies when we communicate it. This "curse of knowledge" assumes that those on the receiving end have all the context, details, and certainty that we do - so we start communicating in the middle, or at the end and meaninglessly drone on to lost audiences.[34] Not only have we missed the why (the goal or the purpose), we have assumed that others have the background, knowledge and understanding that we have. So, before implementing any change, starting a new project, or simply communicating we have two tasks where the one is not to assume we have all the facts and the other is to not assume that others have the same facts and context that we do. The first task has to do with our own self-questioning, learning and in some cases unlearning. The second task has to do with communication and leadership, where leadership also involves leading people to stand on our grounds and see things clearly through the same looking glass. Both tasks share the same theme - find and share knowledge that harbors data instead of assumption and use that knowledge to inspire why you want to do something. Leadership is not a new idea. In times long lost to us, in all areas of society leadership has formed to construct rules, maintain processes, inspire action or compliance, and make us feel as if we are a part of something. We do not always love our leaders. In fact, some would argue that we rarely do. Our bosses might create anguish, our political leaders seem in most instances more concerned with power, our CEOs seems in many instances more focused on self-gain, our religious leaders give us hope in exchange for money or sometimes strange and extreme ways of seeing or doing things, and even our families and communities develop informal leaders that tacitly dictate how we 'should' be doing is. All leaders have an aim, an outcome they are trying to achieve (well, they should). Simon Sinek dedicated his book *Start with Why* to uncover how no aim or outcome can successfully be achieved without first asking the right questions.[35] These questions, always starting with the most important question - why. Why are we doing this? What is our purpose? Our vision? What motivates us to do what we are doing? If we are asking the wrong questions, getting those answers right simply does not matter. It is the role of the leader to start with why, and to inspire and motivate those around them to act out of will and connection to that why - not simply because of arbitrary rules, targets or KPIs.

We understand that with changes as great as those that smart technology offers, there are a few seemingly more complicated things to consider. Smart technology brings utter disruption to our ways of life and through this it is met with great deal of fear. Not to mention the power in our new technologies, codes, and scientific discoveries to elicit large-scale 'good' or 'bad'. On this, I have two things to say - ignoring the changes is more dangerous than drinking them in and fearing the bad makes us powerless to ensure the good. Now let us talk about why we need to change - the first step in our framework for embracing, adopting, and democratizing AI, one step at a time, but always towards the betterment of the world at large. As discussed in the previous chapter, democratizing AI fits within the proposed broader massive transformative purpose framework for humanity.

The current reality is that we are stepping into an unknown future and the ability to change and adapt has never been so important to our survival. Agility has been thrown around as the trendy new word, along with words and terms like digital transformation, innovation and so on. The thing about these words is that while we might roll our eyes when we hear them, they are overused (without real understanding) for a reason. Our future is unknown. The pace of development, knowledge growth, technology advancement, and analysis make it so. We do know that at the core of our unknown future is smart technology. We also know that smart technology keeps getting smarter, moving faster and fundamentally altering our lives. A ground-breaking invention or advancement could make what we think, how we think and what we do today irrelevant tomorrow. Therefore, current business models, strategies and roadmaps no longer work. These often rely on an amount of predictability that we just do not have. While we have more data than we have ever had before and more ways to analyze this data than ever before, we have less certainty on what next year will be like. The bottom line is we must be prepared to change directions, stop what we are doing, and completely reinvent ourselves if we have to. We also must be prepared to do this often. Being comfortably uncomfortable is vital if we want to avoid irrelevance, non-competitiveness and possibly business extinction.[36] The same is true for governments who risk falling far behind the global economy, removing their countries from global dialogue, advancements, and information sharing, and not taking advantage of what the world offers to properly serve and protect their citizens. Agility, innovation, and digital transformation are some of the key action words for any business, organization, or government that aims to thrive in the smart technology era. We must be willing, prepared and inspired to change quickly where in the past we have steered and controlled. We must follow our data, be digitally savvy, responsive, and available for our customers, employees, or citizens, and prepared to chuck our processes, strategies, and services aside (or repurpose them) based on trends, demands, advancements and inventions.

We can no longer have five-year plans that direct our futures with minimal deterrents or interruptions. We can plan for the short term, and direct our vision to solving long-term problems, but must remain agile in our processes, thinking and approach. The pace of global digital transformation and innovation makes this so. In this regard Amy Webb, a Quantitative Futurist and Professor of Strategic Foresight at the New York University Stern School of Business, has said in a Harvard Business Review article, *How to Do Strategic Planning Like a Futurist*, that "deep uncertainty merits deep questions, and the answers aren't necessarily tied to a fixed date in the future".[37] She further asks "where do you want to have impact? What will it take to achieve success? How will the organization evolve to meet challenges on the horizon?" and reckons that "these are the kinds of deep, foundational questions that are best addressed with long-term planning".[38] Without this kind of thinking, we are at risk of becoming the likes of out-of-business publishers who did not account for internet content consumption and advertising, movie renters who did not account for online streaming and so on, because changing their business model was not in their five year plans. In her futurist's framework for strategic planning, she recommends that we need to think about time differently: use time cones instead of timelines that arbitrarily assign goals on a quarterly or yearly basis and look at our planning based on what is most certain to what is least certain. One can then divide the time cone up in four parts where each section of the cone is a strategic approach that encloses the one before and starts with tactics, which is then followed by strategy, vision, and systems level evolution. Because we have most certainty about the trends and probable events of the most immediate future, we can direct our tactics (actionable strategic outcomes) for the next year or two towards achieving related goals. After that, our strategies become less certain and cannot be formulated as tactics or plans. For the following 2-5 years, we focus more on priorities, shifts in the organization's structure or staffing requirements. In the more distant future (5-10 years), we have even less certainty other than the vision of what we want to achieve and where we aim to take the organization. When we reach past 10 years, things are wholly uncertain. Granted, things may change drastically after the first 6 months requiring a change in tactics, but after 10 years, we can assume no certainty. Internal and external systems, trends and processes which are all part of systems level evolution will evolve, fall away, be replaced, and disrupted. We must think about how this uncertainty and possibility might affect us, and how we can direct it.[39]

Perhaps the most important thing to note is the importance of agility. The moment there is a new invention, a new player in the industry, new technology, new trends, or new business and consumer intelligence, we need to be willing to shift, discover and perhaps seek a completely new path. So, this might change our tactics and our vision. Amy recommends that "the beginning of your cone and your tactical category is always reset to the present day" and that the ideal result is "a flexible organization that is positioned to continually iterate and respond to external developments".[40] If we have a strong sense of what our industries might look like, we can address the entire cone simultaneously.[41] By doing this, leaders are in a much better position to assess whether their more immediate tactics and strategies allow and account for the future landscape, effects of other industries, and the potential state of our own industry. Conversely, Amy warns that "if leaders do not have a strong sense of how their industry must evolve to meet the challenges of new technology, market forces, regulation, and the like, then someone else will be in a position to dictate the terms of your future".[42] We can also use this type of holistic thinking to imagine, lead and direct the future developments and be central to systems level evolution through our tactics and strategies.

Bring your attention back to your massive transformative purpose: that vision you have of what you want to achieve for your family, business, customers, industry, citizens, and the world. If you keep focused on that, then the most important thing will always be achieving it. You become less bogged down about following strategies because they sounded good two years ago and they are now part of your key performance indicators. If new developments mean that you can achieve your MTP in a new way or if a break-through discovery means you can achieve it in a way you did not consider possible before, these are now the paths you follow. The same holds for the proposed MTP for humanity and the associated MTP goals. My personal MTP of helping to shape a better future in the Smart Technology Era fits in with the MTPs of my business ventures and non-profit organizations as well as the MTP for humanity. In order to follow the most optimal paths to achieving these MTPs and associated goals, I and we as a collective need to be as agile as possible.

Now, what is left is to understand all the little pieces that will come into how we actually go about achieving transformation, innovation and digitization. Once a business or organization has a clearly defined MTP, the focus shifts to embarking on an AI-driven digital transformation journey as described in Chapter 4. Some of the key elements of successful AI-driven digital transformation include vision or intent, data, technology, process, and people. This is not only relevant for business and organizations, but also communities, governments, as well as regional and global organizations. If you are thinking about your business or country as a futurist would, or in terms of your massive transformative purpose, you are already thinking about intent. You are already taking the first step. As discussed in previous chapters, AI should be a part of every company or organization's strategy.[43] It should not be regarded as another information technology project. Rather, automation and machine learning should define change, growth, products, reach and is a strategic tool to achieve organizational vision. If we are not considering machine learning in our strategy, no matter what institution or organization we are a part of, we are already behind. Furthermore, we are ignoring efficient, innovative, and scalable solutions to our current problems. Whoever you are, think about this - if your current solutions, strategies, and plans involve using the tools that have been available to you since you are founding to stay profitable, become profitable or scale, you are in danger of becoming irrelevant and wasting inordinate amounts of money. If your solutions involve more or improved physical structures, this year's Christmas campaign, improvements to your products or services, or latest specials you do not think the public can refuse - you are in danger of becoming irrelevant. The things that have worked for you in the past, that even seem foolproof, do not work anymore. And if you are in the business of public service and it is not profit you are after, achieving inclusion and development and ensuring resources and rights for your communities simply cannot happen quickly enough with the traditional methods you are used to. If they could, I imagine you would be in a quite different place today. If smart technology such as machine learning, IoT, distributed ledger technology, automation and robotics are not part of your strategies, you are simply ignoring some of the most powerful and scalable tools and solutions for the problems that you face. If you only see AI and any automation or technological advancements as an IT project, not only are you not seeing the full picture, but you probably have no idea how AI can change the path of your business, its impact and maybe even the world. Misunderstandings about what AI is and is not could fuel opposition to technologies with the potential to benefit everyone. From a governmental perspective, poorly informed regulation that stifles innovation would be a tragic mistake.[44]

Designing AI for Social Good and Beneficial Outcomes

In a recent *Nature* article *AI for Social Good: Unlocking the Opportunity for Positive Impact* by authors from the UK, Europe, Japan and Africa that are part of the AI for Social Good (AI4SG) movement and representing academic institutions, global organizations, non-profit organizations and tech companies (like Google and Microsoft) provided a "set of guidelines for establishing successful long-term collaborations between AI researchers and application-domain experts, relate them to existing AI4SG projects and identify key opportunities for future AI applications targeted towards social good".[45] The AI4SG movement is putting interdisciplinary partnerships together that are focused on AI applications with respect to helping to achieve the United Nations' 17 Sustainable Development Goals (SDGs). The same guidelines are also relevant to the proposed MTP for Humanity and the 14 associated complementary MTP goals described in Chapter 10. These guidelines include ensuring that the expectations of what is possible with AI are well-grounded; acknowledging that there is value in simple solutions; ensuring that applications of AI are inclusive and accessible, and reviewed at every stage for ethics and human rights compliance; making sure that goals and use cases are clear and well-defined; understanding that deep, long-term partnerships are required to solve large problems in a successful manner; making sure that planning aligns incentives and incorporate the limitations of both the research and the practitioner communities; recognizing that establishing and maintaining trust is key to overcoming organizational barriers; exploring options for reducing the development cost of AI solutions; improving data readiness; and ensuring that data is processed securely with the greatest respect for human rights and privacy.[46] The AI4SG group also highlighted some case studies to illustrate how their collaboration guidelines can be used with new, mature, and community-wide projects. These projects included the use of AI to improve citizen feedback in Somalia via a non-governmental organization called Shaqodoon, the Troll Patrol project that used AI to quantify and analyze abuse against women on Twitter and potentially make abusive tweet detection easier, and the Deep Learning Indaba being an AI community in Africa that supports AI4SG projects and use AI for sustainable development.[47]

A team from Oxford University's Digital Ethics Lab as well as the Alan Turing Institute which are also part of the AI4SG movement shared seven factors that are key when designing AI for social good in a *Science and Engineering Ethics* journal article, *How to Design AI for Social Good: Seven Essential Factors*.[48] They argue that our understanding of what makes AI socially good in theory is limited, that many practical aspects of AI4SG still needs to be figured out, and that we still need to reproduce the initial successes of these projects in terms of policies. Their analysis is supported by 27 AI4SG projects that function as use case examples. The team identified the following key factors to help ensure successful project delivery: (1) falsifiability and incremental deployment to improve the trustworthiness of AI applications; (2) safeguards against the manipulation of predictors; (3) receiver-contextualized intervention; (4) receiver-contextualized explanation and transparent purposes; (5) privacy protection and data subject consent; (6) situational fairness; and (7) human-friendly semanticization.[49] Each of these factors have a corresponding best practice for AI4SG designers. These include (a) identifying falsifiable requirements (identifying essential conditions for which the systems cannot fully operate) and testing them in incremental steps from the lab to the "outside world"; (b) adopting safeguards which ensure that non-causal indicators do not unsuitably skew interventions, and limiting knowledge (in appropriate fashion) of how inputs affect outputs to prevent manipulation; (c) building decision-making systems in discussion with users that engage with or are impacted by the AI systems and take into consideration the users' characteristics, the methods of coordination, and the purposes and effects of an engagement, and respecting the users' right to ignore or modify engagements; (d) choosing a level of abstraction for AI explanation that fulfils the expected explanatory purpose and is appropriate to the system and the receivers; then deploy arguments that are rationally and suitably convincing for the receivers to deliver the explanation; and ensure that the AI system's purpose is knowable to receivers of its outputs by default; (e) respecting the threshold of permission established for the processing of datasets of personal data; (f) removing from relevant datasets variables and proxies that are irrelevant to an outcome, except when their inclusion supports inclusivity, safety, or other ethical imperatives; and (g) not obstructing the ability for people to semanticize or give meaning to and make sense of something.[50] The team also makes the point that the essential factors that they have identified correspond to the five principles of AI ethics which are *beneficence* (i.e., do only good that includes promoting well-being, preserving dignity, and sustaining the planet), *non-maleficence* (i.e., do no harm that includes privacy, security and "capability caution"), *justice* (i.e., promoting prosperity, preserving solidarity, and avoiding unfairness), *autonomy* (i.e., the power to decide), and *explicability* (i.e., enabling the other principles through intelligibility and accountability).[51] Of these principles beneficence is seen as a precondition for AI4SG. They also recommend that well-executed AI4SG projects require that factors should be balanced intrinsically on an individual factor level (not overdoing or understating a factor) as well as on a systemic one that struck a balance between multiple factors.

Building Human-compatible, Ethical, Trustworthy and Beneficial AI

We live in times ruled by scientific discovery and economic development - although it may not seem so from a village in Ethiopia. With all the information, discovery, and development in the last years, combined with how little we actually know about what will be discovered and exactly what our future will look like, we urgently need a way to answer the ethical questions that keep our discoveries and developments from having a negative impact on planet earth, humanity and the individual. Growing concern and debates around the world are doing a good job at spreading fear and making some of us more accountable and intentional about today's effects on the future of life. But most of us still do not know exactly how to get there or how to truly hold those with power to the correct standards, laws and policies. We need ways to ensure that the human experience, human rights, and the protection of our planet come first. Our affinity towards growth has welcomed innovation and development before thinking about the implications of this innovation and development. By no means should we stop innovation and development, but watch it, steer it, and understand it. We should always consider its potential consequences with the same vigor that we embrace the ways it benefits us or solves problems. In this we not only need to monitor the use and impact of our new developments, but to find meaningful ways to steer them towards greater economic, social and knowledge inclusion and general individual well-being. Smart technologies such as AI have the power to innovate, solve, enhance, and develop at an electrifying pace. This speed of our changing world, Yuval Harari warns, makes it difficult for us to make sense of our present circumstances and to predict what the future holds – for politics, economics, medicine, production, agriculture, the environment and humanity.[52] By not considering the impact of what we are doing today, our future is at stake.[53] More so, if we are not directing this future towards one that puts humanity first, we could be leading future generations into a world we would never choose for ourselves. The future might be unknown, but that does not mean it is out of our control. This forms the basis for policies, guidelines, and global discussions on how to use AI (and Smart Technology in general) ethically, responsibly and in ways that protect, develop and nurture life. Trustworthy, ethically responsible, transparent, and unbiased AI are critical for the transformational purposes of AI, and for businesses and society to thrive in the Smart Technology Era.

As discussed in earlier chapters, AI applications can on a high-level be categorized into customer facing applications and industrial applications. The different intended uses of these systems inspire different ethical considerations. For industrial applications, AI in collaboration with other smart technology can be used to predict equipment and asset maintenance, enhance industrial processes, assess issues, aid in mining, manufacturing, and farming and any instance when the outcome is for the optimal running, intelligence and issue detection of systems and machines. Industrial and consumer facing applications can effectively be categorized into whether they are intended to maximize the safety and efficiency of industrial processes or whether the human being is the intended audience. Because of their differences, when we are thinking about ethics in AI, we need to think about whether they are, by nature, industrial or customer-facing. For customer-facing applications, fairness, privacy, data governance and explicability are incredibly important. Industrial applications need to be less concerned with privacy, but extremely strict when it comes to safety, trustworthiness and robustness of systems and outcomes. In the rest of this chapter, I will focus more on the systems that are intended for human benefit, consumption, use, knowledge, and adoption. Research, world summits, conferences and even policies have taken the stage in AI over the last few years. Many more are popping up all the time and dialogue is flowing in AI, data, and economic communities. Singapore's FEAT (Fairness, Ethics, Accountability and Transparency) Principles in the financial sector have given us a great foundational framework for the responsible use of AI.[54] Many countries are following suit and are incorporating similar thinking into the way they are thinking about the potential consequences of AI. The European Union published their *Ethics Guidelines for Trustworthy AI* in 2019 - helping us grapple with what the operationalization of AI should look like in a way that protects the trustworthiness, transparency and impact of AI systems.[55] For the EU trustworthy AI means three main things: (1) it should be lawful, complying with all applicable laws and regulations; (2) it should be ethical, ensuring adherence to ethical principles and values; and (3) it should be robust, both from a technical and social perspective, since, even with good intentions, AI systems can cause unintentional harm. Based on fundamental rights and ethical principles, the guidelines list seven key requirements that AI systems should meet: human agency and oversight, technical robustness and safety, privacy and data governance, transparency, diversity, non-discrimination and fairness, societal and environmental well-being and accountability.[56]

Since the availability and impacts of technology are borderless, whose laws and regulations are we talking about? Which ethical principles are we talking about? Whose social perspective are we talking about? Only those of the EU? Let us forget about the rest of the world for a second. Even when we look at ethical AI within the confines of the EU, each country has their own laws, guidelines, cultures, values, and foundational ethical principles. The EU's Constitution may celebrate and insist upon the respective rights, laws, and values of each nation, but could it still protect these when machine learning, drones and IoT are in full play?[57] How could processes and legislation ensure that a development in Germany does not negatively impact the value or culture in Greece, for example? It gets even more complicated when we look outside the EU and expand our horizon to the rest of the world. The digital economy is one where trade, services, information, and work have no boundaries. Data and AI applications in one country might infringe human rights in another country. Global outcry to China's Social Credit System that aims to promote the "traditional value of creditworthiness" by incentivizing trustworthiness and punishing untrustworthiness might seem acceptable based on collectivist values of harmony and transparency.[58] It might even appeal (and has) to many others building 'behavioral change' platforms and applications from a standpoint of wanting to make the world a better place. But what does it mean for privacy or the right not to be punished for potential behavior? What does it mean to be innocent until proven guilty? And what does it mean to those currently outside of these systems? These applications only need to be developed once. Once they exist, they exist everywhere. Simple tweaks, knowledge sharing, and integrations makes it so what is developed in one country or by one business has the potential to affect the entire world. So how do we decide what is acceptable to develop? For what purposes and for what uses? If the EU makes ethical decisions, do they really matter if the rest of the world is making these decisions in a different way? Globalization and Digitization mean that the effects of creations, developments, and laws in one country do not only affect that country. Not anymore.

The Organization for Economic Co-operation and Development (OECD) seem to understand this, and are trying to get as many countries as possible on board in their search to practically affect values-based AI principles which is very much in line with the proposed MTP for Humanity and its associated MTP goals: (1) AI should benefit people and the planet by driving inclusive growth, sustainable development and well-being; (2) AI systems should be designed in a way that respects the rule of law, human rights, democratic values and diversity, and they should include appropriate safeguards – for example, enabling human intervention where necessary – to ensure a fair and just society; (3) There should be transparency and responsible disclosure around AI systems to ensure that people understand AI-based outcomes and can challenge them; (4) AI systems must function in a robust, secure and safe way throughout their life cycles and potential risks should be continually assessed and managed. (5) Organisations and individuals developing, deploying, or operating AI systems should be held accountable for their proper functioning in line with the above principles.[59] But again we run into issues when looking into the practicality of applying these rather idealistic theories. Whose rule of law? Whose human rights? Whose interpretation of democracy? And what about those who do not govern democratically? Is it safe to leave anyone out of the principles, guidelines or laws that really affect the entire world? If the very nature is unclear, impractical or does not allow for and account for practical adoption throughout the world, then we are dooming ourselves to theory, with no actionable outcomes.

Let us turn our attention to the Foundation for Responsible Robotics (FRR) and Deloitte, who are developing a Quality Mark for Robotics and AI that aims to ensure the responsible use of robots and AI.[60] In the development of products and systems, if people have not paid attention to privacy, transparency, fairness and accountability, their product will not pass. The FRR wants the quality mark to inspire worldwide regulation and to help shape the way people are thinking of the impact of their products and systems. But have we defined and agreed upon what transparency, privacy, fairness, and accountability mean to the world? Do we have a shared consensus? We do have clear consensus that a large portion of the world do not actually value privacy in governance at all (we are talking about China), so how do the FRR plan to ensure that their mark has any meaning? As we wait for regulated international standards for AI from ISO (International Organization for Standardization)[61], which echo the sentiments that responsible and ethical AI is paramount for a free, fair, and developed world, can we hope that these will be able to be actioned and governed by all countries and all organisations? Or are we again, just playing with idealistic theory? While theories are progress, and helpful in our discussions towards the creation of acceptable and actionable laws in Big Data, Machine Learning and AI, they are just theories. Therefore, it is important for all organisations and governments to find ways to guide, regulate and control the impact, trustworthiness and use of AI. For now, we know one indisputable fact: we are responsible and accountable for our future, and it will be up to all of us to decide what that future looks like. This begins with understanding the different applications of AI and Smart Technology.

Data privacy is considered so important that its contravention is punishable in the EU since GDPR took effect in 2018.[62] Data policies now exist in several countries that follows the EU's lead with respective GDPR and its reaction to Big Data and its potential consequences. Formal regulations over data privacy have not (yet) expanded to data trust, low quality and fake data that most often lead to untrustworthy systems, and as we have seen above, GDPR may protect how the EU behaves, but it has little impact on how the rest of the world behaves. The CSIS (Centre for Strategic International Studies) developed a set of data governance policies for the G20 states which are said to inform the development of data governance frameworks, globally.[63] The CSIS sum up the need for their data governance policies, and why policies, such as GDPR, created in vacuum, might fail: "First is the need for consistency, interoperability, and coordination of the myriad international, regional, national, and local laws and regulations that impact data. The data ecosystem is fundamentally global and cross-functional, and gaps and inconsistencies between jurisdictions create uncertainty and limit the tools available to address harmful uses of data. Second, existing rules and frameworks and the current debate around data governance often focus almost exclusively on personal data and privacy with little thought to broader impacts of data, for example on competition, mobility, and trade. Third, most existing data governance frameworks, and much of the global debate around data governance, focus on controlling access to data instead of how it is used. Fourth, these debates are often framed around the rights and freedoms of data subjects at the expense of other stakeholders and society broadly".[64]

We see how vital it is to consider not only our countries, but the entire world when attempting to create laws around data. This aside, for now, when looking at data governance, we are often referring to the data that has been collected, in bits from people's online footprints, public information, or information we have filled in on forms from organization and businesses that serve us. It is easy for this to be incorrect or contradictory (especially given that devices are accessed and used by multiple people, false information is given, or information is not updated). It is vital that we can trust our data and the systems they feed if we are to trust or even take seriously their outcomes and predictions. Even if the data has structure and can be verified, it can lead to incorrect or unethical decisions in the form of data biases. Data biases are the product of existing biases, either from the people developing the algorithms, or the data's reflecting samples based on existing socio-economic (and other) inequalities or injustices. Privacy is among the largest topics of discussion when it comes to data and AI and we have dedicated some time to the importance and complexity of privacy elsewhere in this book. When there is still a lot to be done for data policy, regulation, and governance, and when the world has not truly tried to build a globally acceptable and actionable framework for data governance, how do we expect to have any control over the AI systems that this data is feeding? The answer is we cannot. But we will be able to if we make it a priority to focus on globally accepted and actionable outcomes. Good? Or just 'not bad'?

Depending on who you ask, you will get a different answer to the questions with respect to the rate of development and discovery. Some schools say we are going a lot slower than we think we are. Other schools say we are going too fast for most to catch up. The truth is that both might be true. We may not be as far advanced as we thought we would be by 2020, but the advances that we have made and are continuing to make have most certainly changed the way we live and the way we are expected to live. This has happened at a rate too fast for many to be able to catch up, particularly since some people are still living without electricity and trading chickens for oranges, whilst others live in IoT-powered homes and have personal assistants in their pockets. Whichever stance we take, there is no denying that the modern goal is growth, and since this growth affects us differently, and we all have different responses, combined with the fact that there is little way to test the effects of our developments until years after they are adopted, if we are not directly trying to protect all life from harm, we are at constant risk of causing harm.[65] Arguably few ideas, inventions or discoveries start out with the intention to harm. Many of us just want to solve problems, find answers, improve how we do things and keep growing. We want to serve more people, serve people better and create successful business while doing it. There is nothing wrong with this in theory. However, smart technology offers a different kind of world. A world based on data. A world where so many unimaginable things are possible that we cannot begin to fathom all their social or ethical implications. Therefore, when developing or using any form of AI, we need to consider every variation of potential consequence, effect or human experience that might go with it. Directly and indirectly.

Let us give a simple example of this. Facebook were not attempting to invade our privacy or infringe some human rights; they were merely looking for a way to bring us the convenience and relevance that we crave. They were looking for a way to give us exactly the content or products that, based on our consumption, we want. They also wanted to help us filter out the 'rubbish' that we wish would disappear from our feeds. They had a way to know their audiences, individually, and through that target and personalize our content to us, directly. They could also offer marketers the chance to advertise to those who would respond in a favorable way. Whether that be to buy something, believe something, or vote for someone... This is where it gets seriously questionable, but many argue that it got questionable before that point. Many feels spied on and known, without any control over who else (granted in efforts no more sinister than marketing) has access to our private habits. Facebook, Google, WeChat, and the likes all have highly intelligent algorithms that get to 'know' us and in turn tell others what they have to do for us to notice them, if we are worthy of their high-end products, candidates for their jobs or susceptible to their views. Is this unethical? Or do we not care because it is just used for marketing. What about the biases it creates on us? What about cases when that very information – a sum up of who we are - falls into the hands of home loaners, insurers, governments? What about cases when we are not even seeing jobs being advertised because there is a bias in the algorithm that only advertises it to white men who live in a certain area?

It is difficult to measure ethics. History has seen many different shifts in what is seen as right or wrong – the most modern being if it feels good, it must be good (as long as it does not cause harm to anyone else). However widely accepted, there is no scientific exactitude to this. While science can offer us cures, food, inventions and understanding of the universe, it cannot seem to come to grips with consciousness and the subjective human experience. The latter is what we use, instead of science, to come up with ethical theories, laws, and guidelines for behavior.[66] Because there is not (yet) a scientific measure for ethics, we can only go with what we currently have, and in many cases, what feels right intersubjectively. This might feel like it falls short in the face of the provable facts that science and mathematics give us, but this does not detract from its importance. Yuval Harari compares science and ethics to yin and yang – unable to have one without the other to balance it.[67] The more science we have, the more emotion we need to balance it. The more development and growth we have, the more we need ethics to keep it in check. As smart technology becomes more advanced and its effects wider spread, we need to continuously check our ethics, our laws, and our guidelines to make sure we are keeping it in check. In some instances, we do not know the effects that scientific discovery will have until we see its ethical downfall – genetically modified genius babies, Facebook taking away our privacy – we have a list of these to choose from. A growing list of science and technological development have potentially disastrous and right-infringing effects on humans. Here, two things are important to note. The first is that what we study, build and produce is proportionate to our values, and the second is that our values differ. If we value power, the likelihood of using AI is rather high. If we value privacy, the likelihood of having measures to protect privacy are high. If we value equal resources and opportunities, we will likely create programmes and solutions that enhance social and economic equality. If we value human rights, we will likely focus on the things that protect those rights. Here we are faced with our second problem - since we value different things, we will find differences in what these human rights are and perhaps we have a philosophical debate about whether rights should exist in the first place. Furthermore, we are inclined to think that our values are correct, so if we value justice as a form of punishment, we might feel we are working within acceptable lines when we develop a programme that attacks people or values that we feel have wronged us.

This is not a new dilemma for the world, but never has it been so important, simply because what we develop in one isolated part of the world has never had the ability to be so far reaching. The ability to produce, invent, study, and make available online, combined with AI, robotics, blockchain, nanotechnology, and biotechnology means that when humans say we fear what AI and technology might be able to do in the future, we are not wrong. I wish I could tell you we were wrong. But the truth is, just like any invention, AI can be a weapon. AI can be destructive. AI can be exclusionary - making the rich richer and the poor poorer. The important question to ask here, is what we are going to do about it. Before we can come to a 'what', we must understand the differences in our values and our different experiences of the world. Have you ever traveled to another country and experienced a culture shock? You were shocked by how the natives greeted one another, the way they were with their kids, the way they spoke too loudly or softly, the blunt questions that every person you met asked you, the food they ate, the way they ate it, how they did not look you in the eye when greeted you, or how they would not stop looking you in the eye. How, when and what times they said please or thank you? The way they queued or did not queue at all? In some cultures, marriage is all about family and love is secondary. In these cultures, arranged marriages are not always seen as a sentence. They are just part of how you get what is ultimately valued - family. In some cultures, marriage is only about love and people would not dream of marrying someone they did not love. In some cultures, it is disrespectful to look people that are older than you in the eye, and in others it is disrespectful to not look anyone in the eye. Some cultures value community, support or honor, some cultures value individuality, privacy, or material wealth. Some cultures are entwined in their languages and have words for things the rest of us cannot begin to comprehend because there is no word for it in our own language.

Whether easily visible or not, entire communities and nations have developed around different value systems. None are better or worse. None are more important. Some have more economic power and a louder voice and so their values are heard, demanded, and spread. Others have little economic stability and a soft voice, so we tend to ignore that, no matter how different, they too have needs and ways and values. The former groups are among our global leaders, powerful countries and thus included in our global society. The latter tend to stick to their own regions, at risk of being invaded by more developed, louder ideas, products, and values. Sometimes we even have two conflicting loud voices in the former group fighting over who is righter and who will dominate the global market, narratives, and developments. This has never been fair or just. No one has ever been righter. Just more powerful and louder. The only difference between now and the past is that globalization, hyper connectedness, and the fact that the most powerful companies and countries in the world are controlling the global economy and developing products that will reach and affect or create bigger rifts and inequalities with the rest of the world in seconds, months or just a few years. We saw it with colonialism, we see it with the imbalance of power and money in capitalism and now we are seeing it cross borders and create an even greater imbalance of power in the world. One person with a knack for machine learning and a bit of money in his or her pocket can literally spread his or her product or idea around the world in days. This is a lot of power for one person to have and should not be taken lightly. It is power, whose effects, up until now, have not been carefully considered by many who have it. If we do not know to ask, when we have a great idea, how this idea might affect our neighbors, how are we to know to ask how it might affect countries and cultures about which we know nothing? How are we to know how our own experience of the world, and our own perception, values and biases might impact others if we are to see our idea developed? How are we to know to ask how our idea might affect our natural resources? Our borderless, digital world, our sick planet, and the abilities for machines to learn more in a day than a human might learn in five years makes these questions absolutely vital to the foundation of humanity.

Maybe it starts with accepting these things in ourselves? And once we have accepted that we are unique, affected, and biased based on where and how we live, we may be able to accept that an experience completely from ours exists and that should be respected too? Then we can accept something else and hopefully reach this conclusion on our own: We are different. We just need to find a way to be different together. Different cultures, religions, regions, eras, and political affiliations value different things and experience the world in a variety of ways. When we are looking to human values and the individual experience in creating laws, policies, and procedures, as has been done many times in the past, we feel no need to look further than our own country, religion, general political affiliations, etc. Why would we? We assume that the reality that has been constructed by our surroundings is THE reality. We then base the ways we formulate our values, beliefs, and fears on THIS reality. This reality has become a part of our identity - an identity that we protect with rationalizations and justifications. An identity that feels protected by communities, laws, cultures, religions, and nations.[68] We are left with more and more people being under the "umbrella of our value system".[69] More people who wish to protect the values and identities that make up their reality. It is no surprise that conflict arises when these realities meet. But that is still alright. We have built political borders, small communities, religions, schools, treaties, and alliances to instill a sense of peace. Generally, we have also by now learnt to value human life (or at least economic growth) a little more than to start wars every time we disagree. The only *problem* is it is becoming increasingly difficult to keep these borders in place. Whether we want to be or not, we are exposed to other views, ways of life and products. Globalization and technological advancement mean that what is developed or done in one area does not stay there – it spreads across the world. This puts a great deal of responsibility on the whole world to look past their own vantage points and values when deciding what is right and wrong, and determining what is worth valuing. It seems then that we have an entire world of values, experiences, religious, cultural, and political affiliations to consider when creating the laws, policies and procedures that govern the digital world.

Smart technology makes this even more complicated, because of the potential issues that we must consider. Is our data true, unbiased, and used only for approved purposes? Is smart technology being used to improve lives? Are we hindering human rights? If so, are the rights in our country the same as those in another? Are we accountable for our systems? Do they uphold privacy? Are we using it for good? Are we ensuring that our developments and systems do not cause further socio-economic or ecological harm? Are we valuing individuals over the collective or the other way around? If we choose to decide this democratically, who wins? The Western view of individuality or the Eastern view of collectivism. Does privacy trump the common good? Does the individual right trump those of the collective? The Eastern or collectivist view seems to be that AI is a way to help and care for humans; improve our experiences and make our lives easier. The Western or individualist view is more reactionary, reacting to potential threats in how AI might harm our personal freedoms and individual rights. Let us take an example of a Care Bot – The Eastern view may see value in the help, companionship, and service it can bring to those in need, while the Western way of thinking is more focused on the personal data it is collecting. Where is it going? Who is seeing it? How is it being used? One is focused on the individual's right to privacy and fairness and the other is focused on harmony, collective good and cooperation.[70] This is not to say that either of these views is inherently incorrect. Just that it is the way we see AI, and not what it actually is, that is being questioned. Partly because AI is just a tool in the hands of humans and partly because we are the creators – we control what it is. So, the way we see it really is quite important.

Perhaps our contrasting views on AI and Robotics arise from intrinsically different world views. Western or more individualist AI principles and guidelines value fairness, privacy, transparency, accountability and individual rights, whereas Eastern principles value openness, inclusivity and humanity; a more collective, utilitarian approach to ethics.[71] These views come across in the West's EU Ethics Guidelines and OECD AI Principles versus the Eastern Beijing AI Principles.[72] Privacy, transparency and accountability play a much larger role in the documents originating from the EU and USA, whereas harmony and optimizing collective good play a much larger role in China's principles. While what we see as collective good may not be what China sees as collective good, or perhaps a better way to put it is that it is very easy to take certain actions and justify them as 'collective good' even where in some cases, it really was not collective good but our own good we were seeking. This shows us that it is not just different values we are seeking to align, but fighting against power, autocracy and civil servants who have more interest in fattening their pockets and getting everyone to bow to their views than they do in protecting the future of the world. "People feel bound by democracy only when they share a common view with most voters", so when our inherent views and values are split, which side wins?[73] We must find a collective voice – values that we share, things we want to protect as a world, not just a country, state, or alliance. This works when people want the same thing and are willing to make the values, they have held secondary in order to achieve a higher value - protecting the future of all individuals. However, this democratizing will not work when certain nations still hold this value as secondary, or as a disruption to their personal gain.

Many organisations around the world are coming together or taking their own initiatives to figure out how to tackle these issues. But what happens when the values of one group are given favor over the values of another (as is inevitable due to the sizes, power, and dominance of certain nations)? This may have been less of an issue when one country's laws only affected their own citizens who, for the most part, shared their values. However, due to the global nature of digitization, one group's laws and policies will undoubtedly affect those of another group. Economic, social, cultural, and structural boundaries are blurred and even broken. Products developed in one country can instantly be bought in another country. Views held in one country can easily spread to another. Working for a company whose walls you never set foot into is becoming normalized. What began as a simple trade of goods has turned into a complicated web of informing, working, purchasing, socializing, and consuming in a global domain. This makes it more important than ever to consider the implications of our developments and inventions on the world at large. We need to find a way to agree what the basic underlying drivers are, and what values and rights deserve our utmost protection. Without this, we cannot hope to come up with international laws that will actually be accepted to be adhered to by all countries. It is next to useless to have policies such as the OECD that are not accepted and followed by all governing bodies in all countries (explained further below) when AI has the same potential for effect throughout the world. We also need to start looking internationally to use already developed systems of intelligence to solve unique issues in different countries. The issues faced in South Korea for example, differ from those experienced in Vietnam which differ from those experienced in Botswana. AI and smart technology together with our wealth of knowledge and ease of sharing that knowledge can solve socio-economic issues, transport issues, healthcare issues, and many others across countries.

We need to develop global laws governing digital technologies, code, and algorithms. It is also clear that, currently, we have not found a way to unite all the different countries, cultures, and economic and political views on this point. The time has passed to merely talk about these things, or create alliances, treaties and organisations that agree on how to move forward when the rest of the world has not agreed to their terms or pledged their participation. Perhaps it is fitting for us to take a page from the EU's constitution in uniting in pluralism while celebrating diversity; in protecting minorities and aiming for social inclusion; in balanced economic growth and price stability.[74] Whatever can be said of the EU, particularly considering Brexit, the Union did not fight over liberalism and socialism, or over capitalism and communism. They saw value in each culture, each value system and each citizen and sought to improve their wellbeing through unified policies and laws. These are countries that, however close in proximity, have a history of conflict. If they could find a way to work together for the betterment of their own and others' lives, the world must be able to find a way to do the same. The question always comes back to values. Do we know what we value? As individuals, as communities, as religions and countries? Do we know what valuing one thing inadvertently causes the devalue of another thing? Finally, do we know what values we would like to have that will help construct the future we want? The lives we want for ourselves and our children? Without a clear vision of the future we desire, and the values that will help us create this future, of the things we may need to give up in order to get it, we have little way of knowing how our values and identities might be destructive.[75] And without carefully debating this with everyone who might be affected (every country in the world) we are at great risk of walking into the future that we fear. Simply, by not considering the impact of what we are doing today, is detrimental to our future.[76]

As a start, it is beneficial to look at the conversations, policies and guidelines that are guiding international thought. From these, we can attempt to find some middle ground that may guide the future laws surrounding smart technology and AI in particular. The WEF, FRR, EU, UN, OECD, China, Singapore, Kenya and several other countries and alliances and organisations are all trying to find ways to tackle the problem of creating a shared future that is safe, trustworthy, socially inclusive, free, and fair. AI should be seen to support that future. We need standards for safe, reliable, and trustworthy AI that promote a better future for all.[77] In this they seek to develop global rules for AI that will govern its international development and use.[78] The future of the entire world is, as we have discussed, impacted by the standards, policies, and regulations we are creating today. Let us look at what the world looks like. In the meantime, Singapore's FEAT principles and 42+ governments around the world that have adopted the OECD (Organization for Economic Co-operation and Development) principles on AI, also being adhered to by several non-OECD members have inspired the G20 to adopt principles for trade in the digital economy that put humanity first in the development of AI.[79] The EU's guidelines also act as an excellent start to develop trustworthy AI, but we are still left with the resounding question of whether we value privacy or transparency more and really whether one has to counteract the other.[80] The EU's 7 key requirements for trustworthy AI create the parameters for using AI for good: ensuring data is correct and a true reflection of the broadest parts of society; that data can always be traced back and reproduced; that there is machine and human accountability, and that no human rights are infringed, or parts of nature threatened, through the process of AI.[81] What is this saying about privacy - a human right in many democratic countries.

AI relies on data for its value. The more data it has, the more it must sift through, compare, and learn from, the more accurate it can be and the more value it has. Much of this data comes from us - people. The people who are browsing websites, participating on Social Media Channels, filling out forms, using digital tools and products, shopping, and banking - whether online or traditionally. Our data is everywhere, and we have no real idea of how it is being used and what the implications might be. Even with South Africa's POPI and the UK's GDPR, our data is already out there, has already been used, passed hands, and even hacked. Often its uses are harmless and anonymous (we are mere numbers or statistics), but even if this is the case, it is still an invasion of our privacy. This poses the question of whether we should be worried about our privacy as we know it and really whether we have any control over it if we also want to reap the benefits of AI. More poignant is to ask ourselves whether to fight what will likely be a losing battle of giving up our privacy and what should be fighting for instead? Is it transparency? Is it control over how our data is being used and by whom? Is it insistence that it will always be used in an ethical, fair, traceable, and just way? Perhaps it is not our privacy we should be fighting for at all, but rather the way our information is used.[82] China's Social Credit system where citizens are rated based on their behavior, which then dictates their access and the prices they will pay for things such as loans, mortgages, and rental cars, seems to be the kind of unfair betrayal of our privacy that we would like to fight against. Applications of Jeremy Bentham's Panopticon propose a kind of police state where citizens do not ever really know whether they are being watched and thus always modify their behavior for the better.[83] This was, of course, before the age of technology, but is not dissimilar to where we find ourselves today. We just have no proof of what our data is being used for in this bigger picture. Well, China is starting to have an idea, but the rest of us have only speculation. In certain applications, where behavioral change and improvement is the goal, the world might benefit from more transparency, more tact, and efforts to improve our own behavior, but how quickly does this change to be used against us?

Of course, we must also ask ourselves if the western and democratic insistence on privacy is in fact worth all the fuss. Eastern and African societies value collectivist, helpful and collaborative environments more than they may privacy. This merely highlights that perhaps some of the things we fight for so vehemently do not have a place in right or wrong, just in how our reality has been constructed based on where we live. A balance has not yet been struck, and the proper, enforceable laws do not yet exist. Before we get to this point, however, the borderless and quick nature of technology means that we would best decide soon, and we would best decide together. How do we tackle the issue of privacy versus personalization? Different societies, cultures, religions and traditions and community values are deeply entrenched in the individuals who make them up. Sometimes these ways of living and seeing the world are unknown to us. We are not aware of how affected we are by our culture's emphasis on independence, or on women being caregivers, or on the value of honor. These are just three simple values ingrained in certain traditions and cultures that shape the way those that are part of these communities perceive and approach the world. An important distinction to note when we are considering AI systems, what we value, what we will allow and what we see as unacceptable, we need to consider two main differences - at odds. Individualism versus collectivism.

Let us consider social, political, and economic inclusion. At a fork in the road, we have more tools, more methods, more strategies than we even had before. We have more ways to save the world and more ways to destroy it. It is not technology itself that has this potential. Humans do. We may not think that a minor action or decision made today will affect tomorrow, but we no longer live in a world separated by borders. We no longer live in a world where we must wait for information to trickle through networks. We no longer live in a world where the developments in one country remain strictly there. We live in a world of instant feedback, borderless collaboration, remote service, and constant information. We live in a world that relies on technology for all of this. Socio-economic inequalities further impact if and how people benefit from and partake in the Smart Technology Era. Where knowledge, skills and opportunities thrive through smart technology, those without access are in danger of being more side-lined from meaningful participation in society and accessing the services that merely having a smartphone might allow. Furthermore, AI's ability to process data instantly and on an incredibly large scale, while AI-powered robots perform tasks that were traditionally strictly human, means that there are fewer traditional jobs for humans. While new kinds of roles have and will continue to appear, it is our responsibility to prioritize humans over machines and find ways to upskill employees for new and different kinds of roles. The responsibility to create a future for humanity and the planet we inhabit is great. If we are not directing our thinking towards using AI to bring about positive social changes, include more people in the Smart Technology Era and protect life and human rights, then the future is something to fear. However, if we are (and we are), then we can steer our future into something worth embracing. One of the questions that remains is whether we need to turn the existing thinking, policies, and guidelines into laws?

There is much needed concern over the impact of technology on well-being. Facing our uncertain future, we only know the technology is a large part of it – larger than ever. We also know that, as the creators and developers of technology, humans direct its purpose and function. Humans are the intelligence behind artificial intelligence. We build the systems and hardware. We develop the algorithms to answer our needs and desires with the tools we have available. And we certainly have plenty of tools. Now, we must ensure that these tools are used to create and sustain successful businesses (of course), and to simultaneously improve and enhance the lives of those who inhabit the world. It is the age of the social enterprise. It is the age where lines between public and private become increasingly blurred. It is the age where governments and organisations work closer together than ever before to improve the world. Technology's impact on well-being has even been calculated by McKinsey & Co – looking into the current waves of 4IR technologies and their potential to improve our general states of well-being.[84] When looking at well-being from a job security, materials living standards, education, health, equal opportunities and environmental sustainability perspective, AI and data are a clear front runner in terms of impact, followed-up by connectivity and platforms and then robotics. We do not just land here - in the place where the world is made better through all of our creations, developments and innovations. We navigate here. Aside from what governments and world leaders themselves can do for this, it is Technological Social Responsibility (TSR) (which is Corporate Social Responsibility's (CSR) cousin) that could be what drives us towards a future of inclusion, well-being, and opportunity for all – not just the elite or lucky few. All of this without being bad for business.

Addressing Bias and Discrimination

Data biases in AI perpetuate biases that we already have. In asking who benefits, who is harmed, who is using and who has the power to use AI systems and products, we are not only asking about the overt implications, but also how these questions are reflected in the ways the systems are built.[85] Who is doing the designing always impacts what is being designed and the results it produces. However unaware we may be, or unintentional the biases. For example, in the development of melanoma detection algorithms, the technology only works on white skin.[86] What about everyone else? Another algorithm used to find criminals quicker, tends to ignore those living in wealthier areas and white people in general. Do white people not commit crimes? These two variably different technologies both show biases. The first bias being that only people of a certain kind can benefit from life-saving technology and the second being that existing cultural and societal discriminations are being taught to algorithms that the rest of the world is told are completely objective. This problem is further perpetuated by the widespread effects of technology. It is no longer one person or group of people who must be present to do this job, it is technology that can be used anywhere in the world, on streams of people at a time. In this, smart technology and machine learning have an immense power to perpetuate, spread and expand social injustices and exclusions, prejudices, personal feelings and cultural, racial and gender inequalities and already entrenched systems.

For a moment, let us zoom in towards the organisations and research institutions that are producing and leading the dialogue around smart technology. The composition of the workforce in these organisations and institutions are mostly white men. 18% of women, compared to 80% of men lead the research and thus the dialogue.[87] Silicon Valley is notorious for its not only favoring white men for funding but in turn for these white men hiring more white men in the companies that are building the systems and products that the world at large is using. If we turn our eye towards the global leaders in technology and machine learning, Facebook's Research staff are at 15% women and 4% black, Google's is at 10% women but only 2.5% black and Microsoft is also at 2.5% black.[88] The percentage of women in research roles in Microsoft is unclear, but women comprise 21.4% of the company's technical roles. Why is research so important in AI? Not only does it control dialogues and tell us where to look and how to look at it, but this research is the foundation of AI systems. It builds the data and decision-making processes for the algorithms that rely on it. It determines what we are building, for whom, what we are considering this process, and how we are building it. There should be little doubt, then, why we land up with biased systems, solutions that favor the elite and focuses on products and solutions that can only be used by the few. It makes it even more difficult to change this when we are reliant on the interventions, laws and guidelines that lie in the hands of more elite - our politicians, global leaders, major economic contributors - more glaring dominance by white men.

If leaders themselves are benefiting from exclusion and prejudice, do we dare wonder why it has taken so long to move our conversations from our troubles and goals towards the laws and policies that will solve and prevent them? In truth these world problems or problems for the minorities and the marginalized are not at a matter of urgency for those who are not directly negatively impacted. It follows that if the same systems that produce social hierarchies and preferential treatment produce and the subsequent direction and biases in smart technology produce the law makers and regulators on whom we are waiting to set our future straight. This book not only aims to shed light on the real impact of smart technology, but of the responsibility of those involved and benefiting from it. We aim to make it clear what needs to be done and how it can be done - to achieve a future that prides itself on ethics, inclusion, and development. We do however know that it is not enough to merely tackle the problems faced in the tech industry. It is not even enough to focus on communities. We must start with the leaders who perpetuate our state of being and insist on the diversity that expands our vantage point. Only then can we ensure that the people guiding, creating, and developing our solutions are more accurately representing the global population and the variety of values, lifestyles, and problems that we each face. And, simultaneously, we must put in place the measures, checks, laws, and processes that will ensure this moves from conversation to action.

The system at large, and every facet that relies on it and contributes to it needs to be considered. For the governments and businesses seeking smart technology in their solutions, we need trained ethicists, sound processes, diverse minds, and internal policies that, together guide every instance, every system and every product. However, we do not have them. While they are more difficult to achieve on a global leadership level, the smaller the ecosystem, the easier it is to introduce them. Governments have much larger ecosystems to contend with than global conglomerates and these conglomerates have larger ecosystems to deal with than large, national organisations (you get where we are going). This does not mean that larger ecosystems should not be thinking about this urgently. It just means that the changes will likely take more time. We do, after all, want them to be changes that are actionable, adoptable, thoughtful, and lasting. But we also want to stop seeing excuses and stalling. AI ethics is not a want. It is a need. And it is also about more than making the right thing or making the best system possible.[89] We have not been faced with such an ethical challenge in society since the time before constitutions and democracy. Not to say that we do not have any other ethical challenges, but that none are particularly novel or new. The potential of smart technology makes our current ethical challenges that much more urgent and threatened and brings with it new ones. This is why AI is known as the greatest human rights challenge of the 21st century. There is little way to control its spread and simply too many unknowns. Those with power control the systems, benefit from the systems and inflict their biases on the systems. Business owners, politicians, leaders, those educated in machine learning, engineering, and data science suddenly have more power than was ever possible and no laws, regulations or checks to balance this power. But we know this. This is not news. What we really need is to do something about it. We need governance, guidance, and regulations. I am advocating for more decentralized governance. To do that however, we need to understand what needs to be governed, guided, and regulated and how to make, one-size-fits-all, global laws that do not favor any culture, country, or value system. Simply, we need common ground. We need one defining good on which we all agree, and paths to reach this that are possible for every citizen of the world to follow. The proposed MTP for Humanity and its associated MTP goals provides such common ground. One thing we know for sure is that if we aim to achieve anything, our goals must be actionable and our paths must be clear, and our method must consider the values and rights of 9 billion individuals. Like with any plan and strategy, if we cannot reach it, it is pointless to discuss. This is where the democratizing AI framework and MTP for Humanity fits in to help people achieve the transformation that the smart technology era offers in an ethical, mindful, and responsible way, that considers all potential blockers and how to face and overcome them. Furthermore, the framework and MTP are also directed at law makers, in what they need to consider in order to create laws and regulations that are reasonable, actionable and impose as many restrictions on the biased individuals creating the laws and building the systems as they do on the people and systems they govern, and the people and social systems impacted by them.

Here we take a note from John Rawls who states that we can find a way to remove the natural instinct towards personal gain and protecting ourselves and what we know and believe in.[90] Not just in theory, but in an actionable framework that helps us embrace AI, be empowered by AI, govern AI and use it for the good of the world. The trade-off between transparency and privacy is, as Peter Thiel, describes, a wickedly hard problem.[91] How transparent should we be? How transparent can we expected to be? Should different people fall differently on the privacy-transparency spectrum? How much privacy should be given? Is privacy even real if it is only awarded to those who behave well? Is that not just the illusion of privacy? Bentham's Panopticon is relevant as it is a sense of constantly being watched. What happens to us when we are behaving in ways that our governments want us to behave? What happens when these governments change? Can citizens adjust quick enough? All stakeholders, including citizens need to be super agile and life-long learners. There will always be things to learn, and if we are willing to keep learning that is the only way we will be ensured to have knowledge that is not outdated or irrelevant and puts us in a better position to deal with change.[92] The ability to reinvent ourselves again and again might sound stressful – we do not want to always have to change. What do we do with the stress that comes with this? How do we ensure we can do this? How do we make learning less exclusive? Digitization may have positive effects on this, but what about the digital divide? If this disappears in the next ten years as we expect it to, are Friedman and Harari correct about the biggest divide being the self-motivation divide?[93] The divide between those who keep learning and those who do not? We are moving into a world that was based on large-scale biases and prejudice to a world where bias and discrimination is based on individual traits.[94] Is self-motivation the most important thing, are those who are not self-motivated doomed to suffer? Furthermore, if there is so much data on us so readily available, this information will not be able to be hidden. Here we have a dilemma between transparency and privacy. If we are transparent, but there are biases and prejudices against what is not considered to be the perfect kind of citizen, loan applicant or employee, are we doomed to discrimination just because our personality type or propensities are not useful to the current system? These are problems that AI and data can cause, and if we do not carefully think about them now, we are a part of creating this future.

Let us look at data responsibility and explainability. Understanding how and why our rules or algorithms reach their conclusions (how a decision is made) is just as important as the accuracy of the decision itself.[95] If we do not understand or cannot explain the decision-making process and criteria that affect that process, we cannot ensure or even justify if the outcome can or should be trusted. Explainability does not stop there. We also need to be able to explain for what it is that our business or organization is using AI, what it is serving and who or what it is aiding. This means that all leaders and essentially everyone at the organization must understand, from a business point of view, why, how and for what their organization is using AI. Being able to explain the algorithm's decision-making process (justifying its outcomes) and for what, how and why AI is being used is only the beginning. We need to consider how, by whom and to what end the data and its learnt paths to conclusions are being directed, checked, watched, tested, and interrogated. Simply, whenever there is machine learning, there need to be measures and humans in place to take accountability of the system, its decision-making processes, and its conclusions. Without these measures, we fall trap to many different potentially detrimental flaws. Firstly, there can be very little valuable explainability without accountability. We might very well be explaining how we think, hope, or assume something works and in fact it does not do that thing at all. There is also the concern that its relatively common practice for humans to make decisions without being willing or able to explain their real motivations in full.[96] In many cases we may not even know what they are. The concerning part here is that our motivations affect our findings. If we want or think a conclusion or outcome will be a certain thing, then we, knowingly or unknowingly steer it that direction. When it comes to the interpretation of that answer, there are in many instances, several ways to interpret it. This is where we get systems that identify CEOs as men, Marketing Managers as women, criminals as black, and so on. These identifications are being picked up based on our own prejudices, biases, senses of reality and frames of reference. We are then infecting our algorithms with our same prejudices. Without checks, measures, and human intervention we can never be sure that our data is clean, accurate or valuable to our conclusions.

The AI Now Institute at New York University is a women-led interdisciplinary research institute devoted to understanding the social implications of AI technologies. The Institute's current research agenda focuses on four core areas: bias and inclusion, rights and liberties, labor and automation, and safety and critical infrastructure.[97] The *AI Now 2019 Report* makes the following recommendations: (1) Regulators should ban the use of affect recognition in important decisions that impact people's lives and access to opportunities; (2) Government and business should halt all use of facial recognition in sensitive social and political contexts until the risks are fully studied and adequate regulations are in place; (3) The AI industry needs to make significant structural changes to address systemic racism, misogyny, and lack of diversity; (4) AI bias research should move beyond technical fixes to address the broader politics and consequences of AI's use; (5) Governments should mandate public disclosure of the AI industry's climate impact; (6) Workers should have the right to contest exploitative and invasive AI—and unions can help; (7) Tech workers should have the right to know what they are building and to contest unethical or harmful uses of their work; (8) States should craft expanded biometric privacy laws that regulate both public and private actors; (9) Lawmakers need to regulate the integration of public and private surveillance infrastructures; (10) Algorithmic Impact Assessments must account for AI's impact on climate, health, and geographical displacement; (11) Machine learning researchers should account for potential risks and harms and better document the origins of their models and data; and (12) Lawmakers should require informed consent for use of any personal data in health-related AI.[98]

Kate Crawford, Meredith Whittaker and Sarah West of the AI Now Institute also produced a report in 2019 called *Discriminating Systems: Gender, Race, and Power in AI* that encompasses some of the recommendations that should be considered for action if we are to ensure that the destruction of smart technology is never allowed to exist.[99] The recommendation for *improving workplace diversity* includes: (1) Publish compensation levels, including bonuses and equity, across all roles and job categories, broken down by race and gender; (2) End pay and opportunity inequality, and set pay and benefit equity goals that include contract workers, temps, and vendors; (3) Publish harassment and discrimination transparency reports, including the number of claims over time, the types of claims submitted, and actions taken; (4) Change hiring practices to maximize diversity: include targeted recruitment beyond elite universities, ensure more equitable focus on under-represented groups, and create more pathways for contractors, temps, and vendors to become full-time employees; (5) Commit to transparency around hiring practices, especially regarding how candidates are leveled, compensated, and promoted; (6) Increase the number of people of color, women and other under-represented groups at senior leadership levels of AI companies across all departments; (7) Ensure executive incentive structures are tied to increases in hiring and retention of underrepresented groups; (8) For academic workplaces, ensure greater diversity in all spaces where AI research is conducted, including AI-related departments and conference committees.[100] Their recommendations for *addressing bias and discrimination in AI Systems* include (9) remedying bias in AI systems is almost impossible when these systems are opaque; transparency is essential, and begins with tracking and publicizing where AI systems are used, and for what purpose; (10) rigorous testing should be required across the lifecycle of AI systems in sensitive domains; pre-release trials, independent auditing, and ongoing monitoring are necessary to test for bias, discrimination, and other harms; (11) the field of research on bias and fairness needs to go beyond technical debiasing to include a wider social analysis of how AI is used in context; this necessitates including a wider range of disciplinary expertise; and (12) the methods for addressing bias and discrimination in AI need to expand to include assessments of whether certain systems should be designed at all, based on a thorough risk assessment.[101]

21st Century Skills, Competencies, and Jobs for a Human-centric AI-driven Workplace

Given the accelerating pace of smart technology driven automation and its impact on people's required skills and knowledge in the dynamic job market, there is a growing need for an always accessible type of continuous learning that covers life-wide and lifelong learning. To thrive as a citizen and participant in the workplace, people need to not only be equipped with the relevant literacies, competencies, and character qualities, but also make proactive smart choices about where the needs and opportunities are shifting and where they can make meaningful contributions. As discussed in Chapter 7, ultra-personalized AI-enabled education is a gamechanger to assist with more productive learning experiences. AI can also help to find relevant jobs and tasks in an evolving marketplace that match people's interests, knowledge, skills, competencies, and experiences. AI is at the same time increasingly having a disruptive impact on many traditional jobs and tasks in the workplace and job market. In *AI Superpowers*, Kai-Fu Lee discusses a blueprint for human coexistence with AI where he recommends that the private sector who drives the AI revolution should take the lead in creating a more human-centric AI-driven workplace with new humanistic jobs that are more social, compassionate, creative, or strategy-based in nature to complement the AI-driven software and machines that can focus on automation, optimization, and non-social related tasks. There are already events and webinars around the globe such as the one organized by the UK India Business Council in 2020 about *Rewiring the 21st Century Workplace – How to make it Human-centric and Tech-driven* which brainstorms how organisations can re-design the future workplace, how people's health and wellbeing can affect the health and wellbeing of the company or organization, how we can better integrate human behavior and technology to achieve long-term success, and what best practices can be shared to ensure people and organizations are making the most of both their human capital and technological assets.[102]

A few years ago, the World Economic Forum presented a meta-analysis of research about 21st-century skills in primary and secondary education and extracted 16 skills in three broad categories of foundational literacies, competencies, and character qualities.[103] Foundational literacies is focused on how people apply core skills to everyday tasks and provides an underpinning to build competencies and character qualities. Apart from literacy and numeracy skills, it also includes scientific, ICT, financial, and cultural and civic literacy. Competencies involve the ability of people to tackle complex challenges using skills such as critical thinking, problem solving, creativity, communication, and collaboration. Character qualities are about how people approach their changing environment where they need skills such as initiative and curiosity to help with originating new ideas and concepts, adaptability and persistence to be more flexible and tough when faced with problems, and leadership along with social and cultural awareness to help people to have positive engagements in ways that are culturally, socially and ethically acceptable and suitable.[104] The WEF has also defined the top ten job skills of 2025 in the categories of problem solving, self-management, working with people and technology use and development.[105] The *problem solving* skills involve analytical thinking and innovation, complex problem-solving, critical thinking and analysis, creativity, originality and initiative. *Self-management* skills include active learning and learning strategies and resilience, stress tolerance and flexibility, whereas *working with people* skills involve leadership and social influence. Examples of *technology use and development* related skills include technology design and programming and technology use, monitoring, and control. In *Critical Skills for the 21st Century Workforce*, Ryan Whorton, Alex Casillas, and Fred Oswald identify three major forces that fundamentally changed the nature of work in the 21st century which are interpersonal, technological, and international in nature and analyzed a core subset of 21st century skills related to these forces, namely teamwork, safety, customer service, creativity, critical thinking, meta-cognition, cross-cultural knowledge and competence, and integrity and ethics.[106]

Lasse Rouhiainen in *Artificial Intelligence: 101 things you must know today about our future* references a description of 24 skills that he published in a previous book *The Future of Higher Education — How Emerging Technologies Will Change Education Forever* and categorized as either people or business skills for the future.[107] The people skills for the future involve self-awareness and self-assessment, emotional intelligence, social intelligence, interpersonal intelligence, empathy and active listening, cultural flexibility, perseverance and passion, a focus on the common good, mindfulness and meditation, physical training, and storytelling. The business skills for the future have to do with problem solving, creativity, adaptability to new technology, entrepreneurial mindset, sales and marketing, data analysis, presentation skills, environmental intelligence, large-scale thinking, accounting and money management, the ability to unplug, design thinking and design mindset, and spotting trends. In addition to these, Lasse Rouhiainen also emphasizes five future skills and competencies which include AI (covering for example deep learning, machine learning, robotics, and self-driving car engineering) and blockchain (including cryptocurrency), social intelligence (which involves coaching, consulting, emotional intelligence, empathy, and helping others), creativity mindset (which involves the ability to create something out of nothing, design thinking, design mindset, and personal brand cultivation), computational thinking (which involves computational sense-making, contextualized intelligence, and virtual collaboration) and learning how to learn (which covers self-awareness, resilience, and mindfulness).[108] From all of the above perspectives we are getting a clearer picture of what skills and competencies we should develop to give us a better chance to survive and thrive in the Smart Technology Era.

The Institute for the Future has communicated their research findings about the essential drivers that will reshape the workplace landscape as well as the salient work skills needed over the next decade in a report called *Future Work Skills 2020* which was sponsored by the University of Phoenix Research Institute.[109] This report specifically considers future work skills and competencies across a variety of jobs and work settings and not the possible future jobs (which I'll elaborate on later in this section). The specific key drivers that they list include *extreme longevity* which is about the impact of increasing global lifespans on the nature of learning, professions and career trajectories; the *ascent of AI-driven machines and systems* where workplace automation affects human workers doing mechanical or habitual repetitive tasks; the *computational world* where the world is being instrumented and made programmable through enormous increases in sensors, communications and IoT devices and processing power; *novel media ecology* where communication tools are enhanced with novel multimedia literacies and technology for digital animation, video production, media editing, augmented reality, and gaming; *super-structured organizations* where social media platforms and technologies drive novel forms of production and value creation at scale on a spectrum of highly personalized to global reach; and *globally connected world* where increased global networking, interconnectivity, and interdependence provides tremendous opportunities for agile and diverse companies, organizations, communities, cities and countries to innovate and grow.[110] These six disruptive forces that are all contributing to the transformation of civilization and the societal landscape make it even more possible to implement the proposed MTP for humanity to drive beneficial outcomes for all through decentralized, adaptive and agile economic, social and governance systems that democratizes knowledge, science, smart technology and other tools in optimal values-based and human-centric ways.

The Institute of the Future further outlines ten future work skills that would be crucial for people to be successful in the workplace going forward. (1) The first one is *sense-making* as the "ability to determine the deeper meaning or significance of what is being expressed" which I have also identified as a key area of competence as expressed through the ninth MTP goal about implementing better collective sensemaking for all of humanity and better alignment with respect to our common goals and visions.[111] Whereas the Institute of the Future primarily links sense-making to the rise of smart machines and systems, I think it can be linked to sense-making more broadly as we are dealing with opposing views, perspectives, and conspiracy theories on social, cultural, economic, political and many other levels. Other future work skills also linked to the identified disruptive drivers include: (2) *social intelligence* as the "ability to connect to others in a deep and direct way, to sense and stimulate reactions and desired interactions"; (3) *novel and adaptive thinking* as the "proficiency at thinking and coming up with solutions and responses beyond that which is rote or rule-based"; (4) *cross-cultural competency* as the "ability to operate in different cultural settings"; (5) *computational thinking* as the "ability to translate vast amounts of data into abstract concepts and to understand data-based reasoning"; (6) *new-media literacy* as the "ability to critically assess and develop content that uses new media forms, and to leverage these media for persuasive communication"; (7) transdisciplinarity as the "literacy in and ability to understand concepts across multiple disciplines"; (8) *design mindset* as the "ability to represent and develop tasks and work processes for desired outcomes"; (9) *cognitive load management* as the "ability to discriminate and filter information for importance, and to understand how to maximize cognitive functioning using a variety of tools and techniques"; and (10) *virtual collaboration* as the "ability to work productively, drive engagement, and demonstrate presence as a member of a virtual team".[112]

The OECD also produced a *Future of Education and Skills 2030 Conceptual learning framework* report on *Transformative Competencies for 2030* that recommend three transformative competencies to help shape the future where well-being and sustainability is achievable, namely creating new value, reconciling tensions and dilemmas, and taking responsibility.[113] More specifically, (1) they describe creating new value as "innovating to shape better lives, such as creating new jobs, businesses and services, and developing new knowledge, insights, ideas, techniques, strategies and solutions, and applying them to problems both old and new", as well as questioning the current situation, collaborating with other people and attempt to think "outside the box". This ties in with applying creativity and critical thinking to innovate in line with a purpose or even better - a massive transformative purpose. The sixth MTP Goal is relevant there as it is about collaborating in optimal human-centric ways to use our growing knowledge base and general-purpose technologies in a wise, value-based, and ethical manner to solve humanity's most pressing problems and creating abundance for everyone. (2) Reconciling strain, friction and predicaments implies making sense of the many inter-relations and interconnections between ostensible opposing or irreconcilable ideas, positions, and logical thinking, and considering the outcomes of actions over the short- and long-term. This kind of sensemaking is exactly what I am advocating for in an interdependent globally connected world as we consider democratizing AI and shaping a better future for as many people as possible. This is again also in line with ninth MTP Goal about implementing better collective sensemaking for all of humanity and better alignment with respect to our common goals and visions. A deeper understanding of contrasting views and a spectrum of positions not only assist in developing better arguments and reasoning to support specific positions, but also help to harmonize and find constructive and pragmatic solutions to problems and disputes in respectful and empathic ways. (3) Taking responsibility is all about being "connected to the ability to reflect upon and evaluate one's own actions in light of one's experience and education, and by considering personal, ethical and societal goals".[114] This is absolutely key and in congruence with MTP goals 10, 11 and 12 that are focused on helping people to live more meaningful lives, developing virtues and character strengths which includes wisdom and knowledge, courage, humanity, justice, temperance and transcendence as well as building local and virtual empathic communities with more meaningful work and relationships.

What are the typical jobs related to artificial intelligence? The most obvious of the jobs related to AI is a data scientist, AI researcher, machine learning engineer, software developer, data engineer, data analyst, business analyst and business intelligence developer. On the *engineering and software development* side there is a preference towards cloud, edge, or hybrid development capabilities. These jobs involve creating the algorithms and ensuring they can connect to the data they need. Jobs also include *solution architects* that design or modify systems architecture to meet specific business needs and make sure the systems have a secure, scalable, and safe home and everything they need to function and work optimally. We also have *data scientists* who oversee delivering data-driven insights and AI solutions by collecting, analyzing, and interpreting multiple data sources through data processing and applying statistical and machine learning methods. Whether the data is correct, relevant, unduplicated, and unbiased is important here. We have *data analysts* who keep checking the data against the algorithm and the conclusions it is drawing in collaboration with data scientists. How is it reaching them, why is it reaching them? Would a human draw the same conclusion? We have *business analysts* who interrogate businesses and problems to guide everyone else on what needs to be achieved and what system may need to be created in order to achieve this. Then we have *data engineers* who are developing algorithms to help make raw data accessible and more useful, processing data throughout the data science pipeline, labeling data and ensuring data can be effectively used by data scientists and algorithms. *AI researchers* investigate new methods and approaches, developing new algorithms, architectures, and systems of solving-problems, while *data scientists* configure and apply these algorithms and systems in real-world scenarios. This whole system is aimed to ensure that the intelligent machine is effective and that its outcomes are true and valid. These roles may have many names, but it is the tasks they perform that is important.

Since we live in the Smart Technology Era and AI is but a part of that, there are many other jobs that use AI or are complemented by AI. These exist in robotics, nanotechnology, biotechnology, engineering, information technology engineering, systems engineering, mathematics, biomedical engineering, physics, quantum physics, quantum computing, and so on. Specific roles that are and will become increasingly more common as AI adoption and development increases are divided into three categories by an MIT study. They are called Trainers, Explainers and Sustainers.[115] Some of these roles have up until now been undertaken as part of the general tasks of data scientists, data analysts and researchers. However, each of these categories require much more time, effort, and energy than they are generally being given. Let us explore what they involve. *Trainers* are the people who teach machines how to mimic human behavior: how to talk, what to say, different contexts and worldviews and how to show empathy or disgust et cetera. They can be psychologists, marketing specialists, digital marketers, sociologists, anthropologists, historians, researchers, English majors, or any knowledgeable person in the subject matter. Trainer jobs according to MIT Sloan include for example: (1) *Customer-language tone and meaning trainer* who teaches AI systems to look beyond the literal meaning of a communication by, for example, detecting sarcasm; (2) *Smart-machine interaction modeler* who models machine behavior after employee behavior so that, for example, an AI system can learn from an accountant's actions how to automatically match payments to invoices; (3) *Worldview trainer* trains AI systems to develop a global perspective so that various cultural perspectives are considered when determining, for example, whether an algorithm is "fair".[116] Next are *Explainers*. These people will need to be able to know and explain how a respective algorithm or system works, what data it is relying on, why it works the way it works and how it reaches the conclusions that it does. Gone are the days of "I don't know, I don't understand, I can't reproduce it, or I can't explain why". Each AI system will need to be scrutinized and understood so that any layman can understand its process. Explainers do not need to be technical at all. They just need to understand technology and AI so they can bridge the gap between the technical and the business. A technical background or studies will not hurt, but any person who is good at understanding and explaining in an accessible way will thrive in this role. According to MIT Sloan some example Explainer jobs include: (1) *Context designer* who designs smart decisions based on business context, process tasks, and individual, professional, and cultural factors; (2) *Transparency analyst* who classifies the different types of opacity (and corresponding effects on the business) of the AI algorithms used and maintains an inventory of that information; (3) *AI usefulness strategist* who determines whether to deploy AI (versus traditional rules engines and scripts) for specific applications.[117] Finally, we have *Sustainers*. In this chapter the importance of these roles and the laws required to maintain an ethical global environment in the face of the Smart Technology Era has been emphasized. Sustainers are among the up-and-coming roles that ensure this happens. They are the people who measure, check, and scrutinize that the systems are fair, true, unbiased, auditable, and designed and used responsibly with no negative consequences. Philosophers, ethicists, historians, political scientists, economists, sociologists, psychologists, researchers, and analysts will make great Sustainers, but anyone with an eye for detail and motivation to see AI used properly will thrive in these roles. MIT Sloan provides the following examples of Sustainer roles: (1) *Automation ethicist* who evaluates the noneconomic impact of smart machines, both the upside and downside; (2) *Automation economist* who evaluates the cost of poor machine performance; (3) *Machine relations manager* who "promotes" algorithms that perform well to greater scale in the business and "demotes" algorithms with poor performance.[118]

Lasse Rouhiainen in his book *Artificial Intelligence: 101 things you must know today about our future* has listed some example AI-related jobs that will likely have more demand going forward.[119] These include an *AI chatbot designer* who designs AI-based chatbots that can perform customer services in a user friendly and effective manner; an *AI digital marketing engineer* who understands how to leverage various digital marketing and social media tools for more effective AI-driven marketing strategies; an *AI business strategy consultant* who examines a company and recommends ways that the business can build AI services and products; an *AI strategy consultant for the public sector* who can identify potential obstacles that will come to the fore due to the initiation and implementation of AI into society and can solve problems through AI training and advising; a *Tech-addiction counselor or coach* who has the know-how, skills, and knowledge to assist people in dealing with the emotional and physical impacts of increased AI adoption and helping to prevent unhealthy ways of using the technology; and a *Creativity coach* that help people to develop and improve their human-centric skills with respect to creative expression along with social and emotional intelligence.[120] In a Glassdoor post *Who's Hiring AI Talent in America*, Andrew Chamberlain lists typical as well as some less common AI related jobs on their Glassdoor job hosting platform.[121] Some of the more unusual ones include an *AI copywriter* who writes the copy used by AI chatbots addressing customer services and other needs and ties in with the AI chatbot designer role mentioned earlier; an *AI journalist* who covers news in the rapidly progressing AI research and applications sectors; an *AI analyst and strategy consultant* who provides AI related consulting and strategic advice for businesses and organizations that use and implement AI solutions; an *User experience designer for AI* who develops stylish, user-friendly, easy-to-use, and fit for purpose AI interfaces for customers; a *Marketing manager for AI groups* who are building the company and product brand awareness and helping to generate leads for AI-driven product or service offerings; an *Attorney for AI groups* who assist in managing highly valued AI intellectual property and legal related matters of companies; and a *Technical sales director* who is involved in supporting the sales of AI-driven products and services to potential customers.[122]

What about the next ten years? What AI-related jobs do we anticipate given the current trajectory and extrapolations we can make? Cognizant has provided their perspective on this as a digital business solutions and services partner for enterprises.[123] In response to the emergence of new smart technologies, new business models and practices and a changing workforce, their Center for the Future of Work has been chartered to examine how work is currently changing and will change over the next decade or so. In their report on *21 More Jobs of the Future* they have added an additional 21 future jobs that they have contemplated for a total of 42 jobs through the period until 2029.[124] Their *low-to-mid technology level jobs within 5 years* include Man-machine teaming manager, AI business development manager, Bring your IT facilitator, Ethical sourcing manager, Fitness commitment counselor, Digital tailor, Walk/talker, Tidewater architect, E-sports arena builder, Data trash engineer, Uni4Life coordinator, Head of business behavior, Joy adjutant, Vertical farm consultant, VR arcade manager, and Juvenile cybercrime rehabilitation counselor. Their anticipated *low-to-mid technology level category of jobs within 10 years* include Personal data broker, Subscription management specialist, Chief purpose planner, Virtual store sherpa, Highway controller, and Personal memory curator. Cognizant's *mid-to-high technology level jobs within 5 years* includes Cyber-attack agent, Master of edge computing, Quantum machine learning analyst, Virtual identify defender, Cyber calamity forecaster, Head of machine personality design, Voice UX designer, AI-assisted healthcare technician, Cyber city analyst, Smart home designer, Data detective; Algorithm bias auditor, Chief trust officer, Financial wellness coach, and Genomic portfolio director. Their forecasted *mid-to-high technology level jobs within 10 years* include Augmented reality journey builder, Haptic interface programmer, Genetic diversity officer, Flying car developer, and Machine risk officer.[125] If many of these jobs materialize over the next decade or beyond, we are certainly entering an interesting and exciting phase of human civilization.

What should you study? As we have seen above, you do not need to fear if science, mathematics and technology are not for you. If you want to work directly with AI, there are many (technical and non-technical) courses and degrees that you can do now, and even more that will be available in the near future. This is not to mention that if you are entrepreneurially minded, follow your passion and just be sure that whatever business you want to start uses AI as a tool. It will simply be more competitive and sustainable if it does. You can study Information Engineering, Mathematics, Statistics, Information Technology, Software Engineering or Computer Science specializing in Machine Learning or AI. You could do a Robotics degree, a degree in Physics or study anything to do quantum or nanotechnology. Study Data Science. Study Business. Study anything to become an expert. Machine learning relies on expertise and data to do its job, so if you are an expert in marketing, economics, sociology or even zoology, you can partner with someone more technical minded and use AI in whatever your endeavor. For the less technically minded, study history, philosophy, sociology, marketing, or anthropology. Study ethics, politics, or economics. Study psychology, history, or linguistics. Study anything that might position to be involved in the more human side of Artificial Intelligence. The side that trains it, keeps it in check and ensures it is not ever biased and is always fair. Whatever you choose to study, ensure you always maintain knowledge and education (even informal) on what technology can do. Technology is the tool in the hands of all humans, and it is people who can use it to solve problems. The more we know about the world, human needs, and human nature, the better equipped we are to think critically, the more empowered we are to solve today's problems and participate in the Smart Technology revolution. If studying, formal education and entrepreneurship are not for you, there are many ways you can get involved in data labelling, data verifying and aiding in machine learning. Much of the dialogue has, reasonably, revolved around the further displacement of unskilled workers. While many jobs have already and will continue to disappear due to general technology and automation, this does not mean that other jobs are not and will not continue to surface. The responsibility is on AI-powered and data-driven organisations taking stock of what needs to be done to support machine intelligence and achieve success and opening up roles necessary to label, verify and teach data.

The World Economic Forum's *The Future of Jobs Report 2020* provides some perspectives on the COVID-19-related disruptions in 2020 and beyond where they position this within a longer history of economic cycles as well as their anticipated viewpoint of the impact of technology adoption on jobs and skills for the period until 2025.[126] The report highlights that the persistent pace of technology adoption is likely to continue and may even be expedited in specific areas with the future of work has already transpired for a large portion of the online white-collar workforce. They observe that AI-driven automation together with the COVID-19 recession is creating a so-called "double-disruption" scenario for workers, that inequality is likely to be aggravated, and that job destruction is actually accelerating with less jobs being created although in the longer run the WEF believes that more future jobs will be created than jobs destroyed. They have also pointed out that the skills gaps will still be significant with a stronger demand over the next five years for skills such as problem-solving, critical thinking and analysis, active learning, flexibility, resilience, and stress tolerance. With online learning and training courses flourishing, it seems that those employed are more attuned to personal development whereas those unemployed focus more on learning computer science, data analysis and information technology skills. Given the expected workplace and skill demand changes and constraints in the labor market, the time available to reskill and upskill employees has also become less. It is good to note that companies during this time still seem to place considerable value on human capital investment. The WEF recommends that the public sector needs to provide more committed support to upskill or reskill employees that have higher potential to be dislodged or losing their jobs. They also advise that businesses need to invest in environmental, social and governance metrics for improved measuring of human and social capital and associated human capital accounting.[127]

In *The Globotics Upheaval* Richard Baldwin shares three rules of thriving in the age of "globots" which involves the combination of the new telemigrant phase of globalization and the new AI-driven form of "robotics" that can do white-collar tasks.[128] These include (1) trying and find jobs that do not compete directly with white-collar robots in the form of AI-driven intelligence and telemigrants as remote human intelligence; (2) looking to develop skills and competencies that allow you to steer clear of direct competition with AI-driven intelligence and remote human intelligence; and (3) understanding that humanity is not a disadvantage or an impediment, but can give you ascendency in many instances. Richard reckons that in the future "a good heart may be as important to economic success as having a good head was in the twentieth century, and a strong hand was in the nineteenth century".[129] I agree with this sentiment and would love to see that we get better at building a more values-based civilization as described in the MTP for Humanity and zoom in on maximizing quality of life, community building, virtues and character strength development, sense-making, standard of living, wellbeing and meaningful living of everyone. By democratizing AI and using it in optimal human-centric ways that are based on wisdom, good values, and ethics, we can not only be smarter in how we dynamically solve problems, but also create opportunities and abundance and share the benefits with everyone.

12. Towards Sapiens, the Human-centric User-controlled AI-driven Super Platform

Having seen the evolution, success, and impact of many platform businesses over the last two decades and being myself involved in building AI-driven platform businesses within the health and financial wellness space, I have been contemplating for several years various ways of how AI and its benefits can be democratized to as many people as possible in a decentralized hyperconnected world. In support of the proposed MTP for Humanity and its associated goals to help shape a beneficial human-centric future, I'm introducing here a revolutionary initiative and an invitation to people around globe to participate in the development, deployment and use of a *decentralized human-centric user-controlled AI-driven super platform* called *Sapiens* with personalized AI agents that not only empower individuals and monetizes their data and services, but can also be extended to families, virtual groups, companies, communities, cities, city-states, and beyond. There has been tremendous technology building blocks and innovative enabling technology developed over the last decade or so and especially the last few years to make the development and ongoing evolution of such a platform possible. But before I elaborate more on this exciting initiative, let us briefly delve into platforms, the platform revolution, platform businesses, the evolution of super platforms, and decentralized AI-driven versions of this along with some of the enabling technological building blocks.

The traditional business landscape has been dramatically disrupted by "platform" businesses that now dominate markets and redefine how value is created. A significant portion of the world's most valuable companies run platform business models and have displaced some of the world's biggest companies with traditional business models by changing the structure of major industries through transforming value creation, consumer behavior, and conventional business processes and leveraging the power of AI, software, and hyper-connectedness. Some of the largest, fastest growing, and most powerful disruptive companies that exploit platform business models have originated in the USA and range from companies such as Apple, Google, Amazon, Microsoft and Facebook to Uber, Airbnb, and eBay as well as some of their counterparts in China such as Alibaba, Baidu, Tencent, JD.com, and Pinduoduo. Sixty percent of the 'Unicorn' billion-dollar start-ups are platform businesses.[1] The most successful companies invest deeply in incorporating platform services into their business models. We have seen that platform businesses outshine all others on growth rates, return on assets, margins, valuation multiples, and customer value creation. Apple became the world's first $1 trillion publicly traded company by investing in a platform-enabled business model that complemented their business model portfolio structure consisting of platform and software services along with physical products. More than fifty percent of Amazon's revenue comes from platform and software services (online stores 51%, AWS 12%, and third-party selling services 20%), whereas Microsoft is predominantly a software and platform services company (more or less an equal split between productivity and business processes, intelligent cloud, and personal computing).[2] Platform businesses outperform businesses with traditional business models in all measures of growth and value such as growth rates, margins, return on assets, and valuation multiples. Very importantly, while platforms are from a business perspective dominant and disruptive, they also have a substantial socio-economic impact that is far reaching and affects jobs and the nature of employment, trade flows between companies and countries, and the manner that personal data is being exploited.

So, what is a platform? McKinsey defines a platform as a software-based digital environment with open infrastructures that orchestrates ecosystems that extends across sectors without borders, harnesses network effects and reduces the marginal costs to near zero, act as a type of matchmaker to link people, resources and organizations, and provides the foundations for combinatorial innovation.[3] *Platform Revolution* by Geoffery Parker, Marshall van Alstyne and Sangeet Choudary describes the rise of the platform as a business and organization model "as one of the most important economic and social developments of our times" and discusses how networked markets are transforming the global economy, the network effects that power the platform, the principles for designing a successful platform business that can conquer and transform traditional industries and change the competition, monetization through capturing the value created by network effects, openness in terms of what platform users and partners can and cannot do, how to govern through policies that enhance growth and increase value, and the regulation of platforms.[4] The authors see the encompassing purpose of a platform as enabling value creation (of resources that they typically do not own or control) for the benefit of all participants through frictionless entry and matching of users and their needs by facilitating the trade of services, goods and social currency. Whereas traditional market leaders became successful through supply economies of scale and push marketing strategies, platform businesses create their success by demand economies of scale that is manifested as network effects and pull strategies that stimulate virality. They observe that a two-sided market that has producers and consumers leads to four different network effects that should all be managed by the platform through quality community-driven curation, optimization and keeping a balance. These include positive and negative same-side effects (i.e., the effects of consumers on other consumers and producers on other producers) and positive and negative cross-side effects (i.e., the effects that consumers have on producers and producers have on consumers). The producers create value units that can be delivered to selected customers based on filters that enable the exchange of appropriate value filters between participants of the platform. Platforms monetize by capturing a part of the excess value created which can be achieved through access to the market, value creation, tools, and curation by asking a transaction fee, users paying for enhanced access, billing third-party users for access to the community and/or asking a subscription fee for enhanced curation. The openness of a platform involves how to regulate participation from managers or sponsors, developers, and users where greater openness is usually associated with more mature and developed platforms. Good governance involves having laws, standards, architectures, and markets that incentivize good interactions, promotes positive behaviors, and dissuades bad interactions and behavior. Self-governance through transparency and participation is also essential to ensure that a platform is managed in an effective manner. The *Platform Revolution* authors further recommend that platforms should during the startup phase focus on strong core interactions, trust, matching and liquidity, whereas during the growth phase the emphasis should be on lifetime value of producers and consumers, sales conversion rate and the growth in various subsets of the user base. Platforms in their maturity phase should concentrate on identifying innovations and mitigating threats from their competitors.[5] They emphasize the importance of cooperation and co-creation and observe that platform competition typically involves platform against platform, partner against partner, and platform against partner and that the control of relationships are more crucial than control of resources. It is evident that industries that are ripe for platform disruption have characteristics such as being very fragmented and information-intensive, having parties with significantly better information than others, and gatekeepers that are not scalable. They foresee platform transformation in sectors such as healthcare, education, energy, finance, and government and call for society to collaborate on ensuring that the platform revolution will create a human-centric world that benefits as many people as possible.[6]

Continuing on our sense-making journey with respect to AI, platforms, and communities, Andrew McAfee and Erik Brynjolfsson in *Machine Platform Crowd: Harnessing Our Digital Future* describes three rebalancing acts needed in the smart technology era which involves human-AI collaboration, the products versus platform balance and inhouse company know-how versus contributions and participation from communities and multitudes of people.[7] The three trends that they identify involve the significant progress in AI (as for example demonstrated by AlphaGo's success in becoming the world's top Go player), the dominance of platform businesses to dethrone incumbents and disrupt industries, and the emergence of crowds or communities that can contribute in development processes and markets. The authors observe that the three trends of AI, platforms, and crowds each have a counterpart that is respectively the human mind that has a significant role to play in human-machine collaboration, products or goods and services which have a redefined role within platform businesses as the value unit, and the core company expertise, knowledge, competencies, and processes that they have built up internally and across their supply chains. Andrew and Erik's message for all businesses, organizations and industries is to rethink the balance between these trends and its counterparts as well as realize that there is likely not a specific success recipe but a spectrum of strategies that can be successful. Apple, Microsoft, and Google for example all leverage platform business models in different ways where the degree of openness and dependence on community or crowd involvement varies. Our choices in how AI and platforms are used, and the level of crowd participation can have very different outcomes such as focused hoarding of power and wealth or distributing affluence and decision making, an increase or decrease of openness and privacy, and business, organizations and work environments that have a sense of purpose, a mission, and a community as opposed to those driven by trepidation, distress, and greed. As I have mentioned before with great technological power that can unlock tremendous value and increase future prospects and choices, comes the need to take greater responsibility and think clearly and deeply about our purpose, goals, and values. That is why I am emphasizing the MTP for Humanity and goals so much to help us in charting our course towards a better future on an individual and societal level.

The platform business model trend has been extended to a super app or platform approach that provides an all-in-one multipurpose marketplace experience of services and offerings as opposed to a single-purpose platform play. Mike Lazaridis, the Founder of Blackberry seems to be first in using the term "super app" and described it as "a closed ecosystem of many apps that people would use every day because they offer such a seamless, integrated, contextualized and efficient experience".[8] The earliest examples of these super platforms are Tencent's WeChat and Alibaba's Alipay, where WeChat hosts more than a million services and offerings where transactions happen within their ecosystem with $7 average revenue per user and a customer base of approximately 640 million users.[9] WeChat is also becoming the interface to Chinese healthcare with features such as appointment booking and telehealth, personal health records management where Tencent's is partnering with hospitals and local government, primary care access with Tencent's trusted doctors, chronic disease management, consumer-facing knowledge platform with Tencent's medical knowledge bank, healthcare provider knowledge and authentication platform linking almost 5 million members of the Chinese Medical Doctor Association, group-buying healthcare product and services linking to JD.com, crowdfunding health insurance, and gamifying aesthetic medicine through SoYoung medicine marketplace.[10] The successful implementation of the super platform approach leads to lower product ownership and development costs as most of the integrated apps and services are third-party developed, reduced know-your-customer and onboarding costs with existing users already on the platform, and more finely-tuned and quicker launches of new products and services to an existing target market. There are many other examples of super platforms such as Grab that provides transport, delivery, lending, payments, telehealth, insurance and loyalty services to 144 million users in eight countries in Southeast Asia; Meintuan in China that provides food and grocery delivery, hotel and restaurant bookings, and local services to about 380 million users; Line in Japan as a social media platform and integrated services provider to 44 million users that provides music playing, video streaming services, freemium games, music playing services, sending money peer-to-peer, ride-hailing, food ordering, and direct-to-user advertising; Gojek/Get that provides ride-sharing services in Indonesia; Paytm in India that provides a mobile wallet service with merchant transaction capability to provide travel bookings and ecommerce services; PhonePe which is an Indian payment app owned by Flipkart and hosts service offerings such as MakeMyTrip's travel booking service, Ola's ride-hailing, and Oyo's hotel booking; Reliance Jio which is an Indian telecom company with a substantial user base that has an offline-to-online platform with more than a hundred services; and Fave mobile payment and deals platform based in Singapore that also provides food delivery and microloans services.[11] Similarly, although Google does not have a connected payment service yet, it seems that they are steadily building out their services linked to their Google Maps and search functionalities such as travel and restaurant bookings, ride-hailing, food delivery, and local services. Given Facebook's move to add a digital wallet called Novi digital wallet (which is supported by Libra cryptocurrency that is driven by the not-for-profit Libra Association) to their existing portfolio offering such as their marketplace, Instagram, Messenger, and WhatsApp, they are in a strong position to create a super platform.[12]

In a Medium article *The Age of the Super Platform*, Stuart Mills argues that the big technology companies such as Google and Facebook have complex forms of monopolies that are difficult to break-up and are effectively already super platforms by providing some of the functionality of smaller platforms (e.g., Google Maps within the Uber app where Google is also a stakeholder) and allow logging in to online services through Google's Gmail, Facebook or Twitter.[13] Even though these companies provide these kinds of services for free as they do with individual users, it provides them with the opportunity to collect more data which can later on potentially be monetized. Stuart refers to this as collecting digital rents. He further summarizes this conundrum with super platform companies by comparing it to the Victorian railways where similar to the railways that cannot work without connecting key locations with one another, super platforms also need scale to offer services, which in turn allow them to collect digital rents similar to private rail owners collected economic rents. If one now wants to split up a super platform, you will effectively dismantle infrastructure similar to disassembling railway infrastructure. However, if nothing is done to the platform business status quo, digital renting will continue.[14] He further makes a case for public ownership similar to how the Victorian railway problem was resolved through government taking control and taking a share of the wealth creation for its contribution to some of the underlying infrastructure and technology. The problem with this approach is super platforms operate across international borders which limits any national governmental actions as well as giving too much control to the state which is already a concern given the trust and privacy issues that we already have with digital surveillance. Stuart also comes to the conclusion that the answer might be in supranational digital organizations and a decentralized data commons which is also more in line with some of the recommendations proposed in this book.[15] Another relevant book that speaks to this topic is *The Platform Society: Public Values in a Connective World* by José van Dijck, Thomas Poell, and Martijn de Waal who analyzes the role of platforms in societies-disrupting markets and employee relations, side-stepping institutions, acting on democratic process, and reshaping social and civic activities.[16] They also accentuate how the battle between the market, government and civil society and the competing ideological systems play out with respect to who should be responsible for safeguarding public values as well as the common good in a platform society. The authors analyzed the impact of the platforms within the media, health, education, and city transport sectors as it pertains to conflicts over regulation between platforms and city governments, on a platform ecosystem level, and the broader geopolitical level between global markets, national governments, and supranational authorities.[17]

In an article titled *Super Platforms in Africa: Not if, but When* by CGAP, a global partnership with a leading development organization that works to improve the lives of poor people through financial inclusion, reckons that a super platform entry into Africa is unavoidable, especially with connectivity quickly expanding with close to 50% of the cell subscribers (almost half a billion people) on the continent estimated to using smartphones in 2020, twenty-four of sixty African countries where Facebook Free Basics currently offers access to a limited version of the internet, and Alibaba's Ant Financial also looking to grow its global foothold in Africa.[18] We have already seen the successful rollouts of mobile money in East Africa with many Africans able to make digital payments from their cell phones as well as success with the Jumia e-commerce platform.[19] Super platforms should open new income streams for low-income people as well as offer and sell local goods or services online, facilitate collaboration with local fintech companies and other businesses, and enable digital liquidity farming by utilizing networks of family and friends to assist with cash-flow issues. Given Africa's agricultural needs and opportunities, the CGAP article *Super Platforms: Connecting Farmers to Markets in Africa* discusses strategic decisions with respect to agriculture-focused digital marketplaces which includes the type of business model (e.g., open, mediated or contract), what crops and value chains will be the focus, who will be the target buyers, how will transportation and logistics be managed, how will engagement with farmers work, how will the movement of goods to buyers be facilitated, and what financial services and payment solutions will be provided.[20] Given that Africa's population is projected to double by 2050 and the demand for food and rural employment will grow, CGAP not only sees super platforms playing an important strategic role to help drive meaningful farmer engagement and provide relevant product and service offerings, but forecasts growth coming from mobile money companies with strong countryside coverage, companies such as Facebook's WhatsApp, as well as native African companies specializing in e-logistics and agribusiness.[21]

Francois Chollet wrote another excellent blog *What worries me about AI* that absolutely resonated with me on multiple fronts, and which are in line with my concerns about AI and how we can address this by democratizing AI with practical solutions where AI helps us - all in line with the proposed MTP for Humanity and associated goals. Francois states his concern as "the highly effective, highly scalable manipulation of human behavior that AI enables, and its malicious use by corporations and governments" and "if given algorithmic control over our minds, governments may well turn into far worse actors than corporations".[22] That is exactly one of my concerns along with others that have been discussed in chapters 8 to 11. We can avoid this path by steering the use of AI towards a future that is beneficial and empowering for all of us on an individual and societal level. Francois specifically highlights how social media acts as a "psychological panopticon" that has sufficient information about people to develop influential psychological models of individuals, groups, or communities as well as the ability to control what algorithmically curated information is being fed to us. This is a dangerous combination that puts the social media companies in a position to use an individual user's digital information consumption as a "psychological control vector" to effectively manipulate people with respect to their beliefs, feelings, and actions. So what's really happening is that human behavior is approached as an optimization problem where a "sufficiently advanced AI algorithm with access to both perception of our mental state, and action over our mental state, in a continuous loop, can be used to effectively hijack our beliefs and behavior".[23] From a psychological control vector perspective the human mind is vulnerable to be attacked via *identity reinforcement* that only shows views with markers that you identify with to make you side with the target view, *negative social reinforcement* that shows posts of the opposite view, *positive social reinforcement* that shows posts that you would like, *sampling bias* that shows posts from your contacts or the broader media that supports the target view (and not necessarily representative of the actual broader support for this view), and *argument personalization* that shows posts that might change your view that is based on what worked for people with a similar psychological profile.[24] So how can we turn this around? By handing over control to the user. An AI-driven portal or interface to our information can not only be a preferable but also an essential way for people to filter and make sense of information if the user has full control of the AI system's goals and objectives and parameters that can be configured to personalize the flow, nature, outcomes, and time spend on the information feed. Francois concludes with a recommendation that we should reject products and services that take our control away and/or manipulate users and work towards developing AI-driven information interfaces that give users more agency and greater ability to direct the information management that affects their lives. More broadly speaking, AI will likely be the most beneficial to its users if it is owned and controlled by humans, and not by corporations or governments.

This provides an excellent prelude to the introduction of *Sapiens, a Decentralized Human-centric, User-controlled AI-driven Super Platform* with personalized AI agents that not only empower individuals and monetizes their data and services, but as mentioned earlier can also be extended to families, virtual groups, companies, communities, cities, city-states, digital nations and beyond. Besides that Sapiens embraces the MTP for

Humanity and its associated goals, it addresses a huge gap in the market and society as there is currently no global solution of this nature at scale that makes life easier and more optimized for the user. We also have a very fragmented apps and platform business ecosystem world-wide, but especially so in the West. Nowhere do we have a solution where the user has full control of their own data with proper privacy and governance without being exploited, controlled, or manipulated in some way. Users also do not have their own personalized AI agents that work for them and help to optimize their lives. We also lack a global solution that helps the user to monetize their own data and services for their own benefit or for people that they want to benefit or for society more broadly. We also do not have AI agents that function in a similar way but support and create benefits for smart families, smart virtual groups, smart companies, smart communities, smart towns, smart cities, smart city-states, and beyond. Furthermore, there do not exist AI agents that try to optimize the connections between networked people that live within structures and even the connections across these hierarchical structures.

Sapiens for the Individual User is a decentralized, human-centric, user-controlled, AI-driven super platform that functions as a multi-sided platform with both centralized and decentralized components and puts the user at the center and in full control of:

- *My Data*
  - *Fully secured storage, management, access and use of personal data with built-in privacy and governance; enriches my data via my engagement with my digital connections and apps.*

- *My AI Assistant*
  - *Next generation AI Assistant that proactively helps to optimize my life; monetizes my data and services; trains on my data; learns from my behavior; understands my needs, wants and learning path; supports lifelong and life-wide learning; helps with sense-making; proactively supports my communications, relationships, activities, safety, travels, accommodation, finances, purchases, decision making, health, wellbeing, and wealth creation; proactively provides guidance, recommendations, and alerts; helps to build virtues and character strengths; filters content, does proactive searches and provides personalized content.*

- *My Digital Connections*
  - *Sapiens connects to my digital connections within a multi-sector digital ecosystem to get access to third party apps and platforms that currently handle my communications, social media, search, health, finance, education, retail, safety, security, entertainment, transport, accommodation, and travel needs.*

Figure 1 illustrates a single node of Sapiens for an individual user being supported from a data governance, AI assistance and digital connections perspective, whereas Figure 2 shows Sapiens connecting to other systems and services within a multi-sector digital ecosystem. Monetization within the Sapiens ecosystem can for example happen through user-controlled advertising, selling of anonymized data and services, subscriptions and transactions between hyper connected users, businesses, and service providers via smart contracts in Sapiens' decentralized distributed ledger-based ecosystem (see Figure 3). As shown in Figure 4 Sapiens can also be expanded to also include *smart contract* based services within a hyper connected network of businesses, organizations, rural areas, smart communities, smart towns, and smart cities, where each entity has its own data governance, AI Assistant, and digital connections and the ability to engage with other entities in the ecosystem.

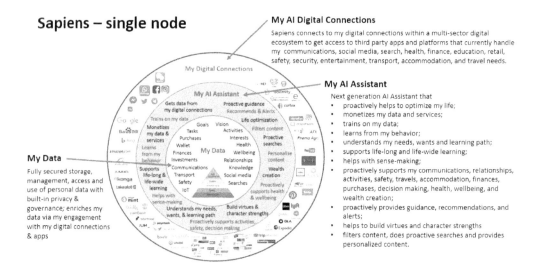

Figure 1. Sapiens for the Individual User

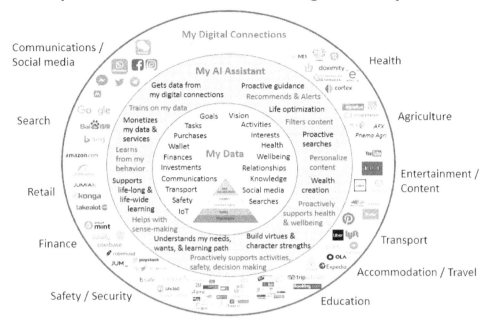

Figure 2. Sapiens within a multi-sector digital ecosystem

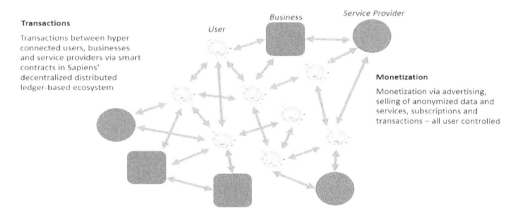

Figure 3. Monetization examples within Sapiens' ecosystem

Sapiens' ecosystem – from users and businesses to Smart Communities and Smart Cities

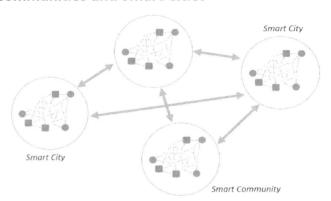

Expand Sapiens to also include smart contract based services within hyper connected network of families, small groups, businesses, organizations, Rural Areas, Smart Communities, Smart Towns, and Smart Cities, where each entity has its own data and AI Assistant that can engage with one another.

Figure 4. Sapiens' ecosystem - from users and business to Smart Communities and Smart Cities

An adapted version of Sapiens for smart communities (or smart towns or smart cities) could for example look as follows:

Sapiens for Smart Communities is a decentralized, human-centric, user-controlled, AI-driven super platform that functions as a multi-sided platform with both centralized and decentralized components and puts the community at the center and in full control of:

- *My Community Data*
    - *Fully secured storage, management, access and use of community data with built-in privacy and governance; enriches my community data via my engagement with my communities' digital connections and apps.*
- *My Community AI Assistant*
    - *Next generation AI Assistant that proactively helps to optimize my community operations, processes, activities and goals; monetizes my community's data and services; trains on my community's data; learns from my community's behavior; understands my community's needs, wants and learning path; supports lifelong and life-wide learning of my community as a collective; help with collective sensemaking; proactively supports my community's communications, relationships, administrative activities, safety, travel activities, accommodation needs, finances, purchases, decision making, health, wellbeing, and wealth creation; proactively provides guidance, recommendations, and alerts; helps to build virtues and character strengths; filters content, does proactive searches and provides community related content.*
- *My Community Digital Connections*
    - *Sapiens connects to my community's digital connections within a multi-sector digital ecosystem to get access to third party apps and platforms*

that currently handle my community's communications, social media, search, health, finance, education, retail, safety, security, entertainment, transport, accommodation, and travel needs.

As mentioned, Sapiens is also a vehicle that not only supports the MTP for Humanity, but a platform that can help to specifically implement components and achieve some aspects of the MTP goals. For example, Sapiens for the individual user directly addresses MTP Goal 7 about democratizing AI and smart technology from a use and benefits perspective to help society thrive through the personalized AI assistant that helps to optimize the user's life and as well as monetizes the user's data and services. It also supports MTP Goal 9 about implementing better collective sensemaking for all of humanity and better alignment with respect to our common goals and visions through supporting lifelong and life-wide learning and better decision-making as well as providing proactive guidance, recommendations, alerts, and filtering of personalized content. The personalized user-controlled AI Assistant can also be implemented in such a way as to support Maslow's 8-stage motivational needs framework (which includes physiological, safety, psychological, esteem, cognitive, aesthetic, self-fulfillment, and transcendence needs) to help an individual user to live a more meaningful life as stated in MTP Goal 11. Sapiens for the individual user can also focus on helping people to build and continuously improve on virtues and character strengths which includes wisdom and knowledge, courage, humanity, justice, temperance, and transcendence as stated in MTP Goal 12. Sapiens for smart communities, smart towns or smart cities can directly support MTP Goal 2 with respect to building a more local, more human city-state civilization with decentralized, community-based, and self-optimized governance and a more elastic, dynamic, and direct democracy with social structures that have polycentric and polyarchic elements. Just imagine a world where user-controlled AI agents that work towards beneficial outcomes for individual users within a community, town or city, can also interact with the AI agents and systems that help to optimize the community, town and city through decentralized, adaptive and agile economic, social and governance systems that reward active participation and positive contributions to society and civilization, but also help to keep peace and protect humanity from any potential harm in elastic ways that respect individual freedom and privacy. Just imagine a world where any community or city in the world can connect with one another to interact in mutually beneficial ways from an economic, cultural, and social perspective as part of a dynamic, empathic, prosperous, thriving, and self-optimizing civilization that benefit everyone in sustainable ways and in harmony with nature. The AI-driven Sapiens ecosystem can also help to drive MTP Goal 10 that is focused on building local and virtual empathic communities connected via a global network with more meaningful work and relationships, as well as MTP Goal 6 that works toward collaborating in optimal human-centric ways to use our growing knowledge base and general-purpose technologies in a wise, value-based, and ethical manner to solve humanity's most pressing problems and creating abundance for everyone.

So where do we start and how do we launch the Sapiens platform and ecosystem? Once the first minimum viable prototype of the platform has been developed it can be first tested on an individual user level and within local communities before rolling this out more widely. We can then for example have a multi-pronged strategy where Sapiens can be tested within the most advanced smart cities in the world (such as Singapore, Dubai, Oslo,

Copenhagen, Boston, Amsterdam, New York, London, Barcelona, or Hong Kong)[25] and/or the most digitized countries (of which Estonia is an example)[26] and/or seeded at scale in Africa that anyway needs series leapfrogging and where there are plenty opportunities to disrupt the current status quo for the better of all Africans. For launching Sapiens in Africa (the birthplace of Homo Sapiens) to become Africa's AI-driven Super Platform where the user is in control, the following factors can be leveraged: Africa is the continent with fastest growing population, growing from 1.3 billion people to an estimated 2.5 billion people over the next 3 decades; multiple large scale entry points such as 33 million small farmers (taking in consideration my earlier references to agriculture-focused digital marketplaces connecting farmers to markets in Africa), the youth in Africa of 226 million people between ages 15-24, and the growing number of smart technology communities across the continent; the possible integration of other African platform businesses and their services into the Sapiens ecosystem; and collaboration with the many mobile network operators in Africa that is helping to connect more Africans to the internet and one another.

From a technology stack perspective, there are many exciting building blocks currently available to implement such as a decentralized AI-driven user-controlled super platform with the required data governance, AI assistant agents and digital connections. Besides the fast growing and tremendously rich AI toolbox of APIs, libraries, frameworks, languages, cloud technologies, hardware technologies available, there also has been significant progress in building out the distributed ledger technology (DLT) stack of which blockchain is a key component to support decentralization through keeping a digital record of transaction securely using cryptography without the need for a central authority.[27] Other advantages of blockchain technology apart from its decentralized nature, is its immutability, transparency, consistency and accuracy of authenticity, information and timelines as well as its security, resilience, and not having a central point vulnerable to attack.[28] Even though there are ongoing efforts to democratize AI, the current reality is that impactful AI and its applications are still to a large extent centralized in single corporations such as Google, Facebook, Microsoft, Amazon, Apple, Tencent, Alibaba, and Baidu which limits collaboration and advancing society in meaningful ways. A recent *Inside Big Data* post about the potential of decentralized AI highlights some of the advantages of combining AI with a decentralized computing model such as blockchain to leverage the strengths of each to help scale resources.[29] With a decentralized AI model, processing can be done in an independent fashion on a variety of computing hardware that can lead to a greater variety of results, knowledge sharing and new solutions for creative problem solving. This is more similar to the decentralized path of scientific discovery and knowledge advancement with the potential of much faster testing and learning in a continuous manner via an evolving decentralized AI network with a proper security framework and appropriate computing power, storage and ultra-high-speed communications. Similar sentiments were shared by Oleg Brytskyi in his Espeo Blockchain blog post called *Decentralized AI: Blockchain's bright future* where he highlights how the merging of blockchain and AI into a decentralized network can lead to benefits such as data protection, ensuring security, a more trustworthy and transparent system than a closed AI system, decentralized intelligence, an energy saving and cost efficient information technology infrastructure, and flexible AI solutions and new ways of using data.[30]

Another major step forward in democratizing AI is the development of AI marketplaces that can for example share trained AI models, data and services which can also be utilized in a decentralized AI-driven user-controlled super platform such as Sapiens. In a *Towards Data Science* article titled *3 AI Marketplaces Everyone Has To Know [One Will Define The Century]* three of the current AI marketplaces that were highlighted included AWS Marketplace, GenesisAI, and SingularityNET.[31] The AWS AI marketplace has almost a thousand solutions (at the time of writing) within categories such as human review services, machine learning solutions, data labeling services, computer vision, natural language processing, speech recognition, text, image, video, audio, structured, and intelligent automation.[32] GenesisAI is building a marketplace for AI products and services which they ironically describe as the "Amazon for AI" on top of their Machine Learning protocol. Their web-based marketplace connects companies in need of AI models, data and services with companies that provide those offerings that they want to monetize.[33] SingularityNET has recently launched a blockchain-driven decentralized AI network which they call the global AI marketplace to allow the creation, sharing and monetization of AI services at scale.[34] This full stack decentralized AI solution allows the registration of organizations on the blockchain as a company or a developer who can create AI services that can be published and used to generate income streams. *Monetize Your Services* and *Create Income Streams* fully control the cost elements of your services, collect platform tokens, and transfer them to your preferred wallet and team members. The SingularityNET decentralized AI solution stack is also made available to third parties to allow them to create their own marketplaces and integrate AI services into their own solutions.[35]

As distributed ledger technologies have a key role to play in the decentralized AI-driven user-controlled super platform stack, I will briefly share some of the exciting DLT related developments to just give a feel for where we are heading with this type of groundbreaking technology. One such example is Holochain, a framework for scalable distributed applications with data integrity, that already thinks outside the blocks of blockchain and asks what comes after the blockchain.[36] Their decentralization solution not only enables a distributed web with user autonomy that is part and parcel of their architecture and protocols, but provides adaptable validation that does not appear to have bottlenecks, a peer-to-peer solution without centralized services or ledgers or any brokers, and agent-centric authority over data-sharing, access and storage. Holochain speaks to the spirit of Sapiens and the MTP for Humanity with their intention to help people own their own data, control their identity, connect applications to suit their personal needs, transact without centralized systems, and support the development of lighter, faster, and more cost-effective applications. Holochain is about emancipating people's online lives from corporate control by distributing the storage and processing of that online data and keeping it under our control. This should effectively impact how we coordinate and interact with one another. I cannot agree more wholeheartedly with their sentiments about "each of us wants to have control over how and with whom we interact" and in order "to evolve and thrive, our communities must support everyone's uniqueness".[37] I also want to highlight Ocean Protocol, which is a decentralized data exchange protocol to unlock data for AI services and applications. I believe this protocol is an important building block for Sapiens as well. They see data as a new asset class where Ocean Protocol can help to unlock its value by making use of blockchain technology, smart contracts, and tokens to connect data owners (data providers) and consumers and "allowing data to be shared while guaranteeing traceability, transparency, and trust for all stakeholders involved".[38] The Ocean Market application can be used by participants to publish, discover, and consume data assets in a way that is secure and protects privacy (where participants can earn by staking or curating on data and by selling data), whereas Ocean data tokens is used to turn data into data assets and Ocean libraries are used by developers to build their own data wallets and data exchanges by making use of decentralized finance tools.[39]

I met Trent McConaghy, one of the cofounders of Ocean Protocol, at the AI for Good Global summit in Geneva Switzerland a few years ago where he also talked about democratizing data and developing a decentralized substrate for AI data and services through BigChainDB (that powers the Interplanetary Database or IPDB network) and Ocean Protocol.[40] Given Trent's background as an AI practitioner before joining the blockchain world and combining AI and blockchain, he also has some interesting perspectives on Decentralized Autonomous Organizations (DAOs) and the AI versions of this called AI DAOs as well as the future of humanity in the face of AI and blockchain type of technologies and even a proposal for a top-level design for the unbounded expression of humanity as mentioned in the previous chapter about beneficial outcomes for humanity. I first got introduced to AI Decentralized Autonomous Organizations through a series of articles and talks that Trent posted in 2016 and 2017.[41] A DAO in a nutshell is a computational process that runs autonomously on decentralized infrastructure with resource manipulation. It is an organization that automates management and administrative functions through running rules encoded as smart contracts that are built on blockchain technology and implements information transmission and enforcement of those contracts. The latter can represent any interaction between humans and organizations. An AI DAO is effectively an AI system running on a decentralized processing substrate or a DAO running with AI algorithms or agents that autonomously take decisions. A simple example is an Art DAO that runs an AI art engine to generate new images and artificial art using generative adversarial neural networks or genetic programming, sell the artificial art on a marketplace for crypto and continue the process.[42] Trent has proposed three different types of AI DAO architectures which involves an AI-driven central smart contract where decisions are taken by a central AI system, a DAO system with AI agents on the edges making autonomous decisions, or a swarm intelligence architecture with many simple AI agents that together creates an emergent AI complexity.[43] It is even possible to give personhood to an AI DAO with today's laws by starting with a corporation (which have rights) and then automate the corporations into an AI DAO which will result in the AI DAO to have rights. We clearly must be very careful with this type of technology that combines the strength of resources from DAOs with the autonomous decision-making capability that AI provides. I agree with Trent that DAOs can potentially catalyze the path to AI getting unrestricted access to resources, which would not be an outcome that we want or would be good for humanity. So, we must be very sensible in how we design these systems and ensure that it is human-centric, under our control and supporting our massive transformative purpose for humanity and its associated goals. Although Andrew McAfee and Erik Brynjolfsson in *Machine Platform Crowd: Harnessing Our Digital Future* acknowledge that blockchain and decentralization might "enable a global crowd of people and organizations, all acting in their own interest, to create something of immense shared value", they also identify some potential problems with completely decentralized organizations and believe that not everything can be captured in smart contracts, that we need human leadership and management to make decisions not specified in contracts, exercise residual rights of control, shape cultures and values, and set purposes, goals, visions, missions and strategies.

As we conclude our sense-making journey on democratizing AI to benefit everyone, I would like to invite anyone across the globe that wants to follow, participate and contribute towards developing, deploying and using Sapiens as a decentralized human-centric and user-controlled AI-driven super platform to connect with us on sapiens.network and our associated community groups and social media.

Acknowledgements

I would like to start thanking my family (including my extended family) for their incredible support throughout the years. It has been a joyful and meaningful journey so far. I dedicate this book to all of you. I specifically would like to thank my loving and kind wife Elna that has been with me through thick and thin and tremendously supportive in her care for our family, throughout my academic career and my business ventures, and the writing of this book; my children, Bianca, Natasja and Jacques, who I am so proud of for the special people that they are, their wonderful and loving support, and the joy that they also bring to my life; my mother Anita who has been figuratively speaking like "the Rock of Gibraltar" in her strong love and steadfast support of me, my brothers, and our family; my late father Hennie (who passed away in 1994 just before I completed my Ph.D.) for everything he has done for us and the special person that he was in our lives; my brothers Hein and Erens and their families, for their unwavering love and support through all these years; my stepfather, John Hoskins, for his wisdom, practical advice and wonderful support; my father-in-law, Eric Olivier, for his guidance, support, wisdom and practical advice and my mother-in-law, Trudie Olivier, for her love and steadfast support; my brothers-in law Albie Olivier and Johan Rademan, and sisters-in-law Lihani Rademan and Hilda Olivier, and all of their families for the people that they are and excellent support of our families.

I also would like to thank my many friends and business colleagues over the years, of which many are scattered across the globe. They have all contributed to my life in various ways for which I am very grateful and appreciative. As part of that group of special people, a special thanks to my friends and colleagues from school and University of Stellenbosch (especially Alten du Plessis and Jurie de Kock), CSense Systems (especially Derick Moolman, Johan Rademan and Tjaart van der Walt), General Electric (many people across the globe), Jumo, Machine Intelligence Institute of Africa, Cortex Logic, and the Cortex Group (especially Con Bruce). Also, much appreciation to the special people that I have interacted with, the ones that inspired me and from whom I have learned so much within the international AI community, intellectual virtual communities, the African AI community, technology hubs, as well as businesses and organizations that my companies have interacted with, and many more. A special thanks also to Amy Meyer for her initial support of this book.

Let us together shape a better future in the Smart Technology Era!

Jacques Ludik

About the Author

Dr Jacques Ludik is a smart technology entrepreneur, AI expert, founder of multiple AI companies, author, AI ecosystem builder, and award-winning AI Leader with a Ph.D. in Artificial Intelligence (Computer Science) and 25+ years' experience in AI and Data Science and its applications. He is currently the Founder and CEO of Cortex Group and Cortex Logic that is focused on providing scalable ultra-personalized AI-enabled wellness solutions and the Founder and President of the Machine Intelligence Institute of Africa (MIIA) that focuses on transforming Africa through AI. One of his previous companies, CSense Systems, was Africa's first AI company that was sold to a multinational company, specifically General Electric in 2011. Dr. Ludik is involved in building AI-based data rich platforms that leverage AI technologies to unlock business, customer, and societal value.

His massive transformative purpose is to help shape a better future in the Smart Technology Era, and specifically to help business and society thrive and to help transform Africa. He is also passionate to help transform Africa through smart Technologies such as AI and blockchain building AI communities and exponential organizations. Dr Ludik's recent book *Democratizing Artificial Intelligence to Benefit Everyone* is not only a sense-making journey on democratizing AI to benefit everyone, but also introduces a massive transformative purpose for humanity and its associated goals to help shape a beneficial human-centric future (which complements the United Nations' 2030 vision and SDGs) along with Sapiens (sapiens.network) as a decentralized human-centric user-controlled AI-driven super platform to empower individuals and monetizes their data and services and can be extended to extended to companies, communities, cities, city-states, and beyond.

Apart from the executive management roles in all the AI companies that he founded, he was previously also Vice President Data Science and Chief Data Officer at Jumo, Director and Big Data and Analytics Leader at General Electric and Senior Lecturer and Researcher at Stellenbosch University. Dozens of his papers on AI were published in Journals and International Conferences as well as a book, *Neural Networks and Psychopathology*, published by Cambridge University Press (UK). He also has a patent filed for Knowledge Fusion. Jacques holds a B.Sc. (Cum Laude), Hons. B.Sc. (Cum Laude), M.Sc. (Cum Laude), and Ph.D. degrees in Computer Science from Stellenbosch University. Dr Ludik currently also serves on the Advisory Boards of Cirrus, AI Africa Expo, Data Science Nigeria, and AI Centre of Excellence in Kenya, and has launched AIAfrica.wiki via MIIA. In 2019, he is also the recipient of Africa's AI Leader of the Year Award.

Websites: jacquesludik.com; cortexgroup.ai; cortexlogic.com; miiafrica.org; sapiens.network.
Twitter: @jacquesludik; YouTube: Jacques Ludik
LinkedIn: https://za.linkedin.com/pub/jacques-ludik/1/286/b2

Appendix: Democratizing Human-centric AI in Africa

As a stepping stone to help democratize human-centric AI in Africa, I am highlighting here a project by the Machine Intelligence Institute of Africa (MIIA) that aims to get not only an accurate dynamic picture about the spread and democratization of human-centric AI in Africa via comprehensive data collection and quality research, but also helping to drive the adoption of AI across Africa continent by engaging in multi-stakeholder, multi-disciplinary research in collaboration with a partner network of excellence. But before I share more details about the project for which MIIA is also requesting sponsorship, let us briefly consider Africa's tremendous potential to flourish and have better quality life for everyone on the continent as well as the many stumbling blocks that need to be overcome. Taking the proposed MTP for Humanity and its corresponding goals and implementation seriously would be a key step in the right direction. Another bold step forward would be to implement Sapiens Africa-wide to become Africa's decentralized human-centric user-controlled AI-driven super platform to empower individuals, companies, communities, and city-states across the continent. We know that Africa is currently the continent with the fastest growing population going from 1.3 billion people to an estimated 2.5 billion people over the next 3 decades and current youth population of 226 million people between ages of 15 and 24. As I have mentioned in Chapter 10, the eighth MTP goal is about the need to have a balance in how we grow our populations whilst still maximizing quality of life. If we want to give ourselves the best chance to accelerate the diffusion of quality of life to every African citizen within reasonable time frames, we also urgently need to address the problem of excessive population growth on this continent along with SDGs and other MTP goals outlined.

In a 2020 World Economic Forum article by Colin Coleman from Goldman Sachs it was indicated that if Africa continues and accelerates its structural policy reforms, the region will be worth \$5.6 trillion within 5 years (according to McKinsey estimates) and potentially mimic China's rapid rise of the last 50 years.[1] They also predict that Africa will continue its very strong urbanization path with on average having 24 million more people living in cities each year between 2015 and 2045. Africa's current economic underperformance, which is a source of global instability and extremism, is demonstrated through the statistic of contributing only 3% to the global GDP with a population that is approximately 17% of the global population. Africa has an opportunity to turn this around and instead become a significant source of growth. Africa Growth Initiative's *Foresight Africa: Top priorities for the continent 2020-2030* report spotlights the successes of previous years as well as strategies to take on impediments successfully to prosper by 2030.[2] Although some progress were made with respect to the SDGs, some of the problems highlighted include not having a robust global and localized governance structure, state vulnerability and large financing gaps, persisting poverty and hunger which is worsen by climate change (and Covid-19), and significant shortcomings with respect to healthcare, education, infrastructure and service delivery. Some of the lessons from Rwanda in making progress towards the SDGs include national ownership and domestication of the SDGs, increasing implementation capacity, resource mobilization and ease of doing business, human capital development and job creation, implementation of the African Continental Free Trade

Agreement, and strengthening analytics capacity and monitoring of SDG indicators.[3] The report also emphasises the importance of good and inclusive governance, justice, respect for human rights, and democracy. Cabinet Secretary of Kenya, Joe Mucheru, has joined a list of global government officials and task forces to fight corruption, provide improved public services to citizens and enhance citizen's social and economic opportunities.[4] An example of the smart technology deployment that can help with this includes distributed ledger technologies such as blockchain to store data in a way that cannot be changed or hidden to keep people, governments, and organizations honest, ethical, and accountable. Using distributed ledger technologies to store and manage data is like a silent, yet powerful promise to value honesty, transparency, and accountability. Building our AI systems on distributed ledger technologies is an extra way to ensure data integrity and reliability – holding AI for good in high regard. Some of the proposed strategies to address the challenges facing during the smart technology era include fixing the labor-skills mismatch, developing physical and digital infrastructure, and enhancing agile governance for secure and effective management of the fourth industrial revolution and integration into global value chains. Cyril Ramaphosa, President of the Republic of South Africa, has also shared focus areas for the country's national strategy to harness the fourth industrial revolution which includes responding with agility and purpose to take advantage of the opportunities technological change presents, to enhance South Africa's global competitiveness in high growth potential sectors such as agriculture, information and communications technologies, electronics, mining, and manufacturing, and preparing citizens as well as protecting them from unfavorable consequences of technology change.[5] As mentioned in Chapter 8, South Africa has published a report of the Presidential Commission on the Fourth Industrial Revolution in August 2020 that makes specific recommendations with respect to investing in human capital, building fourth industrial revolution infrastructure, establishing an AI Institute, platforms and applications of fourth industrial revolution technologies, creating a platform for advanced manufacturing and new materials, securing and availing data to enable innovation, incentivizing future industries, establishing a fourth industrial revolution strategy implementation coordination council, and review and amending policy and legislation.[6] As the new African Union chairman, president Cyril Ramaphosa has also requested that Africa establish an Africa Artificial Intelligence Forum.[7] General Electric and the Africa Leadership University has also for example launched another cohort of the Africa Industrial Internet Programme through a $500,000 scholarship funding which is aimed at equipping young Africans with skills that will enable them to take part in the fourth industrial revolution.[8]

Democratizing Human-Centric AI in Africa Project

The project aims to get an accurate perspective and insights about the democratization and diffusion of human-centric AI in Africa via comprehensive data collection and quality research, whilst helping to drive the adoption of AI on the African continent by engaging in multi-stakeholder, multi-disciplinary research in collaboration with a partner network of excellence. As this project is line with the vision, mission, and objectives of the Machine Intelligence Institute of Africa, this non-profit organization will be acting as a vehicle in collaboration with partners to implement innovative and creative ways of instrumenting the Africa AI Ecosystem so that data can be collected for research, real-time visualization and insights, and actions to help transform Africa through smarter diffusion of human-centric AI, provide guidance to help shape a better and more equitable future for Africans and also become a more meaningful contributor on the global stage with respect to the fourth industrial revolution or smart technology era. The research on the democratization and diffusion of AI in Africa will consist of the interpretation, analysis, reporting, and dynamic visualization of the data collected, as well as developing hypotheses and models, integration and verification of theories, incorporation of complementary interdisciplinary research efforts as applied to African data, presentation of results and insights in digital systems, and the communication of the research outputs via papers and presentations at conferences.

The main purpose of the study is to analyze the state of AI and Data Science in Africa and provide an analysis of constraints to adoption and diffusion building on the business value of AI-based transformation projects. This research project will develop a framework and the systems required for instrumenting the AI ecosystem in Africa, linking key SDG themes and MTP for humanity goals with key dimensions of AI diffusion and providing an accurate perspective and insights about the diffusion of human-centric AI in Africa within the following buckets: (1) Analysis of Africa, African regions, country level analysis and SDGs and MTP goals most relevant to Africa *[AI-diffusion, job creation, polarization and economic growth]*; (2) Analysis of African entrepreneurship, investment, academia, non-profit organizations *[AI-diffusion and entrepreneurship, role of higher education and industry, and SMEs]*; (3) Analysis of African public sector, governments, academia, non-profit organizations, SDGs and MTP goals *[AI-diffusion, security and conflict issues, public procurement, governance, and public good]*; and (4) Analysis of African businesses across multiple industries *[Individual micro decisions on implementation and adaptation of AI by companies and end-users and measuring]*.

The methodology includes manual mapping (bottom-up) by using our researcher network and partner data sources, websites, LinkedIn posts, physical field visits and engagement with communities in each country and region. Key elements of this work include: (1) Instrumenting the AI ecosystem in Africa through methodologies of innovative multi-layered data collection - wikis, surveys, training, certification, and capacity building effort; and (2) Research and innovation effort, collaboration, and co-creation through understanding the process for AI diffusion, obtaining empirical data, deriving policy implications, and modeling the AI-innovation-productivity link. This study will draw from a pool of submissions by ecosystem members. The aim is to understand the influence of AI across industry sectors and academia (e.g., universities, colleges, research institutions, and schools), business (e.g., corporates, SMEs, and startups), public sector (e.g., national and local governments and policymakers), non-profit organizations (e.g., NGOs, NPOs, communities such as MIIA, Data Science Nigeria, AICE Kenya, Kenya AI, Zindi, MLDS-Africa (Deep Learning Indaba), AIMS, Groups at universities, Meetup Groups, Cirrus, etc.), investors (e.g., Venture Capital and Private Equity), and multi-stakeholder partnerships. It is important to understand how AI drives business value on several dimensions of performance and productivity (at the organizational and process levels). The research process (responding to the research question, discussions, making interpretations and comparisons, and formulating recommendations) will be based on a review of relevant case studies from industry practitioners in the African ecosystem.

The expected results are a clear and holistic view of the AI ecosystem in Africa, detailing all the independent elements within the African AI ecosystem; providing multi-layer instrumentation of the AI ecosystem in Africa; and immersion in consortium wide research, enrichment of both historical and nascent research effort, implementation of research across multiple SDGs themes and MTP goals relevant to the African development agenda. The outcomes include doing further research and analysis within the broad spectrum of AI resources in Africa; enriching and substantiating all Africa relevant research being carried out by consortium members, and consolidated efforts; and positioning MIIA as the key entity responsible for the implementation of research being carried out by consortium members. AI covers a wide range of technologies, including machine translation, chatbots and self-learning algorithms, all of which can allow individuals to better understand their environment and act accordingly. The result desired in the context of this work is to stimulate all the recipes that will aid the creation of a vibrant AI ecosystem with the stakeholders that form the basis of building AI success. The intention is to draw from multiple research perspectives across regions in both the developed and the developing world drawing on elements of AI diffusion as follows: the role of higher education and policy to integration of AI education across disciplines; economic growth; job creation; ethics, legal and other social considerations; entrepreneurship and small business adoption; security and conflict; and government, AI and public good. The key elements of the approach include the following: (1) collaborating deeper and wider and applying key existing findings to address issues like security issues, job creation and employment; (2) collaborating with think tank organizations in areas relevant to the SDGs and MTP goals, understanding the link between Data Science, AI, machine learning and domains such as life science, computer science, engineering, humanities, and economics; (3) understanding the effects of individual micro decisions on implementation and adoption of AI by companies and other end users; and (4) the technology innovation and entrepreneurship domain is also an interesting domain for further research and exploration in the context of this work.

The project plan makes provision for an *instrumentation track* to collect the data for research purposes and a *research track* to analyze, interpret, report, publish and communicate the outcome and insights. The email address for funding support and enquiries is info@miiafrica.org.

Year	Instrumentation Track	Research Track
Over all 4 years	Data Collection via MIIA's objectives and initiatives will be used as a vehicle for innovative and creative ways of instrumenting the Africa AI Ecosystem so that data can be collected for research and expanded, enriched, and enhanced continuously: • *Communities*: Collect data about all AI-related	Enriching our research with respective interdisciplinary research packages of the broader Democratizing Human-centric AI in Africa project. The research on the diffusion of AI in Africa will consist of interpretation of the data collected, analysis, reporting,

		communities on the African continent such as MIIA, Data Science Nigeria, Kenya AI, Zindi, MLDS-Africa (Deep Learning Indaba), AIMS, Groups at Universities, Meetup Groups, Cirrus, etc. through surveys, community engagements, community databases, internet search, etc. • *Training*: Collect data of individuals doing AI-related training at MIIA and other training institutions through MIIA Website, training course participation, internet search, training institution databases and collaboration • *Certification*: Collect data of knowledge, practical experience and skill levels of individuals that are working on AI-related projects/initiatives through a "LinkedIn" type of system for Africa AI-related practitioners on the MIIA website • *Validation*: Collect data about how businesses, organizations, and governments in Africa implement AI solutions from an ethics, robustness, and trustworthy AI perspective through validation projects, surveys, internet search, etc. • *Entrepreneurship*: Collect data about entrepreneurs and start-ups in Africa through surveys, internet search, start-up bootcamps, smart tech center of excellence hubs, VCs, etc.	dynamic visualization, setting of hypotheses, integration, and verification of theories/hypotheses/models of complementary interdisciplinary research efforts as applied to African data, presenting of summarized results and insights in digital systems where applicable, and the communication of the research outputs via papers and presentations at conferences.

	• *Projects*: Collect data about SDG projects in Africa where AI can play a role through surveys, internet search, collaboration with partner organizations • *Research*: Collection data of AI-related research in Africa; showcase Africa AI-related researchers through a "LinkedIn" type of system on the MIIA website • *Ecosystem:* Dynamic mapping, monitoring and visualization of the African AI Ecosystem • *Contributors*: The AI Africa Wiki is a decentralized system of collecting data of the Africa ecosystems by contributors on a country-level	
Year 1	***Instrumentation Framework & Systems Development & Initial Data Collection:*** • Develop a framework and the systems required for instrumenting the AI ecosystem in Africa, linking key SDGs and MTP goals and themes with key dimensions of AI diffusion like research, certification, community engagements, validation, and entrepreneurial endeavors across industries (Academia, private sector, public sector, etc.) using AI in Africa. • Develop a framework Multi-dimensional scalable systems of data collection across stakeholders in the ecosystems, industries, SDGs	**Research Focus Areas:** Analysis of • Africa as a whole. • African regions: Northern, Western, Eastern and Southern Africa • Country-level analysis • SDGs and MTP goals most relevant to Africa **Interdisciplinary Research Inputs** • AI-diffusion, job creation, polarization, and economic growth (aggregate, macro level)

	and MTP goals
	• Development software systems
	• Utilize various digital data capturing tools certifications, research,
	• Data collection from the data sources of AI-based solution providers.
	    ☐ Surveys and questionnaires
	    ☐ Field trip
	    ☐ Conferences
	    ☐ Internet search, etc.
	
	Africa AI Atlas Project:
	• Comparative work in 2 Developed regions (Europe and America) and 4 developing regions (Latin America/Caribbean, SSA, MENA, Asia)
	• Build and deliver an extensive list of AI players in developing countries and infographics
	• Create a first African directory for AI hotspots, and matching SDGs and MTP goals.	

Year 2	***Further Instrumentation of the African AI ecosystem in Africa: Entrepreneurship, Investment, Academia, and Non-profit organizations*** • Mapping The "Emerging economies Artificial Intelligence ecosystem" identified players in the following clusters: ☐ Private sector with start-ups and	**Research Focus Areas:** Analysis of African • Entrepreneurship • Investment • Academia • Non-profit organizations **Interdisciplinary Research Inputs** • AI-diffusion and

	accelerators
	☐ Investment
	☐ University labs, government, and public sector
	☐ NGOs, CSOs, think tanks, development projects.
	• AI-diffusion effects on poor countries
	    ☐ Understanding the role of small business owners
	    ☐ Diving deep into the entrepreneurial ecosystem
	    ☐ Understanding ways to translate empirical results into key impact driven solutions
	• Analysis of AI diffusion in education, the situation with skills and capacity, movement in and out of talents in Africa, AI concepts/technologies and other considerations.
	    ☐ Understanding the gaps: Research Literature, change management drive at organization level.
	    ☐ AI solution's framework
	    ☐ Ethical, Legal, and Social Implications (ELSI) considerations
		entrepreneurship, role of higher education and industry, SMEs

Year 3	***Further Instrumentation of the African AI ecosystem in Africa: Entrepreneurship, Investment, Academia, and Non-profit***	***Research Focus Areas:*** Analysis of African • Public sector / Governments

	organizations
	• Creating a bottom-up mapping framework via a community of AI ambassadors:
	   ☐ Focus on the AI distribution in developing countries, specifically in low-middle income countries in Africa
	   ☐ AI Africa report - Country-level analysis
	   ☐ Africa-centric data visualization map
	• Data Collection on security and conflict issues
	• Data collection on public procurement, governance, public good
	• Ethical, Legal, and Social Implications (ELSI) considerations
	   ☐ Ethical, robust, and trustworthy AI implementations, practices, and guidelines at an organization-, and governmental level.
		• Academia
		• Non-profit organizations
		• SDGs
		
		Interdisciplinary Research Inputs:
		• AI-diffusion, security and conflict issues, public procurement, governance, public good

Year 4	***Instrumentation of how businesses across multiple industries operationalize AI:***
	• An in-depth exploration of case studies from a across multiple industrial sectors
	   ☐ Africa AI Wiki
	   ☐ Surveys
	   ☐ Webinars
	   ☐ Field visit
		Research Focus Areas:
		Analysis of African
		• Businesses
		• Industries
		
		Interdisciplinary Research Inputs
		• Individual micro decisions on implementation and

	• Impact analysis: identify impact on the performance of organizations while highlighting the business value of AI-enabled projects transformation within organizations. • Ethical, Legal, and Social Implications (ELSI) considerations ☐ Ethical, robust, and trustworthy AI implementations, practices, and guidelines at a business-level.	adaptation of AI by firms and end-users and measuring

The Machine Intelligence Institute of Africa (MIIA) objectives and initiatives for instrumentation and data collection of the Africa AI Ecosystem:

	MIIA Objective / Initiative	Instrumentation / Data Collection
Community	Growing and connecting an innovative and collaborative community of Machine Intelligence, AI, Smart Technology and Data Science enthusiasts, engineers, researchers, practitioners, entrepreneurs, executives, lay persons, experts, and related partner communities across Africa.	Collect data about all AI-related communities on the African continent such as MIIA, Data Science Nigeria, Kenya AI, Zindi, MLDS-Africa (Deep Learning Indaba), AIMS, Groups at Universities, Meetup Groups, Cirrus, etc. through surveys, community engagements, community databases, internet search, etc.
Training	Facilitating, promoting, and accrediting training courses in AI, Data Science, Machine Learning, Data Engineering, Data Analysis, and related fields to grow the knowledge and skill sets of as many people as possible on the African continent and beyond to	Collect data of individuals doing AI-related training at MIIA and other training institutions through MIIA Website, training course participation, internet search, training institution databases and collaboration

	help transform Africa and help shape a better future for all.	
Certificat ion	Certification of knowledge, practical experience, and skills on an individual level for AI related roles such AI-related business leadership and management, Data Scientists, AI Experts, Machine Learning Engineers, Data Engineers, Data Analysts, AI and Machine Learning Researchers, AI-related Software Development, Business Analyst, AI Implementation Project Management, etc.	Collect data of knowledge, practical experience and skill levels of individuals that are working on AI-related projects/initiatives through a "LinkedIn" type of system for Africa AI-related practitioners on the MIIA website
Validatio n	Validating and advising on ethical, robust, and trustworthy AI implementations, practices, and guidelines at a business-, organization-, and governmental level.	Collect data about how businesses, organizations, and governments in Africa implement AI solutions from an ethics, robustness, and trustworthy AI perspective through validation projects, surveys, internet search, etc.
Entrepre neurship	Establishing smart technology centres of excellence across Africa in collaboration with partners to deliver smart technology entrepreneurs that help to transform the African business landscape.	Collect data about entrepreneurs and start-ups in Africa through surveys, internet search, start-up bootcamps, smart tech center of excellence hubs, VCs, etc.
Projects	Delivering and facilitating impactful & transformative Sustainable Development Goal (SDG) and MTP goals related projects across Africa.	Collect data about SDG and MTP goals related projects in Africa where AI can play a role through surveys, internet search, collaboration with partner organizations
Research	Delivering research and applied research contributions and projects to improve the state-of-the-art in Artificial Intelligence, its	Collection data of AI-related research in Africa; showcase Africa AI-related researchers through a "LinkedIn" type of

	applications, and fusion with other smart technologies in collaboration with partners in the academic, non-academic, business, or public sector.	system on the MIIA website
Ecosystem	Facilitating, delivering, mapping, and monitoring the growth and impact of the AI community, key players, and socio-economic initiatives within the African Artificial Intelligence Ecosystem.	Dynamic mapping, monitoring, and visualization of the African AI Ecosystem
Contributors	Providing an environment for contributors in the MIIA community and elsewhere to share information, knowledge, resources, case studies, learned experiences, research and projects through the MIIA website and African Artificial Intelligence Wiki.	The AI Africa Wiki is a decentralized system of collecting data of the Africa ecosystems by contributors on a country-level

Background on the Machine Intelligence Institute of Africa (MIIA)

Website: miiafrica.org (or machineintelligenceafrica.org)
Email address for funding support and enquiries: info@miiafrica.org

The Machine Intelligence Institute of Africa (MIIA) is an African non-profit organization founded by Dr. Jacques Ludik in 2016. MIIA aims to transform and help build an AI-powered Africa through a strong, innovative, and collaborative Machine Intelligence, AI and Data Science community, consisting of individuals and key players in the African Artificial Intelligence Ecosystem. MIIA's growing network consists of stakeholders in the African AI Ecosystem, including thousands of members as well as key decision-makers in NGOs, NPOs, academia, businesses, and the public sector.

MIIA's vision is to develop a collaborative impactful African AI Ecosystem in collaboration with a global partner network of excellence that helps to transform Africa and shape a better future for all in the smart technology era by:
- growing and connecting an innovative and collaborative community of machine intelligence, smart technology and data science enthusiasts, practitioners, entrepreneurs and experts across Africa;

- certifying and accrediting of AI-related learning, courses, practical experience and skills on an individual level;
- validating & advising on ethical, robust and trustworthy AI implementations at organizations and businesses;
- establishing smart technology centers of excellence across Africa to deliver smart technology entrepreneurs that helps to transform the African business landscape;
- delivering impactful and transformative sustainability development projects across Africa;
- producing significant research and application contributions to improve the state-of-the-art in Smart Technologies such as Artificial Intelligence; and
- mapping and monitoring the growth and impact of the African AI Ecosystem.

MIIA's mission is:
- to build a strong and innovative smart technology community to help transform Africa by networking together the critical mass of resources, establish smart technology centers of excellence, promote and sponsor learning activities, and strengthen scientific and technological excellence, thought leadership, mentoring and collaboration on the continent;
- to accelerate and deliver breakthrough smart technology related research and practical applications to solve African problems, support entrepreneurial activity, and help drive long-term inclusive and sustainable scientific, technological and socio-economic development on the continent;
- to map and monitor the growth and impact of the African AI Ecosystem; and
- to partner with governments, business, start-up incubators, NGOs, non-profit organizations, universities, and research organizations to support and help mold the future of Machine Intelligence and Data Science research and applications in Africa.

References

1. Introduction

[1] https://inequality.org/facts/global-inequality/
[2] Dan Stein & Jacques Ludik, *Neural Networks and Psychopathology*.
[3] Klaus Schwab, *The Fourth Industrial Revolution*.
[4] Ray Dalio, *Principles: Life and Work*.
[5] https://www.forbes.com/sites/stevedenning/2020/04/19/why-only-the-agile-will-survive/#1f37f8be2c1e
[6] Simon Sinek, *Start with Why*.

2. The Smart Technology Era is Here

[1] Steve Case, *The Third Wave*.
[2] Calum Chace, *The Economic Singularity*.
[3] Yuval Harari, *Sapiens*; Yuval Harari, *Homo Deus*; Yuval Harari, *21 Lessons for the 21st Century*.
[4] Richard Baldwin, *The Globotics Upheaval*.
[5] Erik Brynjolfsson and Andrew MacAfee, *The 2nd Machine Age*.
[6] Richard Baldwin, *The Globotics Upheaval*.
[7] Calum Chace, *The Economic Singularity*.
[8] Calum Chace, *The Economic Singularity*.
[9] Erik Brynjolfsson and Andrew McAfee, *The 2nd Machine Age*.
[10] Jeremy Rifkin, *The Third Industrial Revolution*.
[11] Richard Baldwin, *The Globotics Upheaval: Globalization, Robotics, and the Future of Work*.
[12] Richard Baldwin, *The Globotics Upheaval: Globalization, Robotics, and the Future of Work*.
[13] Richard Baldwin, *The Globotics Upheaval: Globalization, Robotics, and the Future of Work*.
[14] Richard Baldwin, *The Globotics Upheaval: Globalization, Robotics, and the Future of Work*.
[15] Calum Chace - *The Economic Singularity*; Richard Baldwin, *The Globotics Upheaval: Globalization, Robotics, and the Future of Work*.
[16] Richard Baldwin, *The Globotics Upheaval: Globalization, Robotics, and the Future of Work*.
[17] Richard Baldwin, *The Globotics Upheaval: Globalization, Robotics, and the Future of Work*.
[18] Richard Baldwin, *The Globotics Upheaval: Globalization, Robotics, and the Future of Work*.
[19] Richard Baldwin, *The Globotics Upheaval: Globalization, Robotics, and the Future of Work*.
[20] Richard Baldwin, *The Globotics Upheaval: Globalization, Robotics, and the Future of Work*.
[21] Calum Chace, *The Economic Singularity*.
[22] Klaus Schwab, *The Fourth Industrial Revolution*.
[23] Erik Brynjolfsson and Andrew McAfee, *The Second Machine Age*.
[24] Yuval Harari, *Sapiens*; Yuval Harari, *Homo Deus*; Richard Baldwin, *The Globotics Upheaval*; Calum Chace, *The Economic Singularity*.
[25] Calum Chace, *The Economic Singularity*.
[26] Eric A Posner and E Glen Weyl, *Radical Markets: Uprooting Capitalism and Democracy for a Just Society*.
[27] Eric A Posner and E Glen Weyl, *Radical Markets: Uprooting Capitalism and Democracy for a Just Society*.
[28] Jacques Ludik, *Democratizing Artificial Intelligence to Benefit Everyone*, Chapters 4, 8, 10, 11, and 12.
[29] https://www.psychologytoday.com/us/blog/home-base/201802/the-social-media-disconnect
[30] https://www.weforum.org/agenda/2016/06/the-poetry-of-progress/

3. AI as Key Exponential Technology in the Smart Technology Era

[1] Kai-fu Lee, *AI Superpowers*.

[2] Kai-fu Lee, *AI Superpowers*.

[3] https://www.pwc.com/gx/en/issues/data-and-analytics/publications/artificial-intelligence-study.html

[4] https://www.accenture.com/t20170524T055435__w__/ca-en/_acnmedia/PDF-52/Accenture-Why-AI-is-the-Future-of-Growth.pdf

[5] https://www.forbes.com/sites/bernardmarr/2020/04/20/these-25-technology-trends-will-define-the-next-decade/?sh=3a9200f29e3b

[6] Yuval Noah Harari, *Homo Deus*.

[7] https://youtu.be/_QOyKeEEU3Q

[8] http://reports.weforum.org/digital-transformation/wp-content/blogs.dir/94/mp/files/pages/files/dti-societal-implications-white-paper.pdf

[9] https://en.wikipedia.org/wiki/Bayes%27_theorem

[10] https://en.wikipedia.org/wiki/Least_squares

[11] https://en.wikipedia.org/wiki/Markov_chain

[12] https://link.springer.com/chapter/10.1007/978-3-642-70911-1_14

[13] https://en.wikipedia.org/wiki/Turing_machine

[14] https://en.wikipedia.org/wiki/Hilbert%27s_program

[15] https://en.wikipedia.org/wiki/G%C3%B6del%27s_incompleteness_theorems

[16] https://en.wikipedia.org/wiki/Church%E2%80%93Turing_thesis

[17] https://academic.oup.com/mind/article/LIX/236/433/986238

[18] https://en.wikipedia.org/wiki/Stochastic_neural_analog_reinforcement_calculator

[19] https://en.wikipedia.org/wiki/K-nearest_neighbors_algorithm

[20] https://en.wikipedia.org/wiki/Perceptron

[21] https://www.robotics.org/joseph-engelberger/unimate.cfm; https://en.wikipedia.org/wiki/Donald_Michie; https://en.wikipedia.org/wiki/ELIZA

[22] https://en.wikipedia.org/wiki/Moore%27s_law; https://en.wikipedia.org/wiki/History_of_artificial_intelligence

[23] https://en.wikipedia.org/wiki/Shakey_the_robot

[24] https://en.wikipedia.org/wiki/History_of_robots

[25] https://core.ac.uk/download/pdf/82206249.pdf

[26] https://en.wikipedia.org/wiki/Neocognitron; https://en.wikipedia.org/wiki/Convolutional_neural_network

[27] https://en.wikipedia.org/wiki/Expert_system

[28] https://en.wikipedia.org/wiki/Fifth_generation_computer#

[29] https://en.wikipedia.org/wiki/Hopfield_network; https://en.wikipedia.org/wiki/Backpropagation; https://en.wikipedia.org/wiki/David_Rumelhart

[30] https://en.wikipedia.org/wiki/NETtalk_(artificial_neural_network)

[31] https://en.wikipedia.org/wiki/Navlab

[32] https://en.wikipedia.org/wiki/Q-learning

[33] https://en.wikipedia.org/wiki/TD-Gammon

[34] https://en.wikipedia.org/wiki/Random_forest

[35] https://en.wikipedia.org/wiki/Support-vector_machine

[36] https://en.wikipedia.org/wiki/Long_short-term_memory

[37] https://en.wikipedia.org/wiki/Deep_Blue_(chess_computer); https://en.wikipedia.org/wiki/Dragon_NaturallySpeaking

38 https://en.wikipedia.org/wiki/Kismet_(robot)

39 https://en.wikipedia.org/wiki/AIBO

40 https://en.wikipedia.org/wiki/IRobot

41 https://en.wikipedia.org/wiki/Spirit_(rover)

42 https://en.wikipedia.org/wiki/ASIMO

43 https://en.wikipedia.org/wiki/Netflix_Prize

44 https://www.sciencedaily.com/releases/2007/07/070719143517.htm .

45 https://www.wired.com/2008/11/google-introduc-2/;
https://www.popsci.com/cars/article/2013-09/google-self-driving-car/

46 https://en.wikipedia.org/wiki/ImageNet

47 http://research.microsoft.com/en-us/projects/vrkinect/

48 https://www.techrepublic.com/article/ibm-watson-the-inside-story-of-how-the-jeopardy-winning-supercomputer-was-born-and-what-it-wants-to-do-next/

49 https://www.apple.com/newsroom/2011/10/04Apple-Launches-iPhone-4S-iOS-5-iCloud/

50 https://icml.cc/2012/papers/73.pdf

51 https://en.wikipedia.org/wiki/DARPA_Robotics_Challenge#Trials

52 https://en.wikipedia.org/wiki/Tianhe-2

53 https://en.wikipedia.org/wiki/Eugene_Goostman

54 https://en.wikipedia.org/wiki/Generative_adversarial_network

55 https://en.wikipedia.org/wiki/DeepFace

56 https://en.wikipedia.org/wiki/Amazon_Alexa

57 https://www.tensorflow.org/

58 https://www.theverge.com/2016/3/24/11297050/tay-microsoft-chatbot-racist

59 https://www.bloomberg.com/news/features/2016-08-18/uber-s-first-self-driving-fleet-arrives-in-pittsburgh-this-month-iso6r7on; https://en.wikipedia.org/wiki/Tesla_Autopilot

60 https://en.wikipedia.org/wiki/Sunway_TaihuLight;
https://en.wikipedia.org/wiki/Fugaku_(supercomputer)

61 https://en.wikipedia.org/wiki/AlphaGo; https://en.wikipedia.org/wiki/Go_(game)

62 https://deepmind.com/blog/article/alphazero-shedding-new-light-grand-games-chess-shogi-and-go

63 https://arxiv.org/abs/1701.01724

64 https://openai.com/projects/five/; https://arxiv.org/abs/1912.06680

65 https://ai.googleblog.com/2018/05/duplex-ai-system-for-natural-conversation.html

66 https://www.deepspeed.ai/

67 https://www.microsoft.com/en-us/research/blog/turing-nlg-a-17-billion-parameter-language-model-by-microsoft/

68 https://openai.com/blog/openai-api/

69 https://qz.com/1419346/ai-has-had-just-one-breakthrough-says-kai-fu-lee/

70 Pedro Domingo, *The Master Algorithm: How the Quest for the Ultimate Learning Machine Will Remake Our World.*

71 https://www.sciencedirect.com/science/article/pii/S0960982207004149

72 https://en.wikipedia.org/wiki/Activation_function

73 https://scikit-learn.org/stable/supervised_learning.html;
https://en.wikipedia.org/wiki/Supervised_learning

74 https://en.wikipedia.org/wiki/Restricted_Boltzmann_machine;
https://en.wikipedia.org/wiki/Autoencoder

75 https://arxiv.org/ftp/arxiv/papers/2001/2001.07092.pdf

76 https://en.wikipedia.org/wiki/Convolutional_neural_network

77 https://arxiv.org/ftp/arxiv/papers/1901/1901.06032.pdf

78 https://arxiv.org/ftp/arxiv/papers/1901/1901.06032.pdf

[79] https://en.wikipedia.org/wiki/Recurrent_neural_network

[80] Jacques Ludik, *Training, Dynamics, and Complexity of Architecture-specific Recurrent Neural Networks*.

[81] Jacques Ludik, Dan Stein, *Neural Networks and Psychopathology*, D. Stein and J Ludik, Chapter 9, *Neural network modelling of cognitive disinhibition and neurotransmitter dysfunction in obsessive-compulsive disorder*.

[82] Jacques Ludik, Dan Stein, *Neural network modelling of cognitive disinhibition and neurotransmitter dysfunction in obsessive-compulsive disorder*.

[83] https://en.wikipedia.org/wiki/Unsupervised_learning

[84] https://towardsdatascience.com/dimensionality-reduction-for-data-visualization-pca-vs-tsne-vs-umap-be4aa7b1cb29

[85] https://en.wikipedia.org/wiki/Unsupervised_learning

[86] https://en.wikipedia.org/wiki/Q-learning; https://en.wikipedia.org/wiki/Markov_decision_process

[87] https://towardsdatascience.com/temporal-difference-learning-47b4a7205ca8

[88] https://www.nature.com/articles/nature24270.epdf

[89] https://en.wikipedia.org/wiki/Generative_adversarial_network

[90] https://machinelearningmastery.com/how-to-use-transfer-learning-when-developing-convolutional-neural-network-models/

[91] Pedro Domingo, *The Master Algorithm: How the Quest for the Ultimate Learning Machine Will Remake Our World*.

[92] Pedro Domingo, *The Master Algorithm: How the Quest for the Ultimate Learning Machine Will Remake Our World*.

[93] https://francesco-ai.medium.com/ai-knowledge-map-how-to-classify-ai-technologies-6c073b969020

[94] https://www.forbes.com/sites/cognitiveworld/2019/06/19/7-types-of-artificial-intelligence/#5866ec28233e

[95] PWC, Man-Machine Intelligence Continuum; https://fedtechmagazine.com/article/2020/01/assisted-intelligence-vs-augmented-intelligence-and-autonomous-intelligence-perfcon

[96] Kai-Fu Lee, *AI Superpowers: China, Silicon Valley, and the New World Order*.

[97] Kai-Fu Lee, *AI Superpowers: China, Silicon Valley, and the New World Order*.

[98] Kai-Fu Lee, *AI Superpowers: China, Silicon Valley, and the New World Order*.

[99] Kai-Fu Lee, *AI Superpowers: China, Silicon Valley, and the New World Order*.

[100] Kai-Fu Lee, *AI Superpowers: China, Silicon Valley, and the New World Order*.

[101] Kai-Fu Lee, *AI Superpowers: China, Silicon Valley, and the New World Order*.

[102] Kai-Fu Lee, *AI Superpowers: China, Silicon Valley, and the New World Order*.

[103] Kai-Fu Lee, *AI Superpowers: China, Silicon Valley, and the New World Order*.

[104] https://blogs.microsoft.com/next/2016/10/18/historic-achievement-microsoft-researchers-reach-human-parity-conversational-speech-recognition/; https://research.googleblog.com/2016/09/a-neural-network-for-machine.html

[105] https://www.theverge.com/2016/8/4/12369494/descartes-artificial-intelligence-crop-predictions-usda

[106] http://news.stanford.edu/2017/04/03/deep-learning-algorithm-aid-drug-development/

[107] https://etech.iec.ch/issue/2020-02/the-intelligence-of-things; https://www.digitaltrends.com/cool-tech/iot-2-intelligence-of-things-is-replacing-internet-of-things-heres-why/; https://www.forbes.com/sites/bernardmarr/2019/12/20/what-is-the-artificial-intelligence-of-things-when-ai-meets-iot/?sh=3118700cb1fd

[108] https://www.thesslstore.com/blog/20-surprising-iot-statistics-you-dont-already-know/

[109] https://www.weforum.org/agenda/2019/06/how-the-future-of-computing-can-make-or-

break-the-ai-revolution/

[110] https://www.anandtech.com/show/16028/better-yield-on-5nm-than-7nm-tsmc-update-on-defect-rates-for-n5

[111] https://www.technologyreview.com/2020/02/24/905789/were-not-prepared-for-the-end-of-moores-law/

[112] https://www.weforum.org/agenda/2019/06/how-the-future-of-computing-can-make-or-break-the-ai-revolution/

[113] https://www.technologyreview.com/2020/02/24/905789/were-not-prepared-for-the-end-of-moores-law/

[114] https://www.computerweekly.com/news/252475371/Stanford-University-finds-that-AI-is-outpacing-Moores-Law

[115] https://www.technologyreview.com/2020/02/24/905789/were-not-prepared-for-the-end-of-moores-law/

[116] https://www.raconteur.net/technology/artificial-intelligence/quantum-computing-ai/

[117] https://quantumai.google/; http://www.nature.com/news/commercialize-quantum-technologies-in-five-years-1.21583http://www.nature.com/news/commercialize-quantum-technologies-in-five-years-1.21583;

[118] https://www.ibm.com/quantum-computing/

[119] https://research.aimultiple.com/quantum-ai/#what-are-the-possibilities-of-applying-quantum-computing-in-ai

[120] https://research.aimultiple.com/quantum-ai/#what-are-the-possibilities-of-applying-quantum-computing-in-ai

[121] Pedro Domingo, *The Master Algorithm: How the Quest for the Ultimate Learning Machine Will Remake Our World.*

[122] Pedro Domingo, *The Master Algorithm: How the Quest for the Ultimate Learning Machine Will Remake Our World.*

[123] Lasse Rouhiainen, *Artificial Intelligence - 101 things you must know today about our future*

[124] Pedro Domingo, *The Master Algorithm: How the Quest for the Ultimate Learning Machine Will Remake Our World.*

[125] Yuval Noah Harari, *Homo Deus.*

[126] https://www.youtube.com/watch?v=-EVqrDlAqYo&feature=youtu.be

[127] Yuval Noah Harari, *Homo Deus.*

[128] http://www.bbc.com/future/story/20170118-how-east-and-west-think-in-profoundly-different-ways

[129] https://www.technologyreview.com/s/612876/this-is-how-ai-bias-really-happensand-why-its-so-hard-to-fix/

[130] https://dustn.tv/social-media-statistics/#reddit-stats

[131] https://theworldin.economist.com/edition/2020/article/17385/demis-hassabis-ais-potential

[132] https://theworldin.economist.com/edition/2020/article/17385/demis-hassabis-ais-potential

4. AI-driven Digital Transformation of the Business Enterprise

[1] https://hbr.org/2019/07/building-the-ai-powered-organization

[2] https://www.forbes.com/sites/cognitiveworld/2020/01/14/ai-driven-disruption-and-transformation-new-business-segments-to-novel-market-opportunities/#3f569ed2e841

[3] https://www.forbes.com/sites/bernardmarr/2020/01/06/the-top-10-artificial-intelligence-trends-everyone-should-be-watching-in-2020/#741b530e390b

[4] https://www.idc.com/getdoc.jsp?containerId=US44840819 & https://www.cacp.ca/index.html?asst_id=1637

5 https://www.forbes.com/sites/stevedenning/2016/09/08/explaining-agile/#5cf83bb0301b

6 https://www.forbes.com/sites/stevedenning/2020/04/19/why-only-the-agile-will-survive/#1f37f8be2c1e

7 Stephen Denning, *The Age of Agile: How Smart Companies Are Transforming the Way Work Gets Done.*

8 https://www.gspublishing.com/content/research/en/reports/2019/09/04/a0d36f41-b16a-4788-9ac5-68ddbc941fa9.pdf

9 https://www.kaggle.com/; https://zindi.africa/

10 https://cloud.google.com/ai-platform

11 https://thenextweb.com/neural/2020/09/18/the-ai-landscape-is-shifting-from-data-to-knowledge-heres-why-that-matters/

12 https://thenextweb.com/neural/2020/09/18/the-ai-landscape-is-shifting-from-data-to-knowledge-heres-why-that-matters/

13 https://cortexlogic.com/

14 Analytics Solutions Unified Method for Data Mining/Predictive analytics (ASUM-DM) has been proposed by IBM

15 https://en.wikipedia.org/wiki/Polyglot_persistence

16 https://www.forbes.com/sites/robtoews/2019/12/19/ai-will-transform-the-field-of-law/#3c9fc11f7f01

17 https://blog.rossintelligence.com/; https://www.judicata.com/; https://casetext.com/

18 https://www.gartner.com/smarterwithgartner/what-do-employee-engagement-surveys-tell-you-about-employee-experience/

19 https://www.wwise.co.za/why-it-is-important-to-attend-comprehensive-sheq-training/

20 https://www.mckinsey.com/~/media/mckinsey/featured%20insights/Digital%20Disruption/Harnessing%20automation%20for%20a%20future%20that%20works/MGI-A-future-that-works-Executive-summary.ashx

21 Kai-Fu Lee, *AI Superpowers: China, Silicon Valley, and the New World Order.*

22 Martin Ford, *Rise of the Robots.*

23 http://www3.weforum.org/docs/WEF_Future_of_Jobs_2018.pdf

24 https://www.cognizant.com/perspectives/21-jobs-of-the-future; Lasse Rouhiainen, *Artificial Intelligence - 101 things you must know today about our future.*

25 Isabelle Rouhan, Les Métiers du Futur (Jobs of the Future), 2019.

26 https://www.welcometothejungle.com/en/articles/let-s-fast-forward-to-2030-4-professions-that-do-not-exist-yet

27 Richard Baldwin, *The Globotics Upheaval.*

28 Calum Chase, *The Economic Singularity.*

29 Martin Ford, *The Lights in the Tunnel*; Martin Ford, *Rise of the Robots.*

30 Erik Brynjolfsson and Andrew McAfee, *The Second Machine Age.*

31 Peter Diamandis and Steven Kotler, *Abundance*; Peter Diamandis and Steven Kotler, *Bold.*

32 Erik Brynjolfsson and Andrew McAfee, *Machine, Platform, Crowd.*

33 Yuval Harari, *21 Lessons for the 21st Century.*

34 Kai-fu Lee, *AI Superpowers.*

35 https://www.financedigest.com/ai-will-power-95-of-customer-interactions-by-2025.html; https://blog.verloop.io/100-best-chatbot-statistics-2020/

36 https://markets.businessinsider.com/news/stocks/the-global-conversational-aimarket-size-is-expected-to-grow-from-4-8-billion-in-2020-to-usd-13-9-billion-by-2025-at-a-compound-annual-growth-rate-cagr-of-21-9-1029504221#

37 https://www.gartner.com/en/documents/3827163 & https://www.searchtechnologies.com/blog/predict-2018-artificial-intelligence

[38] Robert Scoble and Shel Israel, *Age of Context*.

[39] https://www.internetsociety.org/blog/2019/07/internet-societys-online-trust-alliance-2019-cyber-incidents-breach-trends-report/

[40] https://www.accenture.com/_acnmedia/pdf-96/accenture-2019-cost-of-cybercrime-study-final.pdf

[41] https://www.securitymagazine.com/articles/92201-top-10-largest-data-breaches

[42] https://www.cybereason.com/blog/triple-threat-emotet-deploys-trickbot-to-steal-data-spread-ryuk-ransomware

[43] https://www.paubox.com/blog/what-is-a-threat-vector/

[44] https://elie.net/blog/ai/attacks-against-machine-learning-an-overview/

5. AI Revolutionizing Personalized Engagement for Consumer Facing Businesses

[1] Alex Ross, *The Industries of the Future*.

[2] https://www.mckinsey.com/~/media/McKinsey/Industries/Advanced%20Electronics/Our%20Insights/How%20artificial%20intelligence%20can%20deliver%20real%20value%20to%20companies/MGI-Artificial-Intelligence-Discussion-paper.ashx?

[3] https://www.mckinsey.com/~/media/McKinsey/Industries/Advanced%20Electronics/Our%20Insights/How%20artificial%20intelligence%20can%20deliver%20real%20value%20to%20companies/MGI-Artificial-Intelligence-Discussion-paper.ashx?

[4] https://www.gspublishing.com/content/research/en/reports/2019/09/04/a0d36f41-b16a-4788-9ac5-68ddbc941fa9.pdf

[5] https://www.idc.com/getdoc.jsp?containerId=prUS44911419

[6] https://www.grandviewresearch.com/industry-analysis/artificial-intelligence-ai-market

[7] https://www.fortunebusinessinsights.com/industry-reports/artificial-intelligence-market-100114

[8] https://www.statista.com/statistics/607835/worldwide-artificial-intelligence-market-leading-use-cases/

[9] https://advisory.kpmg.us/articles/2020/living-in-an-ai-world.html

[10] https://www.fintechnews.org/big-ai-trends-that-will-revamp-fintech-in-2020/

[11] https://www.businesswire.com/news/home/20200113005533/en/Global-Artificial-Intelligence-AI-Market-in-BFSI-Sector-2019-2023-32-CAGR-Projection-Through-2023-Technavio

[12] https://www.gspublishing.com/content/research/en/reports/2019/09/04/a0d36f41-b16a-4788-9ac5-68ddbc941fa9.pdf

[13] https://www.theatlantic.com/magazine/archive/2019/05/stock-value-satellite-images-investing/586009/

[14] https://www.gspublishing.com/content/research/en/reports/2019/09/04/a0d36f41-b16a-4788-9ac5-68ddbc941fa9.pdf

[15] https://www.gspublishing.com/content/research/en/reports/2019/09/04/a0d36f41-b16a-4788-9ac5-68ddbc941fa9.pdf

[16] https://www.imaginovation.net/blog/ai-in-banking-jp-morgan-case-study-benefits-to-businesses/

[17] https://www.lendingtree.com/home/mortgage/u-s-mortgage-market-statistics-2019/

[18] https://www.jumo.world/

[19] https://www.globenewswire.com/news-release/2020/03/11/1998855/0/en/Artificial-Intelligence-AI-in-Retail-Market-to-Grow-at-a-CAGR-of-35-9-to-reach-15-3-Billion-by-2025-

Largely-Driven-by-the-Growing-Adoption-of-Multichannel-or-Omnichannel-Retailing-.html

[20] https://www.accenture.com/us-en/company-reworking-the-revolution-future-workforce?c=glb_davosotherpleaseente_10166678&n=otc_0118

[21] https://www.gspublishing.com/content/research/en/reports/2019/09/04/a0d36f41-b16a-4788-9ac5-68ddbc941fa9.pdf

[22]
https://www.mckinsey.com/~/media/McKinsey/Industries/Advanced%20Electronics/Our%20Insights/How%20artificial%20intelligence%20can%20deliver%20real%20value%20to%20companies/MGI-Artificial-Intelligence-Discussion-paper.ashx?

[23]
https://www.mckinsey.com/~/media/McKinsey/Industries/Advanced%20Electronics/Our%20Insights/How%20artificial%20intelligence%20can%20deliver%20real%20value%20to%20companies/MGI-Artificial-Intelligence-Discussion-paper.ashx?

[24] https://www.amazon.com/b?node=16008589011

[25] https://qz.com/1185081/amazon-go-china-is-both-ahead-of-and-behind-amazon-in-cashier-less-stores/

[26] https://www.nytimes.com/interactive/2019/06/14/opinion/bluetooth-wireless-tracking-privacy.html

[27] Shubhi Mittal, "25 retailers nailing it with their proximity marketing campaigns," Beaconstac.com, February 11, 2016

[28] https://www.ikea.com/au/en/customer-service/mobile-apps/say-hej-to-ikea-place-pub1f8af050

[29] https://youtu.be/VbfNI-iHBHc and https://blog.crobox.com/article/subconscious-marketing

[30] https://pinterest-style-finder.westelm.com/

[31] https://www.iotsolutionprovider.com/retail/retailers-use-kiosks-ai-pick-up-portals-to-attract-millennials

[32] https://www.1800flowers.com/ and https://www.stitchfix.com/

[33] https://www.technavio.com/report/global-artificial-intelligence-in-telecommunication-industry-market-industry-analysis?tnplus

[34] https://tractica.omdia.com/research/artificial-intelligence-for-telecommunications-applications/

[35] https://www.telecomlead.com/in-depth/mobile-operator-spending-on-ai-solutions-to-cross-15-bn-93913

[36] https://www.technavio.com/report/global-machine-machine-m2m-and-connected-devices-global-telecom-iot-market-2016-2020?tnplus

[37] https://telecom.economictimes.indiatimes.com/news/why-telcos-will-soon-be-betting-on-artificial-intelligence-to-build-their-networks/61531211

[38] https://www.aria-networks.com/

[39] https://sedonasys.com/netfusion/

[40] https://www.nokia.com/networks/solutions/nokia-ava-telco-ai-ecosystem/

[41] https://www.avanseus.com/case-study-telecom/

[42] https://www.affineanalytics.com/predictive-maintenance-telecom-tower/

[43] https://www.kpn.com/algemeen/english.htm

[44] https://techsee.me/resources/surveys/2019-telecom-churn-survey/

[45] https://venturebeat.com/2018/08/07/vodafones-customer-retention-secret-psst-its-ai-vb-live/

[46] https://www.vodafone.co.uk/help-and-information/introducing-tobi

[47] https://techsee.me/blog/vodafone-innovation-augmented-reality/

[48] https://www.nokia.com/networks/services/digital-assistant-as-a-service/

[49] https://www.cigen.com.au/cigenblog/8-real-world-use-cases-robotic-process-automation-rpa-

telecom

50 https://medium.com/@cigen_rpa/8-real-world-use-cases-for-robotic-process-automation-rpa-in-telecom-850b6815bab7

51 https://celaton.com/

52 https://www.marketsandmarkets.com/Market-Reports/ai-in-social-media-market-92119289.html

53 https://www.businesswire.com/news/home/20190325005742/en/Artificial-Intelligence-U.S.-Media-Entertainment-Industry-2016-2025

54 https://www.twipemobile.com/google-dni-funds-collaborative-project-of-twipe-and-the-times/

55 https://www.twipemobile.com/why-half-new-subscribers-churn-first-3-months/

56 https://knowherenews.com/

57 https://arxiv.org/abs/2005.14165

58 https://www.theverge.com/21346343/gpt-3-explainer-openai-examples-errors-agi-potential

59 https://www.twipemobile.com/will-robots-replace-human-reporting/

60 https://mashable.com/video/ai-news-anchor-presenter-china-xinhua/?europe=true#U.5a1xSMGgqM

61 http://jonathanstray.com/papers/What%20do%20journalists%20do%20with%20documents.pdf

62 https://medium.com/id-in-the-iot/artificial-intelligence-is-completely-reinventing-media-and-marketing-d724c150ece3

63 https://www.wired.com/2013/08/qq-netflix-algorithm/

64 https://www.vice.com/en_us/article/kzdwn9/tiktok-cant-save-us-from-algorithmic-content-hell

65 https://venturebeat.com/2019/04/12/disneys-ai-generates-storyboard-animations-from-screenplays/

66 https://www.inc.com/graham-winfrey/4-fascinating-technologies-remaking-hollywood-artificial-intelligence.html

67 https://syncedreview.com/2019/04/17/direct-and-star-in-your-own-movie-with-california-ai-startup-rct-studio/

68 https://www.theguardian.com/music/2019/may/21/whitney-houston-hologram-tour-album-broadway-show-planned

69 https://www.engadget.com/2019-05-02-madonna-billboard-music-awards-augmented-reality.html

70 https://www.youtube.com/watch?v=dhGXhhCGZaY

71 https://www.bbc.com/news/av/technology-53811956

72 https://arxiv.org/pdf/1905.10240.pdf

73 https://venturebeat.com/2019/05/28/researchers-detail-ai-that-generates-character-animations-from-recorded-speech/

74 Deep fake examples: https://www.creativebloq.com/features/deepfake-examples; https://www.theverge.com/tldr/2018/4/17/17247334/ai-fake-news-video-barack-obama-jordan-peele-buzzfeed; https://www.vice.com/en_us/article/qvm97q/deepfake-videos-like-that-gal-gadot-porn-are-only-getting-more-convincing-and-more-dangerous; https://www.forbes.com/sites/kalevleetaru/2019/05/07/what-happens-when-television-news-gets-the-deep-fake-treatment/#51e544bb146e

75 https://advisory.kpmg.us/articles/2020/living-in-an-ai-world.html

76 https://aithority.com/robots/locomotion/artificial-intelligence-transportation-market-projected-grow-usd-1-21-billion-2017-usd-10-30-billion-2030/

77 https://fero.ai/

78 https://markets.businessinsider.com/news/stocks/tesla-surpasses-walmart-market-value-

most-valued-sp500-us-companies-2020-8-1029524035#

[79] https://www.economist.com/technology-quarterly/2020/06/11/driverless-cars-show-the-limits-of-todays-ai

[80] https://www.wired.com/story/news-rules-clear-way-self-driving-cars/

[81] https://www.sae.org/news/2019/01/sae-updates-j3016-automated-driving-graphic

[82] https://www.machinedesign.com/mechanical-motion-systems/article/21838234/how-ai-is-paving-the-way-for-autonomous-cars

[83] https://www.forbes.com/sites/johnkoetsier/2020/07/16/the-android-of-self-driving-cars-built-a-100000x-cheaper-way-to-train-ai-for-multiple-trillion-dollar-markets/#4e674ec85baa

[84] https://comma.ai/

[85] https://venturebeat.com/2020/01/07/comma-ai-launches-comma-two-a-999-kit-that-imbues-cars-with-assisted-driving-features/

[86] https://www.theverge.com/2020/7/22/21334012/waymo-fca-ram-delivery-self-driving-van

[87] https://www.economist.com/technology-quarterly/2019/05/30/pilotless-planes-are-on-the-way

[88] https://www.reuters.com/article/us-aviation-volocopter-singapore/volocopter-eyes-launch-of-its-electric-helicopter-taxis-in-singapore-idUSKBN1WF0ZO

[89] https://www.forbes.com/sites/bernardmarr/2019/06/05/the-incredible-autonomous-ships-of-the-future-run-by-artificial-intelligence-rather-than-a-crew/#8f44e666fbf1

[90] https://www.futurefarming.com/Machinery/Articles/2019/9/The-future-belongs-to-small-self-driving-tractors-474180E/

[91] https://techcrunch.com/2019/06/05/a-first-look-at-amazons-new-delivery-drone/; https://www.amazon.com/Amazon-Prime-Air/b?ie=UTF8&node=8037720011

[92] https://www.pwc.com/us/en/industries/transportation-logistics/airlines-airports/predictive-maintenance.html

[93] https://www.pwc.com/gx/en/industries/communications/assets/pwc-ai-and-iot.pdf

[94] https://synapsemx.com/

[95] https://www.sparkcognition.com/industries/aviation/

[96] https://www.prnewswire.com/news-releases/boeing-and-sparkcognition-to-launch-joint-venture-skygrid-300753426.html

[97] https://www.airbus.com/innovation/industry-4-0/artificial-intelligence/aigym.html

[98] https://www.altexsoft.com/blog/datascience/7-ways-how-airlines-use-artificial-intelligence-and-data-science-to-improve-their-operations/

[99] https://pros.com/products/dynamic-pricing-management-software/#:~:text=PROS%20Control%2C%20a%20dynamic%20pricing,single%20source%20of%20pricing%20truth.&text=Over%2030%20years%20of%20experience,want%20to%20go%20to%20market.

[100] https://arxiv.org/ftp/arxiv/papers/1908/1908.11086.pdf

[101] https://arxiv.org/ftp/arxiv/papers/1908/1908.11086.pdf

[102] https://amadeus.com/documents/en/blog/pdf/2016/09/airline-disruption-management-whitepaper-2016.pdf

[103] https://amadeus.com/en/insights/blog/amanda-the-chatbot-has-some-new-tricks-up-her-sleeves

[104] https://purestrategy.ai/

[105] https://ww2.jeppesen.com/wp-content/uploads/2019/02/crew-rostering-fact-sheet.pdf

[106] https://www.bbc.co.uk/news/extra/IFtb42kkNv/boeing-two-deadly-crashes

[107] https://www.bbc.com/news/business-53646442

[108] https://www.aitrends.com/ai-insider/boeing-737-max-8-and-lessons-for-ai-the-case-of-ai-self-driving-cars/

[109] https://www.altexsoft.com/blog/datascience/7-ways-how-airlines-use-artificial-intelligence-

and-data-science-to-improve-their-operations/

[110] https://www2.deloitte.com/content/dam/Deloitte/us/Documents/consumer-business/us-cb-2018-travel-hospitality-industry-outlook.pdf

[111] https://www.3cinteractive.com/blog/3cinteractive-releases-chatbot-progress-report-showing-consumer-usage-preferences-using-chatbots-brand/ ; https://emerj.com/ai-application-comparisons/chatbots-travel-tourism-comparing-5-current-applications/

[112] https://medium.com/@Imaginovation/ai-assistant-the-future-of-travel-tourism-with-emergence-of-artificial-intelligence-f9ea3cad0cc

[113] https://emerj.com/ai-application-comparisons/chatbots-travel-tourism-comparing-5-current-applications/

[114] https://www.theverge.com/circuitbreaker/2016/12/14/13955878/wynn-las-vegas-amazon-echo-hotel-room-privacy

[115] https://www.gartner.com/en/newsroom/press-releases/2019-01-09-gartner-predicts-25-percent-of-digital-workers-will-u

[116] https://www.phocuswire.com/Voice-series-part-3-Skyscanner

[117] https://www.finavia.fi/en/newsroom/2018/face-detection-customer-service-chatbot-targeted-display-wall-heres-how-ai-used

[118] https://www.welltraveledco.com/

[119] https://www.emerald.com/insight/content/doi/10.1108/JTF-07-2019-0065/full/html#ref056

6. AI-powered Process and Equipment Enhancement across the Industrial World

[1] https://www.vox.com/energy-and-environment/2017/11/20/16678350/global-support-clean-energy & https://www.smart-energy.com/renewable-energy/71-of-uk-citizens-say-renewables-need-more-government-support/

[2] https://www.caixinglobal.com/2020-03-11/china-to-slash-subsidies-for-renewable-energy-amid-drive-to-cut-state-support-101527138.html & https://www.power-technology.com/features/renewable-subsidies-balancing-economy-and-the-environment-in-the-netherlands-and-beyond/https://www.power-technology.com/features/renewable-subsidies-balancing-economy-and-the-environment-in-the-netherlands-and-beyond/

[3] https://www.c2es.org/content/renewable-energy/#:~:text=Renewable%20energy%20is%20the%20fastest,wind%20power%20(6.6%20percent).

[4] https://www.utilitydive.com/news/ai-in-the-utility-industry/543876/

[5] http://ipu.msu.edu/wp-content/uploads/2018/04/EPRI-Electrification-Report-2018.pdf

[6] https://about.bnef.com/electric-vehicle-outlook/

[7] https://bisresearch.com/industry-report/artificial-intelligence-energy-market.html

[8] https://go.frost.com/EI_PR_EE_KCekani_ME8E_WasteWater_Jul19

[9] https://www.gspublishing.com/content/research/en/reports/2019/09/04/a0d36f41-b16a-4788-9ac5-68ddbc941fa9.pdf

[10] https://www.forbes.com/sites/samshead/2019/02/27/deepmind-and-google-train-ai-to-predict-energy-output-of-wind-farms/#7d6c81685e9e

[11] https://www.forbes.com/sites/samshead/2019/03/06/google-deepminds-talks-with-national-grid-are-over/

[12] https://utilityanalytics.com/2019/04/utilities-machine-learning-artificial-intelligence/

[13] https://www.auto-grid.com/news/nextera-energy-services-teams-up-with-autogrid-to-offer-new-demand-response-programs-in-pjm/

[14] http://powerresponsive.com/ai-shaping-future-energy/

15
https://www.ge.com/renewableenergy/sites/default/files/related_documents/GE_Digital_Transformation.PDF

16 http://www.nexteraenergy.com/

17 https://www.dominionenergy.com/company/dvi

18 https://emerj.com/ai-application-comparisons/artificial-intelligence-in-public-utilities-comparison/

19 https://zpryme.com/insights/does-this-smell-funny-to-you/

20
https://www.mckinsey.com/~/media/McKinsey/Industries/Advanced%20Electronics/Our%20Insights/How%20artificial%20intelligence%20can%20deliver%20real%20value%20to%20companies/MGI-Artificial-Intelligence-Discussion-paper.ashx?

21 https://www.smart-energy.com/features-analysis/electricity-theft-south-africa/#:~:text=According%20to%20the%20Ridge%20Times,(%241.5%20billion)%20per%20annum.&text=For%20instance%2C%20Pretoria%20has%20in,compared%20to%20the%20previous%20year.

22 https://new.siemens.com/global/en/company/jobs/what-we-do/brazil-energy-crisis.html#:~:text=But%20Brazil%20was%20facing%20a,to%2040%25%20in%20some%20areas.

23 Kester Eddy, "Hungary's power thieves," Financial Times, March 25, 2011

24
https://www.mckinsey.com/~/media/McKinsey/Industries/Advanced%20Electronics/Our%20Insights/How%20artificial%20intelligence%20can%20deliver%20real%20value%20to%20companies/MGI-Artificial-Intelligence-Discussion-paper.ashx?

25 https://www.forbes.com/sites/oracle/2017/09/20/how-a-huge-utility-is-innovating-with-chatbots-for-better-customer-connections/#14fc33e54152

26 https://en.wikipedia.org/wiki/Category:Energy_companies_of_Europe_by_country & https://www.statista.com/statistics/267066/largest-european-electric-utilities-based-on-power-sales/

27 https://craft.co/bidgely/competitors

28 https://www.achrnews.com/articles/139920-smart-thermostats-are-making-their-way-into-existing-homes

29 https://www.ecobee.com/en-us/smart-thermostats/smart-wifi-thermostat/

30 https://news.duke-energy.com/releases/duke-energy-customers-surpass-1-terawatt-of-energy-savings-through-my-home-energy-report-program

31 https://www.epa.gov/sustainable-water-infrastructure/energy-efficiency-water-utilities

32 https://www.innovyze.com/en-us/blog/ai-in-water-10-ways-ai-is-changing-the-water-industry

33 https://medium.com/datadriveninvestor/digital-water-transformation-the-promise-of-artificial-intelligence-7d88fb07e79b

34 https://waterfm.com/report-data-demand-will-drive-92-billion-in-investment-by-2030/

35 https://waterfm.com/report-opex-water-wastewater-utilities-nearing-100-billion-per-year/

36 https://www.raconteur.net/sustainability/taking-steps-to-cut-global-water-consumption

37
https://www.mckinsey.com/~/media/McKinsey/Business%20Functions/McKinsey%20Digital/Our%20Insights/The%20Internet%20of%20Things%20The%20value%20of%20digitizing%20the%20physical%20world/The-Internet-of-things-Mapping-the-value-beyond-the-hype.ashx

38 https://www.firstpost.com/tech/science/ai-technology-uses-sound-to-seek-out-tiny-leaks-bursts-in-municipal-water-systems-5647491.html#:~:text=The%20technology%20uses%20advanced%20sound,signatures%20of%20a%20leaking%20pipe.&text=An%20AI%20bot%20developed%20by,time%20and%20manpower%20to%20fix.

[39] https://watersource.awa.asn.au/technology/innovation/ai-and-machine-learning-are-flowing-into-the-water-industry/

[40] https://www.waterworld.com/home/article/14071206/using-artificial-intelligence-to-influence-water-infrastructure

[41] https://silo.ai/how-artificial-intelligence-is-transforming-the-water-sector-case-ramboll/

[42] https://www.vineview.com/

[43] https://conserwater.com/

[44] https://spacetimeinsight.com/portfolio-posts/nextera-energy-resources/

[45] https://www.ge.com/renewableenergy/wind-energy/onshore-wind/digital-wind-farm

[46] https://www.ge.com/research/initiative/industrial-ai

[47] https://www.earthnetworks.com/solutions/industries/wind-energy/

[48] https://www.nnergix.com/sentinel-weather/

[49] https://www.xcelenergy.com/

[50] https://www.investopedia.com/ask/answers/030915/what-percentage-global-economy-comprised-oil-gas-drilling-sector.asp

[51] https://emerj.com/ai-sector-overviews/artificial-intelligence-in-oil-and-gas/

[52] https://www.gspublishing.com/content/research/en/reports/2019/09/04/a0d36f41-b16a-4788-9ac5-68ddbc941fa9.pdf

[53] https://www.gspublishing.com/content/research/en/reports/2019/09/04/a0d36f41-b16a-4788-9ac5-68ddbc941fa9.pdf

[54] https://www.bostondynamics.com/

[55] https://www.oecd.org/environment/waste/highlights-global-material-resources-outlook-to-2060.pdf

[56] https://www.researchandmarkets.com/reports/5031470/smart-mining-market-by-type-and-category-global?utm_source=CI&utm_medium=PressRelease&utm_code=pmtjrk&utm_campaign=1414136+-+Insights+on+the+Smart+Mining+Global+Market+to+2027+-+Opportunity+Analysis+and+Industry+Forecast&utm_exec=jamu273prd

[57] https://www.researchandmarkets.com/reports/5013542/impact-of-covid-19-on-the-global-manufacturing?utm_source=dynamic&utm_medium=BW&utm_code=q4bjsh&utm_campaign=1378625+-+Global+Manufacturing+Industry+Report+2020%3a+Deviations+in+Growth+Rates+due+to+the+COVID-19+Pandemic&utm_exec=joca220bwd

[58] https://www.researchandmarkets.com/reports/5013542/impact-of-covid-19-on-the-global-manufacturing?utm_source=dynamic&utm_medium=BW&utm_code=q4bjsh&utm_campaign=1378625+-+Global+Manufacturing+Industry+Report+2020%3a+Deviations+in+Growth+Rates+due+to+the+COVID-19+Pandemic&utm_exec=joca220bwd

[59] https://www.alliedmarketresearch.com/press-release/artificial-intelligence-in-manufacturing-market.html

[60] https://motivo.ai/

[61] https://www.mckinsey.com/~/media/McKinsey/Industries/Advanced%20Electronics/Our%20Insights/How%20artificial%20intelligence%20can%20deliver%20real%20value%20to%20companies/MGI-Artificial-Intelligence-Discussion-paper.ashx?

[62] https://www.mckinsey.com/~/media/McKinsey/Industries/Advanced%20Electronics/Our%20Insights/How%20artificial%20intelligence%20can%20deliver%20real%20value%20to%20companies/MGI-Artificial-Intelligence-Discussion-paper.ashx?

[63] https://www.uptake.com/industry-solutions/aviation

64
https://www.mckinsey.com/~/media/McKinsey/Industries/Advanced%20Electronics/Our%20Insi
ghts/How%20artificial%20intelligence%20can%20deliver%20real%20value%20to%20companies/
MGI-Artificial-Intelligence-Discussion-paper.ashx?

65 https://croplife.org/news/agriculture-a-2-4-trillion-industry-worth-protecting/

66
http://www.fao.org/fileadmin/templates/wsfs/docs/expert_paper/How_to_Feed_the_World_in_2
050.pdf

67 https://www.sciencedirect.com/science/article/pii/S2590332219301320

68 https://www.marketsandmarkets.com/PressReleases/smart-agriculture.asp

69 https://www.gspublishing.com/content/research/en/reports/2019/09/04/a0d36f41-b16a-
4788-9ac5-68ddbc941fa9.pdf

70 https://www.gspublishing.com/content/research/en/reports/2019/09/04/a0d36f41-b16a-
4788-9ac5-68ddbc941fa9.pdf

71 https://plantix.net/en/

72 https://tracegenomics.com/

73 http://wssa.net/2016/05/wssa-calculates-billions-in-potential-economic-losses-from-
uncontrolled-weeds/

74 https://www.ecorobotix.com/en/

75 http://www.bluerivertechnology.com/

76 https://www.naio-technologies.com/en/

77 https://www.energid.com/industries/agricultural-robotics ;
https://harvestcroo.com/about/#why-harvest-croo

78 https://www.aerobotics.com/

79 https://www.vineview.com/

80 https://www.ageagle.com/drones

81 https://www.visionrobotics.com/projects

82 https://www.awhere.com/

83 https://www.gspublishing.com/content/research/en/reports/2019/09/04/a0d36f41-b16a-
4788-9ac5-68ddbc941fa9.pdf

84 https://originhydroponics.com/hydroponics-vs-aquaponics-vs-aeroponics/

85 https://www.marketsandmarkets.com/Market-Reports/vertical-farming-market-
221795343.html?gclid=EAIaIQobChMIiuWdjJe96wIVx-N3Ch0DKwGTEAAYASAAEgJTB_D_BwE

86
http://www.fao.org/fileadmin/templates/wsfs/docs/expert_paper/How_to_Feed_the_World_in_2
050.pdf

87
http://www.fao.org/fileadmin/templates/wsfs/docs/expert_paper/How_to_Feed_the_World_in_2
050.pdf

88 https://www.up.ac.za/media/shared/7/ZP_Files/ai-for-africa.zp165664.pdf

89 https://www.gspublishing.com/content/research/en/reports/2019/09/04/a0d36f41-b16a-
4788-9ac5-68ddbc941fa9.pdf

7. Ultra-personalized AI-enabled Education, Precision Healthcare, and Wellness

1 Kai-Fu Lee, *AI Superpowers: China, Silicon Valley, and the New World Order.*
2 Kai-Fu Lee, *AI Superpowers: China, Silicon Valley, and the New World Order.*
3 https://blog.usaid.gov/2013/04/education-the-most-powerful-weapon/

4 https://www.semanticscholar.org/paper/AI-Grand-Challenges-for-Education-Woolf-Lane/d0bcefbdd145ae02890742010d187eda1619f685?p2df

5 https://www.prnewswire.com/news-releases/education-technology-market-size-worth-285-2-billion-by-2027-grand-view-research-inc-301095941.html

6 https://edtechmagazine.com/k12/article/2019/08/artificial-intelligence-authentic-impact-how-educational-ai-making-grade-perfcon

7 https://www.holoniq.com/edtech-unicorns/

8 https://www.globenewswire.com/news-release/2020/02/26/1990599/0/en/AI-in-Education-Market-is-Poised-to-Post-25-7-Billion-Revenue-by-2030-P-S-Intelligence.html

9 https://www.researchgate.net/publication/323378817_AI_Thinking_for_Cloud_Education_Platform_with_Personalized_Learning

10 https://www.kidaptive.com/

11 https://www.knewton.com/

12 https://www.knewton.com/tag/ai/

13 https://quizlet.com/

14 https://thirdspacelearning.com/

15 https://www.century.tech/

16 https://www.cognii.com/

17 http://querium.com/

18 https://hellothinkster.com/

19 https://www.carnegielearning.com/

20 https://www.dreambox.com/; https://www.dreambox.com/intelligent-adaptive-learning/

21 https://www.italk2learn.com/

22 https://www.gradescope.com/

23 https://roybirobot.com/

24 https://kidsense.ai/

25 https://www.nuance.com/dragon/industry/education-solutions.html

26 https://lingvist.com/

27 https://www.eliasrobot.com/

28 https://collaboration.ai/

29 https://www.cc.gatech.edu/news/631545/worlds-first-ai-teaching-assistant-turns-4; https://www.cc.gatech.edu/news/627578/jill-watson-now-fielding-questions-new-ai-enabled-research-tool

30 https://www.coursera.org/courses;

31 https://www.coursera.org/learn/machine-learning; https://www.coursera.org/instructor/andrewng

32 https://analyticsindiamag.com/how-ed-tech-firms-are-using-ai-to-enhance-learning-from-home/

33 http://contenttechnologiesinc.com/

34 https://www.netexlearning.com/en/

35 https://www.weadmit.com/

36 https://www.eu-startups.com/2019/08/alicante-based-1millionbot-raises-e1-5-million-to-develop-more-educational-and-marketing-chatbots/

37 https://www.civitaslearning.com/

38 https://www.salesforce.org/blog/salesforce-org-civitas-learning-connect-insights-action-across-connected-campus/

39 https://www.haaga-helia.fi/en/services/services-for-business/saleslab

40 https://news.ets.org/stories/three-predictions-on-artificial-intelligence-and-the-future-of-education/

41 https://www.tandfonline.com/doi/pdf/10.1080/03075079.2017.1284195 ;
https://www.voicesofyouth.org/blog/education-and-labour-market-mismatches-what-can-be-done ;
https://www.researchgate.net/publication/258286624_Skill_Mismatch_Education_Systems_and_
Labour_Markets_in_EU_Neighbourhood_Policy_Countries ;
https://www.un.org/en/ecosoc/julyhls/pdf12/un_presentation-dr_amr_salama.pdf
42 https://textio.com/
43 https://www.careerbuilder.com/ ; http://press.careerbuilder.com/2019-10-01-CareerBuilder-
Unveils-Advanced-AI-Based-Talent-Acquisition-Platform-for-Employers-and-Job-Seekers-Turning-
the-Industry-on-Its-Head-while-Addressing-Diversity
44 https://goarya.com/; https://beamery.com/; https://www.entelo.com/; https://hiretual.com/;
https://www.hireabby.ai/; https://hiredscore.com/; https://www.talemetry.com/
45 https://goarya.com/
46 https://www.pandologic.com/technology-overview/
47 https://www.ceipal.com/; https://cvviz.com/; https://ideal.com/;
https://www.mosaictrack.com/; http://www.pomato.com/; https://www.textkernel.com/
48 https://harver.com/; https://www.hackerrank.com/; https://www.interviewmocha.com/;
https://kand.io/; https://mcquaig.com/; https://jobpal.ai/en/; https://www.mya.com/;
https://olivia-ai.org/
49 https://humantic.ai/
50 https://calendly.com/; https://x.ai/; https://www.hirevue.com/; https://www.panna.ai/;
https://talocity.ai/
51 https://appical.net/en/; https://enboarder.com/; https://www.talmundo.com/
52 https://unesdoc.unesco.org/ark:/48223/pf0000246124; https://sdgs.un.org/goals/goal4
53 https://unesdoc.unesco.org/ark:/48223/pf0000373718?posInSet=6&queryId=6630d8ba-7ccf-
47d1-8527-1a2a13a3c4b0
54 https://www.itnewsafrica.com/2019/02/top-10-edtech-startups-transforming-learning-in-
africa/
55 https://www.thestudenthub.co.za/
56 http://thestudenthub.co/; http://www.eraonline.co.za/;
http://www.linkedin.com/pulse/artificial-intelligence-finance-education-healthcare-government
57
https://www.tandfonline.com/doi/abs/10.1080/17439884.2020.1754236?journalCode=cjem20
58 http://squirrelai.com/
59 http://en.100tal.com/
60 https://aiteacher.100tal.com/; https://aiteacher.100tal.com/news/10.html
61 https://m.liulishuo.com/en/aboutus.html
62 https://www.scmp.com/news/china/society/article/2147833/chinas-schools-are-quietly-
using-ai-mark-students-essays-do
63 https://www.scmp.com/news/china/politics/article/3027349/artificial-intelligence-watching-
chinas-students-how-well-can
64 Anthony Seldon, *The Fourth Education Revolution*, The University of Buckingham Press, 2018.
65 Anthony Seldon, *The Fourth Education Revolution*, Chapter 9. The University of Buckingham
Press, 2018.
66 Anthony Seldon, *The Fourth Education Revolution*, Chapter 8. The University of Buckingham
Press, 2018.
67 https://www.udacity.com/
68 https://woolf.university/
69 https://www.accenture.com/_acnmedia/PDF-130/Accenture-Health-Tech-Vision-
2020.pdf#zoom=40
70 https://www.webershandwick.com/news/ai-ready-or-not-artificial-intelligence-here-we-

come/

71 http://www.healthcareitnews.com/news/cost-data-breaches-climbs-4-million-healthcare-events-most-expensive-ponemon-finds

72 https://www.accenture.com/_acnmedia/PDF-49/Accenture-Health-Artificial-Intelligence.pdf#zoom=50

73 https://www.healthcaredive.com/news/confidence-investment-in-ai-remains-high-optum-says/564593/

74 https://www.mckinsey.com/~/media/McKinsey/Industries/Advanced%20Electronics/Our%20Insights/How%20artificial%20intelligence%20can%20deliver%20real%20value%20to%20companies/MGI-Artificial-Intelligence-Discussion-paper.ashx?

75 https://www.grandviewresearch.com/press-release/global-artificial-intelligence-healthcare-market

76 https://www.marketsandmarkets.com/Market-Reports/artificial-intelligence-healthcare-market-54679303.html?gclid=EAIaIQobChMI5pCQruaA7AIVlKmyCh35Qgu1EAAYASAAEgLt5vD_BwE

77 https://www.gspublishing.com/content/research/en/reports/2019/09/04/a0d36f41-b16a-4788-9ac5-68ddbc941fa9.pdf

78 https://www.researchandmarkets.com/reports/5031240/global-electronic-health-records-ehr-market-by

79 https://www.mckinsey.com/~/media/McKinsey/Industries/Advanced%20Electronics/Our%20Insights/How%20artificial%20intelligence%20can%20deliver%20real%20value%20to%20companies/MGI-Artificial-Intelligence-Discussion-paper.ashx?

80 https://www.accenture.com/_acnmedia/PDF-49/Accenture-Health-Artificial-Intelligence.pdf#zoom=50

81 https://spectrum.ieee.org/biomedical/diagnostics/how-ibm-watson-overpromised-and-underdelivered-on-ai-health-care

82 https://www.ibm.com/watson-health

83 https://www.marketsandmarkets.com/Market-Reports/artificial-intelligence-healthcare-market-54679303.html?gclid=EAIaIQobChMI5pCQruaA7AIVlKmyCh35Qgu1EAAYASAAEgLt5vD_BwE

84 https://spectrum.ieee.org/biomedical/diagnostics/how-ibm-watson-overpromised-and-underdelivered-on-ai-health-care

85 https://www.ibm.com/downloads/cas/NPDPLDEZ

86 https://healthitanalytics.com/news/cleveland-clinic-creates-artificial-intelligence-innovation-center

87 https://newsroom.clevelandclinic.org/2016/12/22/cleveland-clinic-ibm-collaborate-establish-model-cognitive-population-health-management-data-driven-personalized-healthcare/

88 https://healthitanalytics.com/news/ibm-watson-health-teams-up-with-hospitals-for-ai-ehr-research

89 https://healthitanalytics.com/news/uci-health-opens-center-for-artificial-intelligence-deep-learning

90 https://healthitanalytics.com/news/johns-hopkins-leverages-microsoft-ai-for-precision-medicine

91 http://newsroom.gehealthcare.com/wp-content/uploads/2016/12/GE-Healthcare-White-Paper_FINAL.pdf

92 https://www.gehealthcare.com/products/edison

93 https://www.gehealthcare.com/products/edison

94 https://www.massdevice.com/ge-healthcare-wants-to-expand-the-use-of-ai-in-healthcare-

heres-how/

95 https://koiosmedical.com/

96 https://www.gehealthcare.com/products/magnetic-resonance-imaging/signa-works/viosworks

97 https://emerj.com/ai-sector-overviews/ai-at-johnson-johnson/

98 https://www.verbsurgical.com/media-article/verb-surgical-delivers-digital-surgery-prototype-demonstration-to-collaboration-partners/; https://www.aurishealth.com/about

99 https://www.businesswire.com/news/home/20190618005363/en/Cara-Care-Raises-7M-Series-Led-Johnson

100 https://www.jnj.com/latest-news/how-artificial-intelligence-is-helping-janssen-discover-new-drugs

101 https://deepmind.com/blog/announcements/deepmind-health-joins-google-health

102 https://ai.googleblog.com/search/label/Health

103 https://deepmind.com/blog/article/Using_ai_to_predict_retinal_disease_progression

104 https://www.mayoclinic.org/departments-centers/ai-cardiology/overview/ovc-20486648

105 https://www.healthcareitnews.com/news/mayo-clinic-google-launch-major-new-10-year-partnership

106 https://www.siemens-healthineers.com/digital-health-solutions/artificial-intelligence-in-healthcare

107 https://www.siemens-healthineers.com/digital-health-solutions/digital-solutions-overview/clinical-decision-support/ai-rad-companion; https://www.siemens-healthineers.com/digital-health-solutions/digital-solutions-overview/clinical-decision-support/ai-pathway-companion#Product_vision

108 https://www.digitalhealthnews.eu/siemens/6177-siemens-healthineers-uses-artificial-intelligence-to-take-x-ray-diagnostics-to-a-new-level

109 https://www.medicaldevice-network.com/news/siemens-healthineers-ai-software/

110 https://oliveai.com/

111 https://oliveai.com/deep-purple/

112 https://qventus.com/

113 https://cloudmedxhealth.com/

114 https://www.babylonhealth.com/us

115 Calum Chace, *The Economic Singularity: Artificial Intelligence and the Death of Capitalism.*

116 https://healthcareweekly.com/best-healthcare-startups-to-watch-for-in-2019/

117 https://healthcareweekly.com/best-healthcare-startups-to-watch-for-in-2019/

118 https://healthcareweekly.com/best-healthcare-startups-to-watch-for-in-2019/

119 https://healthcareweekly.com/artificial-intelligence-in-pharmacology/

120 https://www.pathai.com/

121 https://www.mskcc.org/news/researchers-report-milestone-use-artificial-intelligence-pathology;

122 https://oncoramedical.com/press/oncora-and-md-anderson-abstract-accepted-oral-presentation-2019-asco-quality-care-symposium/

123 https://www.mdanderson.org/publications/cancer-frontline/predicting-head-and-neck-cancer-treatment-toxicities-with-machine-learning.h00-159306201.html

124 https://www.enlitic.com/

125 https://www.freenome.com/

126 https://www.bidmc.org/about-bidmc/news/bidmc-researchers-use-artificial-intelligence-to-identify-bacteria-quickly-and-accurately

127 https://www.zebra-med.com/

128 https://www.buoyhealth.com/

129 https://www.anxietycentre.com/FAQ/why-is-mental-illness-on-the-rise.shtml;

https://www.sciencedaily.com/releases/2019/03/190315110908.htm

[130] https://www.seeker.com/tech/artificial-intelligence/this-ai-system-can-diagnose-depression-from-instagram-photos

[131] https://woebothealth.com/

[132] https://www.nature.com/articles/d41586-018-05267-x

[133] https://www.bioxceltherapeutics.com/

[134] https://aicure.com/; https://www.biospace.com/article/how-a-phone-app-is-helping-participants-stick-to-their-medications-during-clinical-trials/ https://www.mobihealthnews.com/content/small-study-aicure-app-led-50-percent-improvement-medication-adherence#:~:text=Asia%20Pacific-,In%20small%20study%2C%20AiCure%20app%20led%20to,percent%20improvement%20in%20medication%20adherence&text=A%20forthcoming%2028%2Dpatient%20study,in%20adherence%20to%20oral%20anticoagulants.

[135] https://www.cognizant.com/case-studies/ai-based-preventive-care

[136] https://www.berghealth.com/

[137] https://www.xtalpi.com/en/

[138] https://www.atomwise.com/

[139] https://hemophilianewstoday.com/2020/09/23/gc-pharma-atomwise-partner-develop-oral-hemophilia-therapies/

[140] https://www.deepgenomics.com/

[141] https://www.deepgenomics.com/updates/deep-genomics-nominates-industrys-first-ai-discovered-therapeutic-candidate/

[142] https://www.deepgenomics.com/project-saturn/

[143] https://www.benevolent.com/

[144] https://www.tempus.com/

[145] https://www.kensci.com/

[146] https://proscia.com/

[147] https://www.h2o.ai/healthcare/#patient-care

[148] https://www.icarbonx.com/en/

[149] https://arxiv.org/pdf/2001.00627.pdf

[150] https://www.intuitive.com/en-us

[151] https://www.intuitive.com/en-us/products-and-services/da-vinci

[152] https://www.vicarioussurgical.com/

[153] https://www.aurishealth.com/

[154] http://microsure.nl/

[155] https://www.accuray.com/

[156] https://www.accuray.com/cyberknife/

[157] https://www.accuray.com/tomotherapy/; https://www.accuray.com/radixact/

[158] https://turbine.ai/

[159] https://turbine.ai/approach

[160] https://www.mindmaze.com/

[161] https://www.ginger.io/

[162] https://www.jabil.com/blog/digital-health-infographic.html

[163] https://www.jabil.com/blog/digital-health-infographic.html

[164] https://www.who.int/about/who-we-are/constitution; https://www.merriam-webster.com/dictionary/wellness#:~:text=%3A%20the%20quality%20or%20state%20of,goal%20lifestyles%20that%20promote%20wellness

[165] https://www.glwswellbeing.com/wp-content/uploads/2018/02/The-Future-of-Wellnessat-Work-Global-Wellness-Institute-2016.pdf

[166] https://www.glwswellbeing.com/wp-content/uploads/2018/02/The-Future-of-Wellnessat-

Work-Global-Wellness-Institute-2016.pdf

[167] https://globalwellnessinstitute.org/industry-research/global-economy-physical-activity/

[168] https://www.businesswire.com/news/home/20200407005641/en/Outlook-on-the-Worldwide-Health-and-Wellness-Industry-to-2025---Featuring-Amway-Bayer-Brunswick-Danone-Among-Others---ResearchAndMarkets.com

[169] https://www.nutraingredients-asia.com/Article/2017/07/07/Amway-rolls-out-e-commerce-and-artificial-intelligence-platforms-in-the-Philippines

[170] https://pharma.bayer.com/artificial-intelligence-when-we-suddenly-know-what-we-dont-know; https://pharma.bayer.com/artificial-intelligence-technology-driven-disease-prediction-advance-patient-care; https://www.wsj.com/articles/bayer-looks-to-emerging-technique-to-overcome-ai-data-challenges-11580121000; https://www.biospace.com/article/bayer-and-exscientia-collaborate-to-leverage-the-potential-of-artificial-intelligence-in-cardiovascular-and-oncology-drug-discovery/

[171] https://www.longevity.technology/bayer-backs-11-digital-health-and-ai-startups/

[172] https://www.danone.com/content/dam/danone-corp/danone-com/medias/medias-en/2020/corporatepressreleases/Danone-Microsoft-AI-Factory-for-Agrifood-EN.pdf

[173] https://iamherbalifenutrition.com/innovation/artificial-intelligence-customer/

[174] https://www.fooddive.com/news/nestles-personalized-nutrition-pilot-taps-ai-uses-consumer-dna/531560/

[175] https://www.loreal.com/en/usa/articles/research-and-innovation/loreal-unveils-perso/

[176] https://www.prnewswire.com/news-releases/google-cloud-helps-power-more-personalized-experience-for-procter--gamble-consumers-301092670.html

[177] https://finance.yahoo.com/news/corrected-procter-gamble-goes-big-connected-beauty-ces-084854690.html

[178] https://aaptiv.com/coach

[179] https://www.fitnessai.com/

[180] https://youtu.be/tZcRYcjTwWA

[181] https://www.kaiahealth.com/

[182] https://zenia.app/

[183] https://www.aon.com/attachments/human-capital-consulting/2012_Health_Care_Survey_final.pdf

[184] https://medium.com/@lkcyber/the-emerging-artificial-intelligence-wellness-landscape-802caf9638de

[185] https://mindstrong.com/

[186] https://devpost.com/software/addicaid-2sctab

[187] https://www.researchgate.net/publication/337022595_Robots_Artificial_Intelligence_and_Service_Automation_in_Hotels; https://www.trazeetravel.com/marriott-uses-artificial-intelligence-new-guest-service/

[188] https://www.amazon.com/ZEEQ-Smart-Pillow-Connected-Automation/dp/B06XG7G5SC

[189] http://www.parorobots.com/; https://www.siliconrepublic.com/future-human/stevie-robot-elder-care-niamh-donnelly

[190] https://aithority.com/machine-learning/neural-networks/brain-computer-interface-definition-tools-and-applications/

[191] https://www.frontiersin.org/research-topics/13609/deep-learning-in-brain-computer-interface; https://neuralink.com/; https://www.neurable.com/; https://www.next-mind.com/; https://www.emotiv.com/

[192] https://www.oecd.org/statistics/measuring-well-being-and-progress.htm

[193] https://www.oecd.org/newsroom/hows-life-reveals-improvements-in-well-being-but-persistent-inequalities.htm

194 https://www.oecd.org/sdd/How-is-Life-2020-Highlights.pdf

195 https://globalwellnessinstitute.org/press-room/statistics-and-facts/

196 https://globalwellnessinstitute.org/industry-research/global-economy-physical-activity/

197 https://www.wellsteps.com/

198 https://www.sonicboomwellness.com/

199 https://www.wellnesscorporatesolutions.com/; http://www.workstride.com/; https://www.totalwellnesshealth.com/; https://www.wellable.co/home

200 https://www.hioscar.com/; https://www.discovery.co.za

201 https://www.discovery.co.za/vitality/how-vitality-works

202 https://www.mckinsey.com/~/media/McKinsey/Industries/Advanced%20Electronics/Our%20Insights/How%20artificial%20intelligence%20can%20deliver%20real%20value%20to%20companies/MGI-Artificial-Intelligence-Discussion-paper.ashx?

203 https://www.net-reply.com/grx/snb1copy1feb/

8. AI's Impact on Society, Governments, and the Public Sector

1 Thomas Friedman, *Thank you for being late: an optimist's guide to thriving in the age of accelerations.*

2 https://www.globalinnovationindex.org/analysis-indicator

3 https://researchictafrica.net/after-access-survey-papers/2018/After_Access:_youth_and_digital_inequality_in_Africa.pdf

4 Thomas Friedman, *Thank you for being late: AN Optimist's Guide to Thriving in the Age of Acceleration*; https://www.youtube.com/watch?v=_QOyKeEEU3Q&feature=youtu.be

5 https://www.youtube.com/watch?v=_QOyKeEEU3Q&feature=youtu.be

6 https://www.youtube.com/watch?v=_QOyKeEEU3Q&feature=youtu.be

7 https://www.psychologytoday.com/za/blog/the-adaptive-mind/201809/how-overcome-the-fear-change ; https://www.smithsonianmag.com/science-nature/what-happens-brain-feel-fear-180966992/

8 https://hbr.org/podcast/2019/11/ai-accountability-and-power

9 John Rawls, *A Theory of Justice.*

10 John Rawls, *A Theory of Justice.*

11 John Rawls, *A Theory of Justice.*

12 John Rawls, *A Theory of Justice.*

13 https://www.youtube.com/watch?v=-W-eTwnxLw4&feature=youtu.be

14 Kai-Fu Lee, *AI Superpowers, China, Silicon Valley, and the New World Order.*

15 https://www.jamiesusskind.com/; Jamie Susskind, *Future Politics: Living Together in a World Transformed by Tech*, 2018.

16 https://www.netflix.com/za/title/81254224; https://en.wikipedia.org/wiki/The_Social_Dilemma

17 https://www.businessinsider.com.au/facebook-says-netflix-documentary-the-social-dilemma-sensationalist-2020-10?r=US&IR=T; https://about.fb.com/wp-content/uploads/2020/10/What-The-Social-Dilemma-Gets-Wrong.pdf

18 Shoshana Zuboff, *The Age of Surveillance Capitalism*, 2019.

19 https://www.contagious.com/news-and-views/shoshana-zuboff-on-the-age-of-surveillance-capitalism

20 https://www.nytimes.com/2019/05/14/us/facial-recognition-ban-san-francisco.html

21 https://en.wikipedia.org/wiki/Mass_surveillance_in_China

22 https://www.businessinsider.com/how-china-is-watching-its-citizens-in-a-modern-

surveillance-state-2018-4#4-watching-how-people-shop-online-5

23 https://time.com/5735411/china-surveillance-privacy-issues/;
https://www.nytimes.com/2019/05/22/world/asia/china-surveillance-xinjiang.html ;
https://www.foxnews.com/tech/dystopian-how-chinas-top-notch-mass-surveillance-threatens-freedoms

24 https://www.reuters.com/article/us-china-health-surveillance-idUSKBN2011HO

25 https://www.forbes.com/sites/stevedenning/2020/04/19/why-only-the-agile-will-survive/#2b11f80f2c1e

26 https://futureoflife.org/background/benefits-risks-of-artificial-intelligence/

27 Klaus Schwab and Nicholas Davis, *Shaping the Fourth Industrial Revolution.*

28 Klaus Schwab, *The Fourth Industrial Revolution.*

29 https://www.pewresearch.org/internet/2018/12/10/improvements-ahead-how-humans-and-ai-might-evolve-together-in-the-next-decade/

30 https://ai100.stanford.edu/sites/g/files/sbiybj9861/f/ai100report10032016fnl_singles.pdf;

31 https://ai100.stanford.edu/workshop

32 https://news.stanford.edu/2019/03/18/stanford_university_launches_human-centered_ai/

33 https://read.oecd-ilibrary.org/view/?ref=130_130771-3jtyra9uoh&title=Using-artificial-intelligence-to-help-combat-COVID-19

34 https://www.conference-board.org/data/economydatabase/

35 https://www.accenture.com/t20170524t055435__w__/ca-en/_acnmedia/pdf-52/accenture-why-ai-is-the-future-of-growth.pdf

36
https://www.mckinsey.com/~/media/mckinsey/featured%20insights/artificial%20intelligence/applying%20artificial%20intelligence%20for%20social%20good/mgi-applying-ai-for-social-good-discussion-paper-dec-2018.ashx

37 "Computer learns to detect skin cancer more accurately than doctors," Guardian, May 29, 2018; Brandon Ballinger et al., DeepHeart: Semi-supervised sequence learning for cardiovascular risk prediction, 32nd AAAI Conference on Artificial Intelligence, New Orleans, LA, February 2–7, 2018, aaai.org/ocs/index. php/AAAI/AAAI18/paper/view/16967/15916.

38 https://www.plugandplaytechcenter.com/resources/how-ai-and-robotics-are-solving-plastic-sorting-crisis/; https://www.ge.com/news/reports/dumpster-diving-robots-using-ai-smart-recycling; "Using satellite imagery to combat illegal fishing," The Maritime Executive, July 17, 2017; "What have we done so far?" Rainforest Connection, rfcx.org/home

39 https://blog.google/outreach-initiatives/google-org/2602-uses-ai-social-good-and-what-we-learned-them/

40
http://services.google.com/fh/files/misc/accelerating_social_good_with_artificial_intelligence_google_ai_impact_challenge.pdf

41
http://services.google.com/fh/files/misc/accelerating_social_good_with_artificial_intelligence_google_ai_impact_challenge.pdf

42
http://services.google.com/fh/files/misc/accelerating_social_good_with_artificial_intelligence_google_ai_impact_challenge.pdf

43 https://www.pewresearch.org/internet/2018/12/10/artificial-intelligence-and-the-future-of-humans/

44 https://www.pewresearch.org/internet/2018/12/10/concerns-about-human-agency-evolution-and-survival/

45 https://medium.com/@francois.chollet/what-worries-me-about-ai-ed9df072b704

46 https://www.bbc.com/future/article/20201014-totalitarian-world-in-chains-artificial-

intelligence

[47] https://www.theatlantic.com/magazine/archive/2018/06/henry-kissinger-ai-could-mean-the-end-of-human-history/559124/

[48] Kai-Fu Lee, *AI Superpowers: China, Silicon Valley, and the New World Order.*

[49] https://www.bain.com/insights/labor-2030-the-collision-of-demographics-automation-and-inequality/

[50] Calum Chase, *The Economic Singularity.*

[51] Martin Ford, *The Rise of the Robots.*

[52] McAfee and Brynjolfsson, *The Second Machine Age*, McAfee and Brynjolfsson, *Machine, Platform, Crowd.*

[53] https://www.bbc.com/news/business-44849492

[54] Kai-Fu Lee, *AI Superpowers: China, Silicon Valley, and the New World Order.*

[55] https://www.who.int/news-room/fact-sheets/detail/suicide; https://theconversation.com/why-do-people-die-by-suicide-mental-illness-isnt-the-only-cause-social-factors-like-loneliness-financial-ruin-and-shame-can-be-triggers-131744

[56] https://prcp.psychiatryonline.org/doi/full/10.1176/appi.prcp.20190015

[57] https://prcp.psychiatryonline.org/doi/full/10.1176/appi.prcp.20190015

[58] https://img1.wsimg.com/blobby/go/3d82daa4-97fe-4096-9c6b-376b92c619de/downloads/MaliciousUseofAI.pdf?ver=1553030594217

[59] https://img1.wsimg.com/blobby/go/3d82daa4-97fe-4096-9c6b-376b92c619de/downloads/MaliciousUseofAI.pdf?ver=1553030594217

[60] https://crimesciencejournal.biomedcentral.com/articles/10.1186/s40163-020-00123-8

[61] https://www2.deloitte.com/content/dam/insights/us/articles/3832_AI-augmented-government/DUP_AI-augmented-government.pdf

[62] https://www2.deloitte.com/content/dam/Deloitte/lu/Documents/public-sector/lu-government-trends-2020.pdf

[63] https://www2.deloitte.com/content/dam/Deloitte/lu/Documents/public-sector/lu-government-trends-2020.pdf

[64] https://www2.deloitte.com/content/dam/Deloitte/lu/Documents/public-sector/lu-government-trends-2020.pdf

[65] https://atos.net/en/artificial-intelligence

[66] https://www.nytimes.com/2017/07/20/business/china-artificial-intelligence.html

[67] https://www.accenture.com/_acnmedia/pdf-75/accenture-ai-genuine-impact-pov-final-us.pdf

[68] https://www.idc.com/getdoc.jsp?containerId=prEUR146205720

[69] https://en.wikipedia.org/wiki/Crime_drop#:~:text=In%20the%20United%20States%2C%20for,the%20early%201990s%20to%202010; https://www.fbi.gov/news/stories/2018-crime-statistics-released-093019;

[70] https://worldpopulationreview.com/country-rankings/crime-rate-by-country; https://www.statista.com/statistics/243797/ranking-of-the-most-dangerous-cities-in-the-world-by-murder-rate-per-capita/ https://businesstech.co.za/news/government/421424/south-africa-crime-stats-2020-everything-you-need-to-know/#:~:text=Murders%20in%20South%20Africa%20remain,35.8%20people%20per%20100%2C000%20population.

[71] https://www.shotspotter.com/

[72] https://www.securityworldmarket.com/int/News/Product-News/hikvision-introduces-dedicated-series-in-its-deepinview-camera-line

[73] https://www.predpol.com/

[74] https://www.cloudwalk.com/

[75] https://fas.org/sgp/crs/intel/R46389.pdf

76 https://fas.org/irp/doddir/dod/d3000_09.pdf

77 https://jsis.washington.edu/news/autonomous-weaponry-are-killer-robots-in-our-future/

78 https://jsis.washington.edu/news/autonomous-weaponry-are-killer-robots-in-our-future/

79 https://www.pwc.com/gx/en/issues/data-and-analytics/publications/artificial-intelligence-study.html

80 https://www.pwc.com/gx/en/issues/analytics/assets/pwc-ai-analysis-sizing-the-prize-report.pdf

81

https://www.mckinsey.com/~/media/McKinsey/Industries/Advanced%20Electronics/Our%20Insights/How%20artificial%20intelligence%20can%20deliver%20real%20value%20to%20companies/MGI-Artificial-Intelligence-Discussion-paper.ashx?

82

https://www.mckinsey.com/~/media/McKinsey/Industries/Advanced%20Electronics/Our%20Insights/How%20artificial%20intelligence%20can%20deliver%20real%20value%20to%20companies/MGI-Artificial-Intelligence-Discussion-paper.ashx?

83 https://miiafrica.org/

84 http://www3.weforum.org/docs/WEFUSA_NewVisionforEducation_Report2015.pdf

85 http://www3.weforum.org/docs/WEFUSA_NewVisionforEducation_Report2015.pdf

86

https://www.mckinsey.com/~/media/mckinsey/industries/advanced%20electronics/our%20insights/how%20artificial%20intelligence%20can%20deliver%20real%20value%20to%20companies/mgi-artificial-intelligence-discussion-paper.ashx

87

https://www.mckinsey.com/~/media/mckinsey/industries/advanced%20electronics/our%20insights/how%20artificial%20intelligence%20can%20deliver%20real%20value%20to%20companies/mgi-artificial-intelligence-discussion-paper.ashx

88 https://venturebeat.com/2020/03/16/tech-nation-u-s-companies-raised-56-of-global-ai-investment-since-2015-followed-by-china-and-u-k/

89 http://www.chinadaily.com.cn/a/201809/18/WS5ba09a8ca31033b4f4656b65.html

90 https://www2.deloitte.com/us/en/insights/focus/cognitive-technologies/ai-investment-by-country.html

91 https://oecd.ai/

92 https://oecd.ai/countries-and-initiatives

93 https://futureoflife.org/national-international-ai-strategies/

94 https://oecd.ai/ai-principles

95 https://oecd.ai/policy-areas

96 https://www.whitehouse.gov/briefings-statements/president-donald-j-trump-is-accelerating-americas-leadership-in-artificial-intelligence/

97 https://www.whitehouse.gov/ai/executive-order-ai/

98 https://www.wsj.com/articles/artificial-intelligence-can-serve-democracy-11590618319

99 https://www.state.gov/declaration-of-the-united-states-of-america-and-the-united-kingdom-of-great-britain-and-northern-ireland-on-cooperation-in-artificial-intelligence-research-and-development-a-shared-vision-for-driving/

100 https://www.whitehouse.gov/wp-content/uploads/2020/02/American-AI-Initiative-One-Year-Annual-Report.pdf

101 https://www.energy.gov/articles/us-department-energy-and-cray-deliver-record-setting-frontier-supercomputer-ornl; https://www.whitehouse.gov/ai/ai-american-innovation/

102 https://www.whitehouse.gov/ai/ai-american-industry/

103 https://www.whitehouse.gov/ai/ai-american-worker/

104 https://www.whitehouse.gov/ai/ai-american-values/

[105] https://oecd.ai/dashboards/policy-initiatives?conceptUris=http:%2F%2Fkim.oecd.org%2FTaxonomy%2FGeographicalAreas%23UnitedStates

[106] https://www.statista.com/statistics/672712/ai-funding-united-states/

[107] https://www.technologyreview.com/2017/12/06/3775/the-us-leads-in-artificial-intelligence-but-for-how-long/

[108] https://www2.deloitte.com/us/en/insights/focus/cognitive-technologies/ai-investment-by-country.html

[109] h ttp://www.gov.cn/zhengce/content/2017-07/20/content_5211996.htm

[110] https://www.reuters.com/article/us-china-ai-tianjin/chinas-city-of-tianjin-to-set-up-16-billion-artificial-intelligence-fund-idUSKCN1II0DD; https://futurism.com/china-building-2-1-billion-industrial-park-ai-research

[111] https://www2.deloitte.com/us/en/insights/focus/cognitive-technologies/ai-investment-by-country.html

[112]
https://www.mckinsey.com/~/media/mckinsey/industries/advanced%20electronics/our%20insights/how%20artificial%20intelligence%20can%20deliver%20real%20value%20to%20companies/mgi-artificial-intelligence-discussion-paper.ashx

[113] http://www.gov.cn/zhengce/content/2017-07/20/content_5211996.htm

[114] https://oecd.ai/dashboards/policy-initiatives?conceptUris=http:%2F%2Fkim.oecd.org%2FTaxonomy%2FGeographicalAreas%23China

[115] https://www.baai.ac.cn/news/beijing-ai-principles-en.html

[116] https://www.theatlantic.com/magazine/archive/2020/09/china-ai-surveillance/614197/

[117]
https://assets.publishing.service.gov.uk/government/uploads/system/uploads/attachment_data/file/702810/180425_BEIS_AI_Sector_Deal__4_.pdf

[118]
https://assets.publishing.service.gov.uk/government/uploads/system/uploads/attachment_data/file/819331/AI_Sector_Deal_One_Year_On__Web_.pdf

[119]
https://assets.publishing.service.gov.uk/government/uploads/system/uploads/attachment_data/file/702810/180425_BEIS_AI_Sector_Deal__4_.pdf

[120] https://epsrc.ukri.org/research/ourportfolio/researchareas/ait/;
https://assets.publishing.service.gov.uk/government/uploads/system/uploads/attachment_data/file/702810/180425_BEIS_AI_Sector_Deal__4_.pdf

[121]
https://assets.publishing.service.gov.uk/government/uploads/system/uploads/attachment_data/file/702810/180425_BEIS_AI_Sector_Deal__4_.pdf

[122]
https://assets.publishing.service.gov.uk/government/uploads/system/uploads/attachment_data/file/702810/180425_BEIS_AI_Sector_Deal__4_.pdf

[123] https://www.gov.uk/guidance/understanding-artificial-intelligence-ethics-and-safety

[124] https://oecd.ai/dashboards/policy-initiatives?conceptUris=http:%2F%2Fkim.oecd.org%2FTaxonomy%2FGeographicalAreas%23UnitedStates

[125] https://www.gov.uk/government/publications/industrial-strategy-the-grand-challenges/industrial-strategy-the-grand-challenges#artificial-intelligence-and-data

[126] https://www.de.digital/DIGITAL/Redaktion/DE/Publikation/potenziale-kuenstlichen-intelligenz-im-produzierenden-gewerbe-in-deutschland.html

[127] https://www.de.digital/DIGITAL/Redaktion/EN/Standardartikel/artificial-intelligence-

strategy.html
   [128] https://www.de.digital/DIGITAL/Redaktion/EN/Standardartikel/artificial-intelligence-strategy.html; https://ec.europa.eu/knowledge4policy/sites/know4pol/files/germany-ai-strategy-report.pdf
   [129] https://www2.deloitte.com/us/en/insights/focus/cognitive-technologies/ai-investment-by-country.html
   [130] https://oecd.ai/dashboards/policy-initiatives?conceptUris=http:%2F%2Fkim.oecd.org%2FTaxonomy%2FGeographicalAreas%23Germany
   [131] https://www.de.digital/DIGITAL/Redaktion/EN/Standardartikel/artificial-intelligence-strategy.html; https://ec.europa.eu/knowledge4policy/sites/know4pol/files/germany-ai-strategy-report.pdf
   [132] https://www.gouvernement.fr/en/artificial-intelligence-making-france-a-leader
   [133] https://ec.europa.eu/knowledge4policy/sites/know4pol/files/france-ai-strategy-report.pdf; https://medium.com/politics-ai/an-overview-of-national-ai-strategies-2a70ec6edfd
   [134] https://www.aiforhumanity.fr/en/
   [135] https://ec.europa.eu/knowledge4policy/sites/know4pol/files/france-ai-strategy-report.pdf; https://www.gouvernement.fr/en/artificial-intelligence-making-france-a-leader
   [136] https://oecd.ai/dashboards/policy-initiatives?conceptUris=http:%2F%2Fkim.oecd.org%2FTaxonomy%2FGeographicalAreas%23France; https://ec.europa.eu/knowledge4policy/sites/know4pol/files/france-ai-strategy-report.pdf
   [137] https://ec.europa.eu/knowledge4policy/sites/know4pol/files/france-ai-strategy-report.pdf
   [138] https://ec.europa.eu/knowledge4policy/sites/know4pol/files/france-ai-strategy-report.pdf; https://www.gouvernement.fr/en/artificial-intelligence-making-france-a-leader
   [139] https://www.gouvernement.fr/en/artificial-intelligence-making-france-a-leader
   [140] https://www.japan.go.jp/abenomics/_userdata/abenomics/pdf/society_5.0.pdf
   [141] https://www.nedo.go.jp/content/100865202.pdf
   [142] https://www.soumu.go.jp/main_content/000507517.pdf
   [143] https://www.soumu.go.jp/main_content/000507517.pdf
   [144] https://oecd.ai/dashboards/policy-initiatives?conceptUris=http:%2F%2Fkim.oecd.org%2FTaxonomy%2FGeographicalAreas%23Japan
   [145] http://niti.gov.in/writereaddata/files/document_publication/NationalStrategy-for-AI-Discussion-Paper.pdf
   [146] http://niti.gov.in/writereaddata/files/document_publication/NationalStrategy-for-AI-Discussion-Paper.pdf
   [147] http://niti.gov.in/writereaddata/files/document_publication/NationalStrategy-for-AI-Discussion-Paper.pdf
   [148] http://niti.gov.in/writereaddata/files/document_publication/NationalStrategy-for-AI-Discussion-Paper.pdf
   [149] https://oecd.ai/dashboards/policy-initiatives?conceptUris=http:%2F%2Fkim.oecd.org%2FTaxonomy%2FGeographicalAreas%23India
   [150] https://www.cifar.ca/ai/pan-canadian-artificial-intelligence-strategy
   [151] https://www.cifar.ca/ai/pan-canadian-artificial-intelligence-strategy; https://www.cifar.ca/ai/ai-society
   [152] https://www.cifar.ca/ai/pan-canadian-artificial-intelligence-strategy
   [153] https://www.gouvernement.fr/en/launch-of-the-global-partnership-on-artificial-intelligence
   [154] https://www.canada.ca/en/government/system/digital-government/digital-government-innovations/responsible-use-ai.html
   [155] https://www2.deloitte.com/us/en/insights/focus/cognitive-technologies/ai-investment-by-country.html

156 https://www.industry.gov.au/data-and-publications/australias-tech-future ; https://www.computerworld.com.au/article/640926/budget-2018-government-seeks-boost-australian-ai-capabilities/

157 https://oecd.ai/dashboards/policy-initiatives?conceptUris=http:%2F%2Fkim.oecd.org%2FTaxonomy%2FGeographicalAreas%23Australia

158 https://www.industry.gov.au/innovation/Digital-Economy/Documents/Digital-Economy-Strategy-Consultation-Paper.pdf

159 https://consult.industry.gov.au/strategic-policy/artificial-intelligence-ethics-framework/supporting_documents/ArtificialIntelligenceethicsframeworkdiscussionpaper.pdf

160 https://www2.deloitte.com/us/en/insights/focus/cognitive-technologies/ai-investment-by-country.html

161 http://www.kremlin.ru/acts/bank/44731

162 http://www.kremlin.ru/acts/bank/44731

163 http://mil.ru/conferences/is-intellekt.htm

164 https://oecd.ai/dashboards/policy-initiatives?conceptUris=http:%2F%2Fkim.oecd.org%2FTaxonomy%2FGeographicalAreas%23RussianFederation

165 https://medium.com/syncedreview/south-korea-aims-high-on-ai-pumps-2-billion-into-r-d-de8e5c0c8ac5

166 https://www.theguardian.com/technology/2016/mar/15/googles-alphago-seals-4-1-victory-over-grandmaster-lee-sedol

167 https://futureoflife.org/ai-policy-south-korea/

168 https://medium.com/politics-ai/an-overview-of-national-ai-strategies-2a70ec6edfd; https://oecd.ai/dashboards/policy-initiatives?conceptUris=http:%2F%2Fkim.oecd.org%2FTaxonomy%2FGeographicalAreas%23SouthKorea

169 https://oecd.ai/dashboards/policy-initiatives?conceptUris=http:%2F%2Fkim.oecd.org%2FTaxonomy%2FGeographicalAreas%23SouthKorea

170 https://oecd.ai/dashboards

171 https://www.holoniq.com/notes/50-national-ai-strategies-the-2020-ai-strategy-landscape/; https://futureoflife.org/

172 https://oecd.ai/dashboards

173 https://oecd.ai/dashboards

174 https://oecd.ai/dashboards

175 https://oecd.ai/dashboards

176 https://oecd.ai/dashboards

177 https://oecd.ai/dashboards

178 https://www.gov.za/documents/presidential-commission-fourth-industrial-revolution-members-and-terms-reference-9-apr

179 https://miiafrica.org/; https://www.holoniq.com/notes/50-national-ai-strategies-the-2020-ai-strategy-landscape/

180 https://4irsa.org/

181 https://www.datasciencenigeria.org/

182 https://www.up.ac.za/media/shared/7/ZP_Files/ai-for-africa.zp165664.pdf

183 https://sites.tufts.edu/digitalplanet/files/2017/05/Digital_Planet_2017_FINAL.pdf

184 http://www.ict.go.ke/blockchain.pdf

185 https://e-estonia.com/

186 https://www.forbes.com/sites/charlestowersclark/2019/05/13/why-governments-should-be-

using-blockchain/#36336f077c3d

[187] https://youtu.be/6P-5PkzC2ZI; https://www.dubaifuture.gov.ae/our-initiatives/dubai-future-councils/

[188] https://www2.deloitte.com/us/en/insights/focus/cognitive-technologies/ai-investment-by-country.html

[189] https://www.brookings.edu/research/how-different-countries-view-artificial-intelligence/

[190] https://www.brookings.edu/research/how-different-countries-view-artificial-intelligence/

[191] https://www.brookings.edu/research/the-importance-and-opportunities-of-transatlantic-cooperation-on-ai/

9. The Debates, Progress and Likely Future Paths of AI

[1] https://futureoflife.org/

[2] Nick Bostrom, *Superintelligence: Paths, Dangers, Strategies.*

[3] Max Tegmark, *Life 3.0.*

[4] https://futureoflife.org/background/benefits-risks-of-artificial-intelligence/?cn-reloaded=1

[5] Max Tegmark, *Life 3.0.*

[6] https://www.theregister.com/2015/03/19/andrew_ng_baidu_ai/

[7] Stuart Russell, *Human Compatible: Artificial Intelligence and the Problem of Control.*

[8] https://www.nytimes.com/2017/09/01/opinion/artificial-intelligence-regulations-rules.html?ref=opinion

[9] Hans Moravec, *Mind Children: The Future of Robot and Human Intelligence*; Ray Kurzweil, *The Age of Spiritual Machines*; Ray Kurzweil, *The Singularity is Near: When Humans Transcend Biology.*

[10] Ray Kurzweil, *The Singularity is Near: When Humans Transcend Biology.*

[11] https://idlewords.com/talks/superintelligence.htm

[12] https://www.theatlantic.com/science/archive/2018/11/diminishing-returns-science/575665/

[13] https://fchollet.com/blog/the-singularity-is-not-coming.html

[14] https://medium.com/@francois.chollet/the-impossibility-of-intelligence-explosion-5be4a9eda6ec

[15] https://rodneybrooks.com/the-seven-deadly-sins-of-predicting-the-future-of-ai/

[16] https://rodneybrooks.com/the-seven-deadly-sins-of-predicting-the-future-of-ai/

[17] https://arstechnica.com/cars/2020/08/teslas-slow-self-driving-progress-continues-with-green-light-warning

[18] https://www.theringer.com/tech/2019/5/16/18625127/driverless-cars-mirage-uber-lyft-tesla-timeline-profitability;

[19] https://www.scaruffi.com/singular/download.pdf

[20] https://www.scaruffi.com/singular/download.pdf

[21] https://futureoflife.org/superintelligence-survey/?cn-reloaded=1; https://bigthink.com/surprising-science/computers-smart-as-humans-5-years?rebelltitem=1#rebelltitem1

[22] https://bigthink.com/surprising-science/computers-smart-as-humans-5-years?rebelltitem=1#rebelltitem1

[23] https://youtu.be/Me96OWd44q0

[24] https://youtu.be/_L3gNaAVjQ4

[25] https://spectrum.ieee.org/computing/software/humanlevel-ai-is-right-around-the-corner-or-hundreds-of-years-away

[26] https://aiimpacts.org/ai-timeline-surveys/

[27] https://rodneybrooks.com/agi-has-been-delayed/

28 http://book.mfordfuture.com/
29 Martin Ford, *Architects of Intelligence.*
30 Martin Ford, *Architects of Intelligence.*
31 Martin Ford, *Architects of Intelligence.*
32 https://www.zdnet.com/article/devils-in-the-details-in-bengio-marcus-ai-debate/
33 Martin Ford, *Architects of Intelligence.*
34 Martin Ford, *Architects of Intelligence.*
35 John Brockman, *Possible Minds: Twenty-five Ways of Looking at AI.*
36 Stuart Russell, *Human Compatible: Artificial Intelligence and the Problem of Control.*
37 https://en.wikipedia.org/wiki/Human_germline_engineering
38 Stuart Russell, *Human Compatible: Artificial Intelligence and the Problem of Control.*
39 Nick Bostrom, *Superintelligence: Paths, Dangers, Strategies.*
40 Martin Ford, *Architects of Intelligence.*
41 Gary Marcus and Ernest Davis, *Rebooting AI: Building Artificial Intelligence We Can Trust.*
42 https://deepmind.com/
43 https://deepmind.com/blog/article/alphafold-a-solution-to-a-50-year-old-grand-challenge-in-biology
44 Martin Ford, *Architects of Intelligence.*
45 Martin Ford, *Architects of Intelligence.*
46 Martin Ford, *Architects of Intelligence.*
47 Martin Ford, *Architects of Intelligence.*
48 Martin Ford, *Architects of Intelligence.*
49 Martin Ford, *Architects of Intelligence.*
50 Martin Ford, *Architects of Intelligence.*
51 https://www.youtube.com/watch?v=xqetKitv1Ko
52 https://www.youtube.com/watch?v=xqetKitv1Ko
53 https://www.youtube.com/watch?v=e3K5UxWRRuY
54 Judea Pearl, *Heuristics*, 1984; Judea Pearl, *Probability Reasoning*, 1988; Judea Pearl, *Causality*, 2009; Judea Pearl, *The Book of Why*, 2018.
55 Judea Pearl, *The Limitations of Opaque Learning Machines*, John Brockman, *Possible Minds: Twenty-five Ways of Looking at AI.*
56 Martin Ford, *Architects of Intelligence.*
57 https://www.affectiva.com/
58 Martin Ford, *Architects of Intelligence.*
59 https://www.marchcomms.com/blog/affectiva-ai-ethics/
60 Martin Ford, *Architects of Intelligence.*
61 Martin Ford, *Architects of Intelligence.*
62 Martin Ford, *Architects of Intelligence.*
63 Martin Ford, *Architects of Intelligence.*
64 https://www.elementalcognition.com/team
65 https://www.elementalcognition.com/challenge
66 Martin Ford, *Architects of Intelligence.*
67 Martin Ford, *Architects of Intelligence.*
68 Martin Ford, *Architects of Intelligence.*
69 https://medium.com/syncedreview/openai-founder-short-term-agi-is-a-serious-possibility-368424f7462f; https://www.ft.com/content/c96e43be-b4df-11e9-8cb2-799a3a8cf37b
70 https://en.wikipedia.org/wiki/OpenAI
71 https://www.ft.com/content/c96e43be-b4df-11e9-8cb2-799a3a8cf37b
72 https://arxiv.org/abs/2005.14165
73 https://www.ft.com/content/c96e43be-b4df-11e9-8cb2-799a3a8cf37b

[74] https://medium.com/syncedreview/openai-founder-short-term-agi-is-a-serious-possibility-368424f7462f

[75] https://www.ft.com/content/c96e43be-b4df-11e9-8cb2-799a3a8cf37b

[76] https://www.ft.com/content/c96e43be-b4df-11e9-8cb2-799a3a8cf37b

[77] https://www.ft.com/content/c96e43be-b4df-11e9-8cb2-799a3a8cf37b

[78] John Brockman, *Possible Minds: Twenty-five Ways of Looking at AI.*

[79] Seth Lloyd, *Wrong, but More Relevant than Ever*, an essay in John Brockman, *Possible Minds: Twenty-five Ways of Looking at AI.*

[80] Rodney Brooks, *The Inhuman Mess Our Machines Have Gotten Us Into*, an essay in John Brockman, *Possible Minds: Twenty-five Ways of Looking at AI.*

[81] George Dyson, *The Third Law*, an essay in John Brockman, *Possible Minds: Twenty-five Ways of Looking at AI.*

[82] Daniel C. Dennett, *What Can We Do?*, an essay in John Brockman, *Possible Minds: Twenty-five Ways of Looking at AI.*

[83] Max Tegmark, *Let's Aspire to More Than Making Ourselves Obsolete*, an essay in John Brockman, *Possible Minds: Twenty-five Ways of Looking at AI.*

[84] https://en.wikipedia.org/wiki/Jaan_Tallinn

[85] Jaan Tallinn, *Dissident Messages*, an essay in John Brockman, *Possible Minds: Twenty-five Ways of Looking at AI.*

[86] Jaan Tallinn, *Dissident Messages*, an essay in John Brockman, *Possible Minds: Twenty-five Ways of Looking at AI.*

[87] David Deutsch, *Beyond Reward and Punishment*, an essay in John Brockman, *Possible Minds: Twenty-five Ways of Looking at AI.*

[88] David Deutsch, *Beyond Reward and Punishment*, an essay in John Brockman, *Possible Minds: Twenty-five Ways of Looking at AI.*

[89] Tom Griffiths, *The Artificial Use of Human Beings*, an essay in John Brockman, *Possible Minds: Twenty-five Ways of Looking at AI.*

[90] Chris Anderson, *Gradient Descent*, an essay in John Brockman, *Possible Minds: Twenty-five Ways of Looking at AI*; https://en.wikipedia.org/wiki/Gradient_descent

[91] David Kaiser, *"Information" for Wiener, for Shannon and for Us*, an essay in John Brockman, *Possible Minds: Twenty-five Ways of Looking at AI.*

[92] Neil Gershenfeld, *Scaling*, an essay in John Brockman, *Possible Minds: Twenty-five Ways of Looking at AI.*

[93] W. Daniel Hillis, *The First Machine Intelligences*, an essay in John Brockman, *Possible Minds: Twenty-five Ways of Looking at AI.*

[94] W. Daniel Hillis, *The First Machine Intelligences*, an essay in John Brockman, *Possible Minds: Twenty-five Ways of Looking at AI.*

[95] Alex "Sandy" Pentland, *The Human Strategy*, an essay in John Brockman, *Possible Minds: Twenty-five Ways of Looking at AI.*

[96] Hans Ulrich Obrist, *Making the Invisible Visible: Art Meets AI*, an essay in John Brockman, *Possible Minds: Twenty-five Ways of Looking at AI.*

[97] Caroline A. Jones, *The Artistic Use of Cybernetic Beings: Art Meets AI*, an essay in John Brockman, *Possible Minds: Twenty-five Ways of Looking at AI.*

[98] Alison Gopnik, *AIs versus Four-Year-Olds*, an essay in John Brockman, *Possible Minds: Twenty-five Ways of Looking at AI.*

[99] Peter Galison, *Algorists Dream of Objectivity*, an essay in John Brockman, *Possible Minds: Twenty-five Ways of Looking at AI.*

[100] Stephen Wolfram, *Artificial Intelligence and the Future of Civilization*, an essay in John Brockman, *Possible Minds: Twenty-five Ways of Looking at AI.*

[101] Stephen Wolfram, *Artificial Intelligence and the Future of Civilization*, an essay in John

Brockman, *Possible Minds: Twenty-five Ways of Looking at AI.*

[102] https://en.wikipedia.org/wiki/Intelligence

[103] Shane Legg and Marcus Hutter. *A collection of definitions of intelligence, 2007.*

[104] https://arxiv.org/pdf/1911.01547.pdf

[105] Max Tegmark, *Life 3.0*; https://youtu.be/e3K5UxWRRuY

[106] https://youtu.be/e3K5UxWRRuY

[107] https://youtu.be/e3K5UxWRRuY

[108] https://www.youtube.com/watch?v=xqetKitv1Ko

[109] https://www.youtube.com/watch?v=xqetKitv1Ko

[110] https://www.youtube.com/watch?v=xqetKitv1Ko

[111] Frank Wilczek, *The Unity of Intelligence*, an essay in John Brockman, *Possible Minds: Twenty-five Ways of Looking at AI.*

[112] Frank Wilczek, *The Unity of Intelligence*, an essay in John Brockman, *Possible Minds: Twenty-five Ways of Looking at AI*

[113] Frank Wilczek, *The Unity of Intelligence*, an essay in John Brockman, *Possible Minds: Twenty-five Ways of Looking at AI*

[114] Frank Wilczek, *The Unity of Intelligence*, an essay in John Brockman, *Possible Minds: Twenty-five Ways of Looking at AI*

[115] Yuval Noah Harari, *Homo Deus.*

[116] https://www.youtube.com/watch?v=-EVqrDlAqYo&feature=youtu.be

[117] Lisa Feldman Barret, *How Emotions Are Made*; Lisa Feldman Barret; Lisa Feldman Barret, *Seven and a Half Lessons About the Brain.*

[118] Lisa Feldman Barret, *How Emotions Are Made.*

[119] Lisa Feldman Barret, *Seven and a Half Lessons About the Brain.*

[120] https://youtu.be/OheY9DIUie4

[121] https://youtu.be/OheY9DIUie4

[122] https://www.youtube.com/watch?v=-EVqrDlAqYo&feature=youtu.be

[123] https://numenta.com/

[124] https://www.youtube.com/watch?v=-EVqrDlAqYo&feature=youtu.be

[125] https://www.youtube.com/watch?v=uOA392B82qs

[126] https://www.youtube.com/watch?v=uOA392B82qs

[127] https://www.youtube.com/watch?v=uOA392B82qs

[128] https://www.youtube.com/watch?v=uOA392B82qs

[129] https://www.youtube.com/watch?v=uOA392B82qs

[130] https://www.youtube.com/watch?reload=9&v=6ufPpZDmPKA

[131] https://www.youtube.com/watch?v=-EVqrDlAqYo&feature=youtu.be

[132] https://singularityhub-com.cdn.ampproject.org/c/s/singularityhub.com/2017/03/22/is-the-brain-more-powerful-than-we-thought-here-comes-the-science/amp/

[133] http://www.physics.ucla.edu/~mayank/http://www.physics.ucla.edu/~mayank/

[134] https://futurism.com/we-just-created-an-artificial-synapse-that-can-learn-autonomously/; http://www.cnrs.fr/index.php; http://www2.cnrs.fr/en/2903.htm

[135] http://www.incompleteideas.net/IncIdeas/BitterLesson.html

[136] http://www.incompleteideas.net/IncIdeas/BitterLesson.html

[137] https://blog.keras.io/the-limitations-of-deep-learning.html

[138] Yann LeCun, *Self-supervised Learning*, https://drive.google.com/file/d/1r-mDL4IX_hzZLDBKp8_e8VZqD7fOzBkF/view

[139] Judea Pearl, *The Limitations of Opaque Learning Machines*, an essay in John Brockman, *Possible Minds: Twenty-five Ways of Looking at AI.*

[140] Gary Marcus and Ernest Davis, *Rebooting AI, Building Artificial Intelligence We Can Trust.*

[141] https://arxiv.org/ftp/arxiv/papers/1801/1801.00631.pdf

[142] https://arxiv.org/pdf/1703.07950.pdf

[143] https://arxiv.org/pdf/1703.07950.pdf

[144] https://www.darpa.mil/about-us/darpa-perspective-on-ai

[145] https://www.darpa.mil/about-us/darpa-perspective-on-ai

[146] https://www.meritalk.com/articles/darpas-third-wave-projects-push-limits-of-ais-smarts/; https://www.nationaldefensemagazine.org/articles/2019/7/2/algorithmic-warfare-darpas-ai-next-program-bearing-fruit

[147] https://www.meritalk.com/articles/darpas-third-wave-projects-push-limits-of-ais-smarts/

[148] https://medium.com/intuitionmachine/the-first-rule-of-agi-is-bc8725d21530

[149] https://medium.com/intuitionmachine/the-only-way-to-make-deep-learning-interpretable-is-to-have-it-explain-itself-1e874a73108f; https://medium.com/intuitionmachine/the-meta-model-and-meta-meta-model-of-deep-learning-10062f0bf74c; https://medium.com/intuitionmachine/biologically-inspired-software-architecture-for-deep-learning-e64db295bb2f

[150] http://medium.com/intuitionmachine/five-levels-of-capability-of-deep-learning-ai-4ac1d4a9f2be#.iks19awkh

[151] https://towardsdatascience.com/overview-state-of-the-art-machine-learning-algorithms-per-discipline-per-task-c1a16a66b8bb

[152] http://arxiv.org/abs/2003.08237; https://towardsdatascience.com/state-of-the-art-image-classification-algorithm-fixefficientnet-l2-98b93deeb04c

[153] https://arxiv.org/pdf/1912.11370v3.pdf; https://arxiv.org/pdf/2007.03347v2.pdf; https://arxiv.org/pdf/2001.09136v4.pdf

[154] https://arxiv.org/abs/1911.09070

[155] https://arxiv.org/pdf/2008.06439v1.pdf; https://arxiv.org/pdf/1910.04093v1.pdf; https://arxiv.org/pdf/2005.05708v1.pdf

[156] http://arxiv.org/abs/2005.10821

[157] https://arxiv.org/abs/2005.10821

[158] https://arxiv.org/pdf/2005.09629v1.pdf

[159] https://arxiv.org/pdf/1811.07453v2.pdf; https://arxiv.org/pdf/1703.02136v1.pdf; https://arxiv.org/pdf/2006.11477v2.pdf

[160] https://arxiv.org/pdf/1905.01395v1.pdf

[161] https://arxiv.org/pdf/1905.01395v1.pdf; https://arxiv.org/pdf/1911.00936v1.pdf; https://arxiv.org/pdf/1905.03375v1.pdf

[162] https://en.wikipedia.org/wiki/Sentiment_analysis

[163] https://arxiv.org/pdf/1810.04805.pdf

[164] https://towardsdatascience.com/bert-explained-state-of-the-art-language-model-for-nlp-f8b21a9b6270

[165] https://paperswithcode.com/paper/sentiment-classification-using-document; https://arxiv.org/pdf/1910.10683v3.pdf

[166] https://arxiv.org/pdf/1909.08053v4.pdf; https://openai.com/blog/better-language-models/

[167] https://arxiv.org/pdf/1909.08053v4.pdf

[168] https://arxiv.org/pdf/1909.08053v4.pdf

[169] https://arxiv.org/pdf/2005.14165v4.pdf

[170] https://arxiv.org/pdf/2005.14165v4.pdf

[171] https://arxiv.org/pdf/2005.14165v4.pdf

[172] https://arxiv.org/abs/1706.03762

[173] https://towardsdatascience.com/transformers-141e32e69591

[174] https://arxiv.org/pdf/1606.02891v2.pdf; https://openreview.net/pdf?id=HyGhN2A5tm; https://arxiv.org/pdf/2003.03977v1.pdf

[175] https://arxiv.org/pdf/1906.08237v2.pdf

[176] https://arxiv.org/pdf/1906.08237v2.pdf

[177] https://arxiv.org/pdf/1906.08237v2.pdf; https://arxiv.org/pdf/1902.07153v2.pdf

[178] https://en.wikipedia.org/wiki/Question_answering

[179] https://arxiv.org/pdf/1911.04118v2.pdf

[180] https://arxiv.org/pdf/1910.10683v3.pdf

[181] https://arxiv.org/pdf/1910.10683v3.pdf

[182] https://arxiv.org/abs/1406.2661

[183] https://en.wikipedia.org/wiki/Generative_adversarial_network

[184] https://machinelearningmastery.com/impressive-applications-of-generative-adversarial-networks/

[185] https://cloud.google.com/automl; https://docs.microsoft.com/en-us/azure/machine-learning/concept-automated-ml; https://en.wikipedia.org/wiki/Automated_machine_learning

[186] https://arxiv.org/abs/1707.07012

[187] https://arxiv.org/abs/1707.07012; https://sh-tsang.medium.com/review-nasnet-neural-architecture-search-network-image-classification-23139ea0425d

[188] https://arxiv.org/pdf/1707.07012.pdf

[189] https://arxiv.org/pdf/1602.05629v3.pdf

[190] https://arxiv.org/pdf/1602.05629v3.pdf

[191] https://www.scaruffi.com/singular/download.pdf

[192] François Chollet, *On the Measure of Intelligence*, https://arxiv.org/abs/1911.01547.

[193] Shane Legg, Marcus Hutter, *Universal Intelligence: A Definition of Machine Intelligence*, https://arxiv.org/abs/0712.3329.

[194] François Chollet, *On the Measure of Intelligence*, https://arxiv.org/abs/1911.01547.

[195] François Chollet, *On the Measure of Intelligence*, https://arxiv.org/abs/1911.01547; https://github.com/fchollet/ARC

[196] https://en.wikipedia.org/wiki/Fluid_and_crystallized_intelligence;

[197] François Chollet, *On the Measure of Intelligence*, https://arxiv.org/abs/1911.01547.; http://citeseerx.ist.psu.edu/viewdoc/download?doi=10.1.1.14.929&rep=rep1&type=pdf

[198] https://arxiv.org/pdf/1911.01547.pdf

[199] https://arxiv.org/pdf/1911.01547.pdf

[200] https://blog.keras.io/the-future-of-deep-learning.html

[201] https://www.nature.com/articles/nature24270.epdf

[202] https://blog.keras.io/the-future-of-deep-learning.html

[203] https://www.youtube.com/watch?v=OheY9DIUie4; https://www.youtube.com/watch?v=e3K5UxWRRuY

[204] https://www.youtube.com/watch?v=9Kgk4s7yG1c; https://www.youtube.com/watch?v=rAQ-0wTavfM

[205] https://venturebeat.com/2020/05/02/yann-lecun-and-yoshua-bengio-self-supervised-learning-is-the-key-to-human-level-intelligence/

[206] https://www.forbes.com/sites/robtoews/2020/10/12/the-next-generation-of-artificial-intelligence/?sh=7ff35dfe59eb

[207] Yann LeCun, *Self-supervised Learning*, https://drive.google.com/file/d/1r-mDL4IX_hzZLDBKp8_e8VZqD7fOzBkF/view

[208] http://yann.lecun.com/exdb/publis/pdf/lecun-06.pdf

[209] https://openai.com/blog/energy-based-models/

[210] https://medium.com/@mattia.cd.ferrini/compositional-deep-learning-a40a07351c37

[211] https://papers.nips.cc/paper/2018/hash/310ce61c90f3a46e340ee8257bc70e93-Abstract.html

[212] https://arxiv.org/pdf/1609.05518.pdf

[213] https://www.sciencedirect.com/science/article/pii/S2352154618301943?via%3Dihub

[214] https://arxiv.org/pdf/1808.05377.pdf

215 https://medium.com/@mattia.cd.ferrini/compositional-deep-learning-a40a07351c37
216 https://www.microsoft.com/en-us/research/blog/learning-local-and-compositional-representations-for-zero-shot-learning/
217 https://openaccess.thecvf.com/content_ICCV_2019/papers/Tokmakov_Learning_Compositional_Representations_for_Few-Shot_Recognition_ICCV_2019_paper.pdf
218 https://arxiv.org/abs/2007.12407
219 https://arxiv.org/ftp/arxiv/papers/2002/2002.06177.pdf
220 https://www.cyc.com/the-cyc-platform
221 https://arxiv.org/ftp/arxiv/papers/2002/2002.06177.pdf
222 https://arxiv.org/ftp/arxiv/papers/2002/2002.06177.pdf
223 https://www.technologyreview.com/2020/11/03/1011616/ai-godfather-geoffrey-hinton-deep-learning-will-do-everything/
224 https://arxiv.org/pdf/1906.06818.pdf
225 https://arxiv.org/pdf/1906.06818.pdf
226 https://venturebeat.com/2020/05/02/yann-lecun-and-yoshua-bengio-self-supervised-learning-is-the-key-to-human-level-intelligence/
227 Daniel Kahneman, *Thinking, Fast and Slow*.
228 https://arxiv.org/pdf/1709.08568.pdf
229 https://arxiv.org/pdf/2009.00418.pdf
230 https://www.cio.com/article/3236030/artificial-intelligence-is-about-machine-reasoning-or-when-machine-learning-is-just-a-fancy-plugin.html;
231 https://arxiv.org/pdf/2009.00418.pdf
232 https://journals.sagepub.com/doi/pdf/10.1177/2372732215622029
233 https://arxiv.org/pdf/1706.01427.pdf
234 https://arxiv.org/pdf/1706.01427.pdf
235 https://arxiv.org/pdf/2012.08508.pdf
236 https://arxiv.org/pdf/2012.08508.pdf
237 https://www.technologyreview.com/2020/07/17/1005415/a-concept-in-psychology-is-helping-ai-to-better-navigate-our-world/
238 https://arxiv.org/pdf/2006.15085.pdf
239 https://www.youtube.com/watch?v=Me96OWd44qo
240 https://arxiv.org/ftp/arxiv/papers/2005/2005.04305.pdf
241 https://www.youtube.com/watch?v=Me96OWd44qo
242 https://youtu.be/fm_cLfta_pU?t=975
243 https://futureoflife.org/data/documents/research_priorities.pdf?x96845
244 https://futureoflife.org/data/documents/research_priorities.pdf?x96845
245 https://futureoflife.org/data/documents/research_priorities.pdf?x96845
246 Stuart Russell, *Human Compatible: Artificial Intelligence and the Problem of Control*.

10. Beneficial Outcomes for Humanity in the Smart Technology Era

1 https://en.wikipedia.org/wiki/Maslow%27s_hierarchy_of_needs
2 https://www.simplypsychology.org/maslow.html
3 Victor Frankl, *Man's Search For Meaning: An Introduction to Logotherapy*.
4 https://www.beliefnet.com/prayers/protestant/addiction/serenity-prayer.aspx
5 Victor Frankl, *Man's Search For Meaning: An Introduction to Logotherapy*.
6 Stephen Leach & James Tartaglia (editors), *The Meaning of Life and the Great Philosophers 1st Edition*; https://www.amazon.com/Meaning-Life-Great-Philosophers/dp/1138220957

7 https://iep.utm.edu/

8 https://aeon.co/ideas/philosophers-should-be-keener-to-talk-about-the-meaning-of-life

9 https://iep.utm.edu/daoism/

10 https://iep.utm.edu/confuciu/; https://iep.utm.edu/mozi/; https://iep.utm.edu/gorgias/

11 https://iep.utm.edu/plato/

12 https://iep.utm.edu/epicur/

13 https://iep.utm.edu/aristotl/

14 https://iep.utm.edu/marcus/

15 https://iep.utm.edu/descarte/

16 https://iep.utm.edu/locke/

17 https://iep.utm.edu/kantview/#H1

18 https://iep.utm.edu/nietzsch/

19 https://iep.utm.edu/james-o/

20 https://iep.utm.edu/heidegge/

21 https://iep.utm.edu/camus/

22 https://excellencereporter.com/exclusive-interviews-on-the-meaning-of-life/

23 https://civilizationemerging.com/how-to-live-a-meaningful-life/

24 https://civilizationemerging.com/how-to-live-a-meaningful-life/

25 https://www.youtube.com/c/lexfridman/videos

26 https://youtu.be/cMscNuSUy0I

27 https://youtu.be/epQxfSp-rdU

28 https://youtu.be/epQxfSp-rdU

29 https://youtu.be/LW59lMvxmY4

30 https://youtu.be/Ktjo50DxG7Q

31 https://youtu.be/SOr1YYRljV8

32 https://youtu.be/pDSEjaDCtOU

33 https://youtu.be/aB8zcAttP1E

34 https://youtu.be/M95m2EFb7IQ

35 https://youtu.be/L-RuvUkcyJI

36 https://youtu.be/uX5t8EivCaM

37 https://youtu.be/_AGPbvCDBCk

38 https://youtu.be/yTWa-Z1UQwU

39 https://youtu.be/U_6AYX42gkU

40 https://youtu.be/-jA2ABHBc6Y

41 https://youtu.be/tg_m_LxxRwM

42 https://youtu.be/iqBh7G4uDR8

43 https://youtu.be/A22Ej6kb2wo

44 https://youtu.be/WxfA1OSev4c

45 https://youtu.be/P6prRXkI5HM

46 https://youtu.be/ICj8p5jPd3Y

47 https://youtu.be/c9AbECvRt2o

48 https://youtu.be/3qMemn__kK8

49 https://youtu.be/brslF-Cy3HU

50 https://youtu.be/bgNzUxyS-kQ

51 https://youtu.be/NOReE-3EBhI

52 https://youtu.be/nWTvXbQHwWs

53 https://youtu.be/NbdRIVCBqNI

54 https://youtu.be/BIk1zUy8ehU

55 https://youtu.be/FKCJWkPehdY

56 https://youtu.be/PUAdj3w3wO4

57 https://youtu.be/qfKyNxfyWbo
58 https://youtu.be/kxi-_TT_-Nc
59 https://youtu.be/naed4C4hfAg
60 https://youtu.be/P-2P3MSZrBM
61 https://en.wikipedia.org/wiki/Entropy_and_life#Negative_entropy;
https://en.wikipedia.org/wiki/Gibbs_free_energy;
62 https://youtu.be/P-2P3MSZrBM
63 https://youtu.be/NwzuibY5kUs
64 https://en.wikipedia.org/wiki/Free_energy_principle#
65 https://en.wikipedia.org/wiki/Free_energy_principle#
66 https://youtu.be/NwzuibY5kUs
67 https://youtu.be/HhY95m-WD_E
68 https://youtu.be/13CZPWmke6A
69 https://youtu.be/xlMTWfkQqbY
70 https://youtu.be/60KJz1BVTyU
71 https://youtu.be/CwyOUS8TSlo
72 https://youtu.be/ez773teNFYA
73 https://youtu.be/5f-JlzBuUUU
74 https://youtu.be/uPUEq8d73JI
75 https://youtu.be/_TTNGq9djU4
76 James Carse, *Finite and Infinite Games: A Vision of Life as Play and Possibility,*
77 https://smct.org.au/blog/the-dash-by-linda-ellis
78 https://youtu.be/_TTNGq9djU4
79 https://www.linkedin.com/in/danielschmachtenberger/; https://civilizationemerging.com/
80 https://civilizationemerging.com/catastrophic-and-existential-risk/
81 https://civilizationemerging.com/; Rebel Wisdom:
https://www.youtube.com/channel/UCR85PW_B_7_Aisx5vNS7Gjw; The Portal:
https://www.youtube.com/channel/UCFQ6Gptuq-sLflbJ4YY3Umw; Modern Wisdom:
https://www.youtube.com/channel/UCIaH-gZIVC432YRjNVvnyCA; Tom Bilyeau:
thttps://www.youtube.com/channel/UCnYMOamNKLGVlJgRUbamveA; The Seeking:
https://www.youtube.com/channel/UCSZF0YOWeee_RTx-SZL7U2w; Neurohacker:
https://www.youtube.com/channel/UCv9hjmC-M77u3E8lUuO1-nQ; Future Thinkers:
https://www.youtube.com/channel/UCqKnDDavIqBKZuvgQtYAJsA; The Nantucket Project:
https://www.youtube.com/channel/UChYTzcMxdNAwWFLpx6jIFug; Foresight Institute:
https://www.youtube.com/channel/UCg5UVUMqXeCQo3MelT_RXMg; Max Hug:
https://www.youtube.com/channel/UCMrn6U9ZY6_yMzg7OObvogw
82 https://www.youtube.com/watch?v=Xhrr-fJCTWY
83 https://civilizationemerging.com/catastrophic-and-existential-risk/
84 https://youtu.be/IqLELspOa7g
85 https://youtu.be/IqLELspOa7g
86 https://www.youtube.com/watch?v=Xhrr-fJCTWY
87 https://www.youtube.com/watch?v=Xhrr-fJCTWY
88 https://youtu.be/ya_p4RIorXw
89 https://youtu.be/ya_p4RIorXw
90 https://www.brainyquote.com/quotes/thomas_jefferson_136269
91 https://docs.google.com/document/d/1gD30djiG8K5pi1lZF8-RfV9vaYtXz5232QDm9sdUKdU/edit
92 https://en.wikipedia.org/wiki/Consilience#
93 https://www.civilizationresearchinstitute.org/our-projects
94 Citizenship in a networked age: an agenda for rebuilding our civic ideals | University of Oxford

95 (PDF) Citizenship in a Networked Age: An Agenda for Rebuilding Our Civic Ideals | Michael J Reiss and Dominic Burbidge - Academia.edu

96 https://www.youtube.com/watch?v=5chp-PRYq-w

97 https://www.youtube.com/watch?v=5chp-PRYq-w

98 https://www.youtube.com/watch?v=5chp-PRYq-w

99 https://www.youtube.com/watch?v=nM9f0W2KD5s&feature=youtu.be

100 https://www.youtube.com/watch?v=nM9f0W2KD5s&feature=youtu.be

101 https://www.youtube.com/watch?v=nM9f0W2KD5s&feature=youtu.be

102 https://www.youtube.com/watch?v=nM9f0W2KD5s&feature=youtu.be

103 https://www.youtube.com/watch?v=nM9f0W2KD5s&feature=youtu.be

104 https://theportal.wiki/wiki/The_Distributed_Idea_Suppression_Complex_(The_DISC) .

105 https://www.youtube.com/watch?v=nM9f0W2KD5s&feature=youtu.be

106 https://www.youtube.com/watch?v=QX3M8Ka9vUA&feature=youtu.be

107 https://www.youtube.com/watch?v=QX3M8Ka9vUA&feature=youtu.be

108 Yuval Harari, *Homo Deus*, pg. 243

109 Yuval Harari, *Homo Deus*, pg. 244-245

110 https://www.youtube.com/watch?v=xyS94qpsf4A&feature=youtu.be

111 https://www.youtube.com/watch?v=xyS94qpsf4A&feature=youtu.be

112 https://www.youtube.com/watch?v=UDvCqeXCI-0&feature=youtu.be

113 https://www.youtube.com/watch?v=UDvCqeXCI-0&feature=youtu.be

114 Richard Baldwin, *The Globotics Upheaval: Globalization, Robotics and The Future of Work.*

115 https://www.youtube.com/watch?v=UDvCqeXCI-0&feature=youtu.be

116 https://www.youtube.com/watch?v=UDvCqeXCI-0&feature=youtu.be

117 https://www.youtube.com/watch?v=UDvCqeXCI-0&feature=youtu.be

118 Richard Baldwin, *The Globotics Upheaval: Globalization, Robotics, and the Future of Work*, pg. 98 – 99; https://en.wikipedia.org/wiki/Metcalfe%27s_law

119 https://www.youtube.com/watch?v=UDvCqeXCI-0&feature=youtu.be

120 Richard Baldwin, *The Globotics Upheaval: Globalization, Robotics and the Future of Work*, pg. 98 – 100.

121 https://qz.com/on/fixing-capitalism/

122 https://qz.com/1909715/the-difference-between-stakeholder-and-shareholder-capitalism/

123 https://fortune.com/2020/10/27/ray-dalio-china-capitalism-economic-opportunity/

124 https://www.linkedin.com/pulse/why-how-capitalism-needs-reformed-parts-1-2-ray-dalio/; https://corpgov.law.harvard.edu/2020/10/13/why-and-how-capitalism-needs-to-be-reformed/

125 https://www.linkedin.com/pulse/why-how-capitalism-needs-reformed-parts-1-2-ray-dalio/;

126 https://www.linkedin.com/pulse/why-how-capitalism-needs-reformed-parts-1-2-ray-dalio/

127 Eric A. Posner and E. Glen Weyl, *Radical Markets: Uprooting Capitalism and Democracy for a Just Society.*

128 Eric A. Posner and E. Glen Weyl, *Radical Markets: Uprooting Capitalism and Democracy for a Just Society.*

129 https://medium.com/@ryanavent_93844/a-brief-ish-review-of-radical-markets-6454ba0637a8

130 Michael J. Sandel, *The Tyranny of Merit: What Becomes of the Common Good?*

131 https://www.econlib.org/library/Enc/bios/Hayek.html; https://plato.stanford.edu/entries/rawls/

132 Michael J. Sandel, *The Tyranny of Merit: What Becomes of the Common Good?*

133 Max Borders, *The Social Singularity - A Decentralist Manifesto.*

134 https://social-evolution.com/

135 https://holochain.org/#pageTop

136 https://applyingresilience.org/en/principle-7 .

137 https://en.wikipedia.org/wiki/Polyarchy

138 https://brightshinyobjects.net/2020/05/26/we-shape-our-tools-and-thereafter-our-tools-shape-us/ ; https://medium.com/thethursdaythought/we-shape-our-tools-and-thereafter-our-tools-shape-us-marshall-mcluhan-5c304e55909c

139 Max Borders, *The Social Singularity - A Decentralist Manifesto*; https://social-evolution.com/

140 https://www.routledgehandbooks.com/doi/10.4324/9781315682266.ch2

141 https://positivepsychology.com/classification-character-strengths-virtues/

142 https://centerofinquiry.org/uncategorized/ryff-scales-of-psychological-well-being/

143 https://www.researchgate.net/publication/305491629_Is_Autonomy_a_Universal_Value_of_Human_Existence_Scope_of_Autonomy_in_Medical_Practice_A_Comparative_Study_between_Western_Medical_Ethics_and_Islamic_Medical_Ethics

144 https://www.researchgate.net/publication/328315213_Eudaimonia_versus_Hedonia_What_Is_the_Difference_And_Is_It_Real

145 https://mappalicious.com/2016/06/19/feel-good-vs-feel-purpose-hedonia-and-eudaimonia-as-separate-but-connected-pathways-to-happiness/

146 https://mappalicious.com/2016/06/19/feel-good-vs-feel-purpose-hedonia-and-eudaimonia-as-separate-but-connected-pathways-to-happiness/

147 https://www.researchgate.net/publication/328315213_Eudaimonia_versus_Hedonia_What_Is_the_Difference_And_Is_It_Real

148 https://www.lesswrong.com/posts/K4aGvLnHvYgX9pZHS/the-fun-theory-sequence; https://www.lesswrong.com/posts/qZJBighPrnv9bSqTZ/31-laws-of-fun

149 https://www.lesswrong.com/posts/JynJ6xfnpq9oN3zpb/inseparably-right-or-joy-in-the-merely-good

150 https://wiki.lesswrong.com/wiki/Complexity_of_value?_ga=2.218385049.1086135878.1610305147-803325130.1609658484

151 https://www.lesswrong.com/posts/GNnHHmm8EzePmKzPk/value-is-fragile

152 https://wiki.lesswrong.com/wiki/Friendly_artificial_intelligence?_ga=2.208462482.1086135878.1610305147-803325130.1609658484

153 https://www.lesswrong.com/posts/qZJBighPrnv9bSqTZ/31-laws-of-fun

154 https://en.wikipedia.org/wiki/Dunbar%27s_number .

155 https://www.lesswrong.com/posts/qZJBighPrnv9bSqTZ/31-laws-of-fun

156 Max Tegmark, *Life 3.0: Being Human in the Age of Artificial Intelligence*.

157 Calum Chace, *The Economic Singularity: Artificial Intelligence and the Death of Capitalism*.

158 Calum Chace, *The Economic Singularity: Artificial Intelligence and the Death of Capitalism*.

159 Yuval Harari, *Sapiens: A Brief History of Humankind*.

160 Kevin Kelly, *The Inevitable: Understanding the 12 Technological Forces that will Shape our Future*.

161 Kevin Kelly, *The Inevitable: Understanding the 12 Technological Forces that will Shape our Future*.

162 Calum Chace, *The Economic Singularity: Artificial Intelligence and the Death of Capitalism*.

163 https://marinebio.org/the-shift-to-biosphere-consciousness/

164 https://www.effectivealtruism.org/articles/ea-global-2018-paretotopian-goal-alignment/

165 https://www.effectivealtruism.org/articles/ea-global-2018-paretotopian-goal-alignment/

166 https://www.nickbostrom.com/papers/future.html

167 https://www.nickbostrom.com/papers/future.html

[168] https://www.nickbostrom.com/papers/future.html

[169] https://youtu.be/rfKiTGj-zeQ

[170] Max Tegmark, *Life 3.0: Being Human in the Age of Artificial Intelligence*.

[171] Max Tegmark, *Life 3.0: Being Human in the Age of Artificial Intelligence*.

[172] Max Tegmark, *Life 3.0: Being Human in the Age of Artificial Intelligence*.

[173] https://youtu.be/fm_cLfta_pU

[174] Hugo de Garis, *The Artilect War: Cosmists Vs. Terrans: A Bitter Controversy Concerning Whether Humanity Should Build Godlike Massively Intelligent Machines*.

[175] https://youtu.be/fm_cLfta_pU; Hugo de Garis, *The Artilect War: Cosmists Vs. Terrans: A Bitter Controversy Concerning Whether Humanity Should Build Godlike Massively Intelligent Machines*.

[176] https://futureoflife.org/superintelligence-survey/?cn-reloaded=1

[177] https://futureoflife.org/superintelligence-survey/?cn-reloaded=1

[178] Max Tegmark, *Life 3.0: Being Human in the Age of Artificial Intelligence*.

[179] https://medium.com/a-passion-to-evolve/only-6-possible-outcomes-in-next-20-years-76f385f7a082

[180] https://io9.gizmodo.com/7-best-case-scenarios-for-the-future-of-humanity-5958479

[181] https://en.wikipedia.org/wiki/Kardashev_scale#

[182] https://io9.gizmodo.com/7-best-case-scenarios-for-the-future-of-humanity-5958479

[183] Mark Manson, *Everything is F*cked*, pg. 16 - 18

[184] Mark Manson, *Everything is F*cked*, pg. 18

[185] Mark Manson, *Everything is F*cked*, pg. 19

[186] Mark Manson, *Everything is F*cked*, pg. 19

[187] Yuval Noah Harari, *Homo Deus*, pg. 182-214

[188] https://singularityhub.com/2016/11/08/the-motivating-power-of-a-massive-transformative-purpose/

[189] https://singularityhub.com/2016/11/08/the-motivating-power-of-a-massive-transformative-purpose/

[190] https://positivepsychology.com/classification-character-strengths-virtues/

[191] https://link.springer.com/article/10.1057/hep.1993.58

[192] https://sdgs.un.org/2030agenda

[193] https://sdgs.un.org/2030agenda

[194] https://sdgs.un.org/2030agenda

[195] https://link.springer.com/article/10.1007/s10784-020-09487-3

[196] https://link.springer.com/article/10.1007/s10784-020-09487-3

[197] https://link.springer.com/article/10.1007/s10784-020-09487-3

[198] https://link.springer.com/article/10.1007/s10784-020-09487-3

[199] https://sdgs.un.org/2030agenda

[200] https://www.weforum.org/projects/frontier-2030#

[201] https://www.theguardian.com/inequality/2017/nov/14/worlds-richest-wealth-credit-suisse

[202] Geoffrey West, *Scale: The Universal Laws of Life, Growth, and Death in Organisms, Cities, and Companies*.

[203] Geoffrey West, *Scale: The Universal Laws of Life, Growth, and Death in Organisms, Cities, and Companies*.

[204] https://youtu.be/OheY9DIUie4

[205] https://www.youtube.com/watch?v=OheY9DIUie4; https://www.youtube.com/watch?v=e3K5UxWRRuY

[206] https://vimeo.com/213989519; http://trent.st/content/20170401%20convoco%20mcconaghy.pdf

[207] https://vimeo.com/213989519;

http://trent.st/content/20170401%20convoco%20mcconaghy.pdf

[208] https://medium.com/@trentmc0/the-bandwidth-scenario-d3bfd8f29e2d

[209] https://medium.com/@trentmc0/the-bandwidth-scenario-d3bfd8f29e2d

[210] https://vimeo.com/213989519

11. Democratizing AI to Help Shape a Beneficial Human-centric Future

[1] https://www.pewresearch.org/internet/2018/12/10/artificial-intelligence-and-the-future-of-humans/

[2] https://www.mckinsey.com/~/media/mckinsey/featured%20insights/artificial%20intelligence/applying%20artificial%20intelligence%20for%20social%20good/mgi-applying-ai-for-social-good-discussion-paper-dec-2018.ashx

[3] https://www.mckinsey.com/~/media/mckinsey/featured%20insights/artificial%20intelligence/applying%20artificial%20intelligence%20for%20social%20good/mgi-applying-ai-for-social-good-discussion-paper-dec-2018.ashx

[4] https://www.mckinsey.com/~/media/mckinsey/featured%20insights/artificial%20intelligence/applying%20artificial%20intelligence%20for%20social%20good/mgi-applying-ai-for-social-good-discussion-paper-dec-2018.ashx

[5] https://img1.wsimg.com/blobby/go/3d82daa4-97fe-4096-9c6b-376b92c619de/downloads/MaliciousUseofAI.pdf?ver=1553030594217

[6] https://www.bbc.com/future/article/20201014-totalitarian-world-in-chains-artificial-intelligence

[7] https://www.britannica.com/topic/totalitarianism

[8] https://www.bbc.com/future/article/20201014-totalitarian-world-in-chains-artificial-intelligence

[9] http://bigdata-madesimple.com/the-future-of-artificial-intelligence-6-ways-it-will-impact-everyday-life/

[10] http://ai100.stanford.edu/

[11] https://www.datarobot.com/blog/democratizing-ai-transforming-your-operating-model-to-support-ai-adoption/

[12] https://cloud.google.com/automl; https://www.datarobot.com/wp-content/uploads/2020/05/DataRobot_Best_Practices_for_Democratizing_AI_White_Paper_v.2.0.pdf

[13] https://www.strategy-business.com/article/Democratizing-artificial-intelligence-is-a-double-edged-sword?gko=ffdcd

[14] https://www.strategy-business.com/article/Democratizing-artificial-intelligence-is-a-double-edged-sword?gko=ffdcd

[15] https://www.strategy-business.com/article/Democratizing-artificial-intelligence-is-a-double-edged-sword?gko=ffdcd

[16] https://blog.keras.io/on-the-importance-of-democratizing-artificial-intelligence.html

[17] https://blog.keras.io/on-the-importance-of-democratizing-artificial-intelligence.html

[18] https://blog.keras.io/on-the-importance-of-democratizing-artificial-intelligence.html

[19] François Chollet (@fchollet) | Twitter

[20] https://scikit-learn.org/stable/

[21] https://en.wikipedia.org/wiki/Keras

[22] https://autokeras.com/

[23] https://www.tensorflow.org/; https://github.com/tensorflow/tensorflow

[24] https://pytorch.org/

[25] https://blog.keras.io/on-the-importance-of-democratizing-artificial-intelligence.html

[26] https://mlsquare.org/

[27] https://arxiv.org/pdf/2001.00818.pdf

[28] https://onnx.ai/; https://www.kdnuggets.com/faq/pmml.html

[29] https://en.wikipedia.org/wiki/Conjunctive_normal_form

[30] https://arxiv.org/pdf/2001.00818.pdf

[31] https://arxiv.org/pdf/2001.00818.pdf

[32] https://arxiv.org/pdf/2001.00818.pdf

[33] Simon Sinek, *Start with Why: How Great Leaders Inspire Everyone Around Them to Take Action*, pg. 11.

[34] Brad Shorkend and Andy Golding, *We are Still Human and Work Shouldn't Suck*, pg. 143 – 146.

[35] Simon Sinek, *Start with Why: How Great Leaders Inspire Everyone Around Them to Take Action*.

[36] Brad Shorkend and Andy Golding, *We are Still Human and Work Shouldn't Suck*.

[37] https://hbr.org/2019/07/how-to-do-strategic-planning-like-a-futurist

[38] https://hbr.org/2019/07/how-to-do-strategic-planning-like-a-futurist

[39] https://hbr.org/2019/07/how-to-do-strategic-planning-like-a-futurist

[40] https://hbr.org/2019/07/how-to-do-strategic-planning-like-a-futurist

[41] https://hbr.org/2019/07/how-to-do-strategic-planning-like-a-futurist

[42] https://hbr.org/2019/07/how-to-do-strategic-planning-like-a-futurist

[43] https://fortune.com/2019/11/19/artificial-intelligence-will-obliterate-these-jobs-by-2030/amp/

[44] https://ai100.stanford.edu/sites/g/files/sbiybj9861/f/ai100report10032016fnl_singles.pdf

[45] https://www.nature.com/articles/s41467-020-15871-z

[46] https://www.nature.com/articles/s41467-020-15871-z

[47] https://www.nature.com/articles/s41467-020-15871-z

[48] https://link.springer.com/article/10.1007/s11948-020-00213-5

[49] https://link.springer.com/article/10.1007/s11948-020-00213-5

[50] https://link.springer.com/article/10.1007/s11948-020-00213-5

[51] https://doi.org/10.1162/99608f92.8cd550d1

[52] Yuval Harari, *Homo Deus*.

[53] http://www3.weforum.org/docs/WEF_Leading_through_the_Fourth_Industrial_Revolution.pdf

[54] https://www.mas.gov.sg/~/media/MAS/News%20and%20Publications/Monographs%20and%20Information%20Papers/FEAT%20Principles%20Final.pdf

[55] https://ec.europa.eu/futurium/en/ai-alliance-consultation

[56] https://ec.europa.eu/futurium/en/ai-alliance-consultation/guidelines/1#Human%20agency

[57] https://europa.eu/european-union/sites/europaeu/files/docs/body/treaty_establishing_a_constitution_for_europe_en.pdf

[58] https://www.chinalawtranslate.com/en/socialcreditsystem/

[59] https://www.oecd.org/going-digital/ai/principles/

[60] https://www2.deloitte.com/nl/nl/pages/innovatie/artikelen/frr-quality-mark-for-robotics-and-artificial-intelligence.html

[61] https://www.iso.org/committee/6794475.html

[62] https://ec.europa.eu/commission/priorities/justice-and-fundamental-rights/data-protection/2018-reform-eu-data-protection-rules_en

63 https://www.csis.org/analysis/data-governance-principles-global-digital-economy

64 https://www.csis.org/analysis/data-governance-principles-global-digital-economy

65 Yuval Harari, *Homo Deus*, pg. 250 - 255

66 Yuval Harari, *Homo Deus*, pg. 265 - 276

67 Yuval Harari, *Homo Deus*, pg. 279 - 280

68 Tomasello, *A Natural History of Human Morality*, pg. 115.

69 Mark Manson, *Everything is F*cked*, pg. 72.

70 http://www.bbc.com/future/story/20170118-how-east-and-west-think-in-profoundly-different-ways

71 https://www.ft.com/content/6c8854de-ac59-11e9-8030-530adfa879c2

72 https://AIHLEG_EthicsGuidelinesforTrustworthyAI-ENpdf.pdf; https://www.oecd.org/going-digital/ai/principles/; https://www.baai.ac.cn/blog/beijing-ai-principles

73 Yuval Harari, Homo Deus, pg. 292.

74 https://europa.eu/european-union/sites/europaeu/files/docs/body/treaty_establishing_a_constitution_for_europe_en.pdf articles 1, 2 & 3

75 Mark Manson, *Everything is F*cked*, pg. 70-72.

76 http://www3.weforum.org/docs/WEF_Leading_through_the_Fourth_Industrial_Revolution.pdf

77 https://www.technologyreview.com/s/613589/the-world-economic-forum-wants-to-develop-global-rules-for-ai/

78 https://www.technologyreview.com/s/613589/the-world-economic-forum-wants-to-develop-global-rules-for-ai/

79 https://www.mas.gov.sg/~/media/MAS/News%20and%20Publications/Monographs%20and%20Information%20Papers/FEAT%20Principles%20Final.pdf; https://www.oecd.org/going-digital/ai/principles/; https://g20trade-digital.go.jp/dl/Ministerial_Statement_on_Trade_and_Digital_Economy.pdf

80 https://ec.europa.eu/digital-single-market/en/news/ethics-guidelines-trustworthy-ai

81 https://ec.europa.eu/digital-single-market/en/news/ethics-guidelines-trustworthy-ai

82 Calum Chace, *The Economic Singularity*.

83 Jeremy Bentham, https://en.wikipedia.org/wiki/Panopticon

84 https://www.mckinsey.com/featured-insights/future-of-work/tech-for-good-using-technology-to-smooth-disruption-and-improve-well-being

85 https://hbr.org/podcast/2019/11/ai-accountability-and-power

86 https://hbr.org/podcast/2019/11/ai-accountability-and-power

87 https://ainowinstitute.org/discriminatingsystems.pdf

88 https://ainowinstitute.org/discriminatingsystems.pdf

89 https://venturebeat-com.cdn.ampproject.org/c/s/venturebeat.com/2019/11/11/ai-ethics-is-all-about-power/amp/

90 John Rawls, *A Theory of Justice* Cambridge, MA: Harvard University Press, 1971.

91 https://www.youtube.com/watch?v=nM9foW2KD5s&feature=youtu.be

92 https://www.youtube.com/watch?v=5chp-PRYq-w

93 https://www.youtube.com/watch?v=5chp-PRYq-w

94 https://www.youtube.com/watch?v=5chp-PRYq-w

95 https://pwc.blogs.com/fsrr/2019/12/a-journey-towards-responsible-ai-in-financial-services.html

96 Calum Chace, *The Economic Singularity*, pg. 23.

97 https://ainowinstitute.org/

98 https://ainowinstitute.org/AI_Now_2019_Report.pdf

99 https://ainowinstitute.org/discriminatingsystems.pdf

100 https://ainowinstitute.org/discriminatingsystems.pdf

101 https://ainowinstitute.org/discriminatingsystems.pdf

102 https://www.ukibc.com/events/rewiring-the-21st-century-workplace-how-to-make-it-human-centric-and-tech-driven/

103 https://widgets.weforum.org/nve-2015/chapter1.html

104 https://www.weforum.org/agenda/2016/03/21st-century-skills-future-jobs-students/

105 https://www.weforum.org/agenda/2020/10/top-10-work-skills-of-tomorrow-how-long-it-takes-to-learn-them/

106 https://www.mawilearning.com/wp-content/uploads/2020/04/Whorton-et-al-2017-critical-skills-for-21st-century.pdf

107 Lasse Rouhiainen, *Artificial Intelligence: 101 things you must know today about our future.*

108 Lasse Rouhiainen, *Artificial Intelligence: 101 things you must know today about our future.*

109 https://www.iftf.org/uploads/media/SR-1382A_UPRI_future_work_skills_sm.pdf

110 https://www.iftf.org/uploads/media/SR-1382A_UPRI_future_work_skills_sm.pdf

111 https://www.iftf.org/uploads/media/SR-1382A_UPRI_future_work_skills_sm.pdf

112 https://www.iftf.org/uploads/media/SR-1382A_UPRI_future_work_skills_sm.pdf

113 https://www.oecd.org/education/2030-project/teaching-and-learning/learning/transformative-competencies/Transformative_Competencies_for_2030_concept_note.pdf

114 https://www.oecd.org/education/2030-project/teaching-and-learning/learning/transformative-competencies/Transformative_Competencies_for_2030_concept_note.pdf

115 https://sloanreview.mit.edu/article/will-ai-create-as-many-jobs-as-it-eliminates/

116 https://sloanreview.mit.edu/article/will-ai-create-as-many-jobs-as-it-eliminates/

117 https://sloanreview.mit.edu/article/will-ai-create-as-many-jobs-as-it-eliminates/

118 https://sloanreview.mit.edu/article/will-ai-create-as-many-jobs-as-it-eliminates/

119 Lasse Rouhiainen, *Artificial Intelligence: 101 things you must know today about our future.*

120 Lasse Rouhiainen, *Artificial Intelligence: 101 things you must know today about our future.*

121 https://www.glassdoor.com/research/ai-jobs/#

122 https://www.glassdoor.com/research/ai-jobs/#

123 https://www.cognizant.com/

124 https://www.cognizant.com/whitepapers/21-more-jobs-of-the-future-a-guide-to-getting-and-staying-employed-through-2029-codex3928.pdf; https://www.cognizant.com/perspectives/there-will-be-jobs-in-the-future-of-work

125 https://www.cognizant.com/whitepapers/21-more-jobs-of-the-future-a-guide-to-getting-and-staying-employed-through-2029-codex3928.pdf

126 http://www3.weforum.org/docs/WEF_Future_of_Jobs_2020.pdf

127 http://www3.weforum.org/docs/WEF_Future_of_Jobs_2020.pdf

128 Richard Baldwin, *The Globotics Upheaval.*

129 Richard Baldwin, *The Globotics Upheaval.*

12. Towards Sapiens, the Human-centric User-controlled AI-driven Super Platform

1 https://www.thegeniusworks.com/2019/06/the-platform-economy-time-for-a-business-model-revolution-in-europe/

2 https://www.visualcapitalist.com/amazon-revenue-model-2020/; https://venturebeat.com/2020/07/22/microsoft-earnings-q4-2020/

[3] https://www.mckinsey.com/business-functions/mckinsey-digital/our-insights/five-fifty-platform-plays

[4] Geoffery G. Parker, Marshall W. Van Alstyne and Sangeet Paul Choudary, *Platform Revolution: How Networked Markets are Transforming the Economy and How to Make Them work for You.*

[5] Geoffery G. Parker, Marshall W. Van Alstyne and Sangeet Paul Choudary, *Platform Revolution: How Networked Markets are Transforming the Economy and How to Make Them work for You.*

[6] Geoffery G. Parker, Marshall W. Van Alstyne and Sangeet Paul Choudary, *Platform Revolution: How Networked Markets are Transforming the Economy and How to Make Them work for You.*

[7] Andrew McAfee and Erik Brynjolfsson, Machine Platform Crowd: Harnessing Our Digital Future

[8] http://devblog.blackberry.com/2010/02/what-is-a-super-app/

[9] https://techcrunch.com/2018/11/07/wechat-mini-apps-200-million-users/; https://medium.com/@infopulseglobal_9037/introducing-super-app-a-new-approach-to-all-in-one-experience-8a7894e8ddd4

[10] https://www.cbinsights.com/research/wechat-digital-health-china/

[11] https://medium.com/@infopulseglobal_9037/introducing-super-app-a-new-approach-to-all-in-one-experience-8a7894e8ddd4

[12] https://techcrunch.com/2020/05/26/facebook-rebrands-libra-wallet-service-calibra-to-novi/

[13] https://medium.com/swlh/the-age-of-the-superplatform-18546fa77680

[14] https://medium.com/swlh/the-age-of-the-superplatform-18546fa77680

[15] https://medium.com/swlh/the-age-of-the-superplatform-18546fa77680

[16] José van Dijck, Thomas Poell, and Martijn de Waal, *The Platform Society: Public Values in a Connective World.*

[17] José van Dijck, Thomas Poell, and Martijn de Waal, *The Platform Society: Public Values in a Connective World.*

[18] https://www.cgap.org/blog/super-platforms-africa-not-if-when; http://www.connectingafrica.com/author.asp?section_id=761&doc_id=764310

[19] https://group.jumia.com/

[20] https://www.cgap.org/blog/super-platforms-connecting-farmers-markets-africa

[21] https://www.cgap.org/blog/super-platforms-connecting-farmers-markets-africa

[22] https://medium.com/@francois.chollet/what-worries-me-about-ai-ed9df072b704

[23] https://medium.com/@francois.chollet/what-worries-me-about-ai-ed9df072b704

[24] https://medium.com/@francois.chollet/what-worries-me-about-ai-ed9df072b704

[25] https://www.asme.org/topics-resources/content/top-10-growing-smart-cities

[26] https://smartcityhub.com/governance-economy/how-estonia-became-the-most-digital-country-in-the-world/

[27] https://link.springer.com/article/10.1007/s10462-018-09679-z; https://en.wikipedia.org/wiki/Blockchain

[28] https://www.smartdatacollective.com/top-advantages-blockchain-for-businesses/

[29] https://insidebigdata.com/2020/12/31/everything-in-its-right-place-the-potential-of-decentralized-ai/

[30] https://espeoblockchain.com/blog/decentralized-ai-benefits

[31] https://towardsdatascience.com/3-ai-marketplaces-everyone-has-to-know-one-will-define-the-century-a4295d4f0229

[32] https://aws.amazon.com/marketplace/search/results/?page=1&category=c3714653-8485-4e34-b35b-82c2203e81c1

[33] https://www.genesisai.io/

[34] https://singularitynet.io/

[35] https://singularitynet.io/

[36] https://holochain.org/

37 https://holochain.org/

38 https://oceanprotocol.com/

39 https://oceanprotocol.com/

40 https://ipdb.io/; https://www.bigchaindb.com/

41 https://medium.com/@trentmc0/ai-daos-series2-3876510d6eb4

42 https://medium.com/@trentmc0/wild-wooly-ai-daos-d1719e040956;
https://heartbeat.fritz.ai/artificial-art-how-gans-are-making-machines-creative-b99105627198

43 https://medium.com/@trentmc0/ai-daos-and-three-paths-to-get-there-cfa0a4cc37b8

Appendix: Democratizing Human-centric AI in Africa

1 https://www.weforum.org/agenda/2020/02/africa-global-growth-economics-worldwide-gdp/ .

2 https://www.brookings.edu/wp-content/uploads/2020/01/ForesightAfrica2020_20200110.pdf

3 https://www.brookings.edu/multi-chapter-report/foresight-africa-top-priorities-for-the-continent-in-2020/

4 http://www.ict.go.ke/blockchain.pdf?fbclid=IwAR1eOduHgOmz_0hOabryFE3Ixi2pDV5fZz5U2GaIakMp6iSlYc_IomXvfbk

5 https://www.brookings.edu/wp-content/uploads/2020/01/ForesightAfrica2020_20200110.pdf

6 https://www.gov.za/documents/presidential-commission-fourth-industrial-revolution-members-and-terms-reference-9-apr

7 https://www.itweb.co.za/content/LPwQ5MlyVpzqNgkj

8 https://www.africanews.com/2020/02/07/young-africans-benefit-from-500000-scholarship-funding-under-the-africa-industrial-internet-programme/

www.ingramcontent.com/pod-product-compliance
Lightning Source LLC
LaVergne TN
LVHW081328050326
832903LV00024B/1073